THE WORLD SINCE 1945

THE WORLD SINCE 1945

An International History

P. M. H. Bell

BLOOMSBURY ACADEMIC

First published by Hodder Education in 2001

This reprint published in 2010 by:

Bloomsbury Academic

An imprint of Bloomsbury Publishing Plc
36 Soho Square, London W1D 3QY, UK
and
175 Fifth Avenue, New York, NY 10010, USA

CIP records for this book are available from the British Library
and the Library of Congress

ISBN 978-0-3406-6236-6

This book is produced using paper that is made from wood grown in
managed, sustainable forests.
It is natural, renewable and recyclable. The logging and manufacturing
processes conform to the environmental regulations of the country of origin.

Printed and bound in Great Britain by the MPG Books Group

www.bloomsburyacademic.com

This book is dedicated to
John and Stephanie

CONTENTS

LIST OF MAPS

INTRODUCTION

This book presents a compact account and analysis of international affairs between 1945 and 1991, from the end of the Second World War to the close of the Cold War. It deals with international history in its various aspects – relations between governments, the creation of new states through decolonization, the influence of international organizations, the impact of war and economic forces. The significance and fascination of these events need little emphasis. The world was split by the Cold War, and at the same time transformed by the events of decolonization and the emergence of new states in Asia and Africa. Everyone who lived through these changes was affected by them, and those who follow after still feel their effects. To understand them helps us to make sense of the world in which we live.

To deal with so vast a subject in a single volume (even rather a long one) requires a good deal of simplification, with its consequent dangers. Anyone familiar with the detail and depth of historical research knows that simplification can distort a complicated reality. Yet simplification also has its advantages in opening up any subject. Winston Churchill sometimes urged his military advisers not to start by expounding all the difficulties involved in a proposed operation – the difficulties, he said, would speedily argue for themselves. Similarly, in any historical study, it is a good plan to start by simplifying, and we can be sure that the complexities will argue for themselves. To start with the complexities may well mean getting lost straight away! In this book, therefore, complicated matters are dealt with as straightforwardly as possible. Readers will find ample means to pursue them further, starting with the suggestions for further reading at the end of the book.

The structure of the book may need a word of explanation. After a prologue on the Second World War, which set the scene for much that was to follow, the main body of the work is divided into two chronological sections, from 1945 to 1962, and from 1963 to 1991. Within each section, separate parts deal first with the development of the Cold War and then with decolonization and the world outside the Cold War. There is necessarily some overlap between these topics, but each part may be read separately if need be. The main drive of the book is an interlocking explanation of events and their context, with pauses at various points for reflection on the key concepts that have dominated our thinking on international history during this period – the Cold War, détente, the Third World. Finally, as a counterpoint to these main themes the book concludes by examining the underlying forces which have influenced the course of international affairs. It may perhaps be worth emphasizing that our knowledge of events, and the understanding which comes from perspective, are firmer and clearer at the beginning of the period under study than at the end.

Reference notes are used mainly to acknowledge the sources for quotations and statistics.

P. M. H. BELL
Kew, August 2000

ACKNOWLEDGEMENTS

In writing this book I have received much help, which I am delighted to acknowledge here. Not for the first time, my friends David Dutton, Ralph White and John Lukacs have read extensive drafts with care, insight and incisiveness tempered by charity – I have called heavily upon their generosity, and I am deeply grateful for all that they have done. Christopher Hill gave invaluable advice in the early stages of the work. I owe much to Christopher Wheeler, who kindly suggested that I should undertake the book in the first place, and who has shown much patience amid delays, as well as commenting carefully upon the whole draft. The London Library provides immense resources of books and a haven for scholarship, and I am glad to record my gratitude to the Librarian and staff. I would also like to offer my thanks to David Annett, who spared generous amounts of his time to rescue me from computer difficulties.

As always, my greatest debt is to my wife, who read the drafts in their messiest form, helped in all kinds of ways, and has I think suffered more from this book than from any of my earlier ones!

P. M. H. B.
August 2000

Prologue
THE SECOND WORLD WAR
AND ITS CONSEQUENCES

CHAPTER

THE SECOND WORLD WAR AND ITS CONSEQUENCES

The Second World War in Europe and the Pacific – The politics of the Grand Alliance – The Yalta Conference – Europe in ruins – The war and the western European empires – Long-term consequences of the war

The Second World War cast a long shadow. It was a ferocious and complicated conflict, making an immense impact and leaving enduring traces. What was for many years called 'the post-war world' can only be understood by examining the Second World War and assessing its consequences.

◈ The war in Europe

The war in Europe opened with a series of swift and overwhelming German victories, which influenced not only the course of the war but the whole shape of the post-war world. In September and early October 1939, Germany from the west and the Soviet Union from the east defeated and occupied Poland, which was wiped from the map. The two occupying powers then began a process of massacre and deportation which afflicted the Polish people for the next six years, and left enduring memories.

Between April and June 1940 the Germans invaded Denmark, Norway, the Low Countries and France, again with extraordinary success – the defeat of France in six weeks was an astonishing event. These victories established German control over western Europe for the next four years. They confronted the United States with the possibility of German domination of the Atlantic, so that the Americans moved to establish bases to protect their coasts, and to provide the British with war supplies. Stalin congratulated Hitler on his victories, but also sought to secure his position

Previous page: A symbolic moment: American and Soviet soldiers meet on the River Elbe, 27 April 1945. There is already a crack between them – to become the great rift of the Cold War. © AKG

in eastern Europe by annexing the Baltic states (Estonia, Latvia and Lithuania), and the province of Bessarabia from Romania. Across the world, in the Pacific and South-East Asia, Japan was presented with a striking opportunity for expansion, because the capacity of the defeated European powers to protect their colonial territories in the Far East was gravely weakened. The German successes in western Europe thus sent shock waves throughout the world.

Britain held on in the face of German victory, turning increasingly to the Commonwealth and the United States for support, setting a pattern which was to continue after the war. British survival in 1940 was a decisive event. If Hitler had beaten Britain, the course of the war would have been completely changed, and Germany would probably have controlled most of Europe for many years to come. In the event, Britain fought on, becoming a rallying-point for other countries, a base for future offensives, and an inspiration for resistance against Germany in occupied Europe.

In 1941 the Germans resumed their march of conquest. In April and May they invaded Yugoslavia and Greece. Then on 22 June 1941 – one of the most fateful dates in recent history – Germany attacked the Soviet Union. Operation BARBAROSSA was at first another astonishing success. The Germans conquered vast territories and inflicted enormous casualties upon their enemies. At the beginning of December they were within twenty miles of Moscow, but at that stage their advance was stemmed, and the Red Army launched a successful counter-offensive. This was another turning-point in the war. If the Soviet Union had been defeated, and there had been no eastern front after 1941, it is almost inconceivable that the British and Americans could ever have launched a successful invasion of western Europe.

The German victories up to December 1941 and the opposition which they aroused did much to decide the shape of post-war Europe. The Germans defeated most of the countries in western Europe, and overawed the others, so that the western state system could never be the same again. They marched across eastern Europe, conquering territory and massacring or enslaving populations. They made a desert, on which they intended to build a New Order. These German victories in the east, through their scale and their barbarity, evoked a hostile response far more intense than in the west. In the Soviet Union, even people who had every reason to hate Stalin's regime fought the Germans with a deadly ferocity.

The Germans also raised up a formidable coalition against them. Britain, the United States and the Soviet Union formed an alliance which was to win the war and establish the main lines of the post-war settlement. Within German-occupied Europe, small but vitally important groups in every country took up the cause of resistance, which eventually led to political renewal, national self-respect, and a fresh impulse towards European union.

A further and crucial aspect of the Nazi 'revolution of destruction' was the assault upon the Jews. In what the Nazis referred to as the 'final solution of the Jewish problem', begun in 1940, between five and six million European Jews were slaughtered; only some 300 000 survived.[1] Much was known about these appalling events from 1942 onwards, but the full scale and horror of the death camps only emerged into the public gaze at the end of the war, with far-reaching results in the post-war world.

The massacre of European Jews gave a new and desperate resolve to the Zionist movement to create a Jewish state, and attracted an immense wave of support from western governments and public opinion. Thus the Holocaust and the reactions to it provided the final impulse for the creation of the state of Israel in 1948, from which there arose the long conflict between Israel and the Arabs. Moreover, the issue of genocide raised by the Nazi death camps came to haunt the subsequent conduct of international affairs. There was a gnawing sense that governments should have 'done something' (though it was not easy to say exactly what) to save the European Jews, and that in future states should intervene in the internal affairs of other countries when genocide was threatened. Thus a new and complicating element was introduced into world affairs.

The tide of German victories began to ebb in 1942. This was at first by no means obvious. During the summer of 1942 the Germans resumed the offensive in the USSR, advancing to the bend of the Volga at Stalingrad and moving south into the Caucasus. In North Africa Axis forces came within sixty miles of Alexandria. But behind the scenes production figures told a different story. In 1942 American, British and Soviet aircraft production together totalled over 100 000 against Germany's 15 000, and tank production 58 000 against 9000. The Germans later intensified their efforts, but could not catch up.[2] It is true that the mere possession of overwhelming material force does not always guarantee victory, as the later war in Vietnam was to show; but in this case the weight of massive weaponry applied with ruthless determination took effect. On the ground, the Allied victories at Stalingrad (August 1942–February 1943) and El Alamein (end October–early November 1942) showed that the tide had turned.

Thereafter, the Soviets pursued the war on the eastern front with relentless drive and perseverance. They pressed steadily westwards, advancing into the territory of pre-war Poland, reaching the outskirts of Warsaw by the beginning of August 1944. There they halted, in one of the most pregnant pauses of the war, while the Germans annihilated the Polish Resistance in Warsaw. At enormous cost, the Soviets eventually destroyed the German Army on the eastern front. By the end of the war they had occupied the whole of eastern and substantial parts of central Europe, including the great capital cities of Budapest, Vienna, Prague, Warsaw and Berlin.

From these tremendous victories the Soviet Union emerged with a physical grip on half of Europe and unrivalled prestige, which was attached not only to the Soviet armed forces but to the regime which created them. It was the Red Army which triumphed from Stalingrad to Berlin. It was the red flag, with the hammer and sickle embossed upon it, which was raised (in a scene staged for the newsreel cameras) over the Reichstag Building on 1 May 1945. Military victory conferred a new and powerful aura upon the communist regime and upon Stalin as its leader.

At the same time, the British and Americans closed in upon Germany from the south and west. In the south they fought long campaigns in North Africa and Italy, and landed in southern France in August 1944. In the west, Allied forces landed in Normandy in June 1944, liberated France and the Low Countries, and advanced into Germany. They did not attempt to reach Berlin, though the Americans had the opportunity in April 1945, when the Ninth Army was only fifty miles from the German capital. General Eisenhower, the Supreme Commander of the Allied forces in the west, regarded Berlin as a political, not a military target, and halted the attack. He similarly prevented the American Third Army from advancing to Prague, though its troops were already in Czechoslovakia. Churchill, who wanted the Anglo-American forces to meet the Soviets as far east as possible for political purposes, appealed to Truman (who became President of the United States on Roosevelt's death in April 1945) to overrule Eisenhower's decisions, but without success.

The Soviet Union and the United States emerged as the principal victors of the war in Europe. In the west, Britain fought through the whole war from first to last, and until the summer of 1944 Britain and the Commonwealth had more troops engaged in combat with the enemy than the Americans. But after that the balance shifted in favour of the American armies; and American economic and industrial power was always predominant. In the east, the Red Army bore the brunt of the land fighting, suffering and inflicting the heaviest casualties of the whole war. When American and Soviet troops met at Torgau on the river Elbe, on 25 April 1945; and shook hands in genuine greeting as well as for the benefit of the newsreel cameras and press photographers, it was a moment of high symbolic significance. The soldiers of the two great victorious powers shook hands across the corpse of a defeated Germany in the midst of a devastated Europe. Two massive states, each of them in a different way partially but not fully European, would now dominate European affairs.

◆ The Pacific war

The pattern of the war in the Pacific and East Asia was very similar to that of the war in Europe. It began with a phase of Japanese successes and territorial expansion. At the end of 1937, Japan invaded China, and in the next two years occupied the north-eastern part of the country and all its significant ports, without actually finishing off their Chinese opponents. In

1940–41 the Japanese seized the opportunity offered by the defeat of France to occupy French Indo-China. Then in December 1941 and early 1942 they launched a series of sudden and devastating attacks across the Pacific Ocean and South-East Asia. They destroyed the American Pacific Fleet at Pearl Harbour on 7 December; captured Singapore from the British in February 1942, and conquered the Dutch East Indies in March and April. They bombed Darwin, in Northern Australia, on 17 February, with alarming effect. They drove the British out of Burma, and the Americans from the Philippines. The devastating manner and speed of these victories were even more important than the material facts. At Singapore for example a British, Australian and Indian force superior in numbers to its Japanese opponents surrendered ignominiously. European prestige in Asia never recovered from these defeats, and the long-term political effects proved irreversible.[3]

The Japanese thus seized vast territories in East Asia and the South Pacific. Strategically, they hoped to hold these conquests along a defensive perimeter far away from their home islands, making it too difficult and costly for their enemies to recover their lost territories. Notably, the Japanese believed that the Americans would never accept the cost in casualties involved in a long and brutal war.

In the event, the tide turned more quickly than anyone expected. As early as 4–7 June 1942, no more than a month after the peak of Japanese success, the battle of Midway Island shifted maritime superiority back to the Americans, who never thereafter lost it. On the home front, the sheer weight of American war production told inexorably against Japan. In 1942 the United States produced nearly 48 000 aircraft and 1854 major naval vessels; Japan produced nearly 9000 aircraft and 68 major naval vessels. In 1944 the Americans produced over 96 000 aircraft and 2247 major warships; the Japanese figures were over 28 000 aircraft and 248 warships – a remarkable effort, but not enough.[4]

From mid-1942 onwards the Americans pursued two great offensives, one northward from Australia to the Philippines, and the other westward across the Pacific towards Japan. In this Pacific offensive they fought some of the hardest battles of the war to capture small islands. At Iwo Jima in February–March 1945 the Americans lost nearly 6000 killed to overcome a Japanese garrison of 22 000 in an island only five miles long. At Okinawa in April–June 1945 they fought a battle lasting 83 days and costing 12 500 dead to capture an island sixty miles long defended by 77 000 Japanese troops. In each case, the Japanese had to be virtually wiped out – on Okinawa only 7400 survived.[5]

These figures are worth setting out in some detail, because they were those which the American staffs considered as they prepared for an eventual invasion of Japan, and they thus influenced the use of the atomic bombs in August 1945. They also illustrate the extreme savagery of the fighting in the Pacific, which was itself compounded by the appalling Japanese treatment of prisoners of war, news of which became available in the Allied countries as the war went on, and even more as it came to an end. It was a war in which each side regarded the other as inhuman or even sub-human. The Americans put the Japanese in a category lower even than the Germans – Hollywood films during the war showed some 'good Germans' but no 'good Japanese'. Japan represented the 'Yellow Peril', and the Japanese were an inferior race who had achieved astonishing victories by treacherous means. The Japanese considered themselves superior to the whites, and to the Koreans, Chinese, and other 'lesser races' among the Asian peoples. 'Asia for the Asians' was their slogan, but some Asians were more equal than others.

In this far-flung war, there were several minor victors. Britain and the Commonwealth played a significant part. The British contributed a large Pacific Fleet, and the Fourteenth Army under General Slim won hard-fought victories to re-conquer Burma. Until the end of 1943 Australian land forces in the Pacific area far outnumbered the Americans. The Soviet intervention against Japan in August 1945 inflicted heavy losses on the Japanese army in Manchuria. The Chinese fought on from 1937 to 1945, suffering appalling losses (perhaps five million military casualties, dead and wounded), tying down large Japanese forces and eventually emerging on the winning side.

Despite all these other contributions, the principal victor in the Pacific War was the United States. American maritime power dominated the Pacific Ocean, and captured the islands which allowed American aircraft to bomb Japan almost at will. American submarines largely cut off the Japanese home islands from the outside world. Finally, American aircraft dropped the two atomic bombs, on Hiroshima (6 August 1945) and Nagasaki (9 August), and so brought the war to an end. The development of the atomic bomb was the work of scientists from several countries, but it was only American resources which brought the project to a rapid and decisive conclusion. So it came about that while in Europe there were two great victors (the USSR and the USA), in the Pacific there was only one – the United States. Before the Second World War, the United States was a power with interests in the Pacific; after the war, it was for a time the predominant power in the whole Pacific Ocean.

◆ The politics of the Grand Alliance

The 'Grand Alliance' was Churchill's term for the combination of Britain, the United States and the Soviet Union which fought and won the war against Germany, Italy and Japan. The workings of that alliance influenced both the course of the war and its consequences. It won the war, and then its breakdown was followed by the start of the Cold War – which in turn

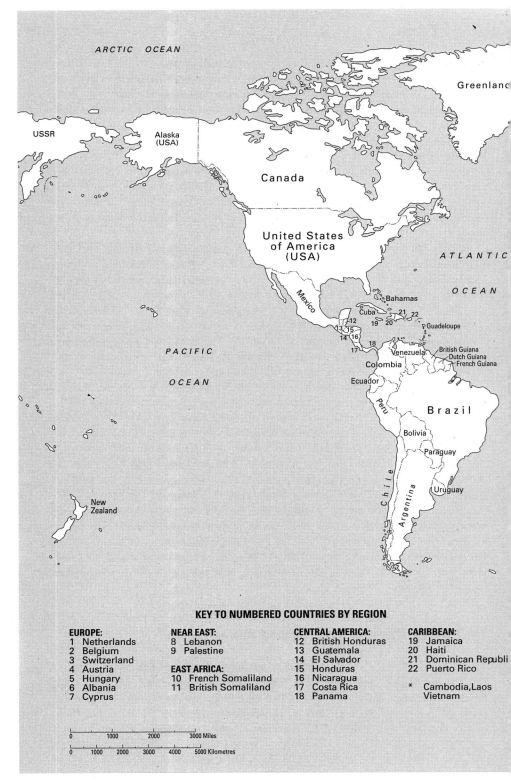

KEY TO NUMBERED COUNTRIES BY REGION

EUROPE:
1 Netherlands
2 Belgium
3 Switzerland
4 Austria
5 Hungary
6 Albania
7 Cyprus

NEAR EAST:
8 Lebanon
9 Palestine

EAST AFRICA:
10 French Somaliland
11 British Somaliland

CENTRAL AMERICA:
12 British Honduras
13 Guatemala
14 El Salvador
15 Honduras
16 Nicaragua
17 Costa Rica
18 Panama

CARIBBEAN:
19 Jamaica
20 Haiti
21 Dominican Republi
22 Puerto Rico

* Cambodia, Laos
Vietnam

The World in 1945

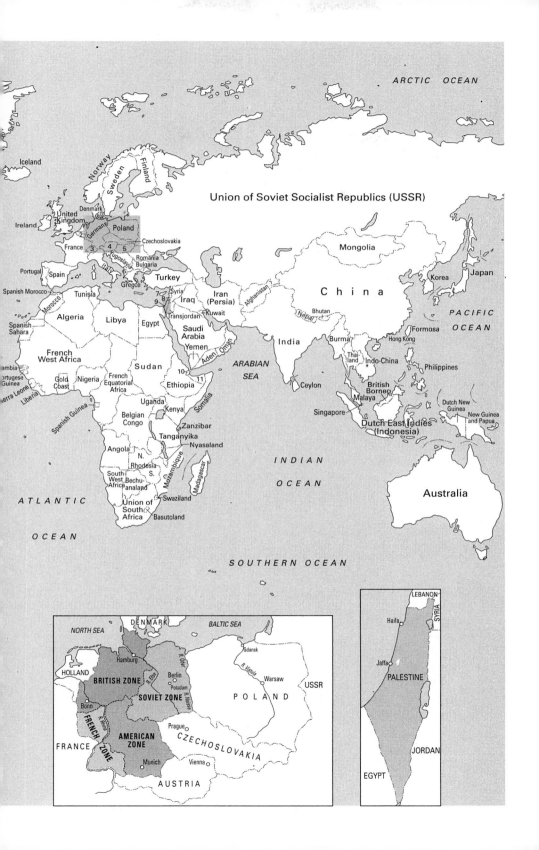

ARCTIC OCEAN

Iceland

Ireland

United Kingdom
Denmark
Germany
Poland
Czechoslovakia

France

Portugal

Spain

Spanish Morocco

Morocco

Tunisia

Algeria

Libya

Egypt

Spanish Sahara

French West Africa

Gold Coast

Nigeria

French Equatorial Africa

Sudan

Ethiopia

Somalia

Uganda

Kenya

Belgian Congo

Zanzibar

Tanganyika

Nyasaland

Angola

N. Rhodesia

Mozambique

Madagascar

S. Rhodesia

South West Africa

Bechuanaland

Swaziland

Union of South Africa

Basutoland

Gambia

Portugese Guinea

Sierra Leone

Liberia

Spanish Guinea

Union of Soviet Socialist Republics (USSR)

Mongolia

Turkey

Greece

Syria

Iraq

Iran (Persia)

Transjordan

Kuwait

Saudi Arabia

Yemen

Aden

Oman

ARABIAN SEA

India

Ceylon

Afghanistan

Nepal

Bhutan

Burma

C h i n a

Korea

Japan

Formosa

Hong Kong

Thailand

Indo-China

PACIFIC OCEAN

Philippines

British Borneo

Malaya

Singapore

Dutch East Indies (Indonesia)

Dutch New Guinea

New Guinea and Papua

INDIAN OCEAN

Australia

ATLANTIC OCEAN

SOUTHERN OCEAN

Romania
Bulgaria
Yugoslavia
Italy

NORTH SEA

DENMARK

BALTIC SEA

HOLLAND

Hamburg

BRITISH ZONE

R. Elbe

Berlin

Potsdam

Gdansk

R. Oder

R. Vistula

Warsaw

USSR

Bonn

SOVIET ZONE

R. Russ

POLAND

FRENCH ZONE

R. Rhine

AMERICAN ZONE

Prague

CZECHOSLOVAKIA

FRANCE

Munich

Vienna

AUSTRIA

LEBANON

SYRIA

Haifa

Jaffa

PALESTINE

JORDAN

EGYPT

has led historians to search for the origins of the Cold War in friction between the partners in the Grand Alliance.

The three allies and their leaders displayed some strange contrasts. President Roosevelt of the United States presented a puzzling mixture of idealism and *realpolitik*. His idealism was genuine, drawing on the long-standing American belief that it was the vocation of the United States to act as a light to guide the world to a better future. He took up the causes professed by Woodrow Wilson in the First World War, proposing a new international organization (the United Nations), and emphasizing the right of peoples to choose their own government. Yet Roosevelt could also be calculating in his aims and ruthless in his methods. For example, when he wanted to secure Soviet entry into the war against Japan, he did not hesitate to hand over various territories (belonging to his allies the Chinese as well as to his enemies the Japanese) to Stalin, with no reference to the rights or wishes of their peoples.

Roosevelt's whole policy during the war shows this combination of idealism and ruthlessness. He genuinely intended to found an international order based on agreement, not on the balance of power. He sought no safeguards against the Soviet Union, because he believed that peace would arise from co-operation between states. On Christmas Eve 1943, Roosevelt, who had just returned from a meeting with Stalin and Churchill at Teheran, broadcast one of his famous 'fireside chats' to the American people. This so-called 'chat' was considered with such care that it went through no fewer than eight drafts before it was delivered; and what the President told his listeners was that the United States and the Soviet Union 'are going to get along very well . . . very well indeed'. There is no doubt that he meant it.[6] His idealism also caused him to oppose imperialism. On 25 May 1942 Sumner Welles, the Deputy Secretary of State, said in a public speech that: 'Our victory must bring in its train the liberation of all peoples . . . The age of imperialism is ended,' and Roosevelt endorsed this statement as authoritative for American policy.[7] Yet this anti-imperialism was highly selective, to be applied to British rule in India and French colonies in West Africa and Indo-China, but not to the American sphere of influence in the Caribbean or even to Soviet domination in eastern Poland. Roosevelt was prepared to regard Stalin with the eye of faith, but the French and British empires with the eye of a demolition contractor – the sites, after all, might be useful to America. It was a strange combination, and it is not surprising that Roosevelt has remained an enigmatic figure.

Roosevelt was a subtle statesman who concealed himself behind a screen of publicity. Stalin shrouded himself in secrecy, but was in many ways straightforward. His means of ensuring the security of the Soviet Union were solidly territorial. When Anthony Eden, the British Foreign Secretary, visited Moscow in December 1941, when the German armies were within a few miles of the city, Stalin calmly presented him with a list of Soviet territorial requirements at the end of the war: nothing less than the frontiers of June 1941, including the former Baltic states of Estonia, Latvia and Lithuania, the former Romanian province of Bessarabia, and the eastern half of pre-war Poland. At the same time, Stalin made it clear that if Britain wanted bases in western European countries, he would have no objection. Later on in the war, at the Yalta Conference, Stalin made it clear that he intended to recover territory lost to Japan by Tsarist Russia in the war of 1904–05, and he contrived to do so. He was also determined to establish spheres of influence beyond the frontiers of the Soviet Union, in both Europe and Asia, to ensure the security of the USSR.

These straightforward territorial ambitions went alongside ideological aims, with which they in no way conflicted. In April 1945 Stalin remarked to the Yugoslav communist Milovan Djilas: 'This war is not as in the past; whoever occupies a territory also imposes on it his own social system. Everyone imposes his own system as far as his army has power to do so. It cannot be otherwise'.[8] This had the merit of simplicity, and it was what happened after the war. Just as trade followed the flag in the nineteenth century, the communist political system followed the Red Army after 1945.

Churchill, the British Prime Minister, was himself very much a man of the nineteenth century, when he had served as a soldier in India and fought at the battle of Omdurman (in the Sudan) in 1898. He was determined to maintain the British Empire. As he remarked in a famous public speech, 'I have not become the King's First Minister in order to preside over the liquidation of the British Empire.'[9] He was also thoroughly imbued with the historic doctrine of the balance of power. He sought to restore France as a great power in Europe to help in counter-balancing the Soviet Union; and if necessary he was even prepared to consider Germany for the same role, after Hitler had been got rid of. Spheres of influence formed a natural part of his thinking, and in 1944 he was perfectly willing to accept that there would be a substantial Soviet sphere in eastern Europe. In Moscow, in October 1944, Churchill proposed to Stalin the so-called 'percentages agreement', suggesting that the Soviet Union should have 90 per cent influence in Romania and 75 per cent in Bulgaria; Britain 90 per cent in Greece; in Hungary and Yugoslavia they should have 50 per cent each – an outline which was later amended to allow the USSR 80 per cent in Bulgaria and Hungary. At the same conference, Churchill was also prepared to put extreme pressure on the Polish government in exile in London to accept Soviet demands that a post-war Polish government should be 'friendly' to the Soviet Union, which in effect meant being in the Soviet sphere. There was no contradiction between this policy and his desire in April–May 1945 that the British and American armies should meet the Soviets as far east as possible, and reach Berlin and Prague before the Red Army. Churchill sought to limit Soviet influence in *central* Europe, even though he accepted it in *eastern* Europe. This hard-headed policy of spheres of influence was understood and accepted by Stalin, but got Churchill into trouble with the Americans. In December 1944 Churchill used force to suppress the communist resistance movement in Greece, which was greeted by complete silence in Moscow, where Stalin kept his side of the percentages agreement, but by vociferous criticism in the United States, where it was seen as British imperialism at work.

After the war, and in the perspective of the Cold War, the internal workings of the Grand Alliance were often presented as a two-sided affair, with the Americans and the British linked together against the Soviet Union. This was gravely misleading. The actual relations of the three powers formed a cat's cradle of criss-cross lines, sometimes bringing any two of the three powers together, and sometimes meshing all three in a complex of common interests.

Anglo-American relations were certainly close. The intensive personal correspondence between Churchill and Roosevelt, and their seven meetings in three and a half years (as against only two jointly with Stalin), created an unusual understanding between the two men. Despite many differences, they worked out a common strategy for the conduct of the war, which was co-ordinated by the American and British Combined Chiefs of Staff – a body unprecedented in the history of war, which met every week continuously from January 1942. The integrated Allied commands (notably those under General Eisenhower, first in North Africa and then for the campaign in north-west Europe) worked with outstanding success. By contrast, the Soviet Union fought an almost completely separate war, conducting its own campaigns with only occasional attempts at co-ordination with the western Allies. This was very largely the result of geography – sheer distance made co-operation almost impossible. Even the journeys involved when Churchill and Roosevelt went to meet Stalin were long and hazardous. To the obstacle of distance was added a good measure of unwillingness to work together. Stalin was secretive by nature and as a matter of policy, and his whole regime operated under a system of obsessive concealment. The Soviet staff never communicated to their allies any information about their order of battle. The British and Americans, for their part, had no wish to disrupt the smooth working of their own integrated commands by bringing in Soviet representatives. For these various reasons, the Americans and British on the one hand, the Soviets on the other, fought separate wars.

But despite the close Anglo-American alliance, their strategic relations were often troubled. The whole question of a cross-Channel invasion of Europe, for example, caused repeated friction. The Americans pressed hard for an early landing in France, first on a limited scale in 1942 and then at full strength in 1943; the British resisted these plans, and secured a number of postponements, partly by insisting on operations in the Mediterranean instead. This long dispute was not concluded until the three-power conference at Teheran at the end of November 1943, when Roosevelt and Stalin together insisted on fixing a firm date for the invasion (May 1944 – it eventually took place on 6 June). In the last resort, therefore, and very strikingly, the issue was settled by an American-Soviet combination against the British. Even in matters of grand strategy, there was no simple Anglo-American line-up to the exclusion of the Soviets.

The diplomatic workings of the alliances were complicated, in various criss-cross patterns. Roosevelt and Churchill worked closely together, but each also sought to get on good terms with Stalin, if necessary at the expense of the other. In May 1943 Roosevelt proposed to Stalin that they should meet somewhere near the Bering Straits, with only small staffs and without the British, so that they could get to know one another. Stalin declined the proposal, on the ground that he was too much engaged in directing military operations; but the point is that Roosevelt made it, and sought to conceal it from Churchill. At the Teheran Conference between the three leaders at the end of November 1943, Roosevelt accepted an invitation from Stalin to stay in the same compound, and went out of his way to court Stalin and remain aloof from Churchill. On the other hand, while Roosevelt *sought* a separate meeting with Stalin, Churchill actually *met* him twice, without the Americans, in August 1942 and October 1944. At the second of those meetings, Churchill secured the 'percentages' agreement about spheres of influence in the Balkans, though he was well aware of Roosevelt's opposition to such arrangements. Both Roosevelt and Churchill had good reasons for their actions. From the American point of view, it was clear that by the end of the war the Soviet Union was going to be a much stronger power than Britain, and would take a vital part in world affairs. It was only prudent to get on good terms with Stalin, and Roosevelt believed that he had the ability, the charm and the bargaining power to do so. Churchill for his part sought to safeguard British interests in the Mediterranean by means of a deal with Stalin on spheres of influence. In these manoeuverings, there was no American-British line-up against the Soviet Union, but rather a series of British and American attempts to get on terms with Stalin, who was in the happy position of being courted by each of his allies in turn.

There were other political difficulties within the Anglo-American alliance, with no reference to the Soviet Union at all. The Americans, with Roosevelt in the lead, were anti-imperialist (or rather, they were against other countries' empires, while affecting not to realize that they had one of their own). Roosevelt was particularly critical of British rule in India, which Churchill was determined to maintain. The United States was opposed to the British Empire tariff system of Imperial Preference, and used the leverage of aid to Britain through Lend-Lease to undermine it. The Americans used their immense advantages in civil air traffic to take over air services previously controlled by British airlines, which largely ceased to operate during the war. American oil companies moved into Saudi Arabia, and began to compete with British oil interests in the Near and Middle East. There was much competition within the Anglo-American alliance.

In all this there is little sign of the Cold War alignments which were to follow. There was a good deal of sparring between all three partners in the Grand Alliance, as each tried to gain advantage in the conduct of the war and in the settlement which would follow; but this sparring was not on simple East–West lines. In practice, the three powers muddled through their mutual disagreements reasonably well, often by postponing the most difficult questions relating to the post-war settlement. This was above all the policy of Roosevelt, who regularly argued that territorial questions should be dealt with at the peace conference, and not in deals between the powers while the war was still going on. Churchill sometimes wished to proceed differently, and to get some aspects of the settlement fixed while he still held some cards. Stalin began by advancing a long list of his territorial demands, but as he grasped that Roosevelt really meant what he said about postponing territorial questions, and as it grew steadily more certain that military victory would enable him to impose his own terms in eastern Europe, Stalin ceased to press these demands. He was prepared to wait, and let victory produce its own rewards.

There were some exceptions to this general rule of postponing territorial questions. One concerned the former Baltic states of Estonia, Latvia and Lithuania, which had been annexed by the Soviet Union in 1940. Early in 1942, the British accepted these Soviet annexations, but the United States did not, and the issue remained formally unsettled as between the USA and the USSR – though Soviet control was firmly established on the ground when the Red Army moved in. A more serious problem arose over Poland. This question had two aspects: what the boundaries of Poland were to be at the end of the war; and what form its government was to take. In October 1939, the Soviet Union had annexed the eastern half of pre-war Poland, along the Molotov–Ribbentrop Line drawn up in the two German-Soviet agreements of August and September 1939. Stalin insisted throughout the war that the Soviet frontiers of June 1941 should be maintained. He also demanded that Poland must have a government 'friendly' to the Soviet Union. These demands were particularly difficult for the British to meet. Poland was Britain's ally, by a treaty signed in 1939. Britain had guaranteed Polish independence (though not territorial integrity), and Polish forces fought alongside the British with great courage and dash throughout the war. The United States had no treaty obligations to Poland, but American principles concerning self-determination and the right of peoples to choose their own government were certainly at stake. (There was no doubt that the Poles would not voluntarily elect a government 'friendly' to the Soviet Union, which meant under Soviet control.) There were also grave moral issues involved. In 1939–41 the Soviets either deported or massacred vast numbers of Poles in the eastern half of the country. The Katyn massacre, in which 4400 Polish officers were murdered by the NKVD (the Soviet security police) and buried in mass graves in April 1940, became a public issue in April 1943, when the Germans publicized their discovery of the graves. Even at the time, the British government was almost completely certain that the Soviets were guilty of this crime, and Churchill communicated the evidence to Roosevelt; but neither was prepared to make an issue of the matter. Later, in August–September 1944, the Red Army stood by on the outskirts of Warsaw while the Germans crushed a rising in the city by the Polish Home Army (the main resistance organization). Stalin even refused to allow American and British aircraft to use airfields under Soviet control to send air-drops of supplies to the Poles. Churchill was convinced that this arose from a deliberate Soviet policy of allowing the Polish anti-communist resistance to be annihilated, and he wished to send assistance, but Roosevelt would do little, permitting only one large-scale American air-drop to Warsaw.

Poland thus presented the gravest of problems, of frontiers, forms of government, and moral issues, on all of which the British and Americans should in principle have opposed the Soviet Union. In practice, neither of

Poland at the end of the Second World War

the western powers chose to risk a break with Stalin over Poland. The importance of the Soviet Union in winning the war and achieving a post-war settlement was so great that other matters had to be set aside. At the Teheran Conference at the end of November 1943, the British and Americans dealt with the major part of the frontier question by accepting the so-called Curzon Line, which was not far from the Molotov–Ribbentrop Line (a name which was tactfully dropped); though the British tried vainly to argue that Lvov – a city to which the Poles attached the highest historic importance – should be placed on the Polish side of the line. Churchill and Roosevelt also agreed that Poland should be compensated for losses in the east by annexing German territory in the west, moving the western frontier of Poland to the line of the rivers Oder and Neisse. (The fact that there were two Neisse rivers, the Eastern and the Western, does not appear to have impinged at that time.) In none of these discussions did the wishes of the populations involved play any significant role, even for Roosevelt. The territorial problems thus moved towards a solution, mainly dictated by the Soviet Union. The question of the future government of Poland remained unresolved until the Yalta Conference in February 1945. The moral issues, raised most prominently by the question of the Katyn massacre, were tacitly set aside. The Polish question perturbed, but was not allowed to break, the wartime alliance.

During the Cold War, there was a natural tendency for historians to seek the origins of that conflict in a line-up of the Americans and British against the Soviets during the Second World War. As we have just seen, this was by no means the case. The three wartime allies formed links and changed part-ners in an intricate pattern, not a simple line-up. On this basis, the Grand Alliance was still in working order at the beginning of 1945, when the lead-ers of the three great Allied powers met at Yalta, a holiday resort in the Crimea, which not long previously had been occupied by the Germans. There, in the almost theatrical surroundings of a palace provided with potted palms for the occasion, Stalin welcomed Roosevelt for his first visit to the Soviet Union, and Churchill on his third.

◆ The Yalta Conference, 4–11 February 1945

Myths cling to the Yalta Conference like barnacles to a wreck. The most powerful has been that at Yalta the 'Big Three' – Roosevelt, Stalin, and Churchill – agreed on a partition of Europe, or even the world. A musical play, *Yalta! Yalta!*, staged at Zagreb in the early 1970s, began with the words: 'In February 1945 the leaders of the three great powers met at Yalta to divide the world'.[10] Musicals may be permitted a dash of fiction, but the same idea may be found in many serious commentaries. It has been almost in vain that historians have pointed out that Yalta divided neither Europe nor the world. The myths cling on, making it all the more important to ask what actually happened at the Yalta Conference.

The first point about Yalta, obvious at the time but easily forgotten in retrospect, was that the war was far from finished. The German armies were fighting hard, and Hitler still hoped that the 'unnatural coalition' ranged against him would break up. In the Pacific, Japan still controlled vast territories, and the Japanese forces were if anything harder to defeat than the Germans. The allies who met at Yalta could not afford to relax their military efforts, nor permit any cracks to appear in their political unity.

It was against this background that Roosevelt, Churchill and Stalin faced the great issues of their conference: (1) to reach agreement on crucial aspects of the United Nations Organization, whose main lines had been sketched out at the Dumbarton Oaks conference in September and October 1944; (2) to settle their policy towards Germany, notably on occupation zones and reparation payments; (3) to deal with the problems of Poland's boundaries and government; and (4) to decide when and on what terms the Soviet Union would enter the war against Japan.

Roosevelt attached particular importance to the United Nations Organization, which he saw as the key to the post-war settlement. The Dumbarton Oaks Conference in 1944, held to draw up an outline for the organization, had left two important questions outstanding: to settle which states were to be members of the United Nations, and to decide on the system of voting in the Security Council, which was to form the main directing body in the organization. As to membership, the United States had proposed the original signatories of the Declaration on the United Nations in 1942, plus eight others, of which six were in Latin America, and thus presumed to be under American influence. The Soviet Union countered by proposing membership for all fifteen of the Soviet Republics, as well as the USSR itself. As to voting in the Security Council, there was general agreement that permanent members of the Council (the great powers) should hold a power of veto, but not on the circumstances in which such a veto should be used. At Yalta, it was agreed that the founding members of the UN were to be states which were at war with Germany at the end of hostilities (which resulted in a rash of declarations of war by countries wishing to secure membership). Stalin agreed to reduce his demand for Soviet membership from sixteen to three (the Soviet Union itself plus the Ukraine and Belorussia). On the matter of voting in the Security Council, Stalin agreed to a proposal by Roosevelt that on matters of procedure a vote by seven out of the proposed eleven Council members would suffice; but that on substantive questions, involving action by the Council, the permanent members should be able to exercise a veto. On both these matters, therefore, Stalin made concessions to the Americans, and Roosevelt secured the sort of arrangements that he wanted. The structure of the United Nations

Organization was agreed on, and a conference to bring it into existence met in June 1945, at San Francisco.[11]

On the German question, much had been decided before the Yalta Conference met. At the Casablanca Conference between Roosevelt and Churchill (January 1943), the American President had announced the policy of 'unconditional surrender' – that Germany, Italy and Japan must accept total defeat, and not negotiate terms on which they would capitulate. The purpose of this was twofold. First, it would avoid the confusion which arose in 1918–19, when Germany agreed to end the Great War on the terms outlined in President Wilson's Fourteen Points, and then was able to claim that the Versailles Treaty did not conform to those Points. This time, there would be no conditions and no room for complaint or evasion. Second, the policy of unconditional surrender (to which Stalin at once adhered) guaranteed the Allies against the possibility of one or more of them making a separate peace with the enemy – a danger which hung over the Grand Alliance for much of its existence. It followed from this that Germany was to be totally defeated and subjected to Allied occupation. During 1944, a European Advisory Commission, made up of American, British and Soviet representatives, agreed that Germany was to be divided into three occupation zones, each garrisoned by one of the great allies, with an Allied Control Council to administer Germany as a whole. Berlin was to be treated as a separate entity, similarly divided into three zones. These decisions left open the question of where Germany's frontiers were to be fixed, and how much territory the country was to lose. (For most of the war there had been general agreement that Germany should be partitioned, or 'dismembered', which was the more ferocious term in common use, but no decision as to how precisely this should be accomplished.) At the Teheran Conference, the three Allies had agreed that the northern part of East Prussia, including Königsberg, should be annexed by the Soviet Union, which was a first step towards resolving this question.

At Yalta, Churchill proposed to change the arrangements for occupations zones to allow France to be included as one of the occupying powers, and to be represented on the Allied Control Council. Somewhat reluctantly, Stalin and Roosevelt agreed to this; though Stalin insisted that the new occupation zone for France must be carved out of the existing American and British zones, leaving the Soviet zone unchanged. The question of German frontiers was taken a step further by an agreement that Poland should annex German territory up to the River Oder; though the Conference failed to agree on whether the frontier should then run along the Eastern or the Western Neisse.

As to reparations, the Soviet Union had a strong claim to the highest possible payments, based on the destruction and losses inflicted by the German invasion. Stalin proposed that reparations should be paid in kind (for example, industrial machinery, minerals, agricultural produce), to a total of $20 billion, of which half should go to the Soviet Union. The British and Americans at first opposed this, arguing that the attempt to extract heavy reparations from Germany after the Great War had proved a disastrous failure. Eventually, Roosevelt (but not Churchill) agreed that a Reparations Commission should meet in Moscow to consider the question, and take the figure of $20 billion (with half for the Soviet Union) as the basis for its discussions. The British objection was overruled, and the Conference thus took a long step towards meeting the Soviet demand.

On the problem of Poland, which took up much of the Conference's time, the question of frontiers was left partially in suspense. The Big Three agreed that the eastern frontier of Poland (i.e. with the Soviet Union) should follow the Curzon Line, leaving Lvov to the USSR but allowing some small variations in favour of Poland. They also agreed that Poland should receive substantial areas of territory in the north (from East Prussia) and in the west, where the River Oder was accepted as one part of the new frontier, which should then follow the line of either the Western or the Eastern Neisse. Stalin advocated the Western Neisse, which would grant Poland a larger share of German territory. Roosevelt and Churchill supported the Eastern Neisse – Churchill remarked that they should not stuff the Polish goose too full. They failed to agree, and the question was left open. (Later, at the Potsdam Conference, the Western Neisse came to be established *de facto* as the frontier of Poland, producing the now familiar Oder–Neisse Line.)

The question of the Polish government proved even more difficult and heavier with consequences. When the Yalta Conference took place, two Polish governments were in existence: the government in exile in London, which was directly descended from the government which had left Poland in October 1939; and the government in Lublin, appointed by the Soviet Union from Polish communists. Britain and the United States recognized the London government; the Soviet Union recognized the Lublin government. Stalin had insisted from 1941 onwards that the Soviet Union must have a 'friendly' government in Poland, for purposes of security on its western frontier. The London government could not be described, by any stretch of the imagination, as 'friendly' to the Soviet Union, which had invaded the eastern part of pre-war Poland in 1939, and then deported and massacred many of its people. On the question of a new Polish government, it was hard to see that any compromise was available; and Stalin held the immense advantage that the Red Army was already in occupation of nearly all pre-war Poland.

The final agreement reached at Yalta was that: 'The Provisional Government which is now functioning in Poland [i.e. the Lublin Government] should . . . be reorganized on a broader democratic basis with the inclusion of democratic leaders from Poland itself and from Poles abroad. This new government should then be called the Polish Provisional Government of

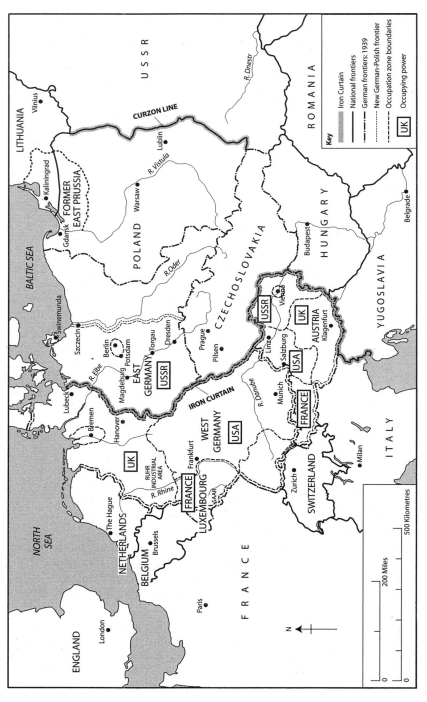

Key

▨	Iron Curtain
——	National frontiers
—··—	German frontiers: 1939
········	New German–Polish frontier
—·—·—	Occupation zone boundaries
UK	Occupying power

Central Europe and the Iron Curtain

National Unity.' This new government was to hold 'free and unfettered elections as soon as possible', on a secret ballot and with all 'democratic and anti-
Nazi parties' having the right to take part.[12] This formulation accepted the
Lublin government as the basis for a new government, and so gave Stalin the
essence of what he wanted. The London government was not even mentioned
by name, though it was understood that its members were included in the
category of 'Poles abroad'. Stalin told the Conference that elections would be
held as soon as the Germans were defeated, but in practice the whole undertaking about 'free and unfettered elections' proved to be no more than a pious
hope. It is hard to believe that experienced statesmen like Churchill and
Roosevelt ever thought it would be otherwise.

In addition to the agreement on Poland, the Conference adopted a
'Declaration on Liberated Europe', put forward by the Americans, in which
the three Allied governments undertook to assist the peoples of liberated
countries (and also former Axis satellite states) to solve their problems by
democratic means, to form interim authorities representative of all democratic elements, and to establish through free elections governments respon-
sive to the will of the people. Stalin accepted this without demur. Molotov,
the Soviet Foreign Minister, grumbled that the Americans were going too
far by insisting on free elections in eastern Europe; but Stalin told him 'We
can deal with it in our own way later. The point is the correlation of
forces.'[13] In practice, Stalin got much the better of the bargain, securing the
sort of Polish government he wanted while conceding only a vague agreement on elections, which need never be kept.

Roosevelt had another vital objective at Yalta: to make certain of Soviet
intervention in the war against Japan, which still seemed likely to be long
and costly. To secure this he had to pay in the hard coin of territory. Stalin
insisted, in strikingly old-fashioned terms, on restoring 'the former rights of
Russia violated by the treacherous attack of Japan in 1904'.[14] Specifically
this meant: the return of South Sakhalin to Soviet sovereignty; the lease of
Port Arthur as a naval base, and recognition of the pre-eminent rights of the
Soviet Union in the neighbouring commercial port of Dairen; the acceptance of pre-eminent Soviet rights in the South Manchurian Railway and
the Chinese Eastern Railway in Manchuria – though China was to retain
sovereignty in Manchuria itself. The Soviet Union was to annex the Kuril
Islands from Japan. The *status quo* in Outer Mongolia was to be preserved
– i.e. the territory was to be accepted as a Soviet sphere of influence. In
return, Stalin undertook to enter the war against Japan three months after
the end of the war against Germany – an engagement which he duly
fulfilled. These terms were agreed upon, even though Manchuria and Outer
Mongolia were territories belonging to China, an ally (supposedly a
favoured ally) of the United States. It was a stern and cold-blooded piece of
power politics; though Roosevelt presumably had no doubt that the gain
was worth the price.

At the time, Yalta was one of those rare conferences where all the principal participants could claim to have attained their main objectives. Churchill gained an occupation zone in Germany for France, which was a step towards the British aim of restoring France as a major power in Europe. Roosevelt gained both his principal objectives: the way was clear to the creation of the United Nations Organization, and Stalin gave a firm undertaking to enter the war against Japan. Stalin secured a favourable agreement on the make-up of the Polish government; an acknowledgement (though not yet full acceptance) of the Soviet claim for $10 billion in reparations from Germany; and a good price in territory and influence for intervening against Japan. All three achieved their common purpose of keeping the alliance together.

This was not the whole story. There were strains in the alliance. Roosevelt's genuine idealism consorted ill with his own practice of power politics, and even worse with Stalin's ruthless concentration on territorial gain. Churchill looked forward with dismay to the possibility of Soviet domination in Europe, with the Americans gone home: 'What will lie between the white snows of Russia and the white cliffs of Dover?' he wondered gloomily soon after his return from Yalta.[15] Stalin kept a wary eye on the possibility that the western powers might make separate agreements with the Germans which would give their forces an easy passage while the Red Army still had to struggle in the east. Moreover, it must be doubted how far Stalin understood Roosevelt's genuine concern with 'democracy' in eastern Europe, so that the two statesmen were storing up difficulties for the future by glibly agreeing on 'free elections' for Poland, and on the high-sounding phrases of the 'Declaration on Liberated Europe'. Still, all alliances work by compromises and evasions, and the Grand Alliance fared not too badly in these respects. At Yalta the great allies were still bound together by the need to win the war, and their three leaders maintained a practical working relationship.

Yalta did not partition the world. It did not even divide up Europe, though it did place Poland firmly in the Soviet sphere of influence. It did not see the beginning of the Cold War, but plotted a feasible course towards bringing the Second World War to a conclusion and setting up a framework for the post-war world. The Grand Alliance was still in being.

◆ Europe in ruins

One of the most obvious consequences of the Second World War was that Europe lay in ruins – often literally so, because the material damage caused by the war was immense. Parts of the Soviet Union had been fought over four times. Warsaw was about three-quarters destroyed, and most of its people killed or dispersed. Germany had been heavily bombed and then fought over; Berlin was a scene of utter devastation. Casualties across the continent had been enormous – even greater than those which had been thought unbearable in the Great War of 1914–18. War-related deaths in Germany were estimated at about 6 500 000, with another 374 000 for Austria, which was part of Germany for the whole of the war. Among Germany's allies, Romania suffered some 500 000 dead and Hungary 430 000 – a high proportion of their populations. Among the victors, a commonly used figure for Soviet war dead is 20 000 000, though other estimates go as high as 25 000 000–27 000 000. Polish losses have been put at 4 123 000, but were almost certainly higher. French losses were approximately 600 000, and those of the United Kingdom 350 000. The war deaths for the whole continent may be computed at a grievous total of something over 36 000 000.[16]

At the end of the war Europe was in a state of economic dislocation and decay. Industrial production across most of the continent was low, and in some places non-existent. Transport was often at a standstill. Agricultural production could not feed the populations – food rations were low, and the northern Netherlands suffered severe famine in the winter of 1944–45. The end of the war brought a movement of peoples such as had not been seen in European history for fifteen hundred years. Between 10 and 12 million Germans (perhaps more) either fled or were driven from territories where they had lived for generations, so that east of the Oder–Neisse Line and in the reconstituted Czechoslovakia only tiny German populations remained.[17] Refugees, survivors of the death camps, slave labourers from the German war economy, and released prisoners of war wandered across lands which were sometimes almost empty of settled population.

In the centre of this ruined continent the soldiers of the United States and the Soviet Union met. The fate of Europe was to be in their hands for a longer time than anyone could then foresee. Meanwhile, the vacuum left by the defeat and destruction of Germany had to be filled, and much would depend on how this was done.

◆ The European empires: Africa

For many years, and in some cases for centuries, European powers had controlled vast empires in Africa, the Middle East and Asia. The Second World War dealt heavy and sometimes fatal blows to those empires, with far-reaching consequences.

Africa south of the Sahara was the area least affected by the war, but did not wholly escape its impact. In British West Africa, Freetown became a major convoy base. The Takoradi air route brought new activity to the Gold Coast and Nigeria, and Americans arrived to run the airfields, bringing new and disturbing influences into the area. African troops from British

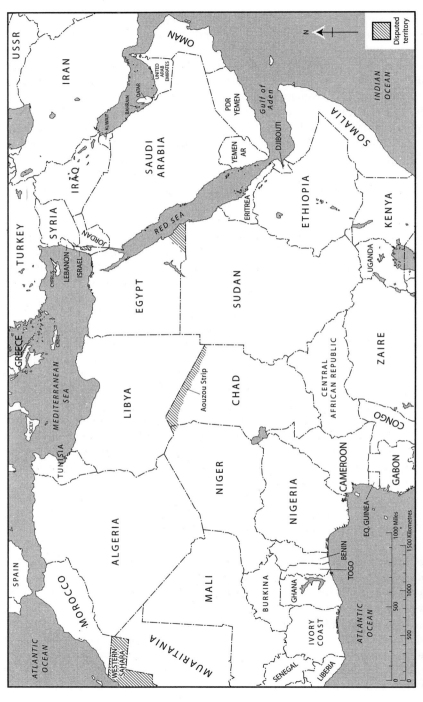

North Africa and the Middle East

colonies in East and West Africa fought in Burma (1943–45), with unsettling effects when they returned home. Several French colonies suffered disturbing conflicts between Vichy and Free French forces. In South Africa, Afrikaner opposition to the war led to increased antipathy to the British connection, and paved the way for later Nationalist successes.

French North Africa suffered a series of shocks in the course of the war. The sudden defeat of France at the hands of Germany in 1940 was a damaging blow to French prestige, though its effects were slow to come to light. Then in November 1942 the Americans and British invaded Morocco and Algeria; the Germans in response occupied Tunisia; and a fierce battle ensued until the German surrender in May 1943. Later, General de Gaulle's Free French movement established its headquarters in Algiers, which became for a time the capital of all French territories at war with Germany. These events disturbed the foundations of French rule in North Africa.

In the protectorate of Tunisia, a new Bey (Moncif) came to the throne in 1942 and began to demand a legislative council and changes in the administrative system. Six months of German occupation (November 1942–May 1943) broke the continuity of French control, and allowed the Bey to appoint his own government. In 1943, the French returned, deposed Moncif Bey and established direct rule, contrary to the terms of the protectorate and to their own previous practice. Also during the war, Habib Bourgiba, the founder and leader of the Neo-Destour nationalist party was released from prison in France by the Germans and returned to Tunisia. He refused to collaborate with the Germans, and appealed for Franco-Tunisian co-operation, but the French continued to ban the Destour party, and in March 1945 Bourgiba left Tunisia for Egypt, where he lived in exile for four years. The war thus undermined French prestige, destroyed the former smooth running of the protectorate, and gave a new impulse to Tunisian nationalism.

In Morocco, which was also a protectorate, the American landings in November 1942 gave the Sultan, Sidi Mohammed Ben Yusef, the opportunity to evade French control for a period. American troops were stationed prominently in parts of the country, and American military missions remained until 1944. In January 1943 President Roosevelt himself visited Morocco to attend the Casablanca Conference with Churchill. He went out of his way to meet the Sultan, and held out hopes of American help in freeing Morocco from the French protectorate. In December 1943 the Istiqlal nationalist party was founded, demanding independence from France and invoking the Atlantic Charter in support of its claims. The Sultan was prepared to work with Istiqlal, forming a powerful alliance. In January 1944 the French tried to suppress the nationalist movement and arrest its leaders, only to find that it was too strong for them, and they had to fall back on concessions. The French hold on the country had been badly shaken.

Algeria was a very different case from Tunisia and Morocco, being in French law a part of France itself, and including about a million

Europeans in a population of about 7 000 000 in 1940. The French administration of the country continued to work effectively until the end of 1942, when it was shaken by the Anglo-American landings in November, by the ensuing campaign in Tunisia, and later by a famine in the winter of 1944–45. By the end of the war, two important shifts of opinion had taken place. First, a small number of politically active Algerians who had earlier advocated assimilation with France and the adoption of French values, turned instead to nationalism or to Islam, or both together. Second, the French population in Algeria had seen their links with France cut, and learned that they could manage alone. Indeed, Algeria became the base for the liberation of southern France in 1944, which conferred a new status upon the country.

It was the Algerian nationalist movement which first made its mark. On 8 May 1945, the day which marked the end of the war in Europe, there were demonstrations and armed insurrection against the French at Setif, in the Constantine district. The rising was crushed with extreme severity, and with Algerian casualties which the French put at 6000, and the Algerians at 45 000. There were no further disturbances for another nine years, but what was to become the Algerian war of independence had begun.

◆ The Middle East

Before the war, the whole of the Middle East was under European control or influence. Syria and the Lebanon were French mandates under the League of Nations, and were treated effectively as French colonies. Palestine was a British mandate, in the throes of a three-cornered struggle between Arabs, Jews and the British. The British tried to govern the territory under the ambiguous terms of the Balfour Declaration of 1917, which undertook to create a 'national home' for the Jewish people in Palestine, without prejudice to the civil and religious rights of the other inhabitants. This was an impossible task. When the British leaned towards the Zionists in matters of immigration and land rights, they faced Arab hostility; when they leaned towards the Arabs, they met Zionist opposition. Just before the war, in 1939, the British had set out a plan proposing to bring the territory to independence in ten years, and restricting Jewish immigration in such a way as to ensure that there would be an Arab majority in Palestine at the end of that time. This proved enough to appease Arab opinion during the war, at the cost of offending the Zionists. Transjordan was an independent state, but under British guidance in foreign relations, and with its army (the Arab Legion) under a British commander. Egypt was independent, but bound by a treaty of 1936 to accept British garrisons and bases in the Suez Canal Zone and Alexandria. Iraq was in a similar position – independent, but under British influence and accepting British bases. Saudi Arabia was independent, but acknowledged the general British influence in the area.

Aden was a British base at the mouth of the Red Sea. Iran, between the Middle East and India, was partially under British influence, with oilfields owned by the Anglo-Iranian Oil Company.

The Second World War transformed this picture. French authority in Syria and Lebanon was first shaken by the defeat of 1940 at the hands of Germany, and later undermined by a long and bitter dispute between de Gaulle and the British, in which the British supported nationalist movements against the French. French forces finally left the two countries in 1947. Superficially, the British fared better than the French. The British campaigns against the Axis in Egypt and Libya were finally victorious, and a rising against British authority in Iraq in 1941 was easily dealt with. But in fact British prestige was badly shaken during the war. In mid-1942 Rommel's Afrika Korps came within 70 miles of the Nile, causing panic among the British in Cairo. The whole area was unsettled by constant warfare, by the movement of vast armies, and by the propaganda war between the two sides. It proved impossible for the British to encourage nationalist movements against the French in Syria and Lebanon without stimulating similar aspirations in Egypt and Iraq, to their own detriment.

The British actually encouraged a move towards unity among the Arab states, hoping to use it for their own purposes. The Egyptian government acted as hosts to two conferences (at Alexandria in 1944 and Cairo in 1945), which agreed to set up the Arab League, comprising seven members: Egypt, Iraq, Lebanon, Saudi Arabia, Syria, Transjordan, and Yemen. A representative of the Palestinian Arabs also attended the conferences. The members of the League agreed to act together in matters of common concern (for example, Palestine and North Africa), and in the United Nations Organization which was then being formed.

The fact that Palestine was one of the matters of prime concern for the Arab League pointed to the most difficult problem in the Middle East: the conflict between Zionists and Arabs in the mandated territory of Palestine. In 1939, the British had set out in a White Paper a plan by which Palestine was to achieve independence in ten years. During that period, Jewish immigration was to be limited to 15 000 per year for the first five years, and then to be subject to Arab agreement, which would almost certainly ensure that there was an Arab majority in the territory when it became independent. This succeeded in its primary purpose of conciliating Arab opinion sufficiently to allow Britain to fight the war with a minimum of Arab opposition. It placed the Jewish Agency (the principal Zionist organization) in a cruel dilemma. They could not afford to see a Nazi German victory in the war; but equally they could not allow the policy of the White Paper to run its course successfully and prevent the emergence of a Jewish state in Palestine. Official Zionist policy therefore became to fight the war as if there were no White Paper, and to fight the White Paper as if there were no war – a remarkable attempt to face both ways which in fact achieved a surprising degree of success. The Zionists were able to take part in the war in co-operation with the British, who used the Haganah (the Zionist armed force) to raise special units in Palestine and in 1944 formed a Jewish Brigade, which served in the Italian campaign, providing valuable experience of modern warfare for its members. The Zionists thus fought the war and improved their own military position at the same time. But meanwhile British policy under the White Paper of 1939 remained unchanged. Restrictions on Jewish immigration into Palestine were enforced as strictly as possible, and the Royal Navy turned back shiploads of Jewish refugees. This became an extraordinarily difficult line to hold as news of the Nazi camps and the annihilation of the European Jews became widely known. Pressure to admit more Jewish immigrants to Palestine increased steadily as the war in Europe drew to an end. It was now the British who faced a virtually impossible dilemma. They had to conciliate Arab opinion, both to conduct the war and to sustain their position in the Middle East when the war was over. To that end, they had to maintain restrictions on Jewish immigration into Palestine. But to restrict immigration became practically difficult and morally intolerable as the fate of the European Jews became obvious. Before the war the British had found the problem of Palestine difficult. By the end of the war it had become impossible. Within two years Britain had to leave Palestine to others, setting the stage for one of the most persistent conflicts of the post-war world.

The Middle East was an important source of oil, the crucial source of energy for all wartime activities. Middle East oil was particularly valuable to the British because they could pay for it in sterling, not dollars. It also became of increasing interest to the Americans, who in 1943 were suffering the first tremors of fear that they might not have enough domestically produced oil. In that year the American government sent a mission to assess the oil potential of Saudi Arabia and other countries in the Persian Gulf area; and one of its members, returning in 1944, told State Department officials that 'The oil in this region is the greatest single prize in all history.' It sounded theatrical, but it proved to be true, and American policy changed accordingly. As early as February 1944 President Roosevelt showed the British Ambassador in Washington a sketch-map of the Middle East, on which the Iranian oilfields were shown as British, those in Iraq and Kuwait were shared between Britain and the USA, and those in Saudi Arabia were American.[18] It was the shape of things to come, and foreshadowed a new American involvement in the Middle East.

Iran was a major source of oil. During the war it also became an important Anglo-American supply route to the Soviet Union. In August 1941, shortly after the German attack on the USSR, Soviet and British forces invaded Iran, with the Soviets occupying the three northern provinces and the British the centre and south of the country. In September the reigning Shah, who had sought to remain neutral and refused passage for British supplies to the Soviet Union, abdicated in favour of his son, the 23-year old Mohammed Reza Pahlavi, whose long and chequered reign was to last until 1979. The Soviet and British occupation continued until the end of the war; by which time the Americans too had some 30 000 troops in the country, mostly involved in transporting supplies to the Soviet Union. In these circumstances, Iranian nationalists remained passive but resentful.

Across North Africa and the Middle East a broadly similar pattern of events emerged. The crushing defeat of France in 1940 shook French authority throughout these areas. Britain, though ultimately victorious, was gravely weakened. The British had been forced into concessions to Arab national-ism; faced an insoluble problem in Palestine; and confronted a new incur-sion of American influence in the Middle East. Everywhere, nationalist movements (nearly all Arab, but in one crucial case Zionist) had gained new strength and exploited wartime opportunities. By 1945 the old order had changed in ways which proved irreversible.

◆ East and South-East Asia

In Asia changes were already under way, and European power under attack, before the Second World War. In China in the 1920s there was a strong nationalist movement, challenging the unequal treaties imposed on the country by the western powers during the nineteenth century. In India, Gandhi and the Congress Party mounted serious opposition to British rule. In French Indo-China and the Dutch East Indies nationalist movements were developing, though so far the position of the colonial powers did not appear seriously threatened.

The Europeans were also under threat from other great powers. Japan had long ago become an Asian power capable of beating the Europeans at their own games of war and commerce; and as early as 1904–05, Japanese victory in war against Russia had been a landmark in relations between Asians and Europeans. The Soviet Union too, with its ideological appeal and its support for anti-imperialist forces of all kinds, was a looming threat to the European colonial powers. The United States hovered uneasily between being an imperial power, with a colony in the Philippines and bases across the Pacific Ocean, and its other role as an anti-imperialist nation and the friend of Asian independence movements.

To these vast areas already in transition, the Second World War brought drastic transformation. In a few months at the end of 1941 and the begin-ning of 1942 the Japanese simply swept aside the British and Dutch forces in Malaya, Singapore, Burma and the East Indies. They drove the Americans out of the Philippines. They had already occupied French Indo-China without even needing to fight. From these defeats the colonial powers could not recover. For many years their position in Asia had relied as much on prestige as on military strength. By 1942 their prestige was shattered, even though their military strength recovered to some degree by 1945.

The Japanese slogan was 'Asia for the Asians', and they encouraged nationalist movements in the territories which they occupied. In Burma, Ba Maw and Aung San, in co-operation with the Japanese, declared independence on 1 August 1943. The Philippines proclaimed independence in October 1943, and declared war on the United States in September 1944. In Indonesia (the former Netherlands East Indies), the nationalist leader Sukarno claimed that Japan's war was also Indonesia's; though independence was not formally proclaimed until 17 August 1945, when the war was over. (Sukarno, who at that moment lost his nerve, was actually compelled to read out the declaration with a pistol held at his head by more ardent nationalists – a strange beginning to what proved to be a long career as ruler of an independent Indonesia.) The Japanese made a gesture towards Indian independence by supporting Subhas Chandra Bose, an opponent of the British, and recruiting an Indian National Army from prisoners of war. This force never numbered more than about 20 000, a tiny number in comparison with the 2 500 000 volunteers in the Indian· Army which fought alongside the British; but it had some symbolic significance.

Japanese policy in the countries which they occupied was ambivalent. Their slogan of 'Asia for the Asians' was sincere; but their main purpose was to create a New Order in East Asia which would be under their own control and serve their own interests. This ambivalence made little difference to the nationalist movements in the long run. There were nationalists who resented merely exchanging one master for another; but in general there was none of the stigma attached to collaboration with the Japanese that clung so damagingly to the 'Quislings' in Europe. The independence movements gained what they could from the Japanese victories, and then seized further advantages from the Japanese defeats. Indeed, in some ways the Japanese themselves, though militarily defeated, achieved what they promised in East Asia. 'Asia for the Asians' eventually prevailed.

The consequences of these events varied widely. The British left India in 1947, but Hong Kong remained a British colony until 1997. The Dutch fought for four years to regain control of the East Indies, and the French for ten in Indo-China, before each gave up. But sooner or later the effects of the Second World War inexorably worked themselves out. The European empires in East and South-East Asia vanished swiftly in some cases and faded away slowly in others; but either way they disappeared.

The war also transformed the structure of power in East Asia and the Pacific. China, though ruined by an eight-year conflict with the Japanese and an apparently endless civil war between the Kuomintang government and the Communists, showed remarkable resilience, and was more of a power to be reckoned with after the war than before. The Soviet Union reasserted itself as a power in East Asia, occupying Manchuria and North Korea, and recovering territories lost in the Russo-Japanese War of 1904–05. Above all, the United States ended the war as the predominant maritime power in the whole of the Pacific, and the conqueror and occupier of Japan. It took some time for the consequences of this to sink into American minds and to emerge in American policy; but ultimately the change was decisive and profound.

◆ Long-term consequences of the war

In the long run, three consequences of the Second World War were to dominate the international relations of the next half-century. First, the United States and the Soviet Union emerged as two superpowers, meeting face to face across the ruins of Europe and Japan. How that meeting would work out was not yet decided in 1945, but in time it was to develop into the Cold War. Second, the European overseas empires, in Africa, the Middle East and Asia were so severely shaken that they were largely to disappear in the course of the next twenty years. The replacement of those empires, often through prolonged wars of succession, was to be another dominant theme of the post-war world. Third, the two atomic bombs dropped on Hiroshima and Nagasaki in August 1945, which brought the Second World War to an end, brought a completely new element into the conduct of international affairs.

All in all, the Second World War produced a radical change in the whole working of international affairs. Between the two World Wars, in the 1920s and 1930s, Europe had largely maintained its predominance, though with the United States and Japan growing in strength and influence. After 1945, a new global order emerged, subject to worldwide influences. The United States and Soviet Union dominated the world as superpowers. The United Nations was to become a genuine world organization, developing in ways which its founders did not foresee. How was the international order to be reshaped to take account of these changes?

◆ Notes to Chapter 1

1. J. A. S. Grenville, *History of the World in the Twentieth Century* (London, revised edn, 1998), p. 284. Grenville comments that historians cannot be sure of the figure *to the nearest million*. See also the article by Martin Gilbert on 'The Final Solution' in I. C. B. Dear and M. R. D. Foot, eds, *The Oxford Companion to the Second World War* (Oxford, 1995), pp. 364–71.

2. Figures in *ibid.*, p. 1060.
3. See below, pp. 29–31, on the effects of these events on the European empires.
4. Dear and Foot, *Second World War*, p. 1060.
5. *Ibid.*, pp. 603–4, 836–7.
6. Ernest R. May, *'Lessons' of the Past: The Use and Misuse of History in American Foreign Policy* (Oxford, 1973), pp.3–4, where the 'chat' is quoted and its preparation described.
7. Henry Kissinger, *Diplomacy* (London, paperback edn, 1995), p. 402.
8. Milovan Djilas, *Conversations with Stalin* (London, Pelican edn, 1969), p. 90.
9. Martin Gilbert, *Road to Victory: Winston S. Churchill, 1941–1945* (London, 1986), p. 254.
10. Timothy Garton Ash, 'A Lesson to Learn from Yalta', *The Times* (London), 11 February 1995.
11. For the setting up of the United Nations Organization, see below, pp. 40–44.
12. US Department of State, *Foreign Relations of the United States: The Conferences at Malta and Yalta, 1945* (Washington, 1955), pp. 971–5.
13. V. Molotov, *Molotov Remembers: Inside Kremlin Politics. Conversations with Felix Chuev*, ed. Albert Resis (Chicago, 1993), p. 51.
14. *Conferences at Malta and Yalta*, p. 984.
15. John Colville, *The Fringes of Power: Downing Street Diaries, 1939–1955* (London, 1985), p. 563, diary entry for 23 February 1945.
16. Figures in Dear and Foot, *Second World War*, p. 290.
17. Henry Ashby Turner, Jr, *Germany from Partition to Unification* (New Haven, 1992), p. 6.
18. Daniel Yergin, *The Prize: The Epic Quest for Oil, Money and Power* (London, 1991), pp. 393, 395.

CHAPTER 2

THE BEGINNINGS OF THE POST-WAR WORLD

Victors and vanquished – The post-war state system – The United Nations – Other international organizations – Economic organization

The most obvious division in the world in 1945 was not between East and West, or capitalism and communism, or between imperialists and the colonial peoples, but simply between victors and vanquished. For a short time, the victors had the opportunity to remake the world. It was no easy task. Much of the world was littered with the ruins of war. Many countries untouched physically by the conflict were still marked by it. Moreover, history does not come to an end, even at a turning-point like that of 1945, and all kinds of issues going back for years and even centuries were bound to reappear. But for a while the board of world affairs was as clear as it was ever likely to be. It was a time of hope and opportunity, as well as ruin and despair. Who were the victors, and what did they try to do with their victory?

◆ The victors

The greatest victor of the Second World War was the United States of America. The USA had been geographically removed from the theatres of war. Japanese bombs fell on Hawaii, and German U-boats played havoc for a time off the east coast, but the vast landmass of mainland America was unscathed. American casualties in the war amounted to 274 000 dead – little more than one-fifth of 1 per cent of the population. The country's economic strength was enormous. Its gold reserves stood at $220 billion, or approximately two-thirds of the world total. The country as a whole had grown wealthier during the war, and the average standard of living of individual Americans was higher than that of any other people. The war effort had mobilized this strength into formidable military power – some

14 800 000 men and women in the armed forces at the end of 1944; a vast fleet, with nearly 68 000 vessels of all types in mid-1945; and an immense air force, including some 3000 heavy bombers. Moreover, the United States was the only country to have manufactured and used atomic bombs.[1]

For Americans, this was a new situation, and their attitudes towards it varied widely. The generation of American leaders hardened in the war was determined that the United States should now act as a world power, and not withdraw into the isolation and neutrality which had been attempted in the 1920s and 1930s. They expected to bring their troops home from Europe, but American bases in the Atlantic and Pacific would be maintained. The USA would take a leading part in the new world organization, the United Nations. American economic interests would be pursued, to ensure that the prosperity attained in wartime was not lost in peace. All this was stern and hardheaded. Yet at the same time the idealism which was so deeply rooted in the American mind was still strong. In 1961, Henry Kissinger (later to become Secretary of State) asked Truman which foreign policy decision he would most wish to be remembered for. Truman's reply was: 'We completely defeated our enemies [in the Second World War] and made them surrender. And then we helped them to recover, to become democratic, and to rejoin the community of nations. Only America could have done that.' This combination of pride in American strength and faith in American virtue was characteristic not only of Truman, but of his fellow-countrymen.[2] There was another strand in American thought and sentiment. Isolationism, though rejected by most American leaders, was by no means dead in the country as a whole. It was very much alive, especially in the Middle West; it was also somewhat confused in its nature, because there were some who wished to be free from entanglements in Europe but were keenly interested in the Pacific and China. In sum, the United States was broadly conscious that it had a new world role, but was by no means sure what it was to be.

The second power among the victors was the Soviet Union. At the end of 1944 the strength of the Soviet armed forces stood at 11 200 000. The Red Army was equipped with some 11 000 tanks and self-propelled guns; the air force totalled 14 500 combat aircraft. These immense forces had played by far the largest part in the defeat of Germany. Soviet power and prestige stood at a pinnacle. But the cost had been enormous – authoritative figures published in 1990 gave a total of 8 668 000 military dead. Estimates for military and civilian casualties together reach a total of some 26 million dead.[3] The comparison with the mere 274 000 fatalities suffered by the United States is astounding – the American losses were barely one-hundredth of the Soviet. To the loss of life was added the immense destruction wrought during the campaigns on the eastern front. The Soviet Union thus displayed the extraordinary spectacle of immense military strength combined with enormous human and material losses.

The USSR was geographically the heir of the old Russian Empire, stretching all the way from eastern Europe to eastern Asia. Its population was varied in character, multi-national and at different stages of economic development. At its head, Stalin saw himself as the successor of the Tsars in his foreign policy – for example, he set out deliberately to recover territory lost in the Russo-Japanese war of 1904–05 and at the end of the Great War, and in 1945 he was looking for that long-standing aim of Russian policy, a base on the straits between the Black Sea and the Mediterranean. But he was also the leader of the world's first socialist state, the base camp for world revolution. His concerns were thus ideological as well as territorial. As two modern Russian historians sum the matter up, he pursued 'the promise of Communist revolutionary universalism combined with the necessities of survival for the Soviet Union, the first and unique "Socialist" empire.'[4] The USSR thus combined great military power with the aspirations and attractions of a socialist ideal.

In 1945, however, Stalin was primarily concerned with the security of the state. He imposed the severest possible control over Soviet territories recovered from the Germans. Prisoners of war released from German captivity were often sent straight to the Gulag (the Soviet slave labour camps) for fear that they had somehow been contaminated by foreign contacts. But this was usually hidden from the outside world, where Stalin appeared as the benevolent patriarch, the hero who had won the war and saved his country, and a world statesman of the first rank.

At the end of the Second World War, there was no certainty that the United States and the Soviet Union would swiftly become enemies. It appears that Stalin regarded Truman as inexperienced (which he was) and weak (which he was not), and thought that he would not last long. There was a brush between Truman and Molotov on 23 April 1945, when the President lectured the Soviet Foreign Minister about keeping agreements. This episode was later seized on by some writers as the beginning of the Cold War, but at the time Molotov and Stalin agreed to keep quiet about it, and Molotov merely recalled many years afterwards that Truman had been 'a bit half-witted'.[5]

Truman, for his part, was not enamoured of the Soviet Union. When Germany attacked the USSR in 1941, he had candidly (if rashly) remarked that the two sides should be encouraged to kill one another off as far as possible – though he did not want to see Hitler win under any circumstances. But when he became President he continued to follow Roosevelt's line of cultivating good relations with Stalin. He declined to visit Britain on the way to the Potsdam Conference, so as not to appear to be 'ganging up' against Stalin He sent Harry Hopkins (Roosevelt's old confidant) to visit Stalin at the beginning of June 1945, with reassuring messages. When Stalin nominated a new Polish government, the United States recognized it quickly (on 5 July 1945), though there had been no free elections and none were in the offing. There were difficulties between the two great powers, but that is the story of all alliances at the end of a war.

Next among the victors stood Great Britain. The British had fought the war from start to finish (which was more than the Soviet Union or the USA had done); they had stood alone against Hitler in 1940, and had not been defeated or occupied; and in 1945 they were still one of the Big Three in world politics. Their casualties (at 350 000 dead, including civilians) had not been heavy when compared with those of 1914–18, or with those of many other belligerents.[6] Yet the nation was weary and exhausted after six years of war, and its economy was at a low ebb. Industrial production had been concentrated on the war effort, and reserves of gold and foreign currency had been run down, so that Britain had to depend on loans to pay for its imports. When American Lend-Lease aid finished with the end of the war, Britain had to ask for loans; the USA lent $3 750 million, and Canada $1.25 million. At that stage, the British expected to come through their economic difficulties and maintain their role as a world power, for which their best chance appeared to lie in the Commonwealth and Empire, and in their predominant position in the Middle East.

France too was among the victors – an occupying power in Germany and Austria, and formally acknowledged as a great power in the new United Nations Organization. This was to a large degree misleading. France was still suffering from the effects of defeat in 1940. Wartime casualties had been heavy, with approximately 600 000 dead (including 360 000 civilians).[7] The French economy was dislocated; food was scarce in the winter of 1944–45; and there were virtually no reserves of gold or foreign currency to pay for imports. France, therefore, like Britain, had to ask for American help, receiving dollar loans in 1946. Despite these difficulties, General de Gaulle, the first Premier of post-war France, was determined that his country should regain an important international position. His successors, though less formidable in personality, remained committed to that aim.

During the war, President Roosevelt liked to talk about the 'Four Policemen' who would keep the peace in the post-war world. The fourth power he had in mind, with the USA, the USSR and Britain, was China. In the event China was in no position to play such a role. A large part of the country had been occupied by the Japanese. Wartime casualties had been heavy – perhaps 1 300 000 dead. The civil war between Chiang Kai-Shek's government and the communists under Mao Zedong had never entirely ceased, even when both were fighting the Japanese, and in the course of the war the communists had increased considerably in strength. The whole country was in a state of disorganization and economic disruption. China was treated by courtesy as a great power, and granted a permanent seat on the Security Council of the United Nations, but in practice was too weak and divided to play an active part in world affairs until its own problems had been resolved.

As the Second World War came to an end, the principal victors met in conference at Potsdam (17 July–2 August 1945). Stalin, Truman, and Churchill (replaced during the conference by Attlee, when the Labour Party won the British general election) grappled with a massive agenda, much of which they dealt with by postponement rather than action. One issue which they could not postpone was that of agreeing on terms for a Japanese surrender. At the time, the United States and Britain were at war with Japan, but the Soviet Union was not, and the Japanese were trying to invoke Soviet mediation to bring hostilities to an end. The three powers agreed on the Potsdam Declaration of 26 July 1945, which called on Japan to declare unconditional surrender. The Declaration also repeated terms laid down in 1943, that Japan must give up all territories acquired since 1914. War criminals were to be brought to justice, and Japanese government was to be democratized, with security for freedom of speech and fundamental human rights. More to the point in military terms, President Truman told Stalin during the conference (14 July) that the United States had developed a weapon of 'unusual destructive force' – meaning the atomic bomb. Stalin was well aware of this from his own sources, notably Klaus Fuchs in the British team of atomic scientists; but he gave no sign, and merely replied 'I hope you will use it on the Japanese.'[8]

The conference spent much time on Germany, to which we will turn in a moment, and on Poland. On the question of Poland's western frontier, which had been left over at Yalta, the Big Three agreed to treat the line of the rivers Oder and Western Neisse as the administrative boundary between Poland and Germany. This led in practice to the Poles taking over all territory up to that line, but left the question of *de jure* sovereignty to be settled at a future peace conference. On the question of the make-up of a Polish government, there was no agreement in principle between the Soviet Union on the one hand and the Americans and British on the other, but in fact the Soviet-controlled government first set up at Lublin became firmly established.

The three powers agreed to set up a Council of Foreign Ministers, of which France was to be a member, to deal with the defeated European countries (Germany, Italy, Bulgaria, Hungary, Romania and Finland), and to prepare peace treaties. This enabled all kinds of contentious issues to be deferred, and ensured that the conference reached a reasonably successful conclusion. The code-name for the conference was TERMINAL, and if not exactly a happy ending for the wartime alliance, it was at least a tolerable one. Yet at the same time there was a sense of unease, at any rate among the western delegates. When Truman left Potsdam, he remarked with feeling that 'he never wanted to live in Europe, and never wanted to go back.'[9]

◆ The vanquished

The principal vanquished powers were defeated, even crushed, to an extent unprecedented in modern times. 'Unconditional surrender' was the doctrine proclaimed by Roosevelt at Casablanca in 1943, and against Germany it was rigorously imposed. The German armed forces were forced to capitulate. Allied armies occupied the whole country. No German government remained. The only effective currency was cigarettes. A modern state had simply ceased to exist.

Germany had temporarily disappeared, but the German Question remained, in various forms. Was Germany to be united or divided? Where were its frontiers to lie? What sort of political system and social organization should be imposed upon it? What scale of reparations should be exacted from Germany, and how were they to be paid? These questions were only partially answered at the Potsdam Conference. The powers agreed that Germany should be administered as a whole, by an Allied Control Council meeting in Berlin, and also be treated as an economic whole. However, each occupying power (USSR, USA, Britain and France) was to carry out the supposedly joint policies in its own occupation zone, which was bound to leave scope for interpretation and differences of practice. Acceptance of the Oder–Neisse line as the Polish administrative border provided a practical, though not a legal, answer to the main frontier question. There was agreement that Germany should be de-Nazified, though not on exactly how this was to be accomplished; and also that new political institutions were to be introduced slowly, starting with the municipalities and local government.

The situation of Japan was equally grave. The state was not utterly dissolved as Germany was, in that the Emperor remained, forming a symbol of continuity with the past. Moreover, some sections within the Japanese government had begun to think the unthinkable even before the war ended, and make preparations for defeat. Even so, Japan was in a calamitous condition. Casualties had been severe – somewhere between 2 350 000 and 2 700 000 killed, including 350 000–393 000 civilians (about 210 000 of them by the two atomic bombs at Hiroshima and Nagasaki).[10] Armies of about 3 000 000 men were scattered over most of the former theatres of war, and were shipped back to islands which were already short of food. The Americans occupied the Japanese mainland, but no one knew how they would use their new authority.

One distinctive feature of the treatment of Germany and Japan at the end of the Second World War was the holding of trials for war crimes. This was not completely new, because after the First World War there had been a low-key trial of a dozen Germans, before a German court. But the trials in 1945 and 1946 were a very different matter. On 8 August 1945 the United

States, the Soviet Union, Britain and France agreed to set up an International Military Tribunal for the trial of the major German war criminals. The indictment, published on 6 October 1945, was drawn up under four main headings: (1) the formulation of a common plan or conspiracy to commit crimes; (2) crimes against peace: the planning, preparation, initiation and waging of wars of aggression; (3) war crimes: violations of the laws and customs of war, including the murder and deportation of civilians, and the wanton destructions of towns or villages; (4) crimes against humanity: the extermination, enslavement or deportation of civilian populations, and persecution on political, racial or religious grounds, whether or not such persecution was in violation of the domestic law of the country where it had taken place. There were difficulties in all these headings. It was not easy to establish what constituted a conspiracy. Most countries made plans for war involving attacks on others – it is the job of military staffs to prepare for war. The Allied bombing offensive had destroyed a number of cities. The Soviet Union (though not on trial) was certainly guilty of exterminating and deporting peoples on a large scale. The trial was held at Nuremberg, in Germany, from October 1945 to October 1946. Of the 22 accused (one of them, Bormann, in his absence), 3 were acquitted, 7 were sentenced to imprisonment for various terms (Hess and Raeder for life), and 12 were sentenced to death. Ten were hanged; Goering committed suicide; Bormann was never apprehended.[11]

The war crimes trial held in Tokyo from May 1946 to November 1948 proved more difficult and controversial. 28 leading Japanese were charged with war crimes, crimes against peace, and crimes against humanity. The Emperor of Japan, Hirohito, was exempted from trial, on the express instructions of General MacArthur, the Allied Supreme Commander and virtual ruler of Japan. The judges failed to achieve unanimity in their verdicts – those from France and the Netherlands recorded dissenting judgements on certain points, while the Indian judge found all the defendants not guilty. As a result of these problems, and also because the sessions went on so long while the world changed around them, the Tokyo war crimes trials made less impact than those held at Nuremberg.

The effect upon the public mind of these trials, and especially that at Nuremberg, had a lasting effect on attitudes towards international affairs in the post-war years. The emphasis on crimes against humanity led to a new sensitivity towards human rights, and an increased concern with events inside other countries, as distinct from the long-standing tradition of minding one's own business. This was also influenced by the role of publicity in international affairs. The reporting, particularly by photographs and newsreel film, of the opening of the German concentration camps in 1945, left a lasting mark on the public mind. The combination of publicity and human rights came to form a new element in world affairs, as we shall see shortly when we turn to the United Nations Organization.

◆ The post-war state system and international organizations

For two centuries or more up to the end of the First World War, European states had dominated world politics, evolving a system of conducting international affairs by means of the balance of power and a series of great treaties which had established a European and world order: Utrecht (1713), Vienna (1815), Versailles (1919).

In 1919 this era was drawing to an end, with the United States playing a new and powerful role at the Paris Peace Conference. In 1945 it had come to an end. There were no longer five or six European great powers, more or less similar in weight and authority, able to balance one another and to control the continent and the outside world. Instead, two superpowers dominated the scene. One, the USA, was much stronger than the other, the USSR; but both stood head and shoulders above the rest. Neither was fully European. The United States had a population which was largely of European extraction, but was far removed from the old continent both geographically and in outlook. The Soviet Union was the successor of one of the old European states, Russia; but it had always been doubtful how far Russia was European, either geographically or in spirit. The indisputably European powers – Britain, France, Germany, Italy – were in decline or eclipse.

The old European state system could no longer regulate its own continent, still less the rest of the world. What was to replace it? During the Second World War, President Roosevelt threw all his energies and authority into creating a new world organization to succeed the old League of Nations, and his policy prevailed. On 1 January 1942, in Washington, Roosevelt, Churchill and the Ambassadors of the Soviet Union and China signed the United Nations Declaration, pledging its signatories to employ all their resources to secure total victory, and not to make a separate peace. This document also created the basis for a new world organization, and gave it a name. Roosevelt introduced the term 'United Nations', instead of 'Associated Powers', and Churchill approved, with an apt quotation from Byron's 'Childe Harold': 'Here, where the sword United Nations drew . . .'[12] The plan was elaborated at a conference of Foreign Ministers (Soviet, American, British and Chinese) at Moscow in October 1943, and at the three-power summit conference at Teheran in November 1943. A conference at Dumbarton Oaks, in New Hampshire in September–October 1944 prepared the main outlines for the proposed United Nations Organization; and the Yalta Conference in February 1945 resolved crucial questions relating to membership and constitution of the new body.[13] The San Francisco conference (April–June 1945) produced the final draft of the United Nations Charter, signed on 26 June by the representatives of 51 states. The fact that this conference began while the war was still in progress in both Europe and the Pacific demonstrated the urgency with which the task was regarded. At the end of the First World War the creation of the League of Nations had been part of the peace settlement; but in 1945 the United Nations Organization was set up before the war was over. If its founders had waited for the peace settlement, the delay would have been infinite and the results incalculable.

The purposes of the United Nations Organization were threefold. The first was to prevent war by means of collective security – that fundamental aim which the League had failed to achieve. If conflicts could not be prevented, the UN would have the lesser but still useful task of containing or resolving them. Second, the Organization was to promote peace by fostering international co-operation in economic and social affairs, in culture and thought. This arose from the widespread belief that the Second World War had arisen partly from economic causes, and partly from perverted ideas which had taken root in the minds of men. Third, under Article 56 of the Charter, the member states of the UN were to promote respect for human rights and universal freedoms for all – again looking back to the 1930s, in the belief that the internal tyranny of Nazi Germany had given rise to its aggressive foreign policy.

To achieve these purposes, the United Nations comprised three main bodies: the General Assembly, the Security Council and the Secretariat. The General Assembly consisted of representatives of all the member states, on a footing of equality – one country, one vote, to meet annually. The Security Council was made up of five permanent members (the United States, the Soviet Union, the United Kingdom, France and China) and six temporary members, elected for two-year terms by a two-thirds majority in the General Assembly. (Later, in 1966, the number of temporary members was increased to ten.) The Security Council was to remain in permanent session. On all substantive matters, the permanent members could exercise a veto – that is, a single negative vote by a permanent member was sufficient to reject a resolution. The Secretariat was the administrative body of the UN, headed by a Secretary-General, appointed by the General Assembly for a five-year term.

◆ The main structures of the United Nations

The Charter of the United Nations included three articles which reserved the rights of individual member states in certain important respects. Article 2(7) laid down that the UN was not authorized to intervene in 'matters which are essentially within the sovereign jurisdiction of any state'. This was difficult to reconcile with Article 56, on promoting respect for human rights; and impeded the discussion of wars or violence *within* states, unless

THE UNITED NATIONS

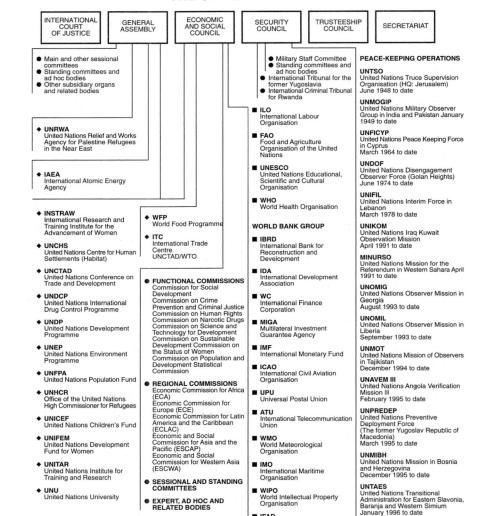

INTERNATIONAL COURT OF JUSTICE	GENERAL ASSEMBLY	ECONOMIC AND SOCIAL COUNCIL	SECURITY COUNCIL	TRUSTEESHIP COUNCIL	SECRETARIAT

● Main and other sessional committees
● Standing committees and ad hoc bodies
● Other subsidiary organs and related bodies

◆ **UNRWA**
United Nations Relief and Works Agency for Palestine Refugees in the Near East

◆ **IAEA**
International Atomic Energy Agency

◆ **INSTRAW**
International Research and Training Institute for the Advancement of Women

◆ **UNCHS**
United Nations Centre for Human Settlements (Habitat)

◆ **UNCTAD**
United Nations Conference on Trade and Development

◆ **UNDCP**
United Nations International Drug Control Programme

◆ **UNDP**
United Nations Development Programme

◆ **UNEP**
United Nations Environment Programme

◆ **UNFPA**
United Nations Population Fund

◆ **UNHCR**
Office of the United Nations High Commissioner for Refugees

◆ **UNICEF**
United Nations Children's Fund

◆ **UNIFEM**
United Nations Development Fund for Women

◆ **UNITAR**
United Nations Institute for Training and Research

◆ **UNU**
United Nations University

◆ **WFP**
World Food Programme

◆ **ITC**
International Trade Centre
UNCTAD/WTO

● **FUNCTIONAL COMMISSIONS**
Commission for Social Development
Commission on Crime Prevention and Criminal Justice
Commission on Human Rights
Commission on Narcotic Drugs
Commission on Science and Technology for Development
Commission on Sustainable Development Commission on the Status of Women
Commission on Population and Development Statistical Commission

● **REGIONAL COMMISSIONS**
Economic Commission for Africa (ECA)
Economic Commission for Europe (ECE)
Economic Commission for Latin America and the Caribbean (ECLAC)
Economic and Social Commission for Asia and the Pacific (ESCAP)
Economic and Social Commission for Western Asia (ESCWA)

● **SESSIONAL AND STANDING COMMITTEES**

● **EXPERT, AD HOC AND RELATED BODIES**

● Military Staff Committee
● Standing committees and ad hoc bodies
● International Tribunal for the former Yugoslavia
● International Criminal Tribunal for Rwanda

■ **ILO**
International Labour Organisation

■ **FAO**
Food and Agriculture Organisation of the United Nations

■ **UNESCO**
United Nations Educational, Scientific and Cultural Organisation

■ **WHO**
World Health Organisation

WORLD BANK GROUP

■ **IBRD**
International Bank for Reconstruction and Development

■ **IDA**
International Development Association

■ **WC**
International Finance Corporation

■ **MIGA**
Multilateral Investment Guarantee Agency

■ **IMF**
International Monetary Fund

■ **ICAO**
International Civil Aviation Organisation

■ **UPU**
Universal Postal Union

■ **ATU**
International Telecommunication Union

■ **WMO**
World Meteorological Organisation

■ **IMO**
International Maritime Organisation

■ **WIPO**
World Intellectual Property Organisation

■ **IFAD**
International Fund for Agricultural Development

■ **UNIDO**
United Nations Industrial Development Organisation

* **WTO**
World Trade Organisation

PEACE-KEEPING OPERATIONS

UNTSO
United Nations Truce Supervision Organisation (HQ: Jerusalem)
June 1948 to date

UNMOGIP
United Nations Military Observer Group in India and Pakistan January 1949 to date

UNFICYP
United Nations Peace Keeping Force in Cyprus
March 1964 to date

UNDOF
United Nations Disengagement Observer Force (Golan Heights)
June 1974 to date

UNIFIL
United Nations Interim Force in Lebanon
March 1978 to date

UNIKOM
United Nations Iraq Kuwait Observation Mission
April 1991 to date

MINURSO
United Nations Mission for the Referendum in Western Sahara April 1991 to date

UNOMIG
United Nations Observer Mission in Georgia
August 1993 to date

UNOMIL
United Nations Observer Mission in Liberia
September 1993 to date

UNMOT
United Nations Mission of Observers in Tajikistan
December 1994 to date

UNAVEM III
United Nations Angola Verification Mission III
February 1995 to date

UNPREDEP
United Nations Preventive Deployment Force
(The former Yugoslav Republic of Macedonia)
March 1995 to date

UNMIBH
United Nations Mission in Bosnia and Herzegovina
December 1995 to date

UNTAES
United Nations Transitional Administration for Eastern Slavonia, Baranja and Western Simium
January 1996 to date

UNMOP
United Nations Mission of Observers in Previaka
January 1996 to date

UNSMIH
United Nations Support Mission in Haiti
July 1996 to date

◆ United Nations programmes and organs (representative list only)
■ Specialized agencies and other autonomous organisations within the system
● Other Commissions, committees and *ad hoc* and related bodies

* Co-operative arrangements between the UN and WTO are under discussion

Published by the United Nations Department of Public Information – DPI/1857 – October 1996 the situation clearly became 'international'. For example, in 1947 and after-wards India claimed that the conflict in Kashmir was an internal matter, on the ground that the province was part of India; but Pakistan argued that the question was an international one. Similarly, France claimed in the 1950s that the war in Algeria was an internal matter, because Algeria was part of France, but other governments argued that the war was one of national liberation, in which the UN could properly intervene. In later years, new states which had previously used the UN to help in their struggle for inde-pendence, took advantage of Article 2(7) to prevent intervention in what had now become their internal affairs. For example, the United Nations from time to time made general declarations denouncing racism and geno-cide, but took no action against the government of Idi Amin in Uganda (1971–79), which expelled Asians from the country and slaughtered thou-sands of people within it. On the other hand, South Africa's internal poli-cies under the *apartheid* regime were deemed to be a danger to peace and the proper concern of the United Nations, meriting the imposition of economic sanctions.

Article 51 of the UN Charter maintained the inherent right of individual or collective self-defence against armed attack; and Article 52 permitted the formation of regional arrangements for the maintenance of international peace and security. Between them, these provisions gave ample scope for the formation of alliances (the North Atlantic Treaty of 1949 is an obvious example) which sometimes proved more effective instruments of collective security than the generalized provisions of the UN Charter.

In subsequent years, the deficiencies and failures of the United Nations became sadly plain. The UN was intended to prevent war, but the half-century following 1945 was marked by almost incessant conflict in many parts of the world. The UN's cultural and economic agencies produced some spectacular failures: UNESCO (the United Nations Educational, Scientific and Cultural Organization) absorbed large funds for small results; the Food and Agriculture Organization proved unable either to predict famines or to cope with them when they occurred; neither made any signif-icant contribution to the peace of the world.[14]

Yet the United Nations survived, and achieved solid if unspectacular successes, largely by accepting the facts of international life. The power of veto exercised by the great powers in the Security Council was simply an acknowledgement that if one of these powers, and especially one of the two superpowers, was opposed to some policy or action, it would not work. Indeed, without the presence of the veto, Stalin would not have permitted the UN to come into existence at all; and the United States had no intention of allowing its vital interests to be endangered by a majority vote – though in 1945 they did not find it necessary to say so. The contradiction between the assertion of human rights on the one hand and the rights of states to control their own affairs on the other, was another necessary compromise, because states would never have accepted an organization with unlimited rights to intervene in their internal affairs.

In the event, the United Nations achieved more than mere survival, and took on a number of major roles in international affairs. First, the Security Council provided a centre for diplomatic activity, sometimes public and confrontational, but often secret and conciliatory. In some of the more glacial periods of the Cold War, the Security Council was almost the only place where American and Soviet representatives could meet regularly and discreetly. Second, the General Assembly became a forum for the expression of views on world affairs, not usually leading to any immediate or practical results, but gradually introducing new climates of opinion, for example on colonialism and international trade. Third, the United Nations undertook peace-keeping operations, the first of which, the UN Truce Supervision Organization, was set up as early as June 1948 to oversee the cease-fire in Palestine between Israel and its opponents. The second was the UN Military Observer Group in India and Pakistan, created in January 1949 to supervise a cease-fire between India and Pakistan in Kashmir. Both were still in existence fifty years later, bearing strange testimony to their success as well as their failure. Cease-fires, by definition, are not peace; but they are in many respects better than war; and these first modest UN contributions to international relations were to have many successors.[15] Fourth, the General Assembly adopted, in December 1948, a Declaration on Human Rights. This was passed without contrary votes, which showed that no government wished openly to oppose the concept; but the Soviet bloc, Saudi Arabia and South Africa abstained – an interesting and disparate combination. Communist governments argued in theory that they held their own view of human rights, different from that of bourgeois states; in practice they continued to impose their own regime of purges, labour camps and the Gulag. Saudi Arabia reserved the rights of Islamic law. South Africa pursued its own policy of *apartheid* and racial discrimination. Other countries doubtless had their reservations but preferred not to express them. In any event, a new and dynamic element was introduced into the conduct of international relations, with far-reaching consequences.

These functions were less dramatic than some of the founders of the United Nations hoped for in 1945, but they were solid and in some respects far-reaching. The organization managed to achieve a life of its own, and exercised a fitful but vital influence in world affairs.

In the immediate post-war period, a number of other international organizations were created, and existing ones changed their character. A new dimension in international politics, and a new density in their tissues, came into being.

The Commonwealth (still called the British Commonwealth of Nations) consisted in 1945 of Great Britain, Australia, Canada, Newfoundland, New

Zealand and South Africa, all independent but united by common alle-giance to the Crown and long habits of co-operation. In 1950 a new depar-ture was made when India (independent since 1947) remained in the Commonwealth when it became a Republic, using the device of recognizing the British monarch as Head of the Commonwealth.. This opened the way for any former British colony to join the Commonwealth on attaining inde-pendence. Nearly all chose to do so, and by 1995 there were 41 members, holding Heads of Government meetings every two years. The Commonwealth, though extremely diverse, retained a considerable degree of cohesion, through similar modes of thought (it was often referred to as a club), and the more practical advantages of the sterling area. This consisted of countries which used the pound sterling as their currency, or to provide reserves for their currency. It was not identical with the Commonwealth – Canada was in the Commonwealth but not in the ster-ling area; Iraq and certain states in the Persian Gulf were at one time in the sterling area but not the Commonwealth. British governments valued the Commonwealth for its prestige as the successor of Empire, and as a means of informal influence; and all the members found enough advantage to keep it in being, though its bonds became increasingly tenuous with the passage of time.

The Arab League (formally the League of Arab States) was founded at a conference in Cairo on 22 March 1945 by Egypt, Iraq, Lebanon, Saudi Arabia, Syria, Transjordan (later Jordan) and Yemen. Representatives of the Palestinian Arabs attended as observers. The form of a League was deliber-ately chosen, as being looser than a federal organization. Its main purposes were to represent the Arab world in the United Nations Organization (whose founding conference was about to meet at San Francisco); to medi-ate in disputes between Arab states; to promote cultural and economic links between the member states; and to act together on the question of Palestine – which meant opposing a Jewish state. The League's headquarters were established at Cairo, with its Council meeting twice a year at various capi-tals. The League has proved long-lived, though Egypt was suspended from membership in 1979, when it signed a peace treaty with Israel, and the headquarters shifted to Tunis.

In the American hemisphere, the International Union of American Republics had been set up as long ago as 1890, changing its name to the Pan-American Union in 1910. In April 1948 a conference in Bogota changed this body into the Organization of American States (OAS), comprising the United States, Canada, and most of the Latin American states, with the lofty but amorphous aims of advancing peace, justice, hemi-sphere solidarity and co-operation, as well as the precise object of defend-ing the sovereignty, integrity and independence of member states. The headquarters of the OAS was to be in Washington, emphasizing the predominant role of the United States; though care was taken that the

Secretary-General should be from Latin America. The Organization consisted of a General Assembly meeting annually, a Permanent Council, and a Conference of Foreign Ministers meeting in case of need. Its actual working became a constant, if often concealed, tug of war between the USA, which used the OAS as a means of exerting its own influence, and the Latin American states, which used it as a means of opposing that influence.

In May 1948, just after the conference of American states in Bogota, the Congress of Europe, with representatives from 24 European countries, met at the Hague to discuss various projects for European unity, ranging from simple co-operation to federal union. This led to the creation of the Council of Europe (1949), which in turn set up a Parliamentary Assembly and a Committee of Ministers to promote greater European unity. A series of moves towards West European integration followed: the Coal and Steel Community, the Defence Community (which broke down), and the Economic Community founded in 1957. The EEC was to prove the most solid and elaborate of all the post-war international organizations, and produced profound changes in western Europe.

The Cominform (Communist Information Bureau), founded in 1947, was a different type of international organization. It was made up, not of states or governments, but of nine European Communist Parties – a truncated version of the old Communist International, which until its formal dissolution in 1943 had united all the Communist Parties of the world in one organization directed from Moscow. The nine parties concerned were those of the Soviet Union, Yugoslavia, Hungary, Romania, Czechoslovakia and Poland (which all had communist governments), together with France, Italy and Belgium (which did not). The founding meeting took place at Szklarska-Poreba, in Poland, under the presidency of Andrei Zhdanov, the Third Secretary of the Communist Party of the Soviet Union and the director of Soviet propaganda policy. Ostensibly, the purpose of Cominform was to promote unity between the member parties by the exchange of information; in practice, the organization was run by the Soviet government for its own purposes.

◆ Economic organization: The Bretton Woods Conference, July 1944

During the Second World War the American government, and especially the Secretary of State, Cordell Hull, believed firmly that the war had largely been caused by the economic conflicts arising from the great depression of the 1930s and subsequent attempts at self-sufficiency and closed trading systems. The United States therefore set out to create a new world trade system, with lower tariffs and convertible currencies. This policy was motivated by a genuine American desire to set the world to rights, and an immense confidence that they could do so. It would also advance the economic interests of the United States, because lower tariffs would favour the most efficient producers, which in 1945 were mostly American, and open up markets to American industries, which were producing more than the domestic market could absorb. In short, the Americans set out to make capitalism work better, and assumed a happy coincidence between the improvement of the world and the advance of American commerce. The Americans regarded this as a natural state of affairs, but others looked on it with a more jaundiced eye.

The Bretton Woods Conference in July 1944, attended by 44 states, prepared the framework for the economic organization of the post-war world. (The Soviet Union attended the conference, but refused to be bound by its conclusions – as did the curious combination of Haiti, Liberia and New Zealand.) The conference set up two new organizations: the International Monetary Fund and the International Bank for Reconstruction and Development. The International Monetary Fund (IMF) was designed to prevent the recurrent pre-war problem of countries running balance of payments deficits which were followed by runs on their reserves of gold or foreign currency. Each member state of the IMF was to pay a subscription according to its economic capacity, one-quarter in gold and three-quarters in currency. The IMF would then, from these reserves, grant governments credits, in the form of drawing rights, to meet deficits in their countries' balance of payments. The International Bank for Reconstruction and Development (later commonly called the World Bank) was founded in order to finance post-war reconstruction. Its funds were to be raised from capital subscribed by member states, and later by its own earnings. As the requirements of post-war reconstruction diminished, the World Bank extended its activities to providing loans for capital investment, and funds to assist economic development in poorer countries. The headquarters of the World Bank were situated in Washington, and all its Presidents have been American.

The Bretton Woods Conference also agreed to establish stable exchange rates, by what amounted to a return to the gold exchange standard for all the participant countries. Each signatory to the Bretton Woods agreement undertook to maintain a stable exchange rate for its currency, using the measurement of either gold or a convertible currency, which was in fact the dollar, using a fixed rate of one ounce of gold to $35. The United States held the greater part of the world's gold reserves, and so was the only state capable of assuring the convertibility of its currency into gold.

This new monetary system gave considerable advantages to the United States. The US dollar had the privileged status of being the equivalent of gold, and thus became a currency which was both national and international. It was convertible anywhere, allowing Americans to purchase goods, services, or property with their own currency. No other currency in the world at that time had such power. But the advantages did not accrue solely to the United States. Stable exchange rates were considered a common interest, much preferable to the monetary confusion of the 1930s. The United States provided stability through the fixed exchange value of the dollar, and other countries on the whole benefited from it. When in 1971 the United States had to abandon the gold standard and allow the dollar to float, the consequences were mixed, and not always to the advantage of those who had previously grumbled at American domination.

The Bretton Woods Conference also proposed the setting up of an International Trade Organization, which was not accepted by the United States Congress. However, in October 1947 a conference of 23 states held in Geneva reached a General Agreement on Tariffs and Trade (GATT), which proposed to introduce systematic tariff reductions by all the members of the conference. GATT became established as an organization, not simply an agreement, while retaining its name and the simple initials by which it has become universally known. Its headquarters were set up in Geneva, with a Director-General and a Secretariat, and its members met once a year, and also in special conferences, to pursue the slow and difficult work of translating a general agreement on tariff reductions into actual changes.

As statesmen looked round in 1945, they could find solid cause for satisfaction. The wartime alliance, despite some friction, was still in working order, and might form the basis for a new power system. A new world organization, the United Nations, had come into being through the initiative of one of the superpowers, the USA, and with the agreement of the other, the USSR. There was an encouraging trend towards regional co-operation in various parts of the world. Vital steps had been taken to restore the world economy, to finance reconstruction, and to stabilize exchange rates. After the havoc wrought by the Second World War, this was a considerable achievement.

◆ Notes to Chapter 2

1. I. C. B. Dear and M. R. D. Foot, eds, *The Oxford Companion to the Second World War* (Oxford, 1995), pp. 290, 1060, 1199; Paul Kennedy, *The Rise and Fall of the Great Powers* (London, paperback edn, 1989), pp. 460–1.
2. Henry Kissinger, *Diplomacy* (London, paperback edn, 1995), p. 425.
3. Dear and Foot, *Second World War*, pp. 1060, 1231–2, 1235; Robert Service, *A History of Twentieth Century Russia* (London, 1997), pp. 286, 295. Figures for civilian casualties vary widely.
4. Vladislav Zubok and Constantine Pleshakov, *Inside the Kremlin's Cold War* (Cambridge, Mass., 1996), p. 12.

5. *Ibid.*, p. 95.
6. Dear and Foot, *Second World War*, p. 290.
7. *Ibid.*
8. Robert H. Ferrell, *Harry S. Truman: A Life* (London, 1994), p. 210.
9. *Ibid.*, p. 209.
10. John Dower, *Japan in War and Peace: Essays in History, Culture and Race* (London, paperback edn, 1996), p. 121; Dear and Foot, *Second World War*, p. 290, gives lower estimates.
11. Table in Dear and Foot, *Second World War*, p. 826.
12. W. S. Churchill, *The Second World War*, Vol. III: *The Grand Alliance* (London, 1950), p. 605.
13. For Dumbarton Oaks and Yalta, see above, pp. 16–22.
14. Rosemary Righter, *Utopia Lost: The United Nations and World Order* (London, 1995), pp. 46, 327 for FAO, *passim* for UNESCO.
15. See the list of UN peace-keeping operations, below, pp. 511–2.

THE FIRST PHASE OF THE
COLD WAR, 1945–1962

THE COLD WAR

Previous page: Crisis point in the Cold War: an American supply plane lands in West Berlin during the Soviet Blockade of 1948–49. The city was supplied by air; the Soviets buzzed American aircraft, but did no more. The Cold War remained cold. © Hulton Getty

CHAPTER 3

THE ANTAGONISTS

The Soviet Union and the United States at the end of the Second World War

In October 1944 President Roosevelt declared that: 'in this global war there is literally no question, political or military, in which the United States is not interested.' In 1946 Molotov, the Foreign Minister of the Soviet Union, asserted that: 'The USSR is now one of the mightiest countries of the world. One cannot decide now *any* serious problems of international relations without the USSR . . .' In these circumstances, the interests of the two states would be almost certain to conflict at some point and at some time.[1] The histories of Athens and Sparta in ancient Greece, Rome and Carthage during the Punic Wars, Hapsburg and Valois in the sixteenth century, Britain and France in the eighteenth century – all showed that it was virtually impossible for two great powers to come into close contact with one another without also coming into conflict. There would have to be some powerful reason if the United States and Soviet Union were to be different. Moreover, it is almost a commonplace that alliances break down when wars come to an end and common enemies are defeated. This had happened to the British and French after the defeat of Germany in 1918. It was almost certain to happen again in the case of the Grand Alliance in 1945, when victory was achieved and differences of view, suppressed or ignored while the war continued, rose to the surface.

In fact, relations between the United States and the Soviet Union were made more difficult because each embodied a creed. The United States was the standard-bearer of democracy, individual liberty and capitalism. The Soviet Union was the world's first and greatest socialist state, committed to building communism at home and displaying the beacon-light of the Workers' Fatherland to communists and sympathizers all over the world.

The two elements of power and ideology were so closely intertwined that it is very difficult to decide which was the more important. On the one hand, if communism had been embodied only in some small state (for example, Albania), the United States would scarcely have been perturbed; so from the American point of view it was communism *plus* power which produced conflict. On the other hand, the Soviet Union was hostile to Switzerland, a small country which offered no threat to Soviet security but epitomized bourgeois values and success; so in this case power was unimportant and ideology was crucial. Between these two extremes there were many variations, and the two elements of power and ideology went together in different proportions.

To the problems arising from power and ideology was added at the end of the Second World War the new fact of *proximity*. The United States and the Soviet Union had lived in the same world for a quarter of a century without being more than distantly hostile to one another, because they were geographically far apart. Their nearest point of contact was at the Bering Straits, where the western tip of Alaska is only eighty miles from the easternmost cape of Siberia; but there was no acute confrontation across those icy waters. It was when the Americans and Soviets met in the middle of Europe that they looked at one another with different eyes and their troubles began.

These three factors of power, ideology and proximity, taken together, made conflict between the Soviet Union and the United States at least probable, and perhaps inevitable. But before going on to examine how the long and complicated struggle which we call the Cold War actually came about, let us pause to look briefly at the two superpowers as they stood in 1945–46.

◆ The Soviet Union

In June 1943 the Soviet Union had adopted a new national anthem, which opened:

> An indestructible union of free republics
> Has forever been welded by Russia the Great.
> Long live the land created by the will of the peoples:
> The united, powerful Soviet Union!

It went on to proclaim that 'Stalin brought us up.'[2] The new anthem thus linked together three great defining features of the state: Russia the Great, the heir of the Tsarist Empire; the Soviet Union, the product of the Bolshevik Revolution; and Stalin, who presented the formidable visage of a Red Tsar.

The mixture was a complicated one, and the inheritance of the country's foreign policy was equally complex, made up of an uneasy combination of expansionist drive and deep-seated insecurity. For centuries Moscow had claimed to be the 'Third Rome' (after Rome itself and Byzantium), with a mission to safeguard the Russian Orthodox religion and the Slav peoples in other countries. In the eighteenth and nineteenth centuries Russia had pushed southwards into the Caucasus and Central Asia, and eastwards through Siberia to the Pacific. Russian armies had imposed order in Budapest in 1849 on behalf of the Hapsburgs, and crushed risings in Poland in 1830 and 1863 on their own account. In theory, the communist regime discarded much of this inheritance, rejecting religion altogether and claiming to rise above race or nationality. But in practice the drive for expansion continued, and retained many of its old features. During the Second World War, Stalin deliberately set out to recover lost Tsarist territory in Poland and the Far East. After the war, the Soviet Army was again to impose order in Budapest in 1956, and to suppress Polish independence.

At the same time, and under both Tsarist and Soviet regimes, insecurity and fear of invasion remained endemic. These fears went far back to the irruption of the Mongols in the thirteenth century (vividly evoked by Eisenstein in the opening scenes of *Alexander Nevsky*), followed by the invasions by Charles XII of Sweden in 1709, Napoleon in 1812, and the Germans in 1917–18. Allied intervention against the Bolsheviks in 1918–20 gave these apprehensions a new, ideological twist. Finally the German assault in 1941 and the great struggle which followed confirmed all these obsessions about foreign invasion and the absolute necessity of security.

Soviet foreign policy thus had deep roots in both a tradition of expansion and a chronic sense of insecurity. It was a difficult combination for the Soviets themselves to manage, and for outsiders to understand.

The nature of the Soviet state which lay behind this foreign policy has been crisply defined thus: 'The USSR was a highly centralized, one-party dictatorship. It enforced a single official ideology; imposed severe restrictions on national, religious and cultural self-expression. Its economy was predominantly state-owned.'[3] All these aspects of the Soviet system had their impact on relations with other countries; but in 1945 the great problem was that the system itself was in disarray. The war had left a trail of material destruction and administrative confusion. Armed opposition to Soviet authority was active in eastern Poland and the Baltic states (annexed in 1939–40), and in the Ukraine, where guerrilla bands held out until the middle of the 1950s. Stalin's answer was severe and large-scale repression. Dissident populations in the Baltic states and Chechneya were deported in large numbers. Something like half the prisoners of war who returned from Germany were put straight into the Gulag or shot out of hand. Party control over literature, science and the arts was tightened. Ideological orthodoxy, which had been somewhat relaxed during the war in order to appeal to Russian patriotism, was sternly reimposed, to ensure internal unity and to eliminate all external influences.

At the head of the state, Stalin emerged from the Second World War with his authority over his own country and the international communist movement virtually absolute. (There were some doubts and discontents in Tito's

Yugoslavia, but these were not yet significant.) The triumphs of 1945 allowed him to shrug off the disasters of 1941; and in the years to come he was untouchable in a way which none of his successors could attain. In this position of supreme authority, he contrived to pursue two purposes: the security of the Soviet state, which he saw largely in territorial terms; and the defence and advancement of socialism. There is no sign that he saw any contradiction between the two. In the pursuit of security he was prepared to do business with all sorts and conditions of men. In 1939 he had met Ribbentrop and made a deal with Hitler. During the war he was on good terms with Churchill and Roosevelt. After the war, he maintained good relations with Chiang Kai-shek and the Chinese Nationalists before, in 1950, welcoming Mao Zedong to Moscow and signing a treaty of alliance with the new Chinese communist government. In these contacts he did not allow considerations of ideology to interfere with the pursuit of the interests of the Soviet state, as these were interpreted from time to time. In the years immediately after the war, he made some public moves away from the revolutionary inheritance of Bolshevism – the title of Commissar for Foreign Affairs was changed to that of Foreign Minister, and even the famous Red Army was renamed the Soviet Army. Yet the Soviet Union still embodied the Bolshevik Revolution, and in 1945 it was still the only socialist state in the world. Its interests were therefore by definition the same as those of international communism, and there was no distinction between them. Two recent historians of Soviet foreign policy, who themselves grew up under Stalin and his successors, were unable to distinguish between ideology and interests of state. Stalin, they concluded, was motivated by twin and inseparable purposes: 'the promise of Communist revolutionary universalism combined with the necessities of survival for the Soviet Union, the first and unique "Socialist" empire.'[4]

On 9 February 1946, Stalin struck a confident note in a speech at the Bolshoi Theatre, in which he claimed that the Second World War had been 'a kind of examination for our Soviet order, for our state, for our Communist Party'. They had passed the test, and victory had demonstrated the superiority of the Soviet order. Yet at the same time the Soviet Union must still press on, to produce 50 million tons of iron, 60 million tons of steel, 60 million tons of petroleum – only thus would the country be safe against all contingencies. He also stressed the importance of science, declaring that Soviet scientists would be able to overtake the achievements of scientists elsewhere.[5] His thoughts doubtless dwelt at that point on the atomic bomb. Stalin had been well informed about the progress of the American atomic project, and received news of an imminent test just before he set off to the Potsdam Conference. Even so, he was badly shaken by the actual explosions at Hiroshima and Nagasaki, and in August 1945 he threw everything into building a Soviet atomic bomb. He put Beria (the head of the NKVD) in charge of a vast project, which moved at headlong speed, so that a bomb was tested as early as 1949. But for the time being, the Soviet Union was behind the United States in a vital area of power and prestige. Stalin put a brave face on it, claiming that the bomb was only intended to frighten those with weak nerves; but in practice his caution, always a marked characteristic of his foreign policy, was reinforced.

Stalin's right-hand man in foreign policy was Vyacheslav Molotov, Foreign Minister from 1939 to 1949. Molotov was an old Bolshevik who never lost his original convictions – 'a man morally committed to the Revolution'.[6] Even when expelled from the Communist Party under Khruschev, he insisted on going personally to the bank every month to pay his party dues, until after twenty-three years he had the satisfaction of seeing his membership formally restored. He took a straightforward view of his work as Foreign Minister. Reflecting in 1974, he remarked: 'My task as minister of foreign affairs was to expand the borders of our Fatherland. And it seems that Stalin and I coped with this task quite well.' And again: 'Stalin often said that Russia wins wars but doesn't know how to avail itself of the fruits of victory . . . But we did well after this war [the Second World War] because we strengthened the Soviet state. It was my main task as minister of foreign affairs to see that we would not be cheated.'[7] On relations with the United States, his views were brisk and matter-of-fact.

> The cold war – I don't like the expression. It sounds like Khruschev's . . . But what does the 'cold war' mean? Strained relations. It was entirely their doing or because we were on the offensive. They certainly hardened their line against us, but we had to consolidate our conquests . . . To squeeze out the capitalist order. This was the cold war. Of course, you had to know when and where to stop. I believe in this respect Stalin kept well within the limits.[8]

There was no rancour in this, and no sense of lost opportunities to maintain good relations between the USA and USSR. The Soviet purpose was 'to squeeze out the capitalist order'; and the Western powers 'behaved the only way they could – as enemies of the Soviet Union and the Socialist way of life'.[9] Molotov made no particular distinction between ideology and power politics, both of which worked in the same direction.

By September 1946 he had taken stock of the situation, in consultation with the Soviet Ambassador in Washington, and reached some general conclusions about relations with the United States. The Americans had abandoned isolation and were set on achieving world supremacy. They would seek to limit or dislodge Soviet influence in eastern Europe and the Middle East, and to establish new bases on the periphery of the Soviet Union. To counter these policies, the best strategy was to exploit contradictions between the imperialist powers, especially the Americans and the British, whose interests were bound to clash in the Middle East, as the

Americans sought to increase their control over the oilfields.[10] At the time these were cautious and not unreasonable calculations, and their conclusions were far from apocalyptic.

Stalin and Molotov were hardened by years of war and political struggle, and were far more experienced than any western statesmen following Roosevelt's death and Churchill's electoral defeat in 1945. Truman especially seemed to them a beginner in international affairs – Stalin called him a 'petty shopkeeper', and Molotov thought him 'a bit half-witted'.[11] They were not afraid of their American opponents, and unlikely to be perturbed by difficult negotiations or verbal confrontations. Their approach was prudent and calculating – as Molotov said, 'you had to know when and where to stop'. The United States was their enemy; but it was an enmity which might last a long time. There was no need to hurry.

◆ The United States

The American political system and tradition were very different from those of the Soviet Union. The United States was founded on the principles of individual liberty and democratic elections for all kinds of office, from the presidency to the local school board. Its vast area was held together by a flexible form of federal government which retained important powers for the individual states of the Union. The American economic system was based on free enterprise, vigorous capitalism and the free market, tempered by limited government intervention and the recent New Deal radicalism of Franklin Roosevelt's presidency. The broad though not unmixed success of this form of government and economics had given the great majority of the American people an enormous confidence in their own country and way of life, recently reinforced by victory in war over Germany and Japan.

The foreign policy of this comparatively new state (just under 170 years old in 1945) comprised different and sometimes contradictory strands. The United States had been created by a long westward expansion from the original thirteen states on the Atlantic coast. This expansion had involved movements of population and settlement on a vast scale. It had also included small wars against the Indians, or Native Americans, and a big war against Mexico in 1846–48, which bore some resemblance to the Russian conflicts with the khanates of Central Asia and the Turks. At the turn of the nineteenth and twentieth centuries there had been no absolutely firm idea of where this expansion should stop. In 1898, in the Spanish-American War, the United States annexed Hawaii in the middle of the Pacific Ocean and the Philippines on the far side of it. By 1945 the Philippines were on the way to independence, but in 1959 Hawaii became a fully-fledged state of the Union. The tradition of expansion, justified by the claim to be working out the 'manifest destiny' of the American people, was very strong.

Yet this expansion was accompanied by an equally powerful tradition of opposition to colonialism as practised by other countries. The United States had come into existence by breaking free from the British Empire, and regarded itself as the natural leader for other peoples rightly struggling to be free. There was also a strong current of even higher idealism, claiming for the United States the role of leading the world to a better form of political and international organization. During the First World War, President Woodrow Wilson embodied this idealism and tried to put it into practice by proclaiming new principles of international conduct and creating the League of Nations to put them into practice.

At that stage he was decisively repudiated by the United States Congress and public opinion, then under the powerful influence of isolationism, which formed yet another strand in the American outlook on foreign affairs. George Washington, the most eminent and influential figure among the Founding Fathers of the United States, had warned his fellow-country-men against the dangers of 'entangling alliances', and his words had made a lasting impression. In the nineteenth century, most immigrants to the USA from Europe wished to leave Europe and its troubles behind them. At the end of the First World War this current of isolationism prevailed over Wilson's internationalist idealism, and at the end of the Second World War there was still, at the very least, a strong instinct to 'bring the boys home'.

All these instincts were real and deep-rooted. They were tempered by a strand of *realpolitik* and power politics, personified about the turn of the century by Theodore Roosevelt but practised by many of his predecessors and successors. The United States treated the Caribbean as its own sphere of predominance; installed an American zone to ensure control of the Panama Canal; and extended its economic influence over much of Central and South America. By the end of the Second World War this predominance in the Western hemisphere was accompanied by the new strategic interests of a superpower, with large armed forces, bases stretched across the Pacific, and the sole possession of the atomic bomb.

Foreign policy was also influenced by the interests of a vast capitalist and free-market economy. As the Second World War ended, the American economy was thriving, stimulated by the almost unlimited demands of war. Yet many Americans were afraid that the wartime boom would collapse into depression, and therefore sought to promote their continued prosperity by securing markets for their exports, raw materials for their industries, and access to oil to meet the growing demand for fuel.

American foreign policy was also subject to the influence of an active and alert public opinion. It was true that the main body of the American public took little or no interest in foreign affairs, except in wartime; but there was a substantial minority that did. Readers of the serious press, especially on the east coast; pressure groups associated with foreign causes such as Zionism or missionary enterprises in China; and the various groups of 'hyphenated Americans' (Polish-Americans, Italian-Americans, Irish-Americans) – all made themselves felt. Newspaper editors and columnists and radio commentators could be highly influential. One example was Walt Lippmann, an outstanding newspaper columnist who became something of an oracle for the American political elite. The Senate Foreign Relations Committee often focussed the opinions of these different groups, and itself brought pressure to bear on the government. The upshot was a complicated mixture of opinions and pressure groups, which no President or Secretary of State could afford to ignore. It was a situation completely unknown in the Soviet Union, and was frequently baffling to Soviet leaders and officials who were accustomed to a very different system of conducting foreign policy. (Indeed, it could sometimes be equally difficult and disconcerting for America's allies.) In 1945–46 American public opinion was highly diverse, and certainly not settled in an anti-Soviet stance. The East Coast press and New Deal activists of the Roosevelt era were still radical in their outlook, and the wartime enthusiasm for the Soviet Union continued well into 1946. It was symptomatic that when Churchill made his speech at Fulton, Missouri, in March 1946, denouncing the iron curtain which had fallen across Europe and appealing for a renewed Anglo-American alliance, he evoked as much hostility as support in the American press and public opinion.

The presence of these different elements – idealism, power politics, economic interests, and the various currents of public opinion – meant that American foreign policy was sometimes uncertain, or even erratic. One set of views or interests could pull against another. For example, American economic interests required sterling to become freely convertible into dollars after the war, to the advantage of American exporters; but when the British introduced convertibility in 1947 its effects were so damaging to the British economy that the United States speedily agreed to the abandonment of the attempt. The value of Britain as an ally for the United States government outweighed the advantages of convertibility for American economic interests. Again, in 1945 American idealism in its anti-imperialist mode led the United States to oppose the return of French forces to Indo-China; but by 1950 the influence of power politics and the new idealism of the Cold War brought the Americans to support the French in their struggle against Vietnamese nationalist and communist forces. The very nature of American politics meant that there were always tensions and disagreements about foreign policy; which made it all the more remarkable when the United States set out to pursue a long-term policy and stuck to it, as it did – despite many ups and downs – during the Cold War.

At the head of the United States government in 1945–46 was President Harry Truman, the former Vice-President, who suddenly acceded to the highest post on the death of Roosevelt in April 1945. He was not a commanding figure in the USA, and virtually unknown in the rest of the world. He was almost totally inexperienced in foreign policy. But he had learned about life and politics in two hard schools. He served as an artillery officer in France in 1918, and he made his way as a politician in the tough world of Kansas City politics, which were run (as was the whole state of Missouri) by the local political boss, Tom Pendergast. It was said that Truman once remarked that Stalin's methods were similar to Pendergast's; which was certainly unfair to Pendergast, but showed that Truman recognized when he had come up against a tough character. In 1945 Truman was feeling his way, but he soon showed remarkable strength of character and powers of decision.[12]

◆ The rivals?

Was it inevitable that these two superpowers, with their different interests and outlooks, would become opponents? The weight of historical precedent, and the pressures created by rivalries of power, interest and ideology and the problems of proximity, all indicated the likelihood of conflict. Yet in 1945 there were significant pointers in the opposite direction.

When Truman became President of the United States, and was taking his bearings in his new responsibilities, he was anxious to follow the lines laid down by Roosevelt in dealing with Stalin, and pursue his predecessor's vision of a new world order. As we have seen, he had previously expressed some hostility to communism and the USSR, but he held no fixed view that the Soviet Union was an enemy, and he was perfectly willing to meet Stalin and get on with him. There were signs that Stalin too wished to avoid direct confrontation with his wartime allies. In Europe, some communist leaders complained that Stalin was keener on reaching agreements with the 'imperialists' than on supporting them. For example, Tito felt he received insufficient support for his territorial demands in Trieste; while in France and Italy fleeting communist ideas of seizing power were firmly checked by Moscow. In the Pacific, a significant issue arose concerning the arrangements for the surrender of Japanese forces in the home islands of Japan. On 16 August Stalin wrote to Truman proposing that Soviet forces should accept the surrender of Japanese troops in northern Hokkaido, the part of Japan nearest to Soviet territory. Truman refused, insisting that Japanese forces on all the home islands should surrender to the Americans. Stalin at first responded by ordering his troops to occupy Hokkaido; but he then countermanded the order on the 22nd, to avoid trouble with the Americans.

Above all, the Potsdam Conference of July 1945 was at least a partial success, if only because the three participants were determined that it should not fail.[13] They still had to finish the war against Japan; they agreed on the outlines of a German policy; and the Americans and British accepted what amounted to a Soviet solution of the Polish question. They agreed to carry forward their co-operation by means of the Council of Foreign Ministers (American, British, French and Soviet), which was to pursue the work begun at Potsdam and prepare peace treaties. All was not well in the wartime alliance, but in many respects it continued to work. In the middle of 1945, the two superpowers had not become antagonists.

In 1945 there was no certainty as to how events would turn out. We now know that the next forty-five years were to be dominated by the struggle between the superpowers which we call the Cold War. A string of questions arises in relation to that development. What was the Cold War, and how did it earn that striking but imprecise designation? How and why did the Cold War come about? Do we know who started it – indeed, does such a question have much meaning in the context of these complicated events? We will examine these questions in the next four chapters, and then reflect on them by trying to fix the outlines of that slippery entity, the Cold War.

◆ Notes to Chapter 3

1. Paul Kennedy, *The Rise and Fall of the Great Powers* (London, paperback edn, 1989), p. 470, juxtaposes the two quotations, and argues that a clash of interests was inevitable.
2. Quoted in Robert Service, *A History of Twentieth Century Russia* (London, 1997), pp. 282, 315.
3. *Ibid.*, p. xxi.
4. Vladislav Zubok and Constantine Pleshakov, *Inside the Kremlin's Cold War* (Cambridge, Mass., 1996), p. 12.
5. David Holloway, *Stalin and the Bomb: The Soviet Union and Atomic Energy* (London, 1994), pp. 148–9.
6. Zubok and Pleshakov, p. 82.
7. V. Molotov, *Molotov Remembers: Inside Kremlin Politics. Coversations with Felix Chuev*, ed. Albert Resis (Chicago, 1993), pp. 8, 53.
8. *Ibid.*, p.59.
9. Quoted in Zubok and Pleshakov, p. 89.
10. Memorandum by Novikov, Ambassador in Washington, as amended by Molotov, 27 September 1946, *ibid.*, pp. 101–3.
11. *Ibid.*, pp. 43, 95.
12. See Robert H. Ferrell, *Harry S. Truman: A Life* (London, 1994), Chapters 4 and 7.
13. On Potsdam, see above, p. 37.

CHAPTER 4

THE BEGINNING OF THE COLD WAR, I: FROM POTSDAM TO THE MARSHALL PLAN, 1945–1947

Conferences and peace treaties – Germany and the German Question – The Soviet Union and Eastern Europe – Turkey and Greece – Kennan's 'long telegram' and Churchill's Fulton speech – The Truman Doctrine – The Marshall Plan – The concept of containment

In the latter part of 1945 the wartime alliance was strained, but still in working order. The victorious powers continued to hold conferences and reach agreement on some issues, though not on all. Europe was not divided on ideological lines. In France and Italy, communists held posts in coalition governments, and there were non-communist ministers in governments in eastern Europe. By 1949 all this had changed. Conferences between the victorious powers had ceased. Representatives of the two superpowers scarcely spoke to one another. In western Europe, the communists had moved into bitter and sometimes violent opposition. The North Atlantic Treaty (April 1949) bound together the United States, Canada and ten European countries in alliance against the Soviet Union. In eastern Europe, Stalinist regimes had been imposed almost everywhere. Europe was divided by an 'iron curtain' of barbed wire, minefields and machine-guns. Across this great divide, the two sides tried to undermine one another by propaganda, espionage and covert operations.

Yet they went no further. American and Soviet tanks confronted one another on occasion. Soviet fighters buzzed American transport aircraft. But the fateful shots were never fired. It was the Cold War, not the Third World War, which began between 1945 and 1949.

These events raise two crucial questions. First, how and why did the superpowers and the European countries move from the position of 1945 to that of 1949? Second, why did hostilities remain 'cold', rather than resulting in the actual fighting which sometimes seemed so close? Discussion of these questions has been much influenced by debates as to who started the Cold War, or who was responsible for it. Schools of thought have arisen among historians, especially in the United States (orthodox, revisionist, neo-revisionist, post-revisionist), holding that the Soviets were to blame, or the Americans, or both at once, or neither.[1] These debates have done much to stimulate research and open up new approaches; but it is best to start here by trying to explain what happened rather than ascribe responsibility. Let us begin by clarifying the course of events, in two stages: first, from the Potsdam Conference to the Marshall Plan (1945–47), and then in the next chapter from the Czechoslovakian crisis of February 1948 to the North Atlantic Treaty in 1949.

◆ Conferences and peace treaties: signs of progress

At the beginning – though this is often forgotten – real progress was made towards a peace settlement in Europe after the Second World War. At the Potsdam Conference in July 1945 the victorious powers made arrangements for the administration of Germany, and fixed a *de facto* frontier between Poland and Germany. It was assumed that peace treaties would be drawn up, as was customary at the end of wars; and the conference agreed to set up a Council of Foreign Ministers to prepare peace settlements with the various former enemy powers: first with Italy, Romania, Bulgaria, Hungary and Finland; and later with Austria and Germany. The Council was to consist formally of the representatives of the United States, the Soviet Union, Britain, France and China; but China played little part and it was understood that France was to be concerned only with the treaties involving Italy and Germany.

There ensued a series of meetings and conferences in 1945–46, as follows:

Council of Foreign Ministers, London, September–October 1945
Foreign Ministers' Meeting (USA, USSR, Britain), Moscow, December 1945
Council of Foreign Ministers, Paris, April–May 1946
Council of Foreign Ministers, Paris, June–July 1946
Paris Peace Conference (21 countries), 29 July–15 October 1946
Council of Foreign Ministers, New York, November–December 1946
Council of Foreign Ministers, Moscow, March–April 1947
Council of Foreign Ministers, London, November–December 1947

The result was a series of five peace treaties, with Italy, Romania, Hungary, Bulgaria and Finland, all prepared at the Paris Peace Conference and formally concluded on 10 February 1947. Peace treaties with Austria and Germany were discussed at the Council of Foreign Ministers in Moscow, in March–April 1947, but without reaching agreement.[2]

Despite these later failures, the peace treaties signed in February 1947 represented a considerable achievement by the victorious powers, and demonstrated that they could still attain a measure of agreement and compromise. They deserve careful attention.

The treaty with Italy included some complicated territorial arrangements. Italy lost the Dodecanese Islands to Greece, and Albanian independence was restored after its annexation by Italy in 1939. Italy also lost territory to Yugoslavia; and the port of Trieste had to be left in dispute, with the United States and Britain supporting the Italian claim to retain it, while the USSR supported the Yugoslav attempt to annex it. A compromise based on zones of administration was reached; but it was not until 1954 that a final solution was reached by which Trieste itself was retained by Italy and the hinterland passed to Yugoslavia. In Africa, Italy had held colonies in Ethiopia, Eritrea, Italian Somaliland, and Libya. Ethiopia had already resumed its independence, which was confirmed by the treaty. But the other three territories presented problems. In 1946 the Soviet Union claimed a mandate over Libya under the aegis of the United Nations, which would have established a Soviet foothold in the central Mediterranean. Britain opposed this, and countered by proposing independence for all three colonies. A decision was postponed, using a formula by which if the four victorious powers (USA, USSR, Britain and France) failed to reach agreement within a year of the Italian peace treaty coming into force, the matter was to be referred to the General Assembly of the United Nations – an early example of the use of the UN as an escape route from a diplomatic impasse. In the event, the four powers did not agree, and the United Nations made a series of rulings by which Italian Somaliland became a UN trust territory in 1950; Libya became independent in 1951; and Eritrea was federated with Ethiopia in 1952 – an arrangement which was later bitterly disputed by an Eritrean independence movement.[3] The treaty also imposed restrictions on Italian internal affairs, by which the Italian government undertook not to allow the resurgence of Fascist organizations; to respect human rights and fundamental freedoms; and to limit the size of its armed forces. Italy was to pay reparations to Yugoslavia, Greece, the Soviet Union, Ethiopia and Albania, in descending order of magnitude.

The other peace treaties imposed a number of territorial changes. Romania lost Bessarabia and northern Bukovina to the Soviet Union, which had annexed these provinces in 1940. Bulgaria retained the southern Dobrudja, even though it had been gained from Romania under a German-imposed treaty in 1940; but returned some Serbian territory to Yugoslavia and Western Thrace to Greece. Hungary returned to the frontiers of 1920, losing (or returning) Transylvania to Romania and southern Slovakia to Czechoslovakia. The Soviet Union secured the right to maintain troops in Hungary and Romania, in order to safeguard communications with its occupation forces in Austria. Finland ceded to the Soviet Union three pieces of territory previously lost in 1940: the port and province of Petsamo in the north; an area in the centre of the border with the USSR; and the Karelian isthmus in the south-east. The Soviet Union secured a lease of the Porkkala–Udd area as a naval base for 50 years – though in fact they were to give it up in 1955. All four countries were to pay reparations of varying amounts to their different enemies.

These were important treaties, dealing with some difficult issues, and involving serious consequences for the countries directly concerned. It is true that they were of less than vital importance for the superpowers, but they still showed what could be achieved by hard and patient negotiation between the victors. Germany presented much more serious problems.

◆ Germany and the German Question

Much of European international politics in the first part of the twentieth century had been dominated by the German Question: what role was this comparatively new, prosperous and powerful country to play in Europe? Twice, in 1914–18 and 1939–45, Germany had fought great wars to establish its dominance over the continent, and in 1945 there was a widespread fear that it might try again. The question of how to prevent such an attempt was crucial, especially to the Soviet Union and France, which had been invaded by Germany, and only marginally less so to Britain. The United States, safe across the Atlantic, took a more relaxed view.

As well as these vital but rather general questions, there were a number of specific matters to be resolved in 1945. Where were the German borders to be fixed? In the west, France claimed that the Saarland should be detached from Germany, preferably to the benefit of France. In the east, the Oder–Neisse line settled at Potsdam was only an administrative device, and a recognized frontier between Germany and Poland remained to be agreed by treaty.

Behind the question of frontiers lay another, and more fundamental, issue: was Germany to be kept in one piece or not? At Yalta, this question was postponed, but the establishment of four occupation zones (Soviet, American, British and French) was agreed on, with a corresponding division of Berlin into four zones. At Potsdam, the Big Three changed their minds on dismemberment, deciding instead to keep Germany in one piece (though diminished in size by loss of territory in the east), and to administer the country as a whole. The four Commanders-in-Chief of the occupation forces would constitute a Control Council, on which each C-in-C would exercise a veto, so that decisions could only be reached unanimously. Similarly, Berlin was to have its central authority, subject to the Control Council.

In principle, the joint administration of occupied Germany required agreement between the occupying powers on the aims which they were to pursue. In practice, this proved to be impossible. The Soviets, seeking both revenge and to make up some of their immense material losses, made the exaction of reparations their first objective, removing equipment, machinery, and even whole factories when they could be found, from their own occupation zone, and whenever possible from the other zones as well – as had been agreed at Potsdam. They also took reparations from current production, both industrial and agricultural, in their own zone. The Americans and British took a very different view. Their occupation zones were densely populated and mainly industrial in their economy, and required imports of food and raw materials. The Americans and British therefore argued that current industrial production should be used to pay for imports, and that some of the agricultural production of the Soviet zone should be used to feed the population of the western zones. In fact, the Americans fed the German population of their zone at their own expense; and in July 1946 the British government introduced bread rationing at home (a measure never found necessary during the war) in order to export wheat to the British zone in Germany. It was a remarkable measure, and one which was not entirely popular with the British people.

In these circumstances, the Americans and British ceased to treat Germany as an economic whole. As early as May 1946 General Clay, the Commander-in-Chief of in the American occupation zone, stopped the despatch of any reparations from the American to the Soviet zone. In July the American and British zones were merged, for purposes of economic administration, into the clumsily named 'Bizonia'. These changes at first arose from the practical necessity of feeding the German population; but the Americans quickly moved on to the more general issue of German economic recovery. In a speech at Stuttgart on 5 September 1946, the Secretary of State, Byrnes, declared that Germany was part of Europe, and the economic recovery of the continent as a whole would be slowed down if Germany was turned into a poor-house. Instead, Germany must be allowed to export enough goods to pay her own way. This was a coherent and sensible course of action; but it was not the policy that had been agreed by the Allies in 1945. In their zone, the Soviets continued to apply the policy of exacting reparations rather than restoring the economy; and the French too stood out of the Anglo-American Bizone and continued to take reparations out of current production until 1947. The economic division of Germany had begun, though it was not based on a division between east and west, but on the differing attitudes of those who had been occupied by the Germans and those who had not.

The political division of Germany also began in 1946. Early that year the Soviet occupation authorities permitted the resumption of political activities within their zone, but insisted on the amalgamation of the Communist and Social Democratic Parties into the Socialist Unity Party, which was simply a front for communist control. In the other zones, political activity was also permitted to resume; and the British and Americans, in their different ways, encouraged the development of a range of political parties. The Communist Party attempted an amalgamation with the Social Democrats, as in the east, but the Social Democrats firmly refused, recognizing a takeover when they saw one. In Berlin the Social Democratic Party and the Socialist Unity Party existed side by side, and their relative popularity was tested in elections for local government and a mayor in October 1946. The result was a substantial victory for the Social Democrats, who were supported by both the British and American occupation authorities. A crucial political division of Germany thus began, with the Soviets insisting on a communist political system in their zone, and the Americans and British developing a multi-party system based on their own form of representative democracy. The French, for their part, were more reluctant than any of the other occupying powers to entrust the Germans with political responsibilities, arguing that caution should be the order of the day. On this matter, as with reparations, the division of opinion among the occupying powers was not between east and west.

By the end of 1946 and the beginning of 1947, the Allied policy towards Germany that had been sketched out at Potsdam had broken down, and the economic and political division of the country was under way. It remained to be seen whether the occupying powers could change the course of events and agree on a new policy. From 10 March to 24 April 1947 the Foreign Ministers of the Soviet Union, the United States, Britain and France met in conference in Moscow, to discuss the preparation of peace treaties with Germany and Austria. They held no fewer than 43 sessions, mainly on reparations and economic questions, but failed to reach agreement on any substantial matter. The participants agreed that there should be a peace conference to draw up a German peace treaty, but not on which countries should be invited – for example, the Soviets proposed to leave out the British Commonwealth states (which had fought throughout the war) and various Latin American countries (which had entered the conflict late in the day). The British and Americans wanted to include both groups. The Soviets insisted on the sum of $10 billion in reparations, to be paid in part from current production in the whole of Germany, as had been agreed at Potsdam. The Americans and British were opposed to the Soviets taking reparations from current production in their zones, now united in the Bizone. On this question, the Soviets were adamant – as Stalin told Marshall face to face, the Americans and British could afford to be generous on reparations, but the Soviet Union could not. On the question of the future government of Germany, the Soviets favoured a centralized government, and claimed a share in the control of the Ruhr. The Americans and British proposed a strong form of federal government, while the French argued for a weak form. In the course of the meetings, the French were forced into what was for them an unwelcome choice. At the start of the conference, the French had hoped to co-operate with the USSR on reparations, on which they held similar views, in return for Soviet support on French claims in the Saarland; but Molotov refused even to discuss the Saarland, and the French Foreign Minister, Bidault, reluctantly concluded that France would have to work with the Americans and British, join the Bizone, and relax its reparations policy. This change, which was implemented by June 1947, established the division of Germany on an east-west basis, which it thereafter retained. It also meant that France had effectively joined the western camp in the developing Cold War.

The Moscow Conference of Foreign Ministers thus failed to make any progress towards a German peace treaty, and confirmed the division of Germany which had been under way for over a year. This division, which was of crucial significance in the whole of post-war international relations, did not come about by agreement between the superpowers, but when it came they acquiesced in it. This created a striking and paradoxical state of affairs which was to persist until 1989. The Soviets and the Americans both said from time to time how desirable it would be to reunite Germany, and how terrible it was that the German people and German families should be divided. The British and French occasionally echoed these sentiments, with varying degrees of conviction. Yet every practical step taken by these various governments confirmed the division of Germany. The western powers worked steadily to integrate West Germany into their own organizations – the North Atlantic Treaty (1949), the European Coal and Steel Community (1950) and the European Economic Community (1957). The Soviet Union created and maintained a communist regime in East Germany, imposed a physical barrier between east and west, and ultimately in 1961 built the Berlin Wall. If we look ahead for a few years, we shall find a series of crises (the Berlin Blockade in 1948–49, the East German rising of 1953, and successive Berlin crises from 1958 to 1961) in which the USA and the USSR both showed that they were prepared to threaten or use force to maintain the existing situation in Germany, but not to change it. The superpowers spoke of a united Germany; but by their actions they made sure that it remained divided

A divided Germany was the most obvious, and in many ways the most perilous, element in the Cold War, raising from time to time the imminent danger of war. Yet what also emerged in Germany was a tacit willingness on both sides to maintain the status quo. The German Question threatened war, and yet it also held the secret of stability and safety.

The division of Germany was the most important event in Europe between 1945 and early 1947, and played the greatest role in the deterioration of relations between the United States and the Soviet Union. But there were two lesser developments which also had their effects, in one case chronic and insidious, in the other acute and incisive. The first was the establishment of a Soviet bloc in eastern Europe; the second was the situation in Greece and Turkey.

◆ The Soviet Union and Eastern Europe

It was Stalin's intention throughout the Second World War to establish a Soviet sphere of influence in eastern Europe, to ensure the security of the USSR and to extend the area of communist control. In 1945–46 this sphere was firmly established. Its core consisted of the Soviet occupation zone in Germany, which later became the German Democratic Republic, and five central and east European states: Poland, Czechoslovakia, Hungary, Romania and Bulgaria. At this stage, there were considerable differences between the regimes operating in these countries. In Poland, the government formed in June 1945 was predominantly communist (14 out of 21 members had been in the Soviet-nominated Lublin government). But the land reform introduced in Poland distributed land in small plots to the peasantry, rather than introducing collectivization. The elections held in January 1947 were accompanied by much intimidation and fraud, but the Democratic Bloc of the communists and their allies still won only 80 per cent of the votes. In Hungary, land redistribution again favoured the smallholders. In the election in November 1945, the Small-holders' Party won 57 per cent of the vote, and the Communist Party only 17 per cent; but the coalition government which followed allowed the communists to control the Ministry of the Interior, and so the security police. In Bulgaria, there was more sympathy for Russia than elsewhere, on traditional grounds; a new constitution on Soviet lines was introduced in 1947, which effectively gave power to the communists under the name of the Fatherland Front. In Romania the Soviets intervened to nominate a government as early as February 1945, but coalition governments survived and the monarchy remained until King Michael was forced to abdicate in December 1947. Czechoslovakia held a key position, because it was a country with a strong parliamentary tradition, and with a President (Edouard Benes) who was determined to co-operate with the Soviet Union on a friendly basis, balancing between east and west. In the first post-war elections, the Communist Party emerged as the strongest single party, with 38 per cent of the vote, which was far from overwhelming. In a coalition government, the Prime Minister, Klement Gottwald, was a communist, but the Foreign Minister was Jan Masaryk, the son of the founder of the Czechoslovakian state and a figure much respected throughout western Europe. As in Hungary, the communists controlled internal security and also the radio.

In four of these countries (Poland, Hungary, Bulgaria and Romania) the communists effectively held political power. Czechoslovakia was the exception, and held a position of particular importance in the eyes of the west.

Throughout the area, the Soviet Union was militarily predominant. Soviet troops were stationed from 1945 onwards in Poland, Romania and Hungary. Czechoslovakia had no Soviet garrison, but was almost entirely surrounded by Soviet-occupied territory. The Soviets thus had at their disposal the ultimate resort to force, which they were later to use in Hungary in 1956 and Czechoslovakia in 1968. There were other important bonds. Over much of eastern Europe, socialism seemed to offer the best way forward – other economic and social systems had been tried and failed, and conservatism had often been discredited by association with fascism. More sinister links were also established. In each country, a secret police force was set up on the pattern of the NKVD and under the command of Soviet officers. Communist leaders in the various countries became dependent on the Soviet Union, which kept them in positions of power, privilege and financial advantage. In April 1947 Rakosi, the Hungarian communist leader, visited Molotov and asked him how long Soviet troops were going to stay in Hungary – not because he wanted them to leave, but because he was anxious for them to remain.

On the edges of this Soviet sphere of predominance there lay debatable lands. In the north, Finland escaped Soviet occupation, and evolved a successful compromise between acceptance of Soviet control in foreign affairs and a full measure of internal freedom.[4] To the south, Tito's government in Yugoslavia could claim to have liberated the country largely by its own efforts in 1944–45; and the Yugoslavs were closely attached to the Soviet sphere in 1945–47 without entirely falling within it. For example, Tito used his own initiative to try to set up a form of confederation between Yugoslavia and other Balkan states in 1946–47, and he provided support for the Greek communists when Stalin did not. In 1948 these differences were to develop into a fatal split between Yugoslavia and the Soviet Union.[5] These two exceptions to the rule of Soviet predominance were to prove of considerable importance in the long run; but in 1946–47 it was the mass of the Soviet bloc which loomed large.

In some ways, there was no great reason for the establishment of this bloc to impinge on Soviet–American relations. The United States had no immediate interests in eastern Europe (though the Polish-American population counted for something in American public opinion). As time went by, it became clear that, while the Americans might grumble about Soviet domination in eastern Europe, they were not prepared to take serious action to disrupt it, and certainly not to risk war. (This was to be demonstrated beyond all doubt by American inaction during the Hungarian uprising against Soviet control in 1956.) Even so, the Soviet bloc was a threatening presence looming over the rest of Europe. It was backed up by formidable armed forces, far stronger than any that could be deployed by any other European power, and greater in numbers than anything the Americans could produce at that time. In retrospect, it has come to appear that there was no serious danger of a Soviet invasion of western Europe. But in 1947 it was natural to ask where the advance of Soviet power was going to stop, and to be alarmed about the possible answers. By the end of that year, the image of the Soviet Union in the west was changing rapidly, from the much-admired wartime ally and the benevolent Uncle Joe to something much more hostile and threatening.

◆ Turkey and Greece, 1945–46

In 1945–46 there was a continuous state of tension, a sort of grumbling appendix of a crisis, in Turkey and Greece. In June 1945 the Soviet Foreign Minister, Molotov, asked the Turkish government for the lease of a base on the straits between the Black Sea and the Mediterranean – a long-standing Russian aim going back to the time of the Tsars. The Turks refused, and nothing happened. In August 1946 the Soviets renewed their request for a base, coupled with a demand for a revision of the rules governing the passage of warships through the straits, laid down by the Montreux Convention of 1936. Again the Turks refused. On this occasion, the United States thought that a Soviet attack on Turkey was likely, and prepared a war plan which included the possibility of using atomic weapons. In the event, and for a second time, nothing happened. At the same time a civil war was continuing in Greece between the government, supported by the British, and communist guerrillas supported by Yugoslavia (though not by the Soviet Union – it appears that Stalin still stood by his agreement made with Churchill in October 1944).

So far, these events were not of decisive importance. The Soviet Union raised demands at the straits, but did not press them; the Americans were sufficiently interested to prepare a war plan which never had to be put into action. The British, for their own purposes in the Mediterranean and Middle East, were willing to sustain the Greek government against the communists, without making the great effort which would be needed to finish the civil war off. The appendix grumbled on, geographically on the margins of Europe and apparently on the margins of everyone's concerns. Yet in 1947 this area was to produce a decisive development in the shape of the Truman Doctrine of March 1947.[6] To see why, we must go back a little in time.

◆ Kennan's 'long telegram' and Churchill's Fulton speech, 1946

At beginning of 1946 American policy towards the Soviet Union was becoming uncertain. Meetings of Foreign Ministers were growing increasingly difficult. Truman felt that Roosevelt's hope of building a *rapport* with

Stalin and bringing the Soviets into the international club was failing, and that he ought somehow to get tougher with the Russians. But no new policy was in prospect.

Early in 1946 two interventions, one private, the other highly public, brought new influences to bear on American policy: George Kennan's 'long telegram' from Moscow (22 February 1946) and Churchill's speech at Fulton, Missouri, on 5 March.

Kennan was a senior diplomat, temporarily in charge of the American Embassy in Moscow in the absence of the Ambassador, Averell Harriman. In February 1946 he received a routine enquiry from the State Department about a particular aspect of Soviet activity. In reply, he took the opportunity to analyse the roots and nature of the whole of Soviet foreign policy, in a telegram of some 8000 words, 'all neatly divided' (in Kennan's characteristic description), 'like an eighteenth-century Protestant sermon, into five separate parts'. Kennan wrote from a long experience of Soviet affairs (he had first been posted to Moscow in the 1930s, at the height of Stalin's purges), and a deep knowledge of the Russian language, literature and history. As early as September 1944 he had pointed out in a memorandum to Washington that the Russians were setting out to establish their own sphere of influence in eastern Europe and parts of Asia, and argued that the United States should respond by drawing a line beyond which they would not allow Soviet power to operate unchallenged. This 'spheres of influence' policy cut no ice in Washington at the time; but the basic idea of drawing a line was to emerge much later as the policy of containment.

In the 'long telegram', Kennan explained that the Soviet leaders worked on the fixed assumption that they were surrounded by capitalist enemies, whom one day they would have to fight (though fortunately the capitalists were also hostile to one another, and their disputes could be exploited). In this hostile world, the security of the Soviet Union could only be achieved by 'a patient but deadly struggle for the total destruction of their rivals'. This belief was dogmatic (and Kennan urged his readers not to underrate the importance of dogma); but it was also deeply rooted in geography and history, which had left the Russian people with a profound sense of insecurity. His conclusion was that: 'Here we have a political force committed fanatically to the belief that with the United States there can be no permanent *modus vivendi*, that it is necessary and desirable that the internal harmony of our society be disrupted, our traditional way of life be destroyed, the international authority of our state broken, if Soviet power is to be secure.' Coping with this challenge was 'undoubtedly the greatest task our diplomacy has ever faced and probably the greatest which it will ever have to face'. Kennan's specific recommendations at the end of this formidable assessment were remarkably slender. He suggested that the American public should be educated in the realities of the situation, and that the United States should put forward to other nations a positive and constructive picture of the world which it would like to see; which amounted to little more than an exercise in propaganda. There were no recommendations for economic or military aid to other countries; nor did Kennan use on this occasion the word 'containment' to describe the nature of his policy.[7]

Robert Ferrell, in his biography of Truman, wrote that the President did not appear to have read Kennan's long telegram; but it made a great impact in the State Department, where opinion was uncertain as to how to interpret Soviet policy and how to respond to it, as the old wartime ally became increasingly difficult to deal with. One official wrote later that 'There was a universal feeling that "this was it" . . .'[8] In April 1946 Kennan was recalled to Washington and appointed to the newly-formed National War College, where he explained his views to influential audiences. Later, he became head of the new Policy Planning Staff in the State Department, and played an important role in formulating the Marshall Plan. What Kennan did was to present, at a crucial psychological moment, a coherent interpretation of Soviet policy, grounded in experience and history. Such an interpretation had been lacking before. Its consequences took effect over time.

Truman may not have read the long telegram, but he certainly heard Winston Churchill's speech at Fulton, Missouri, on 5 March 1946 – indeed he read it and discussed it in advance At the time, Churchill was admirably placed to make the maximum impact without making any formal commitment. He was out of office in his own country, and therefore did not speak for the British government, never mind the American; but he still bore all the immense prestige of his wartime leadership. In his speech, Churchill set out his interpretation of the current situation in Europe in words which instantly became famous: 'From Stettin in the Baltic to Trieste in the Adriatic, an iron curtain has descended across the Continent.' To the east of that line lay the Soviet sphere, subject to an increasing measure of control from Moscow, and where Communist parties had attained a power far beyond their numerical strength in the countries concerned. Churchill was careful to say that: 'I do not believe that Soviet Russia desires war. What they desire is the fruits of war and the indefinite expansion of their power and doctrines.' This presented a danger that could not be removed by a policy of wait and see or by appeasement. The Russians admired strength, and had no respect for weakness. Churchill referred to his own warnings about Germany in the 1930s, when war 'could have been prevented in my belief without the firing of a single shot'. The solution was to achieve 'a good understanding on all points with Russia under the general authority of the United Nations Organization . . . supported by the whole strength of the English-speaking world and all its connections.' Here lay the core of Churchill's thought: that America, Britain and all the English-speaking peoples of the Commonwealth should combine 'in fraternal association' to create a secure peace.[9]

From the whole speech, three points stand out. First, the striking image of 'the iron curtain' was to be part of the common parlance of the next forty years and more, and encapsulated a vital part of the Cold War. Second, the proposal for an association between the United States and Great Britain to oppose Soviet power and doctrine was the basis for a western alliance. And third, often missed by immediate commentators, was the call for a settlement with the Russians. The Fulton speech was the recognition of a threat, a summons to stand up to it, and a proposal to remove it by agreement.

The reception of this speech in the United States was mixed, with hostility probably prevailing over cordiality. Even Truman's position was equivocal – his journey to Fulton with Churchill and his presence on the platform demonstrated support, but he cautiously distanced himself by claiming (wrongly) that he did not know what Churchill was going to say. Even so, Kennan's long telegram in private and Churchill's Fulton speech in public together did much to change the way in which American official and public opinion thought about relations with the Soviet Union, and about foreign policy in general.

Another event, much less conspicuous in the history books, showed that the American government was ready for a change in policy. Towards the end of February 1946 the Turkish Ambassador to the United States died in post, and Truman decided to send his coffin home in an American battleship, the USS *Missouri*, accompanied by two aircraft-carriers and several other warships. This ostentatious display of naval power, far beyond anything required by diplomatic courtesy, was a gesture of support for Turkey against Soviet pressure for a base at the straits. Truman, the man from Missouri, was ready to look tough, and had found an appropriately named battleship to make his point.

These events were all signs of change. Kennan and Churchill put into circulation new and far-reaching ideas. The massive naval escort for the Turkish Ambassador's coffin showed a willingness to challenge the Soviet Union in the distant Mediterranean. But it was not yet clear where this change was leading.

◆ The Truman Doctrine

In the autumn of 1946 Truman was reflecting on his problems with the Soviet Union. On 21 September he wrote privately that: 'We are not going to have any shooting trouble with them [the Russians] but they are tough bargainers and always ask for the whole earth, expecting maybe to get an acre.' At the beginning of 1947, in New Year mood, the President made a list of things he had to do, ending with an exhortation to himself: 'Make it plain that we have no territorial ambitions. That we only want peace, but we'll fight for it!' He was determined that the United States would not be bulldozed, and thought that he could impress this on the Russians, who were bullies who would cave in if you stood up to them.[10] Tough bargaining and refusal to be bulldozed amounted to an attitude, but not yet a policy.

The decisive change came at the end of February 1947. During that month, the British government, in the grip of an acute economic crisis, decided that it must reduce its overseas expenditure. On 24 February Britain informed the United States that it could no longer afford to provide assistance to Greece, and would shortly withdraw British troops from that country. Truman decided at once that the United States must step in to replace Britain; and that they should also extend aid to Turkey. On 27 February he invited leading members of the Congress to the White House, where Marshall, the Secretary of State, expounded the situation thus:

> If Greece should dissolve into civil war it is altogether probable that it would emerge as a communist state under Soviet control. Turkey would be surrounded and the Turkish situation . . . would in turn become still more critical. Soviet domination might thus extend over the entire Middle East to the borders of India. The effect of this upon Hungary, Austria, Italy and France cannot be overestimated. It is not alarmist to say that we are faced with the first crisis of a series which might extend Soviet domination to Europe, the Middle East and Asia.[11]

It was an early statement of what later became known as the 'domino theory', on the analogy of a line of dominoes so placed that if the first were knocked over the rest would follow. Greece and Turkey were the first dominoes. But it was unlikely that such considerations would carry much weight with the remaining isolationists in Congress, to whom Greece and Turkey seemed a very long way off. The Under-Secretary of State, Dean Acheson, therefore added further arguments about protecting the security of the United States and the defence of freedom. Senator Vandenberg, an influential Republican and a former isolationist who had changed his mind, bluntly advised Truman that the best way to persuade Congress to provide the necessary money was to 'scare hell out of the country'.[12]

Truman absorbed all this advice, and when he addressed Congress on 12 March, he specifically requested a bill to provide aid to Greece and Turkey, but he based his appeal on much wider grounds. He declared that a worldwide struggle was in progress between two ways of life, the one based on free institutions and representative government, the other on terror, oppression and the suppression of personal freedoms. He then moved to the heart of his address: 'I believe that it must be the policy of the United States to support free peoples who are resisting attempted subjugation by armed minorities or by outside pressures.' This support should primarily take the form of economic and financial aid, because 'The seeds of totalitarian regimes are nurtured by misery and want.'[13]

Truman's proposal (which at once became known as the Truman Doctrine) came under fire from two directions. In Congress, opponents of the bill to provide aid to Greece and Turkey pointed out that the Greek government was corrupt and that Turkey was by no means a democracy; and it was wrong for the United States to protect countries which were morally unworthy. (The bill passed the Senate by 67 votes to 23, and the House of Representatives by 287 to 107 – large majorities, but far from unanimity.) On the other hand, Kennan in the State Department criticized the proclamation of an apparently universal commitment to 'free peoples' when all that was actually required was limited support to two particular countries.

In practice, the Truman Doctrine proved to be flexible, and not excessively moral, in its application. In the House of Representatives, one member pointed out that nothing was being done for China, where (as in Greece) the government was waging a civil war against communists. But Acheson, speaking for the administration, replied that China, by virtue of its size, was a different case; and that the President had not laid down that the United States must act in the same way in all circumstances. Moreover, Truman had referred in his speech to totalitarian, not communist, regimes, which left some leeway in action. The next year, in 1948, the American government was to extend economic aid to Yugoslavia when it broke away from the Soviet bloc, even though it remained a communist country, on the grounds that it was in American interests to support Tito and weaken the Soviet Union. But despite this flexibility, it remained true that the criticism levelled at the Truman Doctrine from two very different angles presented a problem from which American policy could never escape. An important section of American opinion demanded strict morality in foreign policy; and yet American interests frequently required support for dubious (or even wicked) regimes. It was virtually impossible to satisfy both.

The Truman Doctrine marked a crucial departure in American policy. Aid to Greece and Turkey brought a clear but limited American commitment in the Mediterranean; while the proclamation of support for free peoples, however open to interpretation in practice, was bound to be far-reaching in its implications. Curiously, it did not bring about any immediate change in American relations with the Soviet Union. It elicited no particular response from Stalin, who had never been particularly interested in Greece. A good deal later, in June, he agreed to supply the Greek communists with small arms and ammunition, which was a very limited response. He seems to have regarded Truman's speech largely as a reaction to his own earlier demands on Turkey for a base at the Straits, which in any case he was not prepared to press. The assumption must be that the Truman Doctrine posed no threat to vital Soviet interests. Stalin was to respond very differently to another American intervention later in 1947: the Marshall Plan.

◆ The Marshall Plan, 1947

On 15 April 1947, during the long drawn-out Moscow Conference of Foreign Ministers, the American Secretary of State George Marshall met Stalin. In the course of their conversation, and apparently in a genuine attempt to cheer Marshall up, Stalin remarked that the interminable discussions at the Conference were only the first skirmishes – 'It was necessary to have patience and not become depressed.' Far from being comforted, Marshall was dismayed, and concluded that Stalin intended to let matters drift until Europe disintegrated, and to advance Soviet interests in the resulting chaos. Speaking on the radio after his return to the United States, Marshall said: 'The patient is sinking while the doctors deliberate. So I believe that action cannot await compromise through exhaustion.'[14]

The 'patient' was western Europe, which in the spring of 1947 faced a severe economic and psychological crisis. The winter of 1946–47 had been exceptionally severe, and the harvests for 1947 promised to be poor. In France, the daily bread ration was reduced on 1 May from 300 to 250 grammes – a grim measure for a people dependent on their bread. Food rationing in Britain was more stringent than in wartime. Everyone suffered from the effects of the so-called 'dollar gap' – the inability of Britain, France and other European countries to pay (in dollars or in exports) for their imports from the United States. Psychologically, the crisis was one of exhaustion after six years of war and two of post-war struggle, with no end in sight. In Britain, the political situation under Attlee's Labour government was entirely secure, but France and Italy were in the grip of deep uncertainty, with unstable governments, the break-up of post-war coalitions, and growing Communist parties. In large parts of Europe, economic hardship was already severe, and political upheaval seemed likely to follow.

The sense of crisis was strong, and even before Marshall's return from Moscow with his doleful message that the patient was sinking the American administration was considering ways of meeting it. A joint committee of the State, War and Navy Departments concluded on 21 April that substantial economic aid to Europe was in American interests, and that it would be best arranged through the co-ordination or integration of the different European economies. In May, Marshall set Kennan's newly established Policy Planning Staff to work on the problem, and by 23 May they had produced three key principles for an aid policy. First, the proposal should not be directed against communism as such, but against economic disaster, which would make Europe vulnerable to totalitarian movements generally. Second, a detailed plan for assistance must not come from the United States, but from a number of European states acting jointly. Third, an offer of aid should be open to the countries of eastern Europe and to the Soviet Union; though it should be so formulated that the Soviet satellites could only join by accepting a large measure of economic co-ordination with others. This principle of co-ordination was of crucial importance to the Americans, partly on grounds of efficiency, to prevent a series of competing national demands, and also because it would appeal to public and Congressional opinion.[15]

It so happened that Marshall was to attend the degree ceremonies at Harvard University on 5 June to receive an honorary degree. He informed the President of the university that he proposed to make a few remarks, and perhaps 'a little more', to mark the occasion.[16] In the event, it proved to be surely the most momentous address ever given on a degree day.

In his speech, Marshall referred to the European economic crisis, and pointed out that 'the consequences to the economy of the United States should be apparent to all'. He went on:

> It is logical that the United States should do whatever it is able to do to assist in the return of normal economic health in the world, without which there can be no political stability and no assured peace. Our policy is directed not against any country or doctrine but against hunger, poverty, desperation and chaos. Its purpose should be the revival of a working economy in the world so as to permit the emergence of political and social conditions in which free institutions can exist. Such assistance, I am convinced, must not be on a piecemeal basis as various crises develop. Any assistance that this Government may render in the future should provide a cure rather than a mere palliative.

Any government willing to assist could expect co-operation from the United States; any government which manœuvred to block recovery could expect no help.[17]

Kennan himself described the purposes of Marshall's proposal as being to save European countries from economic disaster, and enable them to live in the future without 'outside charity: (a) So that they can buy from us; (b) So that they will have enough self-confidence to withstand outside pressures.'[18] These objectives have been much scrutinized and debated. Alan Milward has argued, with the benefit of hindsight, that there was in fact no severe economic crisis in western Europe early in 1947, except in the form of a shortage of foreign exchange, which arose from an *increase* in investment and production.[19] This would have cut little ice at the time, though it may well be that the crisis was as much psychological as economic. Others have claimed that the real crisis lay within the American economy, which needed European recovery for its own selfish purposes. There is little point in enquiring whether American motives were self-interested or for the benefit of others, when in practice they were both at once. It was a simple fact that European states could not 'buy American', and so benefit American producers, unless they had enough dollars, or unless their own currencies could be made strong enough to be convertible with the dollar. Equally, American security depended on saving western European countries from political collapse, possible communist insurrection, or perhaps even Soviet invasion. The European countries themselves would benefit from American economic aid and from greater stability. The United States thus pursued its own interests in ways which worked to the advantage of others.

In his speech at Harvard, Marshall launched an idea, not a plan. Everything depended on the reactions to it. The key lay with Britain and France in western Europe, and the Soviet Union in the east. Bevin and Bidault, the British and French Foreign Ministers, met on 17 June, and agreed that Marshall's suggestion should be taken up at once, but differed on the thorny question of whether to invite the Soviet Union to join them. Bidault, for internal French political reasons, wished to bring the Soviet Union in at an early stage. He proposed that the three countries (France, Britain and the USSR) should meet, and then jointly invite other governments to a conference on the American initiative. Bevin was reluctant to bring in the Soviets, believing that they would only make difficulties; but after some demur he agreed to the French idea. Bevin and Bidault together invited Molotov to meet them, and a meeting of the three Foreign Ministers was arranged in Paris on 27 June.

Would the Soviets agree? Indeed, had Marshall been serious in offering aid to the whole of Europe, east as well as west, or did he always expect that the USSR would refuse? It was almost certain that Congress would not vote to provide aid to the Soviet Union. But equally Kennan assured Marshall that the Soviets would not agree to take part in the scheme. The crux lay in the American insistence on economic co-ordination, which effectively presented the Soviets with the choice of either accepting the aid and giving up the exclusive control of their own economy, or refusing economic co-ordination and thus excluding themselves from aid. As Charles Bohlen, a State Department official, said later: 'we gambled that the Soviets could not come in'; so the Americans could make the offer and let the USSR bear the onus of refusing.[20]

At this early stage, the Soviets temporized. Molotov attended the meeting of Foreign Ministers and raised obstacles to the discussion. He proposed that countries requiring aid should draw up separate lists of their needs, rather than co-ordinating their requests and their own contributions as the Americans had asked. If accepted, this would have sunk the whole scheme at once, because co-ordination was an essential condition for the Americans. He also proposed to exclude Germany from the scheme altogether, playing on French fears of German recovery. This too would have stymied the proposal, because Marshall insisted on the inclusion of Germany. In the discussions, Bevin and Bidault stuck together, rejected Molotov's proposals, and insisted that Marshall's scheme must be discussed as it stood. Above all, they held fast to the idea of a co-ordinated programme for aid.

Molotov could not agree to this. On 2 July he declared that the Anglo-French proposals for a co-ordinated programme would lead to a loss of economic independence and were incompatible with national sovereignty. He left the conference and returned to Moscow. Bevin and Bidault were on the whole relieved by his departure, and went ahead on their own. They sent out joint invitations to a general conference on Marshall's proposals, to be held in Paris on 12 July. Twenty-two European governments were invited (excluding the Soviet Union, which had rejected the idea, and Spain, which under Franco was still ostracized from international society).

For a time there was some doubt as to the responses of the east European states. Czechoslovakia and Poland accepted. The Hungarian press agency reported that its government would take part. This state of affairs did not last long. The Soviet government intervened to bring the east European states into line. Poland withdrew quickly, but Czechoslovakia hesitated. On 8–9 July the Czech Prime Minister, Gottwald, and Foreign Minister, Masaryk, visited Moscow, supposedly to discuss their participation in the conference, but were instead instructed not to attend. Between 9 and 11 July, the governments of Yugoslavia, Bulgaria, Czechoslovakia, Hungary, Romania, Poland, Poland, Albania and Finland all declined to attend the conference.

Stalin's reasoning appears to have been simple, and from his own point of view well founded. If the countries of eastern Europe had attended the conference and accepted Marshall aid, they would have had to accept co-ordination in economic planning, and thus been opened to western economic influence, with inevitable political consequences. The Soviet bloc in eastern Europe, built up since 1945, would have been endangered, and probably crumbled away. Moreover, Stalin regarded Marshall's proposals as an attempt to revive German power and direct it against the Soviet Union; which, whatever Marshall's intentions in 1947, was eventually what happened. Looking back long afterwards, Molotov commented that 'if Western writers believe we were wrong to refuse the Marshall Plan, we must have done the right thing . . . The imperialists were drawing us into their company, but as subordinates. We would have been absolutely dependent on them without getting anything useful in return.'[21] The last remark goes too far, in that the eastern bloc might well have received something useful; but it would surely have been at too high a cost from the Soviet point of view.

Sixteen states attended the conference which opened in Paris on 12 July 1947: Belgium, Canada, Denmark, France, Greece, Iceland, Ireland, Italy,

Luxembourg, the Netherlands, Norway, Portugal, Sweden, Switzerland, Turkey and the United Kingdom. Bevin was elected chairman, and Britain and France took the lead in the conference's proceedings, which were remarkably rapid. In five days the conference set up a Committee for European Economic Co-operation, which in two months prepared a joint plan to submit to the United States. Under this plan, an Organization for European Economic Co-operation (OEEC) was to be set up in order to administer Marshall Aid, and also to co-ordinate the assistance given by member states to one another, with the object of restoring the European economy by the end of 1951. The details were worked out during the winter of 1947–48, and the OEEC was formally set up on 16 April 1948, with its headquarters in Paris.

Meanwhile, Truman and Marshall tackled the problem of convincing Congress of the necessity for giving away large sums of American money. Fortunately for them, the Soviets played into their hands. In February 1948, before Congress voted on the legislation for the Marshall Plan, the communists seized power in Czechoslovakia, sending shivers through all of western Europe and across the Atlantic. (See below, pp. 90–91.) The Senate approved the European Recovery Programme on 13 March by a vote of 69–17, and the House of Representatives followed on 2 April by 318–75.

In the event, Marshall Aid continued until 1953, and amounted to a total of nearly $13 billion. It comprised four crucial elements. First, the aid was to be provided mainly in kind, not in cash. Second, there must be co-ordination and self-help among the recipients – the Americans refused to accept piecemeal requests, or applications for help which the Europeans could provide for themselves. Third, the United States was to decide on the commodities which were to be sent free of charge, and also on their use. This was essential to satisfy Congress, which was afraid of waste and fraud. Fourth, the term of the plan was limited to four years, which allowed the Americans to see a limit to their efforts and the Europeans an end to the controls they were accepting.

The chief beneficiaries of Aid and the amounts involved are as follows:[22]

	Amount of aid ($ million)		Amount in gifts
Total	12 992.5		9290
France	2629	(20.3% of total)	
Italy	1434.6	(11%)	
Low Countries	1078.7	(8.3%)	
West Germany	1317.3	(10.1%)	
United Kingdom	3165.8	(24.4%)	

Marshall Aid did not bring immediate results. In France, unemployment almost doubled between 1948 and 1950, rising from 78 000 to 153 000. In Italy, the unemployment figures went down slightly, from 1 742 000 in

1948 to 1 615 000 in 1950.[23] The powerful Communist Parties in France and Italy, which campaigned violently against Marshall Aid, maintained their support among voters. But gradually the programme took effect, especially on the balance of payments problem. To take France as a crucial example, in 1948, Marshall Aid financed 30.1 per cent of French imports; and over the whole period of the aid programme, Marshall Aid financed the equivalent of 69.5 per cent of the total deficit in the French balance of payments.[24] France was thus able to carry out a substantial programme of reconstruction and investment without reducing standards of living, even when reserves of gold and foreign currency were virtually exhausted.

In return for Marshall Aid, the recipient countries had to make certain concessions to American economic policy. They had to adhere to the General Agreement on Tariffs and Trade (GATT), signed on 30 October 1947, and thus accept some lowering of tariffs and phasing out of quotas, which the French in particular found difficult (and to some degree managed to evade). The recipients of Marshall Aid usually had to accept certain types of American exports, whether they wanted them or not, which led to much grumbling, especially in France, about 'chewing-gum imperialism'. It was in the nature of things impossible for aid on this scale to be given without arousing resentment as well as gratitude among those being helped.

But in general the Marshall Plan was a success story, and it has remained a model for all such projects – though one aspired to rather than achieved. Its final success was probably even more psychological than economic The participating countries came to *believe* that there was a way through their difficulties. In July 1947 Kennan wrote that the plan was necessary 'So that they [the European countries] will have enough self-confidence to withstand outside pressures.'[25] That self-confidence was achieved, in full measure, by the time Marshall Aid came to an end.

◆ The concept of containment

In July 1947, a month after Marshall's speech at Harvard which launched the Marshall Plan, the influential American periodical *Foreign Affairs* published an an article (signed only 'X') entitled 'The Sources of Soviet Conduct'.[26] The author was in fact George Kennan, and the article was a reworking, after a year and a half and for a different readership, of the ideas set out in his 'long telegram' of February 1946. His basic theme remained that the Soviet Union, for its own political and ideological reasons, was implacably hostile to the outside world. The aim of its policy was 'to make sure that it has filled every nook and cranny available to it in the basin of world power. But if it finds unassailable barriers in its path, it accepts these philosophically and accommodates itself to them.' It followed therefore that: 'The main element of any United States policy towards the Soviet

Union must be that of a long-term, patient but firm and vigilant containment of Russian expansive tendencies.' The Russians must be confronted with 'unalterable counter-force at every point where they show signs of encroaching upon the interests of a peaceful and stable world'.

Kennan went on to evoke a remarkable vision of the future. At some point there might occur a crisis within the Soviet system, in which leaders tried to win active participation from supporters who had been schooled only in obedience. This would 'disrupt the unity and efficacy of the Party as a political instrument', and as a result 'Soviet Russia might be changed overnight from one of the strongest to one of the weakest and most pitiable of national societies.' Something like this was actually to happen in the late 1980s, when Gorbachev tried to reform the Soviet system, and instead brought about its demise. But in 1947 it seemed a distant, and most likely a vain, hope; and meanwhile Kennan offered only a task with no end in sight, demanding a patience, endurance and flexibility which would test the will and capacity of the American people to the uttermost.

In his memoirs, Kennan complained that the word 'containment' had been turned into the basis of 'one of those indestructible myths that are the bane of the historian'.[27] There was some truth in this, in that the concept of containment was used to attribute coherence to policies which were often improvised rather than systematic. Yet Henry Kissinger was surely right to argue that 'all the various strands of American post-war thought were brought together' in Kennan's article, which for over a generation served as 'the bible of the containment policy'.[28] There are times when an author catches 'a tide in the affairs of men' in a way almost independent of his own intentions. Kennan struck such a time with his 'X' article in July 1947.

The concept of containment was to become the staple of American foreign policy, and proved in the end to be a remarkable success. But almost from the start it came under fire from widely different angles. Some critics argued that 'containment' went too far, and would draw the United States into excessive commitments to all kinds of countries, perhaps of dubious moral standing, and so into positions which would prove untenable. (Vietnam was later to prove a case in point.) Others claimed that it did not go far enough, and that the USA should aim not merely at containment but at liberating countries under Soviet control. There were sceptics who held that containment was mistaken because there was nothing to contain – Soviet policy was motivated by fear, not expansionism. All these viewpoints won support from different sections of American opinion, producing a sustained debate on the conduct of foreign policy. Yet through all the discussions, the basic idea of containment held its own, and elicited a remarkably tenacious response from the American people.

In 1947 the Truman Doctrine and the Marshall Plan marked important practical departures in American foreign policy, and Kennan's 'X' article was published at the precise moment to give these changes a theoretical basis. American policy was assuming a new shape. The latter part of 1947 and 1948 were to see Stalin's response.

◆ Notes to Chapter 4

1. Michael J. Hogan, ed., *America in the World: The Historiography of American Foreign Relations since 1941* (Cambridge, 1995) provides an excellent guide.
2. See below, pp. 70–71 for the Moscow Conference and the German Question.
3. See below, pp. 453–5 for later developments in Eritrea and Somaliland.
4. See below, p. 101 for the Soviet–Finnish treaty of 1948.
5. See below, pp. 99–100 for the Yugoslav–Soviet split.
6. See below, pp. 77–80 for the Truman Doctrine.
7. George F. Kennan, *Memoirs*, Vol. I: *1925–1950* (London, 1967), p. 293. Long excerpts from the telegram are printed, *ibid.*, pp. 547–59.
8. Robert H. Ferrell, *Harry S. Truman: A Life* (London, 1994), p. 248; Louis Halle, *The Cold War as History* (New York, 1967), p. 105.
9. For the Fulton speech, Martin Gilbert, *Never Despair: Winston S. Churchill, 1945–1965* (London, 1988), pp. 192–206; for the New York speech, *ibid.*, pp. 215–17.
10. Ferrell, *Truman*, pp. 249–51.
11. Forrest C. Pogue, *George C. Marshall*, Vol. IV: *Statesman, 1945–1959* (New York, 1987), p. 164.
12. Ferrell, *Truman*, p. 251.
13. Royal Institute of International Affairs, *Documents on International Affairs, 1947–1948* (London, 1952), pp. 2–7.
14. Pogue, *Marshall*, Vol. IV, pp. 191 (Stalin's remarks) and 200 (Marshall's broadcast).
15. This memorandum is in *Foreign Relations of the United States, 1947*, Vol. III, pp. 223–9.
16. Pogue, *Marshall*, Vol. IV, pp. 209–10.
17. Text of Marshall's speech, RIIA, *Documents*, pp. 23–6.
18. Kennan memorandum, 23 July 1947, quoted in Wilson D. Miscamble, *George F. Kennan and the Making of American Foreign Policy* (Princeton, 1992), p. 60; Richard J. Barnet, *Allies: America, Europe, Japan since the War* (London, 1984), pp. 113–14.
19. Alan Milward, *The Reconstruction of Western Europe* (London, 1987), pp. 1–17.
20. Quoted in Diane B. Kunz, *Butter and Guns: America's Cold War Economic Diplomacy* (New York, 1997), p. 34.
21. V. Molotov, *Molotov Remembers: Inside Kremlin Politics*.

Conversations with Felix Chuev, ed. Albert Resis (Chicago, 1993), p. 62.
22. Maurice Vaisse, *Les relations internationales depuis 1945* (Paris, 3rd edn, 1994), p. 19.
23. B. R. Mitchell, *European Historical Statistics, 1750–1970* (London, abridged edn, 1978), pp. 67–8.
24. Hubert Bonin, *Histoire économique de la IVè République* (Paris, 1987), p. 153.
25. Quoted in Barnet, *Allies*, p. 114.
26. 'X' (George F. Kennan), 'The Sources of Soviet Conduct', *Foreign Affairs*, Vol. 25, No. 4, July 1947, pp. 169–82.
27. Kennan, *Memoirs*, Vol. I, p. 356, where he also records that Marshall was shocked by the publication of the article. 'Planners don't talk' was his soldierly comment.
28. Henry Kissinger, *Diplomacy* (London, 1994), p. 454.

CHAPTER 5

THE BEGINNING OF THE COLD WAR, 2: THE PRAGUE COUP TO THE NORTH ATLANTIC TREATY, 1948–1949

Cominform and Czechoslovakia – The Berlin blockade – The Brussels and North Atlantic Treaties – The Two Germanies and the Soviet–Yugoslav split – Reflections on the beginning of the Cold War

The first part of 1947 had seen important American initiatives in policy towards the Soviet Union, in the Truman Doctrine, the Marshall Plan and the formulation of the concept of containment. In the latter part of 1947 and the first half of 1948, Stalin developed his response.

◆ Cominform and Czechoslovakia, 1947–48

The disarray among the eastern European governments on whether or not to attend the Paris conference on Marshall Aid in July 1947 brought Stalin to the point where he could no longer tolerate divergences within the Soviet bloc. He set out to impose order through the familiar instruments of ideology and party discipline. He summoned a conference of communist party leaders at Szklarska Poreba, in Poland, on 22–8 September 1947, under the chairmanship of Zhdanov, the ideological spokesman of the Soviet government. As well as the Soviet Union, there were delegations from the Communist Parties of Bulgaria, Czechoslovakia, Hungary, Poland, Romania and Yugoslavia, and in the west from the French and Italian Parties. Zhdanov's keynote speech to the conference set out the thesis that the world was divided between the imperialist and capitalist camp, led by the United States, and the socialist camp, led by the Soviet Union. He brought home this rather prosaic point by denouncing the Marshall Plan as a programme for the enslavement of Europe. The conference set up the Communist Information Bureau (Cominform), with the ostensible purpose of promoting unity and co-operation between the member parties by exchanging information, and in practice to ensure uniformity under Stalin's control. Its headquarters were to be established in Belgrade.

At that stage, it appeared that Czechoslovakia represented the weakest link in the chain of Soviet control. The Czech representatives at the Szklarska Probeda conference were criticized for their shortcomings in advancing communism, and indeed Czechoslovakia differed markedly from other eastern European countries. There was no Soviet garrison. There was a strong tradition of parliamentary democracy. The President, Edvard Benes, was committed to a pro-Soviet foreign policy, while trying to maintain his country as a bridge between East and West, combining some of the elements of each in its political and economic systems. The Prime Minister, Klement Gottwald, was a communist; but the Foreign Minister was Jan Masaryk, son of the founder of the Czechoslovakian state, and a figure much respected throughout western Europe. Czechoslovakia thus lay within the Soviet sphere but was not fully integrated into it – a balance which was important for the country itself, and for international relations in Europe as a whole. By the beginning of 1948, this sort of balance was no longer acceptable to the Soviet Union.

During 1947 there had been signs that the communists were losing ground, and a public opinion poll in January 1948 put their support at only 25 per cent. The Communist Party reacted by forming, on 20 February 1948, a 'People's Militia', some 15 000 strong, to exert pressure on the streets. On the same day, twelve ministers (out of a total of 26) resigned from the government, hoping to force Benes to form a new administration without the communists, and to call elections, which would reveal the weakness of the Communist Party in the country. But a number of non-communist ministers remained in office, and the communists themselves took the offensive, with street demonstrations and marches by the armed workers of the People's Militia. Gottwald was in constant touch with the Soviet Ambassador; and the Soviet Deputy Foreign Minister, Zorin, on a visit to Prague, promised that the USSR would not allow western intervention. The Soviet Army moved some of its troops in Poland to the Czech border. Benes at first resisted this communist pressure, but on 25 February he gave way and appointed a new government, nominated by Gottwald and consisting of a majority of communist ministers, with a few socialists, and with Masaryk remaining as Foreign Minister. A few days later, on 10 March, Masaryk's body was found beneath a window of the Foreign Ministry building – whether through murder or suicide remained obscure.

In these political changes, the constitutional forms were observed. Benes appointed Gottwald as Prime Minister, and accepted his list of ministers; a majority of deputies in parliament voted in favour of the new government. But these forms did not last long. The former Social Democratic Party was soon absorbed into the Communist Party, and other political parties were placed under communist control. In May 1948 elections produced a communist-dominated legislature, which introduced a new constitution on the Soviet model. Benes resigned as President on 6 June, and died soon afterwards. Czechoslovakia came firmly within the Soviet sphere.

The impact of these events in the West was immense. Stalin may well have thought that he was simply consolidating his grip on a part of what was already his sphere of influence, and in some sense this was true. But in western eyes Czechoslovakia was different from the rest of the Soviet sphere. Britain and France were sharply aware of accusations that they had let Czechoslovakia down in the Munich crisis in 1938; and in March 1939 the German 'coup of Prague' had been the prologue to war in September.

Events in Czechoslovakia thus touched a sensitive nerve. Léon Blum, the veteran French socialist leader, asked how it came about that the socialist and other democratic parties in Prague had melted away so swiftly; and many pointed out in reply that collaboration with the communists was a one-way street, ending in a take-over. The death of Jan Masaryk shocked western opinion. If it was suicide, then Masaryk had despaired of his country under the new regime; if it was murder, it showed how far the communists would go. Either way, the prospects were gloomy. In western Europe, the danger of internal subversion and perhaps war suddenly loomed large. The West responded by drawing together in the Treaty of Brussels, which we will consider in a moment.[1] But soon after the Czechoslovakian coup a new and more dangerous crisis arose over Berlin.

◆ The Berlin blockade, 1948–49

In 1946 the Americans and British had united their occupation zones in Germany into the Bizone; and in 1947 it was decided that all the western zones (but not the eastern) were to receive Marshall Aid. The division of Germany was well under way. Berlin, on the other hand, though divided into occupation zones, was still being administered jointly by the four occupying powers: the USSR, USA, Britain and France. Berlin was thus in a different situation from the rest of Germany, and presented an opportunity to Soviet policy.

It appears that at the end of 1947 Stalin decided to squeeze the western powers out of Berlin. He could see them violating the Potsdam agreements in their zones, so there seemed no reason for him not to do the same in his. On 20 March 1948, at what was expected to be a regular meeting of the Allied Control Council in Berlin, Marshal Sokolovsky (the Commander-in-Chief of the Soviet zone) read at high speed a list of accusations against the western occupying powers, and then left. This proved to be the last full meeting of the Council, though the western commanders continued to meet in the absence of the Soviet representative. On 1 April 1948 Soviet troops stopped the regular American, British and French trains on their way to

Berlin, just inside the Soviet zone, pushed them into sidings, and left them there for over twelve hours before sending them back where they had come from. This was the beginning of a campaign of harassment and delays to western traffic, amounting to a form of limited blockade, which caused inconvenience and irritation, but at that stage not much more.

Meanwhile, the western powers were proceeding with plans to form a new state in West Germany, based upon the three western occupation zones. In June 1948, the United States, Britain and France agreed to unify their zones of occupation, and announced that they were to arrange elections for a constituent assembly, which would then prepare a constitution for a new West German state. They also made secret preparations for the introduction of a new currency, the Deutschmark, in the western zones and in Berlin. These were two crucial steps. The creation of a West German state would conclude the division of Germany; the introduction of the Deutschmark led to an immediate conflict with the Soviet Union.

The new currency was introduced in the western zones on 20 June 1948. On the 23rd, the Soviets introduced their own currency reform in their occupation zone, and declared that it applied to the whole of Berlin. The western powers introduced the new Deutschmark in Berlin on the same day; and it was at once clear that the western currency commanded public confidence and the eastern did not. This proved to be the trigger for drastic Soviet action. On 24 June the Soviet occupation forces halted all rail, road and water traffic between the three western zones and Berlin. Postal services ceased to operate. Electricity supplies to West Berlin from outside were cut off. The blockade of West Berlin had begun.

The introduction of the Deutschmark was the immediate cause of the blockade, because if the new currency were allowed to circulate freely throughout Berlin it would undermine the value of the East German currency and the whole stability of the Soviet zone. But Stalin's underlying intentions in imposing the blockade remain unclear. He had been thinking for some time of squeezing the western powers out of Berlin – perhaps as an end in itself, simply to consolidate the Soviet zone; perhaps to block the creation of a new state in West Germany; perhaps to force a negotiation on a complete German settlement, in his own favour. For any of these purposes, a blockade of Berlin presumably seemed a safe bet: the western powers 'would have to give up either Berlin or their German policy'.[2]

The result was a crisis of a kind not seen since the end of the Second World War. The United States government was convinced that if they gave up West Berlin they would not be able to hold on anywhere else in Europe, if only because no one would *believe* that they would. In any domino theory, West Berlin was a crucial domino, and if it fell the rest of western Europe would fall with it. There was no half-way house.

Truman reacted to this crisis with an astute mixture of determination and caution. He told one adviser on 28 June that 'we were going to stay – period'; but added the next day that he intended to stay 'as long as possible', by which he meant 'short of war'.[3] How could this be done? In principle, there was a way open. In the muddled (and supposedly temporary) agreement achieved at the Potsdam Conference in 1945, there had been no written provision for access to Berlin by the western powers by rail, road or water; but by a curious quirk there was a written agreement on access by three designated air corridors. On 25 June, General Clay, the American Commander-in-Chief, began on his own initiative to send supplies to Berlin by air along these air corridors; and Truman supported this action the next day. But at the time no one considered that this was anything more than a temporary device to gain time for thought. The Americans considered sending a convoy of lorries down one of the roads to Berlin, with an escort of troops and tanks; but they held back. Instead, the air-lift which began as an improvisation was developed into a regular means of supply. The Americans brought aircraft from all over the world; the Royal Air Force made its contribution; a completely new airfield was built in the French sector of Berlin, bringing the number of landing-grounds up to three. The momentum was kept up even during the difficult winter months. In one extraordinary period of 24 hours on 15–16 April 1949, aircraft were landing in Berlin at the rate of almost one a minute, and a total of almost 13 000 tons of cargo was landed. In the whole period of the blockade, there were 277 804 flights, delivering 2 325 809 tons of cargo.[4] The Berliners suffered a hard winter, with barely adequate supplies of coal and long electricity cuts. Food rations were actually increased in the course of the blockade, but remained very tight. All the time, the Soviets watched the aircraft coming in, sometimes 'buzzed' them at close range, but never took the final step of shooting one down.

This was the most acute form of 'cold war'. The Soviet Union and the United States confronted one another on an issue of the utmost importance to them both. They came to the verge of war, but did not cross it. The Americans did not try to force a land passage; the Soviets did not attempt to close the air routes. It was a psychological test of will rather than a direct trial of strength.

The contest went on for ten and a half months, and then ended suddenly, in complete defeat for the Soviet Union. Stalin lifted the blockade on 12 May 1949 without any conditions and without achieving any of his likely objectives. The western powers remained in Berlin, which was now firmly divided into two parts. Progress towards a new West German state continued at a steady pace. Indeed, the Soviet situation became worse, because there emerged a new solidarity between the West Berliners and their former enemies. The American and British air forces which only recently had strained every nerve to bomb Berlin now worked round the clock to bring supplies to that same city – sometimes it was even the same airmen who were involved. Berliners who had survived the air raids now welcomed their former attackers, and endured new hardships with a stoicism which commanded admiration. This was the time when the Berliners worked their passage to respectability in western eyes – a change without which the new West German state, and later the new Western Europe, could never have been achieved.

The significance of the Berlin crisis of 1948–49 cannot be overstated. It was a true crisis, in both senses of that sometimes overused word: it was a time of acute danger, and it was a turning-point in international affairs. The United States displayed immense material strength, technical proficiency and powers of endurance, all deployed in the service of a remarkably sure-footed statesmanship. Britain took its full share, and France, though previously divided from the Americans and British on the question of Germany, rallied to their support. The psychological foundations of a western alliance were laid in this time of trial as they could not otherwise have been. Stalin, for his part, completely miscalculated the reactions of his opponent, and made an immense effort without achieving any result whatsoever – indeed by the end of the blockade his position was actually worse than at the beginning. It was a sign of the extraordinary strength of his position in the Soviet Union and the world in general that he survived this defeat without, so far as can be seen, the slightest loss of prestige or power.

The Czechoslovakian coup of February 1948 and the Berlin blockade of 1948–49 set alarm bells ringing throughout western Europe and the United States. Memories of the 1930s, when Hitler had picked off his enemies one by one until it was almost too late to resist him, were still fresh in everyone's minds. In face of the advance of Soviet power in Czechoslovakia and the tremendous trial of the Berlin blockade, the western powers produced a determined response.

◆ The Brussels and North Atlantic Treaties, 1948–49

In November–December 1947 the Council of Foreign Ministers of the four former wartime allies met for what proved to be the last time, in London. The conference ended in failure on 15 December, marking the end of the mechanism which the Big Three had set up at Potsdam in 1945 to continue their wartime co-operation. For some time there were no more great-power conferences, and the two superpowers virtually ceased to communicate with one another.

The Foreign Ministers' meeting collapsed at a time when communist opposition to the Marshall Plan was at its height, especially in France and Italy. In both countries tension was extreme. In these circumstances, Ernest Bevin, the British Foreign Secretary, believed that western Europe faced an imminent danger of internal communist subversion or external Soviet invasion, or possibly both at once; and he sought for some means to counter the threat. He cloaked his thoughts in obscure phraseology, speaking sometimes of a federation of western Europe, sometimes of a 'spiritual federation of the West'; but his underlying message was plain. The west European states must act quickly to support one another, and they must bring in the Americans, who alone had the military strength to resist the Soviets if it came to the use of force.[5]

The response to Bevin's ideas was at first uncertain. France in particular, with its large Communist Party and a difficult domestic situation, wanted to avoid offending the Soviet Union, and if possible to prevent the final division of Europe into hostile camps. Negotiations to form an alliance between Britain, France, Belgium, the Netherlands and Luxembourg (the Benelux countries) began in February 1948, but made little progress until the bombshell of the Communist take-over in Czechoslovakia at the end of that month. This caused such alarm that a five-power conference of Britain, France and the Benelux countries met at Brussels on 4 March, and on the 17th concluded the Treaty of Brussels, which bound all the participants to come to the help of any one of them if attacked in Europe. The preamble made a token reference to preventing a renewal of German aggression, but the unnamed aggressor envisaged in the treaty was the Soviet Union.

The Brussels Treaty was a gesture rather than a practical step towards security. In military terms, the five treaty powers could not defend western Europe against a Soviet attack. The British and the French, who would provide most of the military strength, knew they would have to bring in the Americans. Bevin had a scheme for three linked defensive alliances: the Brussels Pact, a Mediterranean agreement, and an Atlantic treaty to include the United States. The initiative for what emerged as the North Atlantic Treaty thus came from western Europe

The Americans were already anxious about Europe, in the wake of the communist take-over in Czechoslovakia. Italy seemed the point of greatest danger. Elections were due in April, with the communists and socialists co-operating in the Democratic Popular Front. In the elections of 1946, these two left-wing parties together had polled about a million more votes than the conservative Christian Democrats, and on that analogy it seemed likely that they might win in 1948. The State Department was nervous about the election results, and an academic expert on international relations told the Policy Planning Staff on 1 March that 'If Italy goes Red, Communism cannot be stopped in Europe.'[6] The Americans therefore made every effort to ensure that de Gasperi, the leader of the Chrisian Democratic Party, won the elections. They delivered wheat to prevent a reduction in the bread ration; they encouraged Italian-Americans to write to their relations in Italy and urge them to vote Christian Democrat; they supplied money through the Central Intelligence Agency to the Italian centre parties. The elections took place on 18–19 April 1948, and in the event the Christian Democrats won by a wide margin, gaining 307 seats against 182 for the Popular Democratic Front of Communists and Left-wing Socialists.[7] Yet for some time the sense of crisis had been sharp, and anxiety (in Italy and in the State Department) had been keen.

This sort of anxiety, and clandestine intervention, did not mean that the American government, or the Congress, was eager for a military alliance to protect western Europe. In the State Department, Kennan opposed the idea, arguing that the real danger was political and economic, and must be resisted by political and economic means. More important, the whole idea of an alliance remained alien to American tradition and American instincts – George Washington had warned against 'entangling alliances', and his words still carried weight. The American response to the British and French approaches for an alliance was therefore slow. Secret talks between the Americans, British and Canadians began in Washington on 22 March, and produced a proposal for a North Atlantic Defence Treaty by 1 April. (The 'secrecy' of these talks was badly undermined by the fact that Donald Maclean, a Soviet agent, was a member of the British delegation. Stalin was thus well informed about the negotiations, though it is hard to tell what effect this knowledge had on his policy.)

The discussions on a treaty then stalled. Marshall, the Secretary of State, delayed even setting a date to open negotiations with the Brussels Treaty powers as a whole; and Truman was uncertain as to the best course to adopt. One difficulty was the likelihood of opposition from Congress, but in June this was much diminished by the advocacy of Senator Vandenberg. Vandenberg was a Republican and former isolationist, who in 1948 was working with the Truman administration to devise a bipartisan policy towards Europe. He put before the Senate a resolution which recalled the right of collective self-defence enshrined in the United Nations Charter, and affirmed the desirability of American association with arrangements for such self-defence. His carefully worded resolution, which made no mention of a treaty, an alliance, or Europe, was accepted by the Senate on 11 June by 64 votes to 16. But there remained a wide gap between this and something more precise.[8]

The start of the Berlin blockade on 24 June 1948 brought some sense of crisis, but still no great haste. Talks on a security treaty involving the USA, Canada, Britain, France, Belgium, the Netherlands and Luxembourg began on 6 July, but they moved with painful slowness. The Americans delayed because the next presidential election was due in November, with campaigning taking up the summer and autumn – not the best time to undertake novel and far-reaching commitments. They also insisted that the Congress's constitutional right to declare war must be preserved, so that a treaty should not include any automatic obligation to go to war. The French made difficulties, demanding that Italy should be included among the participants in a treaty, to protect the Mediterranean, and also that the treaty should specifically cover Algeria, which was then legally part of France.

The difficulties on the American side were eventually removed. Kennan reluctantly changed his mind in November 1948. He still believed that the need for a military pact was a purely subjective one, existing only in the minds of the west Europeans; but he came to accept that a treaty would increase European self-confidence, and it should therefore go ahead. The re-election of Truman in November cleared away many domestic political difficulties. As late as 5 February, Senators Vandenberg and Connally were still anxious about infringing the rights and powers of Congress, but eventually a wording was found which combined a commitment to immediate action with respect for the right of Congress to declare war. The French gained both their points, about Italian membership of the treaty and a specific mention that the area covered included Algeria. In a series of meetings in Washington from 14 January to 15 March 1949, agreement on a final draft text was reached. The various governments involved gave their approval, and the North Atlantic Treaty was signed on 4 April 1949. No one could say that the Americans had forced the pace, or leaped hastily to the defence (or the domination) of Europe. But when they did eventually make up their minds, the consequences were far-reaching.

The North Atlantic Treaty was to remain a predominant feature of the international landscape for decades to come. At the time of writing (2000) it is still functioning, despite the demise of its opponent, the Soviet Union. What did the treaty provide for, and what was its significance? The twelve states which signed the treaty in April 1949 were: the United States and Canada in North America; Iceland in the North Atlantic; and in Europe Belgium, Denmark, France, Italy, Luxembourg, the Netherlands, Norway, Portugal and the United Kingdom. The key article of the treaty was Article 5, which stated that an armed attack against one or more of these states would be considered an attack on all. The other member states would then take forthwith such action as each deemed necessary, including the use of armed force. This preserved the rights of the United States Senate, while creating an expectation that in practice an attack on one signatory would result in war with all. Article 6 defined the territories which were covered by the treaty: the territories of the signatories in Europe and North America; the Algerian departments of France; islands north of the Tropic of Cancer (in effect, the Portuguese islands of Madeira and the Azores). This article also extended to any attack on the occupation forces of any of the signatories in Europe, thus covering West Germany and West Berlin, and the western zones in Austria and Vienna. The United States Senate ratified the treaty on 21 July 1949, after twelve days of debate, by 82 votes to 13.[9]

For the United States the treaty was a remarkable departure – the first peacetime alliance in American history. Yet it was not presented as such.

Henry Kissinger commented much later that 'America would do anything for the Atlantic Alliance except call it an alliance'.[10] A State Department memorandum carefully examined various other alliances to show how the North Atlantic Treaty differed from them. The government claimed that it was not a military alliance, but an alliance against war itself. This had the strange consequence that what was essentially an alliance to preserve the balance of power and the security of western Europe was presented primarily in moral terms. In one sense it was an evasion of the issues; yet in a deeper sense it was vital. The North Atlantic Treaty committed the United States to what proved to be a long haul of forty years, which could not have been sustained without a strong sense of moral certainty. For the European members of the alliance, the treaty provided the practical certainty of American protection, a form of insurance policy which added a military element to the economic support provided by Marshall aid. The two together brought a confidence and stability to western Europe which were the foundation for all the progress which followed.

The North Atlantic Treaty said nothing about a North Atlantic Treaty Organization. Not until December 1950 (after the outbreak of the Korean War, to which we shall come in the next chapter) did the signatories of the treaty agree to set up an integrated defence organization, with a command system modelled on the Anglo-American joint commands during the Second World War. The first Supreme Commander was General Eisenhower, who had commanded the Allied Armies in western Europe in 1944–45. This command structure, always headed by an American general, and the presence of American troops on the ground, confirmed the practical expectation that the United States would be involved in any war from the beginning. Thus the North Atlantic Treaty evolved into the North Atlantic Treaty Organization, whose initials, NATO, have entered everyday speech. It had its difficulties. It was a military organization without much military strength on the ground, and without a convincing strategy, because no one really knew how western Europe could be defended against an all-out Soviet attack. Could a Soviet offensive be stopped in the middle of Germany, or on the Rhine; or could the generals only plan for a more orderly repetition of the Dunkirk evacuation of 1940? In the event, this was not put to the test. No Soviet invasion was launched, and it appears that none was seriously contemplated. The true importance of the North Atlantic Treaty was political, and above all psychological. NATO developed into a flexible and durable political instrument, involving the United States in European affairs in a way which ensured stability without complete American predominance. Under the cover of the NATO shield, however inadequate in military terms, the states of western Europe recovered their nerve. Even at the worst of times, there were to be no more alarms like those of 1947 and 1948, when it appeared that everything might dissolve into chaos, and so invite a Soviet attack even if none was actually planned. These advantages were purchased at a certain price in diplomatic rigidity, in that the creation of NATO meant the institutionalizing of the Cold War; but this was a price which proved well worth paying.

◆ The two Germanies and the Soviet–Yugoslav split

In 1948–49 there were two other developments of long-term significance for Europe and for the Cold War. First, the division of Germany was finally sealed by the establishment of two German states, the Federal Republic of Germany in the west and the German Democratic Republic in the east. In 1948, a long conference in London between the three western occupying powers agreed to convoke a constituent assembly to prepare a constitution for a federal and parliamentary West German state. The assembly met in 1948, and formulated a Basic Law for the new state, which came formally into existence in September 1949, with Konrad Adenauer as its first Chancellor. It was not yet fully sovereign, because an Allied High Commission exercised wide control over economic and foreign policy, and it was to remain entirely demilitarized, without armed forces. In the next few years, West Germany in fact moved rapidly towards control of its own economic affairs, but only slowly towards rearmament, which was a highly sensitive issue internally as well as abroad. In the Soviet occupation zone, the creation of an East German state followed some distance behind these developments in the west. The constitution of the German Democratic Republic (GDR) was enacted in October 1949. In contrast to the federal and parliamentary structure of West Germany, the GDR was set up as a centralized socialist state, firmly under the control of the Communist Party, which was itself controlled by the Soviet Union. The two Germanies did not officially recognize one another's existence. Their separation was total, and was marked on the ground, on the eastern side of the boundary, by the physical barrier of the 'iron curtain', a line of barbed wire, minefields and machine-guns. It was striking that the machine guns did not point outwards, to deter attack, but inwards to prevent escape. The barrier was intended to obstruct passage from east to west.

As Germany and Europe thus congealed into two halves, the eastern part showed its first crack. When the Soviet Union set up the Cominform in 1947 to keep the east European states together in ideological unity, the headquarters of the new organization was established in Belgrade. But in 1948 there occurred a grave and bitter conflict between Yugoslavia and the Soviet Union. Yugoslavia was in a different position from the other east European countries, in that Tito's partisans had largely liberated the country themselves, with more help from the British than from the Soviets. Tito was in a strong position, and tended to take his own line in both internal matters and foreign policy. This was unwelcome to Stalin, who in 1948 put heavy pressure on Tito to conform. He accused the Yugoslav Communist Party of deviations from Marxist–Leninist doctrine, and of pursuing a course unfriendly to the Soviet Union. On 28 June 1948 Stalin ordered the expulsion of Yugoslavia from the Cominform; and *Pravda* described Tito as 'the fascist hireling of the USA'.[11] Soviet advisers left the country, and economic assistance was cut off. The whole panoply of Soviet propaganda was directed against Yugoslavia. The trumpets sounded, but the walls did not come tumbling down. Tito defied his new enemies, formerly his friends, and survived. He declared that Yugoslavia would fight if attacked, and threatened to drench the country's soil in blood. Stalin did not attack, though it appears that an invasion plan, including Soviet, Hungarian, Romanian and Bulgarian forces, was prepared in the summer of 1950. Yugoslavia was thus expelled from the Soviet bloc, and lived to tell the tale.

The United States, faced with this new situation, showed a remarkable flexibility. Tito remained a communist, holding an ideology hostile to America and the western world; but he had defied Stalin. In these unexpected circumstances, the United States government adopted a policy of cautious encouragement to Tito, notably in economic relations. Tito for his part – though without making any specific bargain – closed the Yugoslav border with Greece and ceased to send help to the Greek communists. The Soviet bloc had developed a serious split. The Americans were willing to blur the lines of their opposition to communism. The Cold War was going to be a complicated affair.

◆ Reflections on the beginnings of the Cold War

In the years we have just examined, from 1945 to 1949, the wartime alliance between the USA, the USSR and Britain broke down. Conferences between the powers ceased after the London Conference of Foreign Ministers in December 1947. The two superpowers entered a period of strained relations so severe that they ceased to practise all but the most formal diplomatic relations. Most of Europe was sharply divided. The Soviet Union imposed an iron control on most of eastern Europe. The United States, through Marshall Aid and the North Atlantic alliance, established its own sphere of economic and military influence in western Europe. Yet the two sides in this great divide stopped there. They did not go to war. This was the state of affairs which became known as the Cold War: war in so far as there was a condition of intense hostility, but cold in that there was no actual fighting.

The exact nature of this phenomenon of the Cold War will be examined later.[12] Let us look now at the more limited question of how the division of Europe came about, and review the chronological pattern of events.

First, in 1946, the division of Germany began, with the Soviet Union taking the initiative in political affairs by imposing its communist model in the east, and the Americans taking the lead in the economic division of the country. Second, there was a period from February to July 1947 in which the United States formulated a new policy and took the initiative. This was the time of the Truman Doctrine, the launching of the Marshall Plan, and the crystallization of the concept of containment in Kennan's 'X' article. Third, there followed a period in which the Soviet Union imposed rigid control on its sphere in eastern Europe, established Cominform, and took crucial initiatives in the communist seizure of power in Czechoslovakia and the imposition of the Berlin blockade. Fourth, the Czech crisis and the Berlin blockade brought a reaction from the western powers in the form of the Brussels Treaty of 1948 and the North Atlantic Treaty of 1949. The chronological pattern, therefore, was not one in which one side alone took the initiative and set events in motion, but of each side moving at different times, in a form of alternation.

There were two other aspects to these events. First, the division of Europe was not total. There were a number of intermediate countries, not fully within either of the two blocs or spheres of influence. In the north, Finland remained a multi-party liberal democracy and was free from Soviet occupation; but on the other hand it accepted that its foreign policy must not be anti-Soviet. The Finnish government declined to attend the Paris Conference on Marshall Aid. A Treaty of Friendship between Finland and the Soviet Union (6 April 1948) expressed in its preamble the Finnish desire to stand aside from the competing interests of the great powers, and Article III confirmed that neither state would join a coalition directed against the other.[13] In elections in July 1948 not a single communist member was returned, and the communists ceased to take part in government. The Soviet government expressed its concern, but took no action. Next door, Sweden accepted Marshall Aid, but remained neutral in its foreign policy and did not join the North Atlantic Alliance. In the centre of Europe, Switzerland took part in the Marshall Plan but retained its traditional neutrality. Austria was split into four occupation zones, but the division was much less rigid and severe than that imposed in Germany. In the Balkans, Yugoslavia broke from the Soviet bloc without joining the western, and accepted American economic aid while remaining firmly communist. The point about these countries was that none was of sufficient weight to tilt the balance of power, and most were not in a geographically crucial position.

The second point was that the division of Germany and Europe was accepted by the two superpowers, without war and in the course of time by a form of tacit consent. This was a time not only of Cold War but of Cold Peace, which in Europe was to become a very long period of peace indeed. Between 1945 and 1949, this came about without the mutual deterrence of atomic or nuclear weapons which later became so important. There was indeed a military balance, in that the United States possessed atomic bombs but did not use them, and the Soviet Union possessed very large land forces and equally did not use them. But it was probably more important that the two superpowers actually *preferred* the division of Europe, and especially of Germany, to any available alternative. The 'German Question' which had plagued Europe since before 1914, and produced two great wars which had involved both the USA and Russia/the USSR, was resolved – crudely and harshly, but effectively. The division of Germany and of Europe brought a form of stability which was fundamentally acceptable to the two superpowers.

It is thus possible to trace how the Cold War in Europe came about, and draw up a chronology in which the two superpowers alternated in taking decisions which ended by 1949 in the division of the continent. We can also observe and explain the Cold Peace which was established at the same time. There is a natural, and almost irresistible, desire to go on from there to discuss responsibility for these events, and there has in fact been a long-running debate on the responsibility for the Cold War – a new 'war guilt' question. In that case, it is vital to remember (though it is very rarely done) that we must also assess where the credit lies for the establishment of the Cold Peace.[14]

◆ Notes to Chapter 5

1. See below, pp. 94–5 for the Brussels Treaty.
2. J. A. S. Grenville, *History of the World in the Twentieth Century* (London, revised edn, 1998), p. 389.
3. Robert H. Ferrell, *Harry S. Truman: A Life* (London, 1994), p. 258.
4. *Ibid.*, p. 259.
5. Alan Bullock, *Ernest Bevin*, Vol. III: *Foreign Secretary* (Oxford, paperback edn, 1985), pp. 498–500.
6. Arnold Wolfers, quoted in Wilson D. Miscamble, *George F. Kennan and the Making of American Foreign Policy* (Princeton, 1992), p. 104.
7. *Keesing's Contemporary Archives*, 1948, p. 9529.
8. Miscamble, *Kennan*, pp. 163–4.
9. Text of the North Atlantic Treaty in J. A. S. Grenville, *The Major International Treaties, 1914–1973: A history and guide with texts* (London, 1974), pp. 335–7; see also pp. 337, 383–4; Senate vote, D. Cook, *Forging the Alliance: NATO, 1945–1950* (London, 1989), p. 227.
10. Kissinger, *Diplomacy*, pp. 460, 462.
11. Quoted in Robert Service, *A History of Twentieth Century Russia* (London, 1997), p. 310.

12. See below, Reflection, 'What Was the Cold War?', pp. 149–59.
13. Text of treaty in H. M. Tillotson, *Finland at Peace and War* (London, revised edn, 1996), pp. 322–3; see also pp. 246–8.
14. See John Lewis Gaddis, *The Long Peace: Enquiries into the History of the Cold War* (Oxford, 1987) for a full exposition of this idea.

CHAPTER 6

THE COLD WAR: KOREA TO HUNGARY, 1949–1956

Situation at the end of 1949 – The Korean War, 1950–53 – Western
Europe and the German Question – Eisenhower becomes President
– The death of Stalin and crisis in East Germany – Germany and
Austria, 1954–57 – Khrushchev, De-Stalinization and the Hungarian
Rising, 1956

In the latter part of 1949 two events took place which transformed the Cold
War and shifted the balance of power. On 29 August 1949 the Soviets
exploded their first atomic bomb. American intelligence knew of this test
almost at once, and Truman announced the news publicly on 23 September.
Then on 1 October Mao Zedong proclaimed the establishment of the
People's Republic of China. The communists had won the long civil war in
China, and this enormous country (with a population estimated at about
550 million) had joined the communist camp. Communism was not so
much on the march as advancing like an express train.

These events shook the Americans badly. They had expected their
monopoly of atomic weapons to last longer than four years. They had
regarded China as their special *protégé* in Asia. Roosevelt had promoted
China as one of the 'four policemen' who would control the world after the
Second World War. American companies and churches had invested material and spiritual capital in the country. Now the United States had 'lost
China' – or so it was said. The reaction was far-reaching as American public
opinion set out to look for those who had misled – or worse, betrayed – the
country. In the next few years, it was impossible for any American political
leader to appear to be 'soft on communism', and thus repeat the mistakes
allegedly made in China.[1]

This would probably have been true in any case, but the situation was
emphasized and probably prolonged by the intervention of Joseph McCarthy,
Republican Senator for Wisconsin. McCarthy seized on the opportunity
provided by the so-called 'loss' of China to make sensational accusations
about communist agents in the State Department, and communist influence

throughout the country – in Hollywood, the trade unions, the teaching profession and elsewhere. There were in fact a few Soviet agents in sensitive posts, and a handful of communist sympathizers in various places, so that McCarthy was able to feed exaggerated fears on a limited diet of information. But his principal weapon was accusation, with or without evidence, followed by an assumption of 'guilt by association'. He was willing to risk attacking the highest in the land, and those with the highest credentials of patriotism and loyalty – at one point he called for the impeachment of Harry Truman, and even attacked General Marshall, whose record of service to his country was unrivalled. Yet for a few years he touched a nerve in American society, and released fears which in turn grew because he fed them. Even President Eisenhower preferred not to confront him openly. His influence in the Senate and in the country increased until 1954, when he was finally censured by the Senate itself. The phenomenon of McCarthyism was a measure of the shock delivered to the American nervous system by the 'loss' of China.

In face of the Soviet atomic bomb and the Chinese revolution, the National Security Council undertook a review of American interests, dangers and options, and produced a long memorandum (NSC-68, dated 14 April 1950).[2] The Council took the sweeping view that 'a defeat of free institutions anywhere is a defeat everywhere', and illustrated its case by reference to the communist coup in Czechoslovakia in 1948. In itself, Czechoslovakia was of small material importance to the United States; equally, the Soviet Union gained no resources which it did not effectively control before the coup. Even so, 'in the intangible scale of values' the Czechoslovakian coup counted as a loss to the United States. It was by maintaining 'essential values', at home and abroad, that the United States would preserve its integrity and frustrate 'the Kremlin design' to preserve absolute power within the Soviet Union and eliminate all opposition outside it. The authors followed Kennan's earlier papers on containment in assuming that one important purpose of American policy was 'to foster a fundamental change in the nature of the Soviet system'; but meanwhile there would have to be a great military as well as moral effort. The memorandum therefore recommended large increases in American military strength. At the time, it was by no means clear how these were to be paid for, and President Truman deferred approval of the document, which he did not sign until September 1950, by which time events in Korea had given it a new significance.

For Stalin too the Soviet atomic bomb and the Chinese revolution transformed the situation. He had always put a brave face on the American possession of the bomb, claiming that there was no need to be afraid of it; but he could now look the United States in the face as an equal. As for China, his relations with the Chinese communists had often been bad, and he had been willing to work with Chiang Kai-shek when necessary; but he appreciated the potential weight of China in world affairs. In 1948 he said that: 'If socialism is victorious in China and our countries follow a single path, then the victory of socialism in the world will be virtually guaranteed. Nothing will threaten us.'[3] By the end of 1949 that position had been reached. Stalin's assessment was on the optimistic side, but at least he had good grounds for confidence.

Between 1945 and 1949 the centre of the Cold War and of Soviet–American relations was in Europe, and the sharpest crisis arose over Berlin. In 1950 the focus of attention suddenly shifted to Korea, which to most people in America and the Soviet Union was a remote and unknown country.

◆ The Korean War, 1950–53

Japan had annexed Korea in 1910. During the Second World War, at the Cairo conference (December 1943), President Roosevelt and Chiang Kai-shek had declared that the country should be independent when the war was won. As hostilities actually came to an end in the Far East in 1945, much had to be improvised. Soviet troops began to enter Korea from the north on 12 August. American troops did not land in the south until 8 September; and in the meantime the Americans had instructed the Japanese Army to maintain order until their arrival. The Americans and Soviets had agreed, for practical purposes, to divide Korea along the 38th Parallel of latitude, with the Americans occupying the south and the Soviets the north. Under the two occupying powers, a communist government was established in the north under Kim Il Sung, and an authoritarian, anti-communist government in the south under Syngman Rhee. Both Kim and Rhee were intense Korean nationalists, anxious to unite the country, and willing to use force to do so if the opportunity offered. In July 1948 the Republic of Korea was set up in the South, with Syngman Rhee as President; and in the same month the Democratic People's Republic of Korea was created in the North. Both laid claim to the whole of Korea as their territory. Soviet troops withdrew from North Korea in December 1948, and American forces from the South in June 1949; both left behind military missions and advisers. The two Koreas then confronted one another, in a state of profound hostility, and each aiming to unify the country, by force if necessary.

On 25 June 1950 North Korean forces crossed the 38th Parallel and advanced rapidly southwards, carrying all before them in pursuit of what seemed likely to be an instant victory. How did this assault come about?

The plan for an attack on South Korea appears to have originated with the North Korean leader, Kim Il Sung, who put to idea to Stalin in 1949 and asked for his support. Stalin did not take up the proposal at that stage, but

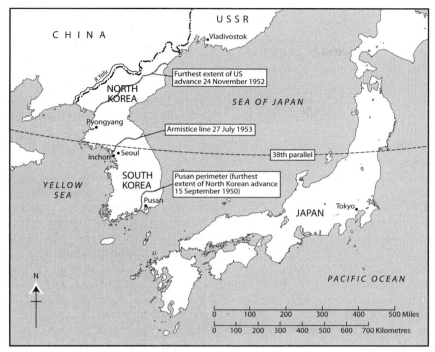

CHINA

USSR

•Vladivostok

R.Yalu

NORTH KOREA

Furthest extent of US advance 24 November 1952

SEA OF JAPAN

Pyongyang•

Armistice line 27 July 1953

Inchon• •Seoul

38th parallel

SOUTH KOREA

Pusan perimeter (furthest extent of North Korean advance 15 September 1950)

YELLOW SEA

Pusan•

JAPAN   Tokyo•

N

PACIFIC OCEAN

0   100   200   300   400   500 Miles

0   100   200   300   400   500   600   700 Kilometres

The Korean War, 1950–1953

he received Kim again in April 1950. This time, Stalin agreed to support a North Korean attack on the South, on certain conditions: the North must be sure of quick success; there must be no likelihood of American intervention; and no escalation into world war. The USSR provided military equipment, and Soviet generals drew up a plan for the offensive, assuming a rapid advance and complete victory in three to four weeks. The date of the attack was set for 25 June in order to finish the campaign before the start of the rainy season.

Thus Kim Il Sung proposed, but Stalin decided. Why did Stalin take up the idea in 1950 when he had left it alone in 1949? The emergence of communist China clearly changed the situation, in at least two ways. First, Stalin did not wish to appear to be holding back the cause of revolution in Asia by restraining Kim Il Sung, especially when Mao might intervene and take the lead; and second the Chinese could now be brought in to share the risk of starting a war in Korea. (Stalin in fact insisted that Kim should only attack South Korea after securing Mao's agreement in person, which he duly did.) The successful Soviet atomic test may also have instilled an extra degree of confidence into Stalin's usually cautious approach. In any case, the risks did not seem great. There was ample reason for Stalin to believe that the Americans would not intervene. In March 1949 General MacArthur, the American commander in Japan, had stated publicly that the American defensive perimeter in the Pacific ran along a string of islands from the Philippines to the Aleutians, excluding Korea. On 12 January 1950 Dean Acheson, the Secretary of State, spoke to the National Press Club in New York, and confirmed existing policy by repeating that the United States would hold a line from the Philippines to the Aleutians, again omitting Korea.[4]

When it came to the point, the United States abandoned all these statements and intervened in Korea almost at once. On 25 June, the day of the North Korean attack, the Americans put a resolution to the Security Council of the United Nations, calling for a cease-fire and the withdrawal of North Korean forces behind the 38th Parallel. The resolution was passed by nine votes to nil, with Yugoslavia abstaining. The Soviet Union, which could have vetoed the resolution, was absent, boycotting meetings of the Security Council in protest against the Council's refusal to allow communist China to take over China's permanent seat. That same evening, Truman ordered American air drops of supplies to the South Koreans, and on 29 June MacArthur was instructed to send air and naval forces to take part in the fighting. On 30 June the order was given to send American troops, and the first contingent arrived by air in Pusan, in the extreme south-east of Korea, on 1 July. Once these troops, at first in small numbers, had been committed, it was impossible to leave them without reinforcements, and the die was cast. Also, under orders issued late on 27 June, the US Seventh Fleet took up station in the Taiwan Straits, to prevent either the Chinese communists or the Nationalists who held Taiwan from exploiting the situation in Korea by making attacks across the straits; this, though superficially even-handed, was directed principally against the mainland Chinese.[5]

American intervention thus came about in a series of steps rather than a single drastic decision; but the results were the same. The Americans found themselves committed to a large-scale war which, as events turned out, was to last for three years. How did this come about? The answers lie as much in instinct as in calculation. By instinct Truman was a fighter, determined not to be pushed around. He also felt strongly that in the 1930s Germany and Japan had been allowed to get away with a series of aggressions which had finally resulted in all-out war. That must not be repeated: there must be no more appeasement. There was also a swift reassessment of the strategic assumptions which had placed Korea outside the American defensive perimeter. The question of whether Japan could be held in face of a hostile Korea (about 100 miles away at the nearest point) was suddenly put with a new urgency, and answered in the negative. This conclusion was made all the clearer by the general American belief that North Korea was simply a Soviet puppet, and that they faced aggression by a single, monolithic communist bloc. Domestic politics and the state of public opinion also played a part: the Truman administration already stood accused of having 'lost China', and could not afford to lose Korea as well. All these motives came together and inspired Truman to decisive action.

The President was also encouraged by a wide measure of international support. The Security Council, in the absence of the Soviet Union, condemned the invasion of South Korea, and the American intervention went forward as a United Nations operation. British troops arrived quickly in Korea, and were soon followed by Australians, New Zealanders and Canadians, forming for the first (and doubtless the only) time in history a Commonwealth Division. France and Turkey provided contingents, and in all sixteen countries provided forces of various types and sizes. Naturally, their motives were not disinterested (the French, for example, were hoping for American help in Indo-China; the Turks were trying to work their passage into NATO); but their presence on 'the battlefield was of great moral and political significance.[6] These details only became clear over time; but from the start Truman was buoyed up by external support.

In July and August, all that the South Koreans and Americans could do was to cling on to a defensive line round Pusan, which seemed likely to be broken at any moment. Then on 15 September MacArthur launched an audacious landing from the sea at Inchon, half-way up the west coast of Korea, threatening to cut off the invading forces in the south. The North Koreans retreated in disorder to avoid encirclement; the South Korean capital, Seoul, was liberated; and the Americans were faced with another crucial decision. Truman's orders to MacArthur at the start of the campaign had been to assist South Korean forces south of the 38th Parallel, which divided the two Koreas. The question now arose of whether to cross that line.

In part this was a practical matter. On the ground, a parallel of latitude has no topographical significance, and troops in close pursuit of a retreating enemy were bound to cross such an artificial line. But local crossings for tactical purposes and a decision to advance far to the north, with the object of occupying the whole of Korea, were two very different issues. The American government and high command considered the question closely; the arguments were finely balanced, but they finally decided to go ahead. The clinching political argument was probably almost a moral one – that to halt on or near the 38th Parallel would check aggression but impose no penalty or punishment upon it. Moreover, the American instinct at that time was that wars were to be won, not drawn. Finally, the striking success of the Inchon landings induced a heady sense of optimism and confidence which helped to carry the day. On 27 September Truman gave permission to MacArthur's forces to cross the parallel, unless there was evidence that this would bring about substantial Soviet or Chinese intervention. This risk was judged to be slight. First South Korean forces, and then on 8 October American troops, crossed the line and moved northwards at great speed, occupying the Northern capital, Pyongyang and then heading full tilt towards the Chinese border on the Yalu River. On 7 October the UN General Assembly passed a resolution proposing to establish 'a unified, independent and democratic government' for the whole of Korea; and on 17 October Truman publicly repeated those exact words.[7] This proved to be a decision even more fateful than the original intervention at the end of June.

For some time the consequences of the American advance remained uncertain. The troops fanned out over the wide spaces of North Korea, their supply lines lengthening and their caution diminishing. On 1 October Kim Il Sung appealed to Stalin for help. Stalin was anxious to keep a low profile, and had earlier ordered Soviet military advisers not to go south of the 38th Parallel and Soviet pilots to conceal their identity. He now declined to commit Soviet troops, and instead asked Mao to send five or six divisions in the guise of 'volunteers'. Mao demurred, arguing that such a force would be enough to provoke the Americans but not enough to stop them; and the result might be an American declaration of war on China, which would bring in the Soviets as well. Stalin replied (5 October) predicting that the Americans would back down in the face of Chinese intervention; but if not, and it came to war, the Soviet Union and China were stronger than their enemies. 'If war is inevitable, let it happen now, and not in a few years . . .'[8] Mao agreed to send nine Chinese divisions, though he asked for Soviet equipment and air cover. But the die was not yet cast. On 12 October Stalin advised Kim Il Sung to get his remaining forces out of Korea to Chinese or Soviet territory; which amounted to telling him to accept defeat. Then, the very next day, Stalin changed his mind, apparently in the certainty that the Chinese were going to fight. Thus up to 12 October the Soviets and Chinese were hesitant and uncertain, and the American estimate that the risk of intervention was slight seemed justified.

Events proved otherwise. Mao was determined not to see the Americans on the Yalu, with their aircraft ranging freely into Chinese airspace. The People's Republic was barely a year old, and could not take such a risk, either materially or in terms of prestige. (The Americans were not the only ones to fear the domino effect of their enemies' victories.) On 19 October 1950 Chinese forces poured south across the Yalu River in large numbers, fighting with astonishing dash and ferocity. They took the UN forces completely by surprise, and drove them back southward in disorder. They crossed the 38th Parallel yet again, and the South Korean capital, Seoul, changed hands for the third time in six months. Not until January 1951 did the Americans and their allies stabilize the front, some 60–70 miles south of the 38th Parallel.

The Chinese intervention changed the character of the war again, and demanded further decisions from the Americans. MacArthur claimed that they must now carry the war to China, by aerial bombardment and naval blockade, and took his arguments to the press and members of the Congress. Truman and the Chiefs of Staff disagreed, and on 11 April 1951 the President dismissed MacArthur from his command – a courageous act, even in a career notable for its courage. This action decided that on the American side the war was to remain limited, a concept previously unknown to American policy and instinct. The Chinese and the Soviets tacitly accepted the same principle. The result was an extraordinary situation. Within Korea the war was fought with the greatest intensity and ferocity. But the fighting was geographically limited to the peninsula itself, with Manchuria remaining a safe haven for the Chinese and Japan for the Americans, Each side accepted limited aims, not attempting complete victory but settling for stalemate. Each side accepted a limitation in weapons, in that neither used the atomic bomb – though Truman publicly referred to it in November 1950, and Eisenhower later hastened the achievement of an armistice by hinting at its use in 1953. Within these limits, neither side gave way. On a number of occasions from July 1951 onwards, Kim Il Sung asked Stalin to make peace, because North Korea was suffering heavily from American air bombardment, but Stalin insisted on holding on, keeping the Americans tied down in Korea and believing that they could not endure the trials of a long and fruitless war. In the United States, the people indeed grew war-weary, but on this occasion they stood firm. Twenty years later Vietnam was to impose a longer and a sterner test.

On the ground, the situation changed yet again in 1951. MacArthur's successor, General Ridgway, undertook a new offensive, recaptured Seoul (which thus changed hands for the fourth time), and pushed the front back northwards to a line running diagonally across the peninsula, mostly just to the north of the 38th Parallel. There it was to remain, though at a continuing cost to both sides. In July 1951 negotiations for an armistice began, but remained stalled for two years, largely as a result of differences on the fate of the prisoners taken by the two sides. The Americans insisted that no prisoners of war, on either side, should be repatriated against their will. The Chinese, supported by Stalin, required that all Chinese and North Korean prisoners must be returned. What was at stake on each side was a propaganda point. The Americans wanted to demonstrate that some of the enemy prisoners did not wish to return to their 'socialist fatherlands'; the Chinese and North Koreans could not risk any such result. The war thus showed its Cold War character. It was a military conflict, recalling the Second World War, and even the trench-lines of the Western Front in 1914–18; but it was also an ideological and propaganda struggle. (As well as the issue of prisoners, communist accusations that the Americans were using germ warfare achieved such success that when General Ridgway was appointed as Supreme Commander for NATO in 1952 he was greeted in Paris by vast crowds shouting '*Ridgway la Peste*' – Ridgway the Plague.) On military terms alone the war could almost certainly have been concluded in 1951; but ideological points kept it going until 1953, with heavy loss of life and widespread destruction.

Ultimately, in 1953, Eisenhower, newly elected President and with his immense prestige as a soldier, brought a new impetus to the negotiations. He was prepared to imply (though he did not directly threaten) an atomic attack against China. He was willing to be tough with Syngman Rhee in South Korea, and with Republican Congressmen at home who opposed an armistice. There was first an exchange of sick and wounded prisoners of war, and finally an agreement that prisoners who did not wish to return to their own countries should present their cases to a Repatriation Commission, made up of representatives of Sweden, Switzerland, Poland, Czechoslovakia and India. An armistice was finally signed on 27 July 1953, at the village of Panmunjom. There was to be a cease-fire along the lines held by the opposing armies on that date, with a narrow demilitarized zone between the two forces. The level of armaments on each side was to be stabilized (a provision which was often disregarded). 22 604 Chinese and North Korean prisoners in United Nations hands were handed over to the Neutral Nations Repatriation Commission; only 137 agreed to repatriation to their own countries, and all the rest chose to go to South Korea or Taiwan. 349 prisoners in Chinese or North Korean hands refused to return to their own countries; these included 325 Koreans, 21 Americans and one Briton.[9] A conference was to meet to work out a lasting settlement. This conference never met. The cease-fire line remained in place, with representatives of the two sides meeting every week to exchange salutes and information (or accusations) about the armistice arrangements. This strange ritual persists to the present time of writing (2000), embalming an aspect of the Cold War at its most rigid.

Casualties in the war were heavy – perhaps about 1.5 million military deaths (most of them Korean), and an unknown number of civilians killed. The Americans lost 33 699 killed and 107 755 wounded; the South Koreans 415 000 killed and 429 000 wounded; the Commonwealth forces 1263 killed and 4817 wounded. The Chinese and North Koreans together were estimated to have lost some 1 500 000 killed and wounded.[10] In Korea, the physical damage was severe, especially in the north, which was heavily bombed. At the end of everything, Korea remained divided along a line not far removed from the 38th Parallel. It had been a tremendous effort, at grievous cost, to leave Korea where it was before. Without a permanent settlement, the peninsula remained a potential point of conflict, either between the two Koreas or between the United States and China. In the event, there was some friction but no further conflict. Not for the first time, the supposedly temporary proved remarkably stable.

Of the great powers engaged in the war, China emerged greatly strengthened. The Chinese had taken on the United States Army in battle, and won.

They had saved North Korea, and emerged as the leading Communist power in Asia. The Soviet Union lost ground during the war, with its influence in North Korea largely supplanted by that of China. But though the Chinese emerged strengthened from the war, they also learned caution. Victory over the Americans had been costly, and far from complete. They fought no more battles against the United States in the years to come, though sometimes they had the opportunity to do so, for example over the islands of Quemoy and Matsu.[11]

The war had profound effects on the United States. Korea was a success for containment, but at a heavy cost in military and economic effort and in sheer endurance. Yet the effort in Korea itself was only part of the story. American defence expenditure as a whole rose from $14.5 billion in 1950 to $49.6 billion in 1953. Between 1951 and 1953 the number of men in the American armed forces roughly doubled. The United States pressed on rapidly with research on a hydrogen bomb; increased the Strategic Air Command; and began to build nuclear-powered aircraft-carriers. In what was technically peacetime the country embarked on military preparations comparable to those undertaken during the Second World War.[12]

The effects of the Korean War were also felt on the other side of the world. There seemed an obvious analogy between a divided Korea and a divided Germany, and fears sprang up of a sudden attack across the iron curtain. After its signature in 1949 the North Atlantic Treaty had remained essentially a notional deterrent, with little military reality on the ground. When the Korean War began this no longer seemed adequate, and the United States began to look for soldiers to man the defences of western Europe. With Britain and France already fully stretched, the only source of new manpower was the former enemy, West Germany. At a NATO meeting on 15 September 1950 Dean Acheson proposed to end the policy of demilitarizing Germany, and to establish West German forces under NATO command. This began a tortuous process, leading through a failed attempt at a European Defence Community to the admission of West Germany to NATO in 1954, with a new army with an eventual strength of twelve divisions. Yesterday's enemies were to become allies. The same was to some degree true of Japan, which during the Korean War became a major source of supplies for the Americans.

In all these ways, the Korean War was a turning point. It extended the Cold War to Asia, and demonstrated how it could unexpectedly explode into actual fighting. Indeed, the Korean battles represented the Cold War at its most ferocious, though without direct Soviet–American conflict. Its effects rebounded back onto the other half of the globe. The transformation of Western Europe, already under way with Marshall Aid, entered a new phase. It is to Western Europe that we must turn next.

◆ Western Europe and the German Question, 1948–53

One of the most remarkable events of the decade following 1948 was the recovery of Western Europe. With help from Marshall Aid, but largely by their own efforts, the west European countries achieved substantial economic growth. At the same time, they developed welfare systems and mixed economies which allowed aspects of capitalism and state control to work side by side, creating a political and social stability which had often been absent in the 1930s. Moreover, there was a new spirit abroad, giving a fresh impulse to the ancient desire to create some form of political union to match Europe's historical and cultural identity.

For a time, this movement towards unity was diffuse. Churchill spoke in Zurich (19 September 1946) of establishing 'a kind of United States of Europe';[13] and he later accepted the honorary presidency of the vast Congress of Europe which met at the Hague in May 1948, acting as a forum for many different brands of the 'European idea'. In May 1950 the French Foreign Minister, Robert Schuman, gave the concept a new and firmer shape. He proposed to end the age-old conflict between France and Germany, and at the same time to take the first step towards a European federation, by creating a European Coal and Steel Community, which would place the whole coal and steel production of member states under a single High Authority, which would represent a small but significant 'pooling' of sovereignty between the member countries. Six West European states (France, West Germany, Italy, the Netherlands, Belgium and Luxembourg) agreed to form this new Community. Britain declined to join, refusing the element of supranational control and pooling of sovereignty represented by the High Authority. In practice, the Coal and Steel Community (which began to operate in 1952) produced only limited results, but its significance lay not in the details but in the wider consequences. A Franco-German association was begun which was to flourish over the next half-century; and the institutions created for the Coal and Steel Community formed the framework for the European Economic Community which followed in 1957. Between them, these two developments were to transform the history of Western Europe.

The immediate next step after the creation of the Coal and Steel Community was an attempt by the same six countries to form a European Defence Community. When the Americans proposed West German rearmament in September 1950, as a consequence of the Korean War, the French were naturally dismayed. They had seen enough of German armies during the last forty years or so (a sentiment in which they were not alone); and yet they were in no position to oppose the American demand outright. They therefore tried to take the sting out of it, and at the same time to advance the integration of western Europe, by accepting German troops only as part of a European Army, in which the Germans would function only in formations of some 5000 men. On this basis (along with other complicated arrangements) a treaty to set up a European Defence Community was signed, on 27 May 1952, by the six countries which already made up the Coal and Steel Community. As a response to the American requirement for German rearmament, this was extremely slow. After almost two years, a complex treaty had been signed which would itself produce after further delay a European Army of untried structures and dubious military value. Eventually the whole scheme collapsed, when in August 1954 the French National Assembly killed the project by failing to ratify the treaty. It was a thoroughly confused and ultimately fruitless exercise, which seemed for a time to have deprived the European idea of its momentum. But throughout these tortuous events the idea of German rearmament slowly advanced and became acceptable; and all the time the institutions of the Coal and Steel Community settled down and assumed a sort of permanence.

In all these developments, the first Chancellor of the new West German state, Konrad Adenauer, played a vital role. Adenauer was 73 when he became Chancellor, yet he was the very opposite of an old man in a hurry. He had seen two World Wars, two German defeats, and two occupations; and he had learned the value of patience. 'I think patience is the sharpest weapon of the defeated. I can wait.'[14] He worked closely with the Americans, without becoming their puppet. He won the confidence of French politicians. He advanced the cause of West German independence, while being prepared to sacrifice a part of that independence to the progress of European integration. By making West Germany a part of both NATO and the European Economic Community, he went far towards providing an answer to the 'German Question' – what was Germany's role in international affairs to be?

To Stalin these events appeared full of danger. He was strongly opposed to the emergence of an independent and armed West Germany; and early in 1952 he launched an attempt to prevent it. On 10 March 1952 he suddenly proposed to revive negotiations for a German peace treaty. The essential stages were to be: First, the creation of a unified Germany, committed to a status of neutrality in its foreign relations; second, the holding of free elections in the new state; finally, this united, neutral Germany would be permitted to maintain its own armed forces. All foreign troops were to withdraw from its territory within a year of its creation.

It is not clear whether this was a serious attempt to resolve the German Problem, or only a tactical move to forestall West German rearmament and stop the progressive absorption of West Germany into western European institutions. In any case, the western powers regarded Stalin's move with deep suspicion. The United States, Britain and France replied quickly (25 March), agreeing to German unification but rejecting neutrality, maintaining that a united Germany should be free to make its own alliances – meaning that it could join NATO. They accepted the idea of free elections, but only on condition that the rights of free speech and assembly should be granted at once in the whole country. There followed an exchange of notes, in which Stalin gradually moved towards the western position; but the affair petered out by the end of 1952. The Cold War pattern was too firmly set to be broken. West Germany was already in existence, and was being integrated with other West European countries through the Schuman Plan. Adenauer was not prepared to throw these advantages into the melting-pot. For the United States, NATO had achieved stability in Europe, which needed to be reinforced by West German rearmament. A united, armed yet neutral Germany would introduce a new and uncertain element – after all, Germany had been united and armed before 1939, and neutrality could be quickly abandoned. Moreover, could Stalin be trusted? Since the Czechoslovakian coup in 1948 most people in the west had concluded that deals with Stalin tended to be one-way traffic, and that Soviet conceptions of 'free elections' were different from those in the west. Recent Stalinist purges in the Communist parties of eastern Europe offered a discouraging prospect. So it came about that Stalin's proposals, which might have led somewhere if made in 1947, merely ran into the sand in 1952. The Cold War had its own momentum, and created situations that were difficult to change. Indeed, both sides had come to prefer the stability they knew to the potential risks of movement.

Yet events were not completely frozen. American presidential elections came round inexorably every four years, and even Stalin was mortal. In January 1953 General Eisenhower took office as President of the United States. In March 1953 Stalin died. Together, these two events brought a new aspect to international affairs.

◆ The opening of the Eisenhower presidency

General Dwight D. Eisenhower, who was elected President of the United States in November 1952 and assumed office in January 1953, had made his reputation first as an Allied Supreme Commander during the Second World War, and later as the first Supreme Commander of NATO forces in Europe. He had an amiable grin, an easy-going public manner and an attractive nickname – 'I like Ike' was one of the simplest and most appealing slogans ever devised for a presidential election campaign.

A man so apparently open and uncomplicated, who yet achieved such remarkable success in military affairs and later in politics, has left historians baffled. Certainly his outward simplicity was misleading. Richard Nixon, who served as his Vice-President, described him as 'complex and devious'. Henry Kissinger, who knew a thing or two about complexity, observed of Eisenhower (along with Reagan) that 'presidents who appear to be the most guileless often turn out to be the most complex.'[15]

Eisenhower cultivated a relaxed style, but worked a good deal harder than he allowed to appear, keeping the key decisions on foreign and military policy in his own hands. He was a soldier who had seen enough of war, and wanted to avoid it in future. He could also be extremely tough-minded – for example, when he decided to bring the Korean war to a compromise conclusion he was prepared to be stern with the Chinese, Syngman Rhee and some of the Congressmen in his own party in order to do so. Like Truman, he was convinced that the policy of appeasement in the 1930s had led to war, and must on no account be repeated. He did not invent the 'domino theory', which had been expounded by Marshall (though without the name) in 1947, but he took it over and attached it firmly to Indochina, with far-reaching consequences.[16] On 4 April 1954 he wrote to Churchill that if the French failed in their Indo-China war 'the consequent shift in the power ratio throughout Asia and the Pacific could be disastrous . . . It is difficult to see how Thailand, Burma and Indonesia could be kept out of Communist hands. This we cannot afford. The threat to Malaya, Australia and New Zealand would be direct.'[17] In practice, his policy was usually more flexible and cautious than this might imply; and he followed the relaxed assumption that most things could be settled by good sense, and that relations with the Soviets were 'a problem to be managed' rather than a crusade against evil.[18]

In this he differed markedly from his Secretary of State, John Foster Dulles, who was a lawyer by training and a Presbyterian by upbringing, with a strong feeling that communism was a form of sin with which there could be no compromise. Dulles talked about rolling back communism and liberating countries trapped in the Soviet bloc – in such a view, containment was not enough. He was thus well fitted for the role of hard man in the Eisenhower administration; and together he and the President made a strong team. Eisenhower could let Dulles take the brunt of criticism abroad, and appear above the fray as the 'reasonable man'. Yet he also benefited from the respect which Dulles could inspire even in his opponents – as Khrushchev wrote in his memoirs, 'Dulles knew how far he could push us, and never pushed us too far.'[19] In practice, Eisenhower was prepared to be flexible in his methods in foreign policy; and despite Dulles's talk of 'rollback' the new administration aimed more at the consolidation than the extension of American commitments.

◆ The death of Stalin and crisis in East Germany

On 5 March 1953, some two months after Eisenhower was inaugurated as President, Stalin died. For a quarter of a century he had dominated the

Soviet Union and the international communist movement. Since the end of the Second World War his prestige had been immense throughout the world, and within the Soviet bloc unassailable. His death opened a new and uncertain era.

On 1 December 1952 Stalin had told a meeting of his immediate entourage: 'When I die, the imperialists will strangle all of you like a litter of kittens.'[20] At the time of Eisenhower's election in November, there had been an alarm in Moscow that the Americans had elected a general in order to wage war; and when Stalin died his successors feared a surprise attack. The Soviet Union was in serious difficulties. Agriculture was failing to meet its targets. The non-Russian nationalities were still refractory. There was unrest even in the camps of the Gulag, which contained about five-and-a-half million prisoners.[21] Stalin's successors were divided among themselves, and none had the grasp of all aspects of policy which Stalin had maintained. Molotov returned to the Foreign Ministry, which he had lost in 1949, and sought to continue Stalin's policies. Malenkov assumed the main public role, and took the opportunity of Stalin's funeral to say that there were no issues in Soviet–American relations which could not be resolved by peaceful means. Beria, the head of the KGB, was in charge of the Soviet atomic and nuclear programme, and well aware that the balance of nuclear power was still very much in favour of the United States. Khruschev, who was eventually to prove the rising star, was not as yet a central figure.

It was the situation in East Germany that brought the divisions within the leadership to a head. In 1952, Stalin had laid down that the East German communist regime should proceed with the 'construction of socialism' (the collectivization of agriculture and Soviet-style control of all industry), with disastrous results. Production of all kinds fell, and there was a stream of refugees to West Berlin. Even the East German communist leader, Ulbricht, warned of the dangers of building socialism without laying proper foundations. In May 1953, the Soviet leaders were divided as to what to do. Molotov was willing to relinquish the policy of 'forced socialism' in East Germany. Beria was prepared to go further, and accept a policy of abandoning socialism itself. Molotov recalled him as saying: 'Why should socialism be built in the GDR [German Democratic Republic]? Let it just be a peaceful country. That is sufficient for our purposes.'[22] Gromyko (later Soviet Foreign Minister) reported Beria as describing East Germany as 'not even a real state. It is only kept in being by Soviet troops.'[23] Malenkov supported Beria, but Molotov would have none of it. For him, East Germany had to be a socialist state, partly as a matter of principle, and partly because he did not believe that a bourgeois Germany would remain peaceful. Khrushchev supported Molotov, and Beria gave way.

In East Germany itself the situation grew worse. On 16 June construction workers in East Berlin opposed new production quotas, and called for a general strike. This news was at once picked up in West Berlin, and broadcast on the American radio there back to the east – an example of the instantaneous effect of modern communications on politics. On 17 June there was a widespread strike in East Berlin, spreading rapidly to other towns in East Germany. Soviet tanks were sent in against the strikers that same afternoon, directed by Beria, who had been sent to Berlin to deal with the crisis, even though he had sought to avoid it. This was indeed a drama. The industrial workers of East Germany, whom the communist regime was supposed to represent, came out on strike against it. The USSR used force to sustain the communist government, which would have fallen without the support of the Soviet tanks. (Beria was right to say that the East German regime depended on the Soviet Army for its existence.) There was a crack in the foundations of Soviet power, though it was to be a long time before the building came down. In the short run, the Soviet Union set out to consolidate the East German state. In 1954 the Soviet government agreed to renounce reparations payments from East Germany (which had still been exacted up to that time), and to write off East German debts to the USSR. The economy began to pull round, and the state itself began to settle down. The country's new status was recognized in 1955, when East Germany became an ally of the Soviet Union and one of the founder members of the Warsaw Pact.[24]

By that time Beria was dead. He was arrested on 26 June 1953, in a daring move by his rivals in the Soviet leadership, and was executed in the following December. Malenkov was forced to give up the post of Premier in January 1955. Khrushchev emerged as the dominant figure in the Soviet government, with far-reaching results.

It is not clear whether the death of Stalin and the uncertainties of his successors offered a serious opportunity to the United States, whether for military action or for some diplomatic initiative. There is no sign that the Americans even contemplated an attack on the Soviet Union, and in any case they were still tied down in Korea. As for diplomacy, when Stalin died Eisenhower had only been President for two months, and the new administration had scarcely played itself in. It appears that little had been done to prepare for the event – Eisenhower remarked that the result of seven years' talk about what would happen when Stalin died was zero.[25] When Churchill urged that the time had come for a new essay in summit diplomacy, his old friend Ike was thoroughly discouraging. The President did make a speech on 16 April 1953, hoping for a new start in Soviet–American relations, and outlining the sort of changes he was looking for – an end to the Korean War, some liberalization in eastern Europe, and a settlement in Austria. The Soviet reply, delivered through the press, was non-committal. Both sides were cautious, and it took some time for changes to develop.

◆ Germany and Austria, 1954–57

It was in 1954 that an attempt was made to deal with the German Question. In February the foreign ministers of the USA, the Soviet Union, Britain and France met in Berlin to discuss the possibility of German reunification, which they had been considering slowly and reluctantly since Stalin had raised the subject in 1952. It was the first such meeting since December 1947, and therefore a remarkable event in itself, and a sign of a thaw in the most severe diplomatic frosts of the Cold War. But though the ministers met and talked, and so restored some of the civilities to international relations, they reached no agreement. In 1952 the Western powers had obstructed Stalin's proposals for reunification, and by 1954 it appears that Stalin's successors had decided that they preferred the division of Germany to the likelihood that a united Germany would turn decisively to the West. The disturbances in East Germany in 1953 had cleared the minds of the Soviet leaders on this issue. So the Berlin conference dispersed without agreement on its main subject, though the ministers agreed to call another conference, at Geneva, on the very different topic of Indo-China, this time with the participation of Communist China – a sign that they were determined to go on talking about *something*, even if Germany had proved a fruitless subject.

In fact, in 1954 the division of Germany was being more firmly sealed by the integration of West Germany into the west European defence arrangements. The proposal made in 1950 to permit West German rearmament in the framework of a European Army finally collapsed in August 1954, but the fundamental problem remained. The North Atlantic alliance did not have enough troops on the ground. Fitzroy Maclean remarked in the House of Commons in May 1952 that NATO was 'like the Venus de Milo, plenty of SHAPE but no arms'.[26] In 1954, NATO disposed of only 20 divisions (five of them American) in the crucial Central European sector, rather than the 30 which were thought necessary. West German rearmament, which was supposed to fill the gap, had not even begun. When the European Army project failed, it was the British Foreign Secretary, Eden, who produced a solution.

In September 1954 Eden visited all the west European capitals, and arranged a conference in London (28 September–3 October) attended by Britain, the six Coal and Steel Community countries, the United States and Canada. The problem was still how to meet the American insistence on German rearmament while allaying the widespread fears of German military resurgence. Eden's solution was to use the existing machinery of the Brussels and North Atlantic Treaties. He proposed that West Germany and Italy should be admitted to the Brussels Treaty and to NATO. West Germany should then form its own army, to be placed in its entirety under an integrated NATO command. (The French, British and other armies only placed a part of their forces under NATO command.) Eden also undertook that Britain would maintain a force of four divisions on the continent of Europe, mainly in West Germany, not to be withdrawn without the agreement of a majority of the states belonging to the Brussels Treaty – a measure aimed as much at reassuring the west Europeans as at deterring the Soviet Army. These proposals were rapidly accepted, and a further conference in Paris (23 October 1954) agreed to remove the remaining restrictions on West German sovereignty. West Germany was to establish an army of up to twelve divisions, and to be admitted to NATO on a footing of equality with the other members of the Treaty.

In the end, the deed was done with surprising ease. The prolonged and obscure wranglings about the European Defence Community had accustomed public opinion to the basic idea of West German rearmament, and diverted attention to the secondary question of how it was to be achieved. When the final agreement was reached, it seemed of a refreshing simplicity after the previous complexities. Moreover, when it came to the point, the West Germans proved less than enthusiastic about forming an army. The old military tradition had died among the defeat and destruction of 1945, and there was much uncertainty as to how (or indeed whether) it should be revived. There was a strong pacifist movement among the younger generations. When conscription was introduced in 1956, the period of service was set at only one year. By 1960 there were only seven West German divisions available for NATO, and the twelve divisions envisaged in 1954 were not attained until 1963.

The whole question of German rearmament, which had seemed to the Americans the answer to NATO's manpower problem, which had caused such agony of mind in western Europe, and aroused so much anxiety in the Soviet Union, proved something of a damp squib on all counts. The Germans were slow to produce their divisions. Their neighbours accepted the fact of a German Army with little fuss. The Soviets rearmed East Germany, and then ceased to worry about the matter. The long-term significance proved to be political rather than military. West Germany advanced to full sovereignty; began to conduct its own foreign policy; and became a full member of NATO. East Germany became a member of the Warsaw Pact when it was formed in 1955. The German Question was being steadily resolved by the consolidation of the status quo, which meant the acceptance of partition.

In 1955 a number of events brought a further relaxation in the tension of the Cold War in Europe. On 15 May 1955 the Austrian State Treaty was signed in Vienna by the United States, the Soviet Union, Britain and France. (It was a 'State Treaty' because Article 1 recognized the re-establishment of Austria as a sovereign state; and it was not strictly speaking a peace treaty, because the former wartime allies had agreed that Austria was not to be regarded as an enemy but as one of Hitler's victims.) The background to this agreement was essentially a bargain by which the Soviet Union secured Austrian neutrality in return for a withdrawal of all occupation forces from the country. Under the treaty, Austria resumed its independent existence within the boundaries of 1 January 1938 (i.e. before the *Anschluss* with Germany), and renounced political or economic union with Germany. All occupation forces were to leave the country before the end of the year. Neutrality was not comprised in the treaty, but was laid down in a constitutional law passed by the Austrian Parliament on 26 October 1955, declaring Austria's perpetual neutrality and prohibiting any military alliance or the establishment of any foreign bases on Austrian territory. These arrangements brought about the first troop withdrawals in central Europe since 1945, including the first retirement by Soviet forces from territory they had occupied. It was true that Austria was a small country, much less important than Germany, where division still prevailed; but even so, the State Treaty of 1955 was a remarkable and encouraging event. The new Austrian status of neutrality was one to which others could aspire, as the Hungarians were to do in 1956.

Paradoxically, one of the immediate consequences of the Austrian treaty was to draw the lines of European alliances more firmly. Until the treaty was concluded, Soviet forces had been stationed in Hungary and Romania, under the terms of the peace treaties of 1947, in order to secure communications with the Soviet occupation troops in Austria. With the end of the Austrian occupation, this technical basis for the presence of the troops in Hungary and Romania came to an end; but the Soviets had no intention of removing their forces. The previous arrangements were therefore replaced by the creation of a new military alliance. On 14 May 1955 the Soviet Union and seven other communist states (Albania, Bulgaria, Czechoslovakia, the German Democratic Republic, Hungary, Poland, and Romania) signed the Warsaw Pact for collective defence. They undertook to consult together on all international questions involving their common interests; and to set up a unified military command, with its headquarters in Moscow. Two formal alliances – NATO and the Warsaw Pact – now confronted one another in Europe.

Yet, almost immediately after the formation of the Warsaw Pact, there took place at Geneva (18–23 July 1955) the first post-war conference of heads of government of the United States, the Soviet Union, Britain and France – the meeting 'at the summit' for which Churchill had vainly pleaded in 1953. On paper, the major issues of the Cold War in Europe (the German Question, European security and disarmament, the restoration of East–West contacts) were on the agenda. In practice little was done about any of them. President Eisenhower made a spectacular move with his 'open skies' proposal for free aerial reconnaissance over the territories of each power bloc; but this was mere window-dressing, and even those who devised it did not expect it to be accepted. There was a complete lack of substantial progress, and yet Western politicians and public opinion claimed to regard the Geneva Conference as a striking success. 'The spirit of Geneva' became the catch-word of the time, and even Foster Dulles, that stern enemy of communism, was prepared to say that Soviet policy was now based on tolerance. On the Soviet side, Khruschev was convinced that Eisenhower (whom he treated as a war veteran like himself) would not permit any serious military conflict to come about – a marked change from the fears which were aroused by Eisenhower's election at the end of 1952. These beliefs, though exaggerated in some respects, had solid foundations. Psychologically, the Geneva Conference was important as a break in the tension of the Cold War. The deep diplomatic frost of the Cold War was breaking up after some six or seven years. The four Foreign Ministers had last met in London in December 1947; they met again in Berlin in February 1954; and then the heads of government met at Geneva in July 1955, to general satisfaction. The way ahead was open, and the start made at Geneva led eventually to Khrushchev's visit to the United States in 1959.

It was significant that the Geneva Conference attempted nothing serious on Germany. German reunification had effectively disappeared from the diplomatic scene. The Soviets tacitly accepted West German rearmament and membership of NATO. Khrushchev, on his way home from Geneva, paused in East Germany and formally recognized the sovereignty of East Germany. A few weeks later, on 9–13 September, he received Chancellor Adenauer on a visit to Moscow, and established diplomatic relations between the Soviet Union and West Germany. The German question, though no one liked to say so, was being settled along the lines of partition and the acceptance of two separate German states.

Of those two states, East Germany was fully absorbed into the Soviet bloc, by the formal machinery of the Warsaw Pact and the powerful presence of a Soviet garrison, while West Germany was becoming steadily more involved in the integration of Western Europe. In 1955 the six member states of the Coal and Steel Community resumed their movement towards integration. A conference of the Six at Messina on 1–2 June 1955 agreed to set up two new European organizations, an Economic Community and an Atomic Energy Community (Euratom). Within a year these proposals were elaborated in detail and embodied in two Treaties of Rome, signed on 25 March 1957, setting up the European Economic Community (EEC) and Euratom. It was plain throughout these negotiations that Chancellor Adenauer was determined to bind the Federal Republic of Germany firmly into the new organization of Western Europe. With every step towards West European integration, the barrier between West and East Germany grew higher, and the division of Germany more pronounced.

◆ Khrushchev, de-Stalinization and the Hungarian Rising, 1956

On 25 February 1956, the Twentieth Congress of the Communist Party of the Soviet Union met in closed session to hear a remarkable speech by Nikita Khruschev, the General Secretary of the Party – the post from which Stalin had ruled the Soviet Union for so long. Now, not quite three years after Stalin's death, Khrushchev launched an astonishing attack on his formidable predecessor. He denounced the great purges of 1937–38 (at least in part); criticized Stalin's failure to foresee the German assault in 1941, revealed something of the deportations carried out within the Soviet Union during the war, and even attacked some of the post-war purges. He traced the root of all these evils to Stalin's 'cult of personality', an explanation which allowed Khrushchev to pass over his own part in the pre-war purges, and to exempt the present leadership from blame, even though they had all worked under Stalin for almost the whole of their political careers. (He also played down the vast scale of the purges, mentioning the death of several thousands of party officials rather than the millions who in fact suffered death or imprisonment in the Gulag.) In addition to these attacks on Stalin, Khruschev took up other themes, of immediate importance in international affairs. He spoke of repairing relations with Yugoslavia, and of the possibility of 'different roads to socialism'. He put a new emphasis on the concept of 'peaceful co-existence', which had long been used in communist foreign policy as a temporary and tactical measure, but which should now become a permanent feature. War between the communist and capitalist camps was no longer inevitable, partly because nuclear weapons would destroy all parties to a conflict, and partly because there were now social and political forces at work in the new states of Asia and Africa which would deter the imperialists from war.[27]

Khruschev's speech was an unprecedented attack on the hitherto untouchable figure of Stalin. It also opened up new vistas for Soviet foreign policy. The possibility of 'different roads to socialism' soon had consequences in Poland and Hungary. The new interpretation of peaceful co-existence raised the possibility of improved relations with the United States. The prominence given to the new states in Asia and Africa signalled a new departure in Soviet relations with the Third World, which Stalin had not attempted to cultivate. In the long run, consequences of the speech were immeasurable, because it began to undermine the legitimacy of the communist system and the Soviet state. Khruschev sought to reassure the Party Congress that criticism of Stalin did not mean an attack on the system. The heritage of Lenin, he declared, remained intact, and the dictatorship of the Communist Party would continue – as indeed it did for another thirty-five years. But the communist system had been so bound up with Stalin, and

Stalin himself so closely linked with Lenin, that in the long run these assurances proved empty. Khrushchev had begun a change which no one knew how to stop.

In the Soviet Union, the speech remained technically secret. Only a short summary was published in the press, and careful briefings were given to Communist Party officials. In practice, reports and rumours circulated freely, and the gist of the speech was widely known. Abroad, translations rapidly appeared in the press. According to some accounts, Khrushchev himself made sure the Americans knew about it by instructing the KGB to pass a copy to the Central Intelligence Agency; according to others, the Israeli secret service, Mossad, sold a copy to the CIA for cash down plus promises for help in the future.[28]

In any case, consequences were not long in following. In April 1956 Khrushchev announced the dissolution of Cominform, as a practical demonstration of opening 'different roads to socialism'. It remained to be seen who would first try to take one of these roads. Not surprisingly, it was the Poles who made a start. In October 1956 Gomulka, who had been purged from the Polish Communist Party in 1951, returned as First Secretary. Rokossovsky, the Soviet Marshal who held the post of Minister of Defence in the Polish government, was dismissed. The Polish Communist Party announced that it was going to follow its own road to socialism. The Soviet government at first responded by making ostentatious preparations for military action. On 19 October Khrushchev flew to Warsaw, with a powerful team from the Soviet leadership – Kaganovich, Mikoyan and Molotov. In the event, Khrushchev and the Poles arrived at a compromise which avoided the use of force. On 20 October the troops which had been ready for action stood down and returned to their barracks. On the 22nd an agreement was concluded by which Gomulka remained as Polish General Secretary in return for undertakings that he would maintain socialism and Polish membership of the Warsaw Pact – a vital reassurance that Poland would not attempt to become neutral. Rokossovsky was not reinstated, and the result was at least a partial success for the Polish Communist Party.

These events were closely followed in Hungary. In recent years the Soviets had intervened repeatedly and arbitrarily in Hungarian affairs. In 1953, after Stalin's death, they dismissed Rakosi (a stern, unbending Stalinist) as head of the Communist Party, and replaced him by Imre Nagy, reputedly a reforming communist. In 1955 the Soviets reversed themselves, dismissing Nagy and restoring Rakosi. In July 1956 Rakosi was again dismissed, and replaced this time by Erno Gero, another hardliner. These frequent interventions aroused much resentment, and made nonsense of any 'Hungarian road to socialism'. Even the partial success of Gomulka in Poland thus appeared all the more significant and attractive.

Public opinion in Hungary began to stir, despite all the difficulties. On

23 October, a demonstration by students and others in Budapest demanded the return of Imre Nagy, the trial of Rakosi, and the withdrawal of Soviet troops from Hungary. This proved to be the start of what soon became an insurrection. On the 24th, Soviet tanks were attacked in the streets of Budapest. Nagy became Prime Minister, intending only to reform the communist system, but he quickly found himself carried away by events and by the demands of the crowds in Budapest. On 30 October Nagy took the drastic step of abandoning one-party rule by forming a new government including Bela Kovacz, of the Small-holders' Party, which had gained a majority of votes in the elections of November 1945. Even so, on the same day, the Soviet government declared publicly that all socialist states should be equal. On the 31st Soviet troops withdrew from Budapest. For a moment it appeared that a compromise was possible.

The Hungarian government then went further. On 31 October Nagy declared that Hungary was to become neutral (on the model provided by Austria in 1955), and was to withdraw from the Warsaw Pact. He also requested the United Nations to recognize Hungary's new status as a neutral state. This brought the Soviet government to the point of decision. It remains uncertain whether the Soviets would have accepted in the long run a return to genuine coalition government in Hungary; though it seems unlikely. It was absolutely certain that they could not accept neutrality in foreign policy and withdrawal from the Warsaw Pact, a precedent which would have resulted in the break-up of the Pact and of the whole Soviet bloc in eastern Europe. At this point therefore the Soviet government hesitated no longer. During the night of 3–4 November the Soviet Army returned to Budapest in irresistible force, crushing all opposition. In the country as a whole, serious fighting went on until 14 November, and sporadic resistance until the end of the month. Casualties have been estimated at 25 000 Hungarians and 7000 Soviet troops killed.[29] The Soviets imposed Janos Kadar as the head of a new government. They promised Nagy safe conduct to Yugoslavia, but instead arrested him when he left the Yugoslavian Embassy. He was later executed. The Hungarian attempt to break free from the Soviet bloc was over.

What was the significance of these dramatic and tragic events? The Hungarian rising was a spontaneous movement, inspired by patriotism and resentment at constant Soviet interference in Hungarian affairs, and drawing together groups and individuals of widely different characters and aims. It owed something, but not much, to encouragement from Radio Free Europe, the American radio station which at the time conveyed the impression that the United States would support a rising. In fact, as an American historian of Hungarian origin has written, it was very much 'a *Hungarian Revolution*', making 'impulsive, at times heroic and even unrealistic demands'.[30] It swept along those were supposed to be in charge of events by its emotional force and exhilarating optimism. Bliss was it in that dawn to be alive; though the dawn proved shortlived, and was followed not by the day but by the dark – or at best twilight.

The Hungarian rising of 1956 was a grave blow to the Soviet Union. The Soviet government first failed to prevent an open insurrection; it then hesitated; and finally demonstrated, with a heavy hand, the limits to the freedom allowed to its satellites, even after the Khruschev speech. In the short term, the lesson was well learned. There was no further trouble in the Soviet bloc until 1968. But in the long run, the consequences of the Hungarian rising had were to prove damaging, perhaps even fatal, to the Soviet system. Much more obviously than in East Germany in 1953, Soviet predominance in Hungary was shown to depend solely upon force, with corrosive effects within the Soviet bloc and among communist supporters in the West, some of whom came to realize (though often with painful slowness) that the Workers' Fatherland was a tyranny.

The Hungarian rising was thus a crisis for the USSR and for communism. Its impact on international affairs was less significant. There was no likelihood of American armed intervention, and thus of general war. On 25 October 1956, Dulles instructed the United States Ambassador in Moscow, Bohlen, to assure the Soviet government that the USA had no vital interests in Central Europe. On the 27th, the Secretary of State said in a public speech that any east European country which broke away from the Soviet Union could count on American *economic* assistance – which by implication excluded military help. On 31 October Eisenhower himself said publicly that the United States was ready to give economic help to new and independent governments in eastern Europe, but did not regard them as potential allies. As a one-time director of the CIA summed it up later, 'President Eisenhower decided that it was tough on the Hungarians, but they weren't worth World War Three.'[31] The often abrasive Dulles made this as clear as did the more emollient Eisenhower. The United States was not going to challenge Soviet predominance in eastern Europe – certainly not by going to war, and in the event not even by economic or diplomatic means. The Soviet government appeared to understand this perfectly well; and the acceptance of the status quo by both sides was a confirmation of the division of Europe, and a sign that the international system there had attained a high degree of stability. But as Europe settled down to its divided state the Cold War spread elsewhere. Stability within conflict was a basic characteristic of the Cold War.

This American passivity in face of what was at least an opportunity to embarrass the Soviet Union arose partly from the fact that 1956 was a presidential election year in the United States, and Eisenhower was seeking re-election as a man of peace. It also owed something to the simultaneous crisis over the Suez Canal – Soviet troops re-entered Budapest on 4 November, and British and French paratroops dropped at the northern end of the Canal on the 5th. The Suez crisis distracted much of the world's attention from Hungary; and the United States and the Soviet Union even found themselves on the same side in opposing the Anglo-French action against Egypt.[32] But it seems certain that, even without Suez, the Americans would have done nothing to save Hungary. On the most basic assessments of risk, the unwritten rules of the nuclear age meant that the Soviets could do as they wished in their own zone.

In the simultaneous crises over Hungary and Suez, it was striking that Asian and African opinion was far more critical of Britain and France over Suez than of the USSR over Hungary. An attack by European imperialists on Egypt was regarded as far worse than an attack by one set of Europeans on another. The Soviet Union gained much credit for its support for Egypt, and this sudden popularity in the Third World contributed to the mood of self-confidence, verging on euphoria, which seems to have gripped Khrushchev towards the end of 1956. At a reception in the Kremlin on 17 November 1956, Khrushchev said to his Western guests: 'If you don't like us, don't accept our invitations and don't invite us to come and see you! Whether you like it or not, history is on our side; we will bury you!' The British Ambassador, who was present, thought that the gist of the remark was 'We shall be at your funeral' rather than 'We shall dig your grave'; but whatever the correct translation, Khrushchev certainly meant that the Soviets were going to win the struggle between capitalism and communism.[33] It was in this mood that Khruschev embarked upon a course which led to crises in Berlin and Cuba, and largely decided the nature of the next phase of the Cold War.

◆ Notes to Chapter 6

1. For the Chinese revolution and American policy towards China, see below, pp. 190–2.
2. For the text of NSC-68, U.S. Department of State, *Foreign Relations of the United States, 1950*, Vol. I, pp. 237–79.
3. Quoted in John Lewis Gaddis, *We Now Know: Rethinking Cold War History* (Oxford, 1997), p. 66.
4. See Peter Lowe, *The Origins of the Korean War* (London, revised edn, 1997), pp. 181–2; Vladislav Zubok and Constantine Pleshakov, *Inside the Kremlin's Cold War* (Cambridge, Mass., 1996), pp. 54–5, 62–4.
5. Robert H. Ferrell, *Harry S. Truman: A Life* (Columbia, Missouri, 1994), pp. 318–19.
6. The strength of the outside contingents in January 1952 stood at: Australia, 2 battalions; Belgium, 1 battalion; Canada, a brigade group; Ethiopia, 1000; France, 1 battalion; Netherlands, 1 battalion; New

Zealand, 1 battalion; Philippines, 5000; Thailand, 4000; Turkey, 6000; United Kingdom, 2 brigades. (Max Hastings, *The Korean War* (London, 1987), pp. 443–4)

7. *Keesing's Contemporary Archives*, 1950, pp. 10996, 11021.
8. Quoted in Zubok and Pleshakov, p. 67; see generally pp. 65–9.
9. Hastings, *Korean War*, pp. 405–6.
10. Casualty figures in *ibid.*, p. 407.
11. For Quemoy and Matsu, see below, pp. 000–00.
12. Paul Kennedy, *The Rise and Fall of the Great Powers* (London, paperback edn, 1989), p. 495.
13. Martin Gilbert, *Never Despair: Winston S. Churchill, 1945–1965* (London, 1988), pp. 265–6.
14. Quoted in Richard J. Barnet, *Allies: America, Europe, Japan since the War* (London, 1984), p. 55.
15. Quoted in Paul Johnson, *A History of the Modern World from 1917 to the 1980s* (London, paperback edn, 1984), p. 461; Henry Kissinger, *Diplomacy* (London, paperback edn, p. 631).
16. For Marshall, see above, p. 78.
17. Peter G. Boyle, ed., *The Churchill–Eisenhower Correspondence, 1953–1955* (London, 1990), p.136.
18. R. A. Divine, *Eisenhower and the Cold War* (Oxford, 1981), p. 11.
19. *Khrushchev Remembers*; with Introduction, commentary and notes by Edward Crankshaw (Boston, 1970), p. 398;. cf. John Lewis Gaddis, *Strategies of Containment* (New York, 1982), p. 162.
20. Khruschev, quoted in Zubok and Pleshakov, p. 145.
21. Robert Service, *A History of Twentieth Century Russia* (London, 1997), pp. 329, 335.
22. V. Molotov, *Molotov Remembers: Inside Kremlin Politics. Conversations with Felix Chuev.* ed. Albert Resis (Chicago, 1993), p. 334.
23. Quoted in Zubok and Pleshakov, p. 161.
24. For the Warsaw Pact, see below, p. 122.
25. Stephen E. Ambrose, *Eisenhower*, Vol. II: *The President* (London, 1984), p. 67.
26. Quoted in David Reynolds, ed., *The Origins of the Cold War in Europe* (London, 1994), p. 16. SHAPE was the acronym for Supreme Headquarters Allied Powers Europe.
27. For Khrushchev's speech, *Khrushchev Remembers*, pp. 559–618.
28. For these two different stories, see Service, *Twentieth Century Russia*, p. 341, and Barnet, *Allies*, pp. 173–4. Perhaps both were true.
29. David Miller, *The Cold War: A Military History* (London, 1998), p. 59.
30. John Lukacs, *A New History of the Cold War* (New York, 1966), p. 357.

31. William Colby, quoted in Gabriel Partos, *The World that Came in from the Cold* (London, 1993), p. 108.
32. For the Suez Crisis, see below, pp. 181–6.
33. Khruschev's remark quoted in Lukacs, *Cold War*, p. 151; cf. Partos, p. 119.

CHAPTER

7

THE COLD WAR, 1957–1962: BERLIN TO CUBA

Khrushchev and Soviet foreign policy – Berlin crisis and the U-2 plane – Kennedy and Khrushchev – Cuba and the Vienna Summit – The Berlin Wall – Cuba missile crisis – State of the Cold War at the end of 1962

The years from 1957 to 1962 were a period of bustle and activity in Soviet foreign policy. Khrushchev was an enthusiastic traveller. In 1954 he visited China. In 1955 he went to Belgrade, and then to Burma, India and Afghanistan. In 1956 he went to England (where he stayed at Claridge's in London and went on a tourist trip to Oxford). In 1959 he became the first Soviet leader to visit the United States, where he conferred with Eisenhower at Camp David and met a farmer in Iowa. Summit conferences took him to Paris and Vienna, and he went to New York to address the United Nations. These were travels which Stalin would never have conceived of, displaying a new awareness of the outside world. Khrushchev set in train crises over Berlin (as Stalin had done in 1948), but also in Cuba (which Stalin would surely have regarded as far too distant to meddle with). He took an ardent interest in the new states of Asia and Africa, believing that the new world could be called into action to upset the balance of the old.

What lay behind this almost frantic activity? What were Khrushchev's ideas on foreign policy? He cut a strange figure – erratic, impulsive and sometimes self-contradictory. At home, he launched into a grandiose scheme to plough virgin lands in Kazakhstan, putting vast areas under cereal cultivation, only to turn much of the territory into a dustbowl and finish with an output lower in 1963 than in 1958.[1] He was self-confident to the point of brashness – on one famous occasion he took off his shoe and banged it on the desk at the General Assembly of the United Nations; yet he was also nagged by fears of falling short of Stalin's immense authority. (During the Hungarian rising in 1956, he imagined people saying that in the old days everyone had obeyed Stalin, but now 'these bastards' had lost

Hungary – which therefore he could on no account afford to do.)[2] He genuinely wanted to improve relations with the United States, and yet he plunged into a challenge to the Americans in the Caribbean.

Among these contradictions, three themes remained constant. First, Khrushchev took his communist faith seriously, and believed that communism would triumph, not just in the Soviet Union but in the world at large. He was fully convinced that the revolutionary potential of the Third World would tilt the balance of world power in favour of the Soviet Union. He confidently planned to overhaul the Americans in milk, butter and meat production by 1961–62, and in industrial output by 1970–75. It seems that he did not really believe in the reality of American prosperity. On one occasion he met Vice-President Nixon for a debate in a model American kitchen, and refused to believe that such kitchens were commonplace in the United States – it must be a put-up job, a sort of Potemkin kitchen. Second, Khrushchev understood that in the new age of nuclear weapons the Soviet Union and the United States could destroy one another and must therefore act with appropriate caution. The safety of his country, and of the revolutionary ideal which he cherished, depended on the two superpowers attaining a level of agreement sufficient to avoid a nuclear war. Third, Khrushchev was increasingly conscious of the dangers arising from the dispute between the Soviet Union and China, which developed from 1956 onwards, introducing a new complication in Soviet foreign policy and in the socialist camp.[3] Despite his impulsiveness, Khrushchev's policy rested firmly on these perceptions.

Khrushchev also introduced an improved system for securing information and advice on foreign policy through various research institutes, dealing with the United States and Canada, the world economy and international affairs, Africa, and the Far East. These bodies provided reports for the International Department of the Central Committee of the Communist Party, headed by Boris Ponomarev, which dealt with policy towards all non-Communist states. In 1957 Molotov, the long-serving and old-style Foreign Minister, conspired to remove Khrushchev from power, failed, and was himself dismissed. (It was a sign of change in the Soviet Union that he survived, and lived quietly in retirement.) Khrushchev appointed as the new Foreign Minister Andrei Gromyko, an experienced diplomat who had been successively Ambassador to the United States, Chief Permanent Delegate to the United Nations, and Ambassador in London. Khrushchev valued his steadfast obedience (he once remarked that Gromyko would 'sit on a block of ice if I tell him to'), but even more his skill and persistence in negotiation.[4] Gromyko's impassivity made an excellent foil to Khrushchev's ebullience, and he was to remain Soviet Foreign Minister from 1957 to 1985, ensuring a long continuity of direction in foreign policy.

◆ Berlin crisis, first phase, 1958–60

In 1957 the Soviet Union launched its first inter-continental ballistic missiles (ICBMs), and in October 1957 put a satellite (the Sputnik) into orbit round the earth. Khrushchev attended the second ICBM launch in person, and boasted in public that the Soviet Union would turn out missiles like sausages. This was bluff. Even two years later, when Khrushchev announced the formation of 'Rocket Strategic Forces', there were only four missiles of the relevant type ready for use. But the confidence behind the bluff was real. Khrushchev believed firmly that the Soviet Union was drawing ahead of the United States in missile technology; and he frightened many Americans into thinking the same thing. The idea of a 'missile gap', to the advantage of the Soviets, took root.

Encouraged by these events, Khrushchev re-opened the question of Berlin, which had slumbered uneasily since the end of the Berlin blockade in 1949. His basic motive seems to have been simple. He remarked on occasion: 'What would you do if you had an aching tooth? You'd have it out.' That was what he felt about Berlin – it was an aching tooth.[5] There were more sophisticated calculations. The lack of a German peace settlement left European affairs in a constant state of instability, which could be ended to Soviet advantage by a new and permanent arrangement in Berlin. The communist leader of East Germany, Ulbricht, grew weary of West Berlin and its display of increasing capitalist prosperity, and wanted to get rid of it. Khrushchev was willing to help him, and so promote the cause of a socialist East Germany. The technical opportunity was always present, because the arrangements for western access to Berlin by land had remained doubtful ever since 1945, and could be called into question at any time. Above all, Khrushchev was convinced that the Americans would not fight over Berlin. He could therefore act boldly yet safely.

On 10 November 1958 Khrushchev made a speech demanding an end to Berlin's status as a city occupied by the four powers, and announcing his intention of handing control over access to East Berlin to the East Germans. On 27 November he followed this up with notes to the United States, British and French governments, declaring the existing four-power agreements on Berlin null and void, and demanding that all occupation troops should leave the city within six months. If they did not, the Soviet Union would unilaterally conclude a peace treaty with the East German government, and hand over control of all movements in and out of East Berlin to the East German authorities. On 10 January 1959 he presented the western powers with a draft treaty setting out a new status for Berlin.

The six-month deadline for the withdrawal of occupation forces from Berlin was a form of ultimatum, with an implied danger of war if the western powers continued to enforce their rights of access to Berlin when the six months were up. The western powers differed markedly in their responses. Eisenhower had no wish to go to war over Berlin, and was prepared to try to find a compromise on the question of access. He proposed (26 November 1958) that the East Germans should simply be regarded as acting as agents for the Soviet Union, which would sidestep the issue of principle involved in East German control of access to Berlin. He was also willing to consider treating Berlin as a 'free city', without occupation forces; though he insisted that the existing rights of the occupying powers should be maintained while negotiations went on. Macmillan, the British Prime Minister, wanted the western powers to accept East German control over the lines of communication, rather than risk using force to maintain their rights of access. He virtually invited himself to Moscow in February 1959 to seek a solution by personal contact with Khrushchev; but without success. In France, de Gaulle had recently become President of the new Fifth Republic. He took a strong line on Berlin, partly because he simply refused to be bullied, but even more because he was determined to stand by West Germany. He was in the course of building a close relationship with Adenauer, who was convinced that Khrushchev's Berlin policy was ultimately designed to undermine West Germany and force the country out of NATO and its role in West European integration. De Gaulle therefore went out of his way to assure Adenauer that France would stand firm about Berlin, if necessary at the risk of war. He refused to look at American and British suggestions for 'exploratory talks' with the Soviets, remarking that there was nothing to explore – only rights to be maintained.

Strangely, Khrushchev made little attempt to exploit these differences between the western powers. He agreed to a meeting of foreign ministers, which convened at Geneva only a fortnight before the six-month deadline was due to expire. The ministers reached no agreement; the deadline arrived; and nothing happened. The Soviets continued to control the access routes to Berlin, and traffic passed as usual. The foreign ministers went on talking until August, and then parted without agreement.

The crisis was not resolved. Khrushchev simply seemed to lose interest in it for a time. Arrangements were now well under way for Khrushchev to visit the United States – an unprecedented journey for a Soviet leader, and one to which he was keenly looking forward. Nothing must be allowed to obstruct it; and for a time the Berlin question was put on one side.

Khrushchev's visit to the United States took place from 15 to 28 September 1959. He made it a family affair, being accompanied by his wife, son, and two daughters, as well as by a party of about a hundred. His talks with Eisenhower did not get very far, because neither was prepared to move from his existing position on disarmament, Berlin or the Middle East; but they got quite far enough on the simple central point that neither of them wanted a war. Most of the visit was public in nature. Khrushchev visited

Washington, New York, Los Angeles, San Francisco, Des Moines and Pittsburgh. He spent a day with Roswell Garst, a farmer in Iowa who had made a name for himself by arranging exchange visits between American and Soviet farmers and had already met Khrushchev in the Soviet Union. The Soviet leader was greeted almost everywhere by large crowds, sometimes enthusiastic and sometimes merely curious. He became involved in heated discussion about the speech in which he had said 'We will bury you', and explained that it was not a matter of physically burying anyone, but of the historical development of society. Still, he insisted that 'Capitalism will be buried and will change to Communism' – which doubtless did not comfort his American audience.[6] The visit produced little substantial result, but it was remarkable that it took place at all.

In the wake of this visit, Soviet–American relations appeared to improve for a time. Two further meetings were agreed on: a four-power summit in Paris in May 1960, to discuss Berlin; and later a journey by Eisenhower to Moscow to repay Khrushchev's visit. But suddenly everything collapsed. On 5 May 1960, on the eve of the Paris summit, the Soviet government released the news that on 1 May they had shot down an American U-2 photographic reconnaissance aircraft in the region of Sverdlovsk, about 1500 kilometres east of Moscow. Such flights had been going on since 1955. In June 1956 Khrushchev had personally told the American Chief of Air Staff, General Twining, to stop sending planes into Soviet air space – 'We will shoot down all uninvited guests'; and in fact the Soviets made some interceptions.[7] There was thus nothing new about this flight, which could have been ignored or dealt with behind the scenes if Khrushchev had so wished. Instead, he chose to make the incident public in the most dramatic way possible, on the eve of the Paris summit. Tactically, he played the game with great skill. On 5 May Soviet officials announced the shooting down of the U-2. The Americans claimed that the aircraft had been engaged in weather reconnaissance and had gone off course. Then on 7 May the Soviets produced the pilot, Gary Powers, with his films, a flight plan, and a 'confession'. The Americans then owned up. On 9 May the Secretary of State, Christian Herter, admitted the facts; and on the 11th President Eisenhower confirmed in public that such flights were made and maintained firmly that they were necessary for American security. Khrushchev, who had by then arrived in Paris for the summit, made his participation in the conference conditional upon an American apology for the operation, the punishment of those involved, and an undertaking not to make any further flights.

Khrushchev thus chose to make a public crisis out of an episode which could easily have been dealt with quietly. Why was this? The answer may lie partly in impulse – Powers' flight took place on May Day, a high point in the Soviet calendar, which Khrushchev took to be a deliberate insult. Tactically, it may be that Khrushchev expected Eisenhower to disown the flight, and so begin the Paris Conference at a moral and diplomatic disadvantage. On the other hand, he may have foreseen that his demands about Berlin were not going to succeed, and so chose to break off the conference on grounds of his own choosing. He was at any rate able to demonstrate that he had not gone 'soft on capitalism' after his visit to the United States in 1959.

In the event, Eisenhower (supported by de Gaulle) refused Khrushchev's demands for an apology, and the Paris Conference collapsed before it began. Yet this proved a strangely hollow crisis, with only limited consequences. Khrushchev scored a propaganda victory, wrong-footing the Americans and damaging their prestige. Eisenhower had to cancel a visit to Japan, for fear of public reaction. On the other hand, Eisenhower's belated frankness in taking responsibility for the flights and his reasoned insistence that they were necessary won him much respect among those who responded in strategic rather than emotional terms. The steadfast support of de Gaulle, who was far from being an automatic supporter of the United States, was particularly significant. Meanwhile, the Berlin question, which Khrushchev had reopened in November 1958 and which was to have been discussed in Paris, remained unresolved.

◆ Khrushchev and Kennedy, 1960–61; The Bay of Pigs and the Vienna Summit

In November 1960 John F. Kennedy was elected President of the United States, defeating Richard Nixon by a very narrow margin in the popular vote. The incoming President was young (only 43), wealthy, charming and largely without experience in world affairs. During his election campaign he had made much play with the 'missile gap', and insisted that American capitalism would build all the defences necessary and promote prosperity as well. He made sure that no one could say he was soft on communism by declaring that 'The enemy is the Communist system itself – implacable, insatiable, unceasing in its drive for world domination . . . a godless tyranny.'[8] Yet at the same time he also insisted on the need for negotiation with the Soviet Union. Kennedy was an unknown quantity – which in a curious way he has remained, suspended between the early adulation of the 'Camelot' era and the later criticisms of poor judgement and lack of real achievement.

Khrushchev took a keen interest in the presidential election, and was privately pleased by Kennedy's victory. In public, the two men opened a long-range verbal bombardment against one another. On 6 January 1961 Khrushchev made a speech predicting that the victory of communism would come, not through nuclear or conventional war, but through wars of national liberation in Africa, Asia and Latin America. Kennedy took this as a direct challenge, and replied in the course of his Inaugural Address as

President, declaring that freedom faced an 'hour of maximum danger', which he assumed the duty of confronting. 'I do not shrink from this responsibility. I welcome it.' America, he proclaimed, would 'pay any price, bear any burden, meet any hardship, support any friend, oppose any foe, to ensure the survival and the success of liberty.'[9] It was an extraordinary commitment, which eventually proved impossible to fulfil. The price of an immense defence budget and the burdens of the Vietnam War were more than the United States was willing to bear. But meanwhile Khrushchev's challenge had been taken up in no uncertain terms.

Behind the scenes there was another story. The Soviet experts estimated that Kennedy was likely to be pragmatic in foreign policy, and would be in favour of talks with the Soviet Union. Khrushchev made a point of consulting the American Ambassador in Moscow frequently, and also opened a new confidential channel to the White House, by-passing the Soviet Ambassador in Washington by using Georgi Bolshakov, nominally the head of the TASS press agency and in fact a colonel in Soviet military intelligence. Bolshakov made contacts with Robert Kennedy, the President's brother (and also the Attorney-General), and with Pierre Salinger, the President's press secretary; so that there were secret communications behind the scenes in marked contrast to the public sparring.

The state of American-Soviet relations thus remained uncertain, when suddenly they were tested at an unexpected point – Cuba. Since becoming independent from Spain in 1898, Cuba had remained very much under the influence of the United States, which took most of its exports and dominated its economy. In the 1950s, the country was run by a dictator, Batista; while in the hills and forests of the interior a young rebel, Fidel Castro, led a resistance movement. In 1957 the American government decided to abandon Batista, and in 1958 suspended its arms supplies to the dictator. Then, towards the end of 1958, they suddenly tried to change course and save Batista, for fear of finding something worse. It was too late. In January 1959, Batista gave up the struggle and fled. Castro and his band of bearded guerrillas came down from the hills and set up a new govenment in Havana. Among them was Ernesto (Che) Guevara, who was to prove one of the most magnetic figures of Third World mythology, and whose portrait was to become an icon for radical youth across the western world.

Castro was strongly anti-American (a trait which was not unknown in Latin America); and it may well be that at that stage he took to communism more as a function of his anti-Americanism than out of conviction. (He maintained diplomatic relations with Franco's government in Spain, which was anathema to most true left-wingers; and in return Spain took no part in the later American-led economic sanctions against Cuba.) In Moscow, there was some reluctance to believe that Castro and Guevara were true Marxists. Curiously (and as it proved disastrously) the Americans deliberately sought to push the Castro regime into close relations with the USSR, in the belief that this would render it unpopular at home and so bring about its fall. For example, the Secretary of State, Herter, preferred Cuba to buy jet fighters from the USSR rather than from Britain, in order to demonstrate Cuban dependence on the Soviet Union – a tactic which he carefully explained to the British Ambassador in Washington. This elaborate policy succeeded up to a point, in that the regime became more radical and developed ties with the Soviet Union; but it failed completely in its main objective. Castro took to courting the Soviets by claiming to be a communist, and established diplomatic relations with the Soviet Union on 7 May 1960; but he remained solidly in power. In Moscow, Khrushchev came to regard Castro and Guevara as heroes, who were bearing the flame of revolution in the centre of the Caribbean. When Khrushchev addressed the UN General Assembly in 1960, he deliberately sought out Castro and hugged him in a demonstration of friendship and support.

The Americans then tried a new tack, and imposed economic sanctions against Cuba. On 8 July 1960 they stopped importing sugar from Cuba, and on 2 August imposed a general economic embargo. At one time, these measures would have been fatal; but Castro could now play the Soviet card. The USSR supplied him with arms, of which the first shipment arrived in September 1960. In November Guevara visited Moscow to sell Cuban sugar to the Soviets. Khrushchev welcomed him warmly; invited him to stand with the Soviet leaders at the great parade on the anniversary of the Bolshevik Revolution; and made sure that the USSR and its east European satellites took all Cuba's sugar exports. For Khrushchev, Castro's success in Cuba came as confirmation of his belief that imperialism would be defeated by revolution in the Third World. If revolution could succeed in America's backyard, its victory was certain.

Thus by the end of 1960 Cuba was part of the Soviet camp, receiving Soviet military assistance and reliant on the Soviet bloc to buy its exports. In dismay, the Americans looked for other means of overthrowing Castro. There was no shortage of Cuban opponents of the Castro regime, some in Florida and others in military-style camps in Guatemala. The CIA set out to recruit a force of exiles to land in Cuba and lead a revolt. When Kennedy took office at the beginning of 1961 this plan was already well advanced. The new President might have dropped it or strengthened it, but in fact he did neither; and he fell between two stools. The so-called Cuban Brigade, operating from Guatemala, landed some 1400 men at the Bay of Pigs on the south coast of Cuba on 17 April 1961. American aircraft with Cuban markings and flown by Cuban exiles made ineffectual bombing attacks on Cuban airfields. No rebellion broke out to support the invaders. The landing force suffered over a hundred fatal casualties, and most were taken prisoner, to be displayed for photographers and film crews. American participation had been clear enough to attract attention, but utterly insufficient to ensure success. The result was not simply failure for the Americans but humiliation.

In Cuba, Castro's authority was consolidated. His prestige was at its height, and he seized the opportunity to crush internal opposition and round up American agents. On May Day 1961 he publicly proclaimed that Cuba was a socialist state, and announced that there was no need to hold any elections, since there was in effect a plebiscite every day in favour of the regime. The Americans in their dismay conceived a series of operations to overthrow or assassinate Castro – including an extraordinary scheme to poison some of his cigars. More seriously, they also attempted sabotage of the Cuban sugar crop and copper mines. (These plans were collectively code-named MONGOOSE, presumably after Kipling's short story in which a brave and tenacious mongoose kills a cobra; but the Americans failed to live up to this example.)

Cuba was now firmly established in the Soviet camp, as much by American errors as by Castro's own policies. The regime became the stan-dard-bearer for socialism in Latin America; and Cuba attained the status of an ally, rather than a mere satellite, of the Soviet Union.

It so happened that on 12 April 1961, a few days before the landing at the Bay of Pigs, the Soviet Union had put the first man into space. Yuri Gagarin became an instant hero, circling the earth under the sign of the hammer and sickle. Khrushchev was thus full of confidence at the time of the American disaster. He had known of the American plan in advance, but kept his own counsel until the day after the attack, when he wrote to Kennedy to declare that the American action threatened the peace of the world, and that Cuba would receive 'all necessary assistance' in repelling the attack. Moreover, he threatened that if the conflict continued in Cuba there might be a new conflagration elsewhere – meaning Berlin.[10] When the Americans did nothing to follow up the landing, Khrushchev had every reason to think that his threats had taken effect.

At the same time as these events in Cuba, the Soviet and American leaders were in contact by secret channels to prepare for a meeting. Khrushchev, buoyed up by successes in space and in the Caribbean, was eager for a meet-ing, and was sure that he faced a weak president whom he could put under pressure. Kennedy, more vaguely, wanted to meet Khrushchev and size him up.

The two leaders met at Vienna on 3–4 June 1961. Khrushchev was ebul-lient, and pleased at being the old hand facing the 'new boy' on the inter-national scene. He lectured the President on the history of the Cold War, and dug into the past to recall the fate of the Holy Alliance, which had failed to hold back revolution in the 1820s. He talked a good deal about the Bay of Pigs, rubbing salt into the wound of the American failure. Kennedy, by contrast, was uncertain and defensive, and failed to impose himself on the discussions. After the meetings, James Reston of the *New York Times* asked Kennedy if they had been pretty rough; and the President replied, 'Roughest thing in my life . . . he just beat hell out of me.'[11] Khrushchev came away convinced that Kennedy was weak. Kennedy concluded that Khruschev was in a mood to take risks. In the course of the meeting, Khrushchev yet again set a six-month deadline on his demands relating to Berlin; and it seemed that this time he meant business.

There was a strange sequel to these events. Kennedy was so dismayed by the almost simultaneous setbacks of the Bay of Pigs and the Soviets putting the first man into space that he sought for some spectacular success to redress the balance. He found the answer in space, and authorized the Apollo moon programme, designed to restore American prestige by landing men on the moon. Some eight years later, on 20 July 1969, the Apollo XI spacecraft came down on the moon, and men took their first lunar walk. It was indeed a remarkable feat; but by that time the situation on earth had changed completely, and the danger to American prestige came from quite a different quarter, in Vietnam.

◆ The Berlin Wall and the end of the Berlin crisis, 1961–62

In 1958 Khrushchev had put the western powers under pressure by provoking a crisis over access to Berlin. But by 1961 it was the Soviet Union and East Germany that were under pressure over Berlin. The East German population was draining away to the west through the city, most of them bound for West Berlin. From 1957 to 1961 the numbers were as follows:[12]

1957	261 622
1958	204 092
1959	143 917
1960	199 188
1961 (to 30/6)	103 159

Both the Soviets and East Germans were alarmed at this migration. Ulbricht, the head of the East German government, asked Khruschev for aid – food, hard currency, and even Soviet 'guest workers'. Khrushchev declined to send workers, and was reluctant to take the drastic step of closing the door, which would amount to admitting that the only way to keep the people of East Germany in their own country was to imprison them.

By July 1961 time was running out. Ulbricht warned the Soviets that if the border in Berlin was kept open, the collapse of the German Democratic Republic was inevitable. The Soviets decided to shut the door. They were prepared to risk the blow to their prestige; and they did not expect any serious reaction from the Americans. (The head of the KGB, Shelepin, put various measures in hand to tie the Americans down elsewhere by inciting trouble in Central America and Africa, spreading rumours of moves to 'liberate' South Korea, Taiwan and South Vietnam, and exaggerating the scale of Soviet nuclear armaments.)[13]

When they reached their decision, the Soviets moved swiftly. Overnight, between 12 and 13 August 1961, East Berlin was cut off from West Berlin by a barrier of barbed wire. Over the next few months this barrier was built up into the Berlin Wall, an ugly obstacle of concrete blocks, some four metres high, and with 300 watch-towers along its 111-kilometre length.

At first, the Americans offered no reaction – it was two days before they even lodged a protest. Eventually, under pressure from Willy Brandt, the Mayor of West Berlin, they sent a symbolic detachment of 1500 troops (accompanied by Vice-President Lyndon Johnson and General Clay, who had been the American Commander-in-Chief in Germany at the time of the Berlin blockade) along the *Autobahn* to West Berlin, thus asserting their right of access. At bottom, it is probable that Kennedy was relieved by the severance of the two Berlins, which offered a way out of the Berlin problem without war. It is hard to see that any other course was open to him without grave risks. As it was, the situation sometimes looked quite dangerous enough. On 22 October East German police tried to stop the American Deputy Commandant from entering East Berlin, causing a difficult incident. On 27 October American and Soviet tanks took up station at Check-Point Charlie, the principal authorized crossing-point between the two halves of the city; the American tanks were carrying equipment suitable for knocking down a wall. The two forces looked at one another for two days, during which the good sense of those on the spot and some intensive diplomacy behind the scenes took the sting out of the situation. In 1962 the Americans were still looking for a compromise on access to West Berlin.

Such a compromise proved to be unnecessary. In January 1963 Khrushchev himself announced that the success of the Berlin Wall made a new settlement about Berlin unnecessary; and he was right. The Wall ended, at one and the same time, the haemorrhage of people from East to West Germany and the Soviet attempt to drive the western powers out of Berlin. It was a grave and self-inflicted blow to Soviet prestige, and a propaganda gift to the West, because nothing could conceal the simple fact that the Wall was built to confine the East Germans in their own country. But the Wall achieved what Khrushchev and Ulbricht hoped: it stabilized the East German state, which began an economic recovery which improved living standards – not up to West German levels, but much higher than they had been before.

The Berlin Wall closed the German Question for many years to come, setting in concrete the division between the two Germanies and the two halves of Berlin until all was changed in 1989. The Wall was a remarkable symbol of the Cold War. It was ugly, brutal and inhuman, cutting a city in two and separating families and friends. It caused grief and hardship; yet

compared to a shooting war it cost few lives. In political terms it represented a crude form of stability.

Yet the Cold War was never stable. When it settled down in one place it
broke out in another; and in 1962 the Cuba missile crisis brought the world
to the verge of actual war.

◆ The Cuba missile crisis, 1962

In early July 1962 Raoul Castro, Fidel Castro's brother and Defence
Minister of Cuba, visited Moscow to initial a secret agreement providing
for the stationing of Soviet missiles in Cuba. In late September and early
October 1962 some 85 Soviet vessels sailed to Cuba carrying 42 intermediate-range missiles with 164 nuclear warheads, and 42 000 Soviet troops to
guard them. The missiles were to be kept under Soviet control; and the
installations which would render them operational were to be completed by
25–7 October.[14]

Why did Khrushchev make this daring move? Its strategic value was
doubtful, and at best temporary. Soviet long-range missiles were already
capable of reaching targets in the United States; and fairly soon the Soviets
would have submarine-launched missiles which would be safer from attack
than land-based rockets in Cuba. In terms of foreign policy it might have
been a bargaining move, enabling Khrushchev to demand concessions elsewhere. In Khrushchev's mood at the time, it may well have been inspired by
genuine commitment to Castro and his revolutionary regime – Cuba had
become to the Soviet Union what Berlin was to the United States, a symbol
of its ideology and prestige. Indeed, it may be that prestige was the key to
the operation, in that Khrushchev may have been aiming to compel the
United States to accept the USSR as an equal – specifically, since the USA
had stationed missiles in Turkey, next door to the Soviet Union, the USSR
could station them in Cuba.

The Soviets made little attempt at concealment; and indeed the voyages
of so many ships and the landing of their cargoes was almost bound to be
observed. But for various reasons, including bad weather over Cuba, it was
not until 14 October that the CIA informed President Kennedy that the
Soviet Union was not only building bases in Cuba (which had been known
for some time) but was installing sites for medium-range missiles. This was
rapidly confirmed by photographs taken by U-2 reconnaissance planes.
How would the Americans react?

In principle, they had several courses open to them. They might accept
the *fait accompli*, do nothing, and await the outcome. In practice, this was
virtually impossible, because no President could show such weakness on a
crisis so close to America's shores. They might negotiate, perhaps through
the United Nations, or through established confidential channels. This

would have the advantage of avoiding an immediate confrontation, but would present the Soviets with the opportunity of spinning out the negotiations until their position in Cuba had become impregnable. On the other hand, the Americans might use force, in different forms. They could bomb the missile sites; but they could not be sure of destroying them all, and it would be dangerous to miss even one or two. They could launch a full-scale invasion, after the style of Normandy in 1944; and in fact the Americans moved large amphibious forces to Florida. But such an operation would involve delay; it would mean direct conflict with Soviet forces, which had always been avoided hitherto; and it might have involved heavy casualties.

In these circumstances, a naval blockade offered an attractive alternative. A blockade would do nothing about the missiles and troops already in Cuba, but would prevent their reinforcement. It would exploit American superiority at sea, where the Soviets were at their weakest; it would gain a little time while making a show of strength; and it would not rule out any of the more drastic options – preparations for invasion or air strikes could still go forward. The Americans opted for a blockade. On 22 October 1962, in a television broadcast, Kennedy announced the presence of Soviet missiles in Cuba, together with 42 000 troops. As a counter-measure, he declared that 'a strict quarantine' would be established round Cuba: with effect from 24 October, 'All ships of any kind bound for Cuba from whatever nation or port will, if found to contain cargoes of offensive weapons, be turned back.'[15] The use of the word 'quarantine' instead of 'blockade' sidestepped questions as to whether a blockade could be established except in time of war, or whether a blockade might in itself be an act of war. It was a subtle choice of word; but the practical consequences were the same. American warships were ordered to take station some 800 miles from the eastern tip of Cuba – a distance later changed to 500 miles, at British suggestion, allowing the Soviet government an extra day to decide on its response. On 23 October Kennedy signed an order putting the 'quarantine' in place with effect from 14.00 hours GMT on the 24th (10.00 hours in Washington, and 18.00 hours in Moscow).

The American warships took up their positions. During the morning of 24 October a number of Soviet vessels were heading for Cuba. The American 'Crisis Committee' which was watching the situation from Washington expected an encounter somewhere between 10.30 and 11.00 a.m. In this respect it was an extraordinarily public crisis. American television showed a Soviet tanker, the *Bucharest*, approaching the 'quarantine' line, with American warships close by. Along with much of the American population, the staff of the Soviet Embassy in Washington gathered round TV sets to watch. The world held its breath. The tanker passed unimpeded, to sighs of relief. But the *Bucharest* carried no missiles. Two other Soviet vessels, the *Gagarin* and the *Komiles* were nearing the American line. At 10.25 a.m. Washington time these ships were reported to have stopped; by

10.30 there were reports that six ships in all had stopped or turned back.[16] The Soviets chose to avoid the confrontation, and sea power had begun its work without a shot being fired.

This was only a temporary respite, leaving the basic situation as it was before. The Soviet missiles already in Cuba were still there, and their installation was still going ahead Even so, a psychological turning-point had been passed, and an opportunity opened for negotiation. The Secretary-General of the United Nations, U Thant, tried to find a compromise in the afternoon of 24 October, sending identical messages to Moscow and Washington, proposing that the Soviet government should cease to send weapons to Cuba and that the United States should lift its quarantine. On the 25th Khrushchev agreed to his part of the bargain (after all, his ships had already turned round); but Kennedy declined (the quarantine was doing its work). Khrushchev then proposed a summit meeting with Kennedy, but the President made no reply.

During the night of 25–6 October, Khrushchev received an erroneous report that the Americans were about to invade Cuba, and began to look for a way out with an anxiety which by some accounts verged on panic. It is striking that throughout this crisis Khrushchev sought to avoid direct confrontation with American forces: he ordered the ships to turn back, and he did not want the troops in Cuba to face an invasion. Meanwhile, the Americans maintained their pressure. On 26 October an American destroyer (appropriately, the USS *Joseph P. Kennedy Jr*) stopped and searched a Lebanese cargo ship, the *Marucla*. After the search, the ship was allowed to sail on; but the Soviets had been warned that the 'quarantine' was still in force. American warships and aircraft ostentatiously increased their surveillance of Soviet submarines in the North Atlantic. Reconnaissance aircraft made low-level flights over Cuba. On the 27th an American U-2 plane was shot down by either Cuban or Soviet anti-aircraft fire. The Cubans publicly took the responsibility, but the Soviet forces in the island were put on high alert. Khrushchev sent their commander an order forbidding any use of nuclear weapons. The risk of war was still acute.

Despite this extreme tension, or perhaps because of it, the outline of a solution began to emerge. During the night of 25–6 October Khrushchev raised the idea that the Americans should remove their missiles from Turkey to balance the withdrawal of Soviet missiles from Cuba. He also sought an assurance from the United States that there would be no invasion of Cuba. During 26 October, the Americans maintained in public that they would not negotiate unless the Soviet missiles were previously withdrawn from Cuba; but they indicated in private that they would not invade Cuba if the missiles were removed, and that American missiles would be withdrawn from Turkey after a suitable delay. In the evening of the 26th Robert Kennedy gave the Soviet Ambassador a firm assurance that the Americans would remove their missiles from Turkey after the proper NATO procedures had been observed. On this basis a bargain became possible.

These confidential exchanges led Khrushchev to broadcast at 17.00 hrs Moscow time on 27 October that he was prepared to withdraw the Soviet missiles from Cuba in return for undertakings that the United States would not invade the island, and that they would remove their own missiles from Turkey. Kennedy made his reply public: he accepted that Khrushchev was to remove the missiles from Cuba; and agreed that the United States would remove the 'quarantine' measures promptly, and would give assurances that there would be no invasion of Cuba. In private, Robert Kennedy assured the Soviet Ambassador that the United States would remove its missiles from Turkey, but he could not make this concession public.

The worst phase of the crisis thus came to an end. The Soviet forces in Cuba rapidly began to dismantle the missile sites. On 20 November Kennedy ordered the lifting of the 'quarantine' (though of course the United States Navy could reimpose it at any time). The Soviet missiles, tactical bombers and land forces (except for a single brigade) left Cuba by March 1963. (The withdrawal of the aircraft and land forces had not formed part of the original bargain, and represented an additional concession by Khrushchev.)

This settlement appeared balanced, but was in practice in favour of the United States. Khrushchev withdrew the missiles from Cuba, and so abandoned a position which he had very publicly taken up. The Americans, on the other hand, had had no intention of invading Cuba except to destroy the Soviet missiles; so when the missiles went they were only giving up something which they did not propose to do anyway. As for the missiles in Turkey, these were Jupiters which were obsolescent, and could be withdrawn without significant strategic effect. Khrushchev thus gave up a prominent venture, to which he had pinned his prestige. The Americans gave up two points which were largely hollow.

The Cuba missile crisis was for a short time intensely dangerous. When Soviet cargo ships approached the American quarantine line no one knew what would happen if an American warship fired on a Soviet vessel, or attempted to put a search party on board against resistance. Again, when the American reconnaissance plane was shot down over Cuba, the Soviets feared some form of retaliation. The two superpowers came near to the brink of war; and they drew back. Nuclear deterrence worked, helped on the American side by the strength and flexibility of sea power.

The shock of these events produced widely different effects on the relations between the superpowers. On the one hand, the American and Soviet leaders were so shaken by their near-disaster that they agreed to improve the speed and reliability of their communications with one another. They installed a so-called 'hot line' (in fact a teletype) between the two capitals, to allow them to communicate directly, securely and almost instanta-neously. This proved to be a psychological gesture rather than a practical measure – the 'hot line' was not used for another five years (by Kosygin during the Middle East crisis of 1967), and then to only modest effect. But after the intensity of the missile crisis, even a psychological gesture had its value.[17] The superpowers also began to move towards a treaty to limit the testing of nuclear weapons in the atmosphere, in which they were joined by Britain but not by France. The Americans and Soviets thus took deliberate steps towards détente – the lessening of tension in the Cold War. On the other hand, the Cuba missile crisis led to an intensification of the arms race. Both superpowers increased their production of nuclear weapons; and the Soviets, conscious that they had been checked and outmanoeuvred by American sea power, set out to build an ocean-going fleet. Thus while moving delicately towards détente the rivals trod heavily towards greater armaments.

In the Cuba missile crisis, the two superpowers confronted one another and negotiated with one another virtually alone. The Americans communi-cated to some extent with their principal NATO allies; Macmillan in Britain and de Gaulle in France tried to influence American policy; but at the height of the crisis there could be no doubt that this was an American affair. Similarly Khrushchev virtually disregarded the Chinese, who were furious at the compromise settlement, which they regarded as a surrender. He also ignored Castro, agreeing to withdraw the missiles and troops without consultation with the Cubans. (Castro, though, struck a blow for self-respect by refusing to allow American inspectors to verify the withdrawal on the ground.)

Of the two, in their lonely eminence, the United States emerged the stronger. Kennedy won immense prestige through his handling of the crisis. He showed firmness in imposing the naval blockade, subtlety in calling it a 'quarantine', and flexibility in seeking a successful compromise – a remark-able performance. Khrushchev, on the other hand, had been rash in taking up a position in Cuba which he could not sustain, and suffered a public defeat when Soviet ships carrying missiles turned back on the high seas rather than test the American blockade. In the personal rivalry with Kennedy, in which Khrushchev had seemed so superior at Vienna in 1961, he was now very much the also-ran. It was not long before he paid the price, being deposed from power in 1964.

But the American success was by no means complete. Cuba remained defiant, a resolute and vigorous enemy of the Americans, a beacon for revo-lution and Left-wing aspirations in Latin America and a lively critic of American policy at all kinds of international gatherings. In the 1970s Cuban expeditionary forces were to intervene in Africa, providing the Soviet Union with an acceptable 'Third World' military arm in countries where Soviet forces would have been less welcome. Castro remained a thorn in the American flesh, defying the might of the United States from a mere ninety miles across the sea. There were only two superpowers, and the USA was the stronger of the two; but a tiny enemy could still flourish in the Americans' own backyard. The facts of power were more complicated than might appear on the surface.

◈ The Cold War at the end of 1962

The Cuba missile crisis showed the two superpowers standing alone, with greater military and nuclear strength than they had ever previously possessed. Yet in many ways their power and prestige were lower than they had been just after the Second World War. In Latin America, American influence was unchallenged at the end of the war, but was successfully defied by Cuba in 1961–62. In 1947 the United States was the saviour of western Europe through the Marshall Plan. By 1962 western Europe was organized in the European Economic Community, which was to a considerable extent directed against the United States; and its most prominent figure, General de Gaulle, was ostentatiously hostile to American influence. At the end of the Second World War, the Americans could play the card of being the liberator of colonial peoples; but by 1962 most of the new countries which had emerged from the ruins of the European empires were fiercely anti-American.

As for the Soviet Union, in 1947–48 its power was supreme in eastern Europe. But its control had been challenged in East Germany in 1953 and Hungary in 1956. In 1961 it had been compelled to admit that the people of East Germany could only be kept in their own country by the Berlin Wall. Yugoslavia had successfully defied even Stalin, and still pursued an independent course. China had become openly hostile to the Soviet Union, creating a rift in the communist world more dangerous and damaging than anything which confronted the United States in western Europe.[18] Even though the Soviet Union enjoyed the admiration of most of the former colonial states, it could prove an expensive and often unrewarding activity to support them.

Each of the superpowers had grown in military strength, and possessed in its nuclear arsenal the means to destroy its opponent beyond hope of recovery. Yet this immense power could not be used, for fear of mutual annihilation, and thus existed in a curious vacuum. In these circumstances, a state of *de facto* stability was established between the two great rivals. They continued to be ideological opponents, conducting a constant propaganda conflict against one another. They were engaged in clandestine combat by espionage and subversion. They pursued arms races of immense complexity and exorbitant expense. Yet they had become, in Raymond Aron's telling phrase, *frères-ennemis* – brothers as well as enemies. They confronted one another, yet they negotiated with one another; and they were prepared to settle down and live with one another, even if it was only on a temporary basis. The Cold War had reached a sort of stalemate. It is time to look back and examine the nature of this strange conflict.

◆ Notes to Chapter 7

1. Robert Service, *A History of Twentieth Century Russia* (London, 1997), pp. 350–2.
2. Vladislav Zubok and Constantine Pleshakov, *Inside the Kremlin's Cold War* (Cambridge, Mass., 1996), p. 184.
3. For Chinese–Soviet relations, see below, pp. 192–9.
4. Anatoly Dobrynin, *In Confidence: Moscow's Ambassador to America's Six Cold War Presidents* (New York, 1995), pp. 32–3, 574–5.
5. Sir Frank Roberts, quoted in Gabriel Partos, *The World That Came in from the Cold* (London, 1990, pp. 39–40.
6. *Keesing's Contemporary Archives*, 1959, pp. 17079–85.
7. Zubok and Pleshakov, p. 159. According to Soviet sources, the Americans lost 130 pilots on reconnaissance over the USSR in the 1950s.
8. Speech by Kennedy at the Mormon Tabernacle, Salt Lake City, quoted in Michael R. Beschloss, *Khrushchev versus Kennedy: The Crisis Years, 1960–63* (London, 1991), p. 25. The parallel with President Reagan's speech referring to the 'evil empire' are close; yet Kennedy's remarks have gone largely unnoticed.
9. Quoted in Thomas C. Reeves, *A Question of Character: A Life of John F. Kennedy* (London, 1991). p. 253.
10. Zubok and Pleshakov, p. 242.
11. Beschloss, *Kennedy versus Khrushchev*, pp. 224–5.
12. David Miller, *The Cold War: A Military History* (London, 1998), p. 342.
13. Zubok and Pleshakov, pp.253–5. The Central American countries named were Nicaragua, San Salvador, and Guatemala; the African countries were Kenya, Rhodesia, and Portuguese Guinea.
14. Dobrynin, *In Confidence*, p. 73; Zubok and Pleshakov, p. 265.
15. Quoted in Beschloss, *Khrushchev versus Kennedy*, p. 484.
16. Christopher Andrew, *For the President's Eyes Only: Secret Intelligence and the American Presidency from Washington to Bush* (London, 1995), p. 296.
17. For the hot-line, see pp. 269–70.
18. For the Sino–Soviet dispute, see pp. 194–9.

REFLECTION

THE COLD WAR IN ITS EARLY PHASES

The study of the Cold War is much plagued by problems of definition. The term itself is a metaphor, necessary but in some ways misleading. It is necessary because we are dealing with a conflict which was not a war in any strict sense of the word. Up to the time of the Second World War, most wars had recognizable beginnings, with the exchange of ultimatums and declarations of war; they comprised direct fighting between the belligerents; and they ended with armistices and peace treaties. The Cold War had none of these characteristics; and above all it involved no direct fighting between the principal antagonists, the United States and the Soviet Union. This unusual sort of conflict therefore required and received a special name.

The term 'Cold War' came into general circulation when Walter Lippman, a highly influential American newspaper columnist, used it as the title of a book in 1947. Before that, George Orwell, writing in prophetic vein in October 1945, had forecast 'a peace that is no peace', in which a great power would be 'in a permanent state of "cold war" with its neighbours.'[1] Since then, the phrase has become an indispensable part of our vocabulary, so that we cannot conceive of describing the history of the second half of the twentieth century without it.

Yet the term remains teasingly imprecise, leaving open a series of questions. When did it start? What was it about? Where was its centre? None of these questions have certain answers; which means that with the Cold War we are dealing with a slippery and uncertain entity – better authenticated than the sea serpent, but nowhere near so certainly classified as the cod.

When did the Cold War start? Some historians have had no hesitation in nominating 1917, when the Bolshevik Revolution in Russia brought into being a socialist state which by its very nature was in fundamental conflict with the bourgeois capitalist countries in other parts of the world; and equally, they were in conflict with it.[2] Others have chosen dates somewhere between 1943 and 1948. Some have discovered an American hostility towards the Soviet Union dating from 1943; others have argued that the Cold War started over Poland between 1943 and 1945; others again have taken the Yalta Conference of February 1945 as the point at which Europe was divided and the Cold War began. There was at one time a strong school of thought that the replacement of Roosevelt by Truman in April 1945 was the decisive turning-point. A selection of other breaking-points have been offered: Stalin's adoption of a hard ideological line in February 1946; the American initiatives in the Truman Doctrine and the Marshall Plan in 1947; the communist coup in Czechoslovakia and the beginning of the Berlin blockade in 1948. Two writers essaying a brief survey of the Cold War in 1988 asserted briskly that 'The Cold War . . . did not begin in earnest until 1948'.[3] There seem to be no later offers; but even so we have a conflict which, according to different versions, started within a bracket of thirty-one years (1917–48), or on a majority verdict five years (1943–48)

What was the Cold War about? It was an ideological conflict between two philosophies and ways of life – communism and a state-controlled economy on the one side, liberal democracy and capitalism on the other. This extended the bounds of the conflict well beyond calculations of power politics. Soviet leaders started from the assumption that 'all other political life-forms were inherently and immutably hostile' – something which was as true for Switzerland, which could present no physical threat to the USSR as it was for the United States.[4] Americans frequently declared that an advance by communism anywhere was a danger to the 'free world'. President Kennedy said on 26 September 1963: 'I know full well that every time a country, regardless of how far away it may be from our own borders – every time that a country passes behind the Iron Curtain the security of the United States is thereby endangered . . . So when you ask why we are in Laos, or Viet-Nam, or the Congo [it is] because our freedom is tied up with theirs.'[5]

Moreover, as an ideological struggle the Cold War was to a considerable degree a conflict *within* countries. For communists, fellow-travellers and many other radicals in the West, the true enemy was American imperialism (which could be economic and cultural as much as territorial), or capitalism in general, or their own bourgeois governments. The most obvious examples were to be found in the ideological traitors, who betrayed their own country not for gain but for their beliefs – for example, the 'Cambridge Comintern' of spies in Britain, notably Philby and Blunt. But sympathy for the Soviet Union was far more widespread than that, and remarkably persistent in intellectual circles. The Soviets gained support from various currents of opinion: anti-fascist, anti-colonialist, anti-capitalist, and anti-American – a remarkable collection of 'antis'! On the other hand, the opponents of communism and the USSR in western Europe came from all parts of the political spectrum, Left as well as Right – in Britain, Bevin as much as Churchill, in West Germany the Social Democrat Ernst Reuter and the Christian Democrat Konrad Adenauer. In eastern Europe, for large numbers of people (sometimes a vast majority, as in Hungary in 1956), the true enemy was the Soviet Union and their own communist governments. Even within the Soviet Union itself nationalists wanted to liberate their own countries (for example, in the Baltic states or the Ukraine), and other dissidents (for example, Sakharov and Solzhenitsyn) opposed the communist regime. These divisions within countries and societies present plain evidence of the ideological nature of the Cold War.

More straightforwardly, the Cold War was also a power struggle between the two superpowers which emerged at the end of the Second World War, the United States and the Soviet Union, which competed for influence or predominance as other great powers had done throughout the history of the world. They formed alliances, collected client states, built up armaments and sought control over raw materials. There was nothing here that statesmen and historians of earlier ages would not have understood; though the struggle was pursued over a wider geographical area than most previous conflicts, and its combination with the ideological rivalry gave it an extra intensity and depth. The particular character of the Cold War arose from the inextricable entangling of the two elements of power politics and ideology. It was as though the struggle between Rome and Carthage had somehow been crossed with that of Reformation against Counter-Reformation.

Where was the centre of the Cold War to be found? The most obvious answer was in Europe, where the heaviest concentrations of armed strength confronted one another and the two ways of life were in close juxtaposition. The iron curtain divided the continent, a constant physical reminder of a deep antagonism. The west European states at first genuinely feared an unstoppable Soviet attack, and long afterwards lived with a lurking anxiety. ('When the Russian tanks roll westward, what defence for you and me?' wrote Philip Larkin once.)[6] The Soviets for their part observed the build-up of American tactical nuclear weapons, which were of immense destructive power beneath their innocuous-sounding name. Perhaps more important, they were constantly afraid of the appeal of western prosperity (most obviously visible in West Berlin) and the infiltration of western ideas, which were excluded as far as possible by a severe censorship and the jamming of radio broadcasts. Europe thus concentrated the issues of power and ideology in a small area and with great intensity. Yet Europe also became the most stable area in the whole of the Cold War. As early as 1948 or 1949, both sides accepted that the division of Europe into spheres of influence was permanent; which suited them not too badly.

While Europe was in some ways the centre of the Cold War, other areas saw far greater movement and violence. The success of the communists in China in 1949 suddenly brought the world's most populous country into the socialist camp. Korea became the scene of a fierce struggle – no question of 'cold war' there, but a full-scale shooting war, with heavy casualties. In Indochina France fought a long and bitter war against nationalist and communist opponents, and the issue appeared so important that the Americans took over the struggle. In Africa, the sudden rush to independence by the European colonies in the early 1960s brought the Cold War into a whole new arena, where the Americans and Soviets competed for influence. A competition for predominance in the emerging Third World became a prominent feature of the Soviet–American conflict. In Latin America, Guatemala was an outpost of the Cold War as early as 1954, and by 1960–62, with the successive crises in Cuba, the continent became of central importance for a short time.

To some degree this shift of activity was superficial. Europe remained the crucial arena, though other continents were the scene of more spectacular conflicts. For the United States, if western Europe were lost and the Atlantic alliance destroyed, the whole of their position would be imperilled; and similarly for the Soviet Union, the loss of eastern Europe would endanger its whole prestige and power – as was to be demonstrated in 1989–91, when the collapse of eastern Europe was followed at once by that of the USSR itself. To lose or gain influence in Korea, Indo-China or the Congo brought dramatic changes on the map and on the surface of events, but was not decisive for either side.

These questions about the nature of the Cold War (when did it begin, what was it about, where was its centre to be found?) have all been complicated by the further issue of who was responsible for it, or in simple terms who started it. For many years this question loomed large in historical discussion of the Cold War in the United States. In the 1950s the predominant school of thought maintained that the cause of the Cold War, and therefore responsibility for it, lay in Soviet expansionism and the drive to dominate Europe, which the United States and its allies had been compelled to resist. This interpretation drew heavily on the supposed lessons of the 1930s, which showed that the attempt to appease Germany and Japan had led infallibly to war. It followed therefore that a new aggressor must be opposed at once. Then in the 1960s and early 1970s there emerged in the USA a so-called 'revisionist' school, taking an almost directly opposite viewpoint. The revisionists argued that it was American intransigence (when Truman replaced the more flexible Roosevelt) or even aggressive intent (for example, when the Marshall Plan threatened to undermine Soviet control in eastern Europe) that aroused Soviet fears, and so provoked the Cold War as a form of reaction. This school of thought gained immense impetus during the American war in Vietnam in the late 1960s and early 1970s, which brought about a critical reappraisal of the whole of American foreign policy in the twentieth century. The question of the origins of the Cold War thus became a matter of American internal politics as well as of historical discussion, and the differing schools were often intransigent in their attitudes and severe in their criticisms of one another. There emerged further variants (neo-orthodox, post-revisionist and others), adding layers of complication, and directing attention as much towards the disputes between historians as towards the events which they were discussing.[7]

Such disputes over responsibility awoke few echoes in the Soviet Union, where there was no doubt among orthodox communists that the capitalists and imperialists were the implacable enemies of the USSR, as they had been since its foundation. Stalin himself, though an experienced practitioner of power politics, assumed that all capitalist powers were at bottom his enemies, even though from time to time they might be accepted as temporary allies. Molotov, who was himself a lifelong communist and a true believer, once reflected: 'What does the cold war mean? Strained relations. It was entirely their doing or because we were on the offensive. They certainly hardened their line against us, but we had to consolidate our conquests.'[8] This showed a sort of resignation about the state of the world and the inevitability of conflict which was in sharp contrast to the American agonizing over responsibility (especially their own responsibility) for the Cold War, which in some ways seemed to go deeper than either history or politics, and draw on well-springs within the American mind.

All in all, historians of the Cold War have been asked to explain too much. The task can be eased, the problems of definition elucidated, and the questions of responsibility brought into better perspective, when we adopt an analytical approach to events, and recognize that the Cold War in the period we have just surveyed, from 1945 to 1962, was not a single entity but several, linked yet separate. These different elements may be plotted on a sort of chart of the Cold War (see Cold War chart).

The first line on the chart represents ideological conflict, and should stretch back to 1917, with something of a break during the Second World War. In the period of the wartime alliance, public opinion in the USA and Great Britain was strongly pro-Russian, and even to some degree pro-Soviet, in the belief that somehow liberal democracy and Soviet collectivism were evolving towards a consensus. The Communist role in resistance movements throughout Europe also attracted widespread support. On the other side, in the USSR, Stalin called on Russian patriotism, evoking the memory of the heroes of the past, like Suvorov and Kutusov; he sought the support of the Orthodox Church; and in 1943 he dissolved Comintern, at any rate on paper. These developments tended to overlay the ideological differences between capitalists and communists; and in western countries there was a strong belief that the old antagonisms were diminishing. This state of affairs did not long survive the war. The ideological conflict resumed almost at once, and was particularly severe in the late 1940s and early 1950s.

The line representing diplomatic relations shows a number of changes. The wartime alliance between the USA, Britain and the USSR produced an effective working relationship, in which the key points were the three summit conferences between the Allied leaders at Teheran, Yalta and Potsdam. There followed, from 1945 to the end of 1947, a period in which the Foreign Ministers of the USA, the USSR, Britain and France continued to meet frequently, though they found it increasingly difficult to reach

Cold war chart, 1945–62

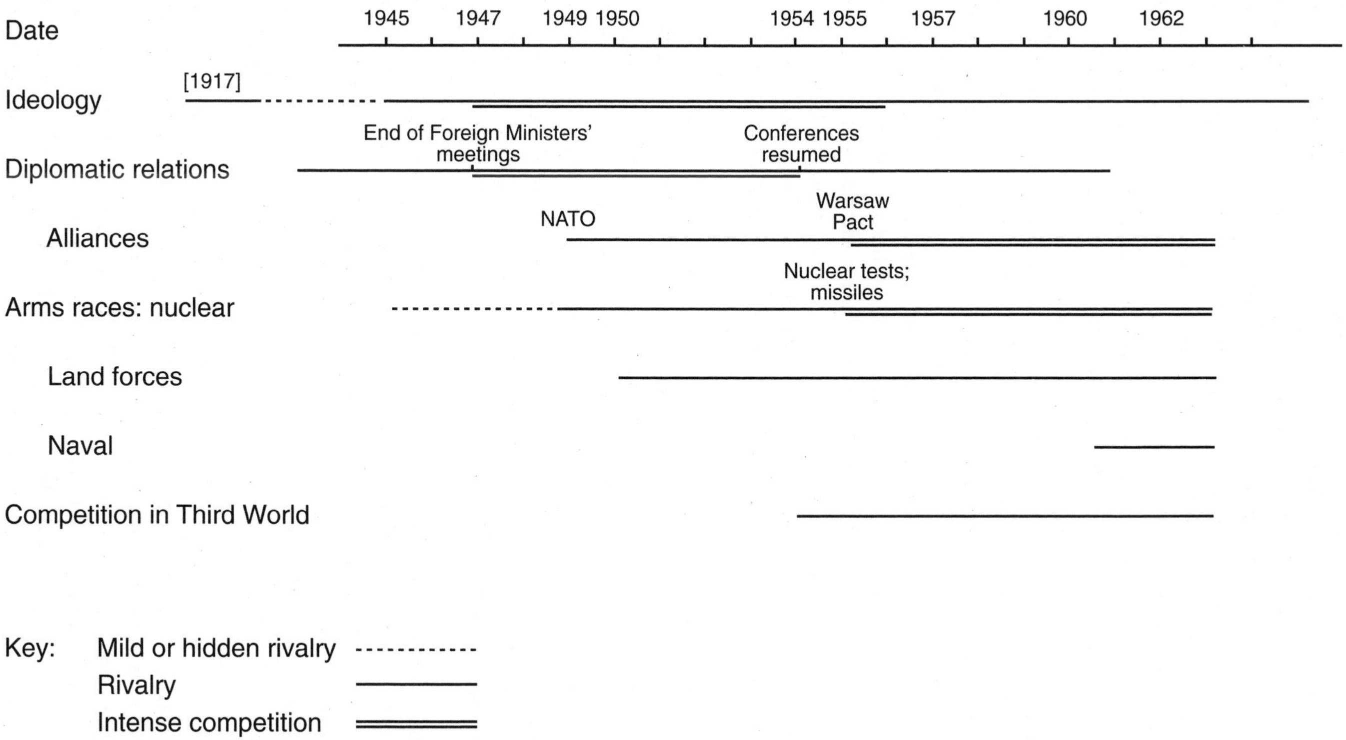

Date	1945	1947	1949 1950	1954 1955	1957	1960	1962

Ideology [1917]

Diplomatic relations

End of Foreign Ministers' meetings

Conferences resumed

Alliances

NATO

Warsaw Pact

Arms races: nuclear

Nuclear tests; missiles

Land forces

Naval

Competition in Third World

Key: Mild or hidden rivalry   ----------

        Rivalry   ————

        Intense competition   ════

agreement. Their last meeting took place in November–December 1947, and broke up amid mutual recriminations without setting a date for a further meeting. Then, for a period of six years, the two superpowers maintained only the most formal and frigid relations. Diplomatic relations were kept up, but that was about all. There were no meetings between the Americans and Soviets at Foreign Minister level; and it was utterly inconceivable that Stalin should visit the United States or Truman go to the Soviet Union. This was the period when the Cold War, in its diplomatic aspect, was at its most severe, and to which the metaphor of frigidity was most applicable.

But this period of deep frost lasted no more than six years. In January 1954 the Foreign Ministers of the USA, the Soviet Union, Britain and France met to discuss the German question. They made no progress, but agreed to meet again to talk about Korea and Indo-China. They reconvened in Geneva in April–May 1954, this time with the addition of the Chinese Foreign Minister. Then in July 1955 there took place the first postwar meeting of heads of government, the Geneva Conference attended by Eisenhower, Khrushchev, Eden and Mendés-France, which was widely welcomed as bringing a marked change in the international climate – 'the spirit of Geneva'. In 1956 Khrushchev and Bulganin visited Britain, and in February 1959 the British Prime Minister, Harold Macmillan, went to Moscow. In September 1959 what would earlier have been unthinkable took place: Khrushchev visited the United States and stayed with Eisenhower in his country retreat at Camp David. 'The spirit of Camp David' followed 'the spirit of Geneva', with a cheering and vivifying effect on the hopes of men. The next two summit meetings were somewhat dampening. The four-power Paris summit of May 1960 broke up almost as soon as it began over the U-2 'spy-plane' episode; and the Khrushchev–Kennedy meeting at Vienna in June 1961 produced some harsh words and no agreements. Then the alarms of the Cuba missile crisis led, not to a breach in relations, but to an intensified determination on the part of the superpowers to keep in touch. The so-called 'secret channel' between them, through the Soviet Embassy in Washington, was formalized; and in 1963 the 'hot line' between the White House and the Kremlin was installed. Later, in 1967, Kosygin (who replaced Khrushchev as leader of the the Soviet Union) visited the United States, and in the early 1970s summit meetings between the leaders of the superpowers were to become annual events. The deep frost of 1948–53 was thus followed by a series of conferences and visits, which continued at a quickening tempo despite persisting ideological opposition and some sharp international crises.

Curiously, these developments in diplomatic relations did not entirely correspond with the next line on the chart, representing the formation of alliances. In 1947–48 there took shape a sphere of Soviet control in eastern Europe, which at that time was not given formal definition in an alliance.

In 1948 the Brussels Treaty between western European states was ostensibly directed against Germany, but in fact against the Soviet Union. In April 1949 the North Atlantic Treaty bound the United States, Canada and a number of western European countries in an alliance for mutual defence against Soviet attack. In 1955 the USSR and six eastern European states signed the Warsaw Treaty, so that Europe and the North Atlantic area were then divided into two alliances, openly directed against one another. These alliances had the strange double effect of embodying antagonism and yet also contributing to the stability which marked the Cold War in the 1950s. The lines between the alliances were made clear, and were respected by both sides. The alliances themselves looked warlike, but they also kept the peace.

The superpowers, and to a lesser extent their allies, were engaged in three different arms races, or more accurately competitions in armaments. The first and most spectacular was the competition in atomic, and later nuclear weapons. The United States first tested an atomic bomb in 1945, and then dropped the only two which have actually been used in warfare. The Soviet Union then threw all its efforts into building its own atomic weapons, and the atomic arms race was under way. The Soviets exploded their first atomic bomb in August 1949. The Americans exploded their first thermonuclear bomb (or hydrogen bomb) in November 1952, speedily followed by the Soviet Union in August 1953. The emphasis then shifted to the means of delivering these weapons, particularly by missiles. The Soviets fired their first successful intercontinental ballistic missile (ICBM) in August 1957, and followed this up by launching a space satellite (the Sputnik) in October. The Americans fired their first ICBM in December of the same year, and followed with a surge of developments, bringing Titan and Atlas ICBMs into service (1959), building Polaris submarines capable of launching missiles from under water (1960), and creating protected launching sites for Minuteman rockets (1962). At the same time, the Soviet Union conducted a series of nuclear tests, culminating in 1961 with the explosion of extremely powerful, multi-megaton bombs. It is striking that the most intense period of this competition in nuclear weapons coincided with the marked *improvement* in diplomatic relations from 1954 onwards. These two aspects of the Cold War, and the lines on the chart representing them, show apparently opposite developments. Only in 1963 did closer diplomatic relations make some impact on the nuclear competition, with the conclusion of a treaty between the United States, the Soviet Union and Britain agreeing to end nuclear tests in the atmosphere (but not underground). But this limited agreement on testing did not mean an end to the competition itself, which continued in the later 1960s with the development of anti-ballistic missiles and of rockets which could carry several warheads on one missile – the so-called MIRVs (Multiple Independently-targeted Re-entry Vehicles).

Competition in conventional land forces (tanks, artillery and infantry – all the formidable armoury of the Second World War, with extra refinements) was not of the same intensity as that in nuclear weapons. The western powers essentially accepted that it was a one-horse race, making no serious effort to match Soviet and Warsaw Pact land strength in Europe man for man or tank for tank. Even so, from 1950 onwards the United States and its allies built up their armies in western Europe. German rearmament got slowly under way. So-called 'tactical atomic weapons', of great power, were deployed to counter Soviet superiority in tanks, guns and men. This competition, in somewhat muted fashion, continued steadily throughout the period we are looking at, despite the summit meetings and the general improvement in diplomatic relations and atmosphere.

Naval rivalry between the superpowers began late. From 1945 to about 1960 the United States had an overwhelming superiority in ocean-going naval forces, and the Soviet Union – a massive land power, with only limited access to the oceans – made no effort to compete. In 1961 the Soviet Union began to build an ocean-going fleet, partly to counter the American development of Polaris missile-carrying submarines – for example, Soviet submarines could defend the homeland by hunting American submarines. In 1962 the blockade imposed by the Americans during the Cuban missile crisis was a striking example of the influence of sea power, and gave a powerful new impulse to Soviet efforts. Moreover, as the Soviet Union developed an active policy in Africa and Asia, it needed a fleet for the old-fashioned purposes of showing the flag and making demonstrations of Soviet power. By 1962–63 a new naval rivalry was under way, at the very time that diplomatic relations between the superpowers were approaching a state of détente. Different aspects of the Cold War were again out of kilter with one another.

Competition in the so-called 'Third World' (Africa, Asia and to some degree Latin America) formed another aspect of the Cold War, and thus another line on the chart. For some time, this was another one-horse race. In January 1949 President Truman announced a plan to help underdeveloped countries, particularly in scientific and industrial projects. Legislation to provide this 'Point Four' aid programme was passed by the United States Congress in 1950, providing funds on the modest scale of $34.5 million.[9] When the Republicans took office in 1953, this form of aid was linked directly to the Cold War, and the Secretary of State, Foster Dulles, made it clear that states which entered into an alliance with the USA would be more generously treated than those which chose to be non-aligned. Even so, there was as yet no competition between the superpowers, because Stalin chose not to compete. Only after his death did Malenkov begin tentative overtures towards Asia and Africa. The Soviets began to provide economic aid to various countries in 1954, and indirect military aid to Egypt in 1955. The competition was curiously lopsided, with the Americans providing more economic aid and the Soviets gaining more political kudos; but either way a new element was added to the Cold War.

The chart, on page 154, shows clearly that when we refer to the Cold War we should always ask *which aspect* of the Cold War we mean. We are not dealing with a single phenomenon, but with several separate conflicts and competitions, with different starting dates and changing degrees of intensity. In the course of a few years, from 1945 to 1962, the issues at stake in relations between the United States and the Soviet Union changed considerably in number and in character. It is particularly striking to observe the brevity of the completely 'frozen' period in diplomatic relations, which lasted only from the end of 1947 to the end of 1953 – about the same length of time as the Second World War. Yet just as that period came to an end, and the leaders of the superpowers started talking to one another, competition in Asia and Africa through aid programmes began. In another three or four years the nuclear arms race entered a particularly intense phase; and a few years later again a naval rivalry which had not existed previously got under way. In these circumstances it is a fruitless endeavour to look for a single or precise beginning of the Cold War – there are a number of beginnings, just as there are a number of relaxations in tension. It is almost equally difficult to try to establish responsibility for the conflict as a whole, because the initiative changed in respect of the various aspects.

The 'Cold War' metaphor is at once a necessity and yet a hindrance to our understanding. We cannot do without it – it is an inescapable part of our vocabulary in describing the events we have been looking at. But it is a hindrance because it gives a misleading impression of a single phenomenon, and above all of something which was frozen and congealed. On the contrary, the Cold War took many forms, and relations between the United States and the Soviet Union, and their respective allies or adherents, were not frozen. They were fluid and shifting, changing their nature and intensity from one period to another, and sometimes showing improved relations in one aspect at the same time as increased hostility in another. There is nothing new about such problems of nomenclature. Historians have long argued that 'imperialism' is no word for scholars to use, because it means too many things to too many people. 'Appeasement' suffers from the same problem, to perhaps a greater degree. But even the most scholarly historians go on using these words, because they have no choice; and the same is true of the Cold War. The best we can do is to remember constantly that the phrase is a metaphor, and that it has several different meanings.

The very name Cold War conveys a chilling sense that something went badly wrong in international affairs after 1945. The superpowers wasted vast resources, took terrible risks and distorted the whole shape of international relations in pursuit of their rivalries. This is largely true; and yet the Cold War also produced some striking positive effects. It closed (certainly for a long time, perhaps permanently) a number of issues which had bedevilled the world for years. The German Question, which had played havoc in Europe since 1870, was settled by partition, imposed and maintained by the rivalry of the superpowers. The Franco-German conflict which had resulted in three great wars came to an end, partly because France and West Germany themselves embarked on the path of reconciliation, but partly also because the United States, in the context of the Cold War, required the two countries to work together and provided the military and economic circumstances which enabled them to do so. In the Pacific, Japan, whose incessant conquests had brought years of conflict to East Asia, was drawn firmly into the American sphere of influence in the Cold War. The Japanese allowed the Americans to defend them, and directed their immense energies to industry and commerce. Both West Germany and Japan, the aggressor states of the 1930s, settled down metaphorically to cultivate their gardens, and thrived within the harsh framework of the Cold War.[10] In Asia and Africa the Cold War provided opportunities for the newly independent states, which could play on the rivalries of the superpowers, to secure economic and military assistance while continuing to pursue their own interests rather than those of their benefactors. It is true that the Cold War caused much damage in the Third World, often exacerbating civil strife (especially in Africa); but it also brought economic advantage and political significance to governments which would otherwise have remained indigent and obscure. The Third World might declare its independence, but when courted by both the superpowers its members were ready to receive favours – though not necessarily to grant them in return.

Finally, the Cold War was also a period of warlike peace. The two superpowers avoided actual war with one another. During the Berlin blockade, the Soviets allowed the western airlift to be carried out without shooting down a single aircraft. In the Korean War, the Americans knew about, but studiously ignored, the missions flown by Soviet aircraft. When both superpowers were equipped with nuclear weapons, the fear of mutual destruction prevented them from taking the final step into war, even when (as during the Cuba missile crisis) they came close to the brink. But they also kept the peace through satisfaction with the status quo. In Europe, the superpowers were content with the partition which was established by 1948. The countries of western Europe also grew content with the status quo. They enjoyed increasing prosperity; a high degree of political stability (even France and Italy, whose governments were often short-lived, achieved an underlying steadiness); and a new social contract based on parliamentary democracy and the welfare state. They had no wish to endanger these assets by war. The peoples of eastern Europe were not content with the status quo, as was shown by revolts in East Germany and Hungary; yet they attained a degree of stability which was to the advantage of many.[11]

The Cold War thus proved in some respects an asset as well as a waste and a threat. It imposed a stability which came as a relief after the turmoil of the 1930s and the Second World War. The new condition of the world, as Raymond Aron summed it up in 1948, was: 'Peace impossible, war improbable'.[12] There were many who were prepared to settle for that.

◆ Notes to Reflection: The Cold War

1. Walter Lippmann, *The Cold War* (New York, 1947); for Orwell, see David Reynolds, ed., *The Origins of the Cold War in Europe* (London, 1994), p. 1.
2. See, for example, André Fontaine, *Histoire de la guerre froide* (2 vols, Paris, 1965, 1967); D. F. Fleming, *The Cold War and its Origins, 1917–60* (2 vols, New York, 1961).
3. For interpretations referred to here, see for example: Gabriel Kolko, *The Politics of War: The World and United States Policy, 1943–1945* (New York, 1968), who goes for 1943 as the start; Adam B. Ulam, *Expansion and Co-existence: Soviet Foreign Policy, 1917–1973* (2nd edn, New York, 1974), p. 378, opting for 1943–45; Daniel Colard, *Les relations internationales de 1945 à nos jours* (6th edn, Paris, 1996), p. 195, goes for Yalta; two Russian writers, Vladislav Zubok and Constantine Pleshakov, *Inside the Kremlin's Cold War* (Cambridge, Mass., 1996) argue for 1946. Charles S. Maier, ed., *The Cold War in Europe: Era of a Divided Continent* (3rd edn, Princeton, 1996), pp. xi, 13, and John Lukacs, *A New History of the Cold War* (New York, 1996) make a strong case for 1947.

   The quotation putting the start confidently in 1948 is from Lawrence Aronson and Martin Kitchen, *The Origins of the Cold War in Historical Perspective* (London, 1988), p. 211.
4. Robert Conquest, *Reflections on a Ravaged Century* (London, 1999), p. 152.
5. Hugh Brogan, *Kennedy* (London, 1996), p. 200.
6. Philip Larkin, *Collected Poems* (London, 1988), p. 172.
7. See the complex and illuminating discussion of the historiography in Michael J. Hogan, ed., *America in the World: The Historiography of American Foreign Relations since 1941* (Cambridge, 1995).
8. V. Molotov, *Molotov Remembers: Inside Kremlin Politics. Conversations with Felix Chuev*, ed. Albert Resis (Chicago, 1993), p. 59.
9. For Point Four, see Truman's Inaugural Address, 20 January 1949, Royal Institute of International Affairs, *Documents on International Affairs, 1949–1950* (London, 1953), pp. 33–8.
10. On this subject, see Maier, *Cold War in Europe*, pp. 16, 191.
11. See *ibid.*, pp.12–25, and Raymond Aron, *Peace and War: A Theory of International Relations* (London, 1967), pp. 159–62.
12. Raymond Aron, *Le grand schisme* (Paris, 1948), title of Chapter 1.

DECOLONIZATION AND WARS
OF SUCCESSION, 1945–1962

While the Cold War was developing, there took place another fundamental change in international relations. Most of the European empires that had controlled Africa and much of Asia in the first half of the twentieth century came to an end. This process was ragged and incomplete. Sometimes the imperial powers fought long and hard before withdrawing, as the French did in Indo-China and Algeria. In other cases, the powers set their own deadlines for departure, and left in haste, as the British did in India, Palestine and much of Africa. Some countries did not give up their empires until much later. Portugal, to all appearances the weakest of the colonial powers, held on to its African colonies with remarkable tenacity. The Soviet Union, which had inherited the Tsarist conquests in the Caucasus and Central Asia, made no retreat from empire at all, and held on until the collapse of the Soviet state itself in 1991.

The process of European expansion, extending over four-and-a-half centuries from about 1500 onwards, had been complicated. The European powers imposed direct or indirect political control over their colonial territories. They promoted trade and investment. They sometimes brought about large-scale European settlement (for example, by the French in Algeria, and the Dutch and British in South Africa). Almost always empire brought the extension of European culture, education and medicine. The end of empire proved equally complicated. Political control was lost or handed over, but economic and military influence often remained; as did important legacies in law, culture and religion. The presence of European settlers produced a series of difficult situations – war in Algeria, *apartheid* in South Africa.

'Decolonization' is a shorthand term covering all these changes. Like many shorthand terms it is misleading but indispensable: misleading because it lumps together all kinds of different events and movements; indispensable because it would be impossibly clumsy to refer to these differences whenever we mention the process as a whole.

Decolonization had profound effects on international relations. The former imperial powers had to change their policies to adapt to the new circumstances. The British, for example, sought a substitute for the Empire in the Commonwealth. The French turned to European integration as a new enterprise to replace the old 'civilizing mission' of empire – though they also contrived to retain a substantial influence in many of their former French colonies. In general, all the former colonial powers were weakened, to the advantage of the superpowers.

On the other side, the newly independent states had to make their way in the world. Almost at once they sought some form of co-operation with their fellows. The Arabs talked of pan-Arab unity and formed the Arab League. The new African governments set up the Organization of African Unity. The Bandung Conference of Afro-Asian states in 1955 aspired to bring together countries across two continents, whether former colonies or not. Yet at the same time the new states often came into conflict with one another, in wars of succession to decide who should inherit the old imperial domains. India and Pakistan, the successor states of British India, embarked on war with each other as soon as they became independent, and have continued the struggle from time to time ever since. In the Middle East, Israel and its Arab neighbours fought long and bitter wars of succession over the old British mandate in Palestine. In Africa there were frequent civil wars to decide who should replace the imperial powers; one of the first was in the former Belgian Congo in 1960–62.

The complicated process of decolonization also became mixed up with the Cold War, sometimes because the superpowers tried to win supporters among the new states, and sometimes because the newly-independent governments themselves joined one or other of the opposing camps, whether out of conviction or in pursuit of gain. The new states all joined the United Nations Organization, where the former colonial countries rapidly attained a majority in the General Assembly, transforming its character and role in world politics.

These vast changes, with their widespread consequences for international affairs, began at the end of the Second World War, and reached a climax in the early 1960s, when many African colonies attained independence and the long war in Algeria came to an end. The following chapters look at various aspects of decolonization and wars of succession in the Middle East, Asia and Africa during that period; and also at the emergence of the Afro-Asian movement and the Third World, which changed the nature and conduct of world affairs.

CHAPTER

8

THE MIDDLE EAST, 1945–1962

The Middle East at the end of the Second World War – The end of the Palestine Mandate: Israel and the Arabs, 1947–49 – The Arab states and Arab nationalism – The Suez Crisis, 1956 – The Middle East after the Suez Crisis

The term 'Middle East' requires definition. In the first part of the twentieth century, it was used in Britain and France to denote a broad area between the Near East and the Far East – which allowed a good deal of latitude, but at least explained the use of the word 'Middle'. The term implies a viewpoint in western Europe, with the observer looking eastwards. From Russia or the Soviet Union, the 'Middle East' is to the south; from India or China it is to the west; from the United States it is a very long way in either direction. 'Near East' has now largely fallen out of use; and in common usage the Middle East comprises the south-east Mediterranean countries, Syria, the Lebanon, Israel and Egypt; then Jordan, Iraq, Saudi Arabia and Yemen; and finally the Persian Gulf states of Kuwait, Bahrain, the United Arab Emirates, Oman and Iran.[1]

This area is inhabited by peoples which are mostly Arabic-speaking in language and Islamic in religion; though the two are by no means identical. Iran is Islamic in religion, but Persian in language. There are other, quite different elements. Lebanon comprises a mixture of Moslems and Christians, speaking both Arabic and French. Israel has a mixed population of Jews and Arabs; and in the early years the Jewish element was very largely made up of European immigrants. The Kurds are mainly Moslem, using their own language; they do not possess their own state, but many aspire to create one.

In these varied circumstances, the term 'nationalism', which dominates much political discussion, is more than usually difficult to define. Nationalism based on language (often used as the basic criterion for nationality) would imply an Arab nation covering most of the Middle East, and perhaps extending along the whole North African coast as far as Morocco. There has indeed been much talk of Arab unity and pan-Arab nationalism; but in practice individual Arab countries have maintained their own identity, and developed a national consciousness based on the unity of the state. Attempts to break away from this pattern – for example, the formation of the United Arab Republic by a union between Egypt and Syria – have proved short-lived.

The states of the Middle East are mainly recent in their formation, mostly dating back to the collapse of the Ottoman Empire at the end of the First World War. (Iran, with its continuous independent existence, forms an important exception.) On the other hand, the Middle Eastern peoples have a long history. The area was the home of ancient civilizations along the Nile, Tigris and Euphrates, at a time when Europe was the home of primitive cultures. It was the birthplace of the great monotheistic religions of Judaism, Christianity and Islam; and the city of Jerusalem is in different ways sacred to all three faiths. In an important sense, the origins of the state of Israel can be traced back to the promise made to Abraham in the Book of Genesis; which is a far cry from modern notions of national self-determination.[2] The Middle East is an area where the present can never be separated from the past.

The Middle East has long exercised a magnetic effect on outside peoples and states, partly for religious reasons, partly as a result of geography, strategy and economics. Geographically, the area is a crossroads, the meeting-point of Europe, Asia and Africa. In the nineteenth century, the Suez Canal made Egypt a nodal point in the maritime communications of the world, and particularly for the British Empire. Early in the twentieth century, oil was discovered in Iran and Iraq, with more to come in Saudi Arabia; and the Middle East thus became vital to a civilization increasingly dependent on petroleum and its products.

For all these reasons (in which history is curiously mixed up with geology), outside powers have repeatedly intervened in the Middle East. Between the two World Wars, Britain and France effectively dominated the area. Britain controlled Egypt, Palestine, Transjordan (later Jordan), and Iraq, and exercised considerable influence in Iran; France ruled Syria and the Lebanon. During the Second World War, the French occupation of Syria and the Lebanon came to an end. Britain and the Soviet Union jointly occupied Iran, and were later joined by American forces, to safeguard a key wartime supply route to the USSR. American oil companies, with support from the United States government, moved into Saudi Arabia and Kuwait. The Middle East was no longer a European preserve, and the pattern of outside intervention was changed. At the same time, the question of creating a Jewish state in Palestine acquired a new urgency and an intense emotional impetus from the Nazi death camps and the massacre of European Jews in German-occupied Europe.[3]

At the end of the Second World War, there were three issues of immediate international importance in the Middle East. First, the British were determined to maintain their influence in the area, and to develop a new framework to protect long-standing interests. Second, there was a difficult problem in Iran, where Britain, the United States and the Soviet Union were in contention. Third, there was an explosive situation in Palestine, which was predominantly Arab in population but where the surviving European Jews now looked for their salvation. The first two issues should be examined now; Palestine requires separate treatment later.

Britain was determined to maintain its influence in the Middle East, for a combination of strategic and economic reasons. The Suez Canal was still the lifeline of Empire; and cheap oil which could be paid for in sterling was a vital economic asset. The British therefore set out to retain their military presence in the area, under the cover of new diplomatic arrangements. In March 1945 the British helped to set up the Arab League, hoping to guide this movement towards Arab unity for their own purposes. They maintained their military base in the Suez Canal Zone in Egypt, and concluded a new treaty with Transjordan (March 1948) permitting British bases to be maintained there. For a time these arrangements worked reasonably well; but they came under increasing pressure from nationalist forces throughout the Middle East.

In Iran three outside powers – Britain, the Soviet Union and the United States – were involved in a muted power struggle that combined British-Russian rivalries going back to the nineteenth century with early exchanges in the Cold War. During the Second World War, the British and the Soviets had occupied the south and north of Iran respectively, and installed a new Shah, Mohammed Reza Pahlavi, in 1941. The Americans later set up a large-scale supply organization in Iran, to send war material to the Soviet Union; and Roosevelt also wanted to demonstrate his anti-imperialism by saving Iran from what he regarded as British exploitation. Iran itself was weak and divided. The new Shah was only twenty-one when he was installed by foreign powers. There was a strong Islamic fundamentalist movement, which opposed all foreign influences. There was a sizeable pro-Soviet communist party, the Tudeh Party. Popular sentiment was anti-foreign, and particularly hostile to the Anglo-Iranian Oil Company, even though in practice a proportion of the Company's profits were being returned to Iran in royalties.[4]

In 1946 there was a trial of strength between the three outside powers. In December 1945–January 1946 the Autonomous Republic of Azerbaijan, and in January 1946 two northern provinces of Iran declared independence, and the USSR took them under its protection. The British, as old hands in the area, were willing to negotiate a deal with the Soviets on a basis of spheres of influence for each country; but the Americans rejected such a compromise, and demanded (6 March 1946) the immediate withdrawal of Soviet forces from Iran. The British supported this demand, in order to keep in step with the Americans. In April 1946 Stalin agreed to withdraw his forces within a month; which he duly did, with the last troops departing during May. But at the same time Stalin sought to maintain Soviet influence by setting up a joint Soviet-Iranian oil company, with a 51 per cent Soviet holding. The Iranian Premier also agreed to appoint three members of the Tudeh Party as ministers in his government. This arrangement did not last. By the end of 1946 the Tudeh ministers had been dismissed; and in 1947 the Majlis, the Iranian parliament, rejected the agreement for a Soviet-Iranian Oil Company. Surprisingly, Stalin accepted this setback without demur – presumably because he had more important things to think about. This left the Americans, and to a lesser extent the British, temporarily victorious in Iran; but for the British it was to be a dangerous victory. If Iran could defy the Soviet Union and reject a Soviet-Iranian oil company, then the obvious next step was to challenge the British and attack the Anglo-Iranian Oil Company – which was in fact what happened in the next few years.

The situation was very much a mixture of past and present, as the British tried to maintain a position they had held since the nineteenth century, and the Americans and Soviets played out moves in the nascent Cold War. In the next ten years, from 1946 to 1956, the international situation in the Middle East was to be drastically transformed, as old influences rapidly gave place to new. Let us start by looking at the struggle for the control of oil resources; then turn to the creation of the state of Israel and the ensuing Israeli-Arab conflict; and then examine the relations between the Arab states themselves before discussing the role of outside powers in all these matters.

◆ Oil in the Middle East, 1946–56

The Second World War and the following years saw an immense rise in world oil production to meet increasing demand; and the share of the Middle East in this production rose dramatically. Production figures, in millions of tonnes, are given below:[5]

	1940	1950	1960
World production	293.2	525.2	1055.9
Middle East production	13.6	87.9	554.

By 1960 the Middle East share thus rose to over a half of the total world production.

About 1950, Middle East oil production was in the hands of American and British oil companies. The Americans operated in Saudi Arabia (Aramco); Kuwait (Gulf Oil); and Iraq (Mobil and Exxon). The British operated in Iran, through the Anglo-Iranian Oil Company. These oil interests were of great importance to both countries. The American oil companies made profits, and the United States government gained tax revenues and political influence. The British paid for Iranian oil at an advantageous price *in sterling* – a crucial matter when dollars were still scarce. Both countries wanted to keep Middle East oil out of Soviet control. The Americans and British both had much at stake, and they both had their problems.

The Americans had to conduct a delicate balancing act between their support for Israel, which offended all Arab states, and their oil interests, which required good relations with a number of Arab countries, notably Saudi Arabia.[6] As early as 1947 and 1948 King Ibn Saud warned the United States that he might cancel the Aramco concession unless the Americans reduced their support for Israel. The threat proved hollow, because Ibn Saud had no intention of cutting off his own major source of income; and in practice he contented himself with pocketing the oil revenues and assuring other Arab countries that the money could be used to assist the fight against Israel. Even so, the Americans were wary, and felt it necessary to reassure the King. In 1950 President Truman wrote to Ibn Saud to assure him that: 'No threat to your kingdom could occur which would not be a matter of immediate concern to the United States.'[7] Though phrased in cautious diplomatic language, this was a far-reaching undertaking to support Saudi Arabia. The Americans were thus committed to a double policy in the Middle East, one pro-Israeli, the other pro-Saudi.

In 1950 the Americans found an ingenious method of increasing the oil revenues of the Saudi government while not diminishing Aramco's profits. On 30 December 1950 Aramco signed an agreement with the Saudi Arabian government, providing for a 50–50 division of profits between the two. At the same time, the United States government agreed to treat Aramco's payments to Saudi Arabia as a tax, which could be set against tax liabilities in the USA. The US government thus accepted a reduction in its tax revenues in order to provide the Saudi government with a larger share of Aramco's profits; and the American taxpayer subsidized both Aramco and indirectly the Saudi government in order to promote United States influence in the Middle East. Similar deals followed for the governments of Kuwait (1951) and Iraq (1952).[8]

In Iran events followed a very different course. In 1949 the Anglo-Iranian Oil Company agreed to pay higher royalties to the government; but this was not enough. In Saudi Arabia there was no parliament, and effectively no public opinion, to obstruct deals of this kind. In Iran nationalist feeling ran high, and the new agreement had to be submitted to the Majlis (the Iranian parliament), and first to its Oil Committee, under the chairmanship of Mohammed Mossadeq. The committee rejected the agreement, and demanded instead the nationalization of the Anglo-Iranian Oil Company.

At that stage, the Iranians were divided among themselves. The Premier, General Razmara, opposed nationalization and was in negotiation with

Anglo-Iranian for a 50–50 agreement on the same lines as that between Aramco and Saudi Arabia. But this was not a time for moderation or for doing deals. In March 1951 Razmara spoke in the Majlis against national-ization, and was assassinated four days later. The Shah was compelled to accept Mossadeq as his successor. Mossadeq was a striking figure – theatri-cal, flamboyant and with an immense popular following. He combined the standing of being a member of an ancient landed family, claiming descent from a former Shah, with the intellectual kudos of having been a Professor of Political Science at Teheran University; and unlike most professors of political science he was a formidable politician. He took office in April 1951, and at once introduced a law nationalizing all the Anglo-Iranian Oil Company's property and assets in Iran, coming into effect on 1 May.

The British government at first considered using force to occupy the Abadan oilfields, but quickly rejected the idea as unworkable. Instead, the government and Anglo-Iranian together organized an international embargo on the purchase of Iranian oil, and Anglo-Iranian brought legal actions against other companies which accepted Iranian oil (which was described as 'stolen') for refinement. The boycott proved a great success. Sales of Iranian oil fell drastically, and production dropped from 32 259 000 tonnes in 1950 to a mere 1 360 000 tonnes in 1952. There was at this stage no solidarity among the oil-producing countries against the oil companies, and Saudi Arabia and Kuwait had no hesitation in increasing their own production to fill the gap.

Despite the success of the embargo, British prestige was badly shaken by Mossadeq's defiance. Moreover, while the American oil companies (with an eye to their own interests) supported the embargo, the United States govern-ment continued its economic assistance to Iran, and tried to mediate in the dispute. In July 1951 the USA sent Averell Harriman, a distinguished polit-ical figure and formerly Ambassador in Moscow, to Teheran to explore terms for an agreement; he stayed for two months, without result. The British too sent an emissary to Iran to get a deal for Anglo-Iranian, without success. They ran up against a brick wall, because Mossadeq was deter-mined to eliminate the Anglo-Iranian Company, not do a deal with it. Instead of negotiating, Mossadeq, on 25 September 1951, gave the last remaining British staff in the Abadan oilfields a week to pack their bags and go. They complied, leaving what remained of British prestige in ruins.

The result was stalemate. The Iranians had nationalized their oil but could not sell it. The British had blocked Iranian oil exports, but had lost all Anglo-Iranian's assets in Iran. This situation persisted until 1953, when the United States government lost patience. On instructions from President Eisenhower, the Central Intelligence Agency (with co-operation with the British intelligence services) organized a coup to overthrow Mossadeq, restore the authority of the Shah and instal a new Premier. The first attempt proved a failure, and the Shah had to leave the country; but then the tables were turned, street demonstrations were organized in favour of the Shah, and Mossadeq in turn took to flight.

Even this drastic intervention could not restore the status quo; and indeed that was not the American objective. Instead, the Americans arranged a new oil settlement in 1954, by which the principle of nationalization was maintained and the National Iranian Oil Company retained ownership of the oilfields and the Abadan refineries; but the purchasing and marketing of the oil was placed in the hands of a new international consortium, in which Anglo-Iranian (renamed British Petroleum) took 40 per cent of the holdings, five American companies shared another 40 per cent, Shell had 14 per cent, and the Compagnie Française des Pétroles 6 per cent.[9] The newly named British Petroleum Company received compensation for its losses, paid not by Iran but by the other companies in the consortium. The immediate result was advantageous to the Americans. American oil companies took a large share in marketing Iranian oil. American political influence became predominant in Iran. In November 1955 Iran joined the Baghdad Pact, the Middle East alliance directed against the Soviet Union. The Americans provided supplies of arms, and the Shah became to a large degree an American *protégé*. The United States thus moved in to exploit what had begun as a British-Iranian crisis. But the foundations of this success proved shaky. So far, the Middle East oil producers had been divided, with Saudi Arabia and Kuwait working against the Iranians. What would happen if they began to work together? On 12 November 1953, the American Ambassador in Teheran, Loy Henderson, wrote that: 'It seems almost inevitable that at some time in the future . . . the Middle Eastern countries . . . will come together and decide upon unified policies which might have disastrous effects upon the operations of the companies.' It was a prophetic observation. Only seven years later, in September 1960, the Organization of Petroleum Exporting Countries (OPEC) was formed. Thirteen years later again, in 1973, OPEC was to shake the world.[10]

◆ The end of the Palestine Mandate: Israel and the Arabs, 1947–49

At the end of the Second World War, the British government still held the mandate for Palestine, which they had accepted from the League of Nations in 1920. The circumstances under which the mandate had to be exercised had been utterly transformed by the massacre of European Jews by Nazi Germany, which generated a renewed and intense determination by the Zionists to achieve a Jewish state. Moreover, there was now a wave of sympathy for the Zionist cause throughout the western world, and particularly in the United States. The British thus came under increasing pressure to permit Jewish immigration into Palestine, and to advance the creation of a Jewish state. But at the same time Arab opposition to Zionism was stiffening. Arab nationalism had been stimulated by the war, and Arab leaders saw no reason why western sympathy for the Jews (or guilt for not saving them from the death camps) should be worked out at Arab expense.[11]

The British thus found themselves in an impossible position, caught between Jews and Arabs on the ground in Palestine and assailed by international (especially American) opinion from the outside. Failing to find any policy which would reconcile these conflicting pressures, and wearying of its thankless, costly and bloody task, the British government decided in February 1947 that it would hand the problem over to the United Nations, and would leave Palestine in May 1948.

The United Nations appointed a Special Committee on Palestine (known by its initials as UNSCOP), which reported in August 1947 in favour of the partition of Palestine into two states, Jewish and Arab, within a joint framework which would maintain their economic unity. The United States and the Soviet Union both supported these proposals, and on 29 November 1947 the General Assembly of the United Nations passed a resolution proposing partition into two states, each of which was to be in three parts, joined only at the corners.

The Jewish Agency, on behalf of the Zionist movement, accepted the proposal, believing that any Jewish state was better than none. The Arab states, and the Grand Mufti of Jerusalem speaking for the Palestinians, rejected the partition plan, refusing to accept any Jewish state, however small. On this fundamental issue of whether a Jewish state should exist or not there was no room for compromise: there could be no half-way house. All attempts at diplomacy had now failed, and this basic question was to be decided by battle.

Fighting began in Palestine before the mandate came formally to an end and the last British forces withdrew. Arab forces, organized from outside by the countries of the Arab League, tried to cut Jerusalem off from other areas of Jewish settlement. The Zionists prepared to set up their state and took control of as much territory as they could. The British mandate ended at midnight on 13–14 May 1948. On 14 May David Ben Gurion proclaimed the state of Israel. On the 15th troops from Egypt, Syria, Lebanon, Transjordan and Iraq advanced into Palestine, ostensibly to protect the Palestinian state as set out in the United Nations resolution of November 1947, but in fact to destroy the state of Israel before it could be properly established. A violent conflict began.

On paper, the odds were heavily against Israel. Five established Arab countries with a combined population of some 40 000 000 were ranged against about 600 000 Israelis and a state which had only just been set up. In practice, the Israelis had a number of advantages. The Jewish Agency had long exercised the functions of a state in embryo. The Haganah (Jewish Defence Force) was some 60 000 strong, well organized and including

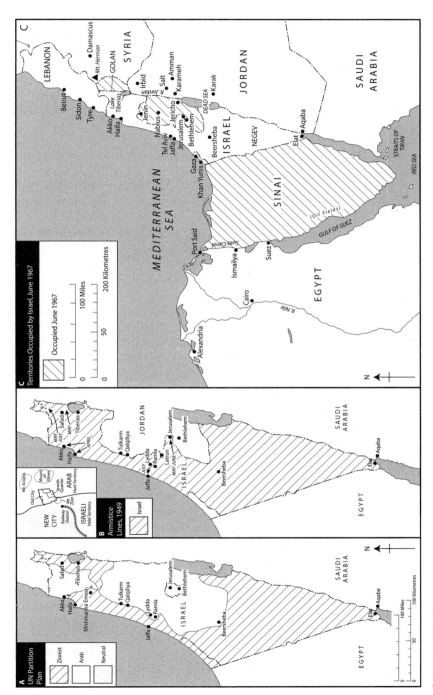

Palestine and Israel

many soldiers with experience from the Second World War. They were short of heavy weapons, and at first had no aircraft at all; but they had plenty of small arms and had recently received supplies of weapons by air from Czechoslovakia – with Stalin's assent. The Israeli forces operated under a single command, and above all they fought with intense spirit and determination. They were assisted by the Irgun Zvai Leumi, a ruthless guerrilla force of some 2000, not under Haganah command but prepared to act alongside it.

The armies of the five Arab states, on the other hand, fought under their own independent commands, and failed to co-ordinate their operations. The Arab governments all pursued their own objectives. Most wanted to destroy Israel; but King Abdullah of Transjordan, whose army (the Arab Legion) was the most efficient fighting force on the Arab side, was prepared to accept a Jewish state in return for territorial gains on the west bank of the River Jordan, and had actually negotiated a deal with the Jewish Agency to that effect before the war began. The Arab states were thus divided, and proved unable to exploit their numerical superiority. The Palestinians themselves were mostly passive, and the militants were ill-organized and split into different factions.

In the fighting from 15 May onwards, the Israelis held off Syrian and Lebanese attacks in the north; checked the Egyptians a few miles from the new capital at Tel Aviv; and held on to part of Jerusalem against the attacks of Transjordan and Egypt. The United Nations arranged a cease-fire on 11 June, which both sides used as an opportunity to regroup and strengthen their positions. The Israelis received their first fighter aircraft, from France. Fighting broke out again on 8 July, and another cease-fire on 18 July was largely ineffective. In October 1948 the Israelis resumed full-scale operations against Egyptian forces in the south, and gained important victories. In December King Abdullah of Transjordan made a separate cease-fire with the Israelis, thus displaying again the lack of unity among the Arab states.

Between February and July 1949 a mediator appointed by the United Nations, Ralph Bunche (an American of immense patience and courage) arranged a series of armistice agreements between Israel and Egypt, Syria, Lebanon and Jordan. (Iraq held out, but was not in direct geographical contact with Israel.) Cease-fire lines were fixed according to the territories held by the various belligerents at the time of the agreements; and these lines became the *de facto* frontiers of the new state of Israel. The successive stages of the fighting had seen a steady growth in the territory occupied by the Israelis. The United Nations plan of November 1947 had proposed an awkwardly shaped Jewish state in three separate pieces, linked only by narrow junctions at the corners. The two cease-fires of 1948 registered some Israeli gains. The armistices of 1949 produced a yet larger territory, but still with a wasp-waist in the centre, where the boundary with Jordan was only fifteen miles from the Mediterranean. Each campaign ended with new Israeli gains, and conversely losses to the Arabs, who had appealed to decision by battle and lost. Instead of the tiny, and possibly unworkable, Jewish state which they had rejected in 1947, they now faced a larger country and a people inspired by the confidence of victory and a sense of achievement. Yet nothing was settled. No peace treaties followed the armistices. The Arab states did not recognize the existence of Israel. The war begun in 1948 was not over.

In the course of these campaigns, a large number of Arab refugees (figures vary widely – perhaps 700 000) left the territories now controlled by Israel. This was partly a simple flight from the war zone; but it was also brought about by a policy of terror on the part of the Irgun Zvai Leumi, operating outside the command of the Haganah. During the night of 9–10 April 1948 a force from the Irgun surrounded the village of Deir Yassin and slaughtered 245 men, women and children.[12] Deir Yassin became a name denoting Israeli terrorism, and assumed symbolic significance in the Arab–Israeli conflict. More refugees fled, congregating in the Gaza strip, on the west bank of the Jordan, and in Lebanon and Syria to the north. The fate of these refugees, often packed into camps close to the lands from which they had fled, was a grim and constant reminder of the human cost of the Arab–Israeli conflict; and also became a part of the conflict in itself. The camps formed a natural recruiting-ground for the militant Palestinian movements which emerged during the 1960s and developed thereafter into the Palestinian Liberation Organization, which assumed many of the aspects of a state in embryo, following with an uncanny similarity the path trodden earlier by the Jewish Agency towards the creation of the state of Israel.

The two superpowers played limited but vital roles in the creation of Israel. The USA and the Soviet Union co-operated to secure the passage of the United Nations resolution on partition. American motives were a mixture of genuine Zionist sympathy and electoral calculation, with an eye on the Jewish vote. Stalin for his part appears to have regarded support for the Zionists as a means of attacking British imperialism; which at the time was a reasonable calculation. At any rate, the Americans and Soviets acted, if not together, at least in parallel. Truman granted *de facto* recognition to Israel on the same day that the new state was proclaimed. The US government provided some financial assistance, and private citizens poured in much more. The Soviet Union went further in technical diplomatic terms, according *de jure* recognition on 18 May, only four days after the proclamation of the state of Israel. The Soviets also permitted the migration of Jews to Israel from the USSR and eastern Europe, and continued the supply of arms from Czechoslovakia up to the end of 1948.

The Arab–Israeli conflict assumed from the start a twofold aspect. It was a conflict between the newly established state of Israel and the surrounding

Arab states; and it was also a conflict between the Israelis and the Palestinians, two peoples claiming one territory. The two aspects overlapped, because the Arab states claimed to be the protectors of the rights of the Palestinians, and especially of the Palestinian refugees, most of whom lived in their territories. But they remained separate. The Arab states were by no means totally committed to the cause of the Palestinians. If the Arab armies had won the war of 1948–49, it is highly unlikely that their leaders would have set up a Palestinian state in its place. Instead, they would probably have divided the territory among themselves, and fallen out over the spoils. Later, the Arab governments were willing to do enough for the refugees to keep the question alive as a propaganda weapon against Israel, but not much more than that. As time went on, some Arab leaders moved towards accepting Israel's existence as a fact, however unwelcome; thus breaking away from the Palestinians, who could accept no such compromise.

At this stage, the Arab–Israeli conflict was not part of the Cold War between the United States and the Soviet Union. Both the Americans and the Soviets were quick to recognize the new state of Israel, and both gave it practical assistance – the Americans by way of funds, the Soviets and their satellites by supplying arms. Later, the Soviet Union was to take up the Arab cause, and the United States was to commit itself fully to Israel; but American-Soviet antagonism played no part in the origins of the dispute, and was never an essential part of it.

After the armistices of 1949, the Arab–Israeli conflict settled down to a period of low-intensity warfare. There were border raids against the Israelis from the refugee camps along the borders; and the Israelis launched their own raids or air strikes in reprisal. There was a continuous propaganda battle in the press and on the airwaves. Arab radio stations, especially in Cairo and Damascus, poured out a constant stream of denunciation against Israel. The Israelis, in a more subtle manner, secured a generally favourable presentation of their country in the mass media of the western countries. At the United Nations, the emerging nations of the Third World were usually sympathetic to the Arab cause, and slowly tilted the balance against Israel. The Arab states themselves nursed their wounds and their hurt pride in a state of angry impotence, until a revolution in Egypt in 1952–53 announced a new radicalism in the Arab camp, and brought Egypt to a position of leadership among the Arab states.

◆ The Arab states and Arab nationalism

The Arab states of the Middle East had much in common: the Arabic language, Islam, and a shared history. They aspired to political co-operation through the Arab League; and in principle they were united in opposition to Israel. But in practice their divisions were often more important than their unity. Islam was divided between modernizers, who sought to compromise with Western or Marxist ideas, and conservatives (notably the Muslim Brotherhood), who rejected the modern world and held to the ancient faith. Arab nationalism was ambiguous in its appeal, meaning on the one hand national independence for separate Arab states, and on the other hand the unity of all Arabs irrespective of state boundaries. Some Arab states were ruled by conservative monarchies; others in the course of the 1950s were taken over by radical regimes advocating modernization, rapid economic development, and often some kind of socialism. The Arabs of the desert (some of whom were rapidly becoming the Arabs of the oilfields), stood in sharp contrast to the Arabs of the cities.

The populations of some of the Middle Eastern states were rising rapidly. The population of Egypt rose from about 16 000 000 in 1937 to 26 000 000 by 1960; that of Syria from 2 500 000 in 1940 to 4 500 000 in 1960; that of Iraq from 3 500 000 in 1940 to 7 000 000 in 1960. The age structure was changing, so that by 1960 in most Arab countries over half the population was under twenty years old.[13] There was large-scale migration from the countryside to the cities, producing large new urban populations. Governments were thus presented with new problems, and sought answers in improved agriculture to feed growing populations; large irrigation projects (for example the Aswan dam in Egypt) to provide water; and state direction of industry to bring work to the cities. All this needed external investment, whether from western Europe, the United States or the Soviet Union. The World Bank agreed to provide finance for the Aswan dam on condition that the USA and Britain also contributed – which they agreed to do in December 1955. The Soviet Union began making loans to Egypt and Syria in the mid-1950s. This built up further tensions in the Arab states, because it emphasized their economic dependence at the very time when they were claiming political independence. The more radical governments asserted themselves by nationalizing foreign companies – most spectacularly in the Iranian nationalization of the Anglo-Iranian Oil Company in 1951, and the Egyptian nationalization of the Suez Canal Company in 1956, which both brought about severe international crises.

In the 1950s Egypt took the lead in finding political solutions to its economic problems. In July 1952 a group of radical army officers, calling themselves the Free Officers, overthrew the government of King Farouk, abolished the monarchy and set up a Revolutionary Command Council to rule the country. General Neguib headed the Council, and became both President and Prime Minister; but the dominant figure in the background was Colonel Gamal Abdel Nasser, who in 1954 took centre stage and replaced Neguib. Nasser proclaimed his modernizing ideas in a book, *The Philosophy of the Revolution* (1954). He appealed to a wide range of opinion by proclaiming an Arab form of socialism, asserting Arab unity against foreign influence, and invoking the support of Islam. The Muslim Brotherhood was not convinced of his sincerity, claiming that Nasser merely used the language of Islam as camouflage for a programme of secularization. In 1954 the Brotherhood tried to assassinate Nasser, but failed; in retaliation, Nasser suppressed the Brotherhood but failed to destroy it.

In foreign policy, Nasser secured the departure of all British forces from the Suez Canal Zone, by means of an agreement which allowed the British to maintain the facilities of their base, using a civilian staff, and to reactivate the base in the event of an outside attack on any Arab state or on Turkey. Egypt and Britain had already agreed in February 1953 that the former Anglo-Egyptian Sudan should be granted immediate autonomy, and achieve self-determination in three years time. The Egyptian government hoped that the Sudan then would opt for union with Egypt; while the British hoped that it would retain links with Britain. In the event, the Sudanese rejected union with Egypt, and opted for independence from both outside powers; and Sudanese independence was proclaimed on 1 January 1956. The outstanding problems in Anglo-Egyptian relations were thus resolved, at least on paper.

But at the same time Nasser set out to undermine the wider British position in the Middle East, and especially to break up the Baghdad Pact, originally concluded in 1955 by Turkey and Iraq, and later joined by Britain, Pakistan and Iran, primarily as a defence agreement against the Soviet Union. Nasser also struck out beyond Middle East politics and established himself on the world stage, taking a leading part in the Conference of Afro-Asian states at Bandung in April 1955.[14] He thus became a world figure, with a prestige which was to stand him in good stead during the Suez crisis of 1956.

Elsewhere in the Middle East, radicalism gained ground. In Syria the newly formed Ba'ath Socialist Party (an amalgamation of the Ba'ath Party founded in 1910 and the more recent Syrian Socialist Party) took power in 1952 on a mixed programme of Pan-Arab nationalism and socialism. Jordan remained a monarchy, and maintained its military treaty with Britain; and its army, the Arab Legion, was still commanded by a British officer, Glubb Pasha. But since the Arab–Israeli war of 1948–49 the country had given shelter to Palestinian refugees roughly twice as numerous as the original Jordanian population, and (alone among Arab countries) had offered them full citizenship. This changed the character of the country, and introduced a new and radical political element. In 1951 King Abdullah was assassinated by a Palestinian youth. His successor, Tallal, abdicated in 1952 in favour of his son, Hussein, who reigned with remarkable tenacity and success until his death in 1998. Iraq too remained a monarchy, with Nuri-es-Said as Prime Minister. The regime remained conservative, and formed the centrepiece of British strategic policy in the area as the focal point of the Baghdad Pact. But opinion in the country was increasingly radical and anti-British, and Nuri's control was shakier than appeared on the surface. In all three countries, President Nasser of Egypt attracted a large and ardent following.

◆ Outside powers and the Middle East

The interests of outside powers in the Middle East were so important that they require separate analysis, even though they have already appeared in this narrative. France, Britain, the United States and the Soviet Union all intervened in the area, often with decisive effect.

France was drawn into the Middle East by its support for Israel; and through the side-effects of the Algerian War. French commitment to the Israeli cause sprang largely from emotional and intellectual origins – the psychological effects of the death camps during the Second World War, and left-wing sympathy with Israel's socialist experiment in the early years of the *kibbutzim*; though these concerns ran alongside the material interests of the French arms industry. The French supplied Israel with its first fighter planes as early as 1948; and in 1955–56 were exporting tanks and aircraft of advanced design (notably the *Mystère* IVA fighter, the key to air superiority over the Egyptians). As for Algeria, the French were involved from 1954 onwards in a war against Algerian nationalists, and they were convinced that their enemies derived crucial support from Egypt.[15] This drew France into even closer co-operation with Israel, in hostility to a common enemy, and was to be a vital element in the Suez crisis of 1956.

British interests in the Middle East were threefold, concerned with strategy, oil and prestige. Strategically, the Suez Canal remained the main artery of British maritime communications to the Persian Gulf, the Indian Ocean and the Far East. The Middle East also provided both a defensive screen against Soviet expansion and a base for air attacks on Soviet oilfields round Baku in the event of war. Oil was vital for the British economy, and Middle East oil had the immense advantage of being paid for in sterling, not dollars. As for prestige, British predominance in the Middle East was generally accepted as being the key to the country's role as a world power, which all British governments (whatever their political complexion) sought to maintain. The equation appeared to be simple: as long as Britain retained her influence in the Middle East through a system of bases and alliances, she was an effective world power; if that influence collapsed, so would the world role. Thus the British bases in Egypt, Jordan and Iraq, and the diplomatic structure of the Baghdad Pact, assumed a symbolic significance which exceeded their practical effects.

American interests in the Middle East were complicated and extensive, even though the area was geographically remote. American oil companies were much involved in Saudi Arabia and Kuwait, and in 1950 President Truman gave Saudi Arabia a guarantee of American support. From 1954 onwards American companies also took a large share in marketing Iranian oil. At the same time the United States was a strong supporter of Israel, which was sustained from the start by American diplomatic recognition, government aid and the gifts of American Jews. Behind this lay an emotional commitment to Zionism on the part of a number of American leaders, and also the calculations of American electoral politics, according to which the Jewish vote could decide election results in the crucial states of New York, Pennsylvania and Illinois. As the Cold War developed, the Americans became determined to keep Soviet influence out of the Middle East. The United States joined the Baghdad Pact in 1958. In 1959 the pact was renamed CENTO (Central Treaty Organization), partly for the practical reason that Iraq was no longer a member and so Baghdad had ceased to be its centre, but also to emphasize the treaty's affinity with NATO. In principle, NATO and CENTO formed a continuous line from Norway to Pakistan, 'containing' Soviet power.

These various American interests and commitments produced some awkward combinations. The Americans supported Israel but also made alliances with some of Israel's enemies. They worked with Britain to oppose the Soviet Union, but did not wish to be associated with British imperialism, which they thought to be morally wrong and politically damaging. The United States thus became involved in a series of balancing acts, supporting Israel but cultivating relations with Saudi Arabia, working with the British but also trying to edge them out. Towards the end of 1955 the Americans were at work, in co-operation with the British, on the highly secret 'Project Alpha', a plan to negotiate a compromise settlement of the frontier between Egypt and Israel. If successful, this might have begun to resolve the Arab–Israeli dispute, and so diminished some of the American problems in trying to befriend both sides; but in the event it came to nothing. The Americans remained deeply enmeshed in these distant and complex problems.

For the Soviet Union, the 'Middle East' was geographically the South – the frontiers with Turkey and Iran, which had been strategically important to Russia under the Tsars and remained so to the USSR. The Soviet Union kept a wary eye on developments in Islam, because the Soviet republics in Central Asia were largely Muslim in population, despite long years of anti-religious propaganda. Apart from this, Stalin appears to have taken no ideological interest in the area. As to oil, the Soviet Union and Romania together produced enough for all the needs of the Soviet bloc, and thus what was a vital issue for other countries was of only marginal interest to the USSR. For these various reasons, the Soviet Union under Stalin did little to develop a Middle East policy, with the exception of its support for Israel in 1948 by diplomatic recognition and the supply of Czech armaments.

After Stalin's death in 1953 his successors became aware of the opportunities to be exploited in the Middle Eastern countries, even if they did not belong to the socialist camp. At the end of 1953 Malenkov opened new contacts with Egypt, and in January 1954 the Egyptian Deputy Defence Minister visited the Soviet Union. In September 1955 Czechoslovakia concluded an agreement (under Soviet auspices) to supply large quantities of armaments to Egypt. The Soviets themselves sold arms to Syria under an agreement of 1954; and they instructed the Syrian Communist Party to co-operate with the Ba'ath Socialist Party, despite their ideological differences. The Soviet Union thus counteracted American and British influence in the Middle East, and infiltrated through the barrier of containment to establish their own links with Egypt and Syria.

In 1956 these different strands in Middle East international politics – oil, the Arab–Israeli conflict, the politics of the Arab states, the interests of outside powers – all came together in the Suez crisis.

◆ The Suez Crisis, 1956

The principal origins of the Suez crisis lay in pressures within Egypt: a rising population to be fed, and the demand for economic as well as political independence. President Nasser set out to build the Aswan dam to control the flow of the Nile and improve irrigation, and also as a prestige project of a spectacular kind. The dam was begun with the promise of financial support from the World Bank, the United States and Britain; but on 20 July 1956 the Americans and British abruptly withdrew their financial support, mainly on the ground that Egypt was becoming too closely involved with the Soviet Union. Neither the United States nor Britain appears to have expected retaliation from Egypt, or indeed serious consequences of any kind. In the event, Nasser reacted quickly and drastically. On 26 July he announced in a radio broadcast that he was forthwith nationalizing the Suez Canal Company, and would use its revenues to finance the building of the dam; though he was careful to offer compensation to shareholders for their losses.

This was a direct challenge to France and Britain. The Suez Canal had been built by de Lesseps, a French engineer, and the headquarters of the Canal Company were in Paris. More important, the French government saw an opportunity to attack Nasser and cut off the aid he was giving to the rebels in Algeria. The British government was the majority shareholder in the Canal Company; about one-third of the ships using the Canal were British; and a large proportion of British oil imports came through the Canal. Moreover, there was a strong sense that the whole prestige of Britain as a great power was at stake. Britain had lost face in the Iranian oil nationalization crisis of 1951. Very recently, on 1 March 1956 King Hussein of Jordan had dismissed Glubb Pasha, the British commander of the Jordanian Army and the embodiment of British influence in the country – an action which the British blamed on the malign influence of Nasser.

The nationalization of the Canal Company seemed to be the last straw. Harold Macmillan, the Chancellor of the Exchequer in Eden's government, wrote in his diary: 'if Nasser "gets away with it", we are done for. The whole Arab world will despise us . . . It may well be the end of British influence and strength for ever.'[16] Such sentiments were common, and a sense of desperation quite disproportionate to the actual dangers involved came to dominate British policy.

Both the French and the British compared Nasser to Mussolini or Hitler, and drew parallels with the situation in the 1930s, when appeasement of dictators had proved disastrous. Anthony Eden and Guy Mollet, the British and French Prime Ministers, both referred repeatedly to this comparison; and a powerful emotional current from the pre-war period thus influenced the policy of both governments.

France and Britain therefore reacted strongly to the nationalization of the Canal Company. In France, Guy Mollet's government decided at once to seize the opportunity to overthrow Nasser and cut off Egyptian help to the Algerians. This would have to be done by force, but they recognized that France was not strong enough to act alone, and would have to work with Britain. The British government was equally determined to overthrow Nasser, by force if necessary, but was uncertain as to how force was to be justified to the British people and to world opinion – a question which hardly worried the French at all.

The British and French went ahead with military plans for an attack on Egypt, though they constantly had to postpone the target date. At the same time efforts were made to find a diplomatic solution to the crisis. A conference of maritime states met in London (16–23 August), and agreed that the Prime Minister of Australia, Robert Menzies, should visit Cairo to persuade Nasser to accept some sort of international body to run the Canal. Menzies arrived in Egypt on 2 September, and left on the 9th, without success. The American Secretary of State, Dulles, then proposed the formation of a Suez Canal Users' Association to manage the Canal and receive its revenues, of which only a proportion would go to Egypt. Eden accepted this proposal rather than break with the Americans; Mollet accepted it, with great reluctance, rather than break with the British. Finally, on 14 September, both the British and French governments agreed to refer the whole question to the Security Council of the United Nations, which began to debate the issues on 5 October.

The French were dismayed by these prolonged delays, and what they regarded as the Hamlet-like hesitations of the British. What they wanted was a bold and rapid attack on Egypt; and they turned increasingly towards the Israelis, as allies who were not afraid of daring and unorthodox action. In mid-October the French and Israelis conceived a plan by which Israel would attack Egypt across the Sinai peninsula, and France and Britain would then intervene, ostensibly to restore peace but in fact to seize control of the Suez Canal. They drew the British in, and three-power conferences between France, Britain and Israel took place at Sèvres, just outside Paris, on 22 and 24 October. They reached an agreement, set out in the Sèvres Protocol of 24 October. Israel was to attack across the Sinai peninsula on 29 October, aiming to reach the Canal on the 30th. That day, the British and French governments would appeal for a cease-fire, and request the Egyptians and Israelis to withdraw ten miles west and east of the Canal respectively. It was assumed that the Israelis would accept, and the Egyptians would refuse (after all, they would be being asked to give up their own territory and surrender control of the Canal, which they had just seized). The British and French would then launch their own military operation on 31 October, supposedly to separate the combatants, but actually to occupy the Canal Zone. The French also concluded another agreement, not mentioned to the British, by which French fighters would defend Israel against air attack, and French warships would protect the Israeli coast.

Eden was desperately anxious to conceal these arrangements, clinging to the justification of military action on the plea of 'separating the combatants'. The French and Israelis, on the other hand, made little attempt at concealment. French warships put into Haifa harbour in full public view; and the French Foreign Minister (Christian Pineau) actually told the American Ambassador in Paris about the Sèvres agreements on 30 October.

On the evening of 29 October the Israelis launched lightning attacks across the Sinai desert. On the 30th the British and French presented their demand that the two sides should withdraw ten miles east and west of the Canal. The Israelis accepted and the Egyptians refused. British and French air attacks on Egyptian airfields began on the evening of 31 October. After a long delay, British and French paratroops dropped at Port Said and Port Fuad, at the northern end of the Suez Canal, on 5 November, and landing forces went ashore on the 6th. They secured a firm lodgement, and were ready to move south along the Canal.

This military success proved short-lived, because the diplomatic balance swung rapidly and decisively against the intervening powers. As early as 31 October the United States and the Soviet Union both presented resolutions to the Security Council of the United Nations, calling on Israel to withdraw from the Sinai, and requesting all states to refrain from the threat or use of force. On 5 November the Soviet government threatened Britain and France with rocket attacks, and Israel with the vague menace of calling the existence of the state into question. In Washington, Eisenhower had always opposed the use of force, and was furious with the British and French for launching their attack – partly because it came on the eve of the election in which he was seeking a second term as President, but mainly because he believed the whole operation would prove disastrous. He was in a powerful position. The British were already looking for a loan from the International Monetary Fund to support the pound, and found that the

Americans would only agree if there was an immediate cease-fire in Egypt. At the same time, Eisenhower threatened to cut off American supplies of oil to Britain and France, which had lost most of their Middle East imports because the Suez Canal was closed.

Under these pressures the British quickly gave way, and the French reluctantly followed. The two governments declared a cease-fire, to take effect at 2 a.m. (local Egyptian time) on 7 November. The British and French troops halted where they stood that night. Later on the same day, under the most severe pressure from the United States, Israel unwillingly agreed to withdraw from the Sinai peninsula, surrendering the gains made during their brilliant campaign. The brief but spectacular Suez War of 1956 was over.

The events were fleeting, but their consequences were momentous. The Suez crisis involved several different aspects. It was part of the widespread decolonization struggle in Asia and Africa. Egypt strove to make good its independence; Britain tried to reassert its predominance in the Middle East; and France sought to win the Algerian War at one remove. In these circumstances, Nasser was able to count on the vigorous support of Third World leaders, especially Nehru, the Prime Minister of India. Suez also provoked a sharp crisis between the western powers, as the United States in the last resort brutally imposed its will on Britain and France. They reacted in very different ways. The British government drew the conclusion that it must never again go against the fundamental wishes of the United States. When Macmillan took over from Eden as Prime Minister in January 1957, he set himself the task of restoring good relations with the Americans, with considerable success but at the cost of a subordination to American policy which was to last for many years. The French reacted very differently. They blamed the Americans for precipitating the crisis in the first place (by pulling out of the Aswan project) and then refusing to support their allies at the crunch. They reacted by pressing ahead with European integration, and by building an independent French nuclear weapon. Britain and France thus embarked on completely different courses. In the Middle East, Suez was a crisis within the already existing Arab–Israeli conflict. The Israelis were at first euphoric over their triumph in the Sinai campaign, and then dumbfounded and bitter at being compelled to give up their gains. They nursed the hope of a second round, which they would not lose. The Egyptians, on the other hand, had conjured a spectacular political success out of military defeat. Nasser emerged as the hero of the Arab world, and Egypt too hoped for another round against the Israelis which would reverse the military verdict of 1956. In this way, the Suez War of 1956 sowed the seeds for the later Middle East war in 1967.

What the Suez War proved *not* to be, to any significant extent, was a crisis in the Cold War. It is true that the Soviet threat (on 5 November) to attack Britain and France with rockets gave an appearance of East-West confrontation; but this was superficial. The first Soviet reaction to the attacks on Egypt by Israel, Britain and France was to move 45 Ilyushin bombers from northern to southern Egypt, out of harm's way; and then to fly them to Syria, completely out of the war zone. At the same time, Soviet and Czech military advisers (380 in number) were moved out of Egypt to the Sudan. On 2 November, the Soviet Foreign Ministry told the Egyptian Ambassador in Moscow that the USSR would mobilize world opinion on Egypt's behalf, but would not provide any military assistance. The Soviets thus took care to keep out of the fighting; and even their threat of rocket attacks on Britain and France was almost certainly bluff because the Soviet rockets of that time had a range of only 400 or 450 miles, and could not reach London or Paris from Soviet territory.[17] At the time the Soviets were heavily preoccupied with the Hungarian rising, which coincided with the attack on Egypt, but they also wanted to make sure that there was no danger of a clash with the Americans. In practice, the two superpowers worked, if not directly with one another, at any rate on the same lines, putting similar resolutions to the Security Council on 31 October.

The Suez crisis revealed much about the new pattern of power and influence in the Middle East. The minor powers, Egypt and Israel, had shown that they could take crucial initiatives, Egypt by nationalizing the Canal Company, Israel by launching the attack in Sinai. But they could not follow them through. Egypt had to be rescued by the United States from invasion by the Israelis, British and French. The Israelis had to yield to American pressure and withdraw from their conquests. The medium-sized powers, Britain and France, proved to have less freedom of action than they had at first believed – though they still had more than the British concluded in the immediate aftermath of the crisis. The coincidence of the Suez crisis and the Hungarian rising showed that opinion in the Asian and African states was more anti-American than anti-Soviet. For the Afro-Asian governments, the attack by the British and French (the European imperialists of old) on Egypt was far worse than the assault by the Soviets on the Hungarians. On 16 November 1956, Nehru (the Indian Prime Minister) explained to parliament that India had not supported a United Nations resolution critical of Soviet action in Hungary because the facts were obscure, and to request free elections supervised by the UN would be a violation of Hungarian sovereignty. The fact that Hungarian sovereignty had already been violated with the utmost brutality by the Soviet Army apparently made no impression upon him. Equally, the American support for Egypt and insistence on Israeli withdrawal from Sinai made little impression on Afro-Asian opinion. It was the Soviets who were regarded as the defenders of Egypt, though in practice they had done very little by way of defence.

It was an odd state of affairs. The United States had acted decisively in the crisis, rescuing Egypt, coercing the British and French, and forcing the Israelis into retreat; and yet for a time they seemed the losers, harried by

Third World opinion, denounced by the French, and drawn increasingly into the treacherous terrain of Middle East politics. Khrushchev, on the other hand, appeared as the victor, advancing Soviet influence in Egypt and the Middle East without undue exertion.

There were two other long-term consequences of the Suez crisis. First, the United Nations Organization, with the USA and the Soviet Union in broad agreement, took effective action. A United Nations force was sent to the Canal Zone to supervise the British and French withdrawal, and remained to oversee the cease-fire line between Egypt and Israel.[18] Second, the Suez crisis sent a shock through all those countries dependent on Middle East oil supplies. The Suez Canal was closed; the Syrians shut off the Iraq Petroleum Company's pipeline to the Mediterranean; the usual supplies were cut off. The Americans and western Europeans responded by organizing an 'oil lift', bringing oil to Europe from the USA and Venezuela instead of from the Middle East. In the long term, Japanese shipyards set about the task of building a new generation of super-tankers, capable of moving vast quantities of oil, not through the Suez Canal or through the Mediterranean at all, but round the Cape of Good Hope. This was a remarkable development – at the time few people thought that such super-tankers could be built; and in the long run it meant that the Suez crisis diminished the importance of the Suez Canal, the very asset that the Egyptians had seized at the start of the crisis.

◆ The Middle East after the Suez Crisis, 1957–62

After the Suez crisis, the Americans increasingly moved into the Middle East to replace the British, whose influence was now much diminished. In January 1957 President Eisenhower proposed to provide military and economic assistance to Middle Eastern countries threatened by communism, whether externally or internally. This plan (the so-called 'Eisenhower Doctrine') was approved by Congress in March, with a vote of 200 million dollars, and authorization for the President to use armed force in case of need. Eisenhower was to put his doctine into practice in Lebanon in 1958.

In the Arab world, Nasser's prestige was at its height. He had emerged victorious against the British and French, and even against the Israelis, whose military success had ended in diplomatic defeat. He was the hero of Arab nationalism, and could advance towards Arab unity. On 1 February 1958 Egypt and Syria proclaimed a union between the two countries, setting up a single state, the United Arab Republic, 'as a preliminary step toward the realization of Arab unity'.[19] But this move was unwelcome to other Arab states which were linked to the West in their foreign policy, depended on oil sales to western countries for their revenues, and distrusted Nasser's radical politics. In Saudi Arabia, King Ibn Saud had no sympathy for Nasser's socialism, and maintained close relations with the United States. In Iraq, the Prime Minister, Nuri es Said, held firmly to his British connections, and the country remained central to the Baghdad Pact. In Jordan, King Hussein survived an attempted *coup d'état* in 1957, and continued to hold the balance successfully in a state divided between the Jordanian and Palestinian sections in the population. On 14 February 1958, Iraq and Jordan proclaimed their own union, in direct opposition to the United Arab Republic of Egypt and Syria.

This union was soon broken. On 14 July there was a revolt in Iraq against the monarchy and Nuri es Said. The King and Nuri were killed, and Iraq swung abruptly from a conservative and pro-western stance to radical nationalism. This tore a hole in the middle of the Baghdad Pact, and thus of the American security arrangements for the Middle East; and did much to explain American intervention in an almost simultaneous crisis in Lebanon.

In May 1958 President Camille Chamoun of Lebanon (a Maronite Christian) proposed to amend the constitution so as to allow himself to serve a second term, endangering the delicate balance of power between Christians and Muslims. There were widespread strikes, and rioting in Beirut and Tripoli; and on 22 May Lebanon appealed to the Security Council of the United Nations, on the ground that armed bands were entering its territory from Syria and that nationals of the United Arab Republic were carrying out terrorist attacks. Chamoun also appealed to the United States, France and Britain for help, without response. After the coup in Iraq, he repeated his appeal to the Americans, who this time responded at once. On 15 July 1958 some 5000 United States Marines landed on the beaches near Beirut (under the interested gaze of holiday-makers who continued to sunbathe and swim among the landing-craft); another 5000 followed later. Almost simultaneously King Hussein of Jordan, afraid of internal unrest and a Ba'athist coup inspired by Syria, appealed to Britain for help; and 2500 British parachute troops were at once despatched to Amman.

These military interventions provoked hostile demonstrations and propaganda opposition in many Arab countries; but no military reaction from the Soviet Union. The USSR was giving Nasser a good deal of support – a loan of $175 000 000 in January 1958, plus another $100 000 000 for the Aswan dam and large supplies of Soviet arms.[20] But they went no further. It appeared that, as long as the Americans did not attempt to reverse the coup in Iraq, the Soviets were prepared to let Lebanon and Jordan alone. After much diplomatic activity, on 21 August 1958, the General Assembly of the United Nations adopted a resolution proposed by a number of Arab governments, piously affirming that the Middle East should be kept out of disputes between the superpowers, and calling for the withdrawal of all foreign troops. The Lebanese internal crisis was temporarily settled at the end of September, when a new President took office, claiming to be neutral between Christians and Muslims. The American forces withdrew from Lebanon by 25 October, and the British troops left Jordan on 2 November.

This slightly mysterious crisis thus came to an end. It was not clear whether either the Lebanon or Jordan had been in serious danger of internal revolt or external intervention, but at any rate the American and British forces stabilized these two states, which held out against the wave of Nasserism which seemed so strong at the time but soon began to ebb. The union between Egypt and Syria, which had been easy to proclaim, could not be consolidated. Most Syrians saw it as an Egyptian take-over, and in September 1961 a new military government repudiated the union and restored Syrian independence. Nasser's influence, which had once seemed virtually unstoppable, receded.

The Middle East settled down to an uneasy calm. The Arab–Israeli conflict continued, at the level of border raids and reprisals. The Arab states refused to recognize the existence of Israel but made no great effort to eliminate it. The Arabs themselves remained divided between the radical nationalist countries, headed by Nasser's Egypt and receiving support from the Soviet Union, and others supported by the United States and the British. The superpowers remained active but cautious. In 1961, under the new leadership of President Kennedy, the Americans set out to improve relations with Egypt, with some modest success; but they could not pursue this policy far without causing problems in their relations with Israel and Saudi Arabia. The Soviet Union, which had always been uneasy about the union between Egypt and Syria, improved relations with both countries after the union broke up.

◆ Notes to Chapter 8

1. See the discussion of the history of the term 'Middle East' in Peter Mansfield, *A History of the Middle East* (London, 1991), pp. 1–2.
2. Genesis, Chapter 13, verses 14–17.
3. For the Middle East during the Second World War, see above, pp. 26–9.
4. Between 1945 and 1950 the Company declared profits of some £250 000 000, of which about £90 000 000 were paid to the Iranian government – Daniel Yergin, *The Prize: The Epic Quest for Oil, Money and Power* (London, 1991), pp. 451–2.
5. Fiona Venn, *Oil Diplomacy in the Twentieth Century* (London, 1986), p. 193, n.3, and the tables on pp. 171–2.
6. For the USA and Israel, see below, pp. 175, 179–80.
7. Quoted in Yergin, *The Prize*, p. 428; see generally pp. 425–8.

8. Details of the 50–50 agreements, Venn, *Oil Diplomacy*, p. 113, and Yergin, *The Prize*, pp. 445–8. A precedent for such a deal, based on US tax concessions, was set in Venezuela in 1948, and a Venezuelan delegation visited the Middle East in 1950 to spread the news. This sort of co-operation later bore fruit in the formation of the Organization of Petroleum Exporting Countries (OPEC).

9. For these arrangements, Venn, *Oil Diplomacy*, p. 116.

10. Quoted in Yergin, *The Prize*, p. 447. For OPEC, see below, pp. 000–00.

11. For Palestine during the Second World War, see above, pp. 000–00.

12. On Deir Yassin, see e.g. David Hirst, *The Gun and the Olive Branch: The Roots of Violence in the Middle East* (London, 1977), pp. 123–9, with evidence that Irgun acted in co-operation with Haganah; and Michael Gilbert, *Israel: A History* (London, 1998), p. 169, and Joseph Heller, *The Stern Gang: Ideology, Politics and Terror* (London, 1993), pp. 207–11, which emphasize the condemnation of the massacre by Ben Gurion and the Jewish Agency.

13. Albert Hourani, *A History of the Arab Peoples* (London, 1991), p. 373.

14. For the Bandung Conference, see below, pp. 247–51.

15. For the Algerian War, see below, pp. 225–31.

16. Quoted in Alistair Horne, *Macmillan*, Vol.II: *1957–1986* (London, paperback edn, 1991), p. 408.

17. Galia Golan, *Soviet Policies in the Middle East, From World War Two to Gorbachev* (Cambridge, 1990), pp. 49–51.

18. For United Nations peace-keeping forces, see below, pp. 510–12.

19. *Keesing's Contemporary Archives*, 1958, p. 16005.

20. Golan, *Soviet Policies*, p. 54.

CHAPTER
9

TRANSFORMATION IN ASIA, 1945–1962

**The Chinese Revolution and the Sino-Soviet alliance – The
Sino-Soviet dispute – The recovery of Japan – India and Pakistan –
Indo-China, The French and the Americans – South-East Asia**

At the end of the Second World War, the vast territories of eastern and
southern Asia were in the midst of immense changes. In China, two great
conflicts had long been in progress: a foreign war against the Japanese, and
a civil war between the Kuomintang (Nationalist) government, under
Chiang Kai-shek, and the communists led by Mao Zedong. In 1945 the
Japanese were defeated, but the civil war resumed with new intensity.
Japan, having long dominated much of Asia, now lay defeated and in ruins,
with its future to be decided by the victors – in practice, by the United
States.

Elsewhere in Asia, the position of the European colonial powers had
been drastically undermined. In India, it was clear that British rule was
coming to an end, but no one knew what would follow it. The Philippines,
Malaya, the Dutch East Indies and Indo-China had all been occupied by the
Japanese, and nationalist movements had grown stronger. The colonial
powers (the USA, Britain, the Netherlands and France) all returned to their
former territories, but found it impossible to restore the status quo. Most
of Asia was in a state of confusion and uncertainty.

◆ The Chinese revolution and its consequences

China was heir to an ancient civilization. When the Chinese referred to their
country as 'The Middle Kingdom', they did not mean that it lay between
other lands but that it stood between earth and heaven, on a higher plane
than that of the barbarians around it. In the nineteenth century they had
been plunged from this charmed and elevated position into defeat and
humiliation at the hands of the Europeans, the Japanese and the Americans,
and had learned to their cost that a superior civilization offered no protection against organized force. China was forced to submit to a series of

unequal treaties, imposing onerous territorial and commercial demands. By 1945 the Chinese, of all political persuasions, were determined to resume control of their own affairs.

On other matters they were bitterly divided. The civil war between Nationalists and communists, which resumed in 1945, lasted for another four years. In 1947 the Nationalists gained some successes; but the tide turned decisively in 1948, when the communists won overwhelming victories. Support for the Kuomintang collapsed, and their troops often deserted or changed sides. By October 1949 the Communists controlled the whole of mainland China, and Mao proclaimed the People's Republic of China on 1 October. Chiang Kai-shek held only the island of Taiwan (Formosa), to which the last Kuomintang forces withdrew in December 1949.

The new regime was headed by one of the most formidable and extraordinary figures of recent history. Mao Zedong had been a founder member of the Chinese Communist Party in 1921; made a reputation for determination and endurance by leading the Long March of the communist army from southern China to the north-west in 1934–35; and then proved his military and political ability by winning the long civil war. At the end of 1949 he became the undisputed dictator of China. He then plunged China into a series of headlong changes. The collectivization of agriculture and nationalization of all industry and commerce (1951–55) was followed by an apparent period of liberalization, when Mao declared 'Let a hundred flowers bloom' (1956–57). But he then proclaimed the 'Great Leap Forward', by which China was to advance to communism in one giant stride, creating self-contained communes all over the country. This proved a total disaster, and Mao himself called it off in July 1959. Soviet advisers in China (some of whom were swept up in the tide and sent to work in the fields) reported with dismay on the disaster; but in much of the world these events were regarded with ardent admiration. When Stalinism fell into disrepute among communist sympathizers and fellow-travellers in the west, Maoism replaced it; and the Chinese model was attractive to some politicians in the Third World.

China thus struck out on new ideological paths; but it also inherited a number of foreign policy issues from the past. In the nineteenth century, foreign powers had imposed their will upon China, by a combination of force and diplomatic settlements which the Chinese referred to as 'unequal treaties'. By such means, for example, Britain had annexed Hong Kong; Russia had taken over vast territories between Lake Baikal and Vladivostok; and the western powers in general had laid down their own terms for trade with China. The Chinese (communist and non-communist alike) were determined to reverse this situation, and to restore the rights, dignity and prestige of their country. The Chinese also faced a difficult situation along most of their borders. It has been calculated that in 1949 China had more contiguous neighbours than any other country in the world, and was involved in frontier disputes with most of them – notably the Soviet Union and India, where the border conflicts were to lead to serious problems.[1]

The new China came into a world dominated by two superpowers, the United States and the Soviet Union. The United States was certainly an enemy. The Americans had supported Chiang, and had opposed the Communist take-over in China, though without managing to prevent it. To the Chinese communists the United States was the principal imperialist power, which by definition could only be hostile. It is just possible that there was a fleeting chance of better relations at the end of 1949, when the Chinese Foreign Minister, Zhou Enlai, approached the Americans with a request for recognition and support for China's admission to the United Nations and membership of the Security Council. This might have offered an opportunity that the Americans failed to grasp; but the Chinese offered little on their side, and were probably only trying to gain time for the new regime to establish itself. In any case, the state of American public opinion would almost certainly have ruled out any agreement. The China lobby, representing important commercial and religious groups which had lost much in China, was strongly opposed to recognizing the new regime. Many Americans also felt, vaguely but strongly, that the United States had 'lost China' to communism, probably as a result of treachery, and that it would be wrong to deal with the new regime.

If the United States was an enemy, was the Soviet Union a friend? Relations between the Chinese communists and Moscow had been poor (and sometimes calamitous) in the 1920s; and in the 1930s the Soviet Union had given more help to the Kuomintang than to the communists. As recently as February 1949 Stalin had advised Mao to settle for something less than complete victory in the civil war – perhaps the formation of a coalition with the Kuomintang, or a partition of China into two halves. On the other hand, Stalin had sometimes recognized the importance of China, saying that if the two countries followed the same path the victory of socialism in the world would be certain. When he received a Chinese communist delegation in July 1949, he was willing to envisage a form of division of labour – the Chinese would lead revolutionary movements in the colonial or semi-colonial countries, while the Soviets dealt with the others.[2] The Chinese communists for their part had fought their own battles and worked out their own version of Marxist doctrine, suitable to Chinese circumstances. Mao was his own man, not Stalin's.

Despite these difficulties, the Chinese had no real choice. They could not stand alone, and the Soviet Union was the only ally available. Mao declared that China would 'lean towards' the Soviet Union and against capitalist imperialism. The phrase was cautious, but Mao's actions were swift. He went personally to Moscow – an immense rail journey as the prelude to what proved a long and difficult visit. He met Stalin on 16 December 1949, but then had to wait in idleness and isolation until 22 January 1950 for a second meeting. Eventually the two sides got down to business, and on 14 February 1950 the Foreign Ministers signed a Soviet-Chinese Treaty of Friendship, Alliance and Mutual Assistance.

The treaty was a simple one, providing for mutual military assistance against aggression by Japan, or any other state that might collaborate with Japan in acts of aggression, which was an indirect reference to the United States. Alongside the treaty, the Soviet Union extended to China a credit of US $300 000 000, at only 1 per cent interest, to be repaid over ten years starting in 1954. The Soviet Union also undertook to restore to China by the end of 1952 the naval base at Port Arthur and the South Manchurian Railway which ran from Port Arthur to Mukden – issues which had been in dispute between the two countries for many years. The Chinese on their part recognized the independence of Outer Mongolia, formerly Chinese territory; which remained allied to the USSR and provided bases for Soviet troops.[3] An economic agreement signed in March 1950 set up three joint Sino-Soviet companies, one to run air services between the two countries, and the other two to exploit deposits of oil, gas and non-ferrous metals in the Sinkiang province of China, an area where the Soviets had long sought to establish their influence. This was disturbing for the Chinese, who had just got rid of western economic predominance by the front door and had no wish to see the Soviets coming in at the back. But on the whole the balance of the various agreements was reasonably favourable to the Chinese. China received the protection of Soviet military power, credit on excellent terms, and the return of Port Arthur. The Soviet Union established its status as senior partner in the new communist alliance, and gained a number of specific though minor advantages.

There was a curious postscript. Stalin sent an ideological expert, Pavel Yudin, to Beijing to supervise an edition of Mao's works and to report on the orthodoxy of his Marxism – a sign of the importance attached to doctrinal and theoretical matters, and of Stalin's fears that Mao (like Tito) might deviate from the paths of orthodoxy. Yudin's report was favourable; but Stalin's fears were not misplaced. Ideology was to prove a dangerous bone of contention between the two regimes.

The impact of the Communist victory in China in 1949 and the Sino-Soviet alliance of 1950 on international relations was enormous. The largest and most populous country in the world had joined the communist camp. (The population of China in 1949 was estimated at 542 millions, though the true figure was unknown.) The two communist giants had formed a military alliance and established a new economic relationship. It became common in later years, in the light of the Sino-Soviet dispute, to point to the differences between the two powers and to claim that no one should have been taken in by the appearance of communist solidarity. But at the time the new alignment was formidable. The communist bloc now stretched in a single mass from eastern Europe to the Bering Straits. It was a vision which struck dismay, sometimes amounting to fear, in the United States, and aroused admiration (again sometimes mingled with fear) over much of Asia. The world had changed with dramatic suddenness.

◈ The Sino-Soviet split

For some time the Sino-Soviet alliance worked well. The two countries co-operated in the Korean War, where the Chinese did the hard fighting and the Soviet Union provided material and diplomatic support; though by the end of the war in 1953 China had replaced the USSR as the main influence in North Korea, which was presumably not Stalin's intention. There was a difficulty when the USSR failed to hand over Port Arthur on the agreed date in 1952; but this was cleared up, and the Soviets left the base by the end of 1955. In 1954 the USSR provided a new loan of US $130 000 000 to China. More important, in 1957 the two countries concluded a military agreement under which the Soviets helped the Chinese to develop nuclear power and atomic weapons. Soviet specialists went to China to advise on nuclear energy (and also to look for uranium). The Chinese began to build their first nuclear reactor, with Soviet help.

But even at this stage there were difficulties. The Soviets took their own view of economic relations with China: the USSR would export manufac-tured goods and expertise, in return for raw materials and foodstuffs. It was an arrangement reminiscent of old-style economic imperialism, and natu-rally resented by the Chinese, who were themselves seeking to lead the former colonial countries in the elimination of imperialism. In 1955 a great Afro-Asian conference met at Bandung, in Indonesia, as a showpiece for the emerging Third World countries.[4] The Soviets angled desperately for an invi-tation, claiming that the USSR was in large part an Asian state – as indeed it was in terms of area. But no invitation arrived. Instead, the Chinese took centre stage at Bandung, scoring a great diplomatic and propaganda success and establishing China as a model for the former colonial states.

In February 1956 Khrushchev's 'secret speech' at the Twentieth Congress of the Communist Party of the Soviet Union brought a new and dangerous friction into Sino-Soviet relations. Khrushchev denounced Stalin's 'cult of personality', and proclaimed the need for peaceful co-existence with the United States. Neither proposition was welcome in Beijing. Mao himself had created a personality cult of enormous proportions, and resented criti-cism even at one remove. As for peaceful co-existence, Mao claimed to be unafraid of nuclear war with the Americans, because there were so many Chinese that enough would survive to win the final victory. (The United States was only a 'paper tiger' anyway.) Moreover, Khrushchev made his speech without even informing, let alone consulting, the Chinese in advance, thus treating them as mere subordinates rather than as powerful colleagues in the world communist movement.

Mao retaliated in kind in 1958. He announced, without consultation with the Soviets, the 'Great Leap Forward' which was to take China to communism in one bound. This was a direct ideological challenge to the Soviet Union, which had been moving towards communism ever since 1917 without ever claiming to have reached the goal. China thus embarked on an ideological conflict with the Soviet Union, which thus far had set the standards for all communist doctrine. The Great Leap Forward proved a disaster, which played into Soviet hands; but the principle remained of crucial importance.

Peaceful co-existence and relations with the Americans also produced a split between China and the Soviet Union in 1958, over the apparently insignificant islands of Quemoy. The Quemoy Islands are a group of twelve small islands, with a total area of only 17.5 square kilometres, about 10 kilometres off the Chinese mainland facing the port of Amoy. Along with the Matsu Islands further north, the Quemoy islands had been held by Kuomintang forces in 1949, and were an irritant to the Chinese because of their proximity to the mainland. In 1954 Chinese artillery bombarded Quemoy and Matsu for a prolonged period, and the Americans responded with a public warning that they would protect the islands against Chinese attack. The Kuomintang thus continued to hold Quemoy and Matsu, with very strong garrisons (65 000 troops in Quemoy), and the Americans were publicly committed to support them. During the night of 22–23 August 1958 Chinese artillery opened a heavy bombardment on Quemoy. The Americans moved warships to the area, but also got in touch with the Chinese through their respective embassies in Warsaw. (The two countries had no diplomatic relations, and therefore had to use indirect channels of communication.) There ensued a strange military and diplomatic quadrille. On 6 October the Chinese announced a cessation of their bombardment, to allow the islands to be provisioned. On 25 October the Chinese Ministry of Defence announced that they would bombard Quemoy on odd dates and observe a cease-fire on even dates, a practice which they proceeded to follow carefully for forty-four days, and then sporadically (and astonishingly) for twenty years.[5] The meaning of these strange manœuvres was that the Chinese had no intention of assaulting the islands (otherwise the Nationalists would not have been allowed to bring in supplies); the purposes of the bombardment were political not military, and were directed against the Soviets more than the Americans. Before the bombardment began, Mao said privately that he intended to send a message to Khrushchev about his relations with the Americans. 'He wants to improve relations with the United States? Good, we'll congratulate him with our guns . . .'[6] On 5 September Zhou Enlai explained to a Soviet emissary that the bombardment was intended to show the Americans that the Chinese

China and her neighbours

were not afraid of war and were still full of hatred for American imperialism. In other words, peaceful co-existence was not on the Chinese menu. On the 7th Zhou told Gromyko, the Soviet Foreign Minister, that China was prepared to face a local war with the United States over Quemoy, and was willing to risk even atomic attack and the destruction of cities. Zhou went on cheerfully to assure Gromyko that the Soviet Union need not take part in the war at that stage; but of course the implication was that the treaty of 1950 would commit the Soviets to the defence of China. Khrushchev waited for twenty days before replying dutifully that an attack on China would be regarded as an attack on the Soviet Union. In fact he had no intention of being drawn into a war with the United States over such a trivial issue as Quemoy. On the contrary, he was determined to improve relations with the Americans, and was already looking forward to visiting the United States the following year. Thus the Chinese used the Quemoy crisis, which was entirely artificial, to put pressure on the Soviet Union to change its policy towards the United States; but Khrushchev refused and held on his course.

The Sino-Soviet alliance was thus subject to a good deal of strain, economic, ideological and diplomatic. In 1959 these problems came to a head. On 20 June 1959 the Soviet Union suddenly denounced the military agreement of 1957 and ordered the withdrawal of its military advisers. In August Khrushchev stopped the despatch of a tactical nuclear bomb which was due to be transported to China. The Soviets had decided that the Chinese were not to be trusted with nuclear weapons. Also in August 1959 an apparently trivial border dispute between China and India produced a severe verbal response from the Soviet Union. Chinese troops crossed the McMahon Line (which the British had established in the nineteenth century as the frontier with Tibet) and attacked Indian Army posts. The significance of this minor incident lay in the Soviet reaction. On 9 September, the Soviet government issued an official statement regretting the dispute between two states which were *both friends of the Soviet Union*, a phrase which put China and India on the same footing, though China was in the socialist camp and an ally of the USSR, while India was a bourgeois democracy and non-aligned. The Chinese were indignant at such treatment, and salt was rubbed in their wounds during Khrushchev's visit to the United States from 15 to 25 September. The very fact of the visit went against Chinese policy; and in the final communiqué Eisenhower stressed the joint responsibility of the USA and the USSR to the world as a whole. It seemed that the superpowers were in league with one another to control the rest of the world – including China.

Meanwhile, the ideological division worsened, with indirect criticisms on both sides. In April 1960 the Chinese condemned Yugoslavia for revisionism, and in reply the Soviets attacked Albania. In November 1960 delegates from no fewer than 81 Communist Parties met in Moscow, in a great conclave, where the Chinese charged the Soviets with revisionism, and Khrushchev denounced the Chinese as left adventurists. Khrushchev rallied the great majority of the parties to his support, though the Albanians joined the Chinese in a strange alliance. This meeting was for long shrouded in secrecy, with news reaching the outside world only sporadically and uncertainly; but it marked a decisive step in the ideological conflict between the Chinese and the Soviets. Khrushchev had attacked the Chinese in a full gathering of the world's Communist Parties, and the Chinese had defied the authority of the Soviet Party. The full significance of this was to emerge later.

In 1962 the Chinese-Indian border dispute broke out again, this time in a serious conflict. In October and November large Chinese forces attacked the Indians, defeated them, and advanced well across the disputed frontier. They then voluntarily retreated to the line which they defined as the true frontier, and declared a cease-fire on 14 November. This time, instead of remaining ostentatiously neutral as he did in 1959, Khrushchev took sides against China and gave firm diplomatic support to India. At the same time, on the other side of the world, the Soviet Union confronted the United States in the Cuba missile crisis, and backed down at the crucial point rather than risk war. From the Chinese point of view, Khrushchev again put peaceful co-existence with the Americans above the solidarity of world communism.

In 1963 the Chinese chose to raise another matter of dispute: their border with the Soviet Union, which from the Chinese point of view was open to question along almost the whole if its immense length. On 8 March 1963 the *People's Daily* (the official Chinese newspaper) published an article listing nine treaties which former Chinese governments had been forced to sign, including the treaties of Aigun (1858) and Peking (1960), by which Russia had acquired a total of 318 000 square miles of Chinese territory, including what was now the port of Vladivostok. The article suggested, rather than stated, that China reserved the right to re-open these questions.[7] This implied threat was held in abeyance; but in the meantime the Chinese demanded that at least these unequal treaties should be properly observed instead of being violated, as they claimed the Soviets were doing along the Amur and Ussuri Rivers. Mao made even more of the issue in July 1964, when he told a visiting delegation of Japanese socialists that the Russians had annexed much territory to which they had no right, in Europe as well as Asia, and he promised to support all countries – including Japan and Germany – which sought to recover their rightful territory. Doubtless he did not actually expect the restoration of the Kuril Islands to Japan, or East Prussia to Germany; but it was a sharp debating point.

The Sino-Soviet dispute thus developed over a number of years at many different points; but its key element was ideological. For Mao, the alliance with the Soviet Union had been *for* socialism as well as *against* the United

States; and he was dismayed by the loss of this ideological solidarity.[8] China could not match the Soviet Union in military strength (especially its nuclear arsenal), and was not a world power on anything like the same scale. What the Chinese could do was to undermine the whole legitimacy of the Soviet system by denying the very principle of its existence, its standing as the guardian of Marxist–Leninist orthodoxy. The Chinese had done this in secret at the Moscow Conference in November 1960. In 1962 Mao publicly denounced the Soviets as revisionist, and on 15 June 1963 the Central Committee of the Chinese Communist Party wrote a formal letter to the Soviet Central Committee, explaining in twenty-five points that the Communist Party of the Soviet Union was no longer pre-eminent in the socialist camp, and that the Soviet Union had become revisionist and the objective ally of the United States. This letter, probably written by Mao and certainly approved by him, was a complete ideological denunciation of the Soviet Communist Party and the Soviet Union itself.

The Sino-Soviet alliance of 1950 had been based on hostility to the United States and a common ideological outlook. By 1963 both these foundations had cracked. The Soviet Union, while remaining fundamentally opposed to the United States, recognized the necessity of avoiding nuclear war and sought to improve relations with the Americans. China on the other hand maintained its hostility and claimed to be perfectly prepared to risk war with the Americans. At the same time, the common ideological ground had dissolved in doctrinal dispute, with the Chinese rejecting the predominance which the Soviets had exercised for so long, and claiming that their own form of communism was a better example for the Third World to follow. The two countries thus moved from co-operation to opposition. In the 1960s the Soviet Union reinforced its armies along the border with China. The Chinese pursued their nuclear programme, testing a nuclear bomb in 1964; and there was no doubt that the most likely target of their weaponry was now the Soviet Union. The alliance of 1950 proved to be remarkably short-lived.

◆ The recovery of Japan, 1945–62

In August 1945 Japan lay in ruins, with its armed forces in dissolution and the state itself apparently in limbo. The Emperor himself and the institution of the monarchy remained, but there was no constitution. The country was ruled by General Douglas MacArthur, the Supreme Commander of the Allied Forces in Japan. MacArthur was advised by a Far Eastern Commission, made up of representatives of eleven states which had been at war with Japan, and by a Four-Power Allied Council (the United States, Britain, China and the USSR); but he could disregard their advice at will. Stalin himself had agreed at the Potsdam Conference that the American

Supreme Commander should act as the sole executive authority for the Allies in Japan, and that is what he proceeded to do. The United States was sometimes outvoted by three to one in the Allied Council, for example on the exaction of reparations, but MacArthur simply ignored them and did as he liked.

In these extraordinary circumstances, two questions arose. What could the Japanese do to restore their own position? And what would the Americans do with their apparently untrammelled authority?

The Japanese were down, but by no means out; and they contrived to secure more control over their own affairs than appeared on the surface. Even before the war ended, groups of civil servants were planning the reconstruction of the economy. On 16 August 1945, the day after the armistice was signed, the Research Group for the Self-Sufficiency of the Japanese Mainland held its first meeting; early in 1946 it reported that high-grade machine tools and ultra-shortwave communications apparatus would be the best way forward – as indeed proved to be the case. There were other vital cases of continuity of administration. The Cabinet Planning Board formed in 1937, when Japan invaded China, continued its work, simply changing its name to the Economic Stabilization Board in 1946 and the Economic Planning Agency in 1955. The Ministry of International Trade and Industry which was set up in 1949 to direct Japan's economic development took over elements from the earlier Ministry of Commerce and Industry and even the wartime Munitions Ministry.[9] Thus the Japanese bureaucracy remained in being, with its eye firmly fixed on economic development as the key to the future.

This was in the background. American power occupied the foreground, and at first it seemed likely to be used with severity. President Truman, writing privately during the Potsdam Conference, described the Japanese as 'savages, ruthless, merciless and fanatic'; which was probably not far removed from general feeling in the United States.[10] In January 1946 MacArthur set up a War Crimes Tribunal, to follow the example of the Nuremberg Trials in Germany. He set out to disarm, demilitarize and democratize Japan – a far-reaching enterprise.

In practice, MacArthur moved cautiously in some respects. The Emperor was not brought to trial, even though in principle the whole war had been conducted under his authority. A number of Japanese were granted immunity from prosecution, and even for those who were tried the Tokyo War Crimes Tribunal proved less drastic in its proceedings than that at Nuremberg. Even so, the Americans imposed sweeping changes in Japan. The new Japanese constitution, prepared in 1946 and entering into force in 1947, was drafted in the Supreme Commander's headquarters, on lines laid down by MacArthur himself. It introduced votes for women; imposed freedom of the press; and recognized the status of trade unions and the right to strike. MacArthur insisted that the constitution should renounce war – an unusual step for a general to take, and a complete departure from Japanese tradition. Article 9 of the constitution was to be so important in Japanese foreign relations that it should be quoted in full.

> Aspiring sincerely to an international peace based on justice and order, the Japanese people forever renounce war as a sovereign right of the nation and the threat or use of force as a means of settling inter-national disputes.

> In order to accomplish the aim of the preceding paragraph, land, sea and air forces, as well as other war potential, will never be main-tained. The right of belligerency of the state will not be recognized.[11]

This article, imposed by American authority, later became a stumbling-block for the Americans themselves. When the United States wanted to rearm Japan, Article 9 could be quoted against them; and when Japanese pacifists opposed an alliance with the United States, they took their stand on Article 9.

Gradually the Americans and Japanese settled down to work together. The Japanese operated with great skill, largely under the direction of Yoshida Shigeru, who was Prime Minister for almost the whole period of the American occupation. Yoshida was a veteran politician (he was 67 when he first became Prime Minister in 1946, and 76 when he finally gave up in 1954). Like Adenauer in West Germany (to whom he was very close in age and temperament), Yoshida was an advocate of patience and caution in dealing with the occupying power. He was willing to accept defeat, but he was determined to preserve Japanese national identity, and to stake the country's future on economic development. He is credited with saying that 'Just as the United States was once a colony of Great Britain but is now the stronger of the two, if Japan becomes a colony of the United States it will eventually become the stronger'.[12] When Prime Minister, he adopted the slight eccentricity of being driven to appointments in an elderly Rolls Royce, and MacArthur at one stage mistakenly thought that he was lazy. In fact, Yoshida ran his government (and the Japanese Liberal Party) with an iron hand, and conducted his relations with the occupying power with a velvet glove. For Japan, he was the right man in the right place at the right time.

Yoshida's first priority was to restore the Japanese economy. In 1945 Japanese foreign trade was virtually non-existent, and overseas supplies of food and raw materials – on which Japan, with its large population and slender domestic resources, was heavily dependent – had dried up. The next two years saw only marginal improvement. Food was scarce and expensive, industrial production low, and exports weak. In 1947 the Americans improved the situation by relaxing their policy on the control of Japanese industry. A group of American businessmen, led by the Chairman of Chrysler, recommended slowing down the efforts to 'deconcentrate' Japanese industry by dissolving the *zaibatsu* – the big conglomerates in industry and banking which had dominated the Japanese economy before and during the war. By a strange irony, a leader of the American car industry thus offered a helping hand to the Japanese firms which were later to invade the American car market.

This change in American policy was the result of the development of the Cold War – 1947 was also the year of the Truman Doctrine, the Marshall Plan and the policy of containment. In the Far East, containment meant keeping Japan out of the Soviet sphere, and ensuring that the Japanese did not turn to communism as a result of economic difficulties. The Japanese and Americans thus began to work together economically. The Japanese built up their foreign trade: their exports reached a value of $174m in 1947; $258m in 1948; and $510m in 1949 – a three-fold increase in three years. The Americans helped by fixing the yen–dollar exchange rate at 360 yen to the dollar, which somewhat undervalued the Japanese currency and so helped exports.[13]

But progress was slow; and it was the Korean War of 1950–53 ('a gift from the gods', as Yoshida called it) which transformed the position.[14] The American government purchased some $500 000 000 worth of war supplies from Japan; and American servicemen in large numbers spent their dollars in the country. It was a crucial impulse for the Japanese economy. Moreover, the Korean War proved a decisive political turning-point. As early as 1949 the American Chiefs of Staff had advocated a limited revival of Japanese military power, and perhaps even an alliance with Japan as a counterweight to the Soviet Union. At that stage the State Department was sceptical; but in the first half of 1950, even before the outbreak of the Korean War, the American authorities had come to agree on the need for some measure of Japanese rearmament. The sudden North Korean attack at the end of June 1950 settled the issue. At once, in July, MacArthur ordered the formation of a 'National Police Reserve' of 75 000 men, which closely resembled a lightly-equipped army; though it was not to serve outside Japan. In 1952 this force was increased in number and equipped with tanks and artillery. In 1954 it was actually called an army, and its strength fixed at 130 000. At the same time a small naval force was set up, and Japanese minesweepers were working with the US Navy off Korea before the end of 1950. In January 1955 an Air Self-Defence Force was added, restoring the full range of the three armed services.[15] The problem of reconciling these changes with Article 9 of the Japanese constitution was dealt with by the legal argument that Japan had never given up the basic right of self-defence, and therefore there was no need to amend the constitution to accommodate purely defensive forces. The degree of rearmament was in any case very limited. Military expenditure remained low, and there was no revival of military sentiment in the country. Indeed, there was sharp opposition from the left wing and many intellectuals, which caused the government to tread cautiously.

The Korean War also brought a Japanese peace treaty. As in the case of Germany, there had been no peace treaty after the Japanese surrender in 1945. As the Cold War developed there seemed little chance that the Americans and Soviets could agree on one; and the communist victory in China added another complication. By 1950 the Americans had begun to think of concluding a separate peace treaty, including most of the former belligerents but excluding the Soviet Union and China. The outbreak of the Korean War brought them to a rather different decision: to try for a peace treaty with Japan, with the Soviets if possible, but without them if necessary; and in any case without the Chinese. The United States and Britain, as two of the most important former belligerents, invited fifty other states which had been at war with Japan to a conference at San Francisco in September 1951. The Soviet Union was invited, and accepted. India, Burma and Yugoslavia were invited but declined. Neither communist nor Nationalist China was invited, which avoided diplomatic problems but had the strange effect of excluding the enemy which Japan had fought longest, from 1937 to 1945. Eventually forty-nine governments were represented at San Francisco. Much work had been done in advance, and the Treaty of San Francisco was concluded on 8 September 1951.

Under this treaty, Japan renounced all claim to territories surrendered at the armistice of 1945, including Korea, Taiwan, the Kuril Islands and South Sakhalin. However, the treaty did not grant possession of Taiwan to China, nor of the Kurils and South Sakhalin to the USSR, so that these territories remained in a sort of legal limbo. The treaty specified that Japan was to pay reparations for damage and suffering caused during the war; but the actual amounts were left open for negotiation between Japan and the countries concerned. Japan was to resume its full sovereignty, and the occupation forces were to withdraw no later than ninety days after the treaty came into effect; but there was a proviso that this did not prevent the stationing of foreign armed forces in Japan under other treaty arrangements. It was in fact carefully arranged that on the same day that the peace treaty was signed a security treaty between the United States and Japan was also concluded, permitting the United States to maintain land, sea and air forces in and about Japan, to defend the country against external attack, and also (if the Japanese government so requested) to put down large-scale riots inside the country which might be caused by the instigation of an outside power – a most unusual function for foreign troops. Japan undertook not to permit any other country to establish bases or station troops on its territory without the consent of the United States. Thus the Americans secured exclusive military use of Japanese territory, and also assumed the defence of Japan against outside attack and, by implication, against internal subversion.[16]

While the peace treaty was under discussion, Australia and New Zealand had made much of their fears of a resurgence of Japanese power. To reassure them, the United States concluded on 1 September 1951 (in advance of the Treaty of San Francisco), a security treaty with Australia and New Zealand (the ANZUS Pact), which committed the USA to the defence of both those countries. This meant that the United States was committed to the military defence of the whole of the South Pacific and Australasia; and that Australia and New Zealand formally turned to the United States for protection, instead of to Britain as in former times. In practice, this had been the case ever since the fall of Singapore in February 1942; but it was still a great departure to acknowledge the change in principle.[17]

The Soviet Union refused to sign the Treaty of San Francisco, because it failed to confirm the annexation of the Kuril Islands and South Sakhalin to the USSR; and because they objected to the parallel arrangements for American forces to stay in Japan. The territorial questions between the USSR and Japan therefore remained unresolved, though the two countries resumed diplomatic relations in 1956, and could at least communicate directly with one another.

After the treaty, relations between Japan and the United States achieved a sort of balance. The Americans tried but failed to get the Japanese to bring their new armed forces up to a strength of 350 000. On the other hand, the Americans successfully insisted that Japan should establish no formal relations with communist China (which the United States did not recognize), and imposed tight restrictions on trade with the Chinese, which Japan would gladly have increased. (In practice, the Japanese found ways round these restrictions, for example by selling goods to Hong Kong for re-export to the mainland.)

Japanese economic development was now well under way. Exports totalled $827 million in 1950; $1.3 billion in 1952; and $2.8 billion in 1957. Imports were higher, and Japan did not record a trade surplus until 1965.[18] In 1955, on American initiative, Japan was admitted to the General Agreement on Tariffs and Trade, the International Monetary Fund, and to the United Nations – a triple recognition of the country's restored standing in world politics.

In 1959 the Japanese sought a revision of the Japanese-American security treaty of 1951, to put the two countries on a footing of greater equality, at any rate in principle. Under the revised treaty, signed on 19 January 1960, the United States retained the use of bases in Japan, but subject to new conditions: they would consult the Japanese government before increasing their forces in Japan, and before making any major changes in their armaments – a veiled reference to nuclear weapons. In fact, after the signature of this agreement, the American forces stationed in Japan were substantially reduced in numbers.

All in all, the new treaty was favourable to Japan, and yet it aroused vigorous opposition and vast street demonstrations in Japanese cities. This opposition sprang from different sources. The very fact of the treaty was resented by patriotic Japanese who did not like to be reminded of their dependence on the Americans. Pacifist and anti-nuclear sentiment, especially among students, was aroused by even a hint of the introduction of nuclear weapons to Japan. The Prime Minister who negotiated the treaty, Kishi, was unpopular with many Japanese because he had been a member of Tojo's wartime government and was thought not to have repented sufficiently. The Lower House of the Japanese parliament voted to accept the treaty, but the street demonstrations grew so large and violent that Kishi had to advise President Eisenhower to cancel a visit which he was due to make to Tokyo, because his safety could not be guaranteed. Kishi himself then resigned from office. After that the opposition died down, and the treaty came into force in June 1960 in comparative calm. But the episode left a lasting impression. Japanese opposition to any revival of militarism, to nuclear weapons, and even to the American alliance, doubtless arose only from a minority in the country as a whole; but it was sufficiently intense and well organized to bring down a Prime Minister and stop a visit by an American President. Both governments trod more cautiously in future.

By 1960, Japan had moved far from the defeat and desolation of 1945, but remained in a curiously ambiguous position. Japan was an ally of the United States, and protected by the American nuclear shield; yet significant sections of Japanese opinion resented dependence on the Americans and were bitterly opposed to nuclear weapons. Japan had made no peace treaty with the Soviet Union. They had no direct relations at all with communist China. Relations with these two great and close neighbouring countries were thus in limbo. By its constitution Japan had renounced war and the use of force to settle disputes; and its post-war governments had set out to pursue economic development as the principal activity of the state. In this the Japanese had the advantage of bearing only a light burden of armaments and military expenditure – in the eyes of their competitors, a 'free ride' at the expense of the Americans who were paying for their own defence and Japan's as well. Japan was a full member of the most important world organizations; on the way to creating a dynamic and prosperous economy; but still militarily weak, with all kinds of inhibitions about the use of military power by the state. It was a strange, partial and ill-defined restoration of Japan's place in the world.

◆ India and Pakistan

On 20 February 1947 the British Prime Minister, Clement Attlee, announced in the House of Commons that Britain intended to effect the transfer of power in India to 'responsible Indian hands' no later than June 1948; but he did not specify whose hands he had in mind. In fact, events moved far more rapidly than Attlee envisaged. It was at midnight on 14–15 August 1947 that Britain handed over power to the two new states of India and Pakistan.

Two crucial developments thus took place at the same time. The British left India in haste, and spared themselves the long and fruitless struggles waged by the Dutch in the East Indies and the French in Indo-China. They achieved this by means of the partition of the former British India, and they were succeeded by two states which from the start were hostile to one another. The British thus avoided a colonial war, but left behind them a war of succession. The background of these events needs explanation.

The Indian nationalist movement was led by the Congress Party, which in the name of Indian independence demanded that the British should 'Quit India'. But the leader of the Muslim League, Mohammed Ali Jinnah, demanded that the British should 'Divide and Quit' – in that order.[19] Division (or partition) meant the creation of a separate state of Pakistan, to be based on the Muslim religion, which Jinnah saw as the key to national self-determination. Jinnah put his case thus in March 1940: 'Hindus and Muslims have two different religious philosophies, social customs, litera-tures. . . . Muslims are a nation according to any definition of the term, and they must have their homelands, their territory and their state.'[20] After prolonged uncertainty, the last Viceroy of India, Mountbatten, and the British government accepted partition in April 1947; and the Congress lead-ers (though not Gandhi) came round to the same position. Their motives were mixed. Vallabhbhai Patel (who ranked with Jawaharlal Nehru in the creation of modern India) explained to Congress on 10 June 1947 that it was necessary to 'cut off the diseased limb and save the main body' – mean-ing that he preferred a cohesive Indian state to one which might overreach itself by trying to include all the Muslim areas.[21] Congress leaders under-stood that events were moving fast, and that they could not delay indepen-dence in order to try to preserve unity. Most shared an underlying belief which they preferred not to avow: that partition would not last. Pakistan would not survive, and if only for economic reasons would soon return to a united India. This proved to be an error; and disappointment bred bitter-ness.

The British devised the final partition in immense haste; and the imme-diate results proved disastrous. In several areas, especially the Punjab, order broke down completely. Some ten to twelve million people left their homes in mass migrations. Hindus and Sikhs fled from the new Pakistan to India; Muslims from India to Pakistan. The total of those killed remains unknown, but was probably not less than a million, and perhaps more.[22] Millions were left displaced and homeless on both sides of the new fron-tiers. The result was a legacy of bitterness and hatred, exacerbated by the widespread belief in both India and Pakistan that the authorities in the other country had welcomed and encouraged the killing in order to consolidate the new order.

Of the two new states, India had a solid political base to build on, and settled down into remarkable internal stability under a federal and parliamentary form of government. Pakistan was in two parts, West and East, separated by about 1000 miles of Indian territory. The West, based on the Punjab and its neighbouring areas, was the seat of the capital and provided most of the army; the East, made up of a large part of Bengal, included a majority of the population. In these circumstances, not surprisingly, stability proved impossible to maintain: the two new countries plunged at once into a state of undeclared war, arising mainly from the events of partition. The founders of Pakistan had wanted their new state to be larger than it was; most Indian leaders had not wanted partition at all, and hoped it would soon come to an end. The massacres and forced migrations of 1947 left deep scars on both sides.

To these general causes of conflict was soon added the specific issue of Kashmir. When the British left India, no fewer than 562 Indian states which had retained their existence under British paramountcy had to choose whether to join India or Pakistan. Almost all achieved a reasonably smooth adherence to one or the other; but there were some difficult cases. In Hyderabad the ruler was a Muslim, and the population mostly Hindu. Adherence to Pakistan was no more than a remote possibility, if only on grounds of distance; but in any case the issue was resolved by Indian forces occupying the state and ensuring that it joined India. In the state of Kashmir and Jammu the opposite situation prevailed: the Maharajah was a Hindu, and the population of some four million was three-quarters Muslim.[23] At the time of independence in August 1947, the Maharajah hesitated, and did not declare for either India or Pakistan. India maintained that the ruler had the right to choose; Pakistan that the population should be consulted. In Jammu, in the north of the state, where the population was only some 60 per cent Muslim, there were attacks by Hindus on Muslims. On the Muslim side, Pathan guerrillas invaded Kashmir, with the support of the nearest Pakistan provincial authorities and at least the connivance of the central government itself. The Maharajah fled to India, where he pledged his adherence in return for military support. Indian troops were airlifted to the capital, Srinagar; and by a treaty signed on 26 October 1947 the Indian government accepted the adherence of Kashmir to India, but undertook that the future of the territory should be settled by its people when law and order were restored. Fighting went on throughout 1948, involving regular forces from India and Pakistan as well as guerrillas. The United Nations arranged a cease-fire on 1 January 1949, and on 5 January the Security Council passed a resolution affirming that a plebiscite was to be held after a UN Commission had ascertained that the cease-fire was effective. A final

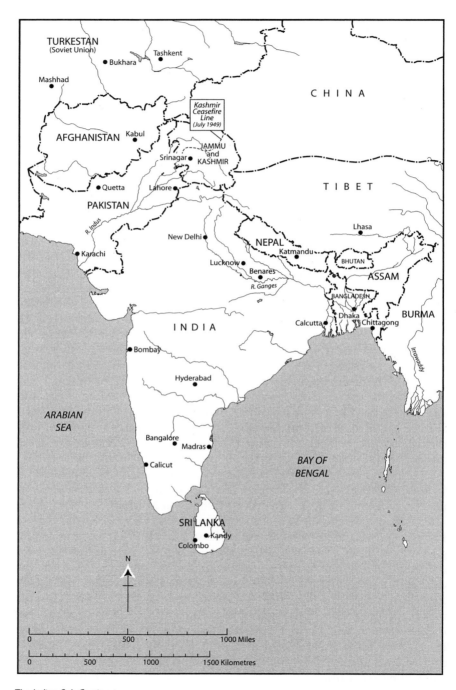

The Indian Sub-Continent

cease-fire line, to be supervised by United Nations observers, was established on 27 July 1949, leaving Pakistan in control of about one-third of Kashmir in the north (including Jammu), and India the other two-thirds, including Srinagar. But no plebiscite to ascertain the wishes of the population ever took place, partly because the Indians feared that the vote would go against them, and perhaps even more because the very existence of the Indian state would be threatened by an example of secession. No permanent settlement was attained; Kashmir was divided along the cease-fire line, not an agreed frontier; and the issue continued to plague relations between India and Pakistan, with fighting breaking out from time to time over the next fifty years.

In their conflict, in which Kashmir was a symbol as well as a cause, both Pakistan and India looked for outside support. Pakistan turned first to the United States, joining the Treaty of Manila (the South-East Asia Treaty Organization) in 1954, and the Baghdad Pact (later the Central Treaty Organization) in 1955. Pakistan was distant from the areas covered by these treaties, but it used them to obtain military equipment from the Americans. India, for its part, turned towards the Soviet Union, receiving economic aid and diplomatic support, and welcoming a spectacular visit from Khrushchev and Bulganin in 1955 – though it continued to proclaim its non-aligned status.

For Pakistan, relations with India almost filled the horizon, and foreign policy was concerned with little else. India, on the other hand, aspired to a wide-ranging role in world affairs, largely through the personality and interests of Jawaharlal Nehru, the country's first Prime Minister. Nehru was a cosmopolitan figure, educated in England at Harrow, Cambridge and the Inns of Court. He absorbed an internationalist mode of thought from progressive friends in Britain; while from Gandhi he learned a philosophy of idealism and non-violence, though he was not himself a pacifist.

Moved by these ideals, drawn from both West and East, Nehru conceived a deep faith in the principles of co-existence – the *panchsheel* which were somewhat incongruously set out in the preamble to a commercial treaty between India and China in April 1954 – an agreement which among other things recognized Chinese suzerainty over Tibet. The principles, five in number, were as follows: mutual respect between states for their territorial integrity and sovereignty; non-aggression; non-interference in the internal affairs of other states; equality in status between states; and peaceful co-existence. These notions breathed a vague goodwill, which the actual conduct of China towards Tibet might well have called into question; but Nehru placed great faith in them, and propagated them further at the Afro-Asian Congress at Bandung in April 1955. Nehru thus became a quintessential Third World figure, deeply versed in the language of non-alignment and anti-colonialism.

At the same time he also played a key role in the Commonwealth, even though it was in some sense a vestige of colonialism, in that it was the heir to the former British Empire. In 1950 India became a republic, and it seemed likely that this would mean leaving the Commonwealth, whose members at the time maintained allegiance to the Crown as a common bond. Nehru was determined that India should remain a member, and largely on his initiative a formula was devised by which member states accepted the British monarch as Head of the Commonwealth while remaining free to become republics if they so wished. This was a crucial device, which allowed the Commonwealth to assume a form which almost any country, whatever its form of government, could accept. Nehru's motives were mixed. He valued the British connection; he wanted to keep level with Pakistan, which intended to remain in the Commonwealth; and he wanted another stage to perform on. In any case, he secured another vehicle for his ambition to be a world statesman as well as Prime Minister of India.

In 1962 the principles of *panchsheel* were abruptly discarded by the Chinese, who had probably not taken them too seriously in the first place. The border between India and Tibet along the McMahon Line, drawn at a conference at Simla in 1914, had long been in dispute; and when the Chinese occupied Tibet in 1950 they revived old claims. On 20 October 1962 Chinese troops attacked the Indians in one of the disputed areas, in Assam, driving them back in disorder. The Indian government was badly shaken, and declared a state of emergency. The Indian forces launched a counter-attack on 14 November, but were again defeated. Nehru, in a state of alarm, appealed urgently for American and British help. Both agreed; though in fact only small quantities of military supplies had arrived by air when the Chinese announced on 21 November that they were ceasing fire along their whole front, and would withdraw to what they insisted was the correct frontier. The Indians lost nearly 1400 killed, 1700 missing and 4000 prisoners, which was a heavy toll for a limited campaign. They suffered a much greater loss in prestige and confidence. Nehru saw his faith in *panchsheel* collapse in ruins, and suffered the humiliation of having to appeal to the Americans for help – at one point he even asked for American transport aircraft plus crews to fly them, to release Indian aircrew for other duties. The lofty Third World leader had stubbed his toe sharply on military realities.

Pakistan seized the opportunity offered by the Chinese-Indian conflict to improve relations with China. In March 1963 the Pakistan government concluded an agreement with China settling their own disputed frontier in north-east Kashmir. The two countries followed this up with military co-operation, enabling Pakistan to strengthen its position against India. On their side, the Chinese were not perturbed by Pakistan's Muslim basis, or by the Pakistani government's hostility to communism within its own borders. On both sides, power politics prevailed: the enemy of my enemy is my friend.

Relations between India and Pakistan and between China and India had only marginal links with other events in international affairs. India and Pakistan pursued their conflict with little reference to the Cold War except when they tried to exploit it, as Pakistan did through the Baghdad Pact and SEATO. China and India carried on a border dispute left over from the age of imperialism. The two superpowers, for their part, were partly influenced by the Cold War, which drew them into issues which they might otherwise have ignored; but their interventions appeared to be scarcely affected at all by ideology. The Americans retained Pakistan as an ally when it came under military rule in 1958. The Soviet Union co-operated with India even though it was a parliamentary democracy led by a bourgeois nationalist. It was the conflict for influence and prestige in the Third World, and to some degree calculations of power politics, which counted for the superpowers.

The Cold War was incidental to events in the Indian sub-continent. The conflict between India and Pakistan which arose out of partition and the Kashmir question was to outlast the Cold War, and proved one of the most durable and irreconcilable problems in the post-war world. By 1998 both India and Pakistan were nuclear powers, on a small but sufficient scale. In 1999 they were still fighting in Kashmir. Yet in all this time the two countries never declared war on one another. For most of the time they were both members of the Commonwealth. They made occasional attempts at reconciliation, which we shall look at in another chapter. It was a strange state of neither war nor peace – oddly characteristic of much of international affairs since 1945.

◆ The French war in Indo-China and the American road to Vietnam

French Indo-China, which brought together Vietnam, Laos and Cambodia in a somewhat artificial union, had been under French control since the 1880s. The Japanese occupied the country from 1941 to 1945, maintaining the formal arrangements of French colonial rule. In March 1945, when the Japanese were losing the war against the western allies, they suddenly dissolved the French administration and declared the independence of Vietnam, under Bao Dai, who had succeeded to the largely empty title of Emperor of Vietnam as long ago as 1926. When Japan surrendered in August 1945 Bao Dai abdicated, and the Vietnamese communist leader Ho Chi Minh formed a new government and declared the independence of the Democratic Republic of Vietnam on 2 September. Meanwhile in France General de Gaulle had maintained throughout the Second World War that the French Empire should remain intact, and he was determined to restore French authority in Indo-China. By the end of 1945 General Leclerc, one of the most distinguished French commanders of the time, was established in

Saigon (in the south of Vietnam) with a force of some 50 000 French troops.

The French and the government of Ho Chi Minh thus found themselves face to face in Indo-China. For most of 1946 the French tried to restore their control over the country by negotiation, aiming at a complicated structure in which a federation of the three Indo-Chinese states (Vietnam, Laos and Cambodia) would be incorporated in the French Union – a device invented by de Gaulle to preserve the essentials of the French Empire under a new name. Ho Chi Minh went to France, and agreement seemed to be close during negotiations at Fontainebleau in September 1946; but in fact the gap between the French intention to restore their control and Ho Chi Minh's determination to achieve genuine independence could not be bridged.

At that stage, the French were well established in southern Vietnam, and the Viet Minh (Vietnam Independence League) in the north. In November 1946 the French decided to use force to defeat the Viet Minh. On 24 November French warships bombarded Haiphong, the main port in northern Vietnam, and French troops landed shortly afterwards. They captured Hanoi, inland from Haiphong, in February 1946.

The French hoped for a rapid victory, but the Viet Minh proved a completely new sort of enemy. Their leader, Ho Chi Minh, had lived the life of a communist conspirator, including some time in the Soviet Union, where he had learned the value of discipline and ruthlessness. He was a skilful political tactician, yet utterly dedicated to his own combination of nationalism and Marxism. He aimed at nothing less than the foundation of a completely independent communist state in Vietnam, and would accept no compromise. He was supported on the military side by General Giap, who was only 34 in 1946 but had already been a communist party member for thirteen years. Giap had fought against the French in the 1930s, and organized resistance against the Japanese during their occupation of Indo-China. He was a hardened fighter, and a skilled guerrilla leader. He commanded the Viet Minh forces throughout the war against the French from 1946 to 1954 (the French had eight different commanders in the same period); and was to do so again during the whole conflict against the Americans. It was a remarkable record.

This combination of communist political discipline and skilful military leadership was at first quite unexpected by the French. The middle-ranking French army officers later conceived a great admiration for their opponents' toughness and dedication, which they set out to emulate; but meanwhile the French authorities were at a loss. The governments of the Fourth Republic in Paris were short-lived and hesitant. They could not decide either to cut their losses and pull out of Indo-China, as the British withdrew from India in 1947, or to commit the whole of French resources to the conflict. The war in Indo-China was fought by regular soldiers and the Foreign Legion (and by large numbers of Vietnamese), not by conscripts, so that most of the French public ignored it for most of the time. French governments usually failed even to ask, never mind answer, the question of what the war was about.

The nearest they came to an answer to this crucial question was the Along Bay statement of December 1947, in which France accepted the principle of Vietnamese independence, followed by an agreement in June 1948 setting up a Vietnamese state, with the Emperor Bao Dai as its head, to which the French promised full independence at some time in the future. This created a strange position in which both the Viet Minh and the French claimed to be fighting for the independence of Vietnam. This played into the hands of the Viet Minh, who obviously meant what they said. The French claims were unconvincing, because Bao Dai was only a puppet and independence – if it ever arrived – would be a sham. Yet at the same time the French undermined their own will to fight, because they had at least to pretend that they were at war only to secure the privilege of leaving the country to Bao Dai.

In these circumstances it was somewhat surprising that the military balance remained fairly even from 1947 to 1949. The French had no difficulty in holding the cities, and most of the countryside in the south. Giap built up his guerrilla forces in the mountains and rural areas of the north. Actual fighting was limited, and the war itself remained self-contained – a colonial war on the French side, a war of liberation for the Viet Minh. At the end of 1949, the communist victory in China transformed the situation. The Chinese provided the Viet Minh with arms (including artillery), and with facilities for training large units ready for a move from guerrilla to open warfare. On the other hand, the French were now able to appeal for American help, on the ground that they were not fighting a colonial war but were engaged in the worldwide struggle against communism. In May 1950 the Truman administration agreed to provide aid to the French in Indo-China; $15 000 000 were provided for the purchase of armaments, lorries and transport aircraft.

This proved to be the crucial first step towards American involvement in Vietnam, which was to last for a quarter of a century and end in disaster for the United States. How did it come about? The immediate reason was the communist victory in China, which convinced the United States government that no further communist expansion could be tolerated. Behind this lay the 'Munich syndrome' – the conviction that appeasement had been fatal in the 1930s and must not be repeated. In February and April 1950 two documents prepared by the National Security Council (NSC-64 and NSC-68) argued that Indo-China was the crucial link in a chain including Thailand, Malaya, the Philippines, Indonesia and Burma; and the breaking of one link would mean the loss of the whole chain. By a change of metaphor, this was to become the 'domino theory' which President

Eisenhower expounded in April 1954, and which had some justification in recent experience.[24] In 1941, after all, the Japanese occupation of southern Indo-China had been followed swiftly by their attacks on Malaya, Singapore, the Philippines and the Dutch East Indies; so in principle the same thing might well happen again.

There were difficulties. The Americans were genuinely committed to anti-colonialism, and they had to find an uneasy compromise between their anti-imperialism and anti-communism. Moreover, they found themselves on a slippery slope. The more they insisted on the crucial importance of Vietnam, the more help the French could ask for. The more help the Americans sent, the more they had to be sure it was used properly. Before the end of 1950 the Americans sent to Saigon a Military Assistance Advisory Group – only a few dozen men, but the vanguard of what was to become a massive army.

There followed a period of intensive fighting in Vietnam. The French gained some victories under the leadership of General de Lattre de Tassigny in 1951; but Giap's forces in the north held their own, not only in guerrilla fighting but increasingly in regular warfare. In 1953 the French government made serious diplomatic moves to end the war, and declared its willingness to grant independence to the three separate states of Indo-China – Cambodia, Laos and Vietnam. A treaty of independence for Laos was actually signed in October 1953, though it included a French undertaking to defend the country against communist attack, which left scope for a continued military presence. In autumn 1953 the French attempted to improve their military position, and so gain better terms in negotiations, by setting up a fortress at Dien Bien Phu, in northern Vietnam, and challenging the Viet Minh to a pitched battle on ground of French choosing. The plan went completely wrong. The position was ill-chosen, in a hollow commanded by surrounding hills. The Viet Minh were equipped with Chinese heavy artillery which played havoc with the French defences. The Americans considered direct military intervention (by means of air bombardment, the despatch of airborne troops, or even atomic attack); but Eisenhower decided against it. After a long siege, the French garrison surrendered on 7 May 1954. It was one of the decisive battles of modern warfare: the victory of an Asian army over a European power in regular combat. In the nineteenth century, European forces – despite occasional disasters – had won their wars over Asian and African opponents. Now the tables were turned. The organization and discipline of the Viet Minh had created a new sort of army; Chinese heavy artillery had changed the balance of armaments; and the stern political will of the Viet Minh prevailed over the uncertainty of governments in Paris. The Viet Minh victory at Dien Bien Phu sent a signal to nationalist movements across the world.

While Dien Bien Phu was under siege, an international conference met at Geneva to reach a negotiated settlement of the Indo-China war. The initiative came from the French. A new and resolute French government under Pierre Mendès-France was determined to end the war as quickly as possible, and secured agreement on a peace conference. The Geneva Conference convened on 26 April 1954, and continued until 21 July. It was attended by nine states: France, Britain, the United States, the Soviet Union, the People's Republic of China, the Democratic Republic of Vietnam (the Viet Minh), Vietnam (the Vietnamese state recognised by the French), Cambodia and Laos. An Indian representative (Krishna Menon) was present, with no official status but acting as an intermediary between the British delegation and the communist states. The fall of Dien Bien Phu on 7 May, when the conference had been at work for less than two weeks, virtually destroyed the French bargaining position. The other participants formed a disparate band – the Americans and Chinese had no diplomatic relations with one another; the two Vietnamese governments were sworn enemies. It was remarkable that the conference achieved any result at all, even though it was only in the form of a series of armistice agreements and accompanying declarations.[25]

Three armistices were signed on 21 and 21 July by the French and Viet Minh high commands, dealing with Vietnam, Cambodia and Laos respectively. These armistices were technically military documents but had important political consequences. The Vietnam armistice established a cease-fire line and a demilitarized zone close to the line of the 17th parallel of latitude, which later became the line of division between North and South Vietnam. Each side was to withdraw its forces to its own side of the cease-fire line, over a period of 300 days. The French were to withdraw their forces from all three states within a period to be agreed. In Vietnam, elections were to be held in July 1956, under the supervision of an international commission, to determine the final status of the country.

The results offered little satisfaction to anyone. For France, the Geneva Conference set the diplomatic seal on military defeat. Yet the result also represented a partial defeat for the Viet Minh, which had aimed at the unification of Vietnam under its own control and had to settle for half. The Chinese pressed this concession upon them, in the belief that a divided Vietnam would offer no danger to Chinese interests. The Viet Minh were thus denied their main objective, and regarded the settlement as merely temporary. Equally the Vietnamese government (effectively the government of southern Vietnam) protested against the armistice terms and reserved its freedom of action. The United States dissociated itself from the later phase of the conference (Foster Dulles, the Secretary of State, actually went home in May, leaving a deputy to represent him). The American government did not sign any of the agreements, and only took note of the final declaration of the conference. Essentially, this very partial settlement only succeeded in bringing the war between the French and the Viet Minh to an end, and allowing the French to make their exit in reasonable order.

The French gradually withdrew from Indo-China, with their last forces leaving in May 1956. The Americans moved in to replace them, supporting the state of South Vietnam which began to develop to the south of the 17th Parallel armistice line. They hoped, with a simple optimism, to build a new democracy in South Vietnam, choosing as their instrument a Catholic politician, Ngo Din Diem. A referendum removed the Emperor Bao Dai (who in any case wisely preferred to live on the French Riviera rather than in South Vietnam); and a republican regime was set up. On 9 April 1956 Diem announced that he was postponing the elections which were due to be held under the Geneva agreements to decide the future of the country, because he had decided that in any election held in Vietnam as a whole the communists would probably win. Senator John F. Kennedy visited the country in 1956, and rashly declared that it was 'a proving ground for democracy in Asia'.[26] The Americans despatched advisers and instructors to set up a new South Vietnamese Army on their own model, equipped and trained primarily for conventional warfare of the kind seen in the Second World War and Korea.

These policies proved ill-conceived. South Vietnam, not surprisingly, failed to produce a democracy on the American model; and the war in which South Vietnam was soon engaged was not a repetition of the Second World War. In 1958 the Viet Cong (the armed forces of the South Vietnamese communists) began an insurrection against the South Vietnamese government by assassinating its officials. In December 1960 the Viet Cong set up the Front for the Liberation of South Vietnam, and embarked on extensive guerrilla warfare, supported and organized from the North, with the aim of destroying the South Vietnamese government and uniting the country under communist rule.

This was not a form of warfare which the Americans had anticipated; but they found themselves committed to it. They had convinced themselves of the crucial importance of South Vietnam, as the domino which, if it fell, would bring down Thailand, Burma, Indonesia, the Philippines and even Australia. They provided increasing amounts of economic assistance to South Vietnam; they despatched more military advisers; and in December 1961 President Kennedy decided to raise the number of American troops in the country to 15 000. It was to prove a fatal involvement.

◆ South-East Asia: Indonesia and Malaysia

Indonesia

The Dutch East Indies, later to become Indonesia, was a vast archipelago of about 3600 islands, stretching over a distance of 3000 miles from east to west. During the Second World War, the Japanese occupied these territories, and gave some encouragement to the Indonesian nationalist movement

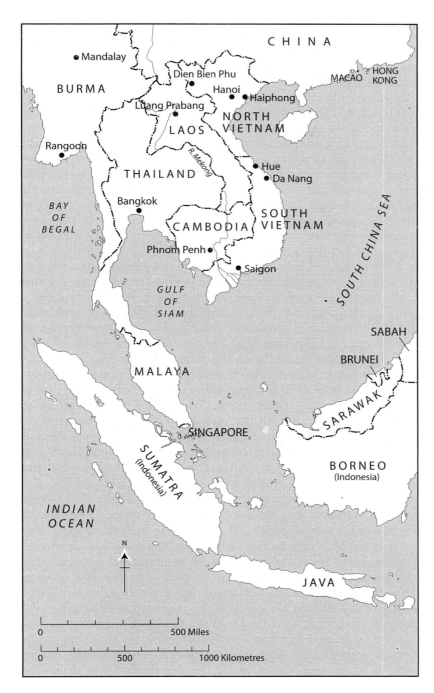

CHINA

Mandalay

Dien Bien Phu

BURMA

Hanoi

Haiphong

MACAO HONG
KONG

Luang Prabang

NORTH
VIETNAM

LAOS

Rangoon

R. Mekong

Hue

THAILAND

Da Nang

Bangkok

SOUTH
VIETNAM

CAMBODIA

BAY
OF
BEGAL

Phnom Penh

Saigon

SOUTH CHINA SEA

GULF
OF
SIAM

SABAH

MALAYA

BRUNEI

SARAWAK

SINGAPORE

SUMATRA
(Indonesia)

BORNEO
(Indonesia)

INDIAN
OCEAN

N

JAVA

| 0 | | | 500 Miles |
| 0 | 500 | | 1000 Kilometres |

South-East Asia

there.[27] When Japan surrendered, the Indonesian leaders Ahmed Sukarno and Mohammed Hatta sought to pre-empt the return of the Dutch by declaring independence on 17 August 1945. When Dutch forces and colonial authorities re-appeared on the scene, they tried a combination of the iron hand and the velvet glove in order to retain at least a part of their former position. There was some heavy fighting between Dutch and nationalist forces in Java in the second half of 1947 and at the end of 1948; but the Dutch concentrated much of their effort on trying to find a compromise by which they could accept some form of Indonesian independence while retaining some influence for themselves. In 1947, for example, they tried to set up a complicated Indonesian Federation, in which some territories would be under their control and others under Indonesian government. While these events were in progress, in September 1948, there was a communist rising against the nationalists in Java, which was violently suppressed by Sukarno's nationalist forces.

In 1949 the United States intervened to break what had become a fruitless deadlock between the Dutch and the Indonesian nationalists. This was a time when American anti-colonial sentiment was still strong; and Sukarno's success against the communists had convinced them that he would be a reliable ally. Moreover, the Marshall Plan was getting under way in Europe, and the Americans had no wish to see the Dutch wasting their share of Marshall Aid in a war in the East Indies. Therefore, the United States put heavy pressure on the Dutch to withdraw, even threatening to cut off Marshall Aid if they did not do so. The Dutch, who were already finding the cost of maintaining their position too great for anything they were likely to secure in return, agreed to a conference with their opponents. In August 1949 the Dutch government and the Indonesian nationalists, led by Sukarno, signed an agreement at The Hague, setting up a Federal United States of Indonesia, together with a Netherlands-Indonesian Union which would save some standing (and some face) for the Dutch. This attempt at a half-way house soon broke down, and at the end of December 1949 the Netherlands accepted the complete independence of Indonesia.

There was an exception. The Dutch held on in Western New Guinea (West Irian), which they rightly claimed had never been administered as part of the East Indies, and was different in ethnic make-up and state of development from the rest of the territory. Indonesia, on the contrary, claimed that it should be the heir to all the former Dutch colonial territories, including West Irian. The Indonesian claim remained largely nominal for some years, until in 1961 the Dutch set up representative institutions in the colony to prepare it for independence. Indonesia then stepped up its diplomatic pressure, and began to take military action, landing troops by sea and air to raise an insurrection. The Americans again intervened to promote the Indonesian cause, and the United Nations was called on to provide the machinery for a transfer of sovereignty. In August 1962, through American mediation, the Dutch and Indonesian governments reached an agreement by which a temporary United Nations administration was to take over the territory in October, and hand over to Indonesia on 1 May 1963. The population of West Irian was then to make a 'free choice' on its future, no later than the end of 1969. This provision was observed, after a fashion, in 1969, not by a plebiscite, but by a gathering of about 1000 representatives of the people, who voted to remain part of Indonesia. This settlement did not prove permanent; but that is another story.

The independence of Indonesia showed some striking features. The role of the United States in intervening on the side of the nationalists, and pressing the Dutch to withdraw, was an example of American anti-colonial sentiment at its most powerful. Indonesia itself went straight from its struggle against colonialism to its own brand of imperialism, claiming West Irian simply as the successor to the Dutch and showing no inclination to allow the population of that territory to decide its own future – except in the most carefully supervised manner.

Malaya

Malaya proved a distinctive case in the history of decolonization. The Malay States were particularly important colonies for Britain in the post-war period, as producers of tin and rubber, whose export earned large sums for the sterling area. Rubber especially was a strong earner of dollars, through exports to the United States. The British sought to maintain these economic advantages while making some concessions to local self-rule by bringing the Malay States together in the Federation of Malaya (February 1948), which preserved British control while permitting considerable autonomy in internal affairs. In June 1948 the Malayan Communist Party (mostly made up of Chinese, not Malays) began an insurrection against British rule, which for over three years gained widespread successes. The insurgents dominated much of the countryside, damaged rubber production, inflicted casualties on civilians and the armed forces, and finally killed the British High Commissioner himself in an ambush.

At this stage, the insurrection showed marked similarities to that in Indo-China, where the French were fighting a losing battle against communist guerrillas. But in Malaya the British succeeded in defeating the insurgents, and in February 1954 the communist commanders had to leave the country and retreat to Sumatra; though the state of emergency declared by the government did not end until July 1960. How was this success achieved? Part of the answer lay in the appointment of General Templer as High Commissioner and Commander-in-Chief in February 1952. Templer adopted a combination of methods – improved intelligence on communist activities; air attacks on guerrilla camps; the introduction of fortified villages to protect civilians against guerrilla attacks; and economic rewards for areas that were declared pacified. Behind these methods, the British were able to exploit a number of general advantages. The guerrilla forces could be cut off from outside support. Malaya's only land frontier was with Thailand, and the Thais were opposed to the guerrillas. Indonesia was willing to support the rebels, but the British could call on their naval power to intercept supplies at sea. The communists were mainly Chinese, and therefore the British were able to appeal for the support of the majority of the population, who were Malays. That appeal was successful because the British convinced the Malays that they seriously intended to hand over power – Malaya actually became independent in August 1957, before the state of emergency came to an end. At the same time, it was agreed that Malaya would remain in the Commonwealth and in the sterling area, so that the most important British economic interests were safeguarded.

This showed that with good military strategy, support from the population, and in favourable geographical circumstances, it was possible for a colonial power to defeat a communist insurrection. The Malayan example naturally attracted much attention, and later encouraged the Americans to believe that they could succeed in Vietnam, where they adopted a number of the methods used by the British – for example, fortified villages and air strikes against guerrilla camps. But the circumstances were very different – the Vietnamese communists had an open frontier with China behind them; there was no split in the population to be exploited; the fortified villages did not work in a different environment; the Americans changed their personnel in Vietnam constantly, and never achieved the continuity which was so important for Templer's operations. The Malayan experience was only partially transferable to Vietnam.

There was a further outcome to these events, in which Indonesia and Malaya came together – or rather, came into dispute. In 1961 the Prime Minister of the independent Malaya, Tengku Abdul Rahman, proposed to form a new Federation of Malaya, Singapore, and the British Borneo territories of Brunei, Sarawak and North Borneo. At the time, this was welcomed by the other parties concerned (notably Lee Kuan Yew, the Prime Minister of Singapore), and by Britain as the former colonial power. Indonesia, the most important neighbouring country, made no objection. But in January 1963, when the Federation of Malaysia had actually been formed, Sukarno denounced it, and announced that Indonesia would adopt a policy of 'confrontation' towards it – which meant in practice diplomatic and economic pressure and some military harassment in the Borneo territories. This was partly a matter of prestige (Indonesia insisted on great power status in South-East Asia, and wanted to be consulted on changes in its area), and partly the result of Sukarno's need for an enemy to hold his disparate country together. The policy of confrontation was a failure. With British military and naval support, the Borneo territories stood firm, and Sukarno himself lost interest as his power at home faded away. Singapore broke away from the Malaysian Federation, for its own reasons, and attained striking economic success in its own right.

The whole story of Indonesia and Malaya (later Malaysia) demonstrates the uncertain nature of the process of decolonization, and the different roles of former colonial powers. In West Irian, the Dutch could only delay the advance of Indonesian expansion. In Malaya, the British defeated a communist insurrection, and then successfully supported the Federation of Malaysia against Indonesian confrontation.

By the early 1960s, the transformation of Asia had produced three grave conflicts. India and Pakistan were locked into a constant hostility. The United States was becoming increasingly involved in Indo-China, where the French had already lost one war. The Chinese-Soviet dispute, in its different aspects of ideology, territory and power politics, was well under way. All these conflicts were to be carried on into the future. The consequences of decolonization had been far from peaceful.

◆ Notes to Chapter 9

1. Harold C. Hinton, 'China as an Asian Power', in Thomas W. Robinson and David Shambaugh, eds, *Chinese Foreign Policy: Theory and Practice* (Oxford, 1994), pp. 349, 352.
2. John Lewis Gaddis, *We Now Know: Rethinking Cold War History* (Oxford, 1997), pp. 66–7.
3. Treaty of 14 February 1950, and attached agreements, J. A. S. Grenville, *The Major International Treaties, 1914–1973* (London, 1974), pp. 370–3.
4. For the Bandung Conference, see below, pp. 247–51.
5. Vladislav Zubok and Constantine Pleshakov, *Inside the Kremlin's Cold War* (Cambridge, Mass., 1996), pp. 227–8
6. Quoted in *ibid.*, p. 221.
7. *Keesing's Contemporary Archives*, 1963, p. 19566.
8. Steven M. Goldstein, 'Sino-Soviet Relations', in Robinson and Shambaugh, p. 237.
9. Ian Nish, 'Preparing for Peace and Survival: The Japanese Experience, 1943–46', Liddell Hart Centre for Military Archives, Annual Lecture, 4 November 1996, published by King's College, London, pp. 10–11; see also John Dower, *Japan in War and Peace: Essays on History, Culture and Race* (London, paperback ed., 1996), p.11.
10. Quoted in *ibid.*, p. 155.
11. Grenville, *Major International Treaties, 1914–1973*, p. 287.
12. Quoted in Robert Harvey, *The Undefeated: The Rise, Fall and Rise of Greater Japan* (London, 1994), p. 339.

13. Figures in Akira Iriye, *Japan and the Wider World* (London, 1997), p. 100.
14. Quoted in Richard J. Barnet, *Allies: America, Europe, Japan since the War* (London, 1984), p. 81.
15. Figures in Harvey, *The Undefeated*, pp. 306–8.
16. Treaty of San Francisco, Grenville, *Major International Treaties, 1914–1973*, pp. 283–6.
17. ANZUS Pact, *ibid.*, pp. 337–9.
18. Iriye, *Japan and the Wider World*, pp. 116–17, 132.
19. Nicholas Mansergh, *The Commonwealth Experience*, Vol. II, *From British to Multiracial Commonwealth* (London, 1982), p. 122.
20. Quoted in *ibid.*, p. 117.
21. Quoted in Michael Edwardes, *Nehru: A Political Biography* (London, 1971), p. 206.
22. Estimates of casualties in Lawrence James, *Raj: The Making and Unmaking of British India* (London, 1997), p. 636.
23. R. J. Moore, *Making the New Commonwealth* (Oxford, 1987), p. 47.
24. For the domino theory, see above, pp. 78, 117.
25. Documents resulting from the Geneva Conference, Grenville, *Major International Treaties, 1914–1973*, pp. 454–62. There were in all three armistice agreements, six unilateral declarations and a Final Declaration.
26. Quoted in Henry Kissinger, *Diplomacy* (London, paperback edn, 1993), p. 639.
27. For the Netherlands East Indies during the Second World War, see above, pp. 29–30.

CHAPTER
10

THE NEW AFRICA, 1945–1962

North Africa – The Algerian War, 1954–62 – Africa south of the
Sahara – The rush to independence – The Congo crisis – South Africa
and apartheid – African unity and conflicts

At the beginning of the twentieth century, the continent of Africa was
almost entirely partitioned between European colonial powers; and at the
end of the Second World War this situation remained unchanged. Britain,
France, Portugal, Belgium and Spain (in rough order of the extent of their
colonial possessions) controlled most of Africa. There were only four independent states – Egypt, Ethiopia, Liberia and South Africa; and of these
Egypt was under British influence and in South Africa power lay in the
hands of a minority of European descent.

The Second World War brought great changes. Axis and Allied armies
fought campaigns across North Africa. Southern France was liberated by an
army from Algeria, largely made up of North African troops. American
influence was felt all over North and West Africa. African mineral resources
(gold, copper, uranium) proved vital for the Allied war effort. Africa was
drawn into the mainstream of wartime strategy. Even so, in 1945 the
European colonial powers believed that the war had been no more than an
interlude, after·which the status quo would be restored in all essentials. The
British government which handed over power in India in 1947 was
convinced that independence for its African colonies lay far in the future.
French governments knew that the Empire had played a crucial role during
the Second World War, and believed that their African colonies formed an
essential support for French power and prestige in Europe. The two countries together held a series of conferences (1947–50) to work out how their
combined African possessions could put them economically on a par with
the American and Soviet superpowers. The assumption was that in Africa
the imperial powers had plenty of time. Other parts of the colonial world,
in India or Indo-China, might be in flames, but most of Africa seemed fire-
proof, and far from inflammable materials.

Events were to prove otherwise.

◈ The Maghreb: French North Africa

French North Africa had felt the direct impact of the war. British and American armies had occupied the area, weakening the authority of the French. President Roosevelt in person had gone out of his way to visit the Sultan of Morocco and encourage the cause of independence. The whole territory, Arabic-speaking in language and Islamic in religion, had links with the Arab countries of the Middle East, and was bound to be influenced by nationalist movements in Egypt and Syria.

The area also had its own political structures. Tunisia and Morocco were not strictly speaking French colonies but protectorates. Their rulers (the Bey of Tunis and the Sultan of Morocco) were under French 'protection'; France controlled all foreign and military affairs and French officials conducted most of the internal administration; but the formal existence of the states was preserved. Algeria on the other hand was in French law a part of France itself, organized into three departments and represented in the French National Assembly. There was no Algerian state, even in shadow form. These somewhat technical differences were to have important effects.

In Tunisia, a nationalist movement had been at work for some years. The Neo-Destour (New Constitution) Party had been founded in 1934, with Habib Bourgiba first as its secretary and later its leader. In 1945 Bourgiba published a proposal for complete union between Tunisia and France, with no reservations or distinctions; but he received no response. From 1945 to 1949 he lived in Cairo and other parts of the Middle East, drawing inspiration from Arab progress there. Back in Tunisia, Bourgiba led the Destour in demands for complete independence, and was arrested and deported in February 1952. There followed a period of rioting, martial law imposed by the French, and widespread insurrection. By 1954 the country was in a state of revolt, with nationalist guerrillas operating in the hills and launching terrorist attacks in the cities. The French Premier, Pierre Mendès-France, who decided to end the war in Indo-China, also resolved to escape from the Tunisian conflict. In July 1954 he undertook to grant Tunisia complete internal autonomy, though retaining for France control of defence, foreign policy and foreign trade. By then, this was too late. The Destour demand was for full independence, which the French (by then engaged in a war in Algeria) were in no position to oppose. On 20 March 1956 the French protectorate, which had been established in 1881, was formally brought to an end. Bourgiba became Prime Minister of the newly independent Tunisia. In 1957 he deposed the Bey, declared the country a republic, and became President – a position which he was to hold for life.

In Morocco a nationalist movement took shape, led by the Istiqlal (Independence) Party, founded in 1943, whose manifesto, published in January 1944, made a bid for American support by invoking the Atlantic

Charter of 1941. The Sultan, Sidi Mohammed ben Youssef, threw his influence behind the independence movement in a speech at Tangier in April 1947, thus linking his traditional authority with the modern appeal of Istiqlal. The French put up a serious resistance, using direct repression and also an alliance with El Glaoui, the Pasha of Marrakesh and leader of the Berbers. They put pressure on the Sultan to break with Istiqlal, without success – the Sultan even used a formal speech from the throne in November 1952 to appeal to Moroccan nationalism. In August 1953 the French lost patience and deposed Mohammed ben Youssef, sending him into exile in Madagascar and replacing him by one of his cousins. This move provoked bomb attacks in the cities and sporadic fighting in the countryside. On 20 August 1955, the second anniversary of Mohammed ben Youssef's deposition, there were attacks on French residents in the mining centres, some by Berbers who had previously supported the French. In France, the will to maintain control over Morocco was withering away. Concessions had already been made in Tunisia, and war had begun in Algeria. The French government was neither able nor willing to make the military effort necessary to assert its control in Morocco. Mohammed ben Youssef was recalled from Madagascar to France, and at the château of La Celle-Saint-Cloud signed an agreement (6 November 1955) with the French government, which in effect (though in tortuous language) conceded independence to Morocco. The Sultan returned to his capital, Rabat, and took the new title of King Mohammed V. The French protectorate was formally brought to an end on 2 March 1956, in the same month as that over Tunisia. The final handover of power was smooth; most French residents remained in the country; and the King retained the authority which he had established by his skilful alliance with the nationalists.

◆ The Algerian War

These events in Tunisia and Morocco were bound to have repercussions in Algeria, which lay geographically between the two and whose population was largely Arab and Muslim. Algeria had no framework as a state like that in Tunisia and Morocco. Before the Second World War War the principal Muslim leader, Ferhat Abbas, who was himself assimilated into French culture, sought greater political rights for Muslims under French rule, not separation for a new Algeria. Wartime experience, and the widespread nationalist ferment of the post-war years, transformed the situation. An Algerian soldier who had fought in the French Army and was personally decorated by General de Gaulle with the *médaille militaire*, Ben Bella, turned completely against the French and became the leading spirit in a nationalist organization. In 1954 the nationalists were encouraged by the French defeat in Indo-China, where Algerian troops served at Dien Bien

Phu and witnessed the French surrender at close quarters. (One of the characteristics of the world after 1945 was the speed with which news travelled, and the swift impact of events half a world away.) By the end of 1954 the Algerian nationalist movement had built up its own organization, the National Liberation Front (*Front de Libération Nationale*, shortened to FLN), whose purpose was to pursue an armed revolt until independence was achieved. Concessions from France or other forms of compromise were not on the agenda. The FLN set up a National Army of Liberation (*Armée Nationale de Libération*, ANL) to act as its military force. On 1 November 1954 (All Saints Day and a French public holiday) the FLN launched a co-ordinated rising, which achieved only limited success and little popular support, but which marked the opening of the Algerian War. A proclamation by the FLN, broadcast on Cairo Radio and distributed in pamphlets across Algeria, declared the aim of national independence – 'the struggle will be long but the outcome is certain.'[1]

The French response was in no doubt. Mendès-France, the Radical Party Premier who had brought the war in Indo-China to an end and gone far to meet nationalist demands in Tunisia, declared in the National Assembly on 20 November that 'The Algerian departments are part of the French Republic.' There could be no comparison with Tunisia – '*Ici, c'est la France*'.[2] Jacques Soustelle, a Right-winger and a Gaullist, declared when he took up his appointment as Governor-General in Algiers that France would no more leave Algeria than she would leave Provence or Brittany. François Mitterrand, later to be the socialist President of France under the Fifth Republic, spoke of one France extending from Dunkirk to Tamanrasset. Across the political spectrum the watchword was the same: Algeria was France. The French backed up their words with force. On 1 November 1954 there were 56 000 French troops in Algeria. By January 1955 there were 83 000; at the end of that year 200 000; and in 1956 the total reached 400 000.[3] Conscripts were sent to Algeria, as they had never been to Indo-China, and the length of military service was increased from eighteen months to two and a half years.

In Algeria itself there was a European population of about a million (called *pieds noirs* – French, Spanish and some Italians) out of a total of some nine million. Most were long settled, sometimes for generations; Algeria was their home. The majority were city workers or poor farmers, with no wealth to fall back on if they left the country. Through their representatives in the National Assembly, the *pieds noirs* could obstruct or overthrow any government which veered towards compromise. The European population of Algeria, and their supporters in France and the French Army, became a third force in the struggle. The National Liberation Front, the French government, and the *pieds noirs* fought a triangular war, made even more complicated by divisions within all three sides.

On the ground, the struggle was ferocious, and by no means uneven. The

Army of National Liberation extended its operations across the country, and launched attacks even in the cities. French paratroops fought a fierce battle in Algiers at the end of 1957, which broke the nationalist hold over the Muslim quarters of the city. But the vast areas of mountainous countryside proved impossible to subdue. In August 1956 the National Liberation Front held a conference in the Soummam valley (east of Algiers, in an area supposedly controlled by the French), and set up new forms of organization, with a new political authority and representatives in all areas to build up the framework of a state – even in some cases raising taxes. The nationalists received help from Egypt, Morocco and above all from Tunisia, which provided a route for arms supplies, a safe haven for hard-pressed guerrillas, and a base for the Algerian leaders. The French in their turn attacked Egypt during the Suez War of November 1956 in the hope of cutting off Egyptian help to the rebels; and in February 1958 French aircraft bombed the Tunisian village of Sakiet, near the border with Algeria.

The war thus became an international issue, which the National Liberation Front had wanted from the beginning. The Front sent observers to the Afro-Asian Conference at Bandung in April 1955, where they were warmly welcomed and won wide support. In September 1955 a group of Afro-Asian countries raised the question of the Algerian war at the United Nations, and on 30 September the General Assembly agreed, by a vote of 28–27, with five abstentions, to place the matter on its agenda. From then onwards the subject came up each year for debate, and France was hard pressed to avoid the passage of condemnatory resolutions proposed by the African and Asian states. In December 1957 the Algerian National Liberation Front was accepted at a new Afro-Asian Conference at Cairo on the same footing as other states. In December 1959 the United Nations General Assembly passed, by a vote of 35–18, with 28 abstentions, a resolution recognizing the right of the Algerian people to independence, and declaring that the Algerian situation was a threat to international peace.[4] These votes could not compel a change of French policy, but they exerted considerable influence, particularly because the two superpowers added their weight. Khrushchev granted *de facto* diplomatic recognition to the National Liberation Front in 1960. In 1961 John F. Kennedy, who had supported Algerian independence in the Senate as early as July 1957, took office as President and put pressure on the French to reach a settlement.

This growing international intervention in the Algerian War, from the Third World, the United Nations and the superpowers – all on the Algerian side – gave the National Liberation Front immense moral support, and condemned France to increasing isolation. It was a sign of the new pressures at work in international affairs, marking a complete change from the 1920s and 1930s, when the colonial powers had conducted their policies largely on their own terms.

In these circumstances, the pressure on France to meet Algerian demands grew steadily stronger. The financial and economic burden of the war was great, and the political and moral strains were even greater. The issue of the use of torture by the French forces in Algeria brought a sharp revulsion against the government, especially among the intellectuals who were so important in French political life. The avowed French aim of the integration of Algeria with France, which would be immensely costly and might well result in a Muslim majority in the combined country within the foreseeable future, became steadily less convincing or acceptable. Public opinion in France swung against the war. But the conflict was not simply one between France and the Algerian nationalists. The Europeans in Algeria (the *pieds noirs*) and some of the military leaders there rejected any thought of a compromise peace. In May 1958 there was a rising in Algiers by a combination of officers and *pieds noirs*, and civil war in France itself seemed imminent. The Fourth Republic foundered, and only the return of General de Gaulle, who managed to avoid civil war by appealing to all shades of opinion, preserved the unity of France.

The Algerian War thus brought down, not just a French government, but the whole regime. De Gaulle returned to power, and set about making a new constitution for a Fifth Republic. At much the same time, in September 1958, the National Liberation Front set up a Provisional Government of Algeria, headed by Ferhat Abbas, who had earlier in his life worked within the French system but had joined the FLN in 1956. There were now two new governments, representing France and Algeria respectively; and the Algerian War assumed more and more the character of a conflict between two states, though one of them was an established entity and the other only striving to come into existence.

De Gaulle took the initiative, intending to surrender what was necessary to get France out of the war, and yet save something from defeat. He publicly accepted the principle of self-determination for the Algerian people on 16 September 1959. In November 1960 he declared that there would be an Algerian Algeria, with its own government, institutions and laws. In January 1961 the French government held a referendum on self-determination in both France and Algeria. In France, 75 per cent of those voting accepted self-determination; in Algeria, 69 per cent. (The National Liberation Front had ordered a boycott of the referendum, but only about 40 per cent of registered voters followed this instruction and abstained.) The double referendum thus accepted self-determination, which in effect meant Algerian independence. The way was open for negotiations to begin between the French government and the Provisional Government of Algeria; and secret meetings began in February 1961.

In Algeria, the *pieds noirs* and part of the French army took desperate measures to stop the negotiations. During the night of 21/22 April 1961 four retired generals launched a coup in Algiers. De Gaulle stood firm, and most of the troops in Algeria were not behind the generals; and the coup collapsed after only three days. It was a severe (though not final) blow to the Europeans in Algeria, and cleared the way further for negotiations.

Negotiations between the French and Algerians began at Evian, on Lake Geneva, on 20 May 1961. The French aims were to secure a special status for the European community in an independent Algeria, with reserved political rights and guarantees; and to establish a special regime for the Sahara, which contained reserves of natural gas and also the site of the French atomic testing ground. The Algerians on the contrary insisted on the unity of the whole Algerian people, with no recognition for separate communities, and on the integrity of Algerian territory within its existing borders – including the Sahara. These differences proved unbridgeable, and the negotiations broke down on 28 July 1961.

In August 1961 the National Council of the Algerian Revolution met in Tripoli; replaced Ferhat Abbas as head of the Provisional Government by Ben Khedda, who had a reputation as a hard-liner; and reiterated its determination to continue the struggle for its fundamental aims: independence, unity, and territorial integrity. The French position on the other hand grew steadily weaker. The French authorities in Algeria had largely lost control of the country. The Algerians obeyed the Provisional Government. Most of the Europeans supported (or at any rate obeyed) a newly formed revolutionary body, the Organization of the Secret Army – *Organisation de l'Armée Secrète*, OAS – which aimed to preserve at least something of a French Algeria.

De Gaulle himself despaired of saving anything from the wreck, accepting that the only option was disengagement, or, in plain terms, surrender. On 5 September 1961 he agreed that the Sahara should belong to Algeria. In November he accepted that the National Liberation Front was supported by the majority of the Algerian population. By February 1962 he had dropped any reference to the co-operation of communities in the new Algeria, and thus tacitly abandoned the claim for a special status and institutions for the European population. Secret contacts between the French and Algerians were resumed during the winter of 1961–62; and final negotiations took place at Evian from 7–18 March 1962. The Evian agreements bringing the war to an end were signed on 18 March.

The first step was a cease-fire, to come into effect on 19 March; the Algerian forces were to remain in their existing positions, and the French to avoid contact with them. The fundamental element in the agreement was the French acceptance of Algerian sovereignty, though under a number of conditions. The French residents in Algeria were to be allowed a three-year period in which to choose Algerian nationality, to remain in the country as foreigners, or to leave. If they decided to leave, they were to be free to take with them their goods and capital. France was to station some troops in Algeria for three years; retain the atomic testing site in the Sahara for five years; and keep the naval base at Mers-el-Kébir for fifteen years. Existing concessions to French companies to exploit oil or gas in the Sahara were to be maintained, and French firms would have preference when applying for new concessions. France and Algeria were to grant each other preferential commercial treatment, and Algeria would remain in the currency zone of the French franc.[5]

In France, these terms were overwhelmingly approved in a referendum held on 8 April 1962. In Algeria, the Army of National Liberation ignored the provision that they should stand fast in their positions at the time of the armistice, and occupied most of the country. The Organization of the Secret Army launched a last outburst of violence, which failed to hold off Algerian independence but struck a death-blow to any slender hopes that the French population might remain in Algeria with some degree of safety. The FLN presented the Europeans with a brutal choice between the suitcase and the coffin, and they packed their suitcases – literally, because only two cases per person were allowed by the new authorities. Over a million people crossed the Mediterranean to France.

The independence of Algeria was officially proclaimed on 3 July. The war had lasted seven and a half years. The economic cost to France and Algeria was heavy, though impossible to estimate with any accuracy, because it lay in the disruption of agriculture, industry and trade as much as in direct expenditure or losses. French casualties were comparatively light – official figures put them at 17 456 military dead, and something over 10 000 European civilians killed. French estimates put the total of Muslim dead at 219 000, of whom 141 000 were killed by the French and the rest by the National Liberation Front. After the war, Algerian governments have put the total of war dead at a round figure of a million.[6] The psychological effects of the long and terrible struggle, in which no quarter was given by either side, were probably more grievous and lasting than the casualties and the material damage.

Almost as soon as the war against the French was over, civil war broke out among the Algerian nationalists, involving fighting as severe as anything during the war against the French and costing perhaps another 15 000 lives. Ben Bella, the founder of the National Liberation Front, denounced the Evian agreements as surrender to the French. With the support of a section of the army, led by Colonel Boumédienne, he overthrew Ben Khedda's provisional government and became President in September 1962. The new government proclaimed itself 'revolutionary', and followed a policy of socialism and nationalization. Ben Bella became increasingly authoritarian, killing his rivals and creating his own cult of personality. He remained in power until 1965, when he was in turn overthrown by a military coup led by Boumédienne. The army took over, imposing a severe military dictatorship.

The Algerian War was an outstanding event in the history of decolonization. It reversed a French conquest and occupation going back over a century, to 1830. The presence of over a million Europeans in Algeria meant that it was a war of decolonization of the most extreme kind, ending in the displacement of a large and long-established population, rather than a few settlers or administrators as was the case in most colonial territories. The war demonstrated the influence of the Afro-Asian movement which took shape at Bandung in 1955, and revealed the new balance of power at the United Nations, where the newly independent states came to outnumber the old and imposed a new order of priorities. A great European power was defeated in what it claimed to be its own territory, after committing the greater part of its armed strength to the conflict. It was a famous victory for the Algerians and the new forces of the Third World. Yet at the end the new state fell into internal strife, ending in a military coup. It was an unhappy precedent for much which was to follow in Africa.

◆ Africa south of the Sahara

At the end of the Second World War the European colonial powers expected to retain their control over Africa south of the Sahara well into the future. The constitution of the Fourth Republic in France set up the French Union, granting the African colonies the status of Overseas Territories of the Republic, with representation in the National Assembly. In effect, French authority remained intact. In Britain, the Labour government of 1945–51 was in principle opposed to imperialism but in practice assumed that the African colonies could only attain independence after a long period of systematic preparation. Belgium and Portugal simply assumed that they would continue to rule their African colonies as usual, and made no preparation for anything else. The colonial powers remained prepared to maintain their authority by force when necessary. The French crushed a revolt in Madagascar in 1947 with great severity. The British fought a long campaign against the Mau Mau insurrection in Kenya from 1952 to 1956. At the same time, both France and Britain put a good deal of effort into the economic development of their colonies, and into education and medical services. The colonial administrations continued to work much as usual.

These expectations of continuity were rapidly revised. Between 1957 and 1964, twenty-seven former colonies in Black Africa (see below) attained independence. In 1960 alone sixteen new African states became members of the United Nations Organization.

These remarkable events arose from a combination of circumstances. Pressure from nationalist movements within the colonies increased steadily. A key example was in the Gold Coast (later Ghana), where the nationalist leader Kwame Nkrumah hustled the British out of their policies of gradualism and into a rapid transfer of power. Once set, this example was almost certain to be followed elsewhere, and Nkrumah himself became a magnetic

Year of independence	British	French	Belgian	Other
1957	Ghana			
1958		Guinea		
1960	Nigeria	Cameroon	Congo	Somalia
		Central African Rep.		
		Chad		
		Dahomey		
		Gabon		
		Ivory Coast		
		Madagascar		
		Mali		
		Mauritania		
		Niger		
		Senegal		
		Togo		
		Upper Volta		
1961	Sierra Leone			
	Tanganyika			
1962			Ruanda	
			Burundi	
1963	Kenya			
	Zanzibar			
1964	Malawi			
	Zambia			

Note: In 1964 Zanzibar joined Tanganyika to form Tanzania.

figure throughout Africa. The Cold War too played its part, as the British sought to bring their West African colonies to independence in order to pre-empt Soviet influence. Perhaps above all, the French and British lost the *will* to maintain their African colonies – France was wearied by the Algerian War, and Britain was shaken by the failure of the Suez expedition in 1956. The imperial idea had lost its attraction, and seemed no longer worth sustaining. The British Prime Minister, Harold Macmillan, summed up these sentiments in a speech to the South African Parliament in Cape Town on 3 February 1960: 'The wind of change is blowing through this continent. Whether we like it or not, this growth of national consciousness is a political fact. We must all accept it as a fact.'[7] Only Portugal, the weakest among the colonial powers in material terms, showed that there was nothing inevitable about events by standing out against the wind of change and holding on to its colonies until the 1970s.

The transformation of the British and French colonial territories followed different paths. The British had prepared their principal West

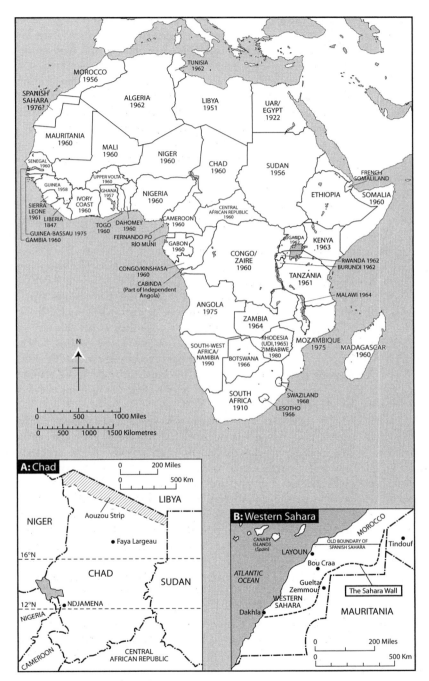

MOROCCO
1956

TUNISIA
1962

SPANISH
SAHARA
1976?

ALGERIA
1962

LIBYA
1951

UAR/
EGYPT
1922

MAURITANIA
1960

MALI
1960

NIGER
1960

CHAD
1960

SUDAN
1956

SENEGAL
1960

GUINEA
1958

UPPER VOLTA
1960

GHANA
1957

NIGERIA
1960

SIERRA
LEONE
1961

IVORY
COAST
1960

LIBERIA
1847

TOGO
1960

DAHOMEY
1960

CAMEROON
1960

CENTRAL
AFRICAN REPUBLIC
1960

ETHIOPIA

SOMALIA
1960

FRENCH
SOMALILAND

GUINEA-BISSAU 1975
GAMBIA 1960

FERNANDO PO
RÍO MUNI

GABON
1960

CONGO/
KINSHASA
1960

CONGO/
ZAIRE
1960

UGANDA
1962

KENYA
1963

RWANDA 1962
BURUNDI 1962

TANZÁNIA
1961

CABINDA
(Part of Independent
Angola)

MALAWI 1964

ANGOLA
1975

ZAMBIA
1964

MOZAMBIQUE
1975

MADAGASCAR
1960

SOUTH-WEST
AFRICA/
NAMIBIA
1990

BOTSWANA
1966

RHODESIA
(UDI,1965)
ZIMBABWE
1980

N

SOUTH
AFRICA
1910

SWAZILAND
1968

LESOTHO
1966

0   500   1000 Miles

0   500   1000   1500 Kilometres

A: Chad

0   200 Miles

0   500 Km

LIBYA

NIGER

Aouzou Strip

Faya Largeau

16°N

CHAD

SUDAN

12°N

NDJAMENA

NIGERIA

CAMEROON

CENTRAL
AFRICAN REPUBLIC

B: Western Sahara

MOROCCO

CANARY
ISLANDS
(Spain)

OLD BOUNDARY OF
SPANISH SAHARA

Tindouf

LAYOUN

Bou Craa

ATLANTIC
OCEAN

Gueltar
Zemmour

The Sahara Wall

WESTERN
SAHARA

Dakhla

MAURITANIA

0   200 Miles

0   500 Km

Africa, showing dates of independence

African colonies for independence by a careful introduction of elected assemblies and responsible government in internal affairs. In 1957 the Gold Coast was the first colony to attain independence, taking the new name of Ghana under the leadership of Kwame Nkrumah. Nigeria, the largest and richest of the West African colonies, followed in 1960, and Sierra Leone in 1961. Each was endowed with a British-style parliamentary system, and Nigeria with a carefully balanced federal constitution. The East African colonies moved more slowly to independence between 1961 and 1963.

Central Africa presented more difficult problems. The British formed the three colonies of Nyasaland, Northern Rhodesia and Southern Rhodesia into the Central African Federation in 1953, but gave up the project in 1963, leaving the colonies to take their separate ways. Nyasaland, where there was almost no British settlement, became independent in 1964 under the name of Malawi and the rule of Hastings Banda, who was to prove one of the most durable of African leaders. Northern Rhodesia, with a European population of about 70 000, also became independent in 1964, taking the name of Zambïa. The situation in Southern Rhodesia was very different. The population of some 3 000 000 in 1960 included a substantial minority of 225 000 Europeans (mostly British) The colony had attained a large degree of autonomy as far back as 1923, and the Europeans controlled the internal politics and the economy of the country. The British government tried to move the colony towards majority African rule, but the white Rhodesians resisted; and in November 1965 the Rhodesian government headed by Ian Smith declared independence unilaterally, opening a crisis which was to last for several years and have international repercussions.

Meanwhile the French African colonies followed a more regular (indeed, more logical) course towards independence. In 1956 the French government introduced a law setting up assemblies in each colony, to be elected by universal suffrage and a single electorate. (Previously there had always been separate representation for Europeans and Africans.) New government councils, responsible to the assemblies, provided internal self-government for each colony. When General de Gaulle came to power in France in 1958, the new constitution of the Fifth Republic set up the French Community, which was intended to maintain the internal autonomy of the colonies while retaining French control over foreign affairs, defence, finance and economic policy. In 1958 de Gaulle offered the African colonies a choice, to be exercised by referendum, between membership of the French Community and complete independence – which would entail the cutting off of all French aid. On 23 September 1958 eleven of the twelve African colonies (including Madagascar) voted for membership of the Community – and to receive continued French aid. Only one, Guinea, led by Sékou Touré, voted for immediate independence.

Yet this success for de Gaulle's policy proved short-lived. It was a sign of the times that the example of independence set by Guinea turned out to be more attractive than the apparently safe and profitable choice made by the majority. There was a telling contrast in the General Assembly of the United Nations, where Guinea was accepted as a full member while the other countries within the French Community were accepted only as observers, forming part of the French delegation. This could not last. As early as 1959 Senegal and the French Sudan (temporarily united as the Federation of Mali) and Madagascar began to negotiate their independence, which they secured in June 1960. All the other former French colonies followed; though all signed treaties with France, and French troops remained stationed in some of the new states.

◆ The Congo crisis

On the whole, this vast transfer of sovereignty from the British and French empires to the new African states was achieved smoothly and in good order. These were days of hope for most of Black Africa. To this general rule the Belgian Congo formed a grievous exception.

The Belgian Congo was a vast territory of about a million square miles (2 350 000 sq km), with a population in 1960 of about 14 000 000, comprising over 200 different peoples and languages. The Belgian administration had a good record in primary education and medical services, but had made no preparations for a transfer of power. There were no African administrators, and the highest rank open to Africans in the *Force publique*, the colonial army, was that of sergeant. In 1956 a committee recommended a move to independence over the next thirty years; but the Belgian government of the day found this timetable too hasty! Events elsewhere in Africa imposed greater speed, but even so when the Belgian government held a conference in Brussels in January 1960 with representatives of Congolese political parties, its intention was to propose independence in four years' time. Before the conference was over, this had come down to six months. The transfer of power was thus attempted at the shortest conceivable notice, and with virtually no preparation.

The independence of the Congo was declared on 30 June 1960, with Joseph Kasavubu as President and Patrice Lumumba as Prime Minister – two men opposed to one another on personal grounds as well as being advocates of different structures for the new state, Kasavubu supporting the dispersal of power and Lumumba centralization. Almost at once the country fell into chaos. As early as 5 July the Congolese troops of the *Force publique* began to mutiny against the Belgian officers who had remained in post. Lumumba appointed a new army commander, General Lundula, and called in Colonel (until recently sergeant) Joseph Mobutu to restore calm in the ranks. But Belgian troops who had remained in bases in the Congo came out (uninvited by the new government) to protect the European population, and parachute troops from Belgium arrived in the capital, Leopoldville. On 11 July the province of Katanga, which with its copper and uranium mines was the richest part of the country, declared its secession and independence under the leadership of Moise Tshombe, a move actively encouraged by the principal mining company, the *Union Minière*. The South Kasai province, another mining area, followed suit and seceded from the Congo on 9 August 1960. The new state was thus breaking up into separate parts, losing its major sources of wealth in the process, and at the same time dissolving into internal disorder.

These events opened a profound and complicated crisis, which at once assumed international dimensions. On 13 July Lumumba appealed to the United Nations against Belgian aggression (because the Belgian troops were acting without Congolese invitation) and to preserve the integrity of the Congo. The Secretary-General of the United Nations, Dag Hammarskjöld, acted with great energy and proposed to the Security Council the formation of a UN force for the Congo. The Security Council authorized the establishment of a United Nations force to maintain law, order and essential services in the Congo, though without specifically mentioning Katanga. The UN was not to become party to any internal conflict, and was to use force only in self-defence – provisions which placed severe limitations on its capacity for action. On 31 July the UN force, made up of contingents from six African countries (Ethiopia, Ghana, Guinea, Liberia, Morocco and Tunisia) and two neutral European states (Ireland and Sweden) began to arrive in the Congo. It reached a total strength of just over 11 000, which was a small number in such a vast country. It did not move against Katanga.

Lumumba then appealed directly to the United States and the Soviet Union for help, and received a quick response from the Soviets, who in September provided transport aircraft to fly 600 Ghanaian troops to Leopoldville to help Lumumba. South Kasai was re-occupied by the Congo, but Katanga remained in secession. Not until 21 February 1961, seven months after the United Nations intervention, were its troops in the Congo formally authorized to use force against Katanga. Even then, the UN representatives on the spot preferred to try diplomatic methods of ending the secession, and Tshombe showed himself adept at gaining time. On 18 September 1961 Hammarskjöld, who was in the Congo in an attempt to resolve the dispute, was killed in an air crash, which deprived the UN actions of the drive and initiative which he had imparted. Finally, in December 1962 United Nations troops and forces of the Congo government moved into Katanga, and Tshombe abandoned his attempt at secession in January 1963. The last United Nations troops left the Congo on 30 June 1964, four years after the force had begun to arrive. They had contributed, though with long delay, to resolving one aspect of the Congo crisis. The break-up of the state by the secession of its richest provinces had been prevented.

Meanwhile,the task of maintaining law and order in a disintegrating country was proving to be a more intractable problem. In August 1960, when the state had been in existence for little more than a month, the President, Kasavubu, tried to dismiss the Prime Minister, Lumumba, who refused to go and in turn asked the Congolese parliament to remove Kasavubu. The new Chief of Staff, Colonel Mobutu, who had built up a base for himself in the army, took advantage of the rivalry to seize power by a coup d'état. Lumumba fled, was captured, and eventually (January 1961) was handed over to his enemies in Katanga, where he was murdered in obscure circumstances. Mobutu broke off diplomatic relations with the Soviet Union and sought help from the United States, receiving clandestine assistance from the CIA. In January 1961 he promoted himself Major-General and assumed command of the army. In February he formally handed power back to President Kasavubu and the civilian authorities; but in practice he retained great influence. In November 1965, after much confusion, Mobutu carried out a second coup d'état, this time installing himself as a military dictator for a supposed trial period of five years. In fact, he remained in power for the next thirty-two years, presiding over the economic collapse of his country (which he renamed Zaire in token of Africanization) and the accumulation of an immense personal fortune.[8]

The international significance of these events was far-reaching: for the United Nations, for the Cold War and for Africa. The United Nations intervened in the crisis largely on the initiative of its Secretary-General, Hammarskjöld, and despatched a substantial force under UN command – a very different situation from that in Korea, where forces flew the UN flag but were under American command. The Charter of the United Nations prohibited intervention in the internal affairs of member states, yet at one time or another the United Nations force in the Congo was engaged in keeping order; helped to bring the secession of Katanga to an end by force; and even on one occasion set up a government by the drastic method of shutting up members of the Congolese parliament together until they produced a set of names for a ministry. A small number of United Nations officials provided a skeleton civil service for the Congo. If this precedent had been followed, the United Nations might have assumed a much more active role in world affairs. In the event, the risks involved in Hammarskjöld's activities (and his death on active service) caused alarm among UN members and in its bureaucracy. Hammarskjöld's successors as Secretary-General were notably more cautious about the use of United Nations forces, and the Organization itself became chary of repeating such drastic intervention in the internal affairs of a member state. United Nations intervention in the Congo thus opened a road which was almost immediately closed again.

At the same time, the Congo crisis brought the Cold War to Africa. In August 1960 the USSR provided aircraft and land transport to help Lumumba; and later the Soviets set up a large Embassy at Leopoldville, full of advisers of various kinds. More important in the long run, the Soviet Union took up the cause of the murdered Lumumba, and elevated him into a left-wing hero and martyr. A Lumumba University was set up in Moscow to educate African students at Soviet expense, and to nurture them in Marxist–Leninist doctrine. The Americans for their part threw their political weight, financial support and the clandestine activity of the CIA behind Mobutu, who claimed to provide a barrier against Soviet influence in the heart of Africa. Other new African states which came into being at the height of the Cold War took to the same game, playing one superpower off against the other to gain prestige and economic advantage. In the short run this brought some striking successes; but in the long run (sometimes not so long) it exacerbated civil strife, diverted effort from serious development, and led to a new form of dependence just as African states were gaining their freedom.

Indeed, for Africa as a whole the Congo set a dismal example of personal rivalries and military coups. The country of Lumumba, Kasavubu and Mobutu became a divided state on the road to disaster. Geographically it lay at the heart of Africa, and it became an example which was all too readily followed.

◆ South Africa and *apartheid*

South Africa had been effectively independent since Britain set up the Union in 1909, and unequivocally so since the Statute of Westminster in 1931. Thus in one sense there was no question of decolonization for South Africa, because it was not a colony. But in fact there was a much deeper and more dangerous question. South Africa maintained a political regime and social system based on white supremacy and racial segregation. The electoral victory of the Afrikaner National Party in 1948 marked a crucial transition from long-standing practice to the systematic imposition of the doctrine of *apartheid* – the separate development of races based on white supremacy. From 1948 onwards, *apartheid* was imposed by legislation which divided the whole population into fixed racial groups, prohibited mixed marriages or sexual relations, allotted specific areas to different races, and provided separate education. Hendrik Verwoerd, who was Prime Minister from 1958 until his assassination in 1966, brought an ardent fervour and a quasi-intellectual rigour to the system.

In different circumstances and at an earlier time, these matters would have been regarded as internal questions for South Africa, of no concern to other countries or to international bodies. Even in the early 1950s, the older members of the Commonwealth (Britain, Australia, Canada, New Zealand) tended to accept the right of South Africa to control its own internal affairs. Even the new members (India and Pakistan) respected this convention by raising the issue of *apartheid* at the United Nations but not at Commonwealth meetings.[9] But this situation was changing rapidly. The concept of universal human rights, adopted by the United Nations in 1948, implied intervention in internal affairs. Moreover, the issue of race was becoming crucial, and the surge of African independence from 1957 onwards meant that it became impossible for a white minority in South Africa to rule over a black majority without challenge from outside.[10]

In these circumstances, South Africa became increasingly isolated. A violent clash at Sharpeville on 21 March 1960, in which the police killed 67 people and wounded 186 during a demonstration against the pass laws, drew condemnation from around the world. South Africa was increasingly criticized even within the Commonwealth, from which the South African government withdrew in 1961, forestalling probable expulsion. At the United Nations, African and Asian countries pursued a campaign of condemnation, supported by the eastern bloc and some western states. In South Africa itself, the African National Congress and its military wing, The Spear of the Nation, became increasingly active, using the shelter of neighbouring African countries.

For a long time this hostility had little direct effect. South Africa produced immense quantities of minerals which were in heavy demand abroad – gold, diamonds, manganese, copper and uranium. Manufacturing industry developed rapidly. With a good deal of investment from Britain and the United States, the South African economy flourished in the 1960s, attracting workers from neighbouring countries despite the conditions imposed under *apartheid*. The South Africans manufactured their own armaments and imported others, maintaining the strongest armed forces on the continent. Strategically, South Africa was the beneficiary of the Cold War and the Suez crisis of 1956, which enhanced the importance of the route round the Cape of Good Hope from the Indian Ocean to the Atlantic. The United States and western European countries wanted to keep the Cape in safe hands; and even *apartheid* South Africa was thought safer than its likely successor.

South Africa came increasingly to resemble a fortress under siege, but the garrison was well supplied, resolute, and not entirely without outside support. The result was a constant international problem, involving states across the world, and generating an intense emotional charge which in the modern world attaches to racial questions more than anything else. In the early 1960s this problem was still in its early stages; its full significance was to appear in the 1970s and 1980s.

◈ The New Africa: African unity and conflicts

The new Africa which took shape in the late 1950s and early 1960s aspired to some form of political unity which would demonstrate African identity and give the continent its distinctive place in the world.

This began at once, with the first appearance of independent Black African states. As soon as Ghana achieved independence in 1957 Kwame Nkrumah took the lead in promoting pan-African unity. In consultation with President Bourguiba of Tunisia, he invited nine independent African states to a conference at Accra. Remarkably, South Africa was among the nine, demonstrating that at that stage, despite nine years of *apartheid*, the South African government was not yet an outcast. In the event the South Africans made their acceptance conditional on the presence of European states with an interest in Africa; a condition which, doubtless foreseeably, proved unacceptable. Delegates of eight countries therefore gathered at Accra from 15 to 22 April 1958 – three from Black Africa (Ghana, Ethiopia and Liberia) and five Arab states (Libya, Morocco, the Sudan, Tunisia and the United Arab Republic of Egypt and Syria). The Algerian National Liberation Front and the Union of Cameroon Peoples attended in an unofficial capacity. The conference denounced colonialism in general and French rule in Algeria in particular. The delegates agreed that all colonial domination in Africa must be ended, though they were willing to contemplate some sort of timetable for the process, on condition that the United Nations Organization and the independent African states were involved as well as the colonial powers. 'Africa for the Africans' was the watchword of the conference, and there was talk of a 'Monroe Doctrine for Africa' to protect the continent from outside intervention. The conference affirmed the principle of economic co-operation; proclaimed the importance of an African identity in cultural affairs; and aspired towards co-operation in education. The delegates agreed to form an African sub-group within the Afro-Asian group already operating at the United Nations. Alongside this emphasis on African unity, the conference also passed a strongly-worded resolution affirming the sovereignty and territorial integrity of all African countries. Newly-gained independence was not to be compromised, and there was already a striking determination to maintain the frontiers which had been imposed on the continent by the colonial powers. The new African states sought unity, but not at the expense of their independence or their territory.

Other meetings followed. An All-African Peoples' Conference at Accra in December 1958 brought together delegations from all kinds of non-governmental bodies (political parties, trade unions, student organizations, associations of intellectuals), aspiring to the liberation of Africa and affirming African solidarity. A Pan-African Peoples' Congress met at Tunis in January 1960, switching the focus to the dangers of neo-colonialism, on the grounds that the imperial powers had granted political independence only to re-introduce economic subordination. Delegates were particularly critical of the terms being discussed at that time for the affiliation of African countries to the recently-formed European Economic Community.

In this way the impulse towards Pan-Africanism was maintained; but at much the same time African states began to form smaller groups, in rivalry with one another. The former British colonies nearly all joined the Commonwealth. (Sudan and British Somaliland were exceptions.) In December 1960 all the former French colonies except Togo, Mali and Guinea formed the Brazzaville Group, working in co-operation with France. In 1961 this group changed its name to the *Union Africaine et Malgache*, and it was later joined by the former Belgian Congo (Congo-Kinshasa, later Zaire). The new African states thus divided along lines of language and the old split between British and French colonies, each with links to the former imperial power. There was also a profound division between the Arab and Muslim countries of North Africa and the mainly Christian states of Black Africa. Nkrumah liked to claim that this was an artificial division, encouraged by the imperialists, and that the Sahara would become a bridge uniting the two parts of Africa; but both geography and history were against him.

Despite these problems, in May 1963 the Emperor Haile Selassie of Ethiopia used his personal prestige and his country's standing as the oldest African independent state to convene a conference attended by thirty independent African states, to set up the Organization of African Unity. The Organization's aims were set out in its charter: to promote the unity and solidarity of the African states; to collaborate in achieving a better life for the African peoples; to defend the sovereignty, territorial integrity and independence of African countries; to eradicate all forms of colonialism from Africa; and to promote international co-operation. These aims were supplemented by a set of principles: the sovereign equality of all member states; non-interference in the internal affairs of states; respect for the sovereignty and territorial integrity of each state; peaceful settlement of disputes; condemnation of political assassination and subversive activities in another state; dedication to the total emancipation of African territories which were still dependent; and non-alignment with regard to all blocs. The Organization was to comprise an Assembly of Heads of State and of Governments, meeting at least once a year; a Council of Ministers to meet at least twice a year; and a Secretariat headed by a Secretary-General. Five specialized commissions were to deal with economic and social questions; education and cultural affairs; health, sanitation and nutrition; defence; and science, technology and research. A Commission of Mediation, Conciliation and Arbitration was to deal with disputes between member states, according to carefully drafted rules. Mediation and arbitration required the consent of all parties to a dispute; conciliation could be initiated by one party, but could only be concluded with the agreement of all the parties. There were no provisions for the enforcement of recommendations made by the Commission, so everything depended on negotiation and agreement.

The founder members of the Organization of African Unity were:[11]

Algeria	Ghana	Nigeria
Benin	Guinea	Rwanda
Burkina Faso	Ivory Coast	Senegal
Burundi	Liberia	Sierra Leone
Cameroon	Libya	Somalia
Central African Republic	Madagascar	Sudan
Chad	Mali	Tanzania
Egypt	Mauritania	Togo
Ethiopia	Morocco	Tunisia
Gabon	Niger	Uganda

The aspirations of this new organization were high, and its structures carefully established. Yet it laid as much emphasis on respect for the sovereignty and territorial integrity of member states as on co-operation between them. The Organization itself reinforced this point in July 1964 by declaring specifically that all member states 'pledge themselves to respect the frontiers existing on their achievement of national independence'.[12] This provision, and the commendable but unusual condemnation of political assassination in the original charter, displayed the nervousness of African states about the fragility of their borders and the possible activities of their neighbours.

There was in fact almost inevitably a contrast between the high ideals and aspirations towards solidarity expressed by the Organization of African Unity and the conflicts which actually arose, both between the new states and within them.

The boundaries drawn by the European powers in Africa were often arbitrary – in extreme cases they were merely straight lines drawn on the map with scant regard for the terrain or its inhabitants. The resulting colonial territories, which later became states, often contained widely different peoples, sometimes hostile to one another. There was therefore every likelihood of frontier disputes between the new states, and of conflicts within them.

Morocco opened frontier disputes with its neighbours as soon as it achieved independence from France in 1956, reviving claims (said to go back 400 years) to the Spanish Sahara, Mauritania and parts of Algeria. In 1957 the Moroccans attempted an invasion of the Spanish Sahara, without success; and in 1963 they attacked the Tindouf region of Algeria, only to be driven back. Some of these claims were later continued in the long dispute over the Western Sahara which persisted through the 1970s and

1980s.[13] When Somalia attained independence in 1960 it laid claim to 'lost territories' in the northern part of Kenya and the Ogaden province of Ethiopia. In March 1963 the Somalis began fighting on the border with Kenya, continuing sporadically until 1967. In February 1964, Somali forces advanced into the Ogaden to enforce their claims there. The Organization of African Unity intervened, and President Abboud of Sudan arranged a cease-fire (30 March 1964) based on the existing frontier. However, the Somalis did not give up their claim, and the conflict later resumed.

As for divisions within countries, Chad, in central Africa, presented a classic case. The population in the north part was Arab, Muslim and largely nomadic; that in the south was black, Christian or animist in religion, and lived mainly by agriculture. The two parts, each with roughly half the total population of 4 500 000, had little in common except the heritage of a French colony. The presence of French troops helped to keep the country together for some years; but when the French garrisons left the north, the National Liberation Front (FROLINAT: *Front de Libération Nationale*) began an insurrection which opened a long, though sporadic, civil war.[14] To the east of Chad, the Sudan (the former Anglo-Egyptian Sudan) was similarly divided between an Arab and Muslim north, which controlled the government in Khartoum, and a black population in the south, mainly Christian or animist. A guerrilla war for secession began in the south in 1963 and continued more or less permanently. Further east again, in the Horn of Africa, Eritrea, a former Italian colony, was incorporated into Ethiopia in 1962; but the Eritrean Liberation Front began a war of secession as early as 1963, and continued the fight with great tenacity.

At the beginning of the 1960s these were only the first stirrings of frontier disputes and claims to secession; others, of greater seriousness, were to follow.

In the years between 1945 and the early 1960s events in Africa moved at remarkable speed, often leaving an impression of confusion. But three great events stand out, with crucial long-term effects on world affairs and international relations. First, the Algerian War of 1954–62 was a momentous war of national liberation. France, formerly a great colonial power, was defeated on what it claimed to be its own home territory. About a million Europeans, many of whose families had been settled in Algeria for generations, were driven out – decolonization in the most emphatic sense of the term. The Algerian independence movement won its struggle by political as much as military means, securing help from other Arab countries and using the leverage provided by the United Nations – a new and unforeseen use for that organization. The second event concerned the United Nations Organization itself, which was transformed by the flood of African states achieving independence. By the end of 1962 no fewer than 33 African states were members of the United Nations. With this change of membership, the United Nations assumed a very different character and role from those fore-seen by its founders in 1945. Thirdly, *apartheid* in South Africa became a new and persistent focus of conflict in Africa, in the United Nations and in the Commonwealth. In all these ways, Africa, which in 1945 had seemed to be on the margins of world affairs, had proved by 1962 to be at the centre of decisive events.

◆ Notes to Chapter 10

1. Quoted in Alistair Horne, *A Savage War of Peace: Algeria 1954–1962* (London, paperback edn, 1987), pp. 94–5.
2. *Ibid.*, p. 98.
3. Figures in Denise Bouche, *Histoire de la Colonisation Française*, Vol. II (Paris, 1991), p. 477.
4. *Keesing's Contemporary Archives*, 1959, p. 16676.
5. See the summary of the Evian agreements in Horne, *Savage War of Peace*, pp. 520–1.
6. *Ibid.*, p. 538. Horne observes that the monthly French military casual-ties, for most months of the war, were fewer than those killed on the roads in France.
7. J. D. B. Miller, *Survey of Commonwealth Affairs: Problems of Expansion and Attrition, 1953–1969* (Oxford, 1974), p. 112.
8. According to the obituary notice on Mobutu in *The Times*, 9 September 1997, the country's per capita income fell by 60 per cent in thirty-two years. *Le Monde*, 9 September 1997, records that Mobutu himself claimed to hold eight milliard dollars in a Swiss bank account.
9. Miller, *Survey*, p. 26.
10. Population of South Africa (in millions):

	1951	1970
Blacks	8.6	15.1
Whites	2.6	3.8
Coloureds	1.1	2.0
Asian	0.4	0.8
Total	*12.7*	*21.5*

(Source: J. A. S. Grenville, *History of the World in the Twentieth Century* (revised edn, London, 1998), p. 781.)

11. Chris Cook, ed., *World Political Almanac* (3rd. edn, London, 1995), pp. 22–3.

12. Quoted in J. A. S. Grenville, *The Major International Treaties, 1914–1973* (London, 1974), p. 483.
13. For the Western Sahara and the Polisario guerrilla war, see below, pp. 458–60.
14. For Chad, see below, pp. 451–3.

CHAPTER 11

THE BANDUNG CONFERENCE, 1955: THE AFRO–ASIAN MOVEMENT AND NON-ALIGNMENT

Origins of the Afro-Asian Movement – The Bandung Conference – Its significance and consequences – The Non-Aligned Movement – The moral high ground

The dissolution of the western empires in the Middle East, Asia and Africa brought into being a large number of newly independent states, stretching half-way across the globe from Morocco to Indonesia, and varying enormously in population, size, economy and culture. In Asia these new states took their place alongside long-established countries which had never lost their independence – Japan, China, Thailand, Afghanistan, Iran, Turkey. All these states had their own interests, and were often in conflict with one another. Yet in spite of their diversity and frequent conflicts, a movement towards some sort of unity between the states of Asia and Africa soon sprang up, and maintained its impetus with remarkable persistence, adding a new and dynamic element to international relations. In this movement, the Afro-Asian Conference held at Bandung in Indonesia in April 1955 played a crucial part, shaping a Third World identity which was to have profound effects on world politics.

This striking and in many ways surprising development had distant origins. As early as 1927 a Congress of Oppressed Peoples had been held at Brussels, financed by the governments of China (then under the Kuomintang) and Mexico, encouraged by the Soviet Union, and attended by a number of left-wing European intellectuals. Those present included a Vietnamese, Nguyen-Ai-Quoc, later known as Ho Chi Minh, and Jawaharlal Nehru, who was to become the first Prime Minister of India.

Nehru never lost this early interest in promoting a widespread anti-colonial movement. In March 1947, even amid all the turmoil of the move to Indian independence and partition, Nehru held an Asian Relations Conference in New Delhi, attended by over 250 delegates from twenty-five Asian countries, who agreed to set up an Asiatic Relations Organization.

This did not actually materialize; but Nehru had signalled his intention of taking the lead in Asian international relations.

In the early 1950s an Arab–Asian group was formed at the United Nations, made up of twelve countries: Afghanistan, Burma, Egypt, India, Indonesia, Iran, Iraq, Lebanon, Pakistan, Saudi Arabia, Syria and the Yemen. Later, Ethiopia and Liberia joined the group, which began to be called Afro-Asian. Its main activities were directed against France in Indo-China and later in Algeria. The war in Indo-China was naturally a major concern for the states of southern Asia, and in April 1954 the heads of government of Ceylon, Burma, India, Indonesia and Pakistan met at Colombo to try to bring the war to an end. In the course of their discussions, the Prime Minister of Indonesia, Ali Sastroamijojo, proposed the idea of a large-scale Afro-Asian conference, with a wide-ranging agenda; and Indonesia was charged with the preparation of such a conference. This was partly a move in Indonesian domestic politics, where the government was in need of a spectacular success; but its aims were much wider than that. In particular Nehru, the Indian Prime Minister, had far-reaching hopes that the Afro-Asian countries could establish a new influence in world affairs.

◆ The Bandung Conference

In December 1954 the five Colombo states (Burma, Ceylon, India, Indonesia and Pakistan) held a meeting at Bogor, in Indonesia, to prepare for the great Afro-Asian conference. Their first problem was simple in form but complicated in substance: who should be invited? In particular, should they invite the Soviet Union, whose territory stretched far into Asia, and perhaps even its individual Asian Republics, which undoubtedly fell within the Asian continent. The Soviets angled hard for an invitation; but Nehru took the lead in excluding them, while making sure that communist China was invited. Other questions arose about invitations for countries which were not yet independent. The organizers agreed to invite the Gold Coast (later Ghana), the Sudan, and the Central African Federation – the last being an unexpected choice, because the Federation was dominated by European minorities, and was vociferously opposed by African nationalists. (In the event, the government of the Federation declined the invitation, anticipating a hostile reception if it attended.) Representatives of a number of liberation movements were also invited as observers.

Finally, representatives of twenty-nine states or aspiring states gathered at Bandung from 18 to 24 April 1955. They varied enormously in almost every respect. China had a population of about six hundred million, Liberia about one million. Japan was the home of an advanced and flourishing industrial economy; Nepal practised the simplest forms of agriculture and forestry. Indonesia, Iran, Iraq and Saudi Arabia were important oil producers; Sudan had almost no natural resources at all. Forms of government included parliamentary democracies, monarchies with varying degrees of power, assorted military and authoritarian regimes, and communist dictatorships. China was the vanguard of an ardent style of revolutionary communism; Japan combined capitalism with a deeply conservative society. In foreign policy, about half the Bandung states were non-aligned or neutralist, and the other half were allies of the superpowers or closely linked to them (see the list below).[1] Some of those attending were open enemies – India and Pakistan, North and South Vietnam.

States attending

Independent states Afghanistan, Burma, Cambodia, Ceylon, China, Egypt, Ethiopia, India, Indonesia, Iran, Iraq, Japan, Jordan, Laos, Lebanon, Liberia, Libya, Nepal, Pakistan, Philippines, Saudi Arabia, Sudan, Syria, Thailand, Turkey, Vietnam (North and South), Yemen

Countries not yet independent Gold Coast (later Ghana)

Observers from Algeria (National Liberation Front), Morocco, Tunisia, Cyprus, Grand Mufti of Jerusalem (Palestine)

Foreign policy status of states (aligned or non-aligned)

Allies of the USA Turkey (NATO), Pakistan (SEATO), Philippines (SEATO), Thailand (SEATO), Japan, South Vietnam

Linked to USA Iran, Saudi Arabia

Allies of Britain Iraq (Baghdad Pact), Turkey (Baghdad Pact), Jordan, Libya

Ally of USSR China

Linked to China North Vietnam

Non-aligned Afghanistan, Burma, Cambodia, Ceylon, Egypt, Ethiopia, India, Indonesia, Laos, Lebanon, Liberia, Nepal, Syria, Yemen. (Note: Ceylon was strongly pro-western, though not strictly an ally of Britain or the USA; Egypt was developing links with the USSR.)

Total number of states in alliances or alignments: 13

Total non-aligned states: 14

The objectives which this heterogeneous group of states gathered to pursue were set out by the five originators of the conference (Burma, Ceylon, India, Indonesia and Pakistan) during their meeting at Bogor in December 1954, as follows. (1) To encourage goodwill and understanding between the nations of Asia and Africa, and to promote their common interests. (2) To examine the social, economic and cultural relations between the states represented at the conferences. (3) To examine problems of particular concern to the peoples of Asia and Africa: national sovereignty, racism and colonialism. (4) To consider the position of Asia and Africa in the world, and how they could contribute to the establishment of peace and international co-operation.

These objectives were general to the point of vagueness, but were no less real or important for that. On the first two issues, the crucial point was that the existing lines of economic and cultural relations, especially for the educated and prosperous elites, often ran between former colonies and the imperial powers – for example, between the Indian sub-continent and Britain. Ties of language, education and culture linked Asian and African elites to Europe more strongly than to neighbours which were geographically closer. The working language of the Bandung conference itself was English – the Asians and Africans could only communicate by means of a European tongue. They therefore sought to create a new network of contacts to promote an Afro-Asian identity, though this proved much easier said than done. The third point – national sovereignty, racism and colonialism – represented the greatest common interest and the most acute point of concern. The new states represented at Bandung were particularly sensitive about their sovereignty, and even the long-established countries (such as China, Thailand or Iran) had recently suffered encroachments on their independence which made them all the more determined to reassert it. The strongest bond between the vastly different countries represented at Bandung was anti-colonialism, and an opposition to racial discrimination which found expression in a sort of racism in reverse. In his opening speech to the conference, President Sukarno of Indonesia deliberately emphasized this issue: 'This is the first inter-continental conference of coloured peoples in the history of mankind.'[2] The fourth and final point represented the conference's greatest hope: to establish a distinct and powerful influence on the affairs of the world, developing the start which had already been made by the Afro-Asian group at the United Nations.

The conference itself was a massive gathering, thriving on oratory and on an active social life. Its chairman was President Sukarno of Indonesia, whose opening speech struck a confident and uplifiting note: 'We, the people of Asia and Africa . . . far more than half the human population of the world, we can mobilize what I have called the *Moral Violence of Nations* in favour of peace.'[3] The other two outstanding figures were Nehru, the Prime Minister of India, and Zhou Enlai, Prime Minister and Foreign Minister of China. Nehru used the conference to persuade Zhou Enlai to commit himself once more to *panchsheel* (the five principles of co-existence): mutual respect between states for their sovereignty and territorial integrity; non-aggression; non-intervention in the internal affairs of other states; equality in status between states; and peaceful co-existence.[4] These principles had previously been set out in the Indian-Chinese commercial treaty of April 1954, and were now repeated in the far wider context of the Afro-Asian conference, which Nehru regarded as a great success. Nehru also sought to urge on the other Afro-Asian leaders his own vague concept of neutralism, and above all to use the conference as the starting-point of a great movement to restore the former colonial peoples to their true place in the world.

Zhou Enlai for his part sought primarily to be reassuring. He explained that China, though communist, was perfectly willing to co-operate with bourgeois nationalists in other countries. He undertook that his government would give no encouragement to subversive activities among the Chinese minorities in South-East Asia. He was generous with assurances that China was willing to condemn all aggression, and ready to settle frontier questions with her southern neighbours peacefully. He mounted a thoroughgoing public relations bid for the leadership of Afro-Asian states; and his 'charm offensive' scored a marked success.

After labouring for seven days the conference achieved a unanimous (though sometimes vague) set of conclusions. The conference called for the establishment of a special United Nations fund for economic development, and urged the World Bank to allocate an increased proportion of its resources to Africa and Asia. It requested the United Nations to ensure stability in commodity prices, to help those countries which were at the mercy of fluctuations in the prices of minerals and foodstuffs. It recommended the establishment of a common policy on the production and sale of oil. These proposals contained the seeds of two important future developments: the claim for a redistribution of resources for the benefit of poorer countries, through the intervention of the United Nations and the World Bank; and the emergence of a common front among oil producers. In practice, when the Organization of Petroleum Exporting Countries (OPEC) was established it produced results far different from anything envisaged at Bandung. The oil producers wanted higher prices, with disastrous effects on many African and Asian countries.[5]

On cultural matters, the conference deplored the ignorance of their own cultural inheritance imposed on Asian and African countries by centuries of foreign domination, and called for the establishment of cultural and educational exchanges between the Bandung countries; though saying little as to how they were to be arranged and paid for. The conference also expressed strong support for human rights and national self-determination. It was the positive duty of all countries which had attained liberation to assist those who were still struggling for it – Morocco, Tunisia, Algeria, Aden, South Yemen, Irian (New Guinea) and the Arab population of Palestine were singled out for particular mention.

This brought the conference to the general question of colonialism and the problems of colonial peoples, which raised a knotty point of definition. What was a colony, and which were the colonial peoples? The Prime Minister of Ceylon, Sir John Kotelawala, argued that the conference should condemn *all* forms of colonialism, specifically including Soviet domination over the countries of eastern Europe; and he gained much support. On 22 April a group of countries made up of Ceylon, Iran, Iraq, Japan, Lebanon, Liberia, Libya, Pakistan, the Philippines, Sudan and Turkey put down a draft resolution condemning all types of colonialism, *and* those international doctrines which adopted the methods of force, infiltration and subversion. This was opposed by China, and also by Nehru, who was anxious to co-operate with the Chinese and did not wish to cause further offence to the Soviet Union, which he had helped to exclude from the conference in the first place. Nehru devised a definition of colonialism which excluded any member of the United Nations from being termed a colony. The result of this was that, since the countries of eastern Europe were all members of the UN, they could not by definition be victims of colonialism. Eventually the conference evaded the issue by adopting a resolution which simply condemned colonialism without attempting to define what it was. In a curious way, this issue produced the most forthright disagreements of the conference, while ending in an evasive conclusion.

The Political Committee of the conference debated the question of Israel and the rights of the Palestinian people, passing a resolution declaring the conference's support for 'the rights of the Arab people of Palestine', and calling for the implementation of United Nations resolutions on Palestine – though without specifying which.[6] In the debate, Nehru condemned Zionism as an aggressive movement, but appealed for understanding of the motives which lay behind it. In general, however, the debate showed the hostility of Afro-Asian governments towards Israel, which was regarded as a new sort of colony created by western imperialism in Asian territory.

Finally the conference set out no fewer than ten principles of co-existence – an improvement, or at any rate an increase, on the original *panchsheel*, which only had five. These ten principles included respect for the sovereignty and territorial integrity of all nations; recognition of the equality of all races and all nations; non-intervention in the internal affairs of other countries; respect for the right of self-defence, individually and collectively; and refusal to join collective defence agreements designed to serve the particular interests of any great power. These last two fitted together only awkwardly, if at all. Turkey, Pakistan and the Philippines voted for the resolution despite being members of the North Atlantic and South-East Asian Treaty Organizations; China voted for it while maintaining its alliance with the Soviet Union. It was just possible for the governments concerned to argue that the alliance in question did not serve the *particular* interests of either the United States or the Soviet Union; but this carried little conviction, and the contradiction between these two principles undermined confidence in the others – like the thirteenth stroke of a clock, which casts doubt on all its predecessors.

◆ The significance and consequences of Bandung

The participants in the Bandung Conference spoke much of Afro-Asian solidarity; but in fact solidarity was sadly lacking, and the divisions between the participants were painfully obvious. Economically, the Bandung states were far too diverse to find interests common to all. Japan, Afghanistan and Liberia, to take three disparate cases, had simply no point of contact. Even when countries could be classified together as primary producers, there was a vast difference between producing oil (Saudi Arabia) and producing jute (East Pakistan). On the foreign policy question of alliances *versus* non-alignment or neutralism, thirteen of the Bandung states had alliances or close ties to one or other of the superpowers, and fourteen did not – giving the benefit of the doubt to Egypt, which was already developing links with the Soviet Union. (See the table on page 248.) The idea of an Afro-Asian cultural identity, or even similarity, was far-fetched.

In view of all these difficulties and divisions, it is remarkable that the Bandung Conference produced any lasting results at all; and yet it did. The Afro-Asian idea was taken up at a vast conference at Cairo (26 December 1957–1 January 1958). The inspiration was the same as at Bandung, but the make-up of the conference was very different. The delegates (some 500 from 46 states or aspiring states) represented not governments but groups and organizations – trade unions, associations of teachers and students, business corporations, as well as some parliamentary representatives and government officials. This time the Soviet Union was represented, sending a delegation drawn mainly from the Central Asian Republics, headed by the President of the Republic of Uzbekistan. Japan sent one of the largest delegations, headed by a businessman and a member of the Japanese parliament, on the look-out for commercial opportunities. The resulting gathering was strongly anti-colonialist, proclaiming the right of self-determination and demanding immediate independence for remaining African colonies, the restoration of Okinawa (still occupied by the Americans) to Japan, and of West Irian to Indonesia. French, British and American imperialism was freely denounced; Soviet imperialism went unremarked. The European Economic Community, just being formed after the signature of the Treaty of Rome in 1957, was condemned as a new form of colonialism. The views expressed at the conference were thus strongly anti-colonial, but by no means non-aligned. The Egyptians (who were the hosts) instilled a positive note by proposing the establishment of an exclusively Afro-Asian Common Market, though without explaining how such disparate economies were to be brought together. The conference ended by setting up a permanent Council of Afro-Asian Peoples, with a secretariat based in Cairo, a newspaper, and the use of two hours daily for broadcasts on Cairo Radio.

An attempt was made to work out the means of economic co-operation at an Afro-Asian economic conference in Cairo in December 1958, again made up of representatives of organizations, not governments, and again including Soviet delegates. The conference recommended the establishment of an Afro-Asian Organization for Economic Co-operation, and the formation of associations among producers of particular commodities – for example, rubber, tin, cotton and tea. A committee met in Bandung in May 1959 to elaborate these proposals; but ran into trouble by deciding to exclude the Soviet Union from the proposed Organization. A further conference on Afro-Asian economic solidarity met in Cairo (30 April–3 May 1960), adopting the compromise of inviting the Soviet Asian Republics but not the Soviet Union itself. No progress was made with the ambitious proposals for economic co-operation, which were in fact impossible of achievement among countries of such different economic levels, needs and forms of organization. This aspect of the Bandung movement thus ran into the sand.

Yet, like a river which goes underground only to reappear, the currents which started at Bandung came to the surface again in various forms, notably in the movement of non-aligned states. At Bandung the concept of non-alignment was only one idea among many, and less important than anti-colonialism or the solidarity of coloured peoples. It later developed a momentum of its own, starting with a strange meeting (18–20 July 1956) at Brioni, an island off the coast of Yugoslavia, between Tito, Nasser and Nehru. They were an ill-matched trio. Tito, the host, was a tough communist dictator and former partisan leader, who had successfully broken with Stalin without joining the western camp, and was looking for another foothold in international affairs. Nasser was a new type of Middle East army officer in politics, recently established as ruler of Egypt and aspiring to become the leader of Arab nationalism. Nehru was a wealthy patrician, a genuine idealist but also an actor constantly in search of a new role on the world stage. Nasser and Nehru had met and impressed one another at Bandung, but Tito's position as host and the site of the meeting in Europe added a different dimension to the meeting. The three together recalled the ten Bandung resolutions; deplored the division of the world into hostile camps; and proclaimed their intention of creating a non-aligned group of states which would form a zone of peace in a troubled world.[7]

It was four years before this initiative produced results, at a conference in Cairo (5–18 June 1960), at which twenty states met to prepare for a full-scale gathering of non-aligned countries. The Cairo conference set out five criteria for non-alignment, which were important as a declaration of principle, though in practice they were often disregarded. (1) States were to follow an independent policy based on peaceful co-existence and non-alignment, or at least be favourable to such a policy – a statement vague enough to include almost anyone. (2) They were to support all movements for national liberation – which maintained continuity with Bandung and with the anti-colonial struggle. (3) They were not to belong to any collective military alliance in the framework of conflicts between the great powers. (4) They were not to conclude any bilateral alliance with a great power. (5) They were not to accept, of their own free will, the establishment on their territory of military bases belonging to a foreign power. These were precise criteria, and were frequently disregarded, as the later history of the movement was to show.

The first Summit Conference of Non-Aligned States met at Belgrade, 1–16 September 1961. Twenty-five states attended:[8]

Afghanistan	Ghana	Saudi Arabia
Algeria	Guinea	Somalia
Burma	India	Sudan
Cambodia	Indonesia	Tunisia
Ceylon	Iraq	United Arab Republic
Congo/Zaire	Lebanon	(Egypt-Syria)
Cuba	Mali	Yemen
Cyprus	Morocco	Yugoslavia
Ethiopia	Nepal	

Bolivia, Brazil and Ecuador were present as observers.

This membership showed that the Cairo principles were applied with a good deal of flexibility. Cuba and Egypt were in close alliance with the Soviet Union. Saudi Arabia was linked to the United States. Cyprus provided military bases for Britain – though technically they were not under Cypriot sovereignty. The conference tried to establish its role in world affairs, giving priority to resolving the superpower conflict between the USA and the USSR and to the problems of colonialism and economic development – the idea of a North-South divide between developed and underdeveloped countries was already present, though the nomenclature had yet to be invented. The conference also discussed whether non-alignment should be a regional movement, following the Afro-Asian pattern laid down at Bandung, or should aim to be worldwide in membership. The very fact of meeting in Belgrade, and the presence of Latin American states, even though mainly as observers, meant that this question had already been answered. The movement was no longer Afro-Asian, but involved states from four continents.

The conference produced lofty resolutions. It was in favour of peace and disarmament; condemned colonialism and racism; and wished to play a role in the settlement of international problems. The participants prepared two identical letters to Kennedy and Khrushchev, warning them of the dangers of nuclear war and urging them to open an East–West dialogue. President Sukarno of Indonesia travelled to Washington, and Nehru and Nkrumah, the President of Ghana, to Moscow, to deliver these letters in person. They were politely received in both capitals, even though Kennedy and Khrushchev might each have pointed out that they were well aware of the perils of nuclear war and were already in contact with one another.

This was highly significant. At Belgrade, the non-aligned states had claimed the moral high ground in world affairs, affirming their impartiality as between the superpowers, and between capitalism and communism; and their claim was tacitly accepted by the Soviet and American leaders. On the issue of colonialism and under-development, the conference went even further, and professed to represent the conscience of the world. There was a great gulf between these lofty claims and the political facts of alignments with the superpowers, and the sometimes questionable demands for economic and financial aid (much of which found its way into the pockets of African and Asian politicians). But at least to some degree the governments and peoples of the superpowers, and the former colonial countries of western Europe, took the non-aligned movement at its own valuation. In the nineteenth century the Europeans had assumed without question that they held the moral high ground, and that they had the right to take their civilization to the rest of the world. By the middle of the twentieth century this position had been largely reversed. The moral claims were made by the Third World, and western Europe and the United States were plagued by guilt. The results of this situation were seen later in the Brandt Commission on the North–South divide, which published its report on development in 1980.[9]

A new element thus appeared in international affairs, and was to show remarkable staying power. In the twenty-one years following the Belgrade Conference in 1964, a further ten conferences of non-aligned countries took place – four in Africa, three in Asia, two in Latin America and one in Europe (Belgrade again, in 1989). The number of states attending grew steadily. The shape of the movement and its precise purposes changed over the years; but its essential components remained the same: anti-colonialism, the economic rights of the poor countries and the primary producers, the moral high ground of non-alignment. A new force was at work in international affairs: the moral and psychological influence of the Third World.

◆ Notes to Chapter 11

1. See G. McT. Kahin, *The Afro-Asian Conference, Bandung* (London, 1956).
2. J. D. Legge, *Sukarno: A Political Biography* (London, 1972), p. 264.
3. *Ibid.*, p. 265.
4. See above, p. 209 for *panchsheel*.
5. See below, pp. 414–23 for OPEC and oil prices.

6. *Keesings Contemporary Archives*, 1955, p. 14184.
7. Brioni communiqué, *ibid.*, 1956, p. 15008.
8. *Ibid.*, 1961, p. 18601.
9. For the North–South issue and the Brandt Report, see below, pp. 514–16.

REFLECTION

THE THIRD WORLD

The term 'the Third World' has attained almost universal currency in descriptions of the world today, and in historical discussions of international affairs since the Second World War. The phrase itself was originated by a French demographer and economic historian, Alfred Sauvy, in an article in a weekly journal under the title 'Three Worlds, One Planet'. Sauvy recalled a pamphlet published by the Abbé Sieyès in 1789, on the eve of the French Revolution, when the French population was divided into three Estates, or social categories: the clergy, the nobility, and all the rest of the population. In his pamphlet, Sieyès asked: 'What is the Third Estate? Everything. What has it been up to now in the political order? Nothing. What does it ask for? To become something.' Sauvy observed that in 1952 the Cold War was raging between the capitalist world and the communist world, but there was also a Third World, economically under-developed, sometimes ignored by both sides and sometimes an object of their conflicts. Like the Third Estate in Sieyès's time, this Third World wanted to *become something*, to attain an importance of its own.[1]

Sauvy's phrase rapidly entered into general circulation. In English, it was granted recognition by *Brewer's Dictionary of Phrase and Fable* (as a phrase, not a fable). The definition was as follows: 'An expression coined in France (*le Tiers-Monde*) and applied to those less developed countries of Africa, Asia and Latin America which are not substantially aligned with the capitalist or communist "worlds" or political groupings.'[2] This definition fastens onto two aspects: non-alignment and economic under-development. Non-alignment, or neutralism, was a prominent concept at the Bandung Conference of Afro-Asian countries in 1955, and became the basis of the movement of non-aligned countries founded at the Belgrade Conference in September 1961. Strictly speaking, this should have ruled out alliances or alignments with either the capitalist world, dominated by the United States, or the communist bloc, controlled by the Soviet Union. In practice, many of the states which claimed to belong to the Third World were in fact aligned, sometimes by formal treaties of alliance, and sometimes by looser but still powerful ties – arms supplies, military 'advisers', foreign bases, or heavy economic dependence. At the Bandung Conference in 1955, thirteen of the twenty-seven independent states present at the conference were firmly aligned with one camp or the other. Later, India developed close ties with the Soviet Union, and Cuba was solidly in the Soviet camp, yet both played leading roles in the Non-Aligned movement.[3] Only Burma took the idea of non-alignment to its logical (if extreme) conclusion, virtually cutting off contacts with other countries and adopting for a time a near-pacifist stance.

The criterion of economic under-development was for a long time as uncertain as that of non-alignment. When the Afro-Asian group took shape at the Bandung Conference in 1955, there was nothing to link together the economic interests of Japan (a highly developed industrial country), Saudi Arabia (a wealthy oil producer) and Nepal or Liberia (poor countries barely on the verge of self-sufficiency). Attempts by the Afro-Asian states to set up some form of Common Market in the late 1950s broke down at once on the unbridgeable gaps between the countries concerned. Gradually a recognizable (though never absolutely clear-cut) line emerged between the industrialized, or industrializing, countries countries on the one hand and those which remained essentially primary producers on the other. At the first United Nations Conference on Trade and Development (UNCTAD), held at Geneva in 1964, the so-called Group of 77 (often abbreviated to G-77) developing countries made common cause on behalf of primary producers and put forward a joint set of economic claims.[4] Even then, primary producers differed widely; and a number of criteria were introduced for the definition of under-development: the proportion of the population engaged in agriculture; average Gross Domestic Product per inhabitant as a measurement of wealth; literacy rates; infant mortality rates and adult expectation of life. These at least provided some definite means of measuring economic development and under-development; but they still revealed not one Third World but several. Four could readily be distinguished: Africa south of the Sahara, which (except for the prosperous but ostracized South Africa) was by far the poorest; East and South-East Asia; the Arab world; and Latin America.[5] But even among these there were wide variations – for example, in the Arab world between Tunisia and Saudi Arabia; or in Latin America between Honduras and Argentina. Thus, while under-development became widely used to define the Third World, it was a simple term which concealed a complicated and divergent reality.

There was another defining feature of the Third World. The Third World was anti-colonialist, and represented the unity of the previously colonized and conquered peoples against the imperialists. Again, the reality behind this apparently straightforward sentiment was far from simple. The elites in former colonies often derived much of their culture from the metropolitan country. For example, they spoke, wrote and thought in English or French; had received a university education in Britain or France; and were widely separated from the mass of the population in their own countries. Moreover, there was a great divide between countries with long histories of civilization and political life (for example, China, India, Iran and Thailand), and other areas where the whole concept of an organized state had been imposed by the colonizing power, and where frontiers were simply lines drawn on maps by European governments in the nineteenth century (as was the case in much of Africa).

There was a further difficulty, because a division into colonialists and colonized implied only two worlds, not three. In the nineteenth century, Russia had been every bit as much an imperialist power as Britain or France, conquering Kazakhstan or Uzbekistan in the same way as the British conquered Zululand or the French invaded Algeria. Similarly, the Americans had fought their Indian wars and conquered territory from Mexico in war. By the middle of the twentieth century, the Soviet Union and the United States both claimed to be anti-imperialist, but showed no sign of giving up Central Asia or New Mexico respectively. Logically the countries of the Third World should have lumped all the imperialists together and denounced them all; but in practice they mostly preferred to ignore the continuing empire of the Soviet Union and concentrated their fire on the west European colonial states and on the economic and cultural imperialism of the United States.

Anti-American sentiment became increasingly important as the concept of the Third World was extended from the Afro-Asians to include Latin America, as occurred in the early 1960s. The Latin American states had certainly been colonies in the somewhat distant past, having achieved their independence from Spain and Portugal at the beginning of the nineteenth century. But in practice the Latin American claim to belong to the Third World in the guise of anti-colonialism was based on resentment against the economic predominance of the United States, not on their status as former Spanish or Portuguese colonies. Here was another element to add to the anti-colonial sentiment which, despite some complications, was probably the simplest and strongest characteristic of the Third World.

Each of these criteria (non-alignment, economic under-development, and anti-colonialism), if applied separately, would produce a different 'Third World'; though it would be possible to draw up a list of countries which at a given date satisfied all three criteria. For the countries involved, this flexibility has had its advantages. A grouping that cannot be strictly defined is easy to belong to, or to slip in and out of without fuss; and this almost infinite suppleness has helped to ensure for the Third World a remarkable longevity. It sometimes appears that a country forms part of the Third World when its government declares that it is. But such variability makes the term 'Third World' a dangerous one for historians. We cannot define it strictly, because it slips through our fingers, or changes according to the criterion we are applying; yet we cannot dispense with it, because it is a part of our vocabulary and almost part of the world in which we live. Since we can neither define it nor do without it, the best we can do is to use it with caution.

There remains a question. It is easy to see why the countries of the Third World (however defined) sought to establish their own identity, and to exert a collective influence on world affairs. But why did the United States and the Soviet Union, operating from a position of power (military, economic and political) regard the Third World as important to them, and sometimes take the countries of the Third World at (or near to) their own valuation? There were a number of solid, practical reasons. Third World countries produced large quantities of oil, raw materials and other commodities. They commanded key points on the world's maritime communications: the Straits of Hormuz in the Persian Gulf, the Suez Canal, and the approaches to the Panama Canal through the Caribbean. The superpowers had their own regional interests which were affected by Third World issues. For example, the republics of Soviet Central Asia were likely to be influenced by developments Afghanistan or Iran; while the United States had substantial economic and strategic interests in Latin America. In the United Nations Assembly, Third World countries could command a majority from about 1960 onwards, with the influx of large numbers of new African states. United Nations resolutions were by no means always carried out, but they were always of propaganda significance, and sometimes had a cumulative effect on issues of substance.

The Cold War added its own weight and intensity to all these matters. At various times both the superpowers thought that the Cold War might be won and lost in the Third World, which led them to intervene in countries (notably in Africa) where they would not otherwise have been concerned, and where they had little or no direct material interest. Behind this lay a deeper ideological issue. Both the United States and the Soviet Union claimed that their system of beliefs was of universal application, and that the whole world would eventually adopt (or at any rate would be better off with) capitalism and American-style democracy on the one hand, or socialism and people's democracy on the other. The Third World movement, with its claims to a separate identity and even to moral superiority, was a challenge to these deeply held assumptions.

Finally, there was in the West a powerful psychological influence: guilt. American governments and liberal public opinion felt guilty about slavery and the position of blacks in American society. An influential section of British public opinion felt guilty about the Empire and the slave trade. This was largely an Anglo-Saxon phenomenon. French governments (of all political complexions) were unperturbed by their imperial past, and worked hard to preserve the remains of the French Empire as Overseas Departments or Territories of France, and to retain a strong French influence in Africa. But in Britain and the United States there prevailed a mixture of guilt and condescension – 'We feel superior even while we beat our breasts', wrote Paul Bauer.[6] It was a powerful combination of emotions, with lasting effects on policy and influential sections of public opinion. For all these reasons, the countries of the First and Second Worlds concentrated much attention on the Third, enhancing its reputation and increasing its influence.

In the early 1960s, it was not yet clear how the Third World was to develop. In the next thirty years or so from the 1960s to the 1980s, three strong tendencies emerged.

First, much of the Third World (Africa, Asia and Latin America) became politically unstable, with frequent insurrections, military coups, and civil wars. Military regimes became common in Africa, and took over in a number of Asian countries; they had long been endemic in Latin America. Taking the standard idea of the three worlds, the First World (led by America and mainly capitalist in its economic organization) proved to be politically stable; the Second World (the Soviet Union and its eastern European satellites) was held together by the strait-jacket of Soviet power, and was stable to the point of immobility; but the Third World, with some notable exceptions was in a constant state of flux.

Second, a number of homegrown Third World ideologies competed for the allegiance of Asian and African countries, and to a lesser degree those of Latin America. Maoist communism flourished in China, made an appeal in Africa and flickered in Latin America, before fading with the reputation of Mao himself after his death. Islam, in an austere and vigorous form, revived in militancy and appeal, notably in Iran, Afghanistan, Pakistan and Algeria. Pan-Arab nationalism ebbed and flowed. All these movements, as Alan Cassels observes, were in part 'expressions of resentment at Western imperialism, stimulated by some degree of racial, anti-white sentiment'.[7]

Third, following the United Nations Conference on Trade and Development in 1964, the economic aspect of Third World identity grew in importance. That Conference set out, as No. XIV of its General Principles, that complete decolonization was the necessary condition for economic development. This was elaborated as a widely-held theory that the 'centre' of the economic system (the industrialized states) exploited the 'periphery' (the Third World), imposing poverty on the deprived nations by an economic system dictated by the demands of the industrialized states This exploitation was achieved by a variety of means: industrialized states bought their raw materials and food cheaply from the primary producers; international companies made profits for themselves, not for the countries where they operated; and indigenous capitalists within the Third World collaborated with foreigners at the expense of their own people. There were many difficulties in this theory, which sought to impose a single pattern on a complex situation. Notably, there were a number of the poorest countries which had almost no international trade (like Ethiopia), or had never been colonies (like Liberia). The export of primary products (for example, rubber from Malaya) or agricultural produce (for example, vegetables from Kenya) was often profitable to the exporting country. Moreover, it was possible to point to an Asian country with very little land, a large and dense population, compelled to import all its oil and raw materials, the home of many international companies, and under colonial rule by a European power, and yet with a thriving economy – Hong Kong. It was also the case that the French-speaking states of West and Central Africa did at least as much to exploit their links with France as the French did to exploit them. Despite these exceptions, dependency theories carried much weight, and became an influential way of describing the Third World.[8]

These developments did not make the concept of the Third World any more coherent in the 1970s or 1980s than it had been in the early 1960s. The descent of several countries in Africa, Asia and Latin America into civil war, military coups and in extreme cases anarchy only emphasized the contrast with stable and orderly countries in the same continents. (For example, in Asia Cambodia was torn by civil war and something near genocide, while Singapore ran like clockwork.) The renewed militancy of Islam sharpened the division in Africa between Muslims in the north and Christians or animists in the south, resulting in constant civil war in Chad and the Sudan. The description of underdevelopment covered an enormous range, from Nepal, Ethiopia and Somalia at one end to Argentina, Brazil and South Africa at the other. It could be said with truth that 'There is no "Third World" interest'. At the United Nations, Third World governments pretend there is; but at home and in practice, they look after their own interests.'[9]

By 1989–91, as first the Soviet bloc and then the Soviet Union itself disappeared, one of the original two 'Worlds' which had given the Third World its name ceased to exist. Despite this, the term 'Third World' marches on, apparently indispensable to our language and thought processes, even though it lacks any precise meaning and the circumstances which gave it birth have ceased to exist. This has the strange consequence that a large part of our vision of international affairs is conceived in terms which amount to fiction.

◆ Notes to Reflection: The Third World

1. *France-Observateur*, 14 August 1952.
2. *Brewer's Dictionary of Phrase and Fable* (2nd edn, London, 1981), p. 1203.
3. See above, p. 248, for the states represented at Bandung and their alignments.
4. For the United Nations Conference on Trade and Development, see below, pp. 514–17.
5. Robert Chapuis and Thierry Brossard, *Les quatre mondes du Tiers Monde* (Paris, 2nd edn, 1997)
6. P. T. Bauer, *Equality, the Third World and Economic Delusion* (London, 1981), p. 84.
7. Alan Cassels, *Ideology and International Relations in the Modern World* (London, 1996), p. 238.

8. Raymond Aron, *Les dernières années du XXe siècle* (Paris, 1984), pp. 66–85; Bauer, *Equality*, pp. 66–85, 185–90 (including the example of Hong Kong); David Landes, *The Wealth and Poverty of Nations* (London, 1998), especially Chapter 25.

9. See the charts in Chapuis and Brossard, pp. 57, 59. The quotation is from Rosemary Righter, *Utopia Lost: The United Nations and World Order* (New York, 1995), p. 20.

PART II

FROM 1963 TO THE END
OF THE COLD WAR

COLD WAR, SECOND PHASE: DÉTENTE, RENEWAL AND THE END

CHAPTER

COLD WAR AND DÉTENTE, 1963–1969

The beginnings of détente – The background to Soviet policy,
1963–68 – American policy and the problem of Vietnam –
Soviet–American relations and the development of détente –
Prague Spring and the Soviet invasion of Czechoslovakia,
1968 – Nixon and a new start, 1969

◆ The coming of détente

The Cuba missile crisis of 1962 was a profound shock to the superpowers. Unlike the Korean War of 1950–53, it was not a confrontation between allies or substitutes, but between the Americans and Soviets themselves, who metaphorically looked straight down the barrels of each other's guns – which were not rifles but nuclear missiles. The experience was salutary as well as alarming, and gave a sharp new impulse to the search for a *modus vivendi* between the superpowers, in the literal sense of finding a means of staying alive.

In 1961, before the Cuba crisis, Raymond Aron had written that the United States and the Soviet Union were *frères-ennemis* – brothers as well as enemies.[1] The crisis brought this paradox home to both governments. They did not cease to be enemies, but they knew that, simply in order to stay alive, they had to co-operate, and to keep in touch with one another. In practical terms, they needed a quicker means of communication in times of emergency. At one point during the Cuba crisis, the Soviet Ambassador in Washington had to send an urgent cipher message to his government, using the services of the American Western Union telegraph office, which actually sent a messenger *by bicycle* to collect the telegram. This touch of absurdity in circumstances of high drama and imminent peril brought home the need for something better by way of communications; and a Soviet–American agreement signed in Geneva on 20 June 1963 provided for the establishment of a 'hot line', which was in practice a direct telephone link between Moscow and Washington, via Helsinki, Stockholm, Copenhagen and London. This was less certain than it appeared – a Finnish farmer once cut the cable in the course of his labours; a second line was therefore installed by way of reinsurance, and eventually a radio-telephone link via satellite was set up.[2] In the event, the hot line was not used until 1967, at the time of the Six-Day War between Israel and the Arabs; but its very existence was significant. At the same time the Soviet Ambassador in Washington, Dobrynin, in co-operation with American officials, developed means of making highly secret contacts between the two governments. Over the next ten years these contacts were to reach the stage where, by Dobrynin's own account, he could say to Henry Kissinger (President Nixon's adviser on foreign policy, and later Secretary of State): 'Come on Henry, this is a bluff, a nonsense. What are you trying to do?'[3] This degree of informality took time to develop, but a start was made in 1963.

The United States and Soviet Union also began to move towards some form of arms control. Along with Britain (at that time the only other nuclear power) they concluded, on 5 August 1963, a limited Nuclear Test Ban Treaty, which committed its adherents to give up the testing of nuclear weapons in the atmosphere, in outer space, or under water. This did not prevent underground tests, and therefore did little to hinder the development of nuclear weapons even by the three signatories; and neither France nor China, which were at work on their own nuclear weapons, acceded to the treaty. Even so, the treaty had a symbolic significance as the first treaty on arms control concluded by the superpowers; and ending tests in the atmosphere was a practical advantage in itself. The agreement was followed by others – the same three powers concluded a treaty on 27 January 1967 providing for the demilitarization of outer space; and on 1 July 1968 the United States and the Soviet Union signed a treaty on the non-proliferation of nuclear weapons, which by 1972 had been joined by a total of 71 states.

The 'hot line' and the Test Ban Treaty of 1963 were limited in their effects, but none the less significant for that. After the brief but alarming paroxysm of the Cuba missile crisis, the Cold War continued, but with an admixture of détente. The word 'détente' itself did not become current until the end of the 1960s, but the fact preceded the name. The problems of definition to which the word gave rise will be examined later (see below, pp. 330–34); for present purposes, it is enough to take it as meaning a relaxation of tension, and a willingness on both sides to look for limited agreements. The reasons for this change were wider than the immediate shock of the Cuba crisis, and may be found in the problems faced by the two superpowers in the 1960s.

◆ The background to Soviet policy, 1963–68

The Cuba crisis ended in a grave setback for the Soviet Union. Khrushchev had ostentatiously despatched missiles to Cuba and then been compelled to withdraw them. Moreover, the defeat appeared worse than it actually was because a part of the deal agreed between Kennedy and Khrushchev remained secret. The withdrawal of Soviet missiles from Cuba was partially balanced by the American undertaking to remove their own missiles from Turkey; but the former was made public and the latter was not. Khrushchev's reputation also suffered through his treatment of Castro, who had bravely thrown in his lot with the Soviet Union and then been left in the lurch. When all was over Khrushchev made amends by inviting Castro to Moscow, providing large quantities of Soviet aid, and ensuring that Cuban exports of sugar and tobacco were purchased by the USSR and the countries of the eastern bloc; but it was impossible to disguise the fact that, at the height of the Cuba crisis, Cuba itself had been a mere spectator. The Soviet Union, though a socialist state, had simply behaved like a great power – no great surprise, perhaps, but disconcerting to many of the Marxist faithful.

The prestige of the Soviet Union, and Khrushchev's own reputation, thus suffered a bad blow. But Khrushchev was a buoyant, resilient character, and at the beginning of 1963 he could find much cause for optimism. The Berlin Wall had averted the collapse of East Germany, which had begun to settle down and even to prosper by its own standards. The upheavals of the 1950s in Poland and Hungary had been weathered, and the east European bloc seemed solid. In 1963 the Bulgarian communist leader, Todor Zhivkov, even sought to have his country incorporated into the Soviet Union – a vote of confidence which the Soviet leadership cautiously declined. Soviet relations with Yugoslavia had improved, though Tito remained resolutely independent. The long-running dispute between the Soviet Union and China was harmful to the socialist camp, but in 1963 Khrushchev had every hope that he could come out on top. Above all, Khrushchev was convinced that the Third World was moving decisively into the Soviet orbit, and that the Cold War would be won in Africa, Asia and Latin America. On the military front, the Soviet Union was increasing and improving its nuclear weaponry, and after 1962 built a great surface fleet, which would carry the Red Flag into the Indian Ocean, the Mediterranean and the Atlantic. The American maritime supremacy which had decided the Cuba missile crisis was being steadily eroded.

The upshot was a sort of balance. On the credit side, the Soviet position had many advantages and offered good reasons for confidence in the future. On the debit side, Soviet prestige had suffered during the Cuba crisis, and the expenditure on armaments bore heavily on the Soviet economy, which failed to develop at the rate which Khrushchev hoped for. The internal political situation also had its difficulties. In 1964 Khrushchev was overthrown, and replaced as Secretary-General by Brezhnev, who proved more cautious than Khrushchev, and much less ebullient in personality. There were disquieting signs of internal opposition to the Soviet system. In 1965 there was a trial of Ukrainian nationalists in Kiev and demonstrations against Soviet rule in Armenia. In September that year the writers Andrei Sinyavski and Yuli Daniel were arrested for circulating *samizdat* publications (a form of clandestine press) critical of the regime. They were sentenced to spells in labour camps in 1966; but the opposition was not silenced. In 1968 a *samizdat* journal, *The Chronicle of Current Events*, began a hazardous but persistent existence, reaching an increasing readership.[4] The Soviet authorities tried to suppress these activities, but without reimposing the full rigour of Stalinist terror. The result was a continuous grumbling against the regime, which posed no serious or immediate threat but appeared to be gathering weight

Soviet leaders were thus confident in their own power and looked forward to the success of the socialist cause – Khrushchev brashly, Brezhnev more circumspectly; but at the same time they were sufficiently conscious of their own economic and political difficulties to try to lighten some of the burdens on the population and offer some material improvements. They were prepared to confront the United States, but they also looked for some measure of détente by means of arms control and limited diplomatic cooperation. In principle this was not new, but only an extension of the long-standing doctrine of peaceful coexistence, which itself signified a continuation of competition with the capitalist camp by other means than those of total opposition. The Cold War and détente could go forward together.

◆ The background to United States policy: the shadow of Vietnam

The United States emerged successful, if shaken, from the Cuba missile crisis; but even so they faced a legacy of problems. During the crisis, America's allies in NATO had been dismayed by the way in which the United States had taken all the crucial decisions; and the European countries sought some means of sharing in choices whose results could mean life and death to them all. To assuage these anxieties, the Americans attempted to remodel NATO, proposing the establishment of a new integrated nuclear force (called rather clumsily the Multilateral Force, or MLF), to be made up of warships from various countries and to include all the British, and a small proportion of the American, nuclear armaments. The missiles carried by the ships of the Multilateral Force would only be used after a unanimous decision by the governments involved, thus giving the Europeans a finger on the nuclear trigger. This complicated proposal was put forward by the Kennedy administration and continued under its successor, and was taken sufficiently seriously for an American warship, the USS *Claude V. Ricketts*, to sail round the Mediterranean with an eight-nation crew to try to prove that it would work. But the scheme was implausible in itself, and in any case left the Americans in charge of the vast majority of their own nuclear weapons – after all, how could it really be otherwise? It died from its own weaknesses by the end of 1964. The Americans retained control of all their weapons; so did the British and French, with their small atomic and nuclear forces. (The British had exploded their first atomic device in 1952, and a nuclear device in 1958; the French tests were in 1960 and 1968 respectively.) In other respects Western Europe was escaping from American influence. France, under the presidency of Charles de Gaulle, pursued an increasingly independent policy, leaving the NATO command structures (though not the treaty itself) in 1966. West Germany began to follow a new course when the long-serving Chancellor Adenauer left office in 1963. The socialist leader Willy Brandt, who became Foreign Minister in 1966, evolved a new policy towards eastern Europe, the *Ostpolitik*, leading towards agreements with Poland, East Germany and the Soviet Union in 1970–72. (See below, pp. 307–10.) In the Middle East, Israel struck out on its own course in launching the Six-Day War against Egypt and Syria in June 1967.[5] There were enough difficulties here for the Americans; but all came to be overshadowed by the problem of Vietnam.

In 1954 the Geneva Conference had agreed to divide North Vietnam from the South along the 17th parallel of latitude, though with the hope of later unification. The United States refused to sign the Geneva agreements; but when the French finally withdrew from Indo-China in 1955 the Americans stepped in to support South Vietnam, building up its armed forces and trying to mould its political system on democratic lines. This intervention was based on the domino theory, which saw South Vietnam as the first in a line of dominos, whose fall would bring down all the rest, as far as Singapore and the Philippines. The Americans at that stage (and for some time afterwards) saw no distinction between communism and Vietnamese nationalism – victory in Vietnam for Ho Chi Minh and the North Vietnamese would mean the advance of world communism, and could not be permitted.[6]

President Eisenhower thus embarked on intervention in South Vietnam; and when Kennedy succeeded him as President in January 1961 he continued the same course. Vietnam was by no means his first priority, and it was not until November 1961 that the new administration decided on its practical policies. The National Security Council ruled out the despatch of combat troops, with the exception of 400 men of the Special Forces (the Green Berets) to train South Vietnamese commandos and undertake small-scale clandestine operations; but agreed to raise the strength of the South Vietnamese army to 250 000, with American equipment. Economic aid to the South Vietnamese government, headed by Ngo Dinh Diem, was to be made conditional upon its making progress towards democracy.

This policy sought to protect South Vietnam, and eventually get the country to stand on its own feet, while limiting the scale of American intervention.

But the limits proved difficult to maintain, and the intervention gradually increased. American 'military advisers', who numbered about 3000 when Kennedy took office, were reinforced to 8000 by the end of 1962. Infiltration by North Vietnamese guerrillas in support of the South Vietnamese communists (the Viet Cong) increased steadily, and the Americans tried to check the flow by using helicopters (flown by American pilots) to harass the Viet Cong's lines of communication. The line between 'advising' and fighting grew blurred, and was frequently crossed. In political affairs, the Americans lost faith in Ngo Dinh Diem, whom they had long supported as a democratic leader who would become the saviour of his country. On 1 November 1963 a group of South Vietnamese generals, with at least the connivance of the American Embassy and CIA officers in Saigon, overthrew Diem's government. Diem himself and his brother, Ngo Dinh Nhu, were both killed. Whether or not the United States government itself was involved (and it appears that Kennedy was genuinely surprised and dismayed by these events), the inevitable result was to draw the Americans increasingly into the intricate and baffling politics of South Vietnam. During the next year, 1964, there were no fewer than seven changes of government in South Vietnam, and the Americans found themselves providing almost the only element of continuity.

When President Kennedy was assassinated on 22 November 1963, his successor, Lyndon Johnson, continued the same policy of limited intervention, though it was already looking threadbare. By then there were about 16 000 American 'military advisers' in South Vietnam; which was beginning to seem either too many or too few. They were too many in that they represented a commitment which would be difficult to escape from without loss of prestige; yet they were also too few, in that they were not producing decisive results.

Thus far, up to the end of 1963 and early 1964, Vietnam had not become a primary concern either for American policy or for American public opinion. Berlin and Cuba far outweighed Vietnam in 1961–62; and in 1963 domestic politics predominated. As for public opinion, the press and television covered Vietnam only cursorily; no TV network was regularly represented in the country before 1965. The public as a whole showed little interest – nearly 800 Americans were killed in Vietnam during Kennedy's presidency, without creating any great stir at home.[7] In the next few years, between 1964 and 1967, this situation changed drastically. American military forces intervened in Vietnam on a large scale, and in consequence the war became a central concern for the American media and public opinion. How did this change come about?

On 4 August 1964 an American warship, the USS *Maddox*, claimed to have been attacked by night in international waters in the Gulf of Tonkin, and to have sunk its attacker (presumed to be North Vietnamese) without trace. President Johnson seized on this mysterious affair to secure the support of Congress in what had so far been very much a presidential involvement in Vietnam. Within three days he secured the passage through Congress of a long resolution (the Tonkin Gulf resolution), concluding that, if the President judged it necessary, the United States was prepared to do all in its power, including the use of its armed forces, to ensure the independence and integrity of South Vietnam and Laos. This resolution, which gave the President virtually a free hand to use force in Vietnam, was passed in the House of Representatives by a vote of 146 to nil, and in the Senate by 88 votes to 2 (both Democrats – Wayne Morse of Oregon and Ernest Gruening of Alaska). This overwhelming support included the 'liberal establishment' of that time – James Fulbright, a distinguished and internationalist Democratic Senator, guided the resolution through the Senate, and in the press the *New York Times* and the *Washington Post* supported it. Public opinion polls were favourable. The later opposition to the war was at this stage unforeseen, and virtually unforeseeable. The consensus behind government policy seemed virtually complete. An American historian, Ernest R. May, wrote in 1973 that: 'Given the assumptions generally shared by Americans in the 1960s, it seems probable that any collection of men and women would have decided as did the members of the Kennedy and Johnson administrations.'[8]

In view of later events, it is necessary to ask why this was so. What were the assumptions shared by Americans in the 1960s? They were doubtless a mixed bag, but their total effect was formidable. American policy-makers were still much influenced by the reaction against the policy of appeasement in the 1930s, and felt that there must be no surrender to aggression – no repetition of the Munich agreement of 1938. This attitude was closely allied to the domino theory – if South Vietnam fell, the rest of South-East Asia would follow; a belief which bore the authority of Eisenhower, who had been a military hero as well as a popular president. To these assumptions Kennedy added his own belief that Khrushchev's emphasis on wars of national liberation meant that guerrilla warfare would be the new test of American strength and determination. The United States must face this test and pass it. For a superpower and the leader of the 'free world', there was no alternative. The whole American stance from the Truman Doctrine to Kennedy's inaugural address led inexorably to the same conclusion. Moreover, behind all these assumptions lay the certainty that the Americans could win the war in Vietnam. They possessed total supremacy in the air, and if necessary could use massive fire-power on land. In the 1960s, American strategic thinking was dominated by a pseudo-scientific approach, strongly advocated by the Secretary for Defence Robert McNamara, in which everything could be calculated in terms of fire-power, bomb-loads and casualty rates (an insistence on 'body counts' later became a feature of American military policy in Vietnam), and too little attention was paid to the imponderable and incalculable issue of morale.

Within a few years, these assumptions lost all their substance, and the arguments came to seem no more than illusions. American intervention in Vietnam appeared at best an enormous mistake, and at worst a crime and offence against all American ideals. We must now recover the certainties of the mid-1960s by an effort which is almost archaeological in its nature: the attitudes have virtually to be dug up. And yet they must be recalled if we are to understand why the American government and people acted as they did.

When the Tonkin Gulf Resolution was passed in 1964 no great change in policy had been decided upon. The resolution conferred wide freedom of action on the President, but he had not yet decided how to use it. Johnson campaigned in the presidential election of 1964 on a platform which included non-escalation of the war in Vietnam. Unhappily, limited intervention still failed to produce results. The Viet Cong guerrillas, supplied and reinforced from the North, continued their operations in South Vietnam. The Americans turned to air power to cut their enemies' communications and destroy their sources of supply. In March 1965 they began the heavy bombing of North Vietnam (grandly code-named 'Operation Rolling Thunder'), directed against factories, military installations and supply routes, and intended more broadly to 'punish' the North Vietnamese for their intervention in the South – though the Americans were careful to keep clear of the Chinese border, and to avoid provoking further Chinese intervention in the war.

This proved to be the beginning of the escalation which had so far been avoided. The American military commanders felt they had to defend the bases from which the bombers operated, and did not trust South Vietnamese troops to do the job. General Westmoreland therefore asked for a force of Marines. President Johnson agreed, and on 8 March 1965 3500 Marines landed at Da Nang, where the main American base was established. They were ostentatiously welcomed with garlands of flowers; but their arrival proved to be the prelude to disaster. More Marines followed, and then infantry from the Army. The air bombardments continued, but they failed to bring the war on the ground to an end. In July 1965 Johnson, along with almost all his close advisers (George Ball in the State Department was a far-sighted exception), concluded that the war would have to be won by despatching large numbers of American troops, not just as advisers or to defend bases, but to fight. The Americans set out to win by wearing down the Viet Cong and North Vietnamese by bombing from the air, by overwhelming fire-power on the ground, and by sheer weight of casualties. It was to be a war of attrition.

They miscalculated completely. As Ho Chi Minh and his military commander, General Giap, knew well, the North Vietnamese were far more willing to take heavy casualties than the Americans were to accept their own, much lighter losses. They had outlasted the French, and were ready to outlast the Americans. Moreover, the North Vietnamese were receiving supplies and equipment from both the Chinese and the Soviets, so that even in material terms they were not totally at a disadvantage. Attrition favoured the North Vietnamese, not the Americans.

In the mid-to late 1960s this was not yet clear. The Americans built up their forces in Vietnam – 184 000 at the end of 1965, 385 000 at the end of 1966, 485 000 at the end of 1967.[9] The American commanders continued to promise victory, though could not yet produce it; indeed, the Americans' own estimates of North Vietnamese infiltration into the South increased steadily. Nonetheless, at the end of 1967 General Westmoreland had convinced himself and his government that victory would be achieved in 1968. It was not.

◆ Soviet–American relations, 1963–67

Thus, in the period following the Cuba missile crisis, the Soviet Union remained committed to competition with the United States, but also had good reasons to pursue a policy of peaceful co-existence by means of arms control and improved communications with Washington. The United States was waging the Cold War with increasing intensity in Vietnam, but was willing to improve relations with the Soviet Union at the same time. The two superpowers therefore manoeuvred rather awkwardly for diplomatic advantage.

After the Cuba missile crisis, Khrushchev revised his opinion of Kennedy, referring to him as another Roosevelt, and looking forward to working with him as joint peace-makers who could cope with the problems of the world. Kennedy's assassination in November 1963 and Khrushchev's removal from office in October 1964 changed all that. Johnson was an unknown quantity to the Soviet leadership; and in 1964 he had to fight a presidential election in which his Republican opponent was Barry Goldwater, who was fiercely anti-communist. Johnson was anxious to maintain the contacts with the Soviet Union which had been established since 1962, but he did not dare to appear less anti-communist than his opponent. He therefore took the precaution of explaining to the Soviet Ambassador, through an intermediary, that during the election campaign he might well have to say unpleasant things about the Soviet regime. He hoped the reasons for this would be understood, and would not mind a certain degree of Soviet criticism in response.

Such distinctions between election rhetoric and serious policy were not always understood in Moscow, where elections were simpler matters; and it well be that the tone of the 1964 presidential election campaign did some harm to American-Soviet relations, despite Johnson's attempt at reassurance. But when the election was over, the Americans were anxious to resume contacts with the Soviet government, not least in the hope that the

USSR might act as an intermediary with North Vietnam. (By this time, thanks to the development of détente, the Americans no longer assumed that communism was a monolithic bloc controlled by the Kremlin, and they were prepared to envisage this sort of role for the Soviet government.) In 1965 the American Secretary of State, Dean Rusk, and the Vice-President, Hubert Humphrey, approached Dobrynin, the Soviet Ambassador, to see whether the two governments could work together towards an agreement in Vietnam. In Moscow, Brezhnev and Gromyko were sympathetic to these approaches, recognizing that in terms of power politics their relations with the United States were more important than Vietnam. But the Soviets too had their political difficulties. If Johnson could not afford to be thought soft on communism, the Soviet leaders could not afford to be thought weak in their anti-imperialism. The Soviet government could not act as mediator between the Americans and North Vietnam (however unofficially) without appearing to betray the communist cause, and thus allowing the Chinese to denounce them. The best they could do was to help North Vietnam without becoming involved in the war, and to keep up their relations with the Americans, which were important (as Gromyko explained in a memorandum for the Politburo in January 1967) in order to avoid nuclear war and to offer protection against 'Chinese adventurism'.[10]

The two superpowers thus found they still had something in common, and showed their determination to remain in contact by holding a summit meeting between Johnson and Kosygin, the Chairman of the Council of Ministers and Brezhnev's principal colleague, at Glassboro on 23–24 June 1967. The Americans issued the invitation, and the Soviets accepted, but Brezhnev thought it best not to attend in person, and Kosygin declined to visit Washington while the Vietnam war was raging. The meetings were therefore held at the small town of Glassboro in New Jersey, which suddenly found itself famous. During the conversations, Johnson tried to persuade the Soviet government to help in negotiations for a settlement in Vietnam by using its influence with the North Vietnamese government. Kosygin refused to commit himself, cautiously saying that he had no authority to deal with the matter, and pointing out that the North Vietnamese often acted independently, without even keeping Moscow informed. For his part, Kosygin tried to focus the discussions on the Middle East, where the Six-Day War (5–10 June) had taken place just before the Glassboro summit began.[11] The conference achieved little in specific terms, but (as was often the case with summit meetings) it was important simply in itself. Johnson and Kosygin made contact. They examined the conflicts in Vietnam and the Middle East together, even if they could do little to deal with them. Before the meetings ended, Kosygin invited Johnson to visit the Soviet Union in 1968. Johnson accepted, and said that he would like to see a summit meeting take place once a year – something which was to be achieved for a period in the 1970s.

The Vietnam war did not prevent the Americans and Soviets from improving their relations in 1967; and indeed from the American point of view it gave an impetus to détente. In 1968 crises struck both the super-powers, the Soviet Union in Czechoslovakia and the United States in Vietnam.

◆ The Prague Spring and the Soviet invasion of Czechoslovakia, 1968

In 1968 there were dramatic events in Czechoslovakia. In 1967 there had been difficulties within the Czecholovakian Communist Party, and between Czechs and Slovaks over the allocation of economic resources. In December Brezhnev, the Soviet leader, had attended a Party meeting and declared that the leadership of the Czechoslovak Communist Party was a question for its own members. After this apparent green light, on 5 January 1968, the First Secretary of the Party (and in effect the ruler of the country), Antonin Novotny, was removed and replaced by Alexander Dubček. For a time Novotny remained in the largely honorary post of President of the Republic; but on 21 March he resigned and was replaced by General Svoboda. Novotny had been an orthodox, Soviet-style communist, content to keep the regime ticking over. Dubček on the contrary wished to embark on reform, though only within the communist system. General Svoboda's surname happened to mean 'freedom'; the day when he took office was by some reckonings the first day of Spring; and he made a point of visiting the grave of Thomas Masaryk, the founder of the Czechoslovakian state. All these things seemed to be portents of change.

Dubček described what he wanted to do in a striking phrase – to create 'socialism with a human face' – which bore the unhappy implication that so far the face of socialism had not been human. He relaxed censorship in March, and abolished it in June. He then called for a Special Congress of the Czechoslovak Communist Party, to meet in September to consider a programme of changes – the introduction of self-management and workers' councils in factories, and possibly the creation of 'interest groups' which could be represented in the communist-controlled National Front, which had ruled the country since 1948, without forming new political parties. In making these proposals, Dubček remained committed to socialism; he retained the directing role of the Communist Party; and he had no intention of abandoning the Warsaw Pact or moving towards neutrality. His programme was popular in Czechoslovakia. Would it be acceptable in Moscow?

The Soviet leaders hesitated for some time, not about aims but about methods. They were agreed that they could not simply stand aside and leave Czechoslovakia to its own devices, thus opening the way for other countries to follow suit. Czechoslovakia must be brought back into line, but opinions were divided as to how this should be done. Andropov, who had been involved in crushing the Hungarian rising in 1956, wanted to use force again. Others wanted to repeat the internal coup of 1948, using Czech communists loyal to Moscow to restore the situation; but they were not sure they could find enough supporters. Brezhnev was apparently uncertain about using force, right up to the last moment.

The Soviet leaders put heavy pressure on Dubček. At the end of July they summoned him to Moscow for a meeting; courageously, he refused to go, insisting that he would talk only on Czechoslovakian territory. Meetings took place on 29 July–1 August, and again on 3 August, when Dubček agreed on a form of words to the effect that his government would not allow anyone to undermine the bases of socialism. But this would not suffice. During the night of 20/21 August 1968 a powerful Soviet army of 29 divisions, with 7500 tanks, invaded Czechoslovakia. They were supported by contingents of troops from East Germany, Poland, Hungary and Bulgaria, to emphasize the international character of the operation. The force was so overwhelming that there was little resistance; but there was fighting in parts of the country, with casualties variously estimated at between 80 and 200.[12] The Soviets could find no collaborators of any influence, so that Dubček was not removed from office. Instead he was compelled to go to Moscow, where on 26 August he accepted the Moscow Protocol, by which communist orthodoxy was to be restored in Czechoslovakia. A new censorship law was imposed in September. Eventually, in April 1969, Dubček was replaced as First Secretary of the Czechoslovakian Party by Gustav Husak. In May 1970 Dubček was expelled from the Communist Party; but he was allowed to live in retirement, in striking contrast to the fate of those who had been purged in earlier times.

The Soviets justified their action in principle by setting out the so-called 'Brezhnev Doctrine' in an article in *Pravda*, the official newspaper of the Soviet Communist Party, on 24 September 1968, under the heading: 'Sovereignty and the international obligations of socialist countries'. The freedom of foreign (i.e. non-Soviet) socialists to determine their own country's path of development must be subordinate to the cause of universal Marxism-Leninism. 'Any decision of theirs must damage neither socialism in one country nor the fundamental interests of other socialist countries nor the world-wide workers' movement. . . . This means that every Communist party is responsible not only to its own people but to all socialist countries and to the entire Communist movement.'[13] In other words, communist countries must subordinate their independence to the interests of communism as a whole, as defined by the Soviet Union.

In 1948 the communist coup in Czechoslovakia had caused widespread alarm and strong international reaction. The invasion in 1968, in striking contrast, caused scarcely a ripple. At the end of July Dean Rusk, the American Secretary of State, let his opposite number, Gromyko, know that the United States had no wish to become involved in events in Czechoslovakia. When the invasion actually took place, the Soviet Ambassador in Washington, Dobrynin, went to see President Johnson at 8 pm on Sunday, 20 August, at the very time when Soviet tanks were moving into Czechoslovakia, to explain the Soviet action. By Dobrynin's account, Johnson displayed no strong reaction, and went on to talk about his proposed visit to Moscow as though there were no difficulty in its going ahead as planned. In western Europe, the former French Premier, Michel Debré, described the Soviet invasion as merely a minor incident on the road to détente. Harold Wilson, the British Prime Minister, who had recently visited Moscow, refused to allow the invasion of Czechoslovakia to interfere with the good relations he was building up with the USSR.

There was in effect no international crisis over the invasion of Czechoslovakia. No one imposed, or even suggested, economic sanctions against the Soviet Union. France postponed (but did not cancel) meetings arranged between French and Soviet ministers. The Security Council of the United Nations passed a resolution on 22 August condemning the armed intervention in Czechoslovakia by the Soviet Union and the Warsaw Pact powers, and calling upon them to withdraw their forces forthwith; but the resolution concluded by merely requesting members of the UN 'to exercise their diplomatic influence' to bring about its implementation. The Soviet Union vetoed the resolution, and there the matter rested.[14]

The reasons for this are not far to seek. The United States was in deep trouble in Vietnam (as we shall see shortly), and hoped that the Soviet Union might help them out. American opinion was increasingly divided over the war in Vietnam, and there was no scope for the United States to take a high moral line about intervention in a foreign country. Moreover, the United States and the Soviet Union actually signed a nuclear non-proliferation treaty on 1 July 1968, and they planned to begin talks on strategic arms limitation, which the Americans had no intention of giving up. Finally, after Dubček himself had yielded to superior force and come to an agreement with his adversary, it would have appeared strange for the western powers to care more for Czech independence than the Czechs themselves did.

It is worth dwelling on the contrast between the western reactions to the Prague coup of February 1948 and the Soviet invasion of Czechoslovakia in August 1968. The coup of 1948 was a communist seizure of power, but involved no invasion by Soviet troops; yet the West responded by the immediate conclusion of the Brussels Treaty and the opening of moves which led to the North Atlantic Treaty in 1949. In 1968 the Soviet Union and four other countries invaded Czechoslovakia, and the Western response was to carry on with business as usual. There could be no clearer indication of the change in the climate of international relations over twenty years. This time, the Soviet Union had intervened to maintain the status quo rather than to change it; and by now the United States had fully accepted Soviet domination in eastern Europe. Moreover, while the Cold War was still on, the advance of détente had taken much of the sting out of the conflict. Relations between the United States (and other western powers) and the Soviet Union had changed out of recognition.

The Prague Spring and the Soviet invasion of Czechoslovakia thus passed with remarkably little disturbance. In Czechoslovakia, the question of how far the regime could be reformed without changing its fundamental nature was never answered. The application of overwhelming force reimposed Soviet control with very little bloodshed. There was no international crisis, but instead a general acceptance that the status quo should be maintained. But there was movement beneath the surface. The Prague Spring stirred a response in other countries, and Dubček's phrase about 'socialism with a human face' was long remembered. Even within the Soviet Union, dissidents protested clandestinely against the invasion. Some twenty years later Mikhail Gorbachev was to raise the question of reforming socialism in the USSR by means of *glasnost* (openness) and *perestroika* (restructuring), reviving the main themes of Dubček's abortive changes in 1968. The events of 1968 in Czechoslovakia left their mark; and Dubček himself was to live to see a happier ending in 1989.

◆ The USA and Vietnam, 1968: the year of crisis

In 1968 the Soviet Union was confronted by a challenge to its authority in Czechoslovakia, and responded with overwhelming military force. In the same year the United States faced a far-reaching crisis in Vietnam and at home, and fell into disarray. During the night of 30–31 January 1968 the Viet Cong guerrillas and forces from North Vietnam launched a surprise offensive against the Americans and South Vietnamese right across South Vietnam. The date chosen was Tet, the Vietnamese New Year, when the South Vietnamese troops were relaxed and off guard; and at the beginning the Tet offensive achieved startling successes. In Saigon, the capital, guerrillas even attacked the American Embassy, various government buildings, and the airport. Gradually the Americans and South Vietnamese recovered; and when the fighting drew to a close at the end of February the Tet offensive had achieved only small gains at the cost of heavy casualties among the attacking forces. But the immediate psychological impression could not be effaced. Instead of the victory which the American commanders had been forecasting for 1968, there were Viet Cong guerrillas firing mortar shells at the US Embassy under the gaze of American reporters and cameramen. The American news media (television, radio and press) conveyed an impression of calamity, invoking comparisons with the French defeat at Dien Bien Phu in 1954. The result was a striking example of how publicity and the mass media can affect policy and strategy. When President Johnson later claimed, correctly, that the Americans had won the battle, hardly anyone believed him. The public impression was overwhelming. The Americans had nearly half-a-million troops in South Vietnam at the end of 1967, and the result was the Tet offensive. Something was disastrously wrong.

In March 1968, when the situation had settled down, the American military commanders in Vietnam, with the support of the Chiefs of Staff in Washington, asked the government for the despatch of a further 206 000 troops. This could only be done by calling up reservists, which had so far been avoided; and the Treasury Secretary, Henry Fowler, pointed out that it would have to be paid for at the cost of other parts of the Defence budget, and probably also by reducing other forms of expenditure. (At the time, the cost of the Vietnam War was being met *in addition to* increased social spending.) The request for 206 000 more troops was refused; and the increase in numbers from 1967 to 1968 was kept to about 50 000 – from 484 000 to 536 000.[15]

The call-up of reserves would probably have proved politically impossible, because the request came at a time of growing domestic opposition to the war. The general consensus when the Tonkin Gulf Resolution was passed in 1964 had been steadily eroded. Opposition had begun on a small scale, among pacifist and left-wing groups, and in universities, and grew as the war went on. In April 1967 there were large-scale organized demonstrations in San Francisco and New York; during the summer the White House was subjected to a form of siege by protestors, so that the President could scarcely leave without a confrontation; and in October there was a vast march on the Pentagon. The East Coast press (notably the *New York Times* and the *Washington Post*) turned against the war. More important for public opinion in general, the presentation of the war on television became more prominent, and shifted from support to neutrality, and in some cases to hostility by 1968. There is much dispute as to how far the mass media, and especially television, *caused* or *reflected* this change. The prevailing academic opinion in the late 1990s was that television did not have a decisive effect. Yet it has also been calculated that before the Tet offensive, editorial comment on television ran about 4–1 in favour of American policy in Vietnam, and afterwards 2–1 against. It is hard to believe that this had no effect, or that the shock administered by the reporting of the Tet offensive passed rapidly away.[16]

In any case, the change in opinion was far from total. The anti-war movement never achieved coherence or permanence in organization. It was not clear that a majority of the American people opposed the war. But it proved to be enough to bring about a decisive change. The crucial factor in the public opinion polls was that President Johnson's personal popularity suffered badly, with an 'approval rating' falling as low as 26 per cent in March 1968.[17] 1968 was a presidential election year; and on 31 March Johnson announced on television that he would not stand for re-election, and would instead devote the remainder of his term of office to a search for peace. It amounted to a surrender by the President, who had previously committed himself to the war.

Articulate American opinion was thus plunged into dispute and dissension. Was the corrupt and dictatorial regime in South Vietnam worthy of American support? What sort of conflict was it that could cause American troops to commit war crimes? (March 1968 was the month of the My Lai massacre, when US troops killed over a hundred people in a village suspected of harbouring Viet Cong guerrillas.) Could the United States 'save Vietnam' by a war which in itself threatened to destroy the country? The unity of American society was undermined by these questions, and American self-confidence (which was perhaps the defining characteristic of the whole country) began to collapse.

The crucial nature of this change may be illustrated by comparison with the situation during the Second World War. The United States fought that war in alliance with the Soviet Union, a totalitarian dictatorship far worse in character than anything to be found in South Vietnam. American troops fought with great ruthlessness, especially against the Japanese. The air force bombed towns flat, regardless of civilian casualties. But hardly anyone protested; and if they did, they gained little support. The crucial issue did not lie in the moral character of America's allies, or the methods of warfare adopted, but in the belief of the American people that the war was necessary and right. When that belief was undermined, as it was over Vietnam, discord and loss of confidence followed. Napoleon is reported to have said that in war three-quarters of the result turned on morale, and material factors counted for only the remaining quarter. The situation of the Americans in Vietnam bore out that verdict.

Failure in self-confidence within the United States was accompanied by a rise in anti-American sentiment outside, where the Vietnam War became a focus and stimulus for an already existing fund of resentment against the USA. In Japan, there was public opposition to American aircraft taking off from Okinawa to bomb North Vietnam. In London, there were repeated demonstrations against the Vietnam War outside the United States Embassy in Grosvenor Square. In Paris, the students who demonstrated and rioted so spectacularly in May 1968 included the Vietnam War among the many objects of their hatred. Even in West Germany, which owed so much to the United States, the press was often severely critical. In all these countries, the pictures displayed on television screens *from American sources* undermined support for the United States even among those normally inclined to be sympathetic. The Americans appeared, on their own testimony, to be 'not only brutal but incompetent'.[18] To some observers the first fault was more significant, and to others the second; together they were almost fatal.

Almost fatal, but not quite. Even in the midst of its difficulties, the United States remained a great power, which governments did not desert even when they were dismayed by some of its actions. Some countries were so closely bound to the United States that they sent troops to fight in Vietnam. Australia contributed a total of 46 000, with a maximum of 8500 serving at any one time. New Zealand sent a small contingent; South Korea a large one – about 300 000 men in all. In Britain, Harold Wilson, the Labour Prime Minister, resolutely refused American pleas to send even a token force of British troops to Vietnam, but he maintained steady diplomatic support, and resisted pressure from his party to condemn American policy in his speeches. The West German government, under Chancellor Kiesinger, remained firm in its public support; and Willy Brandt, the leader of the Social Democratic Party visited Washington to offer his support, though only in private. Japanese governments continued to support the United States, and were not unwilling to accept the advantages which the Americans produced to reward their loyalty. Only in France did the government, under President de Gaulle, express open opposition to American policy in Vietnam – most spectacularly in a speech by de Gaulle himself in Phnomh Penh, the capital of Cambodia, in September 1966. The allies of the United States were dismayed by the American troubles in Vietnam, and disturbed by the reactions of public opinion in their own countries; but their ties with the United States were far too important to be given up.

◆ Nixon and a new start in American foreign policy, 1969

In the American presidential election of 1968, the Republican candidate, Richard Nixon (who had previously been Eisenhower's Vice-President, and had lost the election of 1960 to Kennedy) narrowly defeated his Democratic opponent, Hubert Humphrey. During the campaign, the Soviet leadership was so perturbed by Nixon's reputation for anti-communism that, according to Dobrynin's memoirs, they made a secret offer of help to Humphrey – who at once refused it. If correct, this move was an index of Soviet disquiet at the prospect of Nixon's election.[19]

Such anxiety proved misplaced. Nixon quickly made it clear that he wished to maintain confidential relations with Moscow through Henry Kissinger, his National Security adviser, and Dobrynin, the Soviet Ambassador in Washington. Dobrynin became a frequent visitor to the White House, using the service entrance when he wished to be discreet; and he established a close and confidential relationship with Kissinger. (Nixon was much impressed that nothing ever leaked out from the Soviet Embassy, and doubtless wished, in view of later events, that the White House staff had been equally good at keeping secrets.) Kissinger himself was keenly aware that the United States, weakened by the Vietnam War, would have to rely more than in the past on diplomacy. He set out, by his own account, to find a compromise 'between abdication and overextension'.[20]

The new team in charge of American foreign policy was well suited to seek such a middle road. Nixon, despite his ardent anti-communist past, became primarily concerned with national interests and the balance of power. He placed a portrait of Woodrow Wilson prominently in the Cabinet Room in the White House, but he operated less like Wilson than Talleyrand. Nixon appointed William Rogers as Secretary of State, but in fact his principal adviser on foreign policy was Henry Kissinger, who had himself written a study of the Congress of Vienna, where Talleyrand, the French Foreign Minister, had achieved much for his country from a position of weakness.

Kissinger proved a skilful practitioner of secret diplomacy and power politics. He wrote later, with almost palpable scorn, of those who regarded foreign policy as a subdivision of theology, who hoped the Soviets would be converted, and those who thought it was a branch of psychiatry, who thought they should be made to feel secure. Kissinger, on the contrary, set out with the limited objective of making the Soviet Union a less dangerous enemy.[21]

Nixon expounded his foreign policy in a speech at Guam, in the Pacific, on 25 July 1969. Even in what was to prove the age of the new realism he still used the old nomenclature, and called his policy the Nixon Doctrine; but in fact he was severely practical. In the face of doubt about American steadfastness and strength of will, he reassured his allies that the United States would stand by its treaty commitments. The Americans would continue to provide a nuclear shield against nuclear threats; but they would also expect other countries to provide for their own defence against non-nuclear aggression. With regard to the Soviet Union, the United States would maintain détente, and if possible speed it up. His first priority was arms control, and on 25 October 1969 the American and Soviet governments announced jointly that strategic arms limitation talks (generally known by the acronym SALT) would begin in Helsinki on 17 November. Nixon was in a hurry – he was already a quarter of the way through his four-year presidential term of office, and had to use his time to good effect. His mind was already ranging far ahead, and he had surprises in store.

◆ Notes to Chapter 12

1. Raymond Aron, *Peace and War: A Theory of International Relations* (London, 1966), pp. xi, 536. The French original, *Paix et guerre entre les nations*, was completed in 1961 and published in 1962.

2. See Anatoly Dobrynin, *In Confidence: Moscow's Ambassador to America's Six Cold War Presidents (1962–1986)* (New York, 1995), pp. 96–8, for the episodes of the Western Union cyclist and the Finnish farmer.

3. *Ibid.*, p. 4.

4. For details of *samizdat* and nationalist dissent, see Robert Service, *A History of Twentieth Century Russia* (London, 1997), pp. 381–2, 390–1.

5. For the Middle East and the Six-Day War, see below, pp. 397–400.

6. For the earlier history of US involvement in Vietnam, see above, pp. 213–6.

7. Jacques Portes, *Les Américains et la Guerre du Vietnam* (Paris, 1993), p. 83.

8. Ernest R. May, *'Lessons' of the Past: The Use and Misuse of History in American Foreign Policy* (Oxford, 1973), pp. 120–1.

9. Portes, p. 111, citing *Statistical Abstract of the United States, 1985*, p. 342.

10. Dobrynin, *In Confidence*, pp. 156–8.

11. For the Glassboro summit and the Middle East, see below, pp. 398–401.

12. R. J. Crampton, *Eastern Europe in the Twentieth Century* (London, 1994), p. 336.

13. Alan Cassels, *Ideology and International Relations in the Modern World* (London, 1996), p. 222, citing J. L. Nogee and R. H. Donaldson, *Soviet Foreign Policy since World War II* (New York, 1981), pp. 37–9.

14. *Keesing's Contemporary Archives*, 1968, pp. 22967–72.

15. Portes, pp. 346–7.

16. See the contrasting views in Philip M. Taylor, *Global Communications, International Affairs and the Media since 1945* (London, 1997), pp. 111–15, and Brian Bond, *The Pursuit of Victory: From Napoleon to Sadam Hussein* (Oxford, 1996), pp. 189–90.

17. Portes, p. 189.

18. Richard J. Barnet, *Allies: American, Europe, Japan since the War* (London, 1984), p. 264.

19. Dobrynin, *In Confidence*, p. 176.

20. Henry Kissinger, *Diplomacy* (London, paperback edn, 1995), pp. 703–4.

21. Barnet, *Allies*, p. 297; Kissinger, *Diplomacy*, pp. 709–10.

CHAPTER

13

THE HIGH TIDE OF DÉTENTE, 1969–1975

The problems of the superpowers – The stages of détente and the
end in Vietnam – The limits of détente and the fall of Nixon –
Détente in Europe: Brandt's Ostpolitik – The Helsinki Conference –
Results of détente

The years 1969–75 saw an extraordinary transformation in international relations. In 1971–72 the United States suddenly opened relations with communist China, in a manner inconceivable ten years before. Between May 1972 and November 1974, American and Soviet leaders held no fewer than four summit meetings. In 1973 the Americans accepted defeat in Vietnam, and escaped from a disastrous war by a peace settlement which itself collapsed within two years. At the same time, there was a new flexibility in Europe, where Chancellor Brandt of West Germany launched his *Ostpolitik*, which eventually achieved treaties with the Soviet Union (August 1970), Poland (December 1970), East Germany (December 1972) and Czechoslovakia (December 1973). In 1973 there began the Helsinki Conference on Security and Co-operation in Europe, which concluded in 1975 with an agreement which itself produced some striking long-term consequences. Détente, which had begun hesitantly in the 1960s, now flourished. Something like a Seven Years' Peace succeeded the long period of the Cold War. What lay behind these events, and what were the results of détente in this period? Let us look first at the superpowers and their problems.

◆ The problems of the superpowers

Between 1969 and 1975 the United States faced a series of difficulties. The most obvious was also the most difficult: how to get out of Vietnam without utter disaster. When President Nixon took office, he was confronted by a war which the United States could not win, and was in fact beginning to lose. He had to bring to an end a commitment which three of his predecessors (Eisenhower, Kennedy and Johnson) had repeatedly declared to be vital for the United States and for the whole of South-East Asia. To get out of the Vietnam War while salvaging something of American credibility (on which the whole American position in the rest of the world depended), and to calm the unrest caused by the war within the United States itself was a Herculean task.

Less obviously, the United States also faced an economic crisis. Inflation, the falling value of the dollar, and a deteriorating balance of payments made it increasingly difficult to maintain the Bretton Woods structure, in which the US dollar had assumed the role of the world reserve currency, with a fixed parity against gold at the rate of $35 per ounce of gold.[1] The USA was being steadily pushed towards devaluation of the dollar, which Nixon accepted in August 1971 by abandoning the gold equivalence and floating the dollar. The Americans were also increasingly dependent on imported oil, a situation whose full dangers did not appear until the 'oil shock' at the end of 1973, when the Organization of Petroleum Exporting Countries (OPEC) suddenly trebled the price of oil.[2] The United States had passed from a situation of unchallenged economic supremacy to one of increasing vulnerability.

Just as important as Vietnam and economics, and linked to both, was a crisis of confidence and a failure of will. From 1947 onwards the United States had sustained a political, military and economic world role. Suddenly, in the space of two or three years after 1968, the will to continue this effort sagged. The Vietnam War was the immediate cause of this change, but there was also a long-term weariness under the weight of an apparently endless (and largely thankless) task. What is remarkable is not so much that the Americans grew weary, but that a people with a 'can-do' outlook, keen to see positive results rather than an eternal stalemate, had maintained its effort without flagging for so long. By 1969 and the following years American spirits were failing, and the broad unity of opinion on foreign policy which had prevailed for over twenty years was breaking down.

In all these problems, an improvement in relations with the Soviet Union offered some relief. The Soviets might help to find a settlement in Vietnam. Détente and arms control could diminish the economic burdens borne by the American government and taxpayers. The worldwide confrontation and endurance test of the Cold War might be eased.

On the other side of the fence, the Soviet leaders faced no crisis of the immediacy and severity of Vietnam; and indeed in 1968 they had dealt with dissent in Czechoslovakia with remarkable ease. But they had their difficulties. In foreign policy, the Soviet Union had seen China turn from an ally to an enemy. In a way, the Soviets had 'lost' China, just as the Americans believed that they had 'lost' it in 1949. A hostile China posed a military threat to the Soviet Union along the long land frontier between the two countries. Moreover, China was becoming a nuclear power, and had tested its first nuclear weapon in 1964. The Chinese possessed nothing like the nuclear armoury of the USSR, but enough to be dangerous. (When Brezhnev visited America in June 1973, he told Nixon that China would become a serious nuclear power within the next ten years, and seemed a good deal agitated by this prospect.)[3] Moreover, Chinese ideological independence had split the socialist camp, and deprived the Soviet Union of its prestige as the unchallenged leader of world communism. Even in western Europe, where the Communist Parties had once followed the lead of Moscow without question, changes were afoot. The Soviet invasion of Czechoslovakia had aroused opposition among the West European Communist Parties – even the reliable French had uttered a feeble protest. In the early 1970s the Italian Communist Party, led by Enrico Berlinguer, adopted a policy of 'Euro-communism', meaning mainly support for the European Economic Community and even for NATO. In 1972 the Italian, Spanish and French parties jointly adopted the principles of Euro-communism; though the French soon withdrew into the near-Stalinist attitudes with which they were more at ease. In face of these developments, the Soviets called a conference of 29 European Communist Parties (east and west), which met in East Berlin on 29–30 June 1976. But despite Soviet attempts to restore order to the communist movement, the final document approved by the conference referred to the 'equality and sovereign independence' of all communist parties, and expressed 'respect for their free choice of different roads' to socialism.[4] The socialist camp in Europe was in danger of losing its cohesion.

The Soviet leadership was also in difficulties at home. Stalin's power had been complete and unquestioned, but that of his successors was not. Khrushchev had been overthrown by his opponents. Brezhnev could not always impose his views on the Politburo. The ruling elite was ageing; revolutionary zeal had largely evaporated, and had been replaced by comfort and caution. In some sections of the population dissent was increasing. In 1970 a Human Rights Committee was founded by Andrei Sakharov, Valeri Chalidze and Andrei Tverdokhlebov. Jewish organizations demanded visas for their members to emigrate to Israel – a cause which was to attract support in the United States. Alexander Solzhenitsyn was awarded the Nobel Prize for Literature in 1970, but the Soviet authorities could not risk allowing him to attend the ceremony to receive it. Solzhenitsyn's three volumes on *The Gulag Archipelago*, containing an immense mass of evidence about Soviet purges and prison camps appeared in *samizdat* between 1970 and 1974. Nationalist agitation continued in the Ukraine, and an Estonian National Front was set up in 1971.

The Soviet Union also had its economic problems. There was a sharp contrast between a military sector which produced sophisticated weapons in large quantities, and a civilian sector which failed to produce enough consumer goods for the Soviet people. The USSR could put a man into space, but housewives could not buy simple household equipment. Even according to Soviet official statistics (which outside observers thought optimistic), the rate of economic growth was slackening, as the figures for GNP growth given below indicate.[5]

	1950s	1960s	First half 1970s
Soviet figures	10.2% p. a.	7.1% p. a.	5.7% p. a.
Western estimates	6.7% p. a.	5.4%	4.2%

The Soviet economy was slow in developing the computer – that key to all forms of production and administration and the very symbol of modernity. In 1974, there were an estimated 12 500 computers in the USSR, as against 207 000 in the United States; and by 1977 the figures were 20 000 and 325 000 respectively. In software for use in computers, the Soviets lagged far behind.[6] The Soviet Union therefore became heavily dependent on advanced technology imported from the West. At the same time, Soviet agriculture was in difficulties, despite heavy investment. In the 1970s, the Soviet Union had to import large quantities of cereals, mostly from the United States. It was a costly business. In 1972–73, the USSR was importing wheat from the United States at $59 per metric ton; by 1975–76 the price rose to $153. Yet in October 1975 the Soviet government signed an agreement with the Americans to purchase at least six million tonnes of wheat and corn each year for five years, starting in October 1976, and agreed in advance to meet increases in cost over the period.[7]

The Soviet Union thus became dependent on imports of advanced technology and foodstuffs from the West, and principally from the United States. Increasingly the Soviets had to borrow to pay for these imports. In 1970 the USSR had total hard currency debts of 6.5 billion dollars; by 1975 the figure was 29.6 billion dollars. The countries of the Soviet bloc in eastern Europe also borrowed heavily from the West.[8] This growing economic dependence on the West was a powerful impulse towards political détente, which in turn made it easier for the Soviet Union and its satellites to secure credits for their imports.

In addition to these political and economic reasons for seeking détente with the United States, there appears to have been a deep psychological motive at work. The Soviet leaders sought *acceptance* by the Americans, to be recognized and treated as equals. This influence was to prove particularly strong during the Helsinki Conference which met from 1973 to 1975, where the Soviet Union was anxious to secure formal recognition of the status quo which had prevailed in eastern Europe since 1945, and had been accepted in practice for many years.[9]

The Soviet Union therefore had powerful reasons to seek better relations with the United States. They suffered nothing so severe and damaging as the American trauma over Vietnam, but they faced a combination of political and economic problems which together weighed heavily upon them. On both sides, détente became the order of the day.

◆ The stages of détente and the end in Vietnam, 1971–74

Coup de théâtre: the American 'opening to China', 1971–72

On 9 July 1971 Henry Kissinger, President Nixon's National Security Adviser and closest colleague on foreign policy matters, was on a visit to Pakistan. That morning, Kissinger let it be known that he was unwell and would remain in his room. In fact, he slipped out, and flew in a Pakistani aircraft to China, where he met the Chinese Prime Minister, Zhou Enlai in Beijing. By Kissinger's account, Zhou asked him whether he was 'one of those Americans who refused to shake hands with Chinese leaders' – a reference to John Foster Dulles's refusal to shake hands with him at the Geneva Conference in 1954.[10] This greeting revealed a tenacious memory of a past slight, and was a sign of the frosty and distant nature of Chinese-American relations for the past twenty-two years. The United States had never recognized the communist government which had come to power in China in 1949. The two countries had no diplomatic relations. For some years they exchanged occasional communications through their respective ambassadors in Warsaw; but at the time of the Cultural Revolution in China in 1966 all Chinese ambassadors were recalled from every capital in the world except Cairo, so that even this slender link was severed.

The two countries did not speak to one another; and they were at odds over fundamental issues. They were ardent ideological opponents. To the Chinese, the United States represented all the evils of capitalism and imperialism. Moreover, the Chinese were deeply distrustful of détente between the United States and the Soviet Union, which boded ill for themselves. To the Americans, Chinese communism seemed even worse than the Soviet version, partly because it was more absolute in its nature, and partly because they felt that the 'loss' of China in 1949 had been a betrayal of their goodwill and benevolent intentions towards the Chinese people. More specifically, the United States still recognized the government in Taiwan (headed by Chiang Kai-shek until his death in 1975) as that of China; and until October 1971, on American insistence, Taiwan continued to hold China's permanent seat in the Security Council of the United Nations. The Chinese government, on the contrary, insisted that Taiwan was part of China, and claimed their country's rightful place at the United Nations.

These attitudes presented formidable obstacles to any rapprochement between the two counties. Yet it was in China that Nixon and Kissinger sought a diplomatic opening – perhaps *because* of the difficulties, which would make any success all the more spectacular. They had much to gain if they could pull it off. The Chinese government had provided substantial help to the North Vietnamese, and had thus acquired influence which might now be used to help in ending the Vietnam War. An agreement with China might provide a lever in American relations with the Soviet Union, which would not like to see its two adversaries getting together. Perhaps above all, Nixon hoped for advantage at home, by winning over American opinion – this was a gamble, because the old China lobby and the supporters of Chiang Kai-shek would be offended, but it was a chance worth taking.

Kissinger's visit to Beijing, accomplished in total secrecy, revealed the outline of a possible bargain between the Americans and the Chinese. Kissinger offered to make a public commitment to withdraw all American forces from Taiwan; and in return the Chinese agreed to invite Nixon for a visit to China early in 1972, and to use their influence on the North Vietnamese government to bring about a settlement in the Vietnam War which would be not too disastrous for the Americans.[11] On 15 July 1971 Nixon sprang the news on the American people, and an astonished world, that he was to visit China the next year.

On 17 February 1972 Nixon flew to Beijing. Leaving the aircraft, he made sure to shake hands with Zhou Enlai in full sight of the television cameramen and photographers. Indeed, the whole visit was arranged with an eye to publicity and to make an impact on American public opinion, which was particularly important in the year when Nixon was to stand for re-election. The contacts which had begun in the utmost secrecy were now displayed before the avid gaze of the media. Nixon called on Mao Zedong – a symbolic meeting between the embodiment of capitalist imperialism and the revolutionary icon. (Again, the two leaders shook hands for the benefit of the photographers.) The visit lasted ten days, including much sightseeing and several banquets. Behind the scenes the two sides worked hard to prepare a final communiqué, made public in Shanghai on 27 February 1972.

This document made little attempt to register agreement, but instead stated the two governments' views in separate sections. One of the very few points which they presented jointly was that: 'Neither [country] should seek hegemony in the Asia-Pacific region, and each is opposed to efforts by any other country or group of countries to establish such hegemony.' This was universally understood to refer to the USSR, and represented one of the key elements in the communiqué. On other matters, the two governments agreed to differ. On Taiwan, the Chinese stated that the People's Republic was the sole legitimate government of China, and that Taiwan was part of China; that the liberation of Taiwan was an internal Chinese affair; and that all American forces should be withdrawn from the island. The Americans recognized that all Chinese (in China and Taiwan) maintained that there was only one China, of which Taiwan was a part. They reaffirmed their interest in a peaceful settlement of the Taiwan question by the Chinese themselves; and declared that their ultimate objective was the withdrawal of all American forces from Taiwan. Meanwhile, those forces would be progressively reduced as tension in the area diminished. (This was an indirect reference to Vietnam, and was intended to give China an interest in bringing the war in Vietnam to an end.) On Vietnam itself, the Americans declared that they were searching for peace, while the Chinese firmly supported the Vietnamese people and all oppressed peoples struggling for liberation – they too had an eye to publicity. On Korea, the Americans reiterated their support for the South, while the Chinese backed North Korean demands for unification.[12]

The most remarkable fact about this visit was that it took place at all. Its consequences were mostly worked out slowly, but one became apparent at once. In view of the barely concealed declaration of opposition to Soviet hegemony in Asia and the Pacific, it might have been expected that the new Chinese-American relationship would set back the cause of détente between the United States and the Soviet Union. The reverse proved true – as Nixon and Kissinger had calculated. Within a month of Nixon's broadcast announcing his forthcoming visit to China, the Soviet government invited him to Moscow for a summit meeting which proved to be the first of four such meetings between 1972 and 1974. The *coup de théâtre* of the 'opening to China' thus paid a rapid diplomatic dividend. But it could not save the Americans from the grim reality of defeat in Vietnam.

The end in Vietnam

During 1968 the Americans, government and people alike, came to the conclusion that they must escape from the Vietnam entanglement; but no one knew how. In 1954 the French had found a way out of their Indo-China war by a diplomatic conference, held at Geneva; and the Americans now tried to use the same method, using Paris as the venue. On 16 January 1969 (after innumerable problems of procedure had been overcome) a Vietnam peace conference opened in Paris, attended by four delegations, representing the United States, the South Vietnamese government, the North Vietnamese government, and the rebel movement in South Vietnam, the Front de Liberation National (FNL). Progress was painfully slow, and often non-existent. The two principals (the USA and North Vietnam) were agreed in one respect: the Americans wanted to withdraw their forces, and the North Vietnamese wanted to see them go. But they differed totally on how to achieve this objective. The Americans wanted to withdraw on conditions which would safeguard their protégés in South Vietnam, and salvage at least some part of their own prestige. They therefore required the cessation of supplies and other assistance from North Vietnam to the FNL, and agreement that the future of South Vietnam should be decided by its own people, by means of free elections. They also wanted the North Vietnamese to return American prisoners of war before the United States forces withdrew from Vietnam. The North Vietnamese, on the other hand, demanded the *unconditional* withdrawal of American forces, and the removal of the government headed by Nguyen Van Thieu, whom they regarded as a mere puppet of the Americans. In short, the Americans sought a compromise, but the North Vietnamese intended to win. The Americans thus found themselves at the wrong end of a demand for unconditional surrender, which had been their own watchword during the Second World War.

The American bargaining position was fatally weak. In the field, the morale and fighting power of the American army were deteriorating fast. Most soldiers were sent to Vietnam for only a single year, on a rotation system which meant that every month a unit might send back home one-twelfth of its men, with disastrous results for cohesion and morale. In 1970, there were some 350 court martials for the murder or attempted murder of officers by their own troops. In 1971 it was estimated that 40 000 of the 250 000 American soldiers in Vietnam were using heroin.[13] At home, opposition to the war increased steadily. In October and November 1970 the peace movements organized large-scale demonstrations. Almost every day the television networks transmitted news film, bringing the war into people's homes. This had grave effects, because any attempt by the Americans to put military pressure on the North Vietnamese (for example by attacking North Vietnamese bases in Cambodia, or by bombing North Vietnam) was at once denounced by the peace movement – and the American administration grew very nervous of street demonstrations.

The North Vietnamese and their allies in the National Liberation Front presented a complete contrast. They were resolute in policy, ruthless on the battlefield, and implacable at the negotiating table. They faced heavy casualties without flinching. Ho Chi Minh once said that his forces would if necessary take casualties at a rate of ten to one against, and sometimes they actually did so. Over the whole period of the war the North Vietnamese and Viet Cong armed forces sustained deaths at a rate of almost four to one American and South Vietnamese, and sixteen to one against the Americans alone.[14] This was a stoical endurance which the Americans could not match.

In these circumstances, the United States had almost no military options available. The land war was coming to an end. President Nixon steadily reduced the number of American troops in Vietnam. At the end of 1970 there were 334 600; at the end of 1971, 156 800; and by the end of 1972 only 24 200.[15] In principle the Americans could still use their air power to bomb North Vietnam or mine the ports through which the North

Vietnamese received their supplies; but in practice domestic opposition limited the scope for such operations. The United States was left with only two choices: unconditional withdrawal; or the 'Vietnamization' of the war by shifting the burden of the fighting onto the South Vietnamese while the Americans gradually left the country. The Americans attempted Vietnamization, with only limited success – at the end of March 1972 the South Vietnamese army still needed help from the American air force to fend off a North Vietnamese offensive. Indeed, it was highly unlikely that the South Vietnamese could win the war on their own when they had failed to do so with massive American help – as Le Duc Tho, the principal North Vietnamese negotiator in the peace talks, pointed out to Kissinger.[16]

The American position thus remained desperately weak, until in May 1972 Nixon's visit to China began to produce some diplomatic effects. Secret conversations began between Henry Kissinger and Le Duc Tho, outside the formal sessions of the peace conference, which remained dead-locked. In September the North Vietnamese made a concession by dropping their demand for a date to be set for the complete withdrawal of American forces. On 8 October 1972 Kissinger and Le Duc Tho reached an agreement providing for a cease-fire, the clearing of mines from North Vietnamese ports, the return of prisoners, and measures for the progressive unification of Vietnam by peaceful methods. The North Vietnamese did not insist on the immediate elimination of Thieu's government, which was to remain in being until a government of 'national reconciliation' was formed, comprising representatives of the South Vietnamese Government, the Provisional Revolutionary Government, and neutrals – whoever they might be. Kissinger took these terms to Saigon (19–23 October), only to find that Thieu refused to accept the formation of the three-sided coalition government.

The deadlock was broken when Nixon was re-elected as President in November 1972, with a huge majority, winning 60.7 per cent of the popular vote against McGovern's 37.5 per cent, and carrying every state except Massachusetts. Exploiting his new freedom of action, Nixon ordered the resumption of aerial bombardment of the North, which had been suspended since 23 October. The bombing provoked widespread protests in the United States and elsewhere, but the North Vietnamese resumed negotiations; after which the bombing was again suspended.

This time a conclusion was reached. On 27 January 1973 an agreement to end the Vietnam War was signed in Paris by the four parties to the discussions: the United States and South Vietnamese Government, and North Vietnam and the Provisional Revolutionary Government of South Vietnam. The principal terms were as follows. There was to be an immediate cease-fire from midnight on 27–28 January. Mines were to be cleared from North Vietnamese ports and waterways. All foreign (meaning effectively American) troops and advisers were to withdraw from South Vietnam within sixty days, and foreign bases were to be dismantled within the same period. Captured military personnel and foreign civilians were to be returned within sixty days. On the political side, the South Vietnamese people's right to self-determination was declared to be sacred and inalienable. The two South Vietnamese parties to the agreement (i.e. the existing government and the Provisional Revolutionary Government of South Vietnam), in an extraordinary provision, were to: 'Achieve national reconciliation and concord, end hatred and enmity, prohibit all acts of reprisal and discrimination . . .' They were to set up a National Council of National Reconciliation and Concord, with three elements (government, Provisional Government, and neutral), which was to organize free and democratic elections. The reunification of Vietnam was then to be carried out by peaceful means.

Finally, a Joint Military Commission of the four parties to the agreement and an International Control Commission made up of outside powers (Canada, Hungary, Indonesia and Poland) were to supervise the implementation of the agreement; and an International Conference, meeting within thirty days, was to acknowledge the agreement and guarantee its provisions.[17]

The final agreement was a long and complex document, comprising nine chapters and twenty-three articles. It had taken four years to produce, from the opening of the Paris Conference in January 1969 to its conclusion in January 1973. Most of it proved to be not worth the paper it was written on. The International Conference met in Paris, and its twelve participants solemnly acknowledged, approved and supported the agreements for ending the war in Vietnam; but they did no more. The last American troops left Vietnam on 29 March 1973, which secured one principal North Vietnamese objective. But fighting continued throughout South Vietnam, between South Vietnamese, North Vietnamese and the supporters of the Provisional Revolutionary Government. The cease-fire was not observed, and 'national reconciliation' was a mere mockery. Before the end of 1973 the North Vietnamese launched a general offensive; in 1974 they occupied central Vietnam; and some two years after the signature of the Paris agreement, they overran the whole of South Vietnam. The last Americans left in haste, lifted by helicopter from the roof of the Embassy in Saigon on 21 April 1975. The North Vietnamese occupied Saigon on 30 April 1975, and promptly renamed it Ho Chi Minh City in honour of their greatest hero, who had died in 1969. They had aimed, not at compromise, but at victory; and having achieved it, they registered it on the map.

Cambodia and Laos also fell to the communists. In Cambodia (renamed Kampuchea), the communist Khmer Rouge, supported by the Chinese and the Soviet Union, gained control of the country, and occupied the capital, Phnom Penh, on 17 April 1975. The Khmer Rouge leader, Pol Pot, embarked on a reign of terror which was directed as much against national

Casualties in the Vietnam War, 1964–73[19]

	Killed	Wounded	Missing
USA	57 685	152 303	695
S. Vietnam armed forces	183 528	approx. 500 000	
S. Korea	4407		
Australia	492		
New Zealand	35		
N. Vietnam armed forces, plus Viet Cong	approx. 950 000		
Total Vietnamese	approx. 1 333 000		
Total non-Vietnamese	62 619		

enemies (Vietnamese, Thais, Laotians and even Chinese) as against class opponents. In the next four years, unknown numbers of people (variously estimated at between 1 600 000 and 2 000 000) were slaughtered or systematically starved to death.[18] In Laos, a communist regime was installed by the Pathet-Lao in December 1975.

The effects of the Vietnam War were profound. American casualties were relatively light; Vietnamese casualties were very heavy. In addition to these figures, there were heavy casualties in the Vietnamese population, North and South, and widespread material destruction.

It is worth pausing for a moment to note the comparative impact of these casualties. The United States lost some 58 000 dead out of a population of nearly 200 million – a tiny proportion. Vietnamese military casualties on both sides totalled some 1 133 000 dead out of a population of about 37 million, a proportion of about three per cent. The principal human cost of the Vietnam War was paid by the Vietnamese themselves.

Remarkably, after such an experience, Vietnam emerged as a strong power in its own area. In 1978 the Vietnamese invaded Cambodia/Kampuchea; and in 1979 they successfully resisted a Chinese invasion of their own territory – demonstrating that their victory had been nationalist as well as communist, and that communist states could go to war with one another. Equally remarkably, after Cambodia and Laos passed under communist control, *the other dominos did not fall.* Even Thailand, the closest neighbour to the new Vietnam, remained intact and largely unperturbed. Malaya and Singapore were unaffected. For the Americans, this was comforting in that South-East Asia did not fall to communism, but dismaying in that the domino theory was proved false, and the whole war appeared futile.

In the United States, the war and the defeat had far-reaching consequences. The war divided Americans, in contrast to the unity which they had maintained in earlier conflicts. The divisions did not run along normal political lines, because intervention in Vietnam was the work of four Presidents, two from each party; but between those who supported the war and those who opposed it, and between those who served in Vietnam and those who did not (or even avoided service). The defeat was the first for a country which had long been accustomed to victory (even Korea had been a draw). In its last stages defeat amounted to a humiliation, greater in 1975 with the fall of Saigon than in 1973 at the time of the peace agreement. The morale of the Army suffered gravely, and took a long time to recover. The United States thus reached a position where its own people distrusted any military intervention abroad, and where its Army was in any case crippled by internal difficulties. The strongest single power in the world was going through a crisis of weakness.

Yet there was at least some balancing compensation. American policy emerged from the defeat with a greater realism. The United States was now conscious of the limits of its power. Moreover, American statesmen had come to recognize that the communist bloc was not monolithic, but had divisions of its own which they could exploit. In the circumstances of the new realism, Nixon and Kissinger were able to play the China card in 1971–72. From 1972 onwards they set out to see what advantage could be gained from developing détente with the Soviet Union.

Détente and American-Soviet summit meetings, 1972–74

Détente between the two superpowers had begun in the late 1950s, with the contacts between Eisenhower and Khrushchev, and developed as the two sides came to grasp their common interest in avoiding mutual destruction. In the 1960s American and Soviet leaders had held occasional summit meetings, and concluded agreements on limited aspects of nuclear weaponry, notably the treaty of 1963 prohibiting nuclear tests in the atmosphere. In November 1969 the superpowers had begun strategic arms limitation talks, which proceeded at a technical level and very slowly.

There was thus some basis to build on when in 1971 both governments sought to hurry matters along. Each side had its own reasons for haste. Nixon wanted both the kudos and the solid advantages of an agreement on arms control, and he was desperately anxious to shed his reputation as a man of war in Vietnam by assuming the mantle of a man of peace in relations with Moscow. The Soviet leadership had been shaken by Nixon's announcement that he was to visit China, and moved quickly to ensure that in the new triangular diplomacy they were one of a pair rather than being isolated. They also needed to ease the strain of the arms race – far more than the Americans did, because the strain was greater on their weaker economy. And they too sought to enhance their reputation, as peace-makers and as equal partners with the United States in the management of world affairs.

In October 1971, after a good deal of manoeuvring behind the scenes, the Soviet government formally invited President Nixon to visit Moscow, and he accepted. The date was fixed for 22 May–1 June 1972. At the last minute, in early May 1972, the fate of this meeting hung in the balance as the Soviet leaders debated whether they could receive Nixon in Moscow while the Americans were bombing North Vietnam. (American raids had been resumed on a large scale in April.) Opinions were divided; but Gromyko, the experienced Foreign Minister, wanted the meeting to go ahead, on the ground that to abandon it would mean effectively allowing North Vietnam a veto on Soviet foreign policy. The wider needs of the Soviet Union had to prevail over solidarity with North Vietnam.

Nixon's visit to Moscow was the first to the Soviet capital by an American President. (Roosevelt had been to Yalta, in the Crimea, in 1945; Nixon himself had been to Moscow twice before, once when Vice-President in 1959 and once as a private citizen in 1967.) In his opening remarks, Nixon recalled the wartime conferences and stressed the importance of reaching agreement at the summit. 'If we leave all the decisions to the bureaucrats, we will never achieve any progress,' he said.[20] The lengthy visit (eleven days in all) included some sightseeing and several social events, which had their own value in promoting informal contacts. There were substantial results, notably a Joint Declaration on Principles and two agreements on strategic arms limitation.

The Joint Declaration on the basic principles to be observed in relations between the two countries was phrased in general terms, but was none the less important for that. The first of its twelve points stated that there was no alternative to peaceful co-existence, and that: 'Differences in ideology and in the social systems of the USA and the USSR are not obstacles to the bilateral development of normal relations based on the principles of sovereignty, equality, non-interference in internal affairs and mutual advantage.' The two sides went on to undertake to try to avoid confrontations and to exercise restraint; to exchange views at the highest level; to limit armaments; to promote commercial and economic ties; and to encourage contacts in science, technology and culture. They were careful to emphasize that they made no claims to special rights or advantages, and that their relations were not directed against other countries.[21]

On the question of nuclear weapons, the two sides had to grapple with major changes which had come about during the 1960s, in the two aspects of defence and attack. The defences of both countries had been improved by the introduction of anti-ballistic missiles (ABMs), capable of intercepting enemy missiles in flight, and thus offering some protection against a nuclear attack. At the same time, the attack had also been strengthened by the development of multiple independently targeted return vehicles (MIRVs), missiles carrying several nuclear warheads which could each be directed against a different target. These developments were technically demanding and immensely costly. In Moscow, the two sides grappled with the defensive problem by concluding a treaty on the limitation of anti-ballistic missiles. Each country agreed to maintain only two sites at which anti-ballistic missiles were to be stationed: one to protect their respective capitals, Moscow and Washington; and another elsewhere in the country. Each site was to contain 100 ABMs, thus limiting the two powers to a total of 200 ABMs each. The two sides agreed to verify the execution of the treaty by means of satellite observation; which in itself was a considerable step forward. The principal significance of this treaty was twofold. First, it limited the number of ABMs held by each power, and thus placed some check on the expenditure which they required. Second, the establishment of only two defensive zones left most of each country exposed to attack, so that each side accepted its own vulnerability. By implication, both super-powers recognized the principle of deterrence. The treaty had no time limit, but permitted either signatory to withdraw after six months' notice if it considered that its 'supreme interests' were being jeopardized. This gave an incentive to both powers to conclude a more general arms limitation agreement, so that their supreme interests would not be jeopardized.[22.]

The two sides also reached a further agreement on strategic arms limitation (usually referred to as SALT 1 – Strategic Arms Limitation Talks 1). This did not take the form of a treaty, but was an interim arrangement for five years, limiting the numbers of missile launchers (on land or on board submarines) to those already in existence or under construction. Numbers of offensive weapons, as distinct from the defensive anti-ballistic missiles, were to be limited as follows:[23]

USA: 1054 intercontinental ballistic missiles (ICBMs)
       656 submarine-launched ballistic missiles (SLBMs)
      1710 missiles in total
USSR: 1618 or 1408 ICBMs
      740 or 950 SLBMs
      2358 missiles in total

No limit was placed on the numbers of MIRV warheads, in which arsenal the United States held an advantage; so the apparent disproportion in favour of the Soviet Union was much less significant than it might appear at first sight.

By this agreement the United States accepted that the Soviet Union should have superiority in numbers of missiles, but balanced this by a preponderance in numbers of MIRVs, and by a general technical superiority. Neither side abandoned the development of new types of weapons. In the United States, opponents of the agreement, headed by Senator Henry Jackson (Democrat), claimed that the United states had unwarrantably conceded superiority to the Soviets. In fact, both sides made a virtue of accepting the existing balance, which gave each of them ample strength to inflict catastrophic damage on the other.

Just over a year after the Moscow summit meeting, on 18–25 June 1973, Brezhnev visited Nixon in the United States. In the course of their discussions, the two leaders signed nine separate agreements and declarations, mainly concerning such matters as air services between the two countries, cultural and scientific contacts, and exchange of information on agriculture and the non-military uses of atomic energy. In some circumstances, these might have been regarded as routine, but in the context of the Cold War they illustrated the changes which had occurred in Soviet–American relations. Nixon and Brezhnev also signed an agreement to prevent nuclear war, not only between their own countries but also between either of them and a third power, which implied that the two superpowers together were assuming a directing role in world affairs; which again showed how the nature of their relations had changed.

In the background to these agreements, the informal aspects of the visit went well. Brezhnev went to Camp David for a day or two. Nixon presented him with a Lincoln Continental motor-car, which the Soviet leader drove enthusiastically round the Camp David roads, with the President as his sole passenger. They then went to Nixon's summer residence at San Clemente, California, where they once talked late into the night. In general, Nixon was impressed by the contrast between Brezhnev's demeanour and that of Khrushchev during his visit to America in 1959. Khrushchev, he thought, had been anxious to compensate for weakness by being tough; Brezhnev was confident and relaxed.[24] Nixon now hoped to establish summit meetings as regular annual events, ensuring a constant level of contact and understanding between the two governments; and indeed a third meeting followed almost precisely a year later.

Nixon went to the Soviet Union on 27 June 1974, and stayed until 3 July. The meetings began at the Kremlin, where the two leaders signed an agreement limiting underground nuclear tests, supplementing the Moscow Treaty of August 1963, which had prohibited tests in the atmosphere. Brezhnev then reciprocated Nixon's hospitality in California by taking the President to his own summer retreat in the Crimea. (The meetings in fact took place in Yalta, but Nixon did not want to be associated with the place where Roosevelt was said by his critics to have given away eastern Europe. The Soviets tactfully substituted the name Oreander, after the hotel where Nixon stayed; put up some new signposts; and so avoided the difficulty.)[25] Little was achieved at these discussions, but at any rate the series of summit meetings was kept up, and now appeared well established. Nixon invited Brezhnev to return to the United States in 1975, and the Soviet leader accepted – an arrangement made public in the communiqué at the end of the visit. In fact, Nixon was already gravely damaged by the Watergate affair, and he was compelled to resign from the Presidency on 9 August, just over a month after his return from the Soviet Union.[26] With that change, the pattern was broken.

These three summit meetings between 1972 and 1974 produced significant results, in personal relations, in minor but useful agreements, and in arms limitation. The strategic arms agreements were their most important achievement, and require some further analysis. The agreements registered a rough balance of nuclear strength, in which the two superpowers possessed ample capacity to destroy one another, which was called, in the language of a jargon-ridden age, 'mutual assured destruction', or when abbreviated to its initials – MAD. The USA and USSR were also assured of their superiority over other nuclear powers, though they could not disregard the damage which could be inflicted by even a small number of missiles. The balance of forces may be set out in two ways: numbers of nuclear missiles and bombers (which was not the same as numbers of warheads); and the state of technical innovation in nuclear weapons.

In this balance of terror, the Soviet Union held some advantage in numbers of missiles, but the United States was ahead in the development of MIRVs, whose multiple warheads did much to offset the imbalance in missiles. At the same time, the superpowers put fresh efforts into types of weapons which were not covered by the agreements; and here the

The Nuclear balance

	Nuclear missiles and bombers, 1974[27]				
	USA	*USSR*	*UK*	*France*	*China*
ICBMs	1054	1575	—	—	—
IRBMs	—	600	—	18	c.80
SLBMs	656	720	64	48	—
Bombers, LR	437	140	—	—	—
Bombers, MR	66	800	50	52	100

Innovation in strategic nuclear weapons[28]

Type of innovation	*USA*	*USSR*
Nuclear-powered submarine	1954	1958
First trial of ICBM	1958	1957
ICBM operational	1960	1959
Submarine-launched ICBM operational	1960	1957
ICBM fitted with MIRVs	1970	1974–5
First trial of IM cruise missile	1976	1979
Cruise missiles operational	1983–4	1984–5

Note: ICBM: intercontinental ballistic missile; IRBM:intermediate range ballistic missile; SLBM: submarine-launched ballistic missle; LR: long-range; MR: medium-range; IM: intermediate-range; MIRV: multiple independently targeted return vehicle.

Americans had an advantage in the development of intermediate-range missiles from 1976 onwards.

What the statistics do not show is the relative ease or difficulty with which the two superpowers sustained the competition in armaments. The overall strength and efficiency of the American economy were such that the USA could achieve its nuclear weapons programmes with proportionately less effort and by deploying a smaller proportion of its national resources than could the Soviet Union. On the other hand, the Soviets achieved a prime psychological objective, in that in the arms limitation agreements the United States accepted the USSR as an equal in superpower status. Much later, when the Cold War was over, Yuri Kvitsinsky, a Soviet diplomat and specialist in arms control, told a Western interviewer: 'We were happy that we had achieved parity with the Americans. We had sacrificed maybe the lives of two generations for this task.'[29] When Americans, under Reagan's presidency, withdrew this recognition of equality of status by embarking on the Strategic Defence Initiative, the Soviets were wounded in their self-esteem as well as thrown off balance strategically and economically.

◆ The fall of Nixon and the slow-down of détente

The policy of détente produced considerable achievements, not least by its very existence. A world in which the President of the United States and the leader of the Soviet Union met each year was a safer place than one where they did not even speak to one another. Even so, the policy had many critics in the United States. The new approach to China offended those who still supported Chiang Kai-shek and wanted to have nothing to do with the communists. Many were deeply committed to the ideological struggle against communism, and disliked the increasing co-operation with the enemy. It seemed that détente was pursued by ignoring the issue of human rights within the Soviet Union – for example, Senator Henry Jackson complained that the United Sates was failing to help Jews who wanted to emigrate from the USSR to Israel. Even the arms limitation agreements came under attack for seeming to yield too much to the Soviet Union by way of numbers of missiles.

Such criticisms might have done little damage if it had not been for the Watergate affair, a scandal in internal American politics which swelled to enormous proportions and eventually brought down President Nixon. A burglary in June 1972 at the Democratic National Committee's headquarters in Washington in the Watergate complex of buildings was later shown to have been approved by the then Attorney-General. Officials at the White House, notably Bob Haldeman and John Ehrlichman, who were closely associated with Nixon, made a concerted attempt to conceal what had happened. A Senate committee, and later a special prosecutor, investigated the affair. Eventually, it was demonstrated by tape-recorded conversations that Nixon himself had known about the burglary and its concealment almost from the beginning, and that he had tried to obstruct the Federal Bureau of Investigation's enquiry into the break-in. Articles of impeachment were brought against the President in July 1974; on 5 August Nixon released transcripts of certain highly damaging tape-recordings; and on the 9th he resigned from office, with his reputation in ruins. The Vice-President, Gerald Ford, became President in his stead.

These events absorbed much of Nixon's attention from the spring of 1973 onwards, and gradually undermined his conduct of foreign policy. For a long time, the Soviet government did not grasp the gravity of the affair. The Soviet leaders (who were not unduly perturbed by crimes far worse than burglary) regarded the Watergate affair as an intrigue by Nixon's opponents, who were often also enemies of détente and the USSR. Brezhnev did what he could to sustain Nixon in his trials. On 10 November 1973 he sent the President a personal letter wishing him, 'from the depths of my heart', success in overcoming his difficulties. On 28 May Brezhnev sent Nixon a telegram admitting that he did not really understand what the affair was about, but offering his support in the President's difficulties. By the time of Nixon's visit to the Soviet Union in June–July 1974, it appears that Brezhnev was anxious not to tie the advantages of détente exclusively to Nixon; but he still agreed to meet the President again in 1975.[30]

In the event, the fall of Nixon had serious consequences for Soviet–American relations. Ford, the new President, was a beginner in foreign policy. He had spent some twenty-five years in the House of Representatives, which was by tradition much less concerned with foreign affairs than the Senate. The Soviet Embassy in Washington described him as 'a typical Congressman-patriot of the Cold War era'.[31] On the other hand, Kissinger remained in office as Secretary of State, and sought to continue the policy of détente in which he had played so large a part. Ford agreed to make the attempt, and proposed a meeting with Brezhnev in the Soviet Union, at the unusual venue of Vladivostok.

The Vladivostok summit was short, occupying only two full days (23–4 November 1974). The two leaders worked under handicaps – on the American side obvious, on the Soviet side hidden. Ford was only a stop-gap President, until the next elections came round in 1976. Brezhnev suffered a heart attack on the evening of 22 November, after greeting Ford on his arrival; he recovered well enough to get through the meetings, but this proved to be the beginning of a deterioration in health which was to dog him for the rest of his life. Even so, the Vladivostok conference made some further progress on strategic arms limitation. The two sides agreed to move towards parity in numbers of intercontinental missile launchers, with a total of 2400 each (of which no more than 1320 should be MIRVs). This agreement was to take over from the interim arrangement reached at the first Nixon–Brezhnev summit at Moscow in 1972, which was due to expire in 1977. This represented only a very modest achievement. Parity was not to be reached until 1985, which was a long way ahead; and only at the cost of some increase in numbers of launchers.[32]

The Vladivostok conference was an attempt to prolong détente after the fall of Nixon. But at the same time détente was under threat from within the United States, on the issue of Jewish emigration from the Soviet Union. In October 1972 a trade agreement had been concluded between the USA and the USSR, in which the United States was to grant 'most favoured nation' status to the Soviet Union. (This provision was common in international trade agreements, and ensured that any commercial advantage secured by another state in another agreement should automatically be extended to all countries with 'most favoured nation' status. It thus conferred, not special privilege, but equality within a privileged group.) This agreement had to be ratified by Congress before it came into force; and in March 1973 Henry Jackson in the Senate, and Charles Vanik in the House of Representatives, proposed an amendment to the Trade Reform Bill to prevent any state which restricted emigration from receiving 'most favoured nation' status. The Soviet Union made concessions, removing an 'exit tax' on emigrants imposed in 1972, and secretly offering to permit 50 000 Jews to leave the country each year. This proposal was communicated in confidence to Senator Jackson, who passed it on to the press and demanded an increase to 60 000. This was rejected in Moscow as interference with the internal affairs of the Soviet Union. Finally, Congress passed the Trade Reform Bill with the Jackson–Vanik amendment attached to it. The President signed the Bill in January 1975, but the Soviet Union refused to comply with its terms, and thus the whole trade agreement of October 1972 fell to the ground.

The two governments attempted to maintain that détente as a whole was not affected by this dispute; but in fact Soviet–American relations suffered grave damage. The Soviet Union resented the attempt to interfere in its domestic affairs. In the United States, human rights and Jewish organizations combined in hostility to the Soviet Union. Demonstrations took place outside the Soviet Embassy, and a sustained campaign in the press and on television brought a renewed edge of bitterness to American attitudes to the USSR. In 1975 détente between the superpowers was faltering, and the improved atmosphere generated by the summit meetings was fading. Yet at the same time a movement towards détente in Europe came to a successful conclusion.

◆ Détente in Europe: Germany, 1969–73

For many years Germany lay at the centre of the Cold War, as successive Berlin crises between 1948 and 1961 had demonstrated. By the late 1960s, this was no longer the case. The United States was concentrating its attention on Vietnam. The Soviet Union had achieved stability and increasing prosperity in East Germany by building the Berlin Wall in 1961. Germany had ceased to be the centre of the superpowers' attention.

The German question itself, comprising the relations between the two Germanies, the possibility of unification, and the status of Berlin, seemed to have solidified beyond the possibility of change. Successive West German governments, under three Chancellors – Adenauer (1949–63), Erhard (1963–66), and Kiesinger (1966–69) – bound their country tightly to the West. The Federal Republic was a loyal member of NATO, and remained faithful to the American alliance despite the strains imposed by the unpopularity of the Vietnam War. West German rearmament proceeded steadily, and the new *Bundeswehr* reached a total of 460 000 men, playing a significant role in NATO's strategy. At the same time, West Germany became a leading member of the European Economic Community. With every year that passed, the West German economy was more closely integrated into that of western Europe, and became steadily more prosperous. In 1963 Adenauer and de Gaulle signed the Treaty of Paris, committing their two countries to a close and far-reaching co-operation, so that the 'Franco-German couple' became the most important element in west European politics and the driving force in the EEC.

Thus in western Europe the Federal Republic of Germany pursued a flexible and dynamic policy of alliance in NATO and integration within the EEC. Towards the east, on the other hand, West Germany displayed a total rigidity. In 1955 the West German Foreign Minister, Walter Hallstein, laid down the policy which came to be called the Hallstein Doctrine, by which West Germany refused to recognize East Germany, and undertook to break off diplomatic relations with any government which did so. Dynamism in the west was thus contrasted with complete immobility towards the east.

In the 1960s the situation in western Europe was changed by the attempts of General de Gaulle to break the mould of international politics, and to introduce a new flexibility. In March 1966 he announced the withdrawal of France from the North Atlantic Treaty Organization, though not from the treaty itself. NATO headquarters had to move from Paris, and all foreign troops were to leave France by 1 April 1967. After this bombshell, de Gaulle attempted to improve relations with the Soviet Union (which he preferred to call Russia), in pursuit of his cloudy grand design of a Europe stretching from the Atlantic to the Urals. He visited the Soviet Union in June 1966 to a warm popular welcome. Immediate practical results were not forthcoming, but in the long run and psychologically de Gaulle's initiative loosened the strait-jacket of European diplomacy.

In West Germany, policy began to change at much the same time, under the 'Grand Coalition' government (1966–69), headed by the Christian Democrat Kurt Kiesinger, with the Social Democrat Willy Brandt as Foreign

Minister. In 1967 the Federal Republic established diplomatic relations with Romania and Yugoslavia, even though these countries recognized the East German government; and thus the first departure was made from the strict application of the Hallstein Doctrine. In October 1969 Brandt became Chancellor at the head of a new coalition government formed by the Social Democrats and Liberals. He quickly embarked on a far-reaching new *Ostpolitik* (Eastern policy), aiming at the recognition of East Germany, the acceptance of the Polish frontier along the Oder–Neisse line, and an improvement in relations with the Soviet Union. This was a risky policy in domestic terms, because it meant the formal renunciation of territories which were still 'home' to many people who had been refugees in 1945. But their numbers were diminishing, and there was a change of generations which permitted an acceptance of the status quo which would have been impossible ten or fifteen years earlier. Brandt was also able to secure the backing of Nixon's administration in the United States, which was willing to support a venture which complemented its own policy of détente. Indeed, Nixon found in Brandt's *Ostpolitik* an opportunity to secure a new agreement on Berlin.

In these favourable circumstances, Brandt began his new policy. The final result was to be an intricate series of treaties which had the paradoxical effect of enshrining the existing order and yet starting changes which were ultimately to undermine it. Prosaic and patient diplomatic negotiations led to far-reaching results; and by trying to keep everything the same, much was in the long run transformed.

Brandt began by arranging meetings with the Prime Minister of East Germany, Willi Stoph, first in Erfurt (in East Germany) on 19 March 1970, and then in Kassel (in the West) on 21 May. The public aspects of these meetings were crucial, because they displayed the new situation for all to see, yet they were also risky. In the East, Brandt was greeted by welcoming crowds; in the West, Stoph confronted hostile demonstrators. The contrast might well have brought the new policy to a halt; but it did not. The key to success, as Brandt knew well, lay not in East Germany but in Moscow. The crucial negotiations were those with the Soviet government, leading to the Treaty of Moscow (12 August 1970). In this treaty, the Soviet Union and West Germany agreed that their objectives were peace and the relaxation of tension (apparent platitudes which were in fact of the highest significance); renounced the threat or use of force in their relations with one another; and undertook to respect the territorial integrity of all states in Europe within their existing frontiers, *specifically including* the Oder–Neisse line between Poland and East Germany, and the border between East and West Germany.[33] While this treaty was being negotiated, Brandt made clear that its ratification by West Germany would be dependent on the conclusion of an agreement on the status of Berlin and rights of access to the city; which was a point which Nixon had requested when he gave his backing to the *Ostpolitik*.

West Germany thus accepted the Oder–Neisse line as the western boundary of Poland in a treaty with the Soviet Union. It then became possible to acknowledge the same frontier by direct agreement with Poland. The Treaty of Warsaw (7 December 1970) between West Germany and the Polish government accepted the Oder–Neisse line, confirmed the respect of the two parties for each other's territorial integrity, and affirmed that neither country had any territorial claims against the other. The last of these points marked a crucial renunciation by West Germany of the former German territories that were now part of Poland.[34]

While these negotiations were in progress, the four occupying powers in Berlin (the United States, Soviet Union, Britain and France) began their own discussions in March 1970, and reached a successful conclusion in a Four-Power Agreement on Berlin (3 September 1971). The four governments reaffirmed their existing joint rights in Berlin. The Soviet Union undertook not to impede transport between the Western sectors of Berlin and West Germany, and the access routes were defined in detail. The three Western powers accepted that West Berlin was not a constituent part of the Federal Republic, and would not be governed by it; while the Soviets dropped their claim that West Berlin was part of the territory of the German Democratic Republic.[35] With this agreement, the successive crises over Berlin which had plagued relations between East and West came to an end. The situation which had long been accepted in practice was now formally acknowledged by treaty.

All these agreements together paved the way (though only after difficult negotiations) for the crowning achievement of a treaty between the two Germanies, signed on 21 December 1972. By this treaty, the Federal Republic and the Democratic Republic recognized one another and agreed to exchange diplomatic representatives. They affirmed the inviolability of the existing frontier between them, and declared that the sovereign power of each state was limited to its own territory, which marked the renunciation of the long-standing West German claim to be the rightful representative of the whole German people.[36]

This treaty, and the new atmosphere which it encouraged, brought significant changes in relations between the two Germanies. The West German government financed the maintenance of road and rail communications with West Berlin, across East German territory. There was a large increase in West German economic assistance to the East, which had begun by hidden means under Adenauer's chancellorship. There also developed a strange and secret trade in people. As early as 1963, East Germany had handed eight prisoners over to the Federal Republic in return for payment. This practice then continued sporadically, and after the treaty between the two Germanies attained large proportions, so that by 1989 a total of nearly 250 000 persons had been traded from East to West for payments amounting to some 3.5 billion Deutschmarks.[37]

So it came about that the treaties resulting from Brandt's *Ostpolitik* all confirmed the status quo, and yet in the long run led to change. The apparently limited and legalistic fact that the Germanies recognized one another put the two countries on a different footing, and led to unexpected consequences through increased traffic between them. Thus the road to change was opened by agreements to keep everything as it was. The same proved true of another aspect of détente in Europe: the Helsinki Conference.

◆ Détente in Europe: The Helsinki Accords, 1975

The idea of a general conference on European security and co-operation originated with the Soviet Union. On 5 July 1966 the Warsaw Pact powers, meeting at Bucharest, proposed a conference to discuss European security, to be attended by all European states in order to register their formal acceptance of the existing frontiers and political systems in the continent. For almost two years this proposal remained without a reply from the NATO countries. Then, at a meeting in Reykjavik (25 June 1968), the NATO states put the ball back into the opposite court by proposing a negotiation on mutual and balanced reduction of forces in Europe. This reply was not only extremely slow, but sought to change the subject. The Soviet bloc had wanted primarily to talk about politics, while NATO wanted to talk about military strength.

Half-hearted discussions of these divergent proposals continued, interrupted for a time by the Soviet invasion of Czechoslovakia in 1968, until in 1969 the Warsaw Pact powers twice renewed their appeals for a conference (at meetings in Budapest in March, and Prague in October). The NATO allies, at a meeting in December 1969, approved in principle the idea of a Conference on European Security and Co-operation; but even so it was not until 22 November 1972 that a preparatory meeting, at ambassadorial level, began at Helsinki. Discussions continued until 8 June 1973, dealing with the date and place for the conference; the question of who was to be invited; and what was to be on the agenda. This preparatory meeting finally agreed that the conference should proceed in three stages: first at Helsinki, between Foreign Ministers (3–7 July 1973); second, meetings of experts at Geneva, to prepare detailed draft agreements (these lasted for two years, from 18 September 1973 to 21 July 1975); and finally a meeting (again at Helsinki) of heads of governments or states, to finalize the recommendations made by the officials at Geneva. Thirty-three European states, plus the United States and Canada, were represented at all these meetings. It is scarcely surprising that progress was so slow, and indeed it was remarkable that the whole proceeding was followed through to a final conclusion – in itself a sign of the changed circumstances brought about by détente between the USA and USSR, and by the complex treaties relating to Germany.

The purpose of the Soviet Union in initiating this vast diplomatic effort was to secure public international recognition of the post-war boundaries in Europe, and of the existing order in Europe as a whole. The Soviets had in practice controlled eastern Europe since 1947, and the recent treaties of 1970–72 concerning the two Germanies and Poland had recognized the most contentious frontiers in Europe – yet they still sought the formal acceptance of these facts. The Soviet Union, despite its arbitrary use of power in some respects, attached great importance to formal agreements. The United States, for its part, was at first doubtful as to the value of a Conference on European Security, attaching more importance to the idea of force reductions which had been the original NATO riposte to the Soviet proposals. When the Americans accepted the principle of a Conference on European Security, Kissinger attached no great importance to it, and was not interested in the details. He was prepared to give the Soviets what they wanted by formalizing the status quo in Europe, which had after all been accepted for many a long year; but he seems to have expected little more from the long negotiations. (He had much else on his mind at the time, with the end of the conflict in Vietnam, 1973–75). In the event, both the superpowers were surprised by the outcome. The Soviets achieved their main objective, only to find that other elements had been introduced into the deal. The Americans expected little, and slowly discovered that they had gained much. How did this come about?

The Final Act of the Helsinki Conference, concluded by all 35 governments at the end of July 1975, comprised three sections, often referred to as 'baskets', a curious term conveying the impression that each comprised a somewhat miscellaneous collection of provisions – which was indeed the case. The first 'basket' dealt with questions relating to security in Europe; the second with commercial, industrial and environmental co-operation between the signatories; and the third with co-operation in humanitarian and cultural matters. The contents of this complicated and crucial agreement may be summarized as follows.[38]

First section (basket): Security in Europe

This set out a declaration of principles, accepted by all the signatories for the conduct of their relations with one another, including:

- Acceptance of the sovereign equality of states.
- Rejection of the use or threat of force.
- Acceptance of the inviolability of existing frontiers (this represented the key objective for the Soviet Union).
- Recognition of the territorial integrity of states.
- Peaceful settlement of disputes.
- Non-intervention in the internal affairs of other states.
- Respect for human rights and fundamental liberties, including freedom of thought, conscience, and religious or other convictions.

- Acceptance of equality of rights among peoples, and the right of peoples to self-determination.
- Co-operation between states.
- The carrying out in good faith of obligations assumed in conformity with international law. (This tacitly accepted both the two alliance systems of NATO and the Warsaw Pact, and also the position of neutral states.)

As well as these general principles, this section provided for the exchange of military information, and the signatories agreed to give prior notice of manoeuvres and large-scale movements of troops; to exchange military personnel and arrange visits by military delegations to the other side; and to undertake other measures to increase confidence between the alliances.

Second section (or basket): Co-operation between signatory states

This section set out a programme of co-operation by means of trade agreements (to be based on the 'most favoured nation' principle); co-operation in industrial matters, in science and technology, and in matters concerning the environment, transport, tourism, and migrant workers.

Third section (or basket): Co-operation in humanitarian and cultural matters

In this section, the signatories agreed to increase cultural and educational exchanges, and to improve the circulation of and access to information The agreements specifically undertook to facilitate the dissemination of newspapers and other printed matter, of films, and of broadcast information. They also undertook to develop contacts between individuals, and resolve humanitarian problems – for example, by reuniting families and permitting marriages between citizens of different countries.

Finally, the signatories agreed that the implementation of the Helsinki Accords should be reviewed at a further conference of Foreign Ministers, to meet in Belgrade in 1977.

The Helsinki Accords received only a lukewarm welcome by the two superpowers. In the United States, public opinion was divided and the government unenthusiastic. Wholehearted opponents of communism complained that the agreements abandoned the peoples of eastern Europe to domination by an oppressive regime. Human rights activists claimed that the accords did not go far enough in compelling the Soviet Union to change its policies, for example on emigration. In the administration, Kissinger had never been keen on the Helsinki idea, and Ford was coming near the end of his term as a stop-gap president. In the Soviet Union, the leadership (which had left the details of the negotiations to the Foreign Ministry) was surprised by the contents of the third section, on humanitarian and other questions. A group led by Kosygin and Andropov disliked commitments which might open the way to intervention in the internal affairs of the USSR. Gromyko, the Foreign Minister, argued that the balance of the whole agreement was favourable: Section One scored a major success by securing acceptance of the post-1945 boundaries; and even under Section Three the Soviet government could still decide what constituted interference in internal affairs and act as it thought fit. Brezhnev, anxious to secure a big success in international affairs, supported Gromyko, and the agreement was accepted.[39] In the event, the misgivings of the doubters proved well founded. The text of the Helsinki agreement was published in *Pravda*, giving it wide circulation and the authority of government approval. Dissidents within the Soviet Union later exploited the provisions of Section Three, especially on the diffusion of information; and the government was now too conscious of its reputation abroad to resort to the full machinery of Stalinist repression. In other countries in the Soviet bloc, advocates of human rights (notably Lech Walesa in Poland) claimed the support of the Helsinki agreement for their activities. Quite contrary to the intentions of the Soviet Union, which had been to consolidate the status quo in eastern Europe, the Helsinki Accords in the long term had a destabilizing effect throughout that area, and played a part in the eventual collapse of communism.

As a counterpart to the negotiations on European security and co-operation, the Soviet Union agreed to parallel discussions on mutual and balanced force reductions, which the NATO states had proposed in 1968 and again in 1970. The NATO proposal was to set a maximum of about 700 000 troops on each side in an eastern zone made up of East Germany, Poland and Czechoslovakia, and a western zone comprising West Germany, Belgium, the Netherlands and Luxembourg. Reductions in strength were to be mutual and balanced, but NATO insisted that they should take into account the geographical fact that if American forces left Europe they would have to cross the Atlantic to return, while Soviet forces would merely move into adjoining territories. (In the jargon of the time, this was called the 'geographical asymmetry' between the two sides.) The Soviet Union, for its part, held a considerable superiority in land forces in central Europe, which it saw no sense in giving up without securing some solid compensation.

The two sides were thus a good distance apart. They agreed to convene a Conference on Mutual and Balanced Force Reduction which opened in Vienna on 30 October 1973, attended by seven NATO states (the USA, Canada, Britain, West Germany, Belgium, the Netherlands and Luxembourg) and four Warsaw Pact countries (the USSR, East Germany,

Poland and Czechoslovakia).[40] The Vienna Conference failed to find enough common ground to reach an agreement, but did not close down, clinging on like the ghost of détente until 1989, when suddenly the continent changed around it.

The results of détente

Détente had a chequered career between 1969 and 1975. The Americans and the Soviets in their summit meetings attained a degree of contact, cooperation and personal warmth inconceivable even ten years earlier. The agreements on arms control did not end the arms race, but limited the total numbers of long-range ballistic missiles and anti-ballistic missiles. The ideological aspects of the Cold War did not disappear, but became far less prominent as each side granted the other a sort of acceptance, and even a grudging respect. In Europe, the treaties of 1970–72 between the two Germanies, Poland and the Soviet Union settled frontiers which had been in dispute since 1945; and Berlin, which had been the centre of one crisis after another, was removed from the international agenda. The Helsinki Conference formally endorsed the existing situation in Europe, with all its international frontiers and internal political arrangements. Even the wraith-like Vienna Conference did not actually break down.

These were valuable achievements, especially when compared with the situation during the worst period of the Cold War. Yet by the end of 1975 it appeared that the period of détente was coming to an end. American public opinion came to regard the whole concept as a failure – it was symptomatic that in the presidential election campaign of 1976 Ford instructed Republicans not to use the word 'détente'. There were misgivings in the Soviet leadership about the agreements signed at Helsinki. More widely, the mid-1970s were a time of change. A number of world figures withdrew from public life or died. In May 1974 Willy Brandt resigned as Chancellor of West Germany, after a scandal involving East German espionage. President Nixon resigned from office in August 1974. Brezhnev suffered the first onset of serious illness during the Vladivostok Conference in November 1974. Zhou Enlai died in January 1976, and Mao Zedong in September. At a deeper level, the two superpowers were in a worse case than they had been before embarking on détente. The United States was severely damaged by defeat in Vietnam. The prestige of the presidency, and of the country as a whole, suffered a drastic decline. The value of the dollar had fallen considerably since 1971. The Soviet Union was by no means in such obvious difficulties, but was in the grip of a creeping economic crisis and a growing uncertainty within the regime as to how to tackle it. The mid-1970s had the feel of the end of an era.

◆ Notes to Chapter 13

1. The USA showed a deficit on its balance of payments of $9.83 billion in 1970, and $29.59 billion in 1971 – Diane B. Kunz, *Butter and Guns: America's Cold War Economic Diplomacy* (New York, 1997), p. 114. For Bretton Woods, see above, pp. 47–8.
2. For the 1973 oil shock, see below, pp. 412–19.
3. Stephen E. Ambrose, *Nixon*, Vol. III, *Ruin and Recovery* (New York, 1991), p. 175.
4. *Keesing's Contemporary Archives*, 1976, p. 27954.
5. Figures from Herbert S. Levine, 'Economic Development, Technological Transfer and Foreign Policy', in Seweryn Bialer, ed., *The Domestic Context of Soviet Foreign Policy* (London, 1981), p. 178.
6. Seweryn Bialer, *The Soviet Paradox: External Expansion, Internal Decline* (London, 1986), p. 77.
7. Arcadius Kahan, 'Soviet Agriculture', in Bialer, ed., *Domestic Context*, p. 267.
8. See the table in Paul Marer, 'The Economics of Eastern Europe and Soviet Foreign Policy', *ibid.*, p. 279.
9. For the Helsinki Conference and agreement, see below, pp. 000–00.
10. Henry Kissinger, *Diplomacy* (London, paperback edn, 1995), p. 719.
11. Stephen E. Ambrose, *Nixon*, Vol. II, *The Triumph of a Politician* (New York, 1989), pp. 451–3.
12. Text of Shanghai communiqué, J. A. S. Grenville, *The Major International Treaties, 1914–1973* (London, 1974), pp. 465–71.
13. Gabriel Partos, *The World that Came in from the Cold* (London, 1993), p. 152, Ambrose, *Nixon*, II, p. 418.
14. Ho Chi Minh, quoted in Paul Kennedy, *The Rise and Fall of the Great Powers* (London, paperback edn, 1989), pp. 522–4. For casualty figures, *World Political Almanac* (London, 3rd. edn, 1995), p. 315; see below, p. 298.
15. Jacques Portes, *Les Américains et la Guerre du Vietnam* (Paris, 1993), pp. 346–7, citing *Statistical Abstract of the United States, 1985*, p. 342.
16. Kissinger, *Diplomacy*, p. 684.
17. Text of agreement in Grenville, *International Treaties*, pp. 465–71.
18. Compare J. A. S. Grenville, *History of the World in the Twentieth Century* (London, revised edn, 1998), p. 625, with *Daily Telegraph* obituary of Pol Pot, 17 April 1998.
19. Casualty figures in Cook, *World Political Almanac*, p. 315; Portes, pp. 319, 328, 346–7. Other figures put the North Vietnamese losses at 1.1 million dead.
20. Quoted in Ambrose, *Nixon*, II, p. 545.
21. Text of Declaration in Grenville, *International Treaties*, pp. 520–1.

22. Summary of the treaty, *ibid.*, p. 513.
23. Figures in J. P. D. Dunbabin, *The Cold War: The Great Powers and Their Allies* (London, 1994), p. 176, n. 57. If the Soviet Union built up to the higher number of ICBMs, they were to keep to the lower figure for SLBMs.
24. Ambrose, *Nixon*, II, pp. 173–6.
25. *Ibid.*, p. 371. Nixon himself had joined in the criticism of Roosevelt's actions at Yalta, and so wished to avoid the comparison.
26. For Watergate, see below, pp. 304–5.
27. Figures in Kennedy, *Great Powers,* p. 510.
28. Daniel Colard, *Les Relations internationales de 1945 à nos jours* (Paris, 1996), p. 164.
29. Partos, *World*, p. 215.
30. Dobrynin, *In Confidence*, pp. 302–3, 310–11, 314; Ambrose, *Nixon*, III, p. 373.
31. Dobrynin, *In Confidence*, p. 321.
32. Figures in Dunbabin, *Cold War*, pp. 178–9.
33. Text of treaty in Grenville, *International Treaties*, pp. 293–4.
34. Text of treaty, *ibid.*, pp.294–5.
35. *Ibid.*, p. 276; Henry Ashby Turner, Jr, *Germany from Partition to Reunification* (New Haven, 1992), pp. 155–6.
36. Text, Grenville, *International Treaties*, pp. 296–7.
37. Partos, *World*, p. 49.
38. For the Helsinki Accord, Helsinki Accord, *Keesing's Contemporary Archives*, 1975, pp. 27301–8
39. Dobrynin, *In Confidence*, pp.345–6.
40. Five NATO countries from the northern and southern flanks attended the Vienna Conference as observers: Norway, Denmark, Italy, Greece and Turkey. Similarly Bulgaria, Hungary and Romania, from the Warsaw Pact, attended as observers. France declined to take part, rejecting the whole idea of negotiation between blocs on the ground that it would impede the emergence of a Europe independent of the superpowers.

CHAPTER 14

THE END OF DÉTENTE, 1976–1980

The Carter presidency in the USA – The state of the Soviet Union –
Détente at half-speed: Strategic arms limitation – Détente under
strain: the Soviet Union in Africa – The end of détente: the Soviet
invasion of Afghanistan – Balance sheet for the late 1970s

In November 1976 Jimmy Carter, the Democratic candidate, won the presidential election in the United States, defeating President Ford, who had
succeeded to the office on the resignation of Nixon. The result was a striking change in personalities and attitudes to foreign policy. Ford had continued much of Nixon's policy, and had retained Kissinger, with his approach
based on power politics and secret diplomacy, as Secretary of State. Carter
came to the presidency after serving four years as Governor of Georgia. He
had little experience of Washington politics, and less of world affairs. He
was a man of genuine idealism, determined to break with what he saw as
the cynicism and secrecy of the Nixon–Kissinger era, and restore a foreign
policy based on moral values. This was not a flash in the pan. In a speech
on 22 August 1977, when he had been in office some twenty months, he
still spoke of his determination to solve the global problems of 'nuclear war,
racial hatred, the arms race, environmental damage, hunger and disease' –
a remarkable list, and a perfectly serious intention.[1]

Carter was deeply committed to the concept of human rights, and established a new bureau in the State Department to ensure that they were at the
forefront of American foreign policy. He thus appealed at one and the same
time to liberals who had been offended by Kissinger's realism and to anti-
communists who thought that Kissinger had been too soft on the Soviets
and failed to bring them up to the mark on human rights. Carter appointed
as his National Security Adviser Zbigniew Brzezinski, whose father had
been one of the many Poles who refused to return to their country after the
Second World War, and who was sternly anti-communist. Brzezinski was
willing to continue the diplomatic dialogue with the Soviet government
begun by his predecessors, but set out to use it to press the cause of human
rights in the USSR.

These new departures paid dividends at home, where they allowed

Americans to take pride in a moral foreign policy after the calamities of Vietnam and the *realpolitik* of Nixon and Kissinger. But they raised problems abroad, in the actual conduct of foreign policy as distinct from enunciating its principles. For example, in pursuit of his devotion to human rights, Carter wrote a personal letter to Andrei Sakharov, a leading Soviet dissident, in the naive belief that this would do no harm to American relations with the Soviet Union; but in fact the Soviet government naturally regarded the letter as interference in the internal affairs of the USSR. Carter's high moral tone, amplified by the American mass media, worsened relations with the Soviet Union, where the leadership had grown accustomed to Kissinger's very different approach. The Soviets stiffened their attitude on humanitarian issues when the Belgrade Conference met in 1977 to review and develop the Helsinki Accords, and the conference made little progress.

Elsewhere, the concept of human rights was almost inevitably applied inconsistently, and sometimes to the detriment of American material interests. In Nicaragua, the United States withdrew its support from Somoza (the President, and effectively dictator, of the country from 1974 to 1979), thus assisting in his defeat; only to find that he was replaced by the left-wing Sandinista movement, which was hostile to the United States and had no more respect for human rights than its predecessor. In Chile, the Americans under the Nixon administration had supported General Pinochet, who had overthrown the left-wing President Allende in 1973.[2] Under Carter, the Americans withdrew their support, but Pinochet remained President until 1990, so that the United States gave offence without securing any practical effect. In Iran, the Carter administration continued its assistance to the Shah while criticizing his conduct on human rights, thus weakening his position without gaining any benefit. Indeed, when the Shah was overthrown in 1979 the subsequent regime, under the Ayatollah Khomeini, proved to be fiercely anti-American and without the slightest concern for western interpretations of human rights. Thus a number of Carter's interventions to promote human rights proved at best ineffectual and at worst damaging both to American interests and to the cause they were intended to advance. The result was an impression of muddle and inefficiency which left other governments uncertain as to the real aims of American policy.

At the same time, the Soviet leadership faced its own problems, arising from an odd combination of strength and weakness. The Soviet Union possessed a great armoury of nuclear missiles, and maintained an ocean-going fleet which showed the red flag all over the world. Soviet prestige was high, especially in contrast to that of the United States after Vietnam, and Moscow was able to embark on interventions in Africa and southern Yemen which brought vast territories under Soviet influence, as we shall see later in this chapter. Yet Brezhnev, the Soviet leader, was in increasingly

poor health, suffering successive strokes and often appearing, in his meetings with foreign statesmen, incapable of coherent thought or conversation.
Around him the Kremlin was dominated by old men – the average age of
the Politburo in 1980 was 69.[3] The Soviet leaders knew that the aim set by
Khrushchev, to overtake the Americans in industrial production by the mid-
1970s, was far out of their reach; and Brezhnev no longer referred to it. Yet
they continued to assert, and perhaps believe (as Khrushchev had done),
that the triumph of revolution would come about in the Third World. They
ran ideology in tandem with power politics, creating an uncertainty among
outsiders rather similar to that generated by Carter's ideological forays into
human rights. The two superpowers, though opposed to one another,
continued to be curiously similar in some respects.

The USA and USSR, which had achieved a measure of understanding
and co-operation in the early 1970s, were thus in uncertain positions.
Carter's new administration ran almost carelessly into difficulties through
its own idealism. Brezhnev's Soviet Union had immense prestige and an
apparently free hand in large parts of the world, yet was conscious of its
own economic weakness. Each was tempted into new adventures, the
United States making forays into human rights, the Soviet Union seizing
opportunities in Africa. What was to become of détente in these new
circumstances?

◆ Strategic arms: limitation and new competition

The most tangible successes of détente (as distinct from improvements in
atmosphere and personal relations) had been in strategic arms limitation,
through the SALT I Treaty of 1972 and its extension in the Vladivostok
agreement of November 1974.[4] In March 1977 the Carter administration
put forward proposals for a new agreement on strategic armaments, and the
Secretary of State, Cyrus Vance, visited Moscow on 28–30 March to open
negotiations. The Americans suggested new limits on the numbers of land-
based missile launchers, to be restricted to between 1800 and 2000 for each
country, and also a limitation on the numbers of launchers for MIRV
missiles, with their multiple warheads, to 550 on each side. These proposals
offered substantial advantages to the United States, just over half of whose
missiles were at the time deployed on submarines and therefore not subject
to the proposed limitations on land-based missiles. For the Soviets, on the
other hand, the plan would mean reductions in their existing armaments in
return for cuts by the United States in the future.[5] The Soviet government
therefore refused the American proposals as they stood; but the two governments embarked on negotiations, which after just over two years resulted in
a further Strategic Arms Limitation Treaty (SALT II), signed by Brezhnev and
Carter on 18 June 1979 at a summit meeting in Vienna.

This treaty established a limit of 2400 on all types of strategic delivery vehicles on each side, to be reduced to 2250 by 1981. Within these figures, a limit of 1320 was accepted on each side for the combined total of multiple independently targeted return vehicles (MIRVs) and bombers carrying long-range missiles. Within this figure of 1320, no more than 1200 could be MIRV missiles; so that if one side built up to the limit of 1200 for MIRVs, it could have only 120 bombers, but if it built fewer MIRVs it could have more bombers. The treaty also provided for a system of verification of its observance.[6]

This was at any rate a modest success for strategic arms limitation, after a difficult start. But in other ways the Vienna summit was a failure. There was no personal accord between Brezhnev and Carter. Brezhnev was seriously ill, and confined himself very much to his prepared papers. Carter was afraid of appearing to concede too much after accusing his predecessors of allowing détente to become a one-way street. Before the conference, Senator Henry Jackson had compared Carter's visit to Vienna to Neville Chamberlain's journey to Munich in 1938; and it is said that Carter was so sensitive to this comparison that even though it was raining when he arrived in Vienna he refused to use an umbrella, because in the cartoons of 1938 Chamberlain was always depicted as the man with the umbrella.

Six months after the Vienna summit, in December 1979, the Soviet Union invaded Afghanistan, and Carter refused to submit the SALT II Treaty to the Senate for ratification. But even before that, the state of the strategic arms limitation talks was at best equivocal. The greatest merit of the talks was probably psychological, in the very fact that they took place at all. Their main practical result lay in the acceptance by both sides of a rough balance in the weapons covered by the treaties; but this was still a balance which left each country with ample power to destroy the other. The weakness of the agreements was that they left open the development of other weapons, not covered by the treaties; and the slow pace of negotiation meant that there was plenty of time for such weapons to be produced.

The SALT talks also produced another problem, which eventually developed into an acute crisis. America's allies in western Europe could see the American-Soviet talks going on over their heads and in some respects to their disadvantage. The dangers became plain in 1977, when the Soviet Union began to deploy in central Europe a number of SS-20 missiles, which were mobile, carried three warheads and were of medium range – up to 5000 kilometres. These fell outside the terms of the SALT agreements, which dealt with missiles with a range of 5500 kilometres or above. The SS-20s presented no danger to the United States, which they could not reach; but they could strike targets anywhere in western Europe.

This raised in a sharp form a question which constantly lurked not far beneath the surface in the North Atlantic Alliance. How far would the Americans actually go to protect Western Europe if the United States was not itself under threat? Chancellor Schmidt of West Germany (one of the most faithful members of NATO) expressed his anxiety on this question in a public speech in London (the capital of another loyal member) on 28 October 1977. He evoked responses across most of western Europe, though in differing terms, because the European members of NATO did not know whether to meet the Soviet challenge by resistance or appeasement, by tightening the alliance or by loosening it. Public opinion was stirred, and campaigns for nuclear disarmament revived, particularly in Britain and West Germany, where they were directed against the American and British, not the Soviet, nuclear forces. Amid this confusion a NATO summit meeting was held in Guadeloupe in January 1979, and at least agreed to protest against the Soviet deployment of SS-20 missiles. Finally, after prolonged discussion, NATO agreed in December 1979 on a two-stage policy: to open negotiations with the Soviet Union on the withdrawal of the SS-20s; and if that failed, to station American medium-range missiles in western Europe – specifically, 108 Pershing missiles with a range of 1800 kilometres and 464 cruise missiles with a range of 2500 kilometres, which would be capable of attacking Soviet territory. In the event, negotiations proved fruitless, and the deployment of American missiles began in 1983, amid fervent public protest in Britain and West Germany. A new form of arms race was under way.

Arms limitation thus achieved a modest success in the SALT II Treaty of June 1979; but this proved short-lived when the United States declined to ratify it in December, after the Soviet occupation of Afghanistan. At the same time, a new competition in medium-range missiles stationed in Europe was beginning. The most prominent and definite aspect of détente between the superpowers was breaking down. Meanwhile, in the Third World, hostility was reviving and sharpening.

◈ The Soviet Union and Africa: détente under strain

From 1975 to 1979 the Soviet Union undertook a policy of active intervention in several parts of Africa and the Arabian peninsula.[7] In 1975 the Portuguese withdrew from their colonies in Angola and Mozambique. In Angola they left behind a civil war between rival liberation movements, in which the Soviets supported the Popular Movement for the Liberation of Angola (MPLA), by granting diplomatic recognition to the government which it established, and by the intervention of a large force of Cuban troops (variously estimated at between 20 000 and 36 000), with Soviet arms and supplies. In October 1976 the Soviet Union concluded a treaty of friendship and co-operation with the MPLA government, and Cuban troops remained in the country, though in smaller numbers. In Mozambique the Soviet Union gave diplomatic and economic support to the government formed by the Front for the Liberation of Mozambique (FRELIMO), which was engaged in a civil war against the National Resistance Movement, assisted by the white government in Rhodesia and later by the South Africans. In March 1977 the USSR concluded a treaty with Mozambique, on the same lines as that with Angola.

The Soviet Union also pursued an active policy in the Horn of Africa, in territories close to the Red Sea. In 1974 the USSR signed a treaty of friend-ship with Somalia, and began to train and equip the Somali Army and to build naval facilities at the port of Berbera. In 1977 Somali forces moved into the province of Ogaden in Ethiopia, which Somalia claimed as one of its 'lost territories'. The Soviet Union and Cuba first attempted mediation in this dispute, without success; and then switched support to Ethiopia in 1975. (In September 1974 Haile Selassie, who had been Emperor of Ethiopia since 1930, was overthrown, and a revolutionary regime took over.) The Soviets began to supply arms to Ethiopia, and flew in Cuban troops, numbering about 18 000 by November 1977. By March 1978 these reinforcements had driven the Somalis out of Ogaden. Somalia abrogated its treaty with the Soviet Union and expelled its Soviet military advisers.

The Soviet Union then formally adopted Ethiopia as its protégé in East Africa. In November 1978 the two countries signed a treaty of friendship and co-operation; some 2000 Soviet advisers were established in Ethiopia; and the Ethiopian dictator, Mengistu, embarked on a Soviet-style policy of forced collectivization of agriculture. Cuban troops remained in the country, and took part in the long-running war against Eritrean separatists. For these actions, a valuable base was provided by the People's Republic of South Yemen (formerly the British colony of Aden and its hinterland), where Soviet supplies and Cuban troops landed before going on to Ethiopia. In 1979 the USSR concluded a treaty of friendship with South Yemen.

What lay behind this remarkable surge of activity? A leading – perhaps the predominant – motive was ideological. In the late 1950s and early 1960s Khrushchev had confidently predicted that the struggle for world revolution would be won in the Third World; and in the early 1970s Mikhail Suslov, the member of the Politburo primarily concerned with ideo-logical activity outside the Soviet bloc, argued that support for national liberation movements would lead to the ultimate victory of socialism over imperialism. This ideological struggle was by now not only being waged against the Americans and other imperialists but also against the Chinese, who were competing with the Soviets for the allegiance of African coun-tries. Between 1970 and 1975 the Chinese built the Tanzam railway, between Tanzania and Zambia, designed to free Zambia from its depen-dence on communications through South Africa. Between 1970 and 1977 they gave aid to a total of 29 African countries, as against 22 supported by the Soviet Union (though on a larger scale).[8] From the Soviet point of view, this dangerous Chinese influence had to be countered.

There were other, more specific and practical, reasons for Soviet intervention in Africa. The new ocean-going Soviet fleet needed friendly ports of call. Soviet intelligence agencies wanted to keep track of shipping movements through the Red Sea and round the Cape of Good Hope, which could be achieved from stations in the South Yemen, Mozambique and Angola. The Soviets had some hope of economic advantage, seeking outlets for products which no longer found a ready sale in more sophisticated markets – Angola and Ethiopia actually became members of COMECON. Behind all these motives lay the quest for *status* – the Soviet government was determined to demonstrate that it was a world power, able (like the Americans) to intervene in far-flung corners of the earth.

The Soviets were also greatly encouraged by the fact that the Cubans provided them with an ace, which they could apparently play again and again with undiminished effect. As well as the substantial forces in Angola and Ethiopia, Cuban troops were deployed at one time or another in Mozambique, Tanzania, Congo and Sierra Leone. They were efficient, well accustomed to tropical environments, and above all they were from a Third World country and thus by definition were not imperialists.

The Soviet leaders seemed to be genuinely convinced that their interventions in Africa would not seriously damage their relations with the United States. In private, Suslov assured the Politburo that, by assisting the inevitable process of change in Africa, the Soviet Union was not setting out to undermine American interests there. In public, Brezhnev declared that there was no contradiction between the continuation of détente and the improvement of Soviet relations with countries freeing themselves from colonialism. In any case, it was easy to point out that the Americans themselves intervened all over the world – they had fought a ten-year war in Vietnam, and overthrown President Allende in Chile in 1973; so they had no good ground to complain if the Soviet Union acted similarly. In the late 1970s these assumptions proved reasonably accurate. The Americans were offended by the Soviet actions, and especially by the role played by Cuba – to watch Cuban troops marching over Africa somehow added insult to injury. But the Americans had been so shaken by events in Vietnam that they shrank from any new foreign adventures, and except for some clandestine activities they did little to oppose the Soviets in Africa.

The Soviet Union thus embarked on a series of African adventures, for reasons which seemed sound at the time, and indeed followed almost inevitably from the USSR's position as the leading socialist state. By 1991 the logic seemed much less obvious, and a leading foreign policy expert looked back and asked: 'What the hell did we want to gain in Ethiopia or in Angola or in Ghana?'[9] But in the late 1970s things looked very different. The Soviet Union became an African power of some importance, and succeeded in doing so by straining détente without destroying it. Strangely, the Central Asian country of Afghanistan was to prove a very different matter.

◆ The Soviet invasion of Afghanistan and its consequences, 1979–80

Between 24 and 27 December 1979, some 50 000 Soviet troops were airlifted to occupy Kabul, the capital of Afghanistan. Other forces entered the country by land, and by early 1980 there were between 85 000 and 100 000 Soviet troops in Afghanistan. In the nineteenth century, when Afghanistan was at the centre of the Great Game played between Russia and Britain for the control of Central Asia, the despatch of a Russian army to Kabul would not have been unexpected. Both the British and the Russians sent expeditions to Afghanistan, sometimes with disastrous results. On one occasion, only one man returned alive from a British force which marched on Kabul – which might have given the Soviet General Staff food for thought. In the twentieth century, however, such events seemed to have receded into the remote past, becoming merely the stuff of adventure stories and romantic films. What lay behind the Soviet invasion of Afghanistan, which so abruptly brought the nineteenth century back to life?

In April 1978, an Afghan communist leader, Mohamed Taraki, seized power in Kabul and established a communist government, with Soviet support and – on this occasion – without protest from the United States. In September 1979, Taraki was himself overthrown and murdered by a rival, Hafizulla Amin, who rapidly lost control of the country; in some parts, Afghan troops mutinied and killed their Soviet advisers. In the same year the Ayatollah Khomeini came to power in Iran, founding an Islamic Republic which some Afghans were eager to emulate. The Soviet government was faced by a crisis in a neighbouring country where it had earlier helped to set up a communist government.

During the autumn of 1979 the Soviet leadership discussed the possibility of intervention to restore order in Afghanistan. It appears that Brezhnev opposed military action, as did the Chief of the General Staff, Marshal Orgakov, who knew some nineteenth-century history. But in December a small group made up of Gromyko (the Foreign Minister), Andropov (the head of the KGB) and Ustinov (the Defence Minister) took the interventionist side, and advised Brezhnev that resolute action was necessary if Afghanistan were not to be lost. On 12 December a group of Politburo members met, with Brezhnev in the chair. The triumvirate of Gromyko, Andropov and Ustinov argued that the situation in Afghanistan might be exploited by the USA, China or Iran, and could pose a serious threat to the Soviet Union's southern borders. Ustinov claimed that a military intervention could be carried out rapidly and successfully. Gromyko predicted that there would be criticism from abroad, but thought that it would not last long; in any case, security considerations must be paramount. The meeting decided to send in troops, and the Politburo agreed on 13 December 1979.[10] The troops began to fly in on the 24th.

It thus appears that the main motive for the Soviet action was defensive. The Soviet government applied the Brezhnev doctrine, formulated to justify the occupation of Czechoslovakia in 1968: that no country should defect from the socialist camp once it had joined. (Soviet public statements invoked the cause of proletarian solidarity; though it proved difficult to find many proletarians in Afghanistan.) They were also acting in self-defence, to prevent foreign and above all Islamic influences from gaining ground in Afghanistan – the Soviet Central Asian republics included large Islamic populations, and for Afghanistan to adopt Khomeini's doctrines would be a dangerous precedent. (A sort of Soviet domino theory was at work here, with Afghanistan as the first domino and the later ones in the Soviet Union itself.)

It was also crucial that the Soviet leaders were confident that military operations would be short (perhaps only three or four weeks), and that foreign reactions would be limited and temporary. They were wrong on both counts. The military campaign was to last for over nine years, and foreign reactions were severe and long-lasting.

The Americans reacted with surprising speed and vehemence. As early as 28 December 1979 President Carter used the hot line to Moscow to warn the Soviet leaders that unless they withdrew from Afghanistan they would jeopardize the whole field of Soviet–American relations. In his State of the Union message in January 1980, he declared that a Soviet attempt to gain control of the Persian Gulf would be repelled by any means necessary, including the use of force; and he asserted that the invasion of Afghanistan was the greatest threat to peace since the Second World War – an astonishing claim. Carter even remarked that he had learned more about the Soviet Union in two weeks than in the previous two-and-a-half years. ('Better late than never,' Raymond Aron observed acidly.)[11] Such a response to events in a country which was geographically remote from the the United States, which affected no immediate American interests, and which could not be included in any conceivable definition of the free world or democratic institutions, was astounding. How did it come about?

The answer seems to lie in a strange mixture of simplicity and sophistication. Carter was an idealist who was simply and genuinely appalled by the Soviet invasion – though he doubtless also had half an eye on the presidential election due in 1980. The sophistication came from Brzezinski, the National Security Adviser, who was much occupied with geopolitics. He argued that the Soviet army might move from Afghanistan into Iran, and thus to the Persian Gulf. Moreover, when the invasion of Afghanistan was added to Soviet interventions in Ethiopia and South Yemen, it was possible (with the aid of some imagination and a small-scale map) to discern the two claws of a pincer movement, ready to close around the Arabian Peninsula, the Persian Gulf and the whole of the Middle East oilfields. For the American government, the invasion of Afghanistan thus appeared at one and the same time as a moral issue, a geopolitical threat and a test of willpower. The Soviets for their part could not conceive that Afghanistan could be of vital interest to the United States, and therefore concluded that the Americans were merely seizing on the issue as a pretext to end détente, resume the arms race and organize a propaganda campaign against the USSR.

In fact, the Americans were in deadly earnest. In 1980, within a year from the start of the invasion, the United States imposed a partial embargo on the export of cereals and high technology to the Soviet Union; refused to ratify the SALT II Treaty; boycotted the Olympic Games (held in Moscow in 1980); and sent economic and military assistance to Pakistan, which was encouraging resistance to the Soviet forces in Afghanistan.

Hostile reactions to the Soviet operation were by no means confined to the United States. As early as 3 January 1980 the General Assembly of the United Nations passed a resolution condemning the Soviet invasion of Afghanistan by 104 votes to 18, with 18 abstentions; and on 14 January another resolution calling for the withdrawal of foreign troops was approved by the same majority. The minority of 18, constituting a list of the Soviet bloc and its supporters at the time, was made up as follows: Afghanistan, Angola, Bulgaria, Byelorussia, Cuba, Czechoslovakia, Ethiopia, East Germany, Grenada, Hungary, Laos, Mongolia, Mozambique, Poland, Ukraine, USSR, Vietnam and Yemen.[12] These votes were highly significant, because the General Assembly, dominated by Third World countries, had for some time been anti-American and at least broadly pro-Soviet. From 1980 onwards, annual resolutions calling for the withdrawal of foreign troops were put to the Security Council of the United Nations, accepted by a majority, and vetoed by the Soviet Union. This rallying of opinion against the USSR came partly from the Islamic states. A conference of the Foreign Ministers of Islamic countries, meeting at Islamabad, the capital of Pakistan, in January 1980, unanimously condemned the Soviet aggression against the Afghan people. China also opposed the Soviet invasion and carried a number of Third World states with it.

International opinion as expressed through the United Nations thus moved strongly against the Soviet Union. In immediate practical terms this had little effect, because the USSR ignored votes in the General Assembly, vetoed resolutions in the Security Council, and carried on fighting; but in the long run it undermined the gains which the Soviets had made in the Third World during the 1970s. On the other hand, the United States failed to win solid support among its west European allies. France as usual followed an independent line. Chancellor Schmidt of West Germany was anxious to maintain the advantages of détente, and thought that Carter was exploiting the Afghan issue to secure his own re-election. Neither France nor West Germany would impose economic sanctions on the Soviet Union, and indeed increased their trade with the Soviets to fill the gaps left by American sanctions. The west Europeans declined to follow the American lead in boycotting the Moscow Olympics, and indeed most teams competed as usual.

There was thus some comfort for the Soviets; but all in all it became evident during the course of 1980 that they had made a bad mistake. The Soviet army held Kabul and other towns, but struggled in vain to establish lasting control in the mountainous countryside against determined Afghan guerrillas, supplied from Pakistan. They found themselves in a dilemma, not unlike that which the Americans had faced in Vietnam. They were involved in a guerrilla war which they were unable to win, at the cost of serious casualties and some erosion of morale. Yet they had to persist, because their reputation (both political and military) was at stake. So they continued the war, year after year, in an ultimately disastrous struggle which we must follow in a later chapter. As the war went on, they increasingly drew upon themselves the hostility of Islam, which had previously been directed almost exclusively against the Americans.

Meanwhile, the Americans found themselves with a diplomatic and numerical advantage in the United Nations – an unusual luxury. They could make fine gestures (like boycotting the Moscow Olympics) at no great cost to themselves. And they began to harass the Soviet forces, at a safe distance, by supplying the Afghan guerrillas with arms by way of Pakistan. Like the Soviets using the Cubans in Africa, the Americans could enjoy the benefit of waging war by proxy. In Africa, détente had been severely strained. In Afghanistan, it was broken.

◆ The balance sheet, 1975–80, and the end of détente

Between 1975 and 1979 the balance of power in the Cold War moved steadily in favour of the Soviet Union. The Soviets established their influence in large parts of Africa, and in South Yemen. Even the invasion of Afghanistan went well in its early stages. Pessimistic observers in the West estimated that in five years about 100 million people had come under Soviet influence. On the military front, the SALT treaties had recognized Soviet parity with the USA. In 1977 the Soviets began to deploy SS-20 missiles in central Europe, plunging the Atlantic alliance into uncertainty as to how to respond. A revival of pacifism and campaigns for nuclear disarmament in Britain and West Germany gave the Soviets a propaganda foothold in western Europe which they had lacked for some time. The Soviet government could look on events with some satisfaction – until disaster began to creep up on them in Afghanistan.

At the same time the influence and reputation of the United States were in decline. After the Vietnam War ended in humiliation, the American slogan was 'No more Vietnams', which meant renouncing military intervention almost anywhere in the Third World. American prestige suffered a further blow in Iran in 1979–80. (See below, Chapter 17.) The Shah of Iran, whom the Americans had regarded as a safe ally (safe enough, indeed, to be criticized on his human rights record) was suddenly overthrown in 1979 by the fiercely anti-American Ayatollah Khomeini. The Iranian revolutionaries seized the staff of the US Embassy in Teheran as hostages; and a commando-type raid to rescue them failed disastrously, and almost absurdly, in April 1980. The United States seemed a clumsy and helpless giant, unable to protect even its own diplomatic personnel. It was a time of disaster for the Americans.

Meanwhile, détente was as dead as a doornail. It had been ailing as early as 1974–75, with the fall of Nixon and the limited success of the Vladivostok summit; and it suffered relapses in 1977–78, with Soviet actions in Ethiopia and the deployment of SS-20 missiles in central Europe. The Vienna summit in June 1979, and the SALT II Treaty signed by Carter and Brezhnev, brought only temporary relief. Afghanistan proved the fatal blow. After 1979 there was to be no further summit meeting between the Americans and Soviets until Reagan met Gorbachev at Geneva in November 1985 – a gap of just over six years, in marked contrast to the Nixon–Brezhnev pattern of a meeting each year. It was possible to look back and argue that détente itself had not failed, because for a time it had produced considerable effects. But now it was over. The superpowers were moving into a new period of Cold War, which within a few years was to see a remarkable reversal of fortunes.

◆ Notes to Chapter 14

1. Quoted in Richard J. Barnet, *Allies: America, Europe, Japan since the War* (London, 1984), p. 365.
2. For Chile, see below, pp. 483–4.
3. Robert Service, *A History of Twentieth Century Russia* (London, 1997), p. 404.
4. For the SALT I Treaty and the Vladivostok Conference, see above, pp. 301–6.
5. Figures in Stephen Richard Ashton, *In Search of Détente: The Politics of East–West Relations since 1945* (London, 1989), p. 147; comment in Anatoly Dobrynin, *In Confidence: Moscow's Ambassador to America's Six Cold War Presidents* (New York, 1995), p. 388.
6. Ashton, *Détente*, p. 147; Chris Cook, *World Political Almanac* (3rd

edn, London, 1995), p. 366. Text of agreement in *Keesing's Contemporary Archives*, 1980, pp. 30117–28.
7. See the chapter on Africa, below, pp. 445–68.
8. Philip Snow, 'China and Africa', in Thomas W. Robinson and David Shambaugh, eds, *Chinese Foreign Policy: Theory and Practice* (Oxford, 1994), pp. 286–7; R. K. I. Quested, *Sino-Russian Relations: A Short History* (London, 1984), p. 147.
9. Andrei Alexandrov-Agentov, interview in Gabriel Partos, *The World that Came in from the Cold* (London, 1993), p. 169.
10. Dobrynin, *In Confidence*, pp. 436–40.
11. J. P. D. Dunbabin, *The Cold War: The Great Powers and their Allies* (London, 1994), pp.329–30; Robert Colquhoun, *Raymond Aron*, Vol. II, *The Sociologist in Society, 1955–1983* (London, 1986), p. 557.
12. *Keesing's Contemporary Archives*, 1980, p. 30236.

THE ESSENCE OF DÉTENTE

In 1980 détente was dead. What did it signify while it was alive? The term presents some of the same problems of definition and usage as 'Cold War' and 'the Third World'. We cannot do without it. It was frequently used in the 1960s; became almost omnipresent in the diplomacy of the 1970s; and remains a stand-by for historians to this day. But the word was used in widely different senses by statesmen who pursued policies of détente; it caused some confusion at the time; and it remains difficult to use with precision.

For those familiar with the 'old diplomacy', as practised before 1914, there was no difficulty about the term 'détente'. At that time, French was the language of diplomacy, and détente signified the relaxation of tension between states which had been in dispute about some issue or problem. It was possible for détente (the lessening of tension) to lead to an entente (which meant an understanding or agreement, falling short of an alliance), and so to co-operation; but such a progression was by no means certain.

In the changed conditions after two World Wars, the customs and vocabulary of the old diplomacy fell into disuse, and to a large degree into disrepute. The system of diplomacy which (as many believed) had led Europe into the Great War of 1914–18 and then at least failed to prevent the Second World War seemed to have little to recommend it, and its old-fashioned French terms appeared too refined for the harsh rivalries of the Cold War. Its return to common parlance in the 1960s reflected the need to find a convenient shorthand description for the improvement in relations between the USA and USSR after the Cuba missile crisis; and its adoption in the 1970s as a fashionable term owed much to Henry Kissinger, who, in a previous incarnation, had been a historian of European diplomacy in the age of Metternich, Castlereagh and Talleyrand.[1] Kissinger used the language of the old diplomacy with an authority and conviction which proved infectious. Between 1962 and 1980, most governments came to use the word détente. Even the People's Republic of China, where Mao Zedong had long refused to countenance the term, came round to it by 1980 – just when détente itself was coming to an end.

What did the word mean in the two decades of its heyday? General de Gaulle, the President of France in the 1960s, regarded détente as a policy of improving relations with the Soviet Union and eastern Europe so as to end the division of Europe and escape from the American-Soviet domination of the world. Chancellor Brandt of West Germany, whose *Ostpolitik* was one of the practical forms of détente, also aimed to improve relations with the East, but in his case in order to secure the stabilization of the existing order in Europe, and the acceptance of the partition of Germany which lay at its centre – not to *end* the division of Europe, but to *accept* and even *enshrine* it. These two experienced European statesmen thus used the word détente for widely different purposes. They sought to improve relations, and to relax tension, but with completely opposite ends in view.

De Gaulle and Brandt, though important European statesmen, were secondary figures on the world stage. The principal significance of détente lay in relations between the two superpowers. What did détente signify for the leaders of the Soviet Union and the United States? It appears that for Khrushchev and Brezhnev, the principal Soviet leaders of the 1960s and 1970s, détente was a variant on the old theme of peaceful coexistence, which had always meant the improvement of some aspects of relations with the capitalist powers without abandoning the fundamental struggle between two ways of life, which was a basic tenet of their beliefs. Brezhnev put the matter plainly in 1976: 'détente does not and cannot in the slightest abolish or change the laws of the class struggle'.[2] The class struggle, the conflict of ideas between socialism and capitalism, the economic competition between the two camps, and their rivalry in the Third World – all these were bound to continue. For the Soviet Union to adopt the economic or political ideas of the United States – the free market or American views of human rights – was unthinkable. What the Soviet leadership wanted was a sufficient degree of agreement with the United States to avoid nuclear war – which would be fatal; and to secure some slackening in the nuclear arms race – which was alarmingly expensive. They also sought commercial agreements, for example on supplies of cereals; and access to American science and technology. Less precisely, but crucially in a psychological sense, the Soviets were anxious to secure recognition and acceptance from the United States as an equal partner in world affairs. The summit meetings and strategic arms agreements were designed in large part to make this point, which was one of prestige and esteem. The main areas for détente would thus be nuclear armaments, trade, technology and summit diplomacy, where much might be achieved without prejudice to the fundamental purposes of Soviet policy, which were themselves part of the *raison d'être* of the Soviet state.

The American conception of détente shared some common ground with these Soviet ideas. The Americans were as anxious as the Soviets to avoid nuclear war. In the 1960s they were glad to make a start on arms control with treaties forbidding nuclear tests in the atmosphere and on the non-proliferation of nuclear weapons; and in the 1970s they moved on to strategic arms limitation agreements. From about 1970, facing defeat in Vietnam, the United States saw détente as a means of coping with a position of unaccustomed weakness. Nixon and Kissinger set out to create a new flexibility in diplomacy, improving relations with China and finding room for manoeuvre in a triangular balance of power. Kissinger used the word 'linkage' to describe his method of bargaining with the Soviet Union on nuclear weapons, trade and stability in the Third World. Nixon had a high regard for summit diplomacy as a means of improving the atmosphere of American-Soviet relations – it has been well said that détente was a matter of mood as much as of policy.[3] Moreover, summit meetings, and the carefully managed publicity which surrounded them, also paid considerable dividends in American domestic politics, where Nixon could earn popularity as a peace-maker. There were difficulties, in that détente aroused opposition from American conservatives who thought it meant making undue concessions to the enemy, and from liberals who claimed it did too little to uphold human rights. But on balance there was much domestic advantage in détente, at any rate up to 1974.

Eventually, the idea of 'linkage' broke down. The Soviet Union would not, and indeed could not, give up its basic objectives, and therefore intervened when the opportunity offered to advance the cause of revolution in the Third World, and notably in Africa. In face of this, the Americans came to think that they they were making concessions on the nuclear balance and on trade without being assured of a return.

The United States, equally in pursuit of its own basic convictions, kept reverting to questions of human rights (notably on Jewish emigration from the USSR), which aroused angry Soviet opposition.

For a time both sides secured advantages from détente, which diminished the tension between them and reduced the risks of major conflict. But in the late 1970s the Soviet Union took the risk of screwing up tension in Africa, and finally brought it to breaking-point in Afghanistan. The Soviets overestimated their own strength, and almost certainly under-rated the American capacity to recover from the disaster in Vietnam. The Americans for their part overestimated the effects of personal diplomacy and a change in atmosphere. Both sides gained something from détente, but were in the long run disappointed.

What are we to make of all this, and how in retrospect should we use the term 'détente'? Let us recall Molotov's brisk comment on the Cold War: 'What does the cold war mean? Strained relations.'[4] Détente meant the lessening of those strains – the relaxation of tension. In what aspects of the complicated phenomenon we call the Cold War did this come about in the 1960s and 1970s?

The most obvious relaxation was in diplomatic relations and personal contact between the American and Soviet leaders. In the late 1950s, Eisenhower and Khrushchev had made a start in this, notably by

Khrushchev's visit to the United States in 1959 – a prelude to détente. The 1960s saw the installation of the hot line, and the improvement of confidential relations between the two governments. Between 1972 and 1975 summit meetings were held annually, in each country in turn, achieving a degree of informality and personal contact which would have been unimaginable twenty years earlier. The great frost in personal and diplomatic relations melted away; and even when détente came to an end the ice age did not return.

Another example of lessening tension lay in the partial slackening of the nuclear arms race. The Strategic Arms Limitation Talks, and the agreements to which they led, limited the numbers of long-range ballistic missiles and anti-ballistic missiles, thus striking a rough balance between the two sides. But the gain was only partial, because the competition in nuclear armaments, limited in long-range missiles, re-emerged in the development of medium-range missiles, like a river held back by a dam and finding its way into other channels.

On the other hand, some aspects of the Cold War continued or even intensified during the period of détente. Ideological competition was unavoidable as long as the United States and Soviet Union maintained their essential characteristics, as societies and forms of government; and in some respects the dispute grew keener as the Americans put pressure on the Soviet Union about human rights. (The Helsinki Accords of 1975, which were certainly part of détente, also worsened American-Soviet relations by opening the way to intervention in Soviet internal affairs.) In the Third World, the Soviet Union continued its support for the cause of revolution and wars of liberation, thus increasing their own pressure on the Americans – not least by the use of Cuban intermediaries. Thus some aspects of the Cold War were more acute towards the end of the period of détente than they had been before it began.

During the Cuba missile crisis of 1962 the two superpowers looked into the abyss of nuclear war and knew with an intense certainty that they did not want to go over the edge. They could not make war with one another. Logically, they might have gone to the other extreme and made peace; but that was beyond them, and they did not even want to do it. They were fixed in the mould of competition. So instead they attempted détente, which was a half-way house. Some aspects of the Cold War would yield to a relaxation of tension. The superpowers could talk to one another. Their experts could agree on some limits to nuclear weaponry. The alignments of power politics could be shifted and softened by diplomacy and summitry. But behind these aspects lay an ideological gulf which could not be bridged, and a conflict of civilizations which could not be reconciled. Détente, by its successes and failures, showed with striking clarity which aspects of the Cold War were fundamental, and which were open to alleviation by the relaxation of tensions. We can therefore use the term détente with confidence, in its simple meaning of the easing of strained relations between states; and in so doing we may understand more clearly the essential nature of the Cold War.

◆ Notes to Reflection: The Essence of Détente

1. Henry Kissinger, *A World Restored: Metternich, Castlereagh and the Problems of Peace, 1812–1822* (London, 1957).
2. Quoted in Peter G. Boyle, *American-Soviet Relations: From the Russian Revolution to the Fall of Communism* (London, 1993), p. 186.
3. Stephen Richard Ashton, *In Search of Détente: The Politics of East–West Relations since 1945* (London, 1989), p. viii.
4. V. Molotov, *Molotov Remembers: Inside Kremlin Politics. Conversations with Felix Chuev*, ed. Albert Resis (Chicago, 1993), p. 59.

CHAPTER
15

RENEWED COLD WAR, 1980–1985

The enigma of Ronald Reagan – The Soviet paradox – Confrontation in the Third World – New arms race and Strategic Defence Initiative – Soviet–American relations in the early 1980s

The improvement in Soviet–American relations broadly described by the term 'détente' had ended by 1980. There followed a period of some five years in which relations between the two countries fell into a state of severe and sometimes acute hostility. The United States and the Soviet Union confronted one another at various points across the globe: in Afghanistan, in Africa, in parts of Central America and the Caribbean, and even in Europe, where an apparently permanent stability had been achieved in the 1960s and 1970s. Competition in nuclear armaments, which had been checked though not halted by arms limitation agreements in the 1970s, assumed new dimensions. There was also a marked change in the atmosphere of relations between the United States and the Soviet Union, and in the tone of their exchanges, which reverted to denunciation and denigration.

This period of hostility has sometimes been described as a Second Cold War, or at least a revival of the old Cold War after the armistice represented by détente.[1] There was a new arms race, involving competition in medium-range nuclear missiles stationed in Europe. The deployment of these missiles, both Soviet and American, and the protests against the American missiles in western Europe, produced a heightened tension between governments and a sharpened fear of war in some sections of public opinion. There was a marked cooling in diplomatic relations between the superpowers, with no Soviet–American meetings at summit level and only difficult discussions between Foreign Ministers and ambassadors. In the United States, a new and militant Right wing in domestic politics revived ideological and emotional hostility to communism and the Soviet Union. Whether we call it a Second Cold War or not, it was a time of sharp confrontation between the superpowers.

◆ The enigma of Ronald Reagan

The dates of this period of confrontation, from the end of 1980 to early 1985, coincided with the election of Ronald Reagan as President of the United States, his first term of office, and the opening of his second term. Reagan's election as President was by common consent a turning point in international affairs. Reagan's impact was crucial, yet the man himself remains a mystery, one of the unresolved enigmas of modern politics. The superficial elements of his life and character are simple enough. He was a popular film actor and star of 'B movies' (in the days when any proper cinema programme contained two long items, the main feature and the secondary B-film), with a folksy style and the standard appeal of the hero in old-fashioned Westerns or films about sport. As a politician, he was to exploit this appeal to the full – 'Win one for the Gipper', the key line from a film about American football, became one of his catch-phrases.

He emerged as a political figure as Governor of California, 1967–74. As Republican candidate for the presidency in 1980 he was easily categorized as embodying 'the attitudes and mind-set of small town America' towards the Soviet Union. Observers could collect many examples of his ignorance of history, errors as to current facts, and wild exaggerations.[2] He was an advocate of a strong line in foreign and military policy, claiming that détente had been a one-way street to the USSR's advantage, and calling for the abandonment of SALT II (the second Strategic Arms Limitation Treaty, which had not been ratified by Congress but was being observed by the government). He proposed large increases in military expenditure, and an end to what he saw as the vacillation and weakness of the Carter administration. In the presidential election he defeated Carter soundly, and proceeded by his first appointments to show that he meant business – for example, the new Secretary of State, Alexander Haig, was a former general who took an even sterner line towards the Soviet Union than did Reagan himself.[3] All this seems straightforward enough, and may well be so – it is always possible that the sphinx has no secret behind its weather-beaten face. Yet Henry Kissinger, himself worldly-wise and sophisticated to a degree, writes that 'Reagan's bland veneer hid an extraordinarily complex character', and that by treating everyone with the same bonhomie he kept his own counsel and retained a free hand. The result, in Kissinger's view, was 'an astonishing performance – and, to academic observers, nearly incomprehensible'.[4] Dobrynin, the experienced Soviet Ambassador in Washington, who knew six American presidents, was intrigued by Reagan's contradictory personality, and wrote that 'He grasped matters in an instinctive way but not necessarily in a simple one . . .' On reflection, Dobrynin was sure that 'opponents and experts alike clearly underestimated him.'[5]

Dobrynin also reflected (with some bitterness, because he was himself a believer in secret diplomacy) that Reagan turned foreign policy into a matter of public relations. Yet this was one of the president's great assets. André Fontaine, for a long time editor of *Le Monde* and himself a notable communicator, wrote that Reagan was 'un personnage formidablement médiatique' – a master of the media and of communication, certainly among his own American people.[6] One vital element which Reagan communicated was a sense of *optimism*, at a time when the Americans were desperately anxious for hope and reassurance. His optimism was genuine, not assumed; and there lay one important key to his success, abroad as well as at home. He was prepared to attempt the impossible, in the belief that it could be achieved; and though he was sometimes astonishingly inconsistent, he could carry his contradictions off.[7]

The risks were high. The Soviet leadership was baffled and exasperated by Reagan's early moves. In his first press conference as president, Reagan declared that the Soviets were prepared to commit any crime, to lie and to cheat in order to promote world revolution. Yet at the same time he conveyed a private message to the Soviet Ambassador to explain that he did not mean to give offence, but was only expressing his own deep convictions. It was hard to see whether this was an act of breathtaking naïveté or outright insolence. Dobrynin reflected later that he had thought it impossible to find anything worse than Carter's blundering; but this was indeed worse.[8] In Moscow, the Politburo discussed Reagan's press conference and found his words intolerable.

Reagan's rhetoric, on this and other occasions, was hurtful to Soviet pride and self-esteem. One of the most important results of détente in Soviet eyes had been American acceptance of the USSR as an equal, to be treated with respect. Reagan appeared to be going back on this acceptance, and treating the Soviets as criminals. The most spectacular example of this was his speech on 8 March 1983 to the National Association of Evangelical Christians at Orlando, Florida, in which he referred to 'the aggressive impulses of an evil empire'.[9] This was not intended to be a speech of any particular importance; the Secretary of State (George Shultz, who had succeeded Haig) had not seen the text; and the circumstances of an address to a particular religious group were singularly American. But a President of the United States cannot be simply a speaker at a religious convention; and once the speech was reported it immediately became famous. If any one of Reagan's remarks is still remembered, it is 'an evil empire'. Reagan himself seemed surprised by the stir he had caused; and the Soviet leaders for their part were unduly sensitive in their reactions – after all, their own propaganda against American capitalism and imperialism was by no means mealy-mouthed. But the hazards of conducting foreign policy by this sort of speech-making were great.

It was shortly before this speech, on 15 February 1983, when he had been in office for two years, that Reagan had his first private meeting with the Soviet Ambassador – in itself a sign of the new frost in American–Soviet relations. In their conversation, Reagan made one specific request: that the Soviet government should grant exit visas to seven Pentecostal Christians, who had taken refuge in the American Embassy in 1978 and were still there, unable to leave the country. He claimed that this would be more welcome to the American people than anything else, adding: 'It may sound paradoxical, but that's America.'[10] The Soviet leaders found this a strange and not wholly welcome request; but in April the Pentecostals were allowed to leave the Embassy without fear of arrest, and they were permitted to leave the country in June. It was an odd episode, and together with the 'evil empire' speech is illustrative of Reagan's priorities and methods. In both cases, he had a feel for what would appeal to American opinion. In the one case, he used the bludgeon of strong language, in the other the persuasion of a quiet request; and he used them virtually simultaneously. This might well have proved self-defeating, but in the event Reagan was able to carry it off. He believed that confrontation could lead to conciliation.

Reagan's policy was to pursue apparently contradictory courses. He set out to demonstrate that the United States was prepared to confront the Soviet Union at any point in the world where it was necessary (and at some points where it was not, as we shall see in the case of Grenada). He was resolved to show that the long retreat and uncertainty caused by the Vietnam catastrophe were over. In this way he took the initiative in reviving the Cold War. Yet at the same time he believed that he could persuade the Soviets that the United States was in earnest about making peace, and meant them no harm. Eventually he was able to make these two apparent contradictions come together. Because no one in America could doubt his anti-communism or his devotion to his country, he was able, when the opportunity offered, to go further in negotiation with the Soviet Union than anyone else would have dared to do, and certainly further than any Democratic leader could have done. In 1985 it was to be one of Gorbachev's achievements to grasp that this was so.

◈ The Soviet paradox

The Soviet Union which faced the challenge of the Reagan enigma was itself in a paradoxical situation of manifest strength and largely hidden weakness. In territory and zones of influence, the Soviet sphere (which we might even dare to call an empire) was at its most extensive. The eastern European bloc (Poland, East Germany, Czechoslovakia, Hungary, Romania and Bulgaria) remained intact and under the control of Moscow. Mongolia was firmly in the Soviet camp, with Soviet troops and missiles stationed on its territory. Far afield lay Cuba in the Caribbean and Vietnam in South-East Asia (where Soviet warships had replaced American in the Cam Ranh Bay naval base). Assorted Marxist regimes held power in South Yemen, Ethiopia, Angola and Mozambique. The prestige of the USSR also stood high over a large part of the Third World, and the so-called Non-Aligned Movement was usually non-aligned against the United States and in sympathy with the Soviet Union. There were Communist Parties all over western Europe, particularly strong in France and Italy.

Yet this formidable structure had its weaknesses. In eastern Europe, Poland was showing signs of dissent and revolt. All the Marxist regimes in Africa were challenged by internal and external opposition. A number of Third World countries which had once been close to the Soviet Union had slipped away – notably Egypt, Iraq and to some degree India. The west European Communist Parties were growing independent, in the movement called 'Euro-communism'. China maintained a constant challenge as an alternative leader of the socialist camp, a rival in the Third World, and as a military power, forcing the Soviet Union to station large forces in Asia. At home, the Soviet leadership was suffering from a form of atrophy. In his first term as President, Reagan faced three different Soviet leaders: Brezhnev, who was largely incapacitated by illness long before his death in 1982; Andropov, who was under treatment for a kidney disease and in failing health for most of his short term as General Secretary of the Soviet Communist Party (1982–84); and Chernenko, who was appointed in 1984 at the age of 73, almost because he was 'a man without qualities'.[11] Foreign affairs were mostly in the experienced but elderly hands of Andrei Gromyko, who had been Ambassador in Washington as long ago as 1943 and Foreign Minister since 1957.

These ageing, and in Chernenko's case ineffectual, leaders continued to speak the language of communist ideology, in private as well as in public, with a doubtful degree of conviction but quite enough to colour their view of the outside world and of their own actions. They suffered markedly from the isolation imposed on the Soviet Union by Stalin, and were uncertain in their understanding of the outside world – and not least of the workings of American public opinion. They enjoyed a position of great military strength, with a preponderance of land forces in Europe and ample numbers of nuclear weapons to maintain a balance of terror with the United States.[12] This military power conferred both security and prestige in international affairs; it also placed considerable influence in the hands of the government's military advisers, and the Defence Minister, Marshal Ustinov could normally ensure that his requirements were met. But at the same time these strong military forces had to be maintained by a struggling economy. It has been estimated that in the early 1980s the Soviet Union spent about 14–15 per cent of its gross national product on the armed forces; while in the United States the proportion in the 1970s and 1980s varied between 4 and 6 per cent.[13]

The true state of such affairs is almost impossible to ascertain, because it seems quite likely that no one in the Soviet Union knew the precise state of the economy. Soviet statistics normally exaggerated economic growth, partly through falsification by those anxious to show that they were fulfilling their norms, and partly because the figures took no account of inflation, which officially did not exist. A research economist working for GOSPLAN, the central Soviet planning agency, studied the American Central Intelligence Agency's 'Green Book' on the Soviet economy, and found that its estimates were sometimes only half the official Soviet figures; after some individual research, he thought that even the CIA's figures were occasionally too high. Even the Politburo had no reliable information about the state of the economy. In principle, the whole of production was centralized, so that there were some 25 million types of goods being produced under central control; which in practice led to confusion. The system was far too complicated, and a combination of bureaucracy, inefficiency, lack of incentive and corruption meant that there were never enough consumer goods available, and queues were an inevitable part of life. The Soviet Union fell far behind the United States, Japan and western Europe in its economic growth. In Khrushchev's time, the declared aim of the USSR was to catch up and overtake the United States, but by the early 1980s this had almost disappeared from Soviet propaganda. In fact, the gap between Soviet and United States gross national product grew steadily wider, after being at its narrowest in 1958.[14] The Soviet Union was slow in developing computers and their accompanying technology. The government invested heavily in agriculture, and yet the small plots of land cultivated privately by peasants produced better yields than the collective farms. The Soviet Union imported cereals from the USA and Canada, and dairy produce from the European Economic Community (which thus unloaded a part of its unwanted 'butter mountain'). The imported cereals went largely to cattle, for the production of meat, because Brezhnev set meat consumption as an indicator of the standard of living; but in 1988 meat was rationed in 26 out of 55 regions in the Russian Republic. To pay for its imports, the country was heavily dependent on the export of oil and natural gas, which by 1984 made up 54 per cent of all exports, as against only 18 per cent in 1972.[15] But at the same time, oil production was falling, and Soviet technology proved inadequate to exploit the new oilfields discovered in the frozen tundra of northern Siberia.[16] It was difficult to remain a superpower while labouring under such grave economic handicaps.

Behind these economic difficulties lay ominous trends in the population. Life expectancy was diminishing, in contrast to the situation in all other industrialized countries. In the mid-1960s, average male life expectancy was about 66 years; in 1986 it was only 60. Infant mortality was rising, and the birth-rate was declining, especially among the Russians. In 1980, Russians formed only 52 per cent of the population of the Soviet Union, a proportion which was in decline because of higher fertility rates in the Central Asian republics.[17]

All this added up to a very considerable political and economic crisis within the Soviet Union. There were also accumulating difficulties in the Soviet-controlled zone in eastern Europe. In some respects the countries of eastern Europe had become an economic burden to the Soviet Union. For example, as a result of the five-year agreements setting Soviet export prices, the USSR sold its oil to eastern Europe at lower rates than it could have received on the world markets. The military contribution of the east Europeans through the Warsaw Pact was of uncertain value, because the morale and reliability of the various armies were doubtful. Politically and in all kinds of other ways, often painfully visible to the eye of a visitor, the countries of eastern Europe were 'not a showcase but an eyesore'.[18]

The most immediate danger in 1980–81 lay in Poland. The influence of the Catholic Church as a religious force and a focus for national feeling had remained strong throughout the period since 1945, and received a tremendous impetus from the election in October 1978 of a Polish Pope: Karol Wojtyla, John Paul II. Long ago, in the mid-19th century, the Austrian statesman Metternich lamented in relation to Pius IX that he could have foreseen anything but a liberal Pope; similarly the Soviet leaders were dismayed and baffled by a Polish Pope. In June 1979 John Paul II visited his native land, celebrating mass before crowds numbered in millions, and appealing at one and the same time to the Christian faith, to Polish patriotism and to human rights. His visit came at a time of economic difficulty in Poland, with falling production in industry and agriculture, and was followed by strikes in the shipyards at Gdansk, led by Lech Walesa, himself a Catholic. Walesa and his colleagues formed the trade union Solidarity, independent of the state and the Communist Party, marking an open breach between the great majority of Polish industrial workers and the communist regime. The potential danger to the existing order, not only in Poland but in the whole of eastern Europe, was grave. The Soviet government considered military intervention, as in Czechoslovakia in 1968, moving troops to the Polish border, and even ordering East German forces to the island of Rugen in the Baltic, near Szczecin – formerly Stettin.[19] In the event, they found a Polish intermediary to impose an internal solution. General Jaruzelski, Minister of Defence from 1968 and thus closely associated with the Soviet armed forces, had become Prime Minister and leader of the Communist Party in 1981. On 13 December 1981 he declared martial law, arrested Walesa and other leading members of Solidarity, and revoked most of the concessions earlier granted to the new trade union. This operation proved remarkably successful, partly because the Polish people, expecting a Soviet invasion, were relieved at the intervention of their own forces. But the breach between the majority of the Polish people, led by Solidarity and the Church, and the government remained. The Polish crisis had been suppressed but not resolved, and still threatened danger in the rest of eastern Europe.

Confrontation in the Third World

These Soviet difficulties were by no means obvious to the United States when Reagan was inaugurated as President at the beginning of 1981. Soviet military power was visible and formidable; and for some years the Soviets and their Cuban allies had been scoring a series of successes in Africa. The United States was itself suffering economic problems. At the end of 1980 inflation was running at 17 per cent per year; the federal budget was in deficit by $59.6 billion over the year; and there was a substantial excess of imports over exports. In the next few years, the Reagan administration increased military expenditure and ran even greater budget deficits ($195.4 billion in 1983, $202.8 billion in 1985), and continued to incur high deficits in overseas trade, both of which had to be covered by borrowing from abroad, mainly Japan and western Europe.[20]

Reagan was therefore taking considerable risks, economically as well as politically, in turning to a strategy of confronting the Soviet Union. He was not deterred. He used tough, combative language to show that he meant business, and that the days of soft talk to avoid offending the Soviets were over, and he went into action to oppose Soviet influence right across the globe.

The most vulnerable point for the Soviet Union was Afghanistan. By May 1980 the Soviets had put some 80 000 troops into the country, without subduing Afghan resistance. Large armoured forces and heavy tanks proved to be unsuitable for the terrain. Tajik and Uzbek troops, who were able to communicate freely with the Afghan population, proved unreliable and had to be withdrawn. By the end of 1980 there were over a million Afghan refugees in Pakistan, many of them Pathans, who had no intention of remaining quietly in camps, but were anxious to secure weapons to resume the fight. The reputation of these warriors, well known to the British in times past, might have given the Soviets pause. But even Pathans needed modern weapons.

At an early stage, the Afghan exiles received weapons from Pakistan and China. Under Reagan, the American Central Intelligence Agency began to supply weapons, but were careful to provide only arms originating from the Soviet Union itself or from Warsaw Pact countries, so that the Soviets could not immediately trace them to the United States. The Israelis proved a valuable source, because at various times they had captured large quantities of eastern European weaponry from their Arab opponents. Saudi Arabia was willing to put up money from its oil revenues. Even Egypt joined in the supply of armaments. A very curious informal coalition thus took shape to harass the Soviet forces in Afghanistan.

The result was a savage form of stalemate. The Soviets could not win the war, at any rate with the scale of force they were prepared to use – they never employed more than 150 000 troops in Afghanistan, and the number was usually lower than that. In 1983 Andropov indicated that he was looking for a negotiated conclusion to the war, and concluded a six-month truce with one of the Afghan regional commanders. The next year, after Andropov's death, the Soviet forces tried another tack and launched a big offensive against the guerrillas, with some success. Armoured helicopters were used to pursue the guerrillas far into the hills without fear of reprisals. Victory seemed within sight, but was never quite achieved. But on the other hand there was no danger that the Soviets would lose the war, in the sense of being driven out of Afghanistan. They held Kabul and the country round it; they had a strong base near Herat; and they normally controlled the main roads. Neither side could win; and both suffered from the strain and attrition of prolonged warfare.

In March 1985, after his triumphant re-election to the presidency in 1984, Reagan began to increase the scale and change the methods of American intervention. The United States began to supply the *mujaheddin* (the guerrilla forces) directly with American weapons, and also with hundreds of Tennessee mules – a thoroughly practical contribution to warfare in mountain country. In 1986 the Americans began to provide Stinger missiles, light enough to be carried by one man, and remarkably accurate against helicopters, enabling the Afghans to strike back against the Soviets' best weapon.

The war in Afghanistan also had the political effect of drawing the hostility of Islamic countries down upon the Soviet Union, instead of the United States, which had previously been their principal target. The Organization of the Islamic Conference, which had been formed by 24 Muslim states at a conference in Rabat in September 1969, suspended Afghanistan from membership in January 1980, and gave support to the *mujaheddin*. Every autumn, the General Assembly of the United Nations passed, by large majorities, a resolution calling for the withdrawal of all foreign troops from Afghanistan – on 23 November 1984, for example, the vote was 116–20.[21] These votes dealt a severe blow to Soviet prestige and influence in the Third World, which could normally be relied upon to be broadly pro-Soviet in its sympathies.

Western onlookers were quick to see Afghanistan as the Soviet Union's Vietnam. There were obvious parallels. The Soviets, like the Americans, found themselves fighting an unsuccessful guerrilla war against tough, elusive opponents. Their morale suffered, and there were problems with drugs and desertion (though troops wisely did not desert in Afghanistan itself). There were also differences between the two campaigns, though these proved more superficial than real. The Soviet government, unlike the Americans, maintained a close control over the news media; but nothing could prevent soldiers from talking after their tour of duty, and memorials stood mute in cemeteries – 'Died, fulfilling his internationalist duty'.[22] The

Soviet leaders faced no demonstrations in the streets or university campuses; but even so there was an undercurrent of dismay and gloom in public opinion. The Soviets engaged many fewer troops in Afghanistan than the Americans in Vietnam, and suffered fewer casualties – just over 13 000 killed as against some 58 000; but the debilitating effects of the conflict, the loss of confidence and unity at home and damage to prestige abroad, were very similar.

The parallels were certainly close enough to encourage the Americans, and offer them a piquant pleasure in watching their enemies become involved in problems similar to their own a few years earlier. Moreover, in giving material support the Americans were able to make good use of inter-mediaries; not supplying their own weaponry until 1985, and throughout the campaign Saudi Arabia provided more funds than the United States. Intervention in Afghanistan was by no means confrontation on the cheap – it has been estimated that in eight years the Americans spent some $3 to 3.3 billion;[23] but it involved no American casualties, and consisted largely of ensuring that the Soviets suffered the full consequences of their own mistakes.

In Africa, the Americans had done little to combat Soviet influence during the late 1970s. In 1976 American involvement in Angola had been stopped by Congress, which ruled out any further assistance to opponents of the Soviet-backed government, for fear that Angola should become another Vietnam. Reagan reversed this policy, pursuing active and widespread inter-vention to combat Soviet influence, secure strategic positions, and if possi-ble establish American predominance south of the Sahara. Chester Crocker, appointed by Reagan to control African affairs in the State Department, announced the new American intentions in a speech to ex-servicemen in Honolulu on 29 August 1981, declaring that the United States would confront the Soviet Union throughout Africa, and adding that, even though the *apartheid* regime in South Africa was repugnant to American principles, the Americans would not permit the destabilization of South Africa. This marked an important change from President Carter's emphasis on human rights, and made clear that strategy and economics would predominate. The new emphasis was on the strategic importance of the Cape and the South African production of gold and other minerals, which must not be allowed to fall under Soviet control. The Americans, it is true, hoped to use their support (for example, in the supply of arms) to encourage internal reforms in South Africa, but they did not press the matter very hard.

The principal results of the new policy were felt in Angola, where the Americans resumed clandestine help to UNITA (the National Union for the Total Independence of Angola), which was in revolt against the existing government, itself supported by the Soviet Union and Cuba. The United States also provided secret assistance to South African intervention in

Angola. Eventually, in 1985, Congress went back on its earlier restrictions, and direct American assistance to UNITA was resumed. American intervention in Angola achieved stalemate, not victory; and prolonged the civil war until the Soviet government under Gorbachev became anxious to end its own involvement.

In Central America and the Caribbean, Reagan resumed an active policy against various left-wing regimes and movements which he considered a threat to the United States. His first move was to offer economic assistance, announcing on 24 February 1982 an Initiative for the Caribbean Basin, proposing a programme of financial aid to Caribbean countries, tax incentives for American investors there, and preferential tariffs for exports to the USA. His language was forthright, denouncing 'the poverty and repression of Castro's Cuba, and the tightening grip of the totalitarian left in Grenada and Nicaragua . . . If we do not act promptly and decisively in defence of freedom, new Cubas will arise from the ruins of today's conflicts.'[24] But in the event Congress could not be persuaded to provide the trade preferences and tax incentives, so the Caribbean Initiative had little practical effect. Thus most American energy went into direct action, usually clandestine but occasionally open.

The most dramatic example of clandestine action was in Nicaragua, where Reagan regarded the Sandinista government as providing a bridgehead for the Soviet Union in Central America. The Americans intervened against the Sandinistas by forming, in December 1981, the Contra guerrilla organization (whose formal title was the Nicaraguan Democratic Front), recruited from Nicaraguans who had taken refuge in Honduras. Starting from a few hundreds, the Contras were built up to a strength of some 15 000 by the mid-1980s, armed and supplied by the Central Intelligence Agency. They failed to overthrow the Sandinista regime, but waged a guerrilla war which caused many casualties and inflicted a good deal of economic damage. In June 1984 the United States Congress cut off assistance to the Contras, but the CIA continued its support, securing money from various other sources, including the governments of Saudi Arabia and Brunei, which had no interest in Central America at all, and even from the proceeds of secret arms sales to Iran – a part of the tangled 'Iran-Contra' or 'Irangate' affair. This *imbroglio* has an eerie fascination of its own. Its major significance in the Latin American context is that it shows how far Reagan was prepared to go in his Nicaraguan intervention. At the time, Iran was bitterly, even fanatically, hostile to the United States, and for Reagan to provide the Iranians with weapons seemed unthinkable – it was as though 'John Wayne had been caught selling rifles to the Indians'.[25] In 1986 Congress changed its mind on funding for the Contras, and more orthodox methods of supply were resumed. The Contras never won the guerrilla war, but kept it going until a cease-fire was arranged in 1989. The key to the American intervention in Nicaragua did not lie in any serious

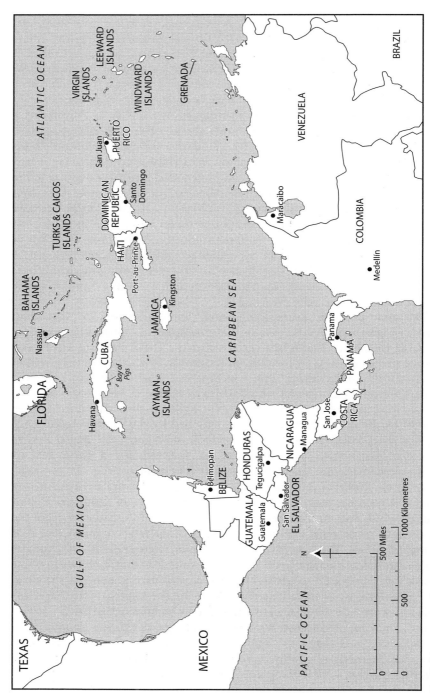

The Caribbean

threat to American interests, but in Reagan's determination to make the country an example of his own determination; and he was prepared to use some extraordinary methods in so doing.

The United States also intervened in El Salvador, a tiny Central American state only 8 200 square miles in extent, with a population of some 5 000 000, which the Reagan administration chose to invest with a crucial significance in East–West relations. In El Salvador the Americans stepped in to support the existing government against a rebellion by the Farabundo Marti National Liberation Front. The United States claimed that the Front was sustained by supplies of arms from Cuba, which itself was acting as a transit station for the Soviet Union – an assertion which, despite much effort, they never actually proved. The Americans helped the Salvadoran army in its battle against the guerrillas, which was pursued with a ruthless disregard for civilian casualties and for what the United States would have regarded in other circumstances as the requirements of human rights.

The extreme case of confrontation in the Caribbean, involving the direct use of force by the United States, took place in Grenada, a tiny island with a population of about 90 000, formerly a British colony and still a member of the Commonwealth. In 1979 a Marxist party led by Maurice Bishop and calling itself the New Jewel Movement (which had nothing to do with jewels, but took its name from an acronym for 'Joined for Welfare, Education and Liberation) seized power in Grenada. Bishop undertook a programme of social reform; he was also an old acquaintance of Fidel Castro, and he concluded a number of agreements with Cuba and the Soviet Union, including one for the building of an airport. The American government believed that the new regime in Grenada formed an extension of Cuban and Soviet influence, and claimed that the airport on the island was to be used for military purposes. In the summer of 1983 Bishop visited Washington in a vain attempt to persuade the Americans of his good intentions. In fact this visit led to his overthrow and murder by members of his own party, who accused him of petty-bourgeois tendencies.

The actual danger to the United States from a small island some 1500 miles distant was miniscule; but the Grenadan coup presented an opportunity for a show of force and decisive action. Four members of the Organization of Eastern Caribbean States (probably not wholly on their own initiative) appealed to the United States for military intervention. The result was an operation on a remarkable scale in proportion to its object. The Americans despatched to Grenada a 79 000-ton aircraft-carrier, two helicopter vessels, a dozen other warships, and a landing force of some 7000 elite troops – marines, paratroops and rangers. To add respectability, this enormous force was accompanied by about 300 soldiers and police from eastern Caribbean islands. The total opposition consisted of about 1000 Grenadan soldiers and 800 Cubans, who were described as either construction workers or paramilitaries according to taste. The Americans landed on 25 October 1983, and the fighting lasted three days, which in view of the overwhelming American superiority was a long time. Casualties were variously estimated at 100–200 Grenadans killed, 50–100 Cubans, and 20–30 Americans.[26] On 27 October President Reagan made a television broadcast declaring that Grenada had been in the process of becoming a Soviet-Cuban colony and a base to export terror. At home in America it appears that this explanation carried much conviction. Elsewhere, Reagan's message was conveyed by the sheer weight of the American assault. The disproportion between the tiny Grenadan forces and the vast American armada may have appeared grotesque or even faintly ludicrous, and it certainly aroused much anti-American feeling abroad. (Even Margaret Thatcher, one of Reagan's firmest supporters, wrote later that she had felt 'dismayed and let down by what had happened'.)[27] But it certainly avoided the error of the half-hearted attack on Cuba at the Bay of Pigs in 1961. The invasion of Grenada undoubtedly used a sledgehammer to crack a nut; but if there were any other potential nuts in the area, they had been warned. The direct consequences were almost nil. The Soviet and Cuban governments protested, but took no action. Most of the American troops departed two months later, leaving a small contingent behind until 1985.

Another strange and striking episode in 1983 showed how far American–Soviet relations had deteriorated, and how strong the spirit of confrontation had become. On 1 September 1983 a Soviet fighter shot down a South Korean B-747 airliner (KAL 007), which was far off course in Soviet airspace over the island of Sakhalin. All on board, 269 passengers and crew, were killed. It was an extraordinary affair, with elements of mystery which have still not been fully cleared up. It appears that the Soviet pilot actually believed that he was facing a military reconnaissance aircraft – though a B-747 should have been recognizable, even at night. On the American side, it was not clear why nothing was done to alert the airliner to its danger. At the time, each side simply denounced the perfidy of the other. In Washington, Reagan and Shultz (the Secretary of State) at once declared that the shooting-down was an act of barbarism and a crime against humanity. Andropov, in a belated statement, claimed that the flight was a provocation organized by American special forces. In other circumstances, the event might have been dealt with differently. The Americans could have refrained from comment until they had secured an explanation; they might even have affected to believe that the Soviet pilot had acted in error. The Soviets might have admitted error and apologized. But in the atmosphere of the early 1980s no such emollient measures were attempted. A calamitous event became a sign of the times.

The thinking behind American confrontation with the Soviet Union in the Third World was set out by the Secretary of State, Shultz, in a speech on 22 February 1985, at the beginning of Reagan's second term as President. The United States aimed to roll back the gains made by the Soviet-supported regimes in Afghanistan, Nicaragua, Angola and Ethiopia (Shultz passed over Cuba in silence). This was a deliberate challenge to the Brezhnev Doctrine, which had claimed that when a country had joined the communist camp it could not be allowed to leave; and Shultz asserted that in the new balance of forces in the world, this challenge could be successful. This policy came to be called in common parlance, though not officially, the Reagan Doctrine. It scored some successes, notably in Afghanistan. It also had its costs, notably in that it damaged the reputation of the United States for fair dealing and good conduct. Clandestine warfare can involve some very dirty dealing. The Iran-Contra affair dragged on, in an obscure and murky fashion, damaging Reagan's own reputation, dividing American opinion, and dismaying America's allies. Intervention in Afghanistan meant supplying some very tough characters with dangerous weaponry which could later be used against anyone. The invasion of Grenada involved an overwhelming use of force against a tiny opponent. Confrontation served its purpose, but the chickens came home to roost for many years to come, in American domestic opinion and in the reactions of America's allies.

◆ New arms races: Euro-missiles and the Strategic Defence Initiative

At the time of this confrontation in the Third World, the United States also undertook two new competitions in nuclear armaments: the deployment of medium-range missiles in Europe, and a completely new defensive programme, the Strategic Defence Initiative.

The situation regarding nuclear missiles in 1980 was that the second Strategic Arms Limitation Treaty (SALT II) had been signed in Vienna in June 1979, but not ratified by the United States Senate as a result of the Soviet invasion of Afghanistan. However, the American and Soviet governments had both undertaken to observe the treaty's terms even though it was not formally in force; which meant that they accepted a rough balance in intercontinental ballistic missiles (ICBMs). The Soviets held about two-thirds of their warheads on land-based missiles, which were accurate in their targeting but vulnerable to a pre-emptive attack. The Americans deployed about two-thirds of their warheads in submarines, meaning that they were less accurate but largely safe from attack. The Soviet Union thus had the more powerful first strike, but the Americans had an almost invulnerable second strike – a true balance of terror.

The SALT II agreement covered missiles with a range of over 5500 kilometres, leaving open the development of missiles with a lesser range. In 1977 the Soviet Union had begun to deploy SS-20 missiles in central and eastern Europe, each armed with three nuclear warheads and with a range of 5000 kilometres. (See above, pp. 320–21.) This opened the possibility of separating the west European NATO countries from their American allies, because the SS-20s could attack targets in western Europe but not in the United States. In 1979 the NATO powers had agreed on a two-stage policy with regard to these medium-range missiles: first, to attempt negotiations with the Soviets for the withdrawal of the SS-20s; and second, if that produced no results, to modernize their own weapons in western Europe – which meant installing American intermediate-range missiles, in the shape of Pershing or cruise missiles.

Negotiations produced no result. At one stage the Soviets proposed a freeze on intermediate-range missiles, which would have left them with their existing superiority, which was unacceptable to the Americans. Then in November 1981 Reagan proposed what he called the Zero Option, under which the Soviets would withdraw their SS-20s in return for the Americans *not* despatching Pershings and cruise missiles to Europe; but this was not acceptable to the Soviets. In July 1982 the principal American and Soviet participants, in the course of a 'walk in the woods' away from the negotiating table, agreed informally to accept 75 missiles on each side; only to find this rejected by the United States government.

The first part of the NATO policy – negotiation – was thus tried and failed. The United States therefore proposed to go ahead with the second part, and deploy their medium-range missiles in western Europe, which in practice meant Britain and West Germany. This step was ardently opposed by nuclear disarmament groups in both countries. In Britain the Campaign for Nuclear Disarmament, which had been quiescent during the 1970s, sprang into renewed life to protest against the arrival of Pershing missiles; and a group of women encamped on Greenham Common, where the first missiles were to be stationed. In West Germany pacifist movements mobilized strongly. French opinion, on the other hand, was little stirred, partly because (under a policy first laid down by General de Gaulle) no American-controlled weapons were accepted in France, and partly because the French simply did not believe there was any real danger. In the event, the British government under Margaret Thatcher disregarded the demonstrators and accepted the missiles. In West Germany, the Christian Democrats won the Bundestag elections in March 1983, ensuring a majority in favour of receiving the American missiles. Public opposition continued, culminating in a week of demonstrations, 15–20 October, in which the Socialists under Willy Brandt joined hands with the Green Party led by Petra Kelly. Despite this, the Bundestag gave its approval on 22 November, by 286 votes to 225; and the first nine Pershing missiles arrived in West Germany the very next day.

While these negotiations and internal western disputes on medium-range missiles were going on, the American and Soviet governments had agreed to attempt a new series of negotiations on long-range missiles, this time under the new acronym START: strategic arms reduction talks. This title included the hopeful notion of reduction in numbers of weapons, whereas earlier negotiations had only aimed at limitation. Negotiations began in June 1982, and proved very difficult, because the Americans began by aiming at cuts in land-based ICBMs, where the Soviets had a marked superiority. The talks had made little progress when the Soviets broke them off in November 1983 in protest at the arrival of the first Pershing missiles in western Europe.

The nuclear arms race, checked during the 1970s by the two SALT agreements, was thus resumed. A completely new element was added to it by President Reagan's announcement, on 23 March 1983, of a new Strategic Defence Initiative (known by the acronym of SDI, and often popularly called 'Star Wars'). This was an extraordinary plan to introduce a comprehensive system for anti-missile defence, using all the resources of space technology (including laser beams and such apparently far-fetched devices as mirrors in space – which helped to confirm the 'Star Wars' image) to provide complete security against nuclear attack. Enemy missiles were to be destroyed at any one of four stages: launch; the start of their trajectory; in flight; or on descent. The aim was to achieve complete destruction. If successful, this would have nullified the existing balance of terror by rendering the United States immune from attack while leaving the Soviet Union exposed; and the Strategic Defence Initiative thus threatened to dissolve all the assumptions which had governed nuclear relations for some thirty years. In practice such an outcome was highly unlikely. There could be no certainty of total success in the destructive process, and since the Soviets had nearly 10 000 warheads, even 99 per cent success would mean that 100 would get through – which would be quite enough. The Strategic Defence Initiative was therefore at best an uncertain device, and many experts thought it a complete waste of effort and money. But it was begun, and the Soviets could not disregard it. They faced an almost impossible dilemma. Strategically, they could not afford to ignore the American programme; economically, they could not afford to match it except at enormous – probably unbearable – cost. It therefore became a major Soviet objective to persuade the Americans to drop the Initiative, or at any rate to limit work on it to the purely theoretical. When the two sides resumed talks on arms limitation in March 1985, the Soviets insisted that any progress must be linked to restrictions on the SDI; the Americans refused, and the talks stalled almost at once.

Thus it came about that in 1986 the nuclear balance remained roughly equal:[28]

	USA	Soviet Union
ICBM-borne warheads	2118	6420
Submarine-launched warheads	5536	2787(+)
Aircraft-borne warheads	2520	680
Total	10 174	9987(+)

But the assumptions which lay behind this balance had now been challenged by the Strategic Defence Initiative, and new uncertainties loomed
ahead.

◆ Soviet–American relations in the early 1980s

In general, the Soviet response to Reagan's strong rhetoric and unrelenting
confrontation was markedly restrained. The Soviet leaders had their own
troubles with the economy at home and the war in Afghanistan abroad, and
they were not inclined to look for further trouble in the Third World. They
repeatedly asked the Americans to resume the dialogue of earlier years.
Andropov, not long after he assumed power, publicly asserted (22
November 1982) that the policy of détente was not yet finished – 'The
future belongs to it'. In June 1983 the American Secretary of State, Shultz,
responded in a statement to Congress which combined a strong line with a
degree of flexibility: 'We now seek to engage the Soviet leaders in a
constructive dialogue . . .'[29]

In 1983 Raymond Aron, an experienced and perceptive analyst of international relations, looked back at his own verdict on Soviet–American relations, pronounced in 1947: 'War improbable, peace impossible'. He
thought that this still held good.[30] Why was this? Both powers were in
immediate material terms satisfied and secure. Neither needed or wanted
more territory. The Soviet Union sought no further territorial gains in
Europe, and the intervention in Afghanistan was not directed towards any
annexations. The United States had no wish whatsoever to extend its own
territory. Both were world powers, with assets which partly balanced one
another: ocean-going fleets, foreign bases, allies or *protégés* in the Middle
East, Africa and Latin America. As nuclear powers, each could destroy the
other but had no intention of doing so.

For all these reasons, war was improbable. Why then did peace appear
impossible? For the Soviet Union, this was partly a matter of ideology. It
was a key element in Marxist–Leninist belief that ultimately the whole
world would become communist, and that the Soviet Union must assist this
process. They no longer thought that war between the two camps was
inevitable (indeed they recognized that it would be suicidal), but the existing order could not be accepted as permanent. Moreover, the Soviet Union
could never *feel* secure, because it faced two enemies, the United States and
China, and was therefore, despite its own vast territory and enormous
strength, an encircled country.

The United States for its part was secure in its own territory and yet
felt vulnerable and endangered by the ideological threat of communism.
In practice, there was not the slightest physical threat, and little commercial loss in proportion to the whole American economy, from (for

example) a Marxist regime in Nicaragua; but the Americans were afraid of contagion. They were conscious of their own recent errors, for example in Iran, and dismayed by the hostility they suffered in much of the Third World. The threat from Islamic regimes, for example those in Iran and Libya, loomed larger than was objectively reasonable. Moreover, the American economy was less overwhelmingly strong than it had been. The United States no longer controlled the world monetary system, as they had done under the Bretton Woods system. The government had to meet its budget deficits in the 1980s by borrowing from its one-time defeated enemies in Japan and West Germany – which was undignified but necessary.

Therefore neither superpower felt fully secure, despite all its territory, resources and military strength. In these circumstances, their mutual hostility became in a curious way a source of stability. The two opponents propped one another up, like heavy-weight boxers after fifteen rounds of a gruelling contest. They had lived with the balance of terror so long that they found it reassuring. The lines drawn between east and west in Europe, embodied in the iron curtain and the Berlin Wall, were accepted by both sides, despite their regular toll in death and suffering. There was a sense in which a peace settlement which involved changes in any of these structures would seem more dangerous than the existing tension. It was not so much that peace was impossible, but that in the constant conflict of the Cold War the two superpowers had already found a sort of peace that arose, not from the absence of conflict, but from its familiar presence.

The confrontation of the renewed Cold War therefore proved to be less dangerous than it sometimes appeared, and relations between the superpowers retained much of their earlier stability. They did not achieve peace, but they stopped a long way short of war. The two countries still regarded one another with a deep suspicion. Many Americans were convinced that the Soviet aim was the final victory of world communism, while well-informed Soviet observers were sure that the Americans sought to impose their own model of capitalism on the rest of the world. (There was indeed something in both these views.) The Soviets disliked the ingrained American habit of lecturing others on morality while themselves assuming complete freedom of action, regardless of principle. The Americans tended to regard Soviet leaders as either fanatics or cynics, neither of whom were easy to deal with.[31]

In these circumstances, war remained improbable despite the constant confrontation of the early 1980s, and peace remained, if not impossible, at least unlikely, because neither side wanted it and there seemed no sufficient reason to change the existing situation. Then suddenly, in the space of five years, everything changed.

◆ Notes to Chapter 15

1. See Fred Halliday, *The Making of the Second Cold War* (London, 1983), and especially the analysis of the characteristics of the Second Cold War on pp. 11–19.
2. Quotation in Peter G. Boyle, *American-Soviet Relations: From the Russian Revolution to the Fall of Communism* (London, 1993), p. 199; comments in Raymond L. Garthoff, *The Great Transition: American-Soviet Relations and the End of the Cold War* (Washington, DC, 1994), pp. 8–13.
3. John Lewis Gaddis, *The United States and the End of the Cold War: Implications, Reconsiderations, Provocations* (New York, paperback edn, 1994), pp. 120–1.
4. Henry Kissinger, *Diplomacy* (London, paperback edn, 1995), pp. 766, 764.
5. Anatoly Dobrynin, *In Confidence: Moscow's Ambassador to America's Six Cold War Presidents, 1962–1986* (New York, 1995), pp. 594, 608; see also generally pp. 594–5, 606–9.
6. *Ibid.*, p. 478; André Fontaine, *Après eux, le déluge: De Kaboul à Sarajevo, 1979–1995* (Paris, 1995), p. 86.
7. Kissinger, *Diplomacy*, p. 772. Kissinger commented that other Presidents had tried confrontation and conciliation by turns; Reagan tried both at once.
8. Dobrynin, *In Confidence*, pp. 484–5.
9. Quoted in Garthoff, *Great Transition*, p. 9. It is worth recalling that John F. Kennedy made very similar remarks in 1960, though as a presidential candidate, not as President. See above, p. 136.
10. Dobrynin, *In Confidence*, p. 518.
11. Seweryn Bialer, *The Soviet Paradox: External Expansion, Internal Decline* (London, 1986), p. 100, borrowing the title of Robert Musil's novel, *The Man Without Qualities*; Robert Service, *A History of Twentieth-Century Russia* (London, 1997), pp. 404–5, 433.
12. In the mid-1980s, the main forces of the Warsaw Pact were estimated at about 6.4 million men, and those of NATO at about 5 million – Paul Kennedy, *The Rise and Fall of the Great Powers* (London, paperback edn, 1989), p. 657. For nuclear weapons, see below, p. 351.
13. Gabriel Partos, *The World that Came in from the Cold* (London, 1993), p. 127.
14. Bialer, *Soviet Paradox*, p. 165.
15. Partos, *World*, p. 131; Service, *Twentieth Century Russia*, pp. 467, 470.
16. Fontaine, *Déluge*, p. 239.
17. Kennedy, *Great Powers*, pp. 641–3.

18. Bialer, *Soviet Paradox*, p.198; see generally pp.196–9.
19. David Miller, *The Cold War: A Military History* (London, 1998), p. 63.
20. Kennedy, *Great Powers*, pp. 680–2.
21. *Keesing's Contemporary Archives*, 1980, p. 32825.
22. Partos, p. 153, quoting interview with Artyom Borovik, a Soviet journalist whose articles about the war were not published until 1987.
23. Samuel P. Huntington, *The Clash of Civilizations and the Remaking of World Order* (New York, 1996), p. 247.
24. *Keesing's*, 1982, p. 31568.
25. A remark by a Chicago lawyer, quoted in Fontaine, *Déluge*, p. 339.
26. Differing casualty figures in Chris Cook, *World Political Almanac* (London, 3rd edn, 1995), p. 326, and Thomas Carothers, *In the Name of Democracy: US Policy toward Central America in the Reagan Years* (Oxford, 1991), p. 112.
27. Margaret Thatcher, *The Downing Street Years* (London, 1993), p. 331.
28. Kennedy, *Great Powers*, p. 51, citing IISS, *The Military Balance, 1985–86*, p. 180.
29. Garthoff, *Transition*, pp. 85–6, 108.
30. Raymond Aron, *Les dernières années du siècle* (Paris, 1984), pp. 165–6.
31. See Bialer, *Paradox*, pp. 346–51, 356–60, for an analysis of American and Soviet misconceptions of one another in the mid-1980s.

GORBACHEV AND REAGAN, 1985–1988: TRANSFORMATION SCENE

**The advent of Gorbachev – Soviet retreat from Afghanistan –
The Gorbachev–Reagan summits – Peace in sight**

◆ The advent of Gorbachev

On 10 March 1985 Konstantin Chernenko, the General Secretary of the Communist Party of the Soviet Union and the effective ruler of the USSR, died at the age of 74. The next day the Politburo nominated Mikhail Gorbachev, its youngest member at the age of 54, to replace him. This was a sudden change of generations in the Soviet leadership. Gorbachev was the first General Secretary to have been born in the Soviet Union rather than Tsarist Russia. He was educated at Moscow University, where he took a degree in Law; entered the Communist Party bureaucracy in his home region of Stavropol; and became a member of the Party Central Committee in 1971. In 1978 he became a member of the Secretariat of the Central Committee, with responsibility for Agriculture; and was promoted to full membership of the Politburo in 1980. This was a rapid rise, but it was achieved through the normal structures of the Party, and under the patronage of Andropov, for a long time head of the KGB. It showed remarkable success as a bureaucrat and politician in the Soviet style; but it was by no means obviously the making of a vigorous reformer.[1]

Gorbachev, writes Robert Service, was 'a Marxist–Leninist believer'. Archie Brown puts it more cautiously: 'He thought of himself as a Marxist – and indeed as a Leninist – but his Marxism was flexible and undogmatic.'[2] He was also an optimist – a vital trait which he shared with Reagan, with whom his relations were to be so important. He thought that the Soviet Union provided a number of services for its citizens (for example, in health and education) which were superior to the equivalents in capitalist countries, and that it was his task to bring other aspects up to scratch. Just as Churchill declared in 1942 that he had not become the King's First Minister in order to preside over the dissolution of the British Empire, so

Gorbachev 'had no intention of presiding over the dissolution of the USSR', or of dismantling the communist system.[3]

He set out instead to reform it. His personal experience and some of his academic studies (he had written a thesis on the economics of milk production) had persuaded him that reform was necessary. When he had been in office for just over a year, the disaster at the Chernobyl nuclear reactor in April 1986 convinced him that reform must be drastic and rapid – Chernobyl revealed a state of affairs which demanded root and branch transformation. Gorbachev therefore pressed forward his twin domestic programme of *perestroika* and *glasnost*. *Perestroika* meant restructuring, and began as an attempt to invigorate the stagnant Soviet economy by decentralization and the introduction of some market forces. But it went further than that. Gorbachev described it as a complete renewal of all aspects of Soviet life, economic, social, political and moral – a sweeping programme. *Glasnost* meant openness in the expression of opinion, relating to current events, contemporary society and Soviet history. *Perestroika* and *glasnost* together raised the fundamental question of whether the system was capable of reform at all, or would have to be abandoned. This was not the original intention. As Gorbachev put it later: 'Just like reformers before me, I thought we had a system that could be improved. Instead, I learned that we had a system that needed to be replaced.'[4] (We may recall what Alexis de Tocqueville wrote in *L'Ancien Régime et la Révolution* in 1856 – that the most dangerous moment for a bad government was usually when it began to reform.)

Internal changes on this scale were bound to have implications for foreign policy. Gorbachev knew that reform at home required a durable peace abroad. He signalled his intention to change foreign policy soon after he took office, by replacing Gromyko as Foreign Minister by Eduard Shevarnadze on 2 July 1985. Gromyko had served as Foreign Minister from 1957, but suddenly found himself 'kicked upstairs' to become President of the Soviet Union. Shevardnadze, like Gorbachev, was a comparative youngster (born in 1928), and virtually without experience in foreign affairs. He represented a new start, and brought to the Foreign Ministry a flexibility which Gromyko could never have provided.

The essential link between reform at home and a new foreign policy lay in the deployment of resources. Gorbachev wanted to reduce the cost of supporting communist regimes in the Third World, and set out to disengage from Soviet commitments in Africa and Afghanistan. More important, he sought to control the defence budget by negotiating arms limitation agreements with the Americans, and if at all possible persuading them to give up or modify the Strategic Defence Initiative, Reagan's astonishing scheme to create a total defence against nuclear attack. The SDI might well prove in the long run to be impossible, but meanwhile the Soviet Union, with its ailing economy, could not attempt to keep up with it.

These were questions of policy and diplomacy. Gorbachev also took a crucial ideological step. In 1985, not long after Gorbachev had become General Secretary, a new Party Programme was being prepared for adoption by the 27th Congress of the Communist Party of the Soviet Union, due to be held in February 1986. Gorbachev deliberately took this opportunity to re-define the concept of 'peaceful coexistence', which since the term had been introduced in the 1920s had been regarded simply as one of the forms of class struggle, so that peaceful coexistence with capitalist states was merely the continuation of hostility by other means. This was now to be abandoned, and peaceful coexistence was to become an end in itself, and part of a genuine co-operation with the United States. The change was accepted by the Party Congress; and though it may have appeared to be no more than the re-definition of a doctrinal point, it marked a fundamental transformation in the basis of Soviet foreign policy.

Gorbachev was adventurous, with a keen and flexible mind. He knew parts of western Europe as a private traveller as well as a Party representative, and was open to its influences. Western leaders – and, as rapidly appeared, the western public – proved equally open to him. Margaret Thatcher, the British Prime Minister, invited him to England in December 1984, before he became General Secretary, and in long talks at Chequers came to the conclusion that he represented something new in Soviet politics. As she remarked to the press at the end of Gorbachev's visit, she liked him and thought he was a man she could do business with.[5] Would Reagan think Gorbachev could do business with the Americans? The omens did not seem favourable. Reagan had committed himself to a policy of confrontation with the Soviet Union, and had not minced his words about that 'evil empire'; though he had never entirely closed the door to negotiations in the future. When Gorbachev came to power, it appears that he was advised to play for safety until Reagan left office. Gorbachev himself thought otherwise. He believed that he had no time to spare, and that he had a good chance of coming to terms with Reagan *because* he had a strong conservative reputation, rather than in spite of it. (There was a parallel with France in the 1960s, where de Gaulle, with his courageous record in two wars against Germany, could go further in reconciliation with the old enemy than anyone else could have done. Similarly Reagan, with his credentials as a 'cold warrior', could be bolder in negotiation with the Soviet Union than any likely successor.) Gorbachev came to think that a personal meeting with Reagan was urgent. There was no need and no time to make all the careful preparations which would be necessary to ensure that a summit meeting would produce solid results, which was the conventional wisdom nurtured by the diplomats on both sides. Arrangements were made behind the scenes, and in July 1985 it was agreed that a summit meeting should take place in November. This was to be the first of four summit meetings which transformed relations between the two countries.

Before discussing these fateful meetings, we must turn to the Soviet retreat from Afghanistan, which was achieved during the same period and was an essential accompaniment to the negotiations at the summit. The Soviet occupation of Afghanistan in December 1979 had been the final blow to the détente between the superpowers, and the Soviet withdrawal was an important element in the restoration of good relations.

◆ The Soviet withdrawal from Afghanistan

When Gorbachev took office, he rapidly decided to reduce Soviet commitments abroad. As early as Chernenko's funeral in April 1985 he warned leaders of the communist states in eastern Europe that in future they would have to take charge of their own affairs – a startling proposition for men set in their ways.[6] By October 1985 he had decided in principle to get out of Afghanistan, though he had not yet worked out how to do it, and he still hoped to save something from the wreck. In particular, he sought to retain at least a neutral (and preferably not Islamic) government in Afghanistan, in order to limit the effects of withdrawal on the Soviet republics in Central Asia.

In May 1986 Gorbachev removed Babrak Karmal, the Secretary-General of the Afghan Communist Party, and replaced him by Mohammed Najibullah, the head of the Afghan equivalent of the KGB. Najibullah, under Soviet instructions, offered concessions to the Afghan resistance, proposing to set up new political parties and introduce a new constitution, but to no avail. In November 1986 Gorbachev resolved upon drastic action. He told the Politburo that the Soviet Union had been fighting in Afghanistan for six years, and unless they changed course they might still be fighting in another twenty or thirty years. He therefore proposed to bring the Soviet troops out within two years, leaving Afghanistan as a neutral state. On 1 January 1987 the Afghan government announced a unilateral cease-fire by its own forces, and declared that it was ready to talk to the resistance. The *mujaheddin* replied that they would continue the armed struggle, and demanded the total, immediate and unconditional withdrawal of all Soviet troops. The Soviets wanted a compromise, but the *mujaheddin* were determined on victory – another parallel with the situation in Vietnam, where the Americans had tried for a compromise and the North Vietnamese had been set on victory.

So the war went on, though Gorbachev continued to try to bring it to an end. On 16 September 1987 the Soviet Foreign Minister, Shevardnadze, gave the American Secretary of State, Shultz, a firm private assurance that Soviet forces would withdraw from Afghanistan, probably within a year. Complicated secret exchanges took place between the USA, USSR and Pakistan, in which the Pakistanis tried to insist that any agreement should involve a new Afghan Provisional Government, rather than the existing government nominated by the Soviets. On 8 February 1988 Gorbachev tried to cut through the tangle by announcing on Soviet television that the Soviet Union would withdraw its troops, starting on 15 May that year, if a political agreement were reached by 15 March. He hoped for, but did not set as a condition, the establishment of an independent and neutral Afghan government.

In March 1988 indirect negotiations between the governments of Pakistan and Afghanistan began in Geneva, using the good offices of the United Nations. On 14 April the Pakistani and Afghan representatives concluded three agreements:the first on non-interference and non-intervention in Afghanistan; the second on the voluntary return of refugees; and the third on the settlement of the situation in Afghanistan. There was to be a phased withdrawal of 'foreign troops' to begin on 15 May and to be completed within nine months. These troops were understood to be Soviet, and this was the key to the whole arrangement.[7] These agreements were guaranteed by American and Soviet representatives, and signed in the presence of the Secretary-General of the United Nations, Perez de Cuellar, but the documents were somewhat opaque and made no explicit reference to the end of hostilities, or to the political future of Afghanistan; and referred only to a 'positive symmetry' in the reduction of outside aid to the two sides in Afghanistan. The American State Department, in a commentary, specified that the Soviet Union had agreed to a complete withdrawal of its forces, and added that if the USSR continued to provide military assistance to its Afghan *protégés*, the Americans would do the same for theirs.

The *mujaheddin* were not directly represented at these negotiations (though Pakistan claimed to represent their interests). They refused to accept the agreements, and declared that they would fight on until the government in Kabul was overthrown. The agreement therefore had only limited effect on the ground (or in the mountains). Its importance lay in the fact that it gave the Soviet Union a way out of the conflict. The Soviet troops began to withdraw on time, on 15 May 1988. The Pakistanis for their part kept up their assistance to the *mujaheddin*, and the Americans continued to channel supplies through Pakistan. Gorbachev turned a blind eye to these events, making threatening remarks about halting the withdrawal of Soviet troops, but taking no action The Soviet withdrawal was virtually complete by 15 February 1989, nine months after the Geneva agreement. They left some troops at their Embassy in Kabul, at Kabul airport, and at their military base near Herat; but that was all. Just over nine years after it began, the Soviet intervention in Afghanistan came to an end.

The cost had been heavy. Soviet casualties, published by the military authorities in Moscow in 1988, were put at 13 310 dead, over 35 000 wounded and 311 missing.[8] The Army suffered a grave blow to its morale, and in some units discipline was badly undermined. The political consequences were far-reaching. Gorbachev had carried out an unprecedented retreat, and had abandoned the claim made in the Brezhnev Doctrine that a communist take-over of power, once achieved, was irreversible. Afghanistan was doubtless an exceptional case, but the example was dangerous. In the Third World, Soviet prestige was badly damaged, as hostile votes in the UN General Assembly showed. More serious still, nationalist sentiment within the Soviet Union was stirred and encouraged by the Afghan resistance, which thus played a part in the dissolution of the Soviet state in 1990–91.

Afghanistan also paid a heavy price. There are no reliable figures for Afghan casualties. Some estimates put the dead at up to a million, though this is almost certainly too high.[9] The Soviet withdrawal was followed by continued fighting. Najibullah's government, which was almost universally expected to vanish when the Soviet troops left, hung on for another three years. (The Americans had been so sure that the government would collapse that they closed their Embassy in Kabul when the Soviets pulled out.) The resistance, whose only unifying element had been opposition to the Soviet occupation, rapidly fell apart into conflicting religious and tribal factions. In 1992 an Islamic Provisional Government was proclaimed, but civil war continued. The great powers were no longer interested.

For the Americans, the war had been a success. They had exploited the Soviet difficulties by limited intervention and the supply of weaponry, costly in money but without risk to American lives. But there were other costs, difficult to estimate but none the less real for that. The Americans had played the role of the sorcerer's apprentice, supporting guerrilla fighters who, after the Soviet withdrawal, maintained their arms depots and training camps for their own purposes. These guerrillas were not only Afghans – about 25 000 volunteers from Islamic countries also took part in the war. Most of them lived to fight another day and against other opponents – including the Americans. The consequences were still being felt ten years or more after the Soviet withdrawal from Afghanistan.

◆ Gorbachev and Reagan: the four summit meetings

While these protracted and often obscure events were taking place in Afghanistan, Gorbachev and Reagan held four summit meetings in a blaze of publicity. These took place in less than three years, following a period of almost six years during which there had been no Soviet–American summits at all. The two statesmen met at Geneva (19–20 November 1985); Reykjavik (11–12 October 1986); Washington (7–10 December 1987); and Moscow (29 May–2 June 1988).[10]

These meetings were in the long run so successful and had such far-reaching consequences that it is easy to forget the difficult circumstances in which they began. At the beginning of 1985 confrontation was still the order of the day in American policy. Reagan, in his State of the Union message to Congress in February 1985, declared that the United States had the right and duty to help everyone fighting for freedom across the globe, from Afghanistan to Nicaragua, and would not betray their confidence. To support them was an act of self-defence.

This was strong stuff. Yet only the next month, in March 1985, George Bush, the American Vice-President, attended the funeral ceremonies for Chernenko in Moscow, bearing an invitation from Reagan to Gorbachev to hold a summit meeting in the United States. For Reagan, this was not out of character. He had from time to time mixed his denunciations of the Soviet Union with expressions of willingness to talk to Soviet leaders. He had written personal letters to Brezhnev and Andropov. This time his simultaneous practice of confrontation and conciliation produced far-reaching results.

Gorbachev, who had himself been looking for a meeting, took up Reagan's proposal for a summit without insisting on agreements being reached in advance on specific issues. He suggested Moscow instead of Washington as the venue, but then both sides agreed on the neutral ground of Geneva. This first Reagan-Gorbachev summit, held on 19–20 November 1985, was an extraordinary affair. Reagan's 'evil empire' speech was still widely remembered. Diplomats and academics doubted his knowledge and judgement in matters of foreign policy. Gorbachev was himself a product of that same 'evil empire', with his thought shaped by Marxism-Leninism; and he was still a beginner in the conduct of foreign affairs. By the standard of earlier summits, when Nixon and Brezhnev had met largely to put the seal on agreements previously drawn up by their officials, the meeting was under-prepared. No joint documents were drafted in advance, and only a very broad agenda was agreed. Yet both leaders wanted their meeting to be a success; and it appears that of the two Gorbachev, despite being twenty years younger and with no fixed term of office to confine him, was the more hurried and the keener that there should be no breakdown.

During the two days of the meeting, Gorbachev and Reagan met four times in private talks, with only interpreters present, instead of the one session of fifteen minutes which had been envisaged. They largely ignored their agenda, and instead 'engaged in a free-form discussion'. Put more simply, they talked to one another.[11] In the event, this worked out rather well. The talk sometimes grew heated, particularly when Gorbachev raised the possibility of the Americans abandoning the Strategic Defence Initiative, which Reagan brusquely refused to consider. But they did not press their differences of opinion to breaking-point, and all in all they got on well together. Reagan had prepared carefully for the summit in his own way. He had rehearsed personal meetings, with a State Department official taking Gorbachev's role. He had even ensured that one meeting would take place in a room with a log fire, so that he and Gorbachev could hold a 'fireside chat'. This scenario was duly used, and the TV cameras conveyed a striking image of cordiality and mutual respect to audiences across the world. One of Reagan's advisers thought they were 'like a couple of fellows who had run into one another at the club and discovered that they had a lot in common'. Gorbachev thought Reagan 'a complex and contradictory person'; Reagan formed a positive impression of Gorbachev, who was clearly very different from any previous Soviet leader.[12] They readily agreed to meet again. Reagan invited Gorbachev to visit the United States; Gorbachev at once accepted and reciprocated with an invitation for Reagan to go to Moscow, which was accepted with equal alacrity.

The result was a triumph of style over substance. Gorbachev's principal substantive objective had been to check the progress of the Strategic Defence Initiative; but on this Reagan yielded nothing. Reagan for his part insisted on discussing trouble-spots in the Third World and human rights in the Soviet Union, but effectively got nowhere. And yet the meeting was an undoubted success. At the end, the two sides issued a joint communiqué, declaring that a nuclear war could not be won and should never be begun; that they recognized the importance of preventing any war between the two countries, whether nuclear or conventional; and that they would not seek to obtain a military superiority over one another. In retrospect this may appear to state the obvious, but after the confrontation of the past five years it was strikingly positive; and it went further than the statements of the previous era of détente by referring to preventing conventional as well as nuclear war. The two sides also agreed to resume strategic arms limitation talks, aiming in principle at a reduction of 50 per cent in their strategic nuclear weapons; which at least held out the hope of substantial progress in the future.

After his return home, Reagan wrote a long letter to Gorbachev in his own hand, recording his warm impressions of the meeting; and Gorbachev replied in similar terms. On New Year's Day 1986, six weeks after the summit meeting, Reagan and Gorbachev broadcast televised messages of goodwill to the Soviet and American peoples respectively – an unprecedented display of public amity and warmth.

Too much can be made of warm impressions. Churchill and Roosevelt in their day both thought that they were on good terms with Stalin, to find that the vision faded in the cold light of dawn. All depended on what was to follow this first contact. In fact there ensued a distinctly rough passage in American-Soviet relations. On 5 April 1986 a bomb exploded in a discotheque in West Berlin, killing an American serviceman. There was evidence of Libyan involvement in this attack, and on 15 April American aircraft bombed Tripoli and Benghazi, attacking mainly military targets but also trying to strike at Gaddafi in person. There were 37 Libyan dead, and the Americans lost an aircraft. At the time, Libya was still a *protégé* of the Soviet Union (though Gaddafi himself was a maverick in international affairs, and did much as he liked). The Soviet Foreign Minister, Shevardnadze, was due to make a visit to the USA to prepare for the next summit meeting; but he cancelled his journey to demonstrate Soviet disapproval of the American raids. At the same time, the arms race looked set to resume. On 27 May Reagan announced that, before the end of the year, the United States would cease to observe the limits set by the SALT II Treaty on numbers of intercontinental ballistic missiles and warheads. The Soviet government replied that if the SALT agreements were not observed it would take all necessary measures to maintain parity in nuclear armaments.

All this looked very unfavourable. But it appears that Gorbachev was growing increasingly anxious about nuclear weapons, perhaps under the shock of the Chernobyl disaster in April 1986. At the end of September he suddenly suggested that he and Reagan should hold, within the next fortnight, what he called a 'preliminary' summit meeting, to try to reach an agreement on medium-range missiles which could pave the way for a formal conference. Reagan agreed, and on 11–12 October 1986 the two leaders met at Reykjavik, in Iceland for what proved an astonishing conference.

Gorbachev offered a number of concessions. On intermediate-range missiles in Europe, he proposed to revive Reagan's 'zero option', suggested in 1981, exchanging Soviet withdrawal of SS-20 missiles for American withdrawal of Pershing and cruise missiles. On long-range nuclear weapons, he proposed a 50 per cent reduction on both sides over a period of five years, and agreed to omit the British and French nuclear weapons from the calculation of totals for these purposes. (Whether or not to count the British and French missiles in with the American totals had long been a point of friction in arms limitation talks.) In return, he asked the Americans to adhere to the provisions of the SALT I Treaty with regard to limitations on anti-ballistic missile defences, i.e. to restrict such defences to the capitals and one other area, which by implication would have prevented the development of the Strategic Defence Initiative, which was to cover the whole territory of the USA. The American delegation countered by proposing to reduce inter-continental missiles to zero within ten years, but to retain the right to install strategic defences against the intermediate-range missiles and bombers which would remain. Gorbachev then made the astonishing proposal of abolishing all nuclear weapons within ten years. Reagan was taken aback, but he had long cherished the apparently impossible aim of doing away with all nuclear weapons; and it appears that for a moment he accepted the proposal. But again the Strategic Defence Initiative (the American scheme to create a total defence against missile attack) proved the stumbling-block. Gorbachev set, as a condition for the abolition of nuclear weapons, a limitation of the Strategic Defence Initiative to laboratory and theoretical work for ten years – i.e. while nuclear weapons were being eliminated. Reagan rejected this condition, and when Gorbachev persisted, the President took a dramatic and unprecedented step. In Kissinger's words, Reagan 'responded in a way no foreign policy professional would have advised: he simply got up and left the room.'[13]

The result was confusion and the total collapse of the summit meeting, in a way which would earlier have been considered a complete disaster. The conventional wisdom had always been that failure could not be admitted, and some pretence of success must always be maintained, for fear of the damage to Soviet–American relations. Yet the Reykjavik summit failed, without fatal consequences. Gorbachev himself did much to save the situation. When he appeared at a press conference before an audience of bewildered and worried journalists, he improvised an explanation of what had happened and managed to sound hopeful – something which his predecessors neither would nor could have done. (Brezhnev at the end of his period in office had been only capable of reading from a prepared script.) Reagan too simply chose to disregard the failure; and it is striking that Gorbachev trusted Reagan more after Reykjavik than before, and his references to the President in private became much more respectful.[14] In retrospect, the failure at Reykjavik was almost certainly fortunate, because the sweeping changes which were almost agreed were improvised, without careful thought as to how they could be achieved. For example, if the United States and Soviet Union had given up their nuclear armaments irrespective of what other powers did, they would have been left without nuclear weapons, while Britain, France and China kept theirs, and India, Pakistan, Israel and South Africa waited in the wings – an unlikely state of affairs.

The immediate aftermath of Reykjavik appeared ominous. The United States carried out two nuclear tests on 3 and 11 February 1987; and on 26 February a Soviet nuclear test ended a moratorium which had lasted since August 1985. But immediately after this explosion, on 28 February 1987, Gorbachev proposed to the Americans a new and separate negotiation on intermediate-range missiles, intended to lead to their dismantling within five years. This represented a marked change in the Soviet approach, which had previously been to link all nuclear issues together. Talks began at Geneva, and in September 1987 the American Secretary of State and the Soviet Foreign Minister announced that they had agreed in principle on a 'zero option' on intermediate-range missiles, meaning not withdrawal but actual abandonment; and also that they would pursue the aim of a 50 per cent reduction in long-range strategic weapons.

This led in turn to the third summit meeting between Reagan and Gorbachev, held at Washington on 7–10 December 1987. By this time, Gorbachev·was at the height of his remarkable popularity in the western world ('Gorby-mania' was the term in vogue), and he received a rapturous welcome in the American capital. The visit was an immense public relations success, and a striking example of Gorbachev's talents as a communicator, which flourished more abroad than at home. All that was required by way of formal business was for the two leaders to sign the Treaty of Washington (8 December), which provided for the destruction within three years of all missiles with a range of between 500 and 5500 kilometres, based on land in Europe and Asia. The treaty thus provided, for the first time, for an actual *reduction* in the number of missiles and weapons, as distinct from earlier agreements which had *restricted* numbers. A whole category of weapons was to be eliminated. The treaty involved substantial concessions on the part of the Soviet Union. Gorbachev dropped his earlier insistence that the Strategic Defence Initiative should be abandoned or restricted as a condition for other agreements. In terms of numbers, the Soviets would give up twice as many missiles as the Americans; though the Soviet SS-20s were becoming obsolete, so the concession appeared greater than it was. The specific mention of the elimination of intermediate-range missiles based in Asia meant that SS-20s could not be re-deployed in Siberia. The treaty specified detailed procedures for verification of the destruction of the weapons – a success for Reagan's constant repetition of the slogan 'trust but verify', which he learned to say in Russian and which gradually made a strong impression on Gorbachev. The procedure for destruction, before the very eyes of inspectors from the other country, marked a concession by both sides, but more for the Soviets than the Americans, who had been less rigid on this issue. Finally, about 4000 American tactical nuclear weapons would remain deployed in West Germany. These could not reach Soviet territory, but represented a considerable threat to eastern Europe and the Soviet forces stationed there.

Despite these substantial concessions by the Soviets, which represented a real advantage for the United States, the treaty was heavily criticized by a number of American Senators, including Dan Quayle (later to be Republican Vice-President under George Bush) and Bob Dole (the Republican candidate for the Presidency in 1996), on the grounds that its terms were too dangerous. It was plain that only Reagan, with his immense prestige in the Republican Party and unrivalled popularity among the American people, could have achieved such a result. Gorbachev too had his difficulties at home with those who thought he had given away too much; but like Reagan he had the authority to carry the agreement through.

The Treaty of Washington was a striking achievement. It was true that the missiles to be eliminated made up only a tiny proportion (4 or 5 per cent) of all the nuclear weapons held by the United States and Soviet Union together; but even so the missiles concerned were those which for a decade had been the most prominent and controversial of all. It was in 1977 that the Soviet Union had announced the deployment of its SS-20s in eastern and central Europe. This had been followed by the arrival, amid intense controversy, of the American Pershings and cruise missiles. Now in 1987 all were to be eliminated. Lord Carrington, who was at first British Foreign Secretary and later Secretary-General of NATO for nearly all this period, later reflected with wry humour that 'Half the time I was trying to get them [the missiles] there, the other half trying to get them out. Much better out than in.'[15]

Only six months after the Washington summit meeting, President Reagan visited Moscow (29 May–2 June 1988). The business aspect of this meeting was limited to the formal exchange of ratifications of the Washington Treaty on Intermediate Range Nuclear Forces, and the opening of negotiations for a reduction of 50 per cent in the two powers' principal nuclear arsenals. The visit's main achievements were in the realms of publicity and propaganda, now exploited by the two leaders working together, not in opposition. Gorbachev and Reagan strolled together through Red Square, talking to passers-by and smiling at babies (if not quite kissing them). Reagan addressed a large audience at Moscow University (where Gorbachev himself had been a student), producing the astonishing picture of the President of the United States speaking beneath an enormous bust of Lenin and before a background of red banners emblazoned with the hammer and sickle. During the visit a ghost from the recent past was laid. Reagan was asked whether he still thought the Soviet Union was an 'evil empire', and replied: 'No. I was talking about another time, another era.'[16] These were not mere trimmings or cosmetic touches. If wars begin in the minds of men, in the striking phrase of the historian Sir Michael Howard, so also may peace begin there. The images of the Gorbachev–Reagan meeting in Moscow spoke directly to the minds of men in both countries. It was not the first visit of an American President to Moscow, but it was the first to achieve a transformation in feelings and attitudes.

While these dramatic summit meetings were in progress, agreements of a less spectacular kind crept up almost unobserved. The United States progressively abandoned the embargoes on trade with the Soviet Union which had been imposed after the invasion of Afghanistan. The Geneva agreement leading to Soviet withdrawal from Afghanistan (see above, p. 360) was signed in April 1988, with the United States and Soviet Union as its sponsors and guarantors. An agreement was reached in New York (December 1988) providing for the withdrawal of Cuban troops from Angola and South African forces from Namibia. In 1989 Vietnam, under pressure from the Soviet Union, withdrew its forces from Kampuchea. This did not mean that peace suddenly prevailed in these areas (civil war continued in Angola and Kampuchea, for example); but the confrontations and wars by proxy between the Americans and Soviets came to an end.

During the Washington summit of December 1987, Reagan said that he could see the possibility, not just of détente, but of peace. For a man who had once regarded détente itself as a one-way street in favour of the Soviet

Union, this was a remarkable vision. By 1988 it appeared to be true, or very nearly so. In December 1988 Gorbachev visited New York to address the General Assembly of the United Nations, and received what was coming to be his usual rapturous reception from American crowds. In his speech to the United Nations he announced a unilateral reduction of 500 000 troops in the Soviet Army, and the withdrawal and disbanding of six armoured divisions stationed in central Europe, thus extending the scope of arms reduction to conventional as well as nuclear forces.[17] By the end of 1988 the end of the Cold War was in sight; though it was not formally and publicly acknowledged until the end of 1989 and early 1990.

The end of the Cold War will be considered later. Meanwhile, what brought about the astonishing transformation which took place between 1985 and 1988? The importance of personalities stands out from the events we have just examined. Gorbachev and Reagan achieved a *rapport* not attained by any of their predecessors, and the successes achieved by 1988 would have been inconceivable without them. But relations between modern states are rarely decided by personalities alone. Other forces were at work, though they are hard to assess with any certainty. In the background to the success of the Reagan–Gorbachev summit meetings lay the legacy of détente from the early 1970s, which secured gains which were not entirely lost even in the years of renewed confrontation. Among these gains were a vast improvement in diplomatic and personal relations; and a change in atmosphere which was strongest at the top, during the Nixon–Brezhnev summit meetings, but permeated much of the relations between the two countries.

There was also a slow and subtle change of generations. Dobrynin, the long-serving Soviet Ambassador in Washington, wrote in his memoirs that if in the late 1980s the Soviet leadership had decided to batten down the hatches and continue the arms race, whatever the cost, the Soviet people would have responded as they did in the Second World War and would have patiently endured the necessary hardships.[18] It may be so. But by 1985 the generation which was hardened in the fires of the Second World War had largely passed away, and their successors had a different outlook. There was a slackening of the ideological impulse, even among Party members. Gorbachev's redefinition of 'peaceful co-existence' to allow for the possibility of permanent reconciliation with the United States was no mere formality. In the United States, Reagan's first term as President had shown that anti-communism was very much alive; but this may well have been more a matter of emotion than ideology, a straw fire rather than a fixed determination. The Americans had sustained the long haul of the Cold War with remarkable persistence; but Vietnam had shown how near they were to cracking in the early 1970s. They rallied, but if there was a chance of peace they were ready to take it.

The revived Cold War of 1980–85 had focused principally on a new arms race in medium-range nuclear missiles, and on confrontation in Africa. But arms control was still in the basic economic interest of both the superpowers, and especially of the Soviet Union, which had fewer resources to take the strain. In this area the United States was able to step up the pressure to a degree which the Soviets found it hard to match. As to Africa, the Soviets had committed themselves for long enough to become disillusioned with the regimes they were supporting. The United States had intervened in the early 1980s to combat Soviet influence, but as the Soviets pulled out the Americans lost interest. It appeared that the Cold War was not after all going to be won or lost in Africa; it merely lost its way there, which was something very different.

Gorbachev and Reagan thus had favourable circumstances in which to work their apparent miracle of transformation. For a few years they were able to work together, and in concord with events. Then suddenly in 1989–91 events seemed to take charge, and governments of all kinds were swept along with them.

◈ Notes to Chapter 16

1. Archie Brown, *The Gorbachev Factor* (Oxford, 1996), Chapter 2, 'The Making of a Reformist General Secretary'.
2. Robert Service, *A History of Twentieth-Century Russia* (London, 1997), p. 443; Brown, *Gorbachev Factor*, p. 32.
3. Service, *Twentieth-Century Russia*, pp. 446–7.
4. Quoted in Brown, *Gorbachev Factor*, p. 95.
5. Margaret Thatcher, *The Downing Street Years* (London, 1993), p. 463.
6. For eastern Europe, see below, pp. 373–6.
7. *Keesing's Contemporary Archives*, 1988, pp. 35970–1.
8. André Fontaine, *Après eux le déluge* (Paris, 1995), p.324.
9. Patrick Brogan, *World Conflicts* (London, 1992), p. 117, notes that estimates of Afghans killed vary from 100 000 to a million, and considers the latter figure too high.
10. Gorbachev and Reagan also met in December 1988, during Gorbachev's visit to New York to address the General Assembly of the United Nations; but this was not a summit conference. Reagan was in the last month of his presidency, and his successor had already been elected. Gorbachev had to cut short his stay in order to visit the scene of a disastrous earthquake in Armenia.
11. The phrase is from Anatoly Dobrynin, *In Confidence: Moscow's Ambassador to America's Six Cold War Presidents* (New York, 1995), p. 592.
12. Raymond L. Garthoff, *The Great Transition: American-Soviet Relations and the End of the Cold War* (Washington, DC, 1994),

pp. 324–5; John Lewis Gaddis, *The United States and the End of the Cold War* (New York, paperback edn, 1994), p. 217; Dobrynin, *In Confidence*, p. 592.

13. Henry Kissinger, *Diplomacy* (London, paperback edn, 1995), p. 783.
14. Brown, *Gorbachev Factor*, p. 233.
15. Quoted in Gabriel Partos, *The World that Came in from the Cold* (London, 1993), p. 235.
16. J. P. D. Dunbabin, *The Cold War: The Great Powers and their Allies* (London, 1994) uses this remarkable picture as the book's front cover; Garthoff, *Transition*, p. 352, for Reagan and the 'evil empire'.
17. *Ibid.*, p. 366
18. Dobrynin, *In Confidence*, p. 611.

CHAPTER 17

THREE YEARS THAT SHOOK THE WORLD, 1989–1991

1989: Lull and landslide – US–Soviet relations – The collapse of Eastern Europe – 1990: Precarious balance: the Soviet Union in crisis – 1991: The end of an era: the break-up of the Soviet Union and the end of Soviet–American relations – The end of the Cold War

The years from 1985 to 1988 had seen a transformation in Soviet–American relations. The next three years brought Soviet–American relations to an end, because the Soviet Union itself disappeared. It was a period of tumultuous change, in which events themselves seemed to take charge, with governments scrambling along in their wake, and peoples suddenly seized control of their own destinies, disregarding governments – whether their own or those of other countries. For much of the time the normal machinery of diplomatic relations continued to work. The American Secretary of State and the Soviet Foreign Minister met frequently (six times in 1989 and 19 in 1990), and with increasing cordiality.[1] Summit meetings between Bush (who was inaugurated as President at the beginning of 1989) and Gorbachev took place each year. Yet for much of the time this machinery appeared to be turning in a void, with the real events taking place in eastern Europe or inside the Soviet Union. It was as though a mighty engine had suddenly been disengaged from the vehicle which it was intended to drive, and the vehicle itself moved under its own volition.

The events of these three years still take the breath away and defy considered historical analysis. Yet in a curious way each year had a character of its own. 1989 started quietly, as the new President of the United States took stock of the situation; but it finished with a sudden deluge of changes which saw the end of six communist regimes in eastern Europe in less than six months. 1990 saw a precarious balance. The Soviet Union was in crisis, on a knife-edge between survival and death, while relations between the Soviet and American governments worked with increasing smoothness. In 1991 the Soviet crisis was resolved: the state broke up. The last Soviet–American summit meeting took place in Moscow, and proved almost irrelevant; the decisive events were taking place elsewhere. The world looked on in amazement, and historians have done much the same. Explanations will take some time to emerge. Meanwhile, let us take one year at a time.

◆ 1989: Lull and landslide

The year began with the inauguration of George Bush as President of the United States. He had been Reagan's Vice-President, and set out to distance himself a little from his predecessor. He also felt that in the last two or three years Reagan had been somewhat carried away by the warmth of his relations with Gorbachev. At any rate, he began his conduct of foreign affairs by ordering a review of policy towards the Soviet Union. This took four months, and ended inconclusively in what Bush described as a policy of 'status quo plus' – a phrase which no one fully understood, but which at any rate erred on the side of caution.[2] Gorbachev, on the other hand, feeling time pressing ever harder upon him, was anxious to move ahead. In the early part of 1989 he visited Britain, France and West Germany, drawing vast and admiring crowds everywhere he went; but these were only the lower slopes – he wanted to get to the summit. Bush, for his part, visited Poland and Hungary in July 1989, keeping a remarkably low profile in unusual circumstances; but there was no sign of his going to Moscow. It was only in July that tentative moves towards a summit meeting began. The meeting itself took place in December, and even then it was carefully called an 'interim summit', to prepare for more serious business the following year.

Meanwhile Gorbachev faced an increasingly difficult situation at home. In March 1989 elections were held to constitute a new Congress of People's Deputies. In this election, 80 per cent of the Communist Party candidates won – which meant that 20 per cent lost, even though they faced no opposition. Voters were permitted to cross out the name of the candidate, and so vote against. No fewer than 38 Provincial Secretaries of the Communist Party were defeated.[3] These were unprecedented events in the history of Soviet elections, which could normally be relied upon to produce the 'correct' results. Economic problems remained not so much unresolved as not tackled. In January 1989 the Politburo decided to retain the system of central price controls; and in March the Central Committee of the Communist Party postponed a decision on the question of land ownership. The nationalities question grew more dangerous. In September 1989 the Ukrainian Popular Front held its first Congress and began to move towards the separation of the Ukraine. On 23 August a vast number of people (estimated at about a million in all) joined hands in a human chain across the Baltic Republics of Estonia, Latvia and Lithuania to protest against the

German-Soviet Pact fifty years before, which had led to the absorption of the three countries into the Soviet Union. This demonstration, extraordinary in its numbers and organization, signalled an ominous revolt against the Soviet state. Nearly two years before, on the 70th anniversary of the Bolshevik Revolution, Gorbachev had claimed that the Soviet Union had resolved the nationalities question. It had not. Instead, the nationalities question seemed likely to dissolve the Soviet Union.

Meanwhile in eastern Europe Gorbachev embarked on far-reaching change. As early as April 1985, during the funeral ceremonies for Chernenko, Gorbachev had told the leaders of the Warsaw Pact countries that in future they were to take control of their own internal affairs. There would be no more Soviet interventions like those in Hungary in 1956 and Czechoslovakia in 1968. They did not believe him.[4] This was not surprising. In view of the Soviet record, it may well be that *no one* would have believed him; and for the east European leaders of that time it was asking the impossible. They had spent all their political lives in the Soviet-dominated system, and the force of habit was strong. When Gorbachev gave them his message in 1985 the following were the rulers of the Warsaw Pact states: Zhivkov in Bulgaria since 1954; Kádár in Hungary since 1956; Ceauşescu in Romania since 1965; Husák in Czechoslovakia since 1969; Honecker in East Germany since 1971; and Jaruzelski in Poland since 1981 – the only recent arrival.[5] None wanted to face the question of whether they could survive without the support – military if necessary – of the Soviet Union.

In the late 1980s there were stirrings in various parts of eastern Europe. In Poland, Solidarity (though legally dissolved) continued its activities underground; and in 1988 the government resigned after a hostile vote in the *Sejm* (the Polish parliament) – an unprecedented event in a communist country. In Hungary in 1988 two non-communist political organizations, the Hungarian Democratic Forum and the Alliance of Free Democrats, were founded. In Czechoslovakia the small but influential Charter 77 group (one of whose founders was the playwright Václav Havel) continued its demands that the government should at least observe its own laws. In 1988 some 400 000 signatures were attached to a petition for greater religious freedom.[6] In early 1989 there were further changes. In February the Polish communist Party agreed to 'round table' talks with other organizations, to discuss the legalization of Solidarity. In March the Polish government stated publicly that the Soviet Union had been responsible for the massacre of Polish officers at Katyn in 1940 – something which the Soviet government had long denied, and which was of intense symbolic importance. In April the government lifted the ban on Solidarity, granted full legal recognition to the Catholic Church, and cancelled the May Day parade – another matter of high symbolic significance. In June elections were held, with half the seats reserved for government candidates but the other half open to contest.

Solidarity won nearly all the contested sets; in the reserved section, only a small minority of the candidates gained the 50 per cent vote necessary for election. It amounted to a total defeat for the Communist Party, and a victory for Solidarity. In Hungary, the Communist Party also used the device of 'round table' discussions with other organizations (July 1989), leading to the rapid disintegration of communist authority. On 7 October the Communist Party formally renounced the doctrine of the dictatorship of the proletariat, thus removing the justification for its own exclusive exercise of power, and opening the way to multi-party politics.

These changes in Hungary had an unexpected and indirect effect in East Germany. In 1988 some 9000 East Germans had taken a roundabout route to the West by spending their holidays in Czechoslovakia or Hungary and then crossing into Austria, which was easier and less dangerous than trying to cross directly from East to West Germany. In August 1989, at the height of the holiday season, another 6000 East Germans took advantage of this route, with thousands more following behind. On 10 September the Hungarians opened the border with Austria, and on the 11th the astonishing number of 125 000 East Germans crossed from Hungary to Austria.[7] It was a strange and impressive movement of people, characterized by the East German Trabant cars which were the common mode of transport. In the same month demonstrations began in East Germany, gathering round the Lutheran churches, particularly in Leipzig, where the numbers grew to about 150 000 each Monday evening. Honecker, by this time 77 years old and set in his ways, refused to change. Gorbachev went to see him on 6–7 October, and talked to him about *perestroika* and the need for reform; but he would not listen. After Gorbachev left, it appeared that Honecker intended to suppress the Leipzig meetings by force, but he was overruled by his own Politburo.

On 18 October Honecker resigned, and was replaced by Egon Krenz, who found himself carried away on a torrent of events. The Soviet troops in East Germany (375 000 in number) stayed resolutely in their quarters, with orders not to intervene. The East German government was on its own; and effectively it gave up. On 8 November the Politburo resigned in a body. On the 9th Krenz announced that requests to leave the country could be presented without giving reasons, and that authorizations would be granted rapidly. Crowds swarmed to the checkpoints, where the frontier police allowed free passage to West Berlin. During the night of 9–10 November parts of the Berlin Wall were knocked down, and East Berliners wandered freely round the other half of their city. These astonishing scenes were broadcast live on television across the whole of Europe and most of the world. In the next few days the East German authorities issued over 7 million visas to their citizens, and it seemed as though half the population was on the move.[8]

These events proved fatal to the communist regimes throughout eastern

Europe. Poland and Hungary had already moved out of communist control. On 10 November Zhivkov was deposed as ruler of Bulgaria. On 17 November a large-scale demonstration (mainly by students) in Prague marked the beginning of what became known as the 'velvet revolution' in Czechoslovakia. In December 1989 Husak resigned and Václav Havel became President of the Republic – no longer a People's Republic. All this took place without the use of force. Only in Romania did the revolution take violent form, ending in the attempted flight, capture and instant execution of Ceauşescu.

The speed of these events beggared belief, though it now appears that the underlying causes had been building up for years. The Helsinki Accords of 1975 had encouraged movements for human rights (especially in Poland and Czechoslovakia) which gradually undermined government authority. Economic hardship increased during the 1980s, when living standards declined over large parts of eastern Europe. The influence of western radio and television was all-pervasive, and especially strong in East Germany, where viewers received West German television in their own language, driving home the contrast in prosperity between the two parts of the country. The relentless change of generations, in contrast to immobile political regimes, affected every country. But behind everything lay the change in Soviet policy. It is possible that Gorbachev could have prevented, or at any rate delayed, the collapse of communist governments by using force at an early stage – perhaps to prevent the Hungarians from opening their frontier with Austria. But he showed no sign of doing so. He had made up his mind and did not go back on his decision. Reform within the Soviet Union would have to be accompanied by reform in the eastern bloc. Perhaps Gorbachev could not have done otherwise even if he had wished, because he had gone so far in his relations with the Americans that he could not afford to offend them by using the old methods and bringing out the tanks. In 1979 the Soviet occupation of Afghanistan had brought the détente of the 1970s to an end. In 1989 Soviet repression in eastern Europe would surely have destroyed the good relations built up since 1985, and taken the Soviet Union back to the days of confrontation – which Gorbachev could not afford to face.

The principal spokesman for the Soviet Foreign Ministry, Gennardy Gerasimov, made light of the new situation, telling journalists at the beginning of November that: 'The Brezhnev Doctrine is dead . . . You know the Sinatra song "My way". Hungary and Poland are doing it their way. We now have the Sinatra Doctrine.'[9] It was a joke which would have been inconceivable even in the previous period of détente; and on a subject which was no laughing matter. Gorbachev appears to have believed that he could let eastern Europe go and still maintain the Soviet Union intact. Events were to prove otherwise.

These extraordinary developments in eastern Europe took place in the interval between the announcement on 31 October 1989 that an 'interim summit' was to take place at Malta, and the actual meeting between Bush and Gorbachev on 2–3 December. Bush was carefully restrained in his reactions to the collapse of the communist regimes and the opening of the Berlin Wall, because he did not seek to add to Gorbachev's difficulties. Gorbachev for his part went out of his way to assure Bush that: 'We don't consider you an enemy any more'; to which he added at another point: 'The world is leaving one epoch, the "Cold War", and entering a new one.' The lively Gerasimov told journalists that: 'We have buried the Cold War at the bottom of the Mediterranean Sea.'[10] By this version, the Cold War was over by the time of the Malta summit; though there were others who regarded the reports of its demise as exaggerated, and later dates of death were to be announced.

◆ 1990: balancing on a tightrope

Gorbachev was staking everything on the reform of the Soviet system, in the hope that he could somehow pull off the success of introducing a socialist market economy without letting the market predominate, permitting greater freedom to the nationalities without conceding independence, and delegating power in a centralized system without leading to disintegration. In 1989 there had already been signs of danger, but he could not stop. He said himself on one occasion: 'I'm doomed to go forward, and only forward. And if I retreat, I myself will perish and the cause will perish too.'[11] It was like riding a bicycle on a tightrope. In 1990 it grew increasingly unlikely that he could succeed, as a threefold crisis developed within the Soviet Union – ideological, economic and nationalist.

In February 1990 Gorbachev prepared a document to be put to the Central Committee of the Communist Party, entitled 'Towards a Humane, Democratic Socialism' – with the unhappy implication that the variety of socialism which had existed in the Soviet Union for the past seventy years or so had been neither humane nor democratic. In this paper, Gorbachev proposed to repeal the article in the Soviet constitution (Article 6 in the Constitution of 1977) that proclaimed the directing role of the Communist Party in the state, and thus secured its political monopoly. In March 1990 the new Congress of Peoples' Deputies approved this recommendation; and soon afterwards elected Gorbachev to the new post of President of the Soviet Union, which was to take precedence over that of General Secretary of the Communist Party – though for some time Gorbachev held both posts together. These changes produced a profound ideological crisis, involving the identity and purpose of the state. Since 1917 the Communist Party had provided the framework of the state, and the *raison d'être* of the Soviet Union had been the building of communism. This framework and *raison d'être* were now removed, with nothing to replace them. At the same time the Soviet economy fell into actual decline, as distinct from its earlier situation of feeble growth. American estimates put the decline in gross national product in 1990 at between 2.4 and 5 per cent; Soviet estimates were more optimistic, but still indicated actual decline.[12]

The movement of nationalities towards independence or separation gathered pace in 1990. Lithuania declared independence on 11 March 1990; Estonia followed on 30 March; and on 4 May Latvia more cautiously declared its intention to become independent. Lithuania suffered a setback. On 18 April the Soviet government cut off oil supplies, and on 30 June Lithuania agreed to suspend its independence for 100 days, though not to give it up. But in June a more serious set of events took place. On 12 June 1990 the Supreme Soviet of the Russian Republic declared its 'sovereignty', i.e. the primacy of its own government over that of the Soviet Union. This action by the largest single Soviet Republic rapidly set off similar declarations by others: Uzbekistan on 20 June, Moldova on 23 June, Ukraine on 16 July, Belorussia on 27 July; with more to follow. The precise meaning of 'sovereignty', as against independence, was uncertain, but the existence of the Soviet Union could scarcely be left dependent on such a refined point of semantics. Gorbachev was still trying to hold the line against unilateral secession from the USSR, but in practice disintegration was setting in.

Against this background, it is almost startling to see Soviet–American relations developing as though nothing much was happening. The long-arranged formal summit meeting between Bush and Gorbachev took place in Washington, 31 May–3 June 1990. The two statesmen signed a total of fifteen agreements, useful rather than spectacular in nature, providing for an 80 per cent reduction in the two countries' chemical weapons; for US exports of grain to the Soviet Union; for a new trade agreement (though this would not be approved by Congress until the USSR had changed its regulations on emigration); and for co-operation on other matters which appeared almost routine, for example on measures against drug trafficking. Privately, Gorbachev made an important concession. He had previously sought to prevent a united Germany (which was already rapidly approaching) becoming a member of NATO; he now assured Bush that the choice as to membership of NATO should be one for the Germans themselves to make – which by implication decided the matter, because the outcome of a German choice was not in doubt. (See below, pp. 378–9 for German unification.) After the summit, Gorbachev visited Minnesota and California, almost on a social basis, greeted warmly by vast crowds and showing once again his golden touch with Western audiences. On 4 June he made a speech at Stanford University, declaring that 'The Cold War is now behind us.'[13]

The truth of this was demonstrated in the frequent meetings between the Secretary of State, Baker, and the Soviet Foreign Minister, Shevardnadze, to discuss a range of problems across the world, with the two increasingly acting as partners even in such sensitive areas as Afghanistan, southern Africa and Korea.[14] The new state of Soviet–American relations was put sharply to the test at the beginning of August 1990. Shevardnadze and Baker met at Irkutsk on 1–2 August; and on 2 August Iraq invaded Kuwait, opening what was to prove a severe crisis in the Persian Gulf, eventually leading to the Gulf War in January–February 1991. Baker and Shevardnadze hastily met again on 3 August, and issued a joint statement to the press condemning the aggression by Iraq. They thus took up a common stance on an issue which in the days of the Cold War would almost certainly have divided them, with the United States supporting Kuwait and the Soviet Union taking the side of Iraq. Moreover they maintained their common front in difficult circumstances during the next few months. On 9 September Bush and Gorbachev met in Helsinki to discuss the crisis, and affirmed their unity in demanding an Iraqi withdrawal (in line with Security Council resolutions). They declared their preference for a peaceful route to withdrawal, but left the way open for other measures to ensure that aggression did not pay. The Soviet Union had long developed close ties with Iraq, and Gorbachev appears to have believed that he could persuade the Iraqi ruler, Saddam Hussein, to withdraw from Kuwait without fighting. The Soviet government made prolonged attempts to bring about such a withdrawal, but without success. Eventually, on 21 February 1991, Gorbachev had to report to Bush that his efforts had failed. Meanwhile the United States, at the head of a coalition including Britain, France and Saudi Arabia, had built up powerful forces in the Gulf; and on 23 February Operation 'Desert Storm' was launched to drive Iraq out of Kuwait by force. The Soviet Union supported this action, though without taking part in it. It was a striking proof of the new relationship between the USA and the Soviet Union.

Amid these rapidly moving events, Europe provided a zone of comparative calm. German unification came about with unexpected speed and smoothness. In March 1990 free elections took place in East Germany for a new People's Chamber. Astonishingly, politicians from West Germany (Chancellor Kohl, the Foreign Minister, Genscher, and the former Chancellor, Brandt) campaigned as though they were on their own home ground, and drew great crowds. A massive 93 per cent of the electorate voted. Parties linked to the West almost swept the board. The conservative Christian Democrats, with some minor allies, won 48 per cent of the votes and 192 of the 400 seats. The Social Democrats gained 22 per cent of the vote, and 88 seats. The Communists (campaigning under the name of the Party of Democratic Socialism) won 16 per cent and 66 seats – a drastic fall after their political monopoly for over forty years.[15] After this election result, unification was certain, though the specific steps presented some difficulties. For over forty years Germany had been divided, with the tacit consent of the United States and the Soviet Union, and the usually unspoken approval of most European states. (There was a joke, which was not altogether a joke, that the French loved Germany so much that they liked to have two Germanies to love.) Unification was not altogether welcome. Britain and France both tried in vain to slow it down. The Soviet Union sought for some time to insist that a united Germany should not be a member of the North Atlantic Alliance; but Gorbachev (as we have seen) tacitly yielded this point during his visit to the United States in June 1990. At a meeting with Chancellor Kohl of West Germany in July, Gorbachev abandoned his opposition to membership of NATO for a united Germany, and in return Kohl undertook to provide credits of 5 billion marks for the Soviet Union. With this obstacle removed, the two Germanies and the former occupying powers (USA, USSR, Britain and France) concluded a treaty, called at the time the Two Plus Four agreement. The treaty laid down that the new united Germany would consist of the two former Germanies and the city of Berlin (thus confirming yet again the Oder–Neisse line as the frontier with Poland). Germany was to be free to join an alliance of its own choice (which in effect meant NATO). The new Germany would be bound by the existing limitations on armaments observed by the Federal Republic (i.e. the renunciation of nuclear, chemical and biological weapons). The Soviet Union undertook to withdraw all its forces from the former East Germany by the end of 1994; and after that date no foreign forces or nuclear weapons were to be stationed in the former East German territory.[16] On these terms, the unification of Germany took place on 3 October 1990. In effect, the German Democratic Republic (East Germany) ceased to exist, and its territory was absorbed into the Federal Republic, whose constitution now applied to the whole country. Berlin was to become the capital of the new state.

The division of Germany between 1946 and 1949 had marked the beginning of the Cold War. The Berlin blockade of 1948–49 and the Berlin crises of 1958–61 had brought some of its tensest and most dangerous moments. The unification of Germany, by the free will of the German people and the consent of the former occupying powers, marked the end of the Cold War in Europe. While the steps towards German unification were being worked out, a meeting of the NATO powers in London on 5–6 July 1990 issued the Declaration of London, which amounted to a declaration of peaceful intentions. The Declaration invited the Warsaw Pact powers to join in reciprocal undertakings of non-aggression, and to agree that the two sides were no longer adversaries. It also undertook to reduce nuclear forces, and to adopt a new strategy for NATO which would ensure that nuclear weapons were absolutely a last resort. At the same time, the meeting invited Gorbachev to address the NATO Council, and proposed that the Warsaw Pact should establish formal liaison arrangements with NATO. The two alliances would thus discuss the state of their forces, armaments and military doctrines, and reach agreement on the reduction of forces in Europe.[17]

The Declaration of London marked a profound change in the strategy and the spirit of the North Atlantic Alliance. The invitation to Gorbachev to address the NATO Council (which was promptly accepted, and followed by a Soviet invitation to the NATO Secretary-General to visit Moscow) was not mere window-dressing but a real change of direction. Yet there was no question of NATO being dissolved. The security which it had preserved for forty-one years, the structures and habits of co-operation which it had established, and the crucial links which it provided between the United States and Europe were so valuable that all members were agreed that it should be preserved.

Earlier in 1990 the Soviet government had proposed to reconvene the Conference on European Security and Co-operation (CESC). This body had been set up by the Helsinki Conference of 1975, in order to oversee the agreements reached there. Gorbachev now proposed to revive the CESC, to provide a meeting-place and framework for the new Europe which was coming rapidly into being. At first, NATO was wary of allowing the Soviet Union too much of a role in the political Organization of Europe; but again the NATO conference in London on 5–6 July 1990 marked a departure. The NATO powers proposed to provide the CESC with permanent structures and new functions, on the lines of Gorbachev's suggestions. On the basis of these proposals, a meeting of the Conference on European Security and Co-operation took place in Paris on 19 November 1990, attended by the United States, the Soviet Union, 34 European states and Canada (in nearly every case by heads of government). The Conference agreed to meet every two years, and to set up permanent organizations – a small secretariat, a body to observe elections in member states, a centre for the prevention of conflicts, and a representative body to act as an 'Assembly of Europe'. This meeting served as a symbolic peace conference after the Cold War in Europe. There had been no declaration of war, and no direct military conflict between the two main antagonists; and similarly there was no great peace treaty to stand in line of succession to Utrecht, Vienna and Versailles. To a Cold War there had succeeded an unofficial peace.

In a striking manner, the membership of the Conference on European Security and Co-operation represented the idea to which Gorbachev had once appealed, of a 'common European home'; and also, looking back to the 1960s, de Gaulle's concept of Europe stretching from the Atlantic to the Urals. The United States and Canada added a reassuring trans-Atlantic presence – Europe had not always been good at conducting its own affairs. One great virtue of the Conference was its inclusiveness: even Albania, usually isolated among European states, attended. Its limitation was that it could operate only by consensus; and its good intentions were later to be severely tested (for example, by conflicts in Yugoslavia) and found wanting. That was in the future. Meanwhile, the Paris Conference of 19 November 1990 offered a hopeful end to a difficult year.

◆ 1991: the end of the Soviet Union, and the end of an era

In some respects relations between the United States and the Soviet Union continued along what had become their normal, co-operative course. In January and February 1991 the Americans and their allies fought the Gulf War against Iraq with the diplomatic co-operation of the Soviet Union. On 30–31 July President Bush visited Moscow for a summit meeting with Gorbachev. They signed the START I Treaty on strategic arms reduction, bringing the totals of long-range nuclear weapons down to roughly the same levels as in 1982, when the negotiations for this agreement had first begun. This was now becoming an issue from the past, as the strategic rivalry between the two countries died away. The same was true of rivalry in the Third World. The two governments had already brought to an end their disputes in Angola and Nicaragua; and at the summit meeting they agreed to convene jointly an international conference on Middle East prob-lems.[18] Bush and Gorbachev also shifted their attention to economic issues, and the formidable problems involved in the integration of the Soviet Union in the international trade system. On this, Bush's approach was notably cautious; he offered little assistance, and did not run the risk of being criti-cized for interfering in Soviet internal affairs. The President was careful to say in public that the transformation of the Soviet economy must come from within.

At the same time, COMECON and the Warsaw Pact came to an end. COMECON (Council for Mutual Economic Assistance) had been founded in January 1949 as a counter to the Marshall Plan in western Europe. It had not been entirely one-sided in its workings, and the Soviet Union had supported the east European economies as well as exploiting them. But its main purpose was always to promote socialist economic integration, and when the east European states adopted market economies after the collapse of their communist regimes COMECON lost its *raison d'être*. It was formally dissolved on 28 June 1991. The Warsaw Pact, which dated from 1955, was wound up at almost exactly the same time, on 1 July 1991. The Soviet government had hoped to preserve some of the political aspects of the Pact, though not its military structures which had subordinated the east European armies to Soviet command. But the new governments in eastern Europe would have nothing to do with half-measures, and the only course was complete dissolution. On the other side, NATO remained in being, but a NATO Council meeting in Rome on 7–8 November 1991 adopted a new document on strategy declaring that the threat of a large-scale attack no longer existed. The NATO powers also invited the Soviet Union and eight other countries (Bulgaria, Czechoslovakia, Hungary, Poland, Romania, Estonia, Latvia and Lithuania) to send their Foreign Ministers to a meeting in Brussels on 20 December, to formulate a declaration on partnership.[19] Thus on the one side the structures of the Cold War (COMECON and Warsaw Pact) vanished, leaving not a wrack behind; and on the other NATO remained in existence but declared that peace had arrived and partnership with the east could begin.

At one time, these events would have been of far-reaching importance. In 1991 they were of small account. The Soviet Union was breaking up. The Gorbachev–Bush meeting in Moscow in July 1991 was the last Soviet–American summit.

At the beginning of the year nothing was certain. The future of the Soviet Union still depended on the attempt at headlong reform which Gorbachev had launched. Various possibilities were still open. Gorbachev might succeed, and preserve the Soviet Union in a new form. Or he might be defeated by internal opponents who wanted a return to sterner measures and a form of Stalinism – after all, Gorbachev was offending all kinds of vested interests, in the Communist Party, the bureaucracy, the armed forces and the KGB. Or there might be some other outcome, which no one could fully foresee, but whose outlines were already visible in the movements towards national independence. In the threefold crisis which the Soviet Union was undergoing – ideological, economic and national – it was the nationalities issue which proved fatal.

In January 1991 it appeared that the Soviet government might act to preserve the state by force. Soviet troops occupied the centres of Vilnius, the capital of Lithuania, and Riga, the capital of Latvia, opening fire against civilians and killing at least 18 people in the two cities. Yet the government also allowed referendums on independence to take place in all three Baltic Republics. On 9 February 1991 the Lithuanians, on an 85 per cent turnout, produced a 90 per cent vote in favour of independence. On 3 March, Latvia and Estonia voted for independence by 74 per cent and 78 per cent respectively.[20] Gorbachev refused to accept these votes, because a referendum on the maintenance of the Soviet Union was due to take place on 17 March. This referendum showed a majority of 76 per cent in favour of maintaining the Union. But this apparently solid result also revealed weaknesses. Six Republics (Estonia, Latvia, Lithuania, Georgia, Armenia and Moldova) refused to take part; and in the Ukraine an additional question showed a majority of 80 per cent in favour of Ukrainian 'sovereignty' at the same time as 70 per cent voted in favour of maintaining the Union.[21] How these votes were to be reconciled remained to be seen. Meanwhile, even to submit the preservation of the Soviet state to popular vote was a sign of uncertainty and weakness.

On 12 June Boris Yeltsin, who had been emerging for some time as a political rival to Gorbachev, was elected as President of the Russian Republic by universal suffrage, winning 57 per cent of the votes cast. Yeltsin thus dominated what was by far the largest republic in the Soviet

Union, and with an electoral mandate which Gorbachev could not match. One of Gorbachev's weaknesses, as he introduced democracy to the USSR, was that he was always less popular at home than he was abroad – 'Gorbymania' was a foreign mood, to which the Soviet peoples proved mostly immune.

In the event, Gorbachev was undermined by a strange and intensely dramatic combination of events. Between 18 and 21 August a group of conspirators attempted to overthrow Gorbachev by a coup d'état, and restore the authority of the Communist Party – the repressive scenario which had always been one of the possible conclusions of the Gorbachev enterprise. Gorbachev himself, who was on holiday in the Crimea, was held under house arrest, while the conspirators declared a state of emergency, claiming that Gorbachev was too ill to exercise his responsibilities. The coup was defeated, partly because Gorbachev himself resolutely refused to sign any documents, partly by the public resistance of Yeltsin, who defied the rebels' tanks in Moscow; and partly through the hesitations of its own leaders.

The coup failed, but it altered the whole course of events. Gorbachev lost his authority, which passed to Yeltsin. On 23 August Yeltsin announced the suspension of all activities of the Russian Communist Party, whose principal members had all supported the coup d'état. The next day Gorbachev resigned as Secretary-General of the Communist Party of the Soviet Union, the post which had for so long been the key position in Soviet politics. His only remaining official function was that of President of the Soviet Union, which was in itself in the process of disintegration. The timing of the attempted coup had been designed to prevent the signing of a new Treaty of Union between the republics, scheduled for 20 August. In fact, while the outcome of the coup was still uncertain, on 20–21 August 1991, Estonia and Latvia declared their independence. They were soon followed by the Ukraine, Belorussia (later Belarus), Moldova and Azerbaijan. On 8 December 1991 the Presidents of Russia, the Ukraine and Belorussia met in conference at Minsk, and declared that the Soviet Union had ceased to exist. They proposed to replace it by an ill-defined Commonwealth of Independent States. On 21 December, by the Treaty of Alma-Ata (the capital of Kazakhstan – a choice symbolic of the new era) a majority of the former Soviet republics agreed to join this Commonwealth. The signatories at that stage were Armenia, Belorussia, Kazakhstan, Kyrgyzstan, Moldova, Russia, Tajikistan, Ukraine and Uzbekistan; Estonia, Latvia, Lithuania and Georgia refused to join.[22]

On 25 December 1991 Gorbachev resigned from the post of President of the Soviet Union, which no longer had any functions. He left the Kremlin, and Yeltsin moved in as President of Russia. The red flag with the hammer and sickle, once a symbol of loyalty for communists across the world as well as for the people of the USSR, was lowered. The new Russian flag, a tricolour with white, blue and red horizontal stripes, was raised in its stead. It was the end of an era.

Formally, the Soviet Union ceased to exist at midnight on 31 December 1991/1 January 1992. One of the two superpowers which had dominated international relations in the second half of the twentieth century disappeared from the map, from the life of states, and from the whole web of world affairs. The consequences of this prodigious event would take a long time to become clear. But one point was plain at once. The end of the Cold War had been announced on a number of previous occasions. A death certificate could now be issued. In 1998 the United States government, under the authority of an Act of Congress, decided to award Cold War Recognition Certificates to all who had served faithfully and honourably during the Cold War era, which was defined as ending on 26 December 1991 – the day after the red flag was lowered over the Kremlin.[23]

◆ Notes to Chapter 17

1. Raymond L. Garthoff, *The Great Transition: American-Soviet Relations and the End of the Cold War* (Washington, DC, 1994), p. 382.
2. Quoted in Peter G. Boyle, *American-Soviet Relations: From the Russian Revolution to the Fall of Communism* (London, 1993), p. 228.
3. Robert Service, *A History of Twentieth Century Russia* (London, 1997), pp. 472–3; Garthoff, *Transition*, p. 390.
4. Service, *Twentieth Century Russia*, pp. 442–3 – a vivid account.
5. List in Gabriel Partos, *The World that Came in from the Cold* (London, 1993), p. 243.
6. R. J. Crampton, *Eastern Europe in the Twentieth Century* (London, 1994), pp. 384–5; see generally pp. 379–85.
7. *Ibid.*, p. 394.
8. André Fontaine, *Après eux, le Déluge* (Paris, 1995), p. 414.
9. Quoted in Boyle, *American-Soviet Relations*, p. 230; cf. Archie Brown, *The Gorbachev Factor* (Oxford, 1996), p. 240.
10. Quotations from Garthoff, *Transition*, pp. 406, 408; Brown, *Gorbachev Factor*, p. 240.
11. Quoted in Service, *Twentieth Century Russia*, p. 486.
12. Garthoff, *Transition*, p. 419, n. 20.
13. *San Francisco Chronicle*, 5 June 1990, quoted in Boyle, *American-Soviet Relations*, p. vii.
14. Baker and Shevardnadze actually used the word 'partners' during their meeting at Irkutsk, 1–2 August 1990 – Garthoff, *Transition*, p. 434.
15. Election results in Henry Ashby Turner Jr, *Germany from Partition to Unification* (New Haven, 1992), pp. 245–6.

16. Summary of terms, *ibid.*, pp. 251–2.
17. *Keesing's Contemporary Archives*, 1990, p. 37599.
18. For Angola, Nicaragua and the Middle East, see below, pp. 457–8, 498–91, 553–5 respectively.
19. *Keesing's*, 1991, p. 38600.
20. Garthoff, *Transition*, p. 453; *Keesing's*, 1991, p. 38419.
21. Garthoff, *Transition*, pp. 455–6; *Keesing's*, 1991, p. 38079.
22. *Ibid.*, p. 38654.
23. Cold War Recognition Web Site, http//cold war. army. mil/. I am grateful to Dr J. R. D. Bell for this reference.

REFLECTION

THE COLD WAR IN RETROSPECT

Historical debate about the end of the Cold War is in its infancy. If historians are still arguing about the reasons for the decline and fall of the Roman Empire after some fifteen hundred years, we can expect no certainty about the decline and fall of the Soviet Union for some time to come. We lack knowledge, and above all we lack perspective on these momentous (and still astonishing) events. But even in these initial stages, two broad questions have emerged to engage attention and discussion. Why did the Cold War end as it did? And what does its end tell us about the nature of the Cold War itself? We can at least open up these questions.

The Cold War ended in a decisive result. At the end of 1991 the United States stood firm, with its territory and institutions intact and its way of life flourishing. The Soviet Union, on the other hand, had disappeared. In 1990 the directing role of the Communist Party·had been removed from the constitution, leaving the country in an ideological vacuum; and by the end of 1991 its territory had been divided among numerous successor states. There is no doubt about the outcome; and it is natural to ask why.

One simple answer is that the United States had won because Reagan's policy of confrontation had placed the Soviet Union under intolerable strain. Broadly speaking, the argument is that the United States had opposed Soviet influence strongly and at every point – in Afghanistan, in Africa and in Latin America. The Americans had embarked on a new build-up of nuclear weapons, notably medium-range missiles in Europe. They had begun the vast enterprise of the·Strategic Defence Initiative, involving sophisticated technological developments and enormous expense. The Soviet Union was thus involved in the twofold strain of conducting several conflicts in Asia, Africa and Latin America and competing in an arms race of immense complexity. At the same time the United States cut off some of the advantages extended to the Soviets under détente – exports of cereals, and access to advanced technology. The cumulative pressure of all these actions proved too much for the Soviet economy and Soviet will-power, and the whole edifice collapsed. The likelihood of this collapse was already visible in 1989, when one observer wrote: 'The Soviet Union is crumbling from within at the same time that its leaders have lost their faith in their revolutionary mission and are preparing to withdraw from the outposts of empire.'[1]

Against this stands a completely different view: that the Soviet Union simply stopped competing in the Cold War, for internal reasons which had little to do with external pressure from the United States. Dobrynin, the long-serving Soviet Ambassador in Washington, claimed that the challenge of a new arms race, and even of the Strategic Defence Initiative, could have been met by the determination of the Soviet people and a bearable increase in defence expenditure. The military burden was not the most important cause of Soviet economic problems, whose roots were to be found in low investment, lack of innovation, and the difficulties of running a closed command economy. 'The fate of the Soviet Union was decided inside our country,' concludes Dobrynin.[2] Shevardnadze, the Soviet Foreign Minister for most of the Gorbachev period, also argued that the decisive changes came from *within* the USSR. He looked back to the Second World War, claiming that it was impossible to break up the Soviet Union from the outside – 'neither Reagan nor Hitler could do it', he said.[3] A careful American analyst, Raymond Garthoff, has reached very similar conclusions, arguing that the Cold War was not won by Reagan's policy of confrontation, the arms build-up and the Strategic Defence Initiative. The key change came within the Soviet Union, when a new generation of Soviet leaders realized that their system had failed at home and that they were not achieving their objectives abroad. Moreover, Garthoff goes a stage further and argues that: 'In the last analysis only a Soviet leader could have ended the Cold War, because the conflict arose essentially from the Marxist–Leninist assumption of a struggle to the end' between two social, economic and political systems. Gorbachev, though remaining a communist, abandoned the idea of inevitable conflict, and so brought the Cold War to an end.[4] Using the metaphor of a race, the Soviet Union stopped running.

These views are not wholly incompatible, and it may well be that some synthesis between them will emerge.[5] External pressures had substantial effects on the Soviet Union. The renewed arms race provided an extra problem for the Soviet economy, which was already in deep trouble. American help for the Afghan guerrillas contributed something to the Soviet defeat in that long-drawn out war, and thus to a weakening of Soviet morale. Moreover, Reagan's policy was not confined to confrontation. He produced a disconcerting mixture of toughness and conciliation, of confrontation and détente – a hard-soft technique familiar in interrogation (and a standard method in Stalin's diplomacy). The effect was to sharpen the choices which Gorbachev already faced: he could take up the American challenge and face the internal consequences of higher military expenditure, or he could seize the chance of détente, improve relations and reap the benefits at home. There was no doubt that he would take the second course. Once Gorbachev had embarked on summit meetings, he found that Reagan's unexpected flexibility gave him an opportunity to pursue his domestic reforms with a dash which he might not otherwise have attempted. It may be, therefore, that Reagan's adaptability played as large a part as his rigidity in the final dénouement.

Moreover, external pressures on the Soviet Union were by no means limited to American government policies. Other influences, more important in their effects on individuals, were at work. The attractions of western prosperity, as against the shortages, queues and general penury of the socialist economies, became increasingly obvious. The contrast was pointed up by the influence of the mass media, with corrosive effects, especially in eastern Europe. Unexpectedly, the pull of material wealth was matched by spiritual influences. The impact of Pope John Paul II, first in Poland and then among all the Catholics of eastern Europe, was not strictly measurable, but no less powerful for that. The appeal of Islam in the Soviet Republics in Central Asia added strength to the forces of separatism.

American pressure, Reagan's flexibility, and contrasting influences of materialism and religion thus all played their part in the end of the Cold War; but the essential point still seems to be that they contributed to a drama which started *within* the Soviet Union. Gorbachev's changes at home, on which he decided before taking any serious steps in foreign or defence policy, were crucial in both the end of the Cold War and the disintegration of the Soviet Union. Without Gorbachev, it is hard to see the Cold War ending in the way, and at the time, that it did; and without the headlong pace of Gorbachev's reforms, the Soviet Union would surely have lasted longer than it did. It was Gorbachev who became the sorcerer's apprentice, unleashing forces over which he had no control. Perhaps above all, two aspects of his policy came together, with disastrous results. By redefining the policy of peaceful co-existence, and accepting the reality of good relations with the United States, he deprived the Soviet Union of that permanent enemy which had justified the economic hardships imposed upon its people. But Gorbachev could not relieve the economic hardships themselves. At one and the same time the enemy vanished and the economy fell into decline. The combination proved fatal.

The likelihood thus far is that the Soviet Union collapsed primarily through internal failures, exacerbated but not created by external pressures. The Cold War ended because the Soviet Union first stopped competing, and then disintegrated, leaving only one of the former antagonists still standing.

Let us turn to the second question: what does the end of the Cold War tell us about the nature of the Cold War itself?

Historians have offered a number of different dates for the beginning of the Cold War, mostly concentrated in a six-year period between 1943 and 1949. The date of its conclusion is almost as uncertain. As early as the Washington summit in December 1987 Reagan said he could see the possibility, not just of détente, but of peace. The Moscow summit in May–June 1988 marked a transformation of attitudes. Gorbachev, at his meeting with

Bush at Malta in December 1989, publicly said that the era of the Cold War was over. He repeated the message in his speech at Stanford on 4 June 1990. The NATO summit meeting in London on 5–6 July 1990 issued a sort of 'declaration of peace', offering friendship to its former enemies of the Warsaw Pact. The meeting of the Conference on European Security and Co-operation in Paris on 19 November 1990, attended by the two major antagonists and every European participant in the Cold War (as well as some neutrals) sketched out a new framework for European co-operation. It was almost a peace conference, of a symbolic kind. Throughout 1990 there was close American-Soviet co-operation, testifying to a new relationship which went further than the earlier state of détente. Finally, at the end of 1991, the Soviet Union itself was dissolved, and the Cold War could definitively be declared at an end. There was thus a period of some four years during which the Cold War was visibly drawing to a close (though successive reports of its demise were self-contradictory), and the Soviet Union was changing its nature and finally found itself in the course of disintegration. The coincidence of these two processes leaves a cloud of uncertainty. How far can we pierce the cloud, and what can we learn from the end of the Cold War?

The Cold War itself was not one but several; or at any rate one conflict with several different aspects: an ideological conflict; frozen diplomatic relations in which the American and Soviet governments scarcely spoke to one another; a confrontation between hostile alliances; arms races, both nuclear and conventional; competition in the Third World; and a bitter conflict of propaganda and cultural rivalry. All these aspects were drawn together in a confrontation of two superpowers unrivalled in strength and the leaders of opposing ideological camps. (See the earlier Reflection on the Cold War, pp. 149–59 above.)

By 1990, most of these aspects of the conflict had either ceased to exist or markedly diminished. Leaving the ideological aspect aside for a moment, diplomatic and personal relations had improved out of recognition. The change which had begun with the thaw of the late 1950s, and then intensified with the Nixon–Brezhnev summits in 1972–74, reached its apogee with the four Reagan-Gorbachev summits in 1985–88. The great freeze of earlier times was forgotten in the warm sunshine of May 1988, when Reagan and Gorbachev strolled together through Red Square. (The fact that it was still Red Square reminds us of the ideological aspect which has yet to be discussed.) The great alliances no longer confronted one another in 1990, when NATO offered its friendship to the Warsaw Pact; though it was not until 1991 that the Warsaw Pact actually ceased to exist. Competition in nuclear armaments, checked by the Arms Limitation treaties of the 1970s before being revived in the early 1980s, had now been halted and put into reverse. One category of weapons, the intermediate-range missiles, had been eliminated, and the two superpowers had agreed to reduce their main nuclear armaments by one-half. This still left them with ample weaponry to destroy one another, but they were no longer competing to add to their stockpiles. Competition in conventional forces had also been halted by Gorbachev's announcement of a unilateral reduction of 500 000 in Soviet land strength. The naval race had always been one-sided, though the Soviet Union retained a large ocean-going fleet. Competition in the Third World had come to an end, as Gorbachev withdrew from Soviet commitments in Afghanistan, Africa and Central America, and the United States lost interest, except in Latin America – and Latin America had been an American sphere of influence long before the Cold War was ever thought of.

All these aspects of the Cold War were over by 1990. What about ideological conflict and two-power confrontation, which were after all the crucial issues? Even by the end of 1989 the ideological conflict was much diminished. On the Soviet side, the formal re-definition of 'peaceful co-existence' in 1986 was of crucial importance in principle. The USSR could now conceive of peace with the capitalist world, and not merely a continuation of the class struggle by other means. The abandonment of the Brezhnev doctrine, first in Afghanistan in 1988 and then (much more important) in eastern Europe in 1989, marked a profound change in practice as well as principle. Under the 'Sinatra Doctrine' (by which everyone 'did it their way'), countries which had been within the socialist camp were allowed to leave it. The USSR remained the Union of Soviet Socialist Republics, but its view of the ideological struggle had changed radically.

American attitudes and ideology had never been strictly laid down after the Soviet fashion. (Despite the American fondness for the word 'doctrine', their thinking was not strongly doctrinal in form.) American opinion was subject to swings of mood, from hostility towards the Soviets to warmth and back again.[6] But the welcome by American crowds to Gorbachev in 1987 and 1988 (part of the 'Gorby-mania' which swept the whole western world), and Reagan's public change of mind on the 'evil empire', marked a significant and lasting shift of opinion. For the Americans, Gorbachev represented a new and different Soviet Union.

At that stage in the Gorbachev–Reagan relationship, neither the Soviet nor the American leader had ceased to believe in their respective ways of life. Gorbachev's intention was to reform the Soviet system and revitalize socialism. Reagan exerted a powerful appeal in small-town America, and was elected (and re-elected) to restore confidence in American values. There was still a deep ideological *difference* between the two men, the two countries and the two systems; but in a way which is hard to define it had ceased to be a *conflict*.

The fundamental characteristic of the Cold War was that it was a struggle involving both ideology and power. The ideological aspect had diminished markedly by the end of 1989, with the Soviet abandonment of the old definition of peaceful coexistence and of the Brezhnev Doctrine. It appeared that both sides had come to accept a genuine peaceful co-existence of two different ways of life. At that stage, the United States and the Soviet Union still remained two superpowers, though with the USA as the stronger of the two. If the normal pattern of two-power rivalry in the past (Athens and Sparta, Rome and Carthage, Hapsburg and Valois, England and France, Germany and France) were to continue, the USA and USSR might well have resumed some form of hostility even after the Cold War had been declared at an end. There can be no certainty about this. Ancient rivalries have come to an end in the past. Franco-British rivalry ended with (or at least was much diminished by) the Entente Cordiale; and Franco-German hostility dissolved in a half-century of close co-operation from 1950 onwards. What would have happened to American-Soviet relations remains unknown, because the matter was never put to the proof. By the end of 1991 the Soviet Union had ceased to exist, and the United States was left alone as the single remaining superpower. Russia, as the largest successor state to the Soviet Union, was a still a great power, with nuclear weapons and large armed forces; but not on the scale of the former USSR; it was also racked by internal disorder and immense economic difficulties.

The Cold War thus came to a blurred end, much in character with its uncertain and fluid shape while it was in progress. By the end of 1989 and early 1990 most of the elements in the Cold War had ceased to exist or diminished in importance. Ideological differences remained, and the potential opposition between two superpowers presented a possible source of difficulty in the future. By the end of 1991 both these elements had also disappeared. In March 1990 the Soviet constitution was amended so as to remove the directing role of the Communist Party, thus removing the state's ideological *raison d'être*. The Soviet Union itself ceased to exist at the end of 1991. Therefore the *ideological* and the *power-political* elements in the Cold War drew (almost staggered) to an end over the same period of time, making it hard for us to distinguish whether one of them was more decisive than the other in the nature of the Cold War itself. We are left with the conclusion that the Cold War was about *ideology plus power*. This is confirmed by a glance at relations between the United States and the remaining communist countries. After 1991, communism still existed in China, Vietnam and Cuba, so there was still an ideological division in the world. But no one called (or calls) relations between the United States and Cuba, or even the United States and China, a Cold War. Ideological conflict alone, it appears, is not enough to make a Cold War.

◆ Notes to Reflection: The Cold War in retrospect

1. For a clear statement that the United States won the Cold War, see Robert Conquest, *Reflections on a Ravaged Century* (London, 1999),

pp.183–4. The quotation is from Patrick Brogan, *World Conflicts* (London, 1989), p. xv.

2. Anatoly Dobrynin, *In Confidence: Moscow's Ambassador to America's Six Cold War Presidents* (New York, 1995), p. 611.

3. Quoted in Gabriel Partos, *The World that Came in from the Cold* (London, 1993), p. 239.

4. Raymond L. Garthoff, *The Great Transition: American–Soviet Relations and the End of the Cold War* (Washington, DC, 1994), pp. 753–4.

5. Partos, *World*, pp. 240–1, gives a sketch of such a synthesis. The essays in Michael J. Hogan, ed., *The End of the Cold War: Its Meaning and Implications* (Cambridge, 1992) show the difficulties involved in reconciling widely different points of view.

6. See Peter G. Boyle, *American–Soviet Relations: From the Russian Revolution to the Fall of Communism* (London, 1993), pp. 272–3.

THE WORLD OUTSIDE THE COLD WAR

Previous page: A different world takes shape outside the Cold War: traditional dress and modern weapons as Iranian women take part in the Islamic revolution that overthrew the Shah, January 1979. A force at once old and new entered world politics. © Hulton Deutsch

CHAPTER
18

THE MIDDLE EAST AND THE
ARAB–ISRAELI CONFLICT, 1963–1979

**Rivalries in the Middle East – The Six-Day War, 1967 – Interval,
1967–73 – The October (Yom Kippur) War, 1973 – OPEC and the oil
weapon – The Egyptian-Israeli treaty – Crisis in Lebanon**

In the mid-1960s the Middle East was the scene of three rivalries: the Arab–
Israeli conflict; disputes between (and within) Arab states; and superpower
rivalry – the extension of the Cold War to the Middle East. All three were
from time to time in suspense, but none showed any sign of being resolved.

The most prominent element was the Arab–Israeli conflict, which was as
severe as ever. Israel had survived a difficult start, and was in many ways
flourishing. The country was an economic success, with gross domestic
product per head rising by 6.5 per cent per year for the five years 1960–64;[1]
the morale and efficiency of the armed forces were high; and there was a
mood of confidence among the population. But the country's existence was
still precarious. The population of Israel was not quite 2 700 000 according to an estimate in 1967, while the population of the neighbouring Arab
states totalled about 40 000 000. Israel's territory was awkward in shape
and difficult to defend, with a wasp-waist only fifteen miles wide between
the Jordanian frontier and the Mediterranean, and a long V-shaped wedge
stretching south to Eilat on the Gulf of Aqaba, giving access to the Red Sea.
Its borders were still only cease-fire lines, established at the end of the
campaigns of 1949 and 1956. None of the adjoining states (Egypt, Jordan,
Syria, Lebanon), nor any other Arab country, had recognized these frontiers, or the existence of Israel. The declared objective of the Arab states,
indeed, was the removal of Israel from the map. In 1964 the Arab League
sponsored the establishment in Jordan of the Palestine Liberation
Organization, bringing together various political groups among the
Palestinian people (mostly refugees) to secure the liberation of Palestine;
which would mean the destruction of Israel.

In this conflict, as long as both sides continued to mean what they said,
there could be no compromise. Either Israel would continue to exist, or it

would disappear. This was an issue which engaged much of the rest of the world, emotionally as well as politically. The United States and western Europe broadly supported Israel, for reasons which arose from memories of the Holocaust as well as from current political calculation. Most of the Third World was hostile to Israel and sympathetic to the Arab states and the Palestinians. The Soviet Union supported some of the Arab states, while remaining cautious about the Palestinians. Whatever happened in the Arab–Israeli conflict could be sure of world attention.

There were also rivalries between the Arab states, less conspicuous but still grave. President Nasser of Egypt, after his success in the Suez crisis of 1956, had become the leader of Arab nationalism and the focus for aspirations towards Arab unity. But his leadership was soon challenged. The United Arab Republic which brought together Egypt and Syria in 1958 broke down in 1961. There were conflicts between radical and conservative elements all over the Middle East. In 1962 civil war broke out in Yemen, with Nasser supporting a group of army officers who proclaimed a republic, while Saudi Arabia and Jordan backed the monarchy. But even radicals were not in agreement with one another. In February 1963 the Ba'ath Party (whose name signified Arab revival, or renaissance) seized power in Iraq, and in February 1966 a new Ba'ath regime took over in Syria. Both these new governments were hostile to Nasser, and claimed that he was not doing enough to liberate Palestine. King Hussein of Jordan survived tenaciously as a monarch amid revolutionary regimes, holding together a divided population of Jordanians and Palestinians. In the Persian Gulf, Saudi Arabia and Iran were opposed in almost every respect. The Saudis were Arabs, the Iranians were Persians or Azeris; the Saudis were Sunni Muslims, the Iranians were mainly Shi-ite; both countries were oil-producers, often in competition with one another; both aspired to be the principal ally of the United States in the area. These various conflicts attracted less attention than that between Israel and the Arabs, but they had far-reaching effects.

The United States and Soviet Union pursued their own policies in the Middle East, in complicated ways. The USA was prepared, in the last resort, to preserve Israel from destruction, by force if necessary. Meanwhile American Jews provided Israel with money and the government sent military equipment. The sale in 1962 of Hawk ground-to-air missiles was particularly important, because France, the Israelis' usual supplier, could no longer provide weapons as effective as those which the Soviets were sending to Egypt. But at the same time the Americans were closely linked to Saudi Arabia, and in the early 1960s were seeking to improve their relations with Egypt; so they were trying to keep a foot in both camps. The Soviet Union, for its part, supported the more radical Arab states. They provided Egypt with tanks and aircraft, and sent advisers and instructors to accompany them. In Iraq, the situation was complicated by problems of ideology. In 1963, the Ba'ath regime persecuted the

Iraqi Communist Party mercilessly (there were reports of some 3000 killed). The Soviets felt bound to react, and suspended deliveries of armaments, as well as giving assistance to Kurdish separatists in northern Iraq. But later they resumed arms supplies, and sent about 1300 Soviet advisers to go with them; and they even provided Iraq with a nuclear reactor.[2] On the other hand, the Soviet Union maintained diplomatic relations with Israel, and offered no support or recognition to the Palestine Liberation Organization. Like the Americans, the Soviets tried to keep their options open. Later, as we shall see, the two superpowers even made some attempt to work together in the Middle East.

◆ The Six-Day War, 5–10 June 1967

In 1967 these three strands in Middle East politics suddenly came together and reached a climax in the Six-Day War between Israel and the Arabs, 5–10 June. This war arose in large part from rivalries between the Arab states; it proved of crucial importance in Israeli-Arab relations; and it drew in both the superpowers. It was a complicated crisis, with far-reaching effects.

Nasser made the first moves, probably because he was being criticized by the Syrians, who claimed that he was not doing enough to deal with the Israelis and liberate Palestine. In May 1967 he set out to demonstrate his belligerence. On 16 May he required the United Nations Emergency Force to leave the Sinai peninsula. This force, of some 3000 men, had been present since the end of 1956, to supervise the cease-fire agreed on at the end of the Suez campaign and to ensure the passage of shipping through the Gulf of Aqaba to the Israeli port of Eilat. Under its terms of reference, the UN Emergency Force could only remain on Egyptian territory with the consent of the Egyptian government, which Nasser now withdrew. At that stage, the Egyptians received inaccurate reports (originating from Soviet Intelligence sources) that Israel was preparing to attack Syria. Nasser therefore moved troops forward into the Sinai peninsula, to show that he was prepared to help the Syrians in case of need. On 22 May he took the drastic step of closing the Straits of Tiran, at the mouth of the Gulf of Aqaba, to Israeli shipping. Then on 30 May Nasser concluded a military agreement with King Hussein of Jordan, placing the Jordanian armed forces under Egyptian command.

It now appears that these bellicose actions were a form of sabre-rattling rather than actual preparations to attack Israel. But at the time their combined effect was ominous, and the closing of the Straits of Tiran was a direct blow to Israeli commerce through the Red Sea. In these circumstances, the Israelis were highly unlikely to wait and see what Nasser intended to do. Some Israelis thought that an Egyptian attack was imminent; others saw an opportunity to get their blow in first. In either case, Israel was bound to mobilize its forces and call up reservists from civilian life. Mobilization brought the economy almost to a standstill, and the armed forces could not be held in a state of alert for very long. They would have go into action, or be stood down even though the situation remained unchanged. The Israeli military commanders urged their government to order a pre-emptive strike against the Egyptians, and during the night of 4–5 June the Prime Minister, Levi Eshkol, agreed. What we know as the Six-Day War began on 5 June 1967.

In the development of this crisis the two superpowers played an ambiguous role. Soviet Intelligence helped to provoke the crisis by passing false information to the Egyptians indicating an imminent Israeli attack on Syria. Yet at the same time the Soviet government warned Nasser not to strike first. Similarly, the Americans (including President Johnson in person) told the Israelis not to attack first. But neither actually prevented its *protégé* from taking action – whether the Egyptians from provocation in the Sinai, or the Israelis from getting their blow in first.

The Israelis struck on 5 June with lightning speed and force. It was a true *blitzkrieg*. Israeli air attacks destroyed the Egyptian air force on the ground. The army invaded Sinai, reaching the Suez Canal in two days. The Israelis briefly offered not to attack Jordan if King Hussein would remain neutral, but the King rejected this proposal. He had committed himself to Egypt and could not withdraw. In any case, to remain neutral might well have provoked civil war at home. On 7 June the Israelis defeated the Jordanian army, which was virtually without air cover, and quickly occupied the West Bank, including the whole of Jerusalem, which had been left divided by the cease-fire line of 1949. This brought all the ancient sites of Jerusalem, notably the Wailing Wall (which was of immense historical and religious significance), under Israeli control. On 9 June the Israelis moved their main forces northwards, attacked Syria, and occupied the Golan Heights, from which the Syrians had overlooked northern Israel, and which now allowed the Israelis to dominate southern Syria. All the forces concerned agreed on a cease-fire arranged by the United Nations on 10 June. This astonishing war – a six-day wonder – was over.[3]

The Soviet Union watched the defeat of Egypt and Syria from the sidelines. The Soviet Mediterranean Fleet kept well away from the fighting zone. When the Israelis attacked Syria, the Soviets made preparations to intervene, painting bombers with Egyptian markings and warning the United States by means of the 'hot line' that they meant business. But they did not follow this up, perhaps because of practical difficulties, perhaps because President Johnson assured them that he was urging the Israelis to call a halt. The only action the Soviets actually took was to break off diplomatic relations with Israel on 10 June, a gesture which showed solidarity with the Arab states without doing the Israelis any immediate harm. The

Americans too did little. The US Sixth Fleet stayed clear of the war zone. American diplomatic attempts to end the hostilities succeeded only after the Israelis had achieved their objectives. While the fighting went on, the super-powers were little more than spectators.

During the war there was a brief glimpse of the shape of things to come. On 7 June 1967, the day after the Israeli attack on Egypt, a meeting of Arab oil ministers, called by Sheikh Yamani of Saudi Arabia, declared an embargo on oil exports to countries friendly to Israel. Saudi Arabia, Kuwait, Iraq, Libya and Algeria prohibited exports to the United States and Britain, and a diminution of those to West Germany. Within two days, the movements of Arab oil had been reduced by about 60 per cent. By coincidence, the Eastern Region of Nigeria declared its independence under the name of Biafra on 30 May 1967, and in the subsequent fighting about half-a-million barrels of oil per day which were normally exported from Nigeria were cut off, adding to the effect of the Arab action. The American government was sufficiently dismayed to set up an Emergency Committee on oil supplies, which in co-operation with the oil companies began to find ways of making up the losses. Stocks were called on; Venezuela, Iran and Indonesia increased their production; and super-tankers which had come into operation since the Suez crisis of 1956 were used to carry supplies to the countries subject to the Arab boycott. In the event, the war in the Middle East was over so quickly that there was no time for the oil weapon to take effect. By July it was plain that the oil-producers concerned were sacrificing their exports and their revenues to no purpose; in August an Arab summit meeting agreed to resume supplies; and the embargo was ended in September. The attempt to use the oil weapon against Israel and its supporters failed; but it was remarkable that it was tried. Six years later an oil embargo was to be repeated, with far greater effects.[4]

The Six-Day War had far-reaching consequences. Israel conquered large territories, in the Sinai peninsula, the West Bank and the Golan heights. Strategically, the country became more secure, with a buffer against Egypt as far west as the Suez Canal, a short eastern frontier along the Jordan, and command of the Golan heights. Psychologically, the capture of the Old City of Jerusalem was of immense importance, and it speedily became apparent that Israel would not (perhaps could not) surrender this gain. The victory gave Israeli morale a tremendous boost, producing a mood of self-confidence which carried the country forward for several years. But at the same time Israel took over a large Arab population in the West Bank which it could not absorb, and which was to become an increasing source of friction and weakness. Israel had won a victory, but at a higher cost than was immediately apparent.

The Arab states, for their part, had suffered a humiliating defeat – the third since 1948. The forces of Egypt, Jordan and Syria had been crushed in six days. Nasser's prestige received a blow from which it never recovered. The oil embargo promised much but achieved little. The armaments supplied by the Soviet Union to Egypt and Syria were destroyed in large numbers, sometimes before getting into action. Jordan received a new influx of about 200 000 Palestinian refugees from the West Bank, adding to the instability of a gravely weakened state.

At the same time, the United States and the Soviet Union had failed to control their supposed 'client states'. The superpowers had neither prevented the war from breaking out nor done much to influence its course. It remained to be seen whether they could do anything to improve the situation when the war was over.

◆ Interlude and attempt at compromise, 1967–73

As the dust settled after the extraordinary events of the Six-Day War, various responses to the new situation emerged. At Khartoum in August 1967 a conference of thirteen Arab states proclaimed defiance in defeat. They rejected any reconciliation with Israel; re-affirmed the principles of non-recognition and no negotiation; and undertook to maintain the rights of the Palestinian people.[5] At the United Nations, on the other hand, the Security Council adopted Resolution No. 242, (22 November 1967), proposed by Britain and supported by both the USA and the USSR, calling for an Israeli withdrawal 'from territories occupied in the recent conflict', and for 'acknowledgement of the sovereignty, territorial integrity and political independence of every State in the area and their right to live in peace within secure and recognized boundaries free from threats or acts of force.'[6] This resolution sought a compromise which would balance Israeli withdrawal from its recent conquests against Arab recognition of the pre-1967 boundaries. The English text contained a hint of ambiguity, referring to 'territories' rather than 'the territories', leaving an opportunity for some adjustment of the pre-Six Day War boundaries. In practice, any such compromise was well out of reach. Israel had no intention of withdrawing from Jerusalem. Sinai, the West Bank and the Golan Heights were all of great strategic value, and the Israelis were highly unlikely to give them up except for some remarkable compensation.

The immediate responses to the Six-Day War thus amounted to defiance by the Arab states, 'what we have we hold' on the part of Israel, and a half-hearted attempt at compromise by the superpowers. Indeed, the superpowers diminished the effects of Resolution 242, and of their co-operation at the United Nations, by their actions in other respects. The Soviet Union urged the Arab states, and especially Egypt, to accept Resolution 242, but at the same time resumed supplies of armaments to make good the losses of the Six-Day War. By the end of 1967 there were 4000 Soviet advisers in Egypt supervising the provision of military equipment. With Soviet encouragement, the Egyptians began raids across the Suez Canal, to make life uncomfortable for the Israelis on the east side of the Canal and in the Sinai peninsula. The Israelis retaliated with bombing attacks on targets in Egypt. The Egyptians appealed for Soviet protection, and in January 1970, after much hesitation, the Soviets agreed to send SAM-3 surface-to-air missiles, with trained personnel to use them, aircraft, and somewhere between 15 000–20 000 military advisers to back up the Egyptian forces. This was an unprecedented step, in that SAM-3 missiles had never previously been deployed outside the Communist bloc.[7] Soviet diplomacy in support of Resolution 242 thus sought to bring the conflict to an end, but Soviet military actions helped to keep it going.

The United States too supported in principle the compromise outlined in Resolution 242, but did little in practice to bring it about. The Americans had no strong motive to put pressure on Israel to withdraw from the conquered territories, and ample domestic reasons (in the shape of the Jewish lobby) not to do so. On balance it seemed best to leave things alone.

Some three years after the end of the Six-Day War passed without any sign of a settlement. Meanwhile, Arab internal divisions grew more severe. King Hussein of Jordan wanted to escape from the impasse, and made several highly secret attempts to reach an agreement with Israel about the West Bank. He met the Israeli Prime Minister, Golda Meir, no fewer than ten times, but without success. On the other hand, the Palestinians tried to renew the struggle in their own way. The Palestine Liberation Organization lost faith in the capacity, or even the desire, of the Arab governments to rescue their land from the Israelis. The Palestinians had to become more militant in their own cause, because no one else was going to act on their behalf. In 1968 Yasir Arafat became Chairman of the PLO, and began a campaign on two fronts. By diplomatic methods (attending international conferences, securing partial recognition from the United Nations, establishing offices which performed some of the functions of embassies in capital cities) he sought to get the PLO accepted as a state in embryo. At the same time the PLO publicized its claims, and showed its determination, by acts of terrorism, notably the hijacking of civilian aircraft in flight – for example, an El Al airliner on 23 July 1968 and a TWA airliner on 29 August 1969.

The principal base of the PLO was in Jordan, where the organization formed almost a state within a state, undermining the authority of King Hussein. Eventually the King refused to tolerate this situation any longer. On 16 September 1970 he proclaimed martial law, and the regular Jordanian army attacked the PLO camps. It took ten days of severe fighting, and heavy casualties on both sides, to break the PLO resistance. At one point Syrian armoured forces moved into Jordan to support the

Palestinians, but soon withdrew. The situation was not completely resolved, and there was more fighting before the last PLO forces left Jordan for Lebanon in July 1971. The PLO called the battle 'Black September'; and an organization bearing that name was formed to take revenge against Jordan as well as to continue the struggle against Israel. (In September 1972 Black September seized the headlines by attacking the Israeli quarters at the Munich Olympic Games.)

There was thus no progress towards compromise on the lines proposed in Security Council Resolution 242. Israel held on to its conquests in the Six-Day War. The Arab states made no move to recognize Israel. The PLO grew more active and more determined, despite its defeat in Jordan. There seemed no way out of the impasse of the Arab–Israeli conflict. Then on 28 September 1970 President Nasser of Egypt died of a heart attack. He was succeeded by the Vice-President, Anwar Sadat, who was prepared to set out on new paths.

◆ The October War, 1973

The new President of Egypt was determined to find a way out of the conflict with Israel. In the long run he was to succeed, and paid for his success with his life. He first attempted to reach a direct, though limited, agreement with Israel. In February 1971 he proposed that the Israelis should make a partial withdrawal from the environs of the Suez Canal, in return for an Egyptian undertaking to reopen the Canal to Israeli shipping. Israel rejected this proposal, insisting on retaining all the territory won in 1967. Sadat then turned to a wider plan, based on a daring and finely-calculated gamble: to build up an Arab coalition strong enough to go to war with Israel, not in search of victory but to achieve a compromise peace. He conceived the idea of a limited war which would bring in the superpowers to impose a new settlement.

Sadat began by the unlikely step of getting rid of his Soviet military advisers. The Soviets were being, from the Egyptian point of view, too cautious. The Soviet government, which was in the middle of its policy of détente with the United States, was anxious to keep the peace in the Middle East, and to discourage the Egyptians from going to war. Even so, it was a bold step for Sadat to demand, on 18 July 1972, the departure of all Soviet military advisers within a week, either taking their equipment with them or selling it to the Egyptian government. In the event, the Soviets took all their equipment, including surface-to-air missiles which were vital for Egypt's air defence. For a time, the breach was complete.

Sadat then sought to strengthen his links with the Arab states. He made a military agreement with Syria – a risky move, because President Assad of Syria did not share Sadat's idea of a limited war, aiming instead at the complete defeat of Israel. Sadat also approached the the oil-producing countries, with a view to reviving the oil embargo which had been briefly imposed in 1967. On 23 August 1973 he visited King Faisal of Saudi Arabia in Riyadh; told him that Egypt was preparing to go to war with Israel; and asked for his help. Faisal agreed to use the oil weapon, but emphasized that it must be given time to take effect.

Thus Sadat elaborated his audacious plan to wage war in order to achieve peace. The upshot was the October War of 6–25 October 1973, which involved a triple crisis. First, there was the war itself, fought by Egypt and Syria (with support from other Arab countries) against Israel. Second, there was a superpower crisis, involving a brief but acute danger of war between the USA and USSR. Third, there was an oil crisis, as the Arab oil-producers combined to cut off supplies to the United States and other countries friendly to Israel.

The Egyptians opened their offensive across the Suez Canal on 6 October, to coincide with the great Jewish fast day of Yom Kippur, the Day of Atonement, when the Israeli troops were preoccupied with their religious duties. The attack achieved complete surprise, and destroyed some 300 Israeli tanks on the first day. The Syrians launched a simultaneous attack on the Golan Heights, with immediate success. Iraq contributed three divisions, and Jordan two armoured brigades, so that the Arab states achieved an unusual degree of unity. The Israelis rallied, and counter-attacked against the Syrians and their allies on 12 October; on the 15th they launched a daring attack across to the western side of the Suez Canal, surrounding the Egyptian Third Army and threatening to destroy it completely. At that point the Americans and Soviets intervened to check the fighting. Brezhnev, the Soviet leader, invited Henry Kissinger to Moscow (20 October); the two superpowers agreed to present a joint resolution to the UN Security Council calling for a cease-fire; and they brought pressure to bear on their respective *protégés* in the conflict. A cease-fire was declared on 22 October, but broke down on the same day that it began. After an acute crisis between the Soviets and Americans, and a fresh Security Council resolution, a new cease-fire was agreed between all the belligerents on 24 October.

On the ground, the result amounted to a draw. The Egyptians had captured territory on the eastern side of the Suez Canal, while the Israelis had countered by crossing over to the western bank. The Syrians had gained ground on the Golan Heights, and then been forced to retreat. Losses were heavy for such a short campaign. Israeli casualties were 2812 killed and some 7500 wounded. The Egyptians lost about 5000 killed, 12 000 wounded, and 8000 prisoners; the Syrians 3000 killed, 6000 wounded and 500 prisoners; the other Arab forces involved lost 340 dead and about 1000 wounded.[8] It was a costly draw, but for the Egyptians it was enough.

The second crisis arose between the superpowers while the fighting was going on. At first, the Soviet Union and the United States played little part. The Soviets did not want war, but did nothing to prevent it, even though it appears that they received advance information about the Egyptian intentions. The United States, distracted by the aftermath of the Vietnam War and paralysed by the Watergate affair, were taken by surprise. They were shaken by the early Israeli defeats, and quickly provided the Israelis with new equipment, flown out in unmarked El Al civilian aircraft. On 12 October the Israeli Prime Minister, Golda Meir, made an urgent personal appeal to Nixon, claiming that the survival of her country was at stake. The Americans responded by organizing a massive airlift using their own military transport aircraft. There was a brief attempt at concealment, but many of the planes came in to land at Israeli airfields in broad daylight on 14 October, in full view of anyone who cared to watch.

The Israelis used the new American equipment in their counter-attack across the Suez Canal; and it became the Soviets' turn to fear the defeat of their ally. When the brief cease-fire on 22 October broke down, the Soviets prepared to intervene directly in the battle. Reports reaching the Americans during the night of 24–25 October indicated that Soviet airborne divisions were about to set off for the war zone. In alarm, the US government ordered all its forces (including nuclear forces) onto a state of war alert. Despite the existence of the 'hot line', and the recent advances of détente, they took this drastic step without informing the Soviet Union – though of course the Soviets knew soon enough. The Soviets did not respond with a war alert of their own; but even so the two superpowers were brought much nearer to a confrontation than either wished to go over a crisis which was to them of no more than secondary importance. Kissinger got in touch with Brezhnev on 25 October; the Soviets agreed not to send troops to Egypt; and the Americans rescinded the war alert. On the same day, the two governments introduced a second cease-fire resolution at the Security Council, and succeeded in bringing the fighting to an end.

Even so, neither superpower came well out of the crisis. The Soviets offended Egypt and Syria by working with the Americans to bring about the two cease-fires. The Americans alarmed their allies in western Europe by going onto nuclear alert without consultation; and some NATO countries retaliated by refusing fuelling facilities to American aircraft *en route* for Israel. Yet neither superpower did anything irretrievable, and finally they worked together to bring the fighting to an end, which was more than they had achieved in previous Arab–Israeli wars.

The third crisis arose from the Arab states' use of the oil weapon. This developed only slowly. It was not until 16 October, ten days after hostilities had begun, that delegates from six oil-producing states of the Persian Gulf (Abu Dhabi, Iran, Iraq, Kuwait, Qatar and Saudi Arabia) met in Kuwait, and raised the price of their oil from $3.20 to $5.11 per barrel, an increase of some 70 per cent. On the same day, King Faisal of Saudi

Arabia asked the United States to stop all deliveries of arms and military equipment to Israel. As we have seen, the Americans disregarded this request. Indeed, on 19 October Nixon publicly asked Congress to appropriate $2.2 billion for assistance to Israel. On 20 October Saudi Arabia placed a total embargo on all oil exports to the United States, and also announced a reduction of 10 per cent in its oil production. Libya, Algeria and most of the Gulf states followed at once, stopping oil exports to the United States.

On 4 November the oil ministers of the Arab states agreed on an immediate reduction of 25 per cent from the level of production in September, and further 'rolling cutbacks' of 5 or 10 per cent of production each month. They also extended and refined the embargo on oil exports, by defining three categories of states, as follows. (1) 'Hostile' states, i.e. those with close ties with Israel, to which no oil was to be exported; these comprised the United States, the Netherlands, Portugal, South Africa, Rhodesia and at first Japan. (2) 'Friendly' countries, which had adopted pro-Arab or anti-Israeli policies, which were to receive supplies at the same level as before the embargo was imposed; these included Britain, France, Spain, and Belgium. Japan, by a rapid adjustment of its attitude to Israel, secured a transfer to this group. (3) 'Neutral' states, whose supplies were to be subject to a 25 per cent reduction, plus another 5 per cent in December. Finally, on 23 December 1973, the Gulf oil states increased their prices yet again, this time to $11.60 per barrel, which meant that the price had more than tripled since mid-October.

The policies of the Gulf states were not completely united, in that neither Iraq nor Iran joined in the cut-backs in production, and Iraq drew up its own list of countries to be boycotted; but even so the effect of the measures was formidable. Before October 1973, the United States had imported 1.2 million barrels of oil per day from the Arab states; by February 1974 this had fallen to 18 000 barrels per day, which was almost nothing. The Netherlands, which had very little to do with the Middle Eastern crisis, normally imported about 70 per cent of its oil from the Arab states, and was reduced to bringing in supplies from Belgium, which was on the 'friendly' list, or West Germany, which was among the 'neutrals'. Meanwhile, every country in the world outside the Soviet bloc (which produced its own oil supplies) suffered the effects of a tripling of the price of oil.[9]

The oil weapon, though powerful, was slow in coming into action and (despite the distinction drawn between friendly, hostile and neutral states) somewhat indiscriminate in its effects. It became detached from the October War, which was over before the oil embargoes began to bite; and its major effects were felt far outside the Middle East, and in unexpected ways, which we will examine in the next chapter.[10]

◆ Aftermath of the October War and the Egypt–Israel peace treaty, 1979

In the October War of 1973 the Arab states achieved a remarkable degree of unity. Egypt, Syria, Jordan and Iraq all took part in the fighting, and co-ordinated their plans successfully at the start of the conflict. The oil-producing countries, which were mostly conservative monarchies, rallied to the support of the front-line states, which were mostly left-wing and moderniz-ers. From the Maghreb, far distant from the fighting zone, Morocco sent troops and Algeria joined in the oil embargo. Much would depend on whether this unity could be maintained. The war had also restored Arab military pride, after the disasters of earlier conflicts against Israel. This time the Arab armies, and especially the Egyptians, had fought on level terms. Sadat was now in a position to negotiate with Israel from a position of at least some strength; which had been his principal aim in going to war in the first place. The Israelis, on the other hand, had been badly shaken. The immense self-confidence which had led them to reject any compromise after the Six-Day War had been dented, and they became more willing to nego-tiate with their enemies. How negotiations could begin, and whether they could succeed, remained to be seen.

When Sadat first planned to make war in order to move towards peace, he recognized that the superpowers would have to be drawn in to achieve successful negotiations. Even after the changes brought about by the October War, the involvement of the superpowers proved a slow and diffi-cult business.

The October War brought a significant shift in Soviet policy. Up to that time, the Soviets had seen much advantage from the continuance of the Arab–Israeli conflict, which had given them opportunities for political intervention in the region, and direct leverage through the supply of arms to the Arab states. The October War had shown the limits of their influ-ence on the Arab countries, and had produced the sudden threat of war with the United States. The Soviets now began to press for a Middle East settlement, on conditions satisfactory to themselves. Their position was that an agreement should be reached with full Soviet involvement (not just that of the United States); and that it should be a comprehensive settle-ment, including the Palestinians. This was an important development. Even before the war, in 1973 the Soviets had begun to refer to Palestinian 'national rights', and in September 1974, Podgorny (the President of the Soviet Union) publicly advocated the creation of a Palestinian state. (The Soviet government gave permission for a PLO office to be set up in Moscow in 1974, though it did not actually open until 1976.) By 1977 the USSR had arrived at a design for a Middle East settlement, based on four main points: Soviet–American co-operation in negotiations; Israeli withdrawal from all territories conquered in 1967 and afterwards; the recognition of the independence, integrity and security of all states in the region, including Israel; and the acceptance of the Palestinian right to an independent state on the West Bank. The United States, on the other hand, regarded a Middle East settlement as their own affair, conducting negotiations with Israel and Egypt in 1975–76 to the exclusion of the Soviet Union.

In the autumn of 1977 Soviet and American policies briefly seemed to come together. In September the Soviet Foreign Minister, Gromyko, went to New York on his annual visit to the United Nations General Assembly, in the course of which he conferred with the American Secretary of State, Cyrus Vance. On 1 October Gromyko and Vance together publicly proposed to convene a conference at Geneva in December, under joint American-Soviet chairmanship, to be attended by all the states concerned plus the Palestine Liberation Organization, with the aim of reaching a comprehensive Middle East settlement which would ensure the legitimate rights of the Palestinian people. The proposed presence of the PLO, and the reference to the rights of the Palestinians, offended the Israelis, who vehemently opposed the project. In the United States, President Carter was heavily criticized for conceding too much to the Palestinians and the Soviets. He retreated from the proposed conference, and instead returned to the concept of single-handed American mediation between Israel and Egypt, appealing directly to Sadat to make some dramatic gesture to stimulate negotiations.

This appeal fell on willing ears, and yielded dramatic results. Sadat was already in direct clandestine contact with the Israelis, discussing a settlement to be based on Israeli withdrawal from Sinai in return for diplomatic recognition by Egypt and guarantees of security. He publicly proposed, on 9 November 1977, the daring plan of a personal visit to Israel, and the next day the Israeli Prime Minister, Menachim Begin, invited him to address the Knesset (the Israeli parliament) in Jerusalem on 20 November 1977. This astonishing occasion, unthinkable four or five years earlier, proved an immense psychological success. It was an act of the highest courage on both sides. On the Israeli side, it is likely that only Begin, with his record as leader of the Irgun Zvai Leumi against the British and his recent toughness in dealing with Palestinian attacks, could have arranged the visit. Sadat, by going to Jerusalem and talking to the enemy, took his life in his hands, and later lost it – he was assassinated in 1981 by a group of Islamic terrorists. Sadat's very appearance in the Knesset, and the emotional effect of his speech, made a tremendous impact. The substance of his exchanges with Begin proved a different matter. In brief, Sadat offered Israel recognition and peace; but he referred to peace with *all* the Arabs, including the Palestinians, and required Israeli withdrawal from *all* territories conquered in 1967. This proved too much to ask of the Israelis. Direct negotiations between Egypt and Israel revealed that the Israelis wished to retain the whole of the West Bank (including Jerusalem), and to keep a considerable military presence in Sinai. This fell far short of Sadat's aims, and discussions reached an impasse by July 1978. It appeared that Sadat's visit to Jerusalem might be no more than a striking gesture.

At that point the United States intervened. President Carter persuaded Begin and Sadat to come to Camp David in September 1978 to negotiate an agreement with American help and mediation. After much difficulty, they reached an agreement (17 September) by which Israel was to withdraw from Sinai over a period of three years, in return for recognition of Israel as a state and free use of the Suez Canal and the Straits of Tiran by Israeli shipping. In addition, Israel agreed to begin negotiations with Egypt (and if possible Jordan) to establish some form of Palestinian autonomy (not independence) in the West Bank and the Gaza Strip. (This was a narrow band of territory on the Mediterranean coast, largely inhabited by Palestinian refugees, which had been occupied by the Israelis since 1967.) Both Egypt and Israel reserved their positions on the question of Jerusalem, which in fact the Israelis intended to retain. These arrangements were to be embodied in a formal peace treaty within three months.

This timetable proved too ambitious, but with persistent American mediation Egypt and Israel concluded a peace treaty in March 1979, comprising the essentials of the Camp David agreement. It was the first peace treaty between Israel and an Arab state, and as such a remarkable departure; but its effects proved limited. Sadat found himself ostracized by the other Arab states for breaking the front which they had previously maintained intact. Israel was reluctant to make any substantial progress towards Palestinian autonomy, and that part of the peace agreement remained largely unfulfilled, which stored up trouble for the future.

◆ Crisis in Lebanon, 1975–78

As the Arab–Israeli conflict eased in one area, Egypt, it intensified in another, Lebanon. Lebanon was a small state, with a population of about 2 500 000 in 1967, overwhelmingly Arab but divided by religion into about three-quarters Moslem (both Sunni and Shi-ite) and one-quarter Maronite Christian. For many years a political balance was maintained by an informal arrangement that the President should normally be a Christian, the Prime Minister a Sunni Moslem, and the Speaker of the Assembly a Shi-ite Moslem. This worked well, and Lebanon achieved a high degree of stability and prosperity in an area not noted for either. There was a problem in foreign relations, in that Syria never granted diplomatic recognition to Lebanon, because in the period of the League of Nations mandate France (the mandatory power) had transferred territory from Syria to Lebanon; but for some time this dispute lay dormant.

In 1970–71 large numbers of Palestinians, driven out of Jordan by King Hussein, moved to Lebanon, where they they created the same sort of situation as had existed in Jordan. They set up their own camps and bases, amounting to a state within a state; they made raids across the border into Israel, attracting Israeli reprisals; and they disturbed the delicate three-sided political balance. In April 1975 a right-wing Christian group, the Phalangists, attacked Palestinian camps, inflicting heavy casualties. The Palestinians were supported by left-wing Lebanese Moslems, and fighting became widespread, amounting to a civil war in Lebanon. In April 1976 President Frangie, a Maronite Christian, appealed to Syria for help – though reluctantly, and under some pressure from Damascus. On 1 June a Syrian force, with tanks and air support, moved into Lebanon, growing to a strength of about 40 000 during the next few months and occupying most of the country. The Israelis declared a 'Red Line' in south Lebanon, to the north of their border, beyond which they warned the Syrians not to advance. In this southern strip, the Israelis intervened clandestinely to help the Phalangists against the Palestinians.

In October 1976 the various parties achieved a cease-fire in the civil war; and on 17–18 October a conference of Arab states at Riyadh agreed to set up a joint Arab force, called the Arab Deterrent Force, to ensure observance of the cease-fire.[11] This force was mainly Syrian in composition – 25 000 out of a total of 30 000; so that the new arrangement amounted in effect to another form of Syrian occupation.

The cumulative effect of these events was a drastic loss of Lebanese independence, and what amounted to a partition of the country between the Syrian-occupied north (the major part of Lebanese territory) and an area in the south where the Palestinians, Phalangists and Israelis fought sporadically with one another. Parts of the country were reduced to anarchy and ruin. In these events the superpowers took little part. The Americans limited themselves to urging restraint on the Israelis, with limited success; the Soviet Union protested against the Syrian occupation of Lebanon, but took no action to prevent it.

During 1977 the PLO established itself more firmly in southern Lebanon, and launched raids into Israel. The Israelis, as always, retaliated. On 10 March 1978 the PLO extended its operations by making a seaborne landing on the Israeli coast at Herzliyyah (a few miles north of Tel Aviv), attacking a bus and killing 35 people. This time, the Israelis reacted on a large scale, seizing the opportunity to invade southern Lebanon, up to the line of the River Litani, with a force of some 25 000 troops. They avoided the cities (leaving Tyre alone), but occupied the countryside, with help from the Phalange militias.

Curiously, this Israeli invasion evoked only a limited response fom the Arab states – perhaps because Lebanon had already been partitioned. The Syrians, with troops in northern Lebanon, simply held their ground, though they allowed Iraqi volunteers to pass through to help the Palestinians. The

Lebanese government appealed to the UN Security Council, which on 19 March 1978 passed a resolution (No. 429) requiring complete Israeli withdrawal from Lebanon, to be supervised by a United Nations force. At this stage, the role of the superpowers was vital. The United States voted for the resolution, even though it was directed against Israel; the Soviet Union abstained, which was enough to ensure that the resolution passed. More important, it was put into effect. In June 1978 the United Nations Interim Force (4000 in number, rising to 6000) entered southern Lebanon, with the double task of supervising the withdrawal of the Israelis and helping to restore Lebanese control in the area. Neither could be entirely achieved. The Israelis withdrew as the UN troops arrived; but they continued to give clandestine support to the Christian militias, now calling themselves the South Lebanon Army. The PLO retained its bases.

Lebanon remained divided. In the south the PLO continued to act independently. Syrian troops dominated the greater part of the country, to the north. The problem was damped down but not resolved by the intervention of the United Nations Interim Force. The Lebanese crisis was not resolved, and was to break out again in 1982, with another Israeli invasion of southern Lebanon.

◆ The situation in 1979

Among the three main elements in Middle Eastern international relations, the character of the Arab–Israeli dispute changed considerably between 1963 and 1979. First, the Six-Day War of 1967 gained Israel a larger territory with shorter boundaries, but left a legacy of greater internal insecurity through the inclusion of a large Arab population. Later, the Egyptian-Israeli treaty of 1979 was a fundamental change, marking the end of the total refusal by all Arab states to accept even the existence of Israel. A shift in Arab attitudes had begun. But as that shift developed, the burden of total opposition to Israel was increasingly taken up by the Palestine Liberation Organization, which became more militant and achieved wider recognition. A settlement of the Arab–Israeli dispute thus came nearer in one respect, with the signature of the Egyptian-Israeli treaty; but receded in another, with the development of the PLO.

Divisions and conflicts within the Arab world were as severe at the end of the period as at the beginning. President Nasser's widely acknowledged leadership among the Arab states faded with the Egyptian defeat in the Six-Day War 1967, and vanished with his death in 1970. Egypt, Syria and Iraq competed with one another on roughly equal terms as modernizing and in some sense socialist regimes. In their socialist aspirations, and their comparative poverty, all three stood in opposition to the conservative and oil-rich monarchies of Saudi Arabia and the Gulf states. Lebanon, once an island of stability and prosperity, had been torn apart by Syrian occupation in the north and warring factions and Israeli invasion in the south.

The two superpowers continued to intervene in the Middle East, mostly in opposition to one another but sometimes in co-operation. Broadly, they supported opposite sides in the Arab–Israeli conflict. The Americans were fundamentally committed to Israel, and rallied quickly to the Israelis' rescue in the October War of 1973. Soviet support for Egypt, Syria and Iraq ebbed and flowed over time, but was always there. On the other hand, neither the USA nor the USSR could control the actions of what were often wrongly described as their 'client states'. In 1967 the Americans warned the Israelis not to strike first against Egypt, but they still went ahead. After the Six-Day War, the two superpowers agreed on Security Council Resolution 242, proposing an Arab–Israeli settlement on the basis of Israel surrendering territory in return for recognition, but they were unable to impose it upon the antagonists. In 1972 the Egyptians expelled their Soviet advisers, and Sadat pursued his plans for a war of his own devising. There was no real pattern in superpower policies. At bottom, both the USA and the USSR sought peace in the Middle East; but at times they also encouraged war by maintaining their supplies of armaments. At no time did they control events, and the conflicts in the Middle East were far from being simply an extension of Soviet–American rivalry. The problems were more complicated than that, and all the more difficult to resolve.

◆ Notes to Chapter 18

1. *Oxford Economic Atlas of the World* (4th. edn, Oxford, 1972), p. 169.
2. Galia Golan, *Soviet Policies in the Middle East, from World War Two to Gorbachev* (Cambridge, 1990), pp. 164–5.
3. For casualties, see Chris Cook, *World Political Almanac* (3rd. edn, London, 1995), p. 293.
4. Figures on the effect of the oil embargo in Daniel Yergin, *The Prize: The Epic Quest for Oil, Money and Power* (London, 1991), pp. 555–7. For the 1973 oil embargo, see below, pp. 413–15.
5. Resolutions of the Khartoum summit, *Keesing's Contemporary Archives*, 1967, pp. 22275–6.
6. *Ibid.*, 1968, p. 22473. The French text of the resolution removed the ambiguity by using the definite article – 'les territoires'.
7. Golan, *Soviet Policies*, p. 73.
8. Casualty figures in Cook, *World Political Almanac*, p. 294.
9. Fiona Venn, *Oil Diplomacy in the Twentieth Century* (London, 1986), p. 146; Yergin, *Prize*, p. 606.
10. See below, pp. 416–19, for discussion of the 'oil shock'.
11. *Keesing's*, 1976, p. 28122.

CHAPTER 19

THE TWO OIL SHOCKS: MIDDLE EAST, 1973–1974, IRAN 1979–1980

Conditions for the oil shocks – The oil weapon in action – Consequences of the first oil shock – The Iranian revolution, 1979 – The second oil shock

The conflicts in the Middle East produced drastic side-effects in the 'oil shocks' of the 1970s, whose consequences were so far-reaching that they require separate examination. In the 1960s the the western industrialized countries had grown accustomed to cheap oil as the indispensable fuel for their flourishing economies. At the beginning of October 1973 the price of a barrel of oil stood at $3.00 per barrel. Late in 1973, during the October War between a number of Arab states and Israel, the Arab oil producers increased their prices, which reached $11.65 per barrel in December, thus almost quadrupling in three months. In 1979–81 there was a revolution in Iran and war broke out between Iraq and Iran, and the price of oil soared again, reaching $34 per barrel in 1981.[1] The value of the dollar had diminished in the meantime, so these figures for 1973 and 1981 cannot be precisely compared; but in any case the rise was enormous. For countries almost addicted to petroleum, it was a body blow which shook the whole of society. The shock waves ran through the world economy, leaving almost no part of it unaffected.

◆ Conditions for the oil shock

To make such events possible, certain conditions had to prevail. Dependence on imported petroleum had to be firmly established, especially in the United States; the oil-producers had to achieve sufficient unity to act together; and the producers had to develop the determination to *use* their economic power, even at risk to themselves. At the end of 1973 these conditions were all present.

In the early 1970s the industrialized world became heavily dependent on oil. In 1950, oil made up 37.8 per cent of the total usage of energy in the world, as against 55.7 per cent provided by coal, the great fuel of the nineteenth and early twentieth centuries. By 1972 the share of oil and natural gas together had reached 64.4 per cent of the total energy used in the world, and meanwhile that total itself had *tripled*.[2] Aircraft, diesel locomotives and oil-burning ships; the chemical industry with its ever-growing production of plastics; heating and lighting – all consumed vast quantities of oil. For the individual and the family, the private car had become commonplace, first in the United States and then in the rest of the world, which had overtaken the Americans in numbers of cars by 1970, as the figures given below indicate.[3]

Year	Passenger car registrations, in millions		
	USA	Rest of World	Total
1950	40.3	12.7	53.0
1960	61.7	36.8	98.3
1970	89.2	104.2	193.4

These changes had vital political as well as economic consequences. Flourishing economies and growing wealth among individuals brought optimism and self-confidence to the West as a whole. Until the early 1970s, the United States could sustain the cost of the Cold War and grow more prosperous at the same time. Western Europe developed elaborate and expensive systems of social security, creating an attractive alternative to the appeal of communism. The economic miracles achieved in West Germany, France and Italy gave a great impetus to the movement for European unification. Oil consumption and political success went hand in hand: oil provided cheap energy, which promoted economic growth and prosperity, which in turn supported western political stability and success.

All this depended mainly upon oil from the Middle East. As early as 1948 the United States, though still a great oil-producer, had become a net importer of oil. At that stage, the Americans purchased most of their imported oil from Venezuela, which was geographically close and strategically secure. Even so, the American government was sensitive to the strategic implications of dependence on imports. In March 1959 President Eisenhower imposed a quota system, limiting oil imports to nine per cent of total annual consumption. This system worked, with some alterations and increasing difficulty, until 1973. American domestic oil production declined from 1970 onwards, and in April 1973 President Nixon abandoned the quota system and accepted unlimited oil imports. In that year, imports reached 36 per cent of total American oil consumption.[4] This provided the first condition for the oil shock. The United States was utterly dependent upon oil in its economy and way of life, and by 1973 was one-third dependent upon imports. Other western countries, though smaller consumers of oil than the Americans, were even more vulnerable, because they had no domestic supplies at all.

Could the oil-producers work together to exploit this situation? During the 1950s the governments of oil-producing states, notably Venezuela and the Arab countries, had begun to consult together on how best to deal with the oil companies. As their oil revenues increased, through higher production and better terms conceded by the oil companies, governments took a closer interest in the oil prices on which their income depended, and which were still fixed solely by the oil companies. In August 1960 Standard Oil suddenly announced a reduction of 14 cents per barrel (amounting to 7 per cent) in the price of their Middle East oil; and other oil companies followed suit. The result was a sharp loss of revenue for the producing countries, imposed by the oil companies without consultation or even advance warning. The oil-producing countries, which had been grumbling for some time, were jolted into action. Representatives of five states (Iran, Iraq, Kuwait, Saudi Arabia and Venezuela) met in Baghdad on 8 September 1960, and on the 14th concluded an agreement to set up an Organization of Petroleum Exporting Countries (OPEC), in order to co-ordinate their oil policies, protect prices, regulate production and generally combine against the oil companies. The five founders were joined by Qatar (1961), Indonesia and Libya (1962), Abu Dhabi (1967), Algeria (1969), Nigeria (1971) and Ecuador (1973), bringing the total to twelve members by the crucial year of 1973.[5]

For some years, OPEC was content with modest gains, maintaining oil prices despite an excess of supply over demand, and increasing governments' shares in the profits, which by 1970 reached a proportion of about 70/30 as between governments and companies.[6] The oil companies for their part became careful to consult governments about their actions, and made no further attempt to reduce prices; on the other hand they refused to negotiate with OPEC as a body, only with individual governments. This balance was accepted by both sides, and neither the oil companies nor OPEC sought a confrontation.

In 1967, during the Six-Day War, a number of Arab oil-producing countries, including Saudi Arabia, attempted to use the oil weapon by imposing an embargo on oil exports to countries supporting Israel. This alarmed the Americans briefly, but Iran and Venezuela (OPEC members which took no part in the embargo) made up for the cuts imposed by the Arab states. The war ended quickly, and in September 1967 the embargo was called off. In September 1968 the Arab members of OPEC formed their own structure, the Organization of Arab Petroleum Exporting Countries, giving themselves a freer hand.

OPEC thus provided the oil-producing countries with the means for joint action, but for some years they made only limited use of it. Then developments in Libya brought a decisive change. Oil was first discovered in Libya in 1959, and within ten years Libyan oil production was greater than that of Saudi Arabia. In 1969 a coup led by Colonel Gaddafi over-threw the Libyan monarchy, and the new Revolutionary Command Council set out to increase its oil revenues by putting pressure on the oil companies to increase prices. Occidental, a small company which was almost entirely dependent on its Libyan output, agreed; and other companies followed. This Libyan success roused other members of OPEC to think about increasing prices rather than simply maintaining them. In December 1970, at a meeting in Caracas, OPEC began to discuss putting oil prices up. In 1971 the Libyans nationalized the oil companies operating on their territory, without resistance and with no difficulty in selling their production. The oil-producers grew confident. Gaddafi had given a bold lead, and others were willing to follow. Across the political spectrum, from the Revolutionary Council in Libya to the monarchy of Saudi Arabia, there was a new determination to act.

◆ The oil weapon in action, 1973

During the Arab–Israeli War in October 1973, the oil-producing states of the Persian Gulf agreed to use the oil weapon on behalf of the Arabs. (See above, pp. 404–5.) Between October and December 1973, the Gulf states adopted a three-pronged strategy. They introduced, as we have seen, two steep increases in prices, taking the price per barrel from $3.00 per barrel to $11.65. Four of the six states (Abu Dhabi, Kuwait, Qatar and Saudi Arabia) undertook progressive reductions in production. A selective embargo was imposed upon exports, designed to strike hardest at the countries most sympathetic to Israel, and principally the United States, whose imports of Arab oil were reduced from 1.2 million barrels per day to a mere 18 000 by February 1974.[7] As to cut-backs in production, in early October 1973 the production of the four countries concerned was 20.8 million barrels per day; in December, when production reached its lowest point, it was 15.8 million – a reduction of 5 million barrels per day. In the event, Iran and Iraq, which did not join in the programme, increased their production by a total of 600 000 barrels per day, reducing the net loss to 4.4 million barrels per day. This amounted to only about 9 per cent of the total world oil production outside the Soviet Union; but this limited loss was compounded by alarm among the oil-consuming countries, amounting on occasion to panic; so that the effects were greater than the simple figures might have indicated.[8]

Such were the immediate effects of the three-pronged oil weapon. Other and wider consequences were to follow, among oil-producers and consumers alike.

◆ Consequences of the oil shock: the oil-producers

Eight years before these events, in 1965 the Organization of Petroleum Exporting Countries had established its headquarters in Vienna, where it took over a set of offices whose principal tenant had previously been the American oil company Texaco. The Texaco Building in Vienna was renamed the OPEC Building.[9] Within a few years this change of name assumed a symbolic quality: the influence of OPEC supplanted that of the oil companies. In the new wave of confidence inspired by Libya, even the conservative oil states nationalized their oil industries. In 1974 the Kuwaiti government acquired a 60 per cent holding in the Kuwait Oil Company, jointly owned by British Petroleum and the Gulf Oil Company; in 1975, Kuwait simply took over the remaining 40 per cent, awarding a mere $50 million in compensation instead of the $2 billion demanded by BP. In 1976 Saudi Arabia took over the ownership of all ARAMCO's assets in the country. In the Middle East as a whole the oil now belonged to the governments, not the oil companies. They quickly reaped vast profits.

With the near-quadrupling of Middle East oil prices at the end of 1973, the revenues of the oil-producing states increased dramatically:

Revenues of oil-producing states (in US $ billions)[10]		
State	1973	1978
Saudi Arabia	4.35	36.0
Kuwait	1.7	9.2
Iraq	1.8	23.6
Libya	2.2	8.8

Suddenly, the oil-producing countries of the Middle East had vast incomes to dispose of. They spent heavily – on armaments, skyscrapers, airports, motor vehicles, and luxury imports of all kinds. (This flood of expenditure had the curious effect of permitting the industrialized countries to recoup some of the losses imposed by high oil prices by selling their products to the oil-producers.) But even when they had spent all they could, the oil states still had enormous sums to invest. Vast quantities of so-called 'petrodollars' became available to Western banks, with results on the world economy which we shall look at shortly.

The oil weapon thus enriched the oil states dramatically; but it achieved only limited success in assisting the Arab cause against Israel. The major effects of the oil weapon came too late to affect the issue of the October War on the battlefield. In March 1974 President Sadat of Egypt, who had done much to bring the oil embargo into action, asked for it to be ended. It had served its purpose, not by defeating the Israelis in the field, but by shaking the morale of the Americans; and Sadat now wished to play the diplomatic card and bring in the United States to achieve the settlement with Israel which had always been his main aim. At a meeting on 18 March 1974, the Arab oil ministers agreed to suspend the embargo, which was formally ended in July 1974.

By that time, the oil weapon was already suffering from the law of diminishing returns. The economic recession caused in the industrialized countries by the oil shock automatically reduced the demand for oil. Non-OPEC suppliers (for example Mexico) increased their production. The British and Norwegian oilfields in the North Sea were being hastily developed, and came into production by 1975. By the 1980s the proportion of world oil exports provided by the OPEC countries had fallen to about 40 per cent, as against 90 per cent at the time of its foundation.[11] Divisions arose within OPEC itself. Some countries (Nigeria, Algeria and Iran) needed all the revenue they could get in order to spend it on their own immediate needs, while others (Saudi Arabia, Kuwait and Libya) were quite happy to leave their oil in the ground and sell it another day – or even another decade. Saudi Arabia was a conservative monarchy, dependent on American military support, and certainly not anxious to ruin the western economy. Libya, on the other hand, was a revolutionary state, strongly anti-American and quite happy to contemplate the wreck of the capitalist system. Between spenders and savers, conservatives and revolutionaries, there was little common ground. The mid-1970s were OPEC's golden age, but golden ages never last, and this one was very short. Still, the oil-producers flourished while the sun shone, and remained much better off even when it began to set. What was the fate of the oil-consumers?

◆ Consequences of the oil shock: the oil-consumers

Every country in the world was an oil-consumer of some kind, though the extent of their consumption differed widely. All had to face the consequences of the immense increase in oil prices at the end of 1973.

The United States tried at first to take a strong line. Since OPEC was using collective action, the obvious answer was collective opposition – a coalition of consumers against producers. The Americans called an Energy Conference at Washington in February 1974, to discuss means of dealing with the crisis, and try to prevent countries doing separate deals with the Arab states. This proved impossible. Arab oil ministers were conspicuous visitors at a summit meeting of the European Economic Community at Copenhagen in December 1973, and western European countries moved to protect their own interests. The French Foreign Minister, Michel Jobert, visited Iraq to make special arrangements for French oil supplies. Britain made its own deals with Iran and Kuwait. Japan was acutely conscious that its thriving economy depended on imported oil, and sought to placate the

Arabs. The Americans themselves broke away from the ranks they were trying to form, and made their own approaches to Saudi Arabia.

Despite these difficulties and divisions, the Washington Energy Conference met, with some success. In November 1974 an International Energy Agency was set up by the United States and fifteen other countries (France was a conspicuous absentee, preferring to play its own hand), to make plans to counteract the influence of OPEC and organize the distribution of oil in any future crisis. Individual countries also took their own measures. In the United States, Congress agreed in 1974 to the building of a pipeline from Alaska to the main part of the country, which had previously been rejected on environmental grounds. By 1978 this pipeline was carrying over a million barrels of oil per day.[12] In 1979 the Carter administration secured the passage of a National Energy Act, in an attempt to regulate the consumption of energy – largely in vain, because it was almost impossible to persuade Americans to use less petrol. In practice, despite the rise in oil prices, American oil imports continued to increase. France embarked on an ambitious nuclear power programme, which in the long run drastically reduced French dependence on oil. Britain exploited its own oilfields in the North Sea, and became self-sufficient in oil by the end of the 1970s. Japan introduced so-called 'knowledge-intensive' industries, based on computers and micro-chips, to replace or supplement those which were heavily dependent on oil. Brazil began a nuclear programme, and in 1975 concluded a contract with West Germany for the purchase of eight nuclear reactors.

The industrialized countries thus sought to reduce their dependence on imported oil, but no one could escape the effects of the drastic rise in oil prices, which affected every country and almost every individual. Western Europe was badly hit, because it had grown accustomed to uninterrupted economic growth, accompanied by moderate inflation, since the time of the Marshall Plan. In 1974–75 countries suffered economic decline, accompanied by high inflation (25 per cent in Britain in 1975), producing the unprecedented phenomenon known to economists as 'stagflation' – a stagnant economy plus rampant inflation. Widespread unemployment and industrial strife followed almost inevitably. The United States suffered in the same way, though less severely; and even the Japanese economy faltered.

In this crisis, President Giscard d'Estaing of France invited the leaders of five other industrialized countries to a meeting at Rambouillet in November 1975, to discuss means of dealing with their common problems. These six states (Britain, France, West Germany, Italy, Japan and the United States) added Canada to their number in 1976, thus becoming the Group of Seven, usually abbreviated to G-7. The Group met annually, becoming a fixed part of the international scene. Its actual achievements were limited, because despite the arrangements for consultation countries continued to fend for themselves in an emergency. In 1979, for example, the United States took its own measures to tackle inflation by a sharp rise in interest rates. This drew capital to the United States, raised the value of the dollar on the international exchanges, and in turn contributed to a worsening of the depression in western Europe.

From these events the Soviet Union stood somewhat aside. The sharp increase in oil prices at the end of 1973 was an asset to the USSR as a major oil-producer and exporter, but to a lesser degree than might have been expected. The Soviet Union sold a large proportion of its oil exports to the east European countries of COMECON, at prices which were fixed in advance at the average of the previous five years on the world markets. This arrangement flattened out the effects of the sudden fourfold price increase at the end of 1973 by distributing it over five years. This shielded the east European states from the sudden shock which struck all the other oil-consumers, but prevented the Soviet Union from reaping the extra profits from its oil exports. The Soviets continued to sell oil to the COMECON countries at much less than the new world price, and thus deprived themselves of hard currency which they could have earned by sales to other parts of the world.

◆ The Iranian revolution, 1979

Iran held a detached position in Middle East politics. Iran was not an Arab country, and was detached both emotionally and by distance from the Arab–Israeli conflict. Geographically it faced north towards the Soviet Union and Central Asia as well as south to the Persian Gulf. Politically and strategically it could balance between the United States and the Soviet Union, though leaning more towards the former than the latter. In the 1970s Iran moved to the centre of affairs, as an oil-producer, as a military power, and finally as the home of an Islamic revolution.

At the end of 1973, Iran joined the Arab oil states in raising the price of oil, but declined to take part in the progressive cuts in production inaugurated by the Saudis. The Shah of Iran wanted to maintain production, and to exploit the increase in oil revenues, partly for his own wealth and glory, but also to turn his country into a modern state and the leading power in its area. When British forces withdrew from the Persian Gulf in 1971 (to the dismay of the smaller Gulf states, which even offered to put up the money to persuade them to stay), the Shah seized the opportunity to put Iran forward as the new military guardian of the area, a claim which was quickly accepted by the United States.

The Americans provided Iran with large quantities of military equipment, building the country up as the principal military power in the Gulf area, a solid bastion against the Soviet Union and a counter-balance to the radical Arab regimes in Iraq and Syria. This policy presented problems. Iran and the United States held opposite views on oil prices – Iran wanted to push them up, the Americans wanted to bring them down. There was also the issue of human rights. The Shah directed an autocratic regime, with little regard for civil liberties. In the early 1970s this consideration had not greatly perturbed Henry Kissinger, who thought primarily in terms of power; but it counted a great deal more when President Carter took office at the beginning of 1977 with a genuine concern for human rights. Even so, neither problem seemed beyond resolution. OPEC imposed only two price increases between 1974 and 1977, raising the price of oil from $10.84 per barrel at the end of 1973 to $11.46 in 1975 and $12.70 in 1977. Making allowances for inflation, the real price of oil was about 10 per cent lower by 1978 than it had been in 1974 – perhaps no great comfort for the motorist at the petrol pump, but satisfactory for the United States government.[13] As to human rights, the Iranian record did not prevent the Secretary of State, Cyrus Vance, visiting Iran in May 1977 and assuring the Shah of continued American support. When the Shah himself visited Washington in November 1977, there was much trouble with hostile demonstrators, but there still seemed scope for a bargain by which Iran would keep oil prices steady and the Americans would not press too hard on human rights – after all the United States supported several regimes in the Third World with worse records than that of Iran.

This sort of arrangement seemed all the more likely because the Shah himself was balancing carefully between the United States and the Soviet Union. From the 1960s onwards Iran had maintained generally good relations with the USSR. Brezhnev visited Teheran in 1963, and promoted various trade agreements. In 1966 and 1968 the Soviet government advanced large credits to Iran, helping to build steel factories at Isfahan (which the Americans refused to finance), and to construct a pipeline to carry gas to the USSR. By 1978 the USSR was supporting a total of 147 projects in Iran, making the country one of the largest recipients of Soviet aid.[14] The Soviets also provided substantial quantities of arms to Iran, and made no fuss when the Shah arrested communists. Thus the Shah steered a course between the two superpowers, with considerable success.

What he failed to do was to safeguard his own position at home. He over-reached himself, and showed signs of megalomania, by holding extravagant celebrations at Persepolis, claiming to be the heir of the glories of the ancient Persian Empire. He combined severe suppression of political opposition with a fatal tolerance of dissent among religious leaders. He underestimated the power of Islam, putting his faith in modernization and secularism, and pressing forward with a programme of radical measures to transform Iranian society on American or European lines. He put too much reliance on American support, not realizing that in the last resort the Americans would abandon him.

The Shah was eventually overthrown at the beginning of 1979 by a revolutionary Islamic movement led by the Ayatollah Khomeini, working from his exile in France and demonstrating the power of an ancient religion combined with modern communications. Khomeini recorded his messages, which were copied onto innumerable cassettes and then broadcast on sympathetic radio stations and carried into Iran itself in numbers which no border or airport controls could stop. The result was one of the most astonishing upheavals of modern times. Day after day, hundreds of thousands of demonstrators packed the streets of Teheran, shouting 'Death to the Shah'. It was even said that the profile of Khomeini's face could be seen on the surface of the moon. In the face of this massive popular movement, the Shah finally rejected the drastic use of force (which might well not have availed in any case), and left the country on 16 January, after appointing a new Prime Minister, Shahpour Bakhtiar, with a a mandate to introduce liberal democracy. This was implausible, probably impractical, and quite certainly too late. On 1 February 1979 the Ayatollah Khomeini arrived in Teheran on a special flight arranged by Air France. He was welcomed by enormous crowds, and at once proclaimed an Islamic republic, with himself at its head. A new political phenomenon was loosed upon the world.

The shock waves were felt in all directions. The United States rapidly became Iran's prime foreign enemy – the 'great Satan', in the vocabulary of the Islamic revolution. When the American government, after much hesitation, allowed the exiled Shah (who was suffering from cancer) to enter the United States for medical treatment (October 1979), there was a furious response in Teheran. On 4 November a crowd stormed the American Embassy, capturing 63 members of its staff and holding them as hostages to force the United States to return the Shah to Iran to stand trial. (In fact, he went first to Panama, and then to Egypt, where he died in July 1980.) President Carter retaliated against the hostage-taking by freezing Iranian assets in the United States, and by stopping all imports of Iranian oil (though the Iranians had no difficulty in finding other customers). In April 1980 the Americans attempted to rescue the hostages by means of a commando-style airborne operation, which failed miserably when three of the eight helicopters which were intended to lift out the embassy personnel broke down. The failure had a touch of the absurd about it which added to the American humiliation.

The new situation in Iran brought some advantages for the Soviet Union. Iran left the Central Treaty Organization, the alliance which was intended to contain Soviet power from the south; and Khomeini's government shut down American intelligence operations in Iran. But on balance the Iranian revolution was damaging for the Soviets. They had waited too long before switching their support to Khomeini. The new Islamic Republic, and the wave of religious fervour which it touched off, threatened the stability of Soviet Central Asia, where there were large Moslem populations. The new

Iranian government even denounced the Soviet Union as imperialist – getting in ahead of Ronald Reagan. The Soviet Union was hesitant in its response; and indeed the Iranian revolution left both the superpowers uncertain and ineffectual in face of events which were outside their normal experience and which they did not fully understand.

◈ The second oil shock and its consequences

The Iranian revolution speedily produced a second oil shock. The fall of the Shah and the early confusion of the new regime caused a fall in Iranian oil production; and although Saudi Arabia and other countries increased their output to fill the gap, panic seized the markets in face of the unknown. The oil companies competed to build up stocks, pushing up prices. In September 1980 war broke out between Iraq and Iran, initially over the line of the frontier between the two countries along the waterway of the Shatt al-Arab. But it was also a war of religion and politics, because the Ayatollah Khomeini had condemned the Ba'athist regime in Iraq, headed by Saddam Hussein, as hostile to Islam. Iraqi forces invaded Iran, and each side bombed the other's oilwells and refineries. The conflict became a war of attrition, one of the fiercest in modern times, with heavy casualties on both sides.[15] It lasted for eight years, until the two sides made a peace of exhaustion in 1988. Meanwhile, an early effect of the war had been to reduce the oil production of both countries. Iranian production was nearly 156 million tonnes in 1979, and not quite 65 million in 1981; Iraqi production was 169 million tonnes in 1979, and only 43 million in 1981.[16]

The consequences of these events were far-reaching. At the beginning of 1979 the price of oil stood at $13 per barrel; in 1981 it reached $34.[17] When we recall that at the beginning of October 1973 the price had been a mere $3 per barrel, the combined effects of the two oil shocks become dramatically plain. In nine years the price of oil had increased more than tenfold.

The second oil shock reinforced the effects of the first on the world economy. Oil-consumers grappled with the new costs of paying for their imports. All over the world, oil prices carried almost all other costs up with them, with harsh consequences for the poorest countries and individuals. The western industrialized countries, which had been adjusting to the new situation since 1974, were in the best position to cope. Western Europe had new supplies of oil from the North Sea, and was developing nuclear power. The United States and Japan succeeded in resuming economic growth in the early 1980s, but other countries faced increasing difficulties. In East Asia, the rapidly developing 'tiger economies' in Taiwan, Singapore and South Korea (which imported all their oil) were hard hit. South Korea borrowed heavily to pay for its oil imports, but the others came through their difficulties largely by their own efforts. In Latin America, Brazil and Argentina, countries of immense economic potential, borrowed to meet their oil bills, and incurred enormous debts. The gravest effects of all were suffered by the poorest countries of the Third World, which imported all their energy and had to borrow to pay the new oil prices, even though they were already heavily in debt. By 1979 Zaire, a country in desperate circumstances, had accumulated debts of $3 billion. By the early 1980s, so far from showing any recovery from the oil shocks, a whole range of Third World countries, from the potentially prosperous to the utterly poor, had contracted debts on which they could not pay the interest, and repayment was out of the question. This situation threatened not only the indebted countries, but also the banks and governments which had provided loans which would never be repaid.[18] Less severe problems of debt even struck some of the oil-producing countries. Mexico, Venezuela and Indonesia used their increased revenues to such poor effect that they too had to borrow. Indonesia borrowed about $6 billion, and then defaulted on its debts. In 1982 Mexico and Venezuela both introduced drastic programmes of deflation to reduce their debts and improve their balance of payments.

The most extraordinary effects of the oil shocks arose from the use made of the immense new revenues which accrued to most of the oil-producing countries, and especially the Arab oil states. In 1974–77, after the first wave of price increases, it was estimated that the Arab oil-producers held about half the world's liquid currency reserves. Even when they indulged in the most extravagant expenditure (as they sometimes did) they simply could not spend the wealth at their disposal. At that time, they had no banking system of their own, and therefore invested their surpluses in the commercial banks of the United States and western Europe – the very countries against which the oil weapon had been directed in the first place. Vast sums in 'petrodollars' thus returned to the industrialized countries. The banks in turn made large loans to Third World countries to pay their oil bills. It was a bizarre cycle, whose consequences we shall encounter repeatedly in later chapters. The early purposes of the Arab oil weapon were entirely lost to sight. Even the Arab oil revenues became so huge that no one knew what to do with them. The western banking system, which gained most of the Arab investments, lost them again in the bottomless pit of Third World debt. In the heady days of October 1973, when the Arab states set out to use the oil weapon in the war against Israel, such results had been utterly unforeseen.

◆ Notes to Chapter 19

1. For the October War, see above, pp. 402–5; for oil prices, see below, p. 422.

2. Maurice Vaisse, *Les relations internationales depuis 1945* (Paris, 3rd edn, 1994), p. 105.
3. Daniel Yergin, *The Prize: The Epic Struggle for Oil, Money and Power* (London, 1991), p. 837, note 12.
4. *Ibid.*, pp. 538–9, 567.
5. Chris Cook, *World Political Almanac* (3rd edn, London, 1995), pp. 29–30. Gabon became an associate in 1973, and a full member in 1975.
6. Fiona Venn, *Oil Diplomacy in the Twentieth Century* (London, 1986), p. 131.
7. *Ibid.*, p. 146; see also above, p. 405.
8. Production figures in Yergin, *The Prize*, pp. 614–16.
9. *Ibid.*, p. 633.
10. Albert Hourani, *A History of the Arab Peoples* (London, paperback edn, 1992), p. 421.
11. Peter Mansfield, *A History of the Middle East* (London, 1991), p. 291.
12. Yergin, *The Prize*, pp. 665–6.
13. Figures in *ibid.*, p. 646.
14. Galia Golan, *Soviet Policies in the Middle East, from World War Two to Gorbachev* (London, 1990), p. 180.
15. Cook, *Almanac*, p. 296, estimates the casualties at approximately 600 000 killed on the Iranian side and 400 000 on the Iraqi.
16. Venn, *Oil Diplomacy*, p. 176.
17. Figures in Yergin, *The Prize*, pp. 685–7.
18. See Raymond Aron, *Les dernières années du siècle* (Paris, 1984), pp. 47–8; and Paul Johnson, *A History of the Modern World, From 1917 to the 1980s* (London, paperback edn, 1984), pp. 669, 671.

CHAPTER 20

THE RISE OF ASIA, c.1962–1990

Japan as an economic superpower – China in ferment – Chinese power and foreign policy – Dormant crises in Taiwan and Korea – India and Pakistan

By the 1960s, the countries of East Asia were well established in their new forms. There were three great regional powers: Japan, China and India, each conscious of its long history and ancient civilization as well as its modernity. Japan had recovered from the disasters of 1945, and had begun an intense industrial and commercial growth which was to make it the world's most advanced and prosperous economy. China was still full of revolutionary dynamism, and also a growing military power, capable of confronting its former ally and mentor, the Soviet Union. India was the predominant power in its own subcontinent, a leader of the Afro-Asian and non-aligned movements, and an influential member of the Commonwealth. Each of these three powers was free, to a considerable degree, to chart its own course in international affairs, influenced but not dominated by the Cold War between the superpowers. Pakistan was in a different position, as a substantial power in its own region, but with its horizons almost entirely dominated for most of the time by its rivalry with India.

Two international organizations drew together certain Asian countries. The Treaty of Manila (1954) had set up, on American initiative, the South-East Asia Treaty Organization (SEATO), comprising Australia, France, New Zealand, Pakistan, the Philippines, Thailand, the United Kingdom and the United States. This alliance was essentially American in inspiration, and only three of its eight members were Asian. The Association of South-East Asian Nations (ASEAN), on the other hand, was entirely Asian in membership. It was founded at a conference in Bangkok in August 1967, attended by representatives from Indonesia, Malaysia, the Philippines, Singapore and Thailand, in order to promote economic, political and cultural co-operation between its member states. A Secretariat was established at once, but it was nine years before the first meeting of heads of government took place in February 1976, demonstrating a lack of urgency and drive behind the high-sounding aspirations of the Association. If Asian states were to co-operate,

SEATO was quite inappropriate, because it was scarcely Asiatic. ASEAN was Asiatic, but largely passive. In fact, leadership in Asia fell to individual states, among which Japan and China formed a striking contrast.

◆ Japan: an economic superpower

In December 1960 the Japanese Prime Minister, Ikeda Hayato, proclaimed the objective of doubling the country's national income in ten years. Many a government has wished for the same sort of thing; but Japan delivered the goods, and more. In 1960 the Japanese gross national product (GNP) was $33.3 billion (about 1/16th of that of the United States); in 1970 it was $203.4 billion (1/5th of the American GNP). Making allowances for inflation, Japan had achieved a rate of growth of 10 per cent per year, the United States 3 per cent.[1] Japanese industries produced goods of high quality, in vast quantities and at competitive prices. Older industries like steel-making and ship-building thrived. Car production increased at a dizzying rate – an average of 29 per cent per year between 1966 and 1972. By 1979 Japan was producing more watches than Switzerland, at 60 million per year as against 50 million.[2] At the same time new industries flourished. Transistor radios, television sets, all kinds of electrical goods, cameras and musical instruments met the demands of a new consumer society over much of the world. In 1965 Japan achieved a surplus of exports over imports for the first time since the Second World War. In the 1960s, the exchange value of the yen was fixed at the rate of 360 to the dollar, a comparatively low rate which helped to keep down the price of Japanese goods in foreign markets.[3]

The 1970s brought a check to this prodigious economic growth. In 1973 the United States government took the dollar off the gold standard and allowed it to float, meaning in fact devaluation. For the Japanese this meant a rise in the exchange value of the yen, putting up the cost of their exports. Between the end of 1973 and 1981 the two oil shocks increased the price of oil tenfold. Japan was entirely dependent on imported oil, and the cost of all its products was pushed up as a consequence.[4] Inflation rose, and the economy faltered badly. From 1974 to 1981 the Japanese trade balance went back into deficit. But Japanese industry responded boldly and flexibly. Car manufacturers turned high petroleum prices to their advantage by building small cars with low petrol consumption. Honda's scooters and light motor-cycles, already bought by youthful drivers all over the world, became even more attractive. Industries of all kinds introduced new methods of production, using computers, the microchip and automation to diminish demands on energy. By 1982 Japanese external trade was again showing a surplus of exports over imports. In 1987 Japanese income per head of the population was for the first time higher than that in the United States, at $19 553 as against $18 570. In the same year the trade surplus reached almost $100 billion, providing Japan with vast sums to spend and invest abroad. Japanese tourists travelled in vast numbers, estimated at about 4 million in 1980 and 8 million in 1988. Japanese overseas investments reached a total of $132.8 billion in 1987.[5] Japanese firms established themselves in western Europe, and investment in US government bonds helped to finance the American budget deficits of the 1980s.[6] Japanese car manufacturers competed successfully with the big American automobile firms, which complained of unfair competition. It was indeed true that American exporters found it very hard to sell in the Japanese market, partly because of formal restrictions, and partly because the Japanese simply preferred to buy their own goods.

These developments were often called the Japanese 'economic miracle', but they owed nothing to the miraculous. The government, through the Ministry for International Trade and Industry, provided some degree of central guidance (on the lines of the *dirigisme* practised in France), for example by financing research. Many Japanese attained high levels of personal savings, which were channelled through insurance companies and banks into investment in industry. Income tax was low, partly because Japan spent little on defence and armaments. In 1983 Japanese expenditure on defence was $11.6 billion, while that of the United States was $239 billion, an average of $98 per head of the population in Japan as against $1023 in the USA.[7] The Japanese workforce was well educated (notably in engineering), hard-working and adaptable. The people as a whole demonstrated an extraordinary determination, which persisted far longer than the period of recovery after the Second World War, and carried Japan through the setbacks of the 1970s. In that respect there was an element in the Japanese economic success which, though not miraculous, arose from intangible factors of traditions and national characteristics.

Japan thus achieved immense commercial success, becoming the second economic power after the United States, and in some respects even more successful than the Americans. But it did not become a great military power. Article Nine of the Japanese constitution actually prohibited the country from going to war or maintaining armed forces – though in fact what were carefully called self-defence forces were established.[8] Later, the Americans often claimed that the Japanese were getting a 'free ride', protected by American power and thus able to concentrate all their resources on economic growth. They pressed the Japanese to take greater responsibility for their own defence, with some success. In 1978 the Japanese government agreed to take over the cost of maintaining American forces in Japan. During the 1980s Japanese expenditure on defence increased considerably in amount, but only slightly as a proportion of gross national product – from 0.90 per cent in 1980 to 1.01 per cent in 1988.[9] The demands of defence on the Japanese economy thus remained low.

The Japanese armed forces remained comparatively small, and were

organized primarily for defensive purposes. Japan had no nuclear armaments. Pacifist, or at any rate pacific, sentiments were widespread, the
inheritance of defeat in 1945 and of the experience of Hiroshima and
Nagasaki, where Japan had suffered the explosion of the only atomic
weapons so far used in war. Governments and public opinion alike trod
cautiously in military matters. In consequence, Japan remained only
partially armed and showed little desire to use the armaments it had.

Japan was largely isolated from other countries in East Asia by the legacy
of the past, and especially of the Second World War in the Pacific. Japanese
governments were reluctant to pay reparations to countries which they had
occupied during the war. Eventually, they agreed on reparations to the
Philippines, Indonesia, Burma and Vietnam, but ensured that these should
partly take the form of credits which had to be spent in Japan itself. Korea,
which had been annexed to Japan from 1910 to 1945, remained a sore
spot, and diplomatic relations between Japan and South Korea were not
established until 1965. There was thus no question of the Japanese forming
any kind of links with East Asian states, perhaps on the lines of the
European Economic Community, to strengthen their hand against the great
powers. They had to pursue their own policy, in a difficult geographical
situation where the interests of the United States, the Soviet Union and
China met and often conflicted.

The essential element of Japanese policy throughout this period
remained the alliance with the United States. This was by no means a one-
way street. Japan depended on the Americans for its security; but the United
States for its part relied on Japan as an essential link in the containment of
both the Soviet Union and China. American bases in Japan and Okinawa
played a crucial role in Cold War strategy, and were regularly used during
the Vietnam War. The alliance had its troubles, especially with regard to
China. For many years the Americans insisted that Japan should follow
their lead and not recognize the communist government in Beijing. Then in
1972 the United States suddenly threw its policy into reverse. President
Nixon made his dramatic visit to China, and diplomatic relations were
established between the USA and China. All this was begun in total secrecy.
The Japanese were neither consulted nor informed, and had to scramble
along behind as best they could. The Japanese Prime Minister, Tanaka,
visited China in September 1972, and the two governments established
diplomatic relations.[10]

The Americans thus played their own diplomatic hand in relations with
China; but at the same time the Japanese held the economic cards. As we
have seen, Japanese firms competed successfully in American markets, and
in the 1980s the Japanese invested heavily in the United States, in industry,
real estate and government bonds. In a curious combination, Japan was
militarily and diplomatically dependent on the United States, but was also
a successful economic rival.

Japanese relations with the Soviet Union remained difficult. The two countries resumed diplomatic relations in 1956, but did not conclude a peace treaty to put a formal end to the hostilities opened in 1945. This was partly because they were on opposing sides in the Cold War, but they were also separated by a territorial dispute. Under the Yalta agreement of February 1945, the Soviet Union had annexed the Kuril Islands (to the north of Japan) at the end of the Second World War. Japan continued to claim sovereignty over the four southernmost of these islands (Habomai, Shikotan, Kunashiri and Etorofu, under their Japanese names). The Soviet Union rejected this claim (as did the succeeding government of the Russian Republic when the Soviet Union was dissolved in 1991), and the dispute remained unresolved. Japanese relations with China slowly improved after the two states recognized one another in 1972. In August 1978 they concluded a Treaty of Friendship, including a clause agreeing to oppose any country which sought to establish its hegemony in East Asia or the Pacific – meaning the Soviet Union.

By the 1980s, Japan had become immensely prosperous, and had largely re-established itself as an independent entity in international affairs. Militarily the Japanese were still dependent on the United States, but they had the capacity to increase their military strength if they chose to do so. They pursued their own economic policy, when necessary in rivalry with the United States. The country's status, sometimes disparagingly described as an economic giant and a political dwarf, certainly appeared anomalous. Yet in practice it worked well enough. Japan was a model of economic growth and political stability. Its foreign policy was cautious and inactive; but then the Japanese had had their fill of boldness and action earlier in the century. They were ready to follow Guizot's advice to the French in the 1840s: *enrichissez-vous* – grow rich.

◆ China in turmoil

China rejected the capitalist pursuit of riches, and instead followed a course of continuous revolution and upheaval. In 1958–60 Mao Zedong had attempted the Great Leap Forward, which was intended to attain communism in one bound, but in fact ended in disaster and famine. In 1966 Mao proclaimed the Great Proletarian Cultural Revolution, in which the 'Red Guards' (mostly students and teachers) attacked all manifestations of Chinese tradition, but also the Communist Party bureaucracy, bourgeois revisionism, Khrushchev-style revisionism – anything that Mao chose to denounce. The result was later called in China the 'Ten-Year Catastrophe'.[11] It began with a period of chaos (1966–68), amounting in parts of the country to civil war, and ended only by the use of the army to impose order. Another phase of the Cultural Revolution followed in the early 1970s. Several million students, teachers and members of the professions were then sent into the countryside to live the life of peasants. In 1975 Zhou Enlai, the Chinese Prime Minister, declared a fresh change of direction – the pursuit of modernization in agriculture, industry, defence and science. Mao died in 1976, and there followed a power struggle between Deng Xiaoping on the one hand and the extreme left-wing Gang of Four (including Mao's widow, Jian Quing) on the other. Deng won. The Gang of Four were put on trial, and Jiang Quin was condemned to death – a sentence which was commuted to life imprisonment. Deng then attempted to combine communist dictatorship with economic reform, with some success. But discontent and opposition developed, with demands for political reform and democracy. In April and May 1989 vast student demonstrations filled Tiananmen Square, in Beijing, until the army moved in to drive out the demonstrators with heavy casualties. These violent changes and internal conflicts meant that for much of the time Chinese attention was directed inwards, and the country was largely cut off from the rest of the world.

Beneath these upheavals, a certain massive stability prevailed. China was an enormous country, with vast resources and potential. It occupied a vast area (about 3 745 000 square miles). It had the largest population of any country in the world, estimated at 720 millions in 1967 and over 900 millions in 1978. It possessed great natural resources (coal, iron ore and other metals, and even oilfields which were coming into production in the 1960s), which conferred a high degree of economic independence. But these resources were not translated into production or commerce. In 1977 China produced 24 million tonnes of steel; Japan produced 102 million tonnes. In the same year, Chinese external trade was worth $14.3 billion; Japanese external trade $151.3 billion.[12]

China was a strong military power. It possessed nuclear weapons, the 'Second Artillery', first publicly referred to in 1967 – the year when the Chinese exploded their first hydrogen bomb. By 1980 they had some 30–40 medium-range ballistic missiles; about 70 missiles with a range of 2500 km, and three inter-continental missiles with a range of 7000 km. All of these could reach targets in the Soviet Union; and the few long-range missiles could strike at either the USSR or the USA. The weakness of the Chinese nuclear force lay in its lack of anti-missile defences, which made it vulnerable to a first strike. China did not launch a successful submarine-borne ballistic missile until September 1988. The Chinese Army (the People's Liberation Army) was immensely strong in numbers – some four million men in 1977–78, including 12 armoured and 136 infantry divisions, though its supply and transport services were weak, making large-scale operations outside China difficult to conduct.[13] Chinese troops had a high reputation for courage and fighting spirit. They had won striking victories over the Americans in Korea in 1950–51, though at a heavy cost in casualties; and in

1962 Chinese forces had inflicted a sharp defeat on the Indians in a border conflict in the Himalayan mountains. Chinese military power was acknowledged by the Soviet Union in a thoroughly practical manner: the number of Soviet divisions stationed on the border with China rose from 21 in 1969 to 30 in 1970 and 44 in 1971.[14]

Communist China was also a revolutionary power, a rival to the Soviet Union for the leadership of the communist world and an inspiration to many in the Third World. Mao Zedong proclaimed that the pattern of the communist victory in China, where revolution in the countryside had surrounded and crushed the cities, would be repeated in the world at large. The whole Third World amounted to a vast 'countryside', which would eventually defeat the industrialized states in a sort of planetary war of liberation. The prestige of China as a revolutionary power, and of Mao as the leader of socialism in an Asiatic style, stood high. The 'Thoughts of Chairman Mao', gathered together in a Little Red Book produced in vast numbers and many languages, attained a wide circulation, and attracted many western as well as Third World intellectuals. Maoist parties and guerrilla groups sprang up in many countries. Even after Mao's death the vision did not entirely fade away.

For China, ideology and foreign policy were closely linked. In both respects, the long-lasting conflict with the Soviet Union loomed large. In the 1960s and 1970s the Chinese continued to dispute the predominance of the USSR in the Communist Parties of the world. On 14 July 1964 the Chinese Communist Party issued a statement denouncing Khrushchev's phoney communism. During the Cultural Revolution, the Soviet Embassy in Beijing was the target of Chinese demonstrations, and the Ambassador himself was insulted in the street. Even more daringly, Chinese students in Moscow staged a demonstration (25 January 1967) in support of the Cultural Revolution, only to be dispersed by the Soviet police; many of the Chinese were later expelled. Mao criticized the Soviet occupation of Czechoslovakia in 1968, and it appears that the Chinese actually feared that the Brezhnev Doctrine, declaring that no socialist state could be allowed to leave the socialist camp, might be applied against them. In April 1969 the Ninth Congress of the Chinese Communist Party adopted a report which subjected the Soviets to the full litany of abuse – revisionist renegades, social imperialists and social fascists, and collaborators with the American imperialists!

During the 1960s, border disputes between the two countries continued. In 1964 the Chinese government published a new map of territories which had been seized by the imperialists, including the Soviet Far Eastern provinces and parts of the Soviet Republics of Kazakhstan, Kirghizia and Tajikistan. An official spokesman for the Chinese government declared in 1968 that there had been over 5000 frontier incidents, provoked by the Soviet Union. On the Soviet side, *Pravda* produced the more detailed counter-accusation that the

Chinese committed 488 violations of the frontier between June and September 1969. In 1969 there was serious fighting along the Ussuri River, and Chinese artillery fired on Soviet vessels on the Amur River. At that stage, it appears that the Soviet government seriously considered the likelihood of war, and made preparations for air attacks on Chinese bases, including nuclear installations. In October 1969 talks began between the two governments on the border problems, but the Chinese insisted that, as a prerequisite for any progress, all forces should be withdrawn from the disputed territories. Since these were all within the USSR, the withdrawals would have been made solely by the Soviets; who naturally refused to comply.

The Sino-Soviet dispute extended into Africa. In 1963–64 Zhou Enlai led the first large-scale Chinese mission to Africa, visiting ten countries, offering economic aid and also military assistance through the provision of arms and training at the Chinese military academy. Between 1970 and 1975 the Chinese financed and helped to build the Tanzam railway, from Tanzania to Zambia, after both the Soviet Union and the United States had declined to subsidize this venture. In 1976 Chinese aid to Africa reached $100.9 million, though it later declined to only $13.8 million in 1982.[15] Much of this Chinese assistance was intended to oppose Soviet influence in Africa; though the Chinese also used it to gain votes from African countries in favour of Chinese entry to the United Nations. In most cases, the Chinese did little to advance the cause of communism, preferring to support African nationalism in the belief that the continent was not yet ready for communism. Their attitude was also complicated by a deep-seated sense of historical and racial superiority to African peoples. (Interestingly, very different sentiments prevailed in the Middle East, where the Chinese sometimes referred to the Jews as 'the second great race' – though they still provided arms for the Palestine Liberation Organization.[16])

In Indo-China, the Chinese and Soviets were in principle on the same side, supporting North Vietnam against the Americans, but in practice they were often opposed to one another. In 1965–68 the Chinese stationed some 320 000 regular troops in North Vietnam, with anti-aircraft artillery and supplies.[17] By this means they hoped to limit Soviet influence as well as to help the North Vietnamese, but with only limited success. When Vietnam was finally unified in 1975, it remained an ally of the Soviet Union, providing a base for the Soviet fleet at Camh Ranh. The Chinese then sought to prevent Vietnamese influence from extending to neighbouring countries. They tried to maintain Laos as a neutral state, but the Vietnamese established control there in 1976. In Cambodia, the Chinese supported Prince Sihanouk against the Khmers Rouges, but again without success – with help from Vietnam, the Khmers Rouges dominated the country and set up the Republic of Kampuchea in January 1979. In February 1979 China retaliated by invading Vietnam, but had to withdraw within a month, suffering some 20 000 casualties and accomplishing nothing.[18]

The Chinese also opposed the Soviet Union in the Indian sub-continent, by supporting Pakistan against India. The Soviet Union maintained close relations with India in the 1960s and 1970s, and China therefore assisted Pakistan, without regard to ideological considerations. This support was necessarily limited. In 1971 China was unable to intervene, other than diplomatically, in the India–Pakistan war in which Pakistan lost its eastern territories (which became Bangladesh).[19] But during the 1970s China developed close military relations with Pakistan, and in 1989 the two countries concluded a ten-year agreement on arms supplies, under which the Chinese provided Pakistan with missiles and assistance with its nuclear programme. China also co-operated with Pakistan to oppose the Soviet forces in Afghanistan in the 1980s. China (like the United States, but less conspicuously) supplied the Afghan rebels with arms by way of Pakistan, and thus made their own contribution to the Soviet defeat.

However, it was also in the 1980s that the Chinese-Soviet dispute moved towards a resolution. In 1982 Brezhnev made two conciliatory speeches, at Tashkent (24 March) and Baku (26 September), saying that the Soviet Union recognized China as a socialist state and had no territorial claims upon it. In October 1982 the Deputy Foreign Ministers of the two countries met in Beijing, and the Chinese put forward three conditions for the improvement of relations: Soviet withdrawal from Afghanistan; the withdrawal of Soviet forces from the Chinese border, particularly in Outer Mongolia; and the withdrawal of Vietnamese forces (with Soviet backing) from Kampuchea.

When Gorbachev came to power in the Soviet Union, relations with China were not at the top of his agenda, but the Soviets and Chinese pursued negotiations on these points for some years. Eventually, on 15–18 May 1989, Gorbachev visited Beijing. The timing could not have been more difficult, because the Chinese government was confronting student demonstrators who occupied Tiananmen Square. Gorbachev's motorcade could not pass along the main streets of Beijing, and the Soviet leader could not even enter the Great Hall of the People by the main doorway. Even so, Gorbachev and Deng held a meeting, and issued a joint communiqué on 18 May, setting out a new framework for Chinese-Soviet relations which largely met the three Chinese conditions. The Soviet Union had already withdrawn from Afghanistan, for its own good reasons (the last troops had left in February 1989). Gorbachev now also assured the Chinese that Soviet troops would eventually withdraw from Mongolia. The two sides discussed Kampuchea (where they supported rival governments), without reaching agreement. Relations between the Soviet and Chinese Communist Parties were to be resumed, which marked a significant ideological concession by both sides.

In these meetings, Gorbachev had his hands full with reforms in the Soviet Union, the problems of eastern Europe and relations with the United

States. The Chinese government had to conduct the meetings in difficult, even humiliating, circumstances, as a result of the demonstrations in the heart of Beijing. The final result was favourable to the Chinese, marking a considerable success. For thirty years China had confronted the military power and the ideological authority of the Soviet Union, and had finally achieved an advantageous settlement.

China was also able to deal with the United States on a footing of something like equality. In 1971–72 the United States came courting for Chinese co-operation to get them out of the war in Vietnam. Kissinger visited China in total secrecy in 1971, and President Nixon in a glare of publicity in 1972, but the purpose was the same in each case. The Americans needed Chinese help, and the Chinese made them pay – though, as it turned out, mostly in promises. The main point at issue was the status of Taiwan. Ever since 1949, when Chiang Kai-shek had retreated to Taiwan from the mainland of China, the USA had continued to recognize the Taiwan government as the government of China, and insisted that Taiwan should hold the Chinese seat on the Security Council of the United Nations. In October 1971 the United States withdrew its opposition to Chinese membership of the United Nations, and the People's Republic replaced Taiwan on the Security Council. This American concession was thus in the bank before President Nixon's visit to China in February 1972. At the end of that visit, the two governments issued a joint communiqué at Shanghai, in which the Chinese government stated firmly that the People's Republic was the only legal government of China, and that Taiwan was one of its provinces. The Americans for their part acknowledged that all Chinese maintained that there was only one China, and undertook that they would ultimately withdraw all their forces from Taiwan. Negotiations on Taiwan continued when the Vietnam War ended, and in a further joint communiqué in December 1978 the United States agreed to break off diplomatic relations with Taiwan, and end its defence agreement, while China renounced the use of force to restore Taiwan to unity with the mainland. The Americans actually withdrew their Ambassador from Taiwan in January 1979, and withdrew their forces from the island by the end of the year. China thus gained much in principle in its negotiations with the United States; though in the event Taiwan proved able to survive the diplomatic breach with the Americans and maintain its independence, so that the practical advantage to China proved limited.

As a consequence of their improved relations with the United States, the Chinese undertook negotiations with Japan, and after six years (1972–78) the two countries signed a Treaty of Peace and Friendship, including a clause (which was understood to be directed against the Soviet Union) opposing any country which sought to impose hegemony in Asia and the Pacific. In practice, in the 1970s and 1980s, there was no completely predominant power in the area. The United States controlled the Pacific Ocean by sea and air power, effectively unchallenged despite the growing Soviet fleet. The Soviets maintained powerful forces in Central Asia and Siberia, confronting the Chinese along their long frontier; and exercised considerable influence through their relations with India. Japan was by far the strongest economic power in Asia, but remained militarily weak. China did not quite fulfil its potential in any direction. It was a strong military power, within strict limits. It could hold its own in negotiation with the superpowers, without attaining the same rank. It claimed influence in the communist camp and in parts of Africa, without securing many followers. What emerged in this period was a rough balance of power and interests between the USA, the Soviet Union, Japan and China, with none of them playing a predominant role.

◆ Taiwan, Korea and the Pacific Island States

Within the area of East Asia and the Pacific there were two unresolved conflicts, Taiwan and Korea; and also a remarkable phenomenon of modern international relations, the microstate. These three situations presented lingering or potential problems.

We have just seen how, in 1979, the United States withdrew diplomatic recognition, and its armed forces, from Taiwan. The Chinese government insisted that Taiwan was part of China, but undertook not to use force to make good its claim. This difficult and anomalous situation still prevails (writing in the year 2000). In 1981 the Chinese government proposed that Taiwan should become part of China, but with a special status which would include maintaining its own armed forces and separate economic and social organizations. A modified form of this proposal was advanced in 1984, when China reached an agreement with Britain that in 1997 the British colony of Hong Kong should return to China under an arrangement providing for the maintenance of two political and economic systems within one country. The Chinese then suggested that this solution (one country, two systems) could also be applied to Taiwan. Neither proposal made any headway with the government of Taiwan. The island became increasingly isolated diplomatically – in 1984 it was only recognized as a state by twenty-three governments. Taiwan was not a member of the United Nations, nor of the Association of South-East Asian Nations (ASEAN). It had no allies, and very few friends, though the United States and France continued to supply armaments and warships. Yet it survived politically and prospered economically. In 1991 Taiwan, with a population of just over 20 000 000 exported goods worth 76 billion dollars; China, with a population of perhaps 1200 million, exported 72 billion dollars' worth.[20] It was a striking demonstration of what could be achieved by commercial enterprise without formal international links.

But the status of Taiwan remains in dispute, and its future in doubt. In 2000 the country's electorate rejected the Nationalist party (the heirs of Chiang Kai-shek) which had governed the country since 1949, and elected a government with a mandate to declare formal independence from China. (Previous governments had simply claimed to *be* China.) The Chinese warned against any such step, and threatened military action. The possibility of war remained.

In Korea, the armistice signed in 1953 at the end of the Korean War remained in force. No peace settlement was attained, or even seriously attempted. North and South Korea confronted one another across the cease-fire line, which became an almost impenetrable barrier between the two states, making the iron curtain in Europe seem positively porous by comparison. In North Korea, Kim Il Sung maintained a strict communist dictatorship. In the South, Park Chung Hee established his personal autocracy, ruling from 1962 until his assassination in 1979. The economies of the two countries took very different courses, with the South developing more rapidly than the North from a level which in 1969 was very similar. South Korea received much American and Japanese investment. Ship-building, steel and textiles all flourished, competing successfully against their rivals in western Europe. South Korea, like Taiwan, became one of the 'tiger economies' of Asia.

GNP per head in North and South Korea, in US dollars[21]		
Date	North	South
1969	216	208
1975	398	532
1984	965	1707
1992	1064	5569

The two governments made tentative contact with one another through the International Red Cross in 1971, and in 1972 set up a committee of co-operation, with the declared intention of moving towards unification. These contacts were broken off by North Korea in 1973, and resumed in 1984. At that stage, North Korea proposed a form of federation between the two states, but the South prevaricated, and no change resulted. In 1990 the Prime Ministers of the two countries met in conference for the first time, but without result. The two governments were deeply suspicious of one another, fearing that unification would mean simply a take-over by one or the other. The population of South Korea greatly outnumbered that of the North (by 29 million to 13 million in 1967, and by 42 million to 22 million in 1992), so the danger that the North would be overwhelmed by union with the South was obvious. On the other hand, the South Korean government feared the tight communist organization of the North. In 1988 South Korea gained a prestige victory by holding the Olympic Games at Seoul; but the population of South Korea showed increasing discontent with its own authoritarian government. There were occasional outbreaks of hostilities between the two states – warships exchanged shots as late as 1999; and the situation remained one of unresolved crisis.

In the Pacific Ocean there occurred a striking development, which may contain the seeds of future difficulties. It is a feature of modern world affairs that a number of very small countries, barely able to meet what would earlier have been the criteria for statehood, have come into independent existence. Since the 1970s, the Pacific has seen the advent of the microstate. A succession of islands and archipelagos, formerly colonies, attained independence: Samoa with a population of 197 000 in 1993; Vanuatu (formerly the New Hebrides) with 157 000; Tonga with 103 000; Kiribati (formerly the Gilbert Islands) with 76 000; Tuvalu (formerly the Ellice Islands) with 10 000; Nauru with 10 000 (all figures for 1993). These tiny states all enjoy formal independence, but are in practice protected by the United States Navy, or sometimes by the former imperial power. All have rights, under the international law of the sea and the ocean-bed, to vast tracts of ocean and whatever lies beneath it, which might at some stage prove more valuable or more contentious than their governments can cope with. The development of the microstate is a modern phenomenon whose consequences have yet to be worked out.

◆ India and Pakistan

The Indian sub-continent (including India, Pakistan, Sri Lanka and after 1971 Bangladesh) formed a largely self-contained region, with its own pattern of international relations and less impact on the rest of the world than was at one time expected. India in particular seemed destined for a great role in world affairs. It was the home of ancient civilizations. It had a large and growing population – some 511 million in 1967, 600m in 1978, 874m in 1993. Despite occasional turbulence, it achieved remarkable political stability, based on federal and parliamentary institutions. It possessed a strong, efficient and non-political army, built on the traditions of the old British Indian Army. India's first Prime Minister, Jawaharlal Nehru, took a leading role in the Afro-Asian movement founded at Bandung in 1955, in the movement of non-aligned states, and in the Commonwealth. In the 1970s India took the first steps towards becoming a nuclear power, carrying out a nuclear explosion in 1974. (The Indians finally produced a nuclear weapon in 1998.)

Yet despite its high aspirations and considerable achievements, India never quite emerged as a great power on the world stage. In 1962 the Indians fought a brief but disastrous border war with China, which damaged both Nehru's reputation as a statesman and the prestige of the Indian Army. Influence in the Third World and the non-aligned movement passed to more radical leaders, like Boumedienne in Algeria and Castro in Cuba. The Commonwealth diminished in importance. India devoted much diplomatic effort to its relations with the Soviet Union, leading to the conclusion of a Treaty of Friendship in 1971, providing for consultation in the event of an external threat; but in this association India was the junior partner. India developed its industries, following Soviet-style Five-Year Plans which tended to fall short of their objectives. Agricultural production increased, but did little more than keep pace with the growing population. By the early 1990s India was broadly self-sufficient in food, but only at a very low level for a large part of the population. Intense poverty prevailed over much of the country.

India thus had its own internal problems, and became a great power only within the sub-continent. Indian foreign policy was largely taken up by the long and inconclusive conflict with Pakistan, in which Kashmir was the principal bone of contention. As we have seen (above, pp. 207–9), at the time of partition Kashmir was predominantly Muslim in population, but its Hindu ruler had opted to join India. After 1947, India held most of the province, and Pakistan occupied areas in the north and west. India promised a plebiscite, which never took place; and the two parts of Kashmir remained separated by a cease-fire line supervised by the United Nations. The volatile nature of this situation, and the violent emotions involved, were vividly illustrated in December 1963, when a holy relic (a hair from the beard of the Prophet Mohammed) vanished from a mosque in Srinagar, the capital of Kashmir. Rumours spread that the relic had been stolen by a former Chief Minister of Kashmir, Bakshi Ghulam Mohammed, and there were vast demonstrations demanding its return. The relic was in fact restored, in mysterious circumstances, on 3 January 1964; but by that time the demonstrations had gathered momentum, and changed their object to the release of Sheikh Abdullah, an important Kashmiri Muslim leader who had been imprisoned by the Indians for many years. There were attacks on Hindus in East Pakistan, and on Muslims in parts of India. The Security Council of the United Nations debated Kashmir yet again, to no effect. The disappearance of the relic, which was itself a focus for intense religious and nationalist emotions, released forces which had little to do with the calculations of statesmen; and the episode furnishes a powerful demonstration of the difficulties inherent in the Kashmir question and the whole India–Pakistan conflict.[22]

In 1965 open warfare between India and Pakistan broke out in a different area. In April there was fighting in the Rann of Kutch, an area of salt marshes on the border between the two countries to the south-east of the Indus delta. The territory was of no value in itself, and indeed was under water for parts of the year; and the issues involved were not material but matters of prestige and national sensitivity. A cease-fire came into force from 1 July, but the conflict quickly shifted to Kashmir. Muslim irregulars attacked Indian-held territory in eastern Kashmir on 5 August; and troops of the Pakistan Army crossed the cease-fire line on 1 September. On the 6th Indian forces began a counter-offensive towards the Pakistani city of Lahore. (One of the features of the Kashmir conflict is that important Pakistani cities – Lahore, Rawalpindi, and the new capital, Islamabad – lie close to the disputed region.) China intervened indirectly in the conflict on 16 September, by choosing that moment to demand that India should dismantle certain fortifications on the Himalayan border between the two countries, presenting the Indians with the potential threat of a war on two fronts. At that stage both the Soviet Union and the United States warned the Chinese against taking military action, and the incident passed. On 23 September yet another cease-fire was arranged by the United Nations, and the Indian and Pakistani forces returned to their respective positions. The Indians published casualty figures of 2212 killed, 7636 wounded and some 1500 missing, testifying to the severity of the fighting.[23]

After this conflict, the Soviet Union (which still maintained close relations with India) attempted the role of mediator. Kosygin, the Soviet Prime Minister, invited the Indian Prime Minister (Lal Shastri) and the President of Pakistan (Field Marshal Ayub Khan) to a meeting at Tashkent, in Soviet Central Asia, where the two leaders conferred from 4–10 January 1966. It was a remarkable scene. The very name of Tashkent recalled the Great Game played between Russia and Britain in the nineteenth century for the control of Central Asia. Kosygin took the role of mediator in the Indian sub-continent in a way that the Tsars might well have envied. But the results were slender. Shastri and Ayub Khan cautiously agreed that their countries would not use force against one another, which seemed hopeful in principle but implausible in practice. They also undertook to resume negotiations about Kashmir, which had proved a fruitless task in the past. A final grim element of drama was added when Shastri suddenly died of a heart attack at the conclusion of the conference.

One of the signatories of the Tashkent agreement thus died almost as soon as the ink was dry, and was succeeded by Indira Gandhi, Nehru's daughter. The other principal participant in the conference, Ayub Khan, found himself the target of discontent at home, partly because he had failed to achieve success against India, and was eventually compelled to resign in 1969. He was replaced by another military ruler, General Yahya Khan. The Tashkent agreement did not survive these changes, and by the end of 1971 the two countries were again engaged in conflict, this time over the secession of East Pakistan (Bangladesh) from Pakistan itself.

At the time of its creation in 1947, Pakistan was a state in two parts, separated by about 1000 miles of Indian territory. To keep the two parts of the country together was certain to be difficult, and proved to be impossible.

The capital was in West Pakistan (in Karachi up to 1959, and then in Rawalpindi pending the building of a new capital city at Islamabad), which meant that the West did better in government jobs and expenditure. The Army was mostly recruited from the 'martial races' of the West, where its main bases were also established. The East provided most of Pakistan's exports, principally jute; but jute was suffering from increasing competition from artificial fibres, and was a wasting asset. Much of the territory of East Pakistan, which included about half the delta of the River Ganges, was regularly subject to severe flooding and periodical famines; and the people felt forgotten or disregarded by the distant government in the West. During the 1960s, political protest against neglect by the central government was organized by the Awami League, led by Mujibur Rahman, demanding at first autonomy for East Pakistan in a new federal system, and later complete independence.

In 1970 the nagging discontent in East Pakistan came to a head through a combination of natural disasters and the calling of a parliamentary election, which was intended to bring to an end a period of military rule. Bengal suffered severe floods in the summer of 1970, followed by a cyclone on 13 November. The Pakistani government was slow in responding to these emergencies, strengthening the Awami League's case for independence. In December 1970 the elections took place throughout Pakistan. In the East, the Awami League swept the board, winning 161 seats out of 162. In the West, the Peoples' Party, led by Zulfiqar Ali Bhutto, won 83 seats out of 138. The combined result gave the Awami League a majority of the 300 members of the Assembly, and Mujibur Rahman had every expectation of becoming Prime Minister. In fact, the existing military government under General Yahya Khan refused to convene the new Assembly and retained power for itself. In March 1971 Rahman and the Awami League called a general strike in East Pakistan, demanding independence. Troops of the Pakistan Army occupied the university in Dacca, the principal city in the East, and attempted to suppress the Awami League. On 26 March Rahman declared the independence of the new state of Bangladesh. He was at once arrested, and the Pakistani Army attempted to suppress the independence movement, inflicting heavy casualties among the population. Vast numbers of refugees (variously estimated at between seven and ten million, mostly Hindus) crossed the border into India.

What was in principle an internal crisis for Pakistan was in fact of intense concern to India. The influx of refugees from East Pakistan created immediate practical problems. Much more seriously, in the context of the long-standing conflict between India and Pakistan, the crisis presented India with an almost irresistible opportunity to exploit Pakistan's difficulties. In fact, the Indians provided help for Awami League resistance against the Pakistan Army, but the government hesitated for some eight months before intervening directly and on a large scale. Eventually at the end of November

1971 the Indian Prime Minister, Indira Gandhi, formally requested the Pakistan government to release Rahman from imprisonment, and Indian regular troops crossed the border into East Pakistan. On 3 December 1971 Pakistan responded by attacking India from the West and bombing Indian airfields. The next day Indian forces, about 160 000 strong, advanced into East Pakistan, and reached the outskirts of Dacca on 14 December. The Indians set up a Provisional Government of Bangladesh, and the Pakistani forces in the territory surrendered on 16 December.

While these events were taking place, the great powers manoeuvred on behalf of the opposite sides. China had long supported Pakistan against India, and had just attained a stronger diplomatic position since its admission to the United Nations and the Security Council in October 1971. The United States had also normally sided with Pakistan, and at this very time, with Pakistani help, was in the midst of negotiations with China which were to lead to President Nixon's visit there in February 1972. In these circumstances, the Americans and Chinese formed an unlikely combination in support of Pakistan. On 4 December the United States put to the Security Council a resolution calling for an immediate cease-fire in East Pakistan, which would have had the effect of halting the Indian advance into the territory. The Soviet Union vetoed it. A similar resolution was then put to the UN General Assembly, where the veto did not apply, and was carried on 8 December, with a majority of the 'non-aligned' states voting in its favour – and thus against India, which had put great efforts into forming the non-aligned movement. Behind the scenes, President Nixon put pressure on the Soviet Union by threatening to cancel his summit meeting with Brezhnev arranged for 1972. He also ostentatiously despatched the aircraft-carrier *Enterprise* to the Gulf of Bengal to show the flag and imply the possibility of American intervention against India. In secret, the Chinese agreed not to intervene militarily in support of Pakistan, and the Soviets undertook to restrain India from attacking West Pakistan or Kashmir. Under these various pressures and agreements, a balance of sorts was struck. On 17 December Yahya Khan accepted the UN resolution on a cease-fire (which by that time made no practical difference in East Pakistan/Bangladesh, because the Pakistani troops there had already surrendered on the 16th). On the same day Yahya Khan resigned as Prime Minister, and was replaced by Zulfiqar Ali Bhutto, who at once accepted the independence of Bangladesh. India thus secured an important victory, and East Pakistan became Bangladesh; but West Pakistan remained intact.

The crisis thus ended in victory for India; and independence for Bangladesh. Pakistan suffered a severe defeat, and lost the eastern part of the country that had come into being with such difficulty and suffering in 1947; but in the long run it gained from its new coherence as a single geographical unit.

The Indian government concluded a treaty with Bangladesh on 19

March 1972, guaranteeing the new state against external attack – a psychological rather than a practical assurance, since Bangladesh's only immediate neighbour was India itself. The Prime Ministers of India and Pakistan, Indira Gandhi and Zulfiqar Bhutto, met at Simla on 2 July 1972, and signed an agreement to maintain peaceful co-existence between their two countries, to resolve differences by peaceful means, and to respect the existing cease-fire line in Kashmir. Shortly after this, Bhutto told the Pakistani Assembly that Pakistan could not secure self-determination for the people of Kashmir; which in practice though not in principle amounted to a retreat from Pakistan's claims on the subject. In August 1973 India and Pakistan concluded a Repatriation Agreement, providing for the return of some 90 000 Pakistani prisoners of war and civilian internees to Pakistan, and for Pakistan to accept an unspecified number of emigrants from Bangladesh who did not wish to remain in the new state.

Pakistan was unable to prevent the international acceptance of the new state of Bangladesh. The Commonwealth admitted Bangladesh to membership in 1972, and Pakistan resigned in protest. Admission to the United Nations, which was dependent on a vote in the Security Council, was held up by Chinese veto, but only until 1974. At home, Bangladeshis found that independence solved none of their problems. Rahman's attempt to combine parliamentary democracy, socialism and economic development failed. He resorted to a form of dictatorship in 1975, but was displaced by a military coup later in the year, and then murdered.

India and Pakistan both went through a period of internal difficulties. In March 1977 the Congress Party lost a parliamentary election in India for the first time, and Indira Gandhi resigned. Her successor, Morarji Desai, pursued a policy less favourable to the Soviet Union. Mrs Gandhi returned to power in 1980; but was assassinated in 1984. In Pakistan Zulfiqar Bhutto was overthrown by the Army in July 1977, and General Zia Ul-Haq was installed as President. He imposed martial law, and set about turning Pakistan (which had long been described as an Islamic republic) into a thoroughgoing Islamic state. Bhutto, charged with corruption and the rigging of elections, was executed. The two states, despite their limited agreements in 1972–73, remained fundamentally at odds, over Kashmir and over the whole basis of their relations in the sub-continent. Both made steady progress in manufacturing nuclear weapons, which they tested in close succession in 1998.

India also intervened, though in a very different way, in the internal struggle which wracked Sri Lanka from 1977 onwards. The Tamil people formed a minority of about 15–16 per cent of the population in Sri Lanka, mostly concentrated in the north of the country round the city of Jaffna. Rioting in Jaffna in August 1977 caused 125 deaths, and marked the beginning of a conducted a long separatist campaign among the Tamils, led by a guerrilla army calling themselves the Tamil Tigers. The insurrection persisted into the 1980s, causing much anxiety in India, where there was a substantial Tamil population in southern India, across the Palk Straits from Sri Lanka. The Indian government feared that the movement for Tamil independence in Sri Lanka, if successful, would have repercussions in India. India therefore supported the Sri Lankan government in its long struggle against the Tamil Tigers, and also tried to find a compromise solution to the conflict. In July 1987, the Indian Prime Minister (Rajiv Gandhi) concluded an agreement with Sri Lanka by which India would send troops to help to defeat the guerrillas, and Sri Lanka undertook to establish a Tamil homeland with a large measure of autonomy. In the event, the Indian Peace-Keeping Force grew to some 50 000 men, without defeating the rebels or keeping the peace; and eventually the Sri Lankan government grew weary of the presence of foreign troops and asked for their withdrawal. The Indian troops left in 1990, and Rajiv Gandhi was killed in October 1991 by a bomb handed to him within a bunch of flowers by a suicide assassin working on behalf of the Tamil Tigers. The Tamil war continued, and by 1993 had caused an estimated 30 000 dead on both sides.[24]

The conflict between India and Pakistan persisted, and by 1987 was in its fortieth year. It was still continuing in 2000, far outliving the Cold War, which the participants had from time to time exploited for their own purposes. On a much smaller scale, the Tamil insurrection in Sri Lanka had by 2000 also persisted for nearly a quarter of a century. In both cases, the fundamental issue was one of national identity, powerfully reinforced in the case of Pakistan by religion. Pakistan was created in 1947 on the claim for an Islamic homeland, and the country has grown more strongly Islamic over the years. India has remained a secular state, with a large minority of Muslims in its population; but many Indians have continued to resent the very existence of Pakistan. Kashmir has remained the symbol of the struggle between the two states, not its cause. Over territory, compromise is always possible; but symbols are another matter altogether.

◆ Notes to Chapter 20

1. Akire Iriye, *Japan and the Wider World* (London, 1997), p. 147.
2. Paul Johnson, *A History of the Modern World: From 1917 to the 1980s* (London, paperback edn, 1984), p. 720.
3. Iriye, *Japan and Wider World*, p. 147.
4. For the oil shocks and oil prices, see above, pp. 412–23.
5. Iriye, *Japan and Wider World*, pp.182–3.
6. Paul Kennedy, *The Rise and Fall of the Great Powers* (London, paperback edn, 1989), p. 601.
7. *Ibid.*, p. 604.
8. For the Japanese constitution, see above, pp. 200–1.

9. Iriye, *Japan and Wider World*, p. 180.
10. For the change in American policy towards China, see above, pp. 292–4.
11. Edwin W. Moise, *Modern China: A History* (London, 1986), p. 174.
12. François Joyaux, 'Réflexions sur la "puissance" de la Chine populaire', *Relations Internationales*, No.17, Spring 1979, p. 66.
13. *Ibid.*, pp. 66–7. William T. Tow, 'China and the International Strategic System', in Thomas W. Robinson and David Shambaugh, eds, *Chinese Foreign Policy: Theory and Practice* (Oxford, 1994), p. 148.
14. François Fejto, *Chine–URSS: De l'alliance au conflit, 1950–1977* (Paris, 1977), p. 468.
15. Philip Snow, 'China and Africa', in Robinson and Shambaugh, p. 306.
16. L. C. Harris, 'China's Relations with the Middle East', *ibid.*, p. 324.
17. David Shambaugh, 'Sino-American Relations', *ibid.*, p. 201.
18. Chris Cook, *World Political Almanac* (London, 3rd edn, 1995), p. 321.
19. For Bangladesh and the conflict of 1971, see below, pp. 439–42.
20. Gerald Segal, *The World Affairs Companion* (revised edn, London, 1993), p. 40.
21. J.-B. Duroselle, *Histoire diplomatique de 1919 à nos jours* (Paris, 11th edn, 1993), p. 881; Segal, *World Affairs Companion,* p. 180.
22. Michael Edwardes, *Nehru: A Political Biography* (London, 1971), p. 327.
23. Cook, *Almanac*, p. 316.
24. *Ibid.*, p. 319.

CHAPTER

21

THE FATE OF AFRICA, c.1962–1990

African aspirations and problems – Conflicts in Africa – Nigeria and Biafra – Chad – The Horn of Africa – Western Sahara – African economic problems – Outside powers and Africa

◆ African aspirations

1960 was widely acclaimed as the 'Year of Africa', as one country after another emerged from colonial status to independence. In the few years between 1957 and 1962 the greater part of the continent was emancipated from European rule and set off hopefully towards a revived African civilization and a new role in the world. The 32 states whose representatives met at Addis Ababa in May 1963 to found the Organization of African Unity set themselves far-reaching aims: to promote African unity and solidarity; to co-ordinate their political, economic, cultural, health, scientific and defence policies; and to eliminate colonialism in Africa.[1]

The continent had strong foundations for economic prosperity. Africa possessed great mineral resources: gold and diamonds; coal, oil and uranium – the old and new fuels; copper, cobalt, chrome, iron ore, manganese, bauxite and phosphates. In the 1980s, it was estimated that Africa was producing 64 per cent of the world's manganese, 50 per cent of its gold, and 30 per cent of the uranium in the non-communist countries. African agriculture produced important crops for export – cocoa, coffee, vegetable oils and tobacco. The prospects for economic development seemed favourable.[2]

The new African states looked forward to a dynamic role in international affairs. The Afro-Asian congress at Bandung in 1955, though held before the great majority of African states had attained independence, showed the way forward. The first summit conference of non-aligned countries, held at Belgrade in September 1961, included 11 African states out of a total of 25. The second summit conference, at Cairo in October 1964, comprised an African majority (29 out of 47). Out of ten non-aligned summit conferences between 1961 and 1989, four were held in Africa (in

Cairo, Lusaka, Algiers and Harare). These meetings were frequently concerned with an African issue – the elimination of the *apartheid* regime in South Africa; and also with the question of how to restructure the world economy to meet the needs of primary producers and poor countries, which included most African states.

The new Africa thus began with great hopes, and made its mark in the councils of the non-aligned movement. But for the most part the period after the 'year of Africa' and the foundation of the Organization of African Unity was a time of difficulty and disillusionment.

◆ African problems

The new Africa comprised a large number of states, rising to 52 by 1992 (including island states in the Indian Ocean – Comoros, Mauritius, Seychelles – which chose to join the Organization of African Unity). Most of the new states inherited the frontiers drawn by the colonial powers in the nineteenth century, and attained little internal cohesion, being divided along tribal or ethnic lines or by religious differences. Language, which in Europe was often the foundation of nationality, could play no such role in Africa. Africa south of the Sahara included an estimated 1300 indigenous languages in a population of about 460 millions in 1980. Cameroon alone, for example, with a population of 7 663 000 in 1976, comprised some 230 languages; though it was held together, and communicated with the outside world, through the use of French.[3] Indeed, the European languages introduced by the colonizing powers – especially English and French – maintained cohesion over large areas of the continent, though at the cost of some rivalry between the English and French-speaking groups.

Hopes for political stability, often encouraged by the institutions left behind by the colonial powers, were quickly disappointed. In January 1963 the army overthrew the government in Togo, and the President, Sylvanus Olympio, was killed. A series of other military coups speedily followed – in Congo (Brazzaville) and Benin in 1963; Gabon in 1964 (French troops restored the government, but that only amounted to military intervention of a different kind); Congo and Dahomey in 1965; the Central African Republic, Upper Volta and Ghana in 1966. The last of these was a particular blow to British hopes in Africa. Ghana (formerly the British colony of the Gold Coast) had been guided to independence by carefully designed stages, and its first Prime Minister, Kwame Nkrumah, was widely admired as a model African statesman of the new generation. But Nkrumah first made himself a dictator, and then in 1966 was overthrown by the army, dying in exile in 1972. In the late 1960s Nigeria and Sierra Leone, which had begun their independent existence with high hopes, each suffered three military coups. By 1975 it was calculated that 20 out of 41 former colonies in Black Africa were under military rule or military influence. In the thirty years from 1960 to 1990, there were 80 successful coups d'état in Africa.[4] All across Africa authoritarian governments prevailed, of various kinds – military, imperial, Marxist, African socialist, or simply tyrannical. A severe but well-informed observer counted in 1990 25 military and 19 civilian dictatorships.[5]

It is worth describing three of these dictatorships briefly, to illustrate what was happening in large parts of Africa. Sese Seko Mobutu seized power in the Congo (later Zaire) by a military coup in 1965, and ruled the country until 1997. He was a champion of African authenticity, replacing all European place-names by African ones, and taking a new African name for himself. He plunged the country into economic chaos and poverty, yet he himself amassed an enormous personal fortune, much of it safely stowed in Swiss bank accounts. Despite this, Zaire was sustained by repeated loans from the International Monetary Fund and the World Bank, usually extended on conditions for reform which were never fulfilled. He played a significant role in African politics, becoming President of the Organization of African Unity in 1967. He claimed to be anti-communist and a bastion of stability in Central Africa ('It is me or chaos,' he is reported to have exclaimed) to secure aid from the Americans. He was sustained to the last by the French government, with which he played the card of *Francophonie* – he was, after all, the leader of a vast French-speaking country. When Mobutu was finally defeated and overthrown by a revolt in 1997, Zaire had been reduced to economic ruin and political chaos.[6]

Jean Bedel Bokassa was head of the army in the Central African Republic, formerly the French colony of Ubangi-Chari. He seized power and declared himself President for life in 1966, and proclaimed himself Emperor in 1977, with an astonishing coronation ceremony partly modelled on that of Napoleon. Bokassa enriched himself by fraudulent dealings in gold and diamonds, and committed multiple murders. Yet he was sustained in power by France, and was entertained in Paris by President Giscard d'Estaing, to whom he gave a present of diamonds which later became notorious. He was finally overthrown in 1979 by French troops, who restored the previous president, David Dacko.

In Uganda, Idi Amin (the army commander, who like Mobutu had risen from the ranks) seized power in 1971. He expelled the Ugandan Asians, who ran most of the commercial life of the country – a racist move which was popular among much of the population, but proved an economic disaster. He attempted to turn Uganda into an Islamic country, though Muslims made up only a small proportion of the population, and murdered an Anglican archbishop. The number of Ugandans killed under his regime was variously estimated at between 100 000 and 300 000. His 8-year tyranny was arbitrary, murderous and occasionally absurd – during the October War in the Middle East in 1973, he claimed to have played a decisive role in the Egyptian victories by his own daring operations behind the Israeli lines. Amid all this, and when his record was well known, he was elected President of the Organization of African Unity, and played host at its meeting in Kampala in 1975, which was attended by all member states except three. At the beginning of his rule the British government continued to supply Uganda with arms, and they permitted a regular supply of luxury goods (notably whisky) to be flown from Stansted until his fall from power. Amin finally over-reached himself by attempting to seize territory from the neighbouring state of Tanzania. He was then resisted by President Nyerere, and overthrown by a Tanzanian army which invaded Uganda and entered Kampala as liberators. Amin took refuge, first in Libya and then in Saudi Arabia, where he lived in comfortable exile.[7]

These three were extreme examples of tyranny, but they involved elements which recurred frequently across the continent: the seizure of power by the head of the army, large-scale murder, and disastrous damage to the economy. Amin's actions against the Asians were also plainly racist in character. Yet each of these tyrants was accepted by other African rulers and by the Organization of African Unity, and sustained to a greater or less extent by western powers – France (Mobutu and Bokassa), Britain (Amin) and the United States (Mobutu). Together, they brought disaster on the reputation of the new Africa – though even together they inflicted far fewer deaths than Stalin or Pol Pot.

Strikingly, what none of them did was to conquer territory from a neighbouring country (Amin's one attempt at this was his undoing), or to lose territory from his own. Mobutu wrecked Zaire economically, but it passed geographically intact to his successor; and the same was true of Bokassa and Amin. The basic rule of African international politics, and the founding principle of the Organization of African Unity, was the preservation of the territorial integrity of existing states. The cohesion of most African states was so fragile that no government wished to set a dangerous example of conquest or secession. This did not prevent Africa from becoming the scene of a large number of conflicts, between and within states.

◆ African conflicts

In the three decades between 1960 and 1990 Africa suffered conflicts of various kinds – wars between states, civil wars, and sometimes a mixture between the two. A somewhat arbitrary count arrives at a total of 24 such conflicts:[8]

Sudan, civil war, 1955–present
Congo–Zaire, civil war with outside intervention, 1960–67
South Africa, liberation struggle by African National Congress, 1961–94

Angola, war of liberation, 1961–75
Somalia–Kenya, border conflict, 1963–67
Guinea–Bissau, war of liberation, 1963–74
Algeria–Morocco, border conflict, 1963
Eritrea–Ethiopia, war of secession, 1963–91
Somalia–Ethiopia, border conflict, 1964 and 1977–78
Mozambique, war of liberation, 1964–74
Rhodesia/Zimbabwe, war of liberation, 1965–79
Chad, civil war with outside intervention, 1965–88
Namibia, war of liberation, 1966–90
Nigeria–Biafra, civil war (failed war of secession), 1967–70
Burundi, civil war, Hutu against Tutsi, 1972–present
Angola, civil war with outside intervention, 1975–present
Western Sahara (Polisario, Morocco, Mauritania), 1975–91
Mozambique, civil war with outside intervention, 1976–92
Zaire, invasion by rebels from Angola, 1977–78
Libya–Egypt, border raids, 1977
Uganda–Tanzania (resulting in overthrow of Amin), 1978–79
Somalia, civil war with outside intervention, 1981–present
Liberia, civil war, 1989–93
Rwanda, civil war, 1990–present

Among these conflicts (which were of very different scale and intensity), six were wars of liberation against a colonial power or against white governments (in Rhodesia and South Africa); twelve were civil wars, often with outside intervention; and six were wars between states, usually over borders and territory. Let us look at certain examples, which illuminate various aspects of the African situation.

◆ Nigeria–Biafra, 1967–70

One of the most serious of these African conflicts was that in Nigeria from May 1967 to January 1970, which (like the American Civil War in the nineteenth century) was a war of secession, and therefore either a civil war or a war between states depending on the date and one's point of view. Nigeria was one of the most populous African states, and at the time of independence one of the richest, with a thriving export trade in cocoa and vegetable oils, and production of crude oil averaging 7 753 000 metric tons for the years 1963–65, mostly from the Eastern Province.[9] Britain, the colonial power, left behind a federal system of government, comprising three provinces: the north was mainly Hausa in its population and Moslem in religion; the south-west mainly Yoruba and Christian; and the east mainly Ibo and Christian (largely Catholic). In January 1966 the Federal Prime

Minister, Abubakar Tafewa Balewa, was assassinated, and the army took power under the leadership of General Ironsi, who suppressed political parties and embarked on a policy of centralization. In July 1966 Ironsi himself was assassinated, and replaced by another soldier, Colonel Gowon. Ibos living in the North were killed in large numbers, and many took refuge in the Eastern Province, among their own people. Gowon abandoned Ironsi's short-lived policy of centralization and went instead for greater division, setting up (May 1967) a new federation consisting of twelve provinces instead of three, dividing the Ibos of the former Eastern Province between several of the new regions. Colonel Ojukwu, an Ibo officer and military governor of the Eastern Province, opposed the new division of the country, which would subvert Ibo autonomy and remove the province's control over its oil revenues. Ojukwu declared the independence of the Eastern Province, under the name of Biafra, on 30 May 1967.

The subsequent war lasted two-and-a-half years, with casualties (military and civilian) estimated at some 600 000 killed.[10] For nearly a year the struggle was fairly even, but in 1968 the Nigerians began to prevail, capturing the main Biafran port and oil centre at Port Harcourt on 20 May. Biafran resistance then persisted, but under increasing difficulties, through 1969. Finally Ojukwu left the country on 8 January 1970, leaving his successor, General Effiong, to ask for terms. The last Biafran troops surrendered on 15 January 1970.

During the war, much turned on the attitudes of outside states, in Africa and elsewhere. In Africa, only four governments (Tanzania, Zambia, Gabon and Ivory Coast) recognized Biafra as an independent state. All the other members of the Organization of African Unity refused to do so, mainly on grounds of self-preservation – if the principle of secession from one of the new African states were once accepted, there was no telling where it would stop. Outside Africa, the Soviet Union and Britain were quick to declare their support for the Nigerian government, and to supply it with arms and other assistance. The Soviets were trying to increase their influence in West Africa; Britain, as the former colonial power, wished to maintain its own creation in Nigeria, and was also in competition with the Soviet Union – the British government was well aware that if it did not provide armaments to Nigeria, the Soviets would. The United States refused to sell arms to either side, and eventually declared its opposition to secession – but not until June 1968, when the fall of Port Harcourt showed that Nigeria was likely to win. The French government sympathized with Biafra, mainly in the hope of diminishing British influence in West Africa. In July 1968 President de Gaulle said publicly that he was in favour of resolving the conflict on the basis of self-determination, which would have met Biafran wishes. For much of 1968 the French flew supplies of arms to Biafra by way of Gabon and the Ivory Coast, former French colonies which had recognized Biafra; but France stopped short of granting its own recognition. China also sympathized with Biafra, on the simple ground that the Soviet Union was backing Nigeria, but to little practical effect. Biafra was also supported by South Africa, Rhodesia and Israel – all opposed, for their own reasons, to the majority of African states. Biafra thus secured some recognition and outside help, but never enough to turn the conflict into an international war. It remained a war of secession which ultimately failed. The outcome was a victory for the status quo, which suited the great majority of African states. If the result had gone the other way, and a precedent for successful secession had been set, the consequences might have been far-reaching. For Nigeria the cost of victory was high, and the country suffered economic and political damage whose effects persisted for many years. For Africa as a whole, the attitude of other countries to the war was a striking demonstration that the principle of self-determination applied only to liberation from the colonial powers or white rule, not to separation from a new African state.

◆ Chad

The former French colony of Chad became independent in 1960. It was a large and sparsely-populated country, with some 2 675 000 people in a territory of 496 000 square miles. It was a poor country, with a short life expectancy among its people, a small GNP and little foreign trade, mostly with France.[11] There was little to be gained in Chad; though in French eyes the country had a significant place in recent history, as the first colony to join de Gaulle and the Free French in 1940. The new state consisted of two contrasting parts: the north was Arab and Muslim in population, and nomadic in way of life; the south was black in population, Christian or animist in religion, and practised agriculture, producing cottonseed and groundnuts.

The northern Arabs were afraid of domination by the more populous south, which also included the capital, Fort Lamy (later N'Djamena), and in 1965 the National Liberation Front (FROLINAT) began an armed rebellion in the north. In 1968 French forces intervened to defeat the rebellion. In 1973 Libya, an Islamic state under the leadership of Colonel Gadaffi, intervened to support the Muslims in northern Chad. Libya also occupied the 'Aouzou Strip', a disputed territory of some 70 000 square miles on the border between Libya and Chad. This territory was disputed for historical reasons dating back to the colonial period. In January 1935 the French Premier, Pierre Laval, in negotiations with Mussolini, the Italian dictator, had agreed to cede the Aouzou strip to the Italian colony of Libya; but Italy never took the formal step of annexing the territory, and its exact status remained in doubt. Gadaffi considered himself the heir to the Italian colony; and his claim was inspired by the further incentive that the Aouzou

Strip might contain deposits of uranium. Libya was in fact something of a rogue state, and Gaddafi an erratic leader. He came to power in 1969, when he was only 31. At different times he intervened on behalf of Muslim rebels in Chad, Tunisia, Sudan, and as far afield as the Philippines. He proclaimed unions between Libya and a series of other states – Egypt, Tunisia, Mauritania, Chad and Morocco; though none of these achieved any reality. His intervention in Chad was a part of this idiosyncratic and erratic behaviour, in which economic advantage played only a small part.

In 1975 a military coup in Chad brought in a new government, supposedly of national reconciliation; but the National Liberation Front, now with Libyan support, continued its rebellion. French troops again intervened, confining the revolt to the northern areas. In 1979 Nigeria, which shared a short boundary with Chad and sought to counter Libyan influence, attempted mediation between the different parties, but without success.

There followed a period of sporadic conflict, from 1980 to 1988, with the civil war continuing, accompanied by Libyan intervention in the north and French in the south. In 1980 French troops withdrew from Chad, and a new government was formed under Goukouni Oueddi, the military commander of the National Liberation Front. Goukouni concluded a treaty with Libya, and in October 1980 asked for Libyan troops to defeat what had now become a rebellion in southern Chad, led by Hissein Habré. Gaddafi sent a force of 15 000 men, and in January 1981 Libya and Chad announced a union between the two countries. In practice this led nowhere, and in September 1981 the Libyan forces actually withdrew from Chad without bringing the civil war to an end. In 1983 the Organization of African Unity accepted Habré as head of government in Chad, but this had no effect in the country, where the conflict continued. Libyan troops returned to the north, and the French sent 3000 men to check their advance. The United States also sent help to Habré (in order to oppose the Libyans); and Zaire, under Mobutu, also despatched a small force. The result was a division of Chad, roughly along the 16th parallel of latitude, with a separate government in each zone, supported by different foreign backers.

In September 1984 the French and Libyans agreed on the simultaneous withdrawal of their forces from Chad. The French left (though only as far as the neighbouring Central African Republic). The Libyans stayed, and in 1986 the French returned. That year, Goukouni was wounded in a quarrel with Libyan soldiers, and his followers changed sides and joined Habré's forces in the south. At that point, Gadaffi appeared to lose interest, and most of the Libyans withdrew from northern Chad, though not from the Aouzou Strip. In 1987 the Organization of African Unity arranged a ceasefire, and in 1988 Habré's government and Libya opened diplomatic relations with one another. Finally, in 1994, Libya withdrew even from the Aouzou Strip, and acknowledged the Chadian claim to the area.

In this long and confused struggle no one gained any advantage. Chad was poorer in 1990 than when it became independent in 1960, partly through the effects of war and partly through the advance of desertification. Yet determined groups in Chad itself had sustained the conflict, and at various times no fewer than five outside countries intervened in the war. French intervention, which lasted longest, arose mainly from motives of prestige. Africa offered France the opportunity to play the role of a great power, and to check the advance of Libyan power in Africa seemed a fine gesture. Libyan intervention itself lasted for fifteen years (and in the Aouzou Strip for twenty), inspired by motives part religious, to some degree economic, and perhaps above all the result of Gaddafi's own restless and volatile personality. The United States intervened briefly, in order to oppose Libya. Nigeria opposed the growth of Libyan influence for the sake of its own security, not least because the large Muslim population of northern Nigeria might attract Gaddafi's attention. Mobutu sent troops to demonstrate his own importance, and to please the French and Americans.

Chad thus provided, in small compass, a striking example of Africa's international problems. It was a desperately poor country, made up of two halves with almost nothing in common, prone to internal dissension and unable to sustain a stable government. Outside powers (African as well as western) intervened for their own purposes, helping to keep the conflict going without bringing it to a decisive conclusion. Even the end appeared to come through Gaddafi losing interest rather than anything more positive.

◆ The Horn of Africa: Somalia, Ethiopia, Eritrea

In East Africa, the so-called Horn of Africa protrudes in a great promontory between the Indian Ocean and the Red Sea. In 1960 the area was dominated by two principal states, Ethiopia and Somalia. The ancient Empire of Ethiopia, ruled by Haile Selassie, had retained its independence for almost the whole of the colonial period, and had a large population (estimated at 21 800 000 in 1961, rising to 55 140 000 in 1992). Somalia was a new country, formed in 1960 by a union between the former colonial territories of Italian and British Somaliland. (Djibouti, the former French Somaliland, became independent only in 1977.) It had a thinly scattered population of about 2 000 000, mostly nomadic; and a large number of Somalis lived in Kenya and Ethiopia, across frontiers which were often ill-defined on the ground. The new Somali government laid claim to neighbouring territories with Somali populations; and a commitment to recover these 'lost territories' was written into the constitution.

There was a minor conflict between Somalia and Kenya over the northern frontier districts of Kenya, beginning in 1963 and ending in 1967, when the two countries came to an agreement to accept the existing frontier. The Somali claims to the Ogaden province in Ethiopia produced a much more serious and lengthy conflict. Somali forces first moved into the Ogaden in 1964; but the Organization of African Unity scored one of its early successes, in which President Abboud of Sudan, acting on behalf of the OAU, arranged a cease-fire along the line of the existing frontier.

Somalia's aspirations then lay dormant until February 1977, when a guerrilla organization called the Front for the Liberation of Western Somalia began a rising in the Ogaden, openly supported by the Somalis. At that stage, Somalia was a *protégé* of the Soviet Union, which since 1974 had been training and arming the Somali army, and using Berbera as a naval station. Colonel Mengistu, the left-wing military ruler of Ethiopia (who had deposed Haile Selassie in 1974) appealed for help from the USA, but was turned down. Mengistu then turned to the Soviet Union, in the first instance for diplomatic assistance. The USSR and Cuba tried to mediate, without success. At the end of July 1977 Somali forces entered the Ogaden province and advanced towards the important city of Harer. The Soviet Union then abruptly changed sides, began to supply arms to Ethiopia, and flew Cuban troops into the country. By November some 18 000 Cubans had arrived, along with Soviet tanks, aircraft and missiles, to join the fight against the Somalis. Somalia retaliated by breaking off diplomatic relations with the Soviet Union and Cuba, and expelling its Soviet military advisers. On the ground, the Somalis were defeated, and withdrew from the Ogaden by March 1978.

The Soviet Union then established Ethiopia as a client state and the main base for its influence in East Africa. On 20 November 1978 the Soviet Union and Ethiopia concluded a Treaty of Friendship and Co-operation. Some 2000 Soviet advisers set to work in Ethiopia. Large quantities of Soviet military equipment (estimated at about eleven billion dollars-worth) was shipped into the country. Mengistu embarked on a Soviet-style programme of forced collectivization of agriculture.[12] The United States, on the other hand, remained largely inactive, until Reagan embarked on his policy of confrontation with the Soviets during the 1980s. In 1982 the Ethiopians moved outside their own territory by supporting a rebellion against the Somali government; the Somalis appealed for American help, which was provided at once. The revolt was defeated, and the Americans established a foothold in Somalia.

But at that stage the conflict between Somalia and Ethiopia faded away, and the American foothold proved useless and even dangerous, because Somalia itself disintegrated. During the 1980s the Somali National Movement fought a guerrilla war in the north of the country (the former British Somaliland). Another group, the Somali Patriotic Movement, began a revolt in the south in 1989. The Somali National Congress (formed in 1990) also opposed the existing (though by then largely powerless) Somali government headed by Siad Barre. The three groups briefly co-operated to drive out Siad Barre in January 1991, but speedily resumed fighting among themselves. The northern territory declared itself independent in May 1991. Somalia ceased to have any effective administration; warlords ran their own territories; and famine spread through the land, caused by a combination of warfare, the breakdown of order, and drought. By the end of 1991 deaths from starvation ran into hundreds of thousands. At that stage, the United Nations and the United States attempted to intervene, but with little success.

There was another long conflict in the Horn of Africa – the Eritrean war of secession against Ethiopia. Eritrea, formerly an Italian colony, was administered by the British after the Second World War, until it was incorporated into Ethiopia in 1952. In 1963, the Eritrean Liberation Front began a guerrilla campaign against the Ethiopians, which continued at low intensity for many years. In 1977, with Ethiopian forces distracted by the conflict against Somalia, the Eritrean separatists took control of most of the country except for Asmara, the capital. In 1978, with the help of Cuban troops and Soviet material, the Ethiopians restored control, but without finally defeating the Eritreans. Fighting continued through the 1980s, and the Eritreans were assisted by the outbreak of a separatist revolt in the Tigray Province of Ethiopia. The two guerrilla movements, Eritrean and Tigrean, gained increasing successes. The Soviets and Cubans pulled out as Gorbachev reduced his foreign commitments. Mengistu's government in Ethiopia fell in May 1991; and Eritrea declared its independence later that year. The new state was accepted as a member of the United Nations in 1993. Eritrea thus succeeded where Biafra had failed in 1967–69, and fought the only successful war of secession in Africa so far. The independence of Eritrea marked the only departure from the principle that, whatever else happened in Africa, boundaries remained intact. Even this apparent exception, however, actually restored the old colonial boundary between Eritrea and Ethiopia; so in practice it may be that the rule was not broken but reinforced. The boundary itself remained in dispute, and was the scene of heavy fighting between Ethiopians and Eritreans as recently as the year 2000.

The two long wars together (Somalia against Ethiopia, Ethiopia against the Eritreans) showed the difficulties which could arise when boundaries were arbitrary, or imposed the rule of one people upon another. The wars were fought with great tenacity (especially by the Eritreans), and at immense cost, in direct casualties and because warfare contributed to famine. Large-scale Soviet and Cuban intervention proved decisive against the Somalis, but not against the Eritreans. Of the two wars, one ended in the virtual disintegration of an African state (Somalia), and the other in the emergence of a new one (Eritrea).

◆ Angola: a war of succession

Portugal possessed two vast African colonies, Angola and Mozambique; and though the Portuguese were in many ways the weakest among the old imperial powers, they held on to their empire the longest. Only in 1974, with a revolution in Portugal and the fall of the authoritarian regime founded by Salazar, did a new Portuguese government decide to give up its African colonies. The new government agreed in January 1975 that Angola would become independent by November; and the specific date was set for 11 November 1975.

Angola duly became independent, but there was no clear successor to the Portuguese to govern the new state. Since 1961 nationalists had fought guerrilla campaigns against Portuguese rule, led by three separate organizations: the Popular Movement for the Liberation of Angola (MPLA); the National Front for the Liberation of Angola (FNLA); and the National Union for the Total Independence of Angola (UNITA). The MPLA was a left-wing group of Marxist inspiration, with its main strength in the centre of Angola, including the capital, Luanda. As well as its campaign in Angola, it aimed at liberating Namibia (Angola's southern neighbour) from South African control. In 1975, before the Portuguese departed, the MPLA asked the Soviet Union for direct military assistance. The Soviets declined, but brought in the Cubans to act on their behalf. The first Cuban troops arrived in July 1975, building up to about 3000 by September, with some Soviet advisers. The FNLA was strong in the far north of Angola, and was supported at various times by the USA, Zaire (with Mobutu acting, as in Chad, to demonstrate his own importance and to please the Americans), and the Chinese, who were as usual ready to help anyone who opposed the Soviets. UNITA drew its strength from the Ovimbudu people, which made up perhaps 40 per cent of the total population; it received assistance from the USA and (more important) South Africa, which in November 1975 sent about 2000 troops into southern Angola to assist UNITA and to protect the northern border of Namibia.

In November 1975, as the Portuguese left, two governments claimed the succession: the MPLA, and a combination between the FNLA and UNITA. The MPLA, supported by Cuban troops (reaching perhaps 20 000 by January 1976), controlled the capital, Luanda, and most of the country. It was recognized as the government of Angola by the Soviet Union and the countries of the east European bloc, and by about one-third of all African states. In February 1976 Portugal, the former colonial power, also recognized the MPLA government; and in the same month the Organization of African Unity accepted it as a member. The rival government, set up by UNITA and the FNLA, achieved no foreign recognition at all. The South Africans withdrew their forces in January 1976; and on 27 January the

United States Congress, fearing that Angola would become another Vietnam, ended all assistance to the FNLA and UNITA by the Clark Amendment to legislation under which foreign aid was provided. The furthest the United States would go in formal opposition to the MPLA government was to refuse recognition as long as Cuban troops remained in the country. The issue seemed decided, with the MPLA as the clear winner.

It was not. UNITA, with a solid base among the Ovimbudu people and a determined leader in Jonas Savimbi, continued to hold out and wage a guerrilla war against the new government. The South Africans sent troops back to Angola in 1978. When Reagan became President of the United States in 1981, the Americans resumed clandestine intervention in Angola. In 1985 Congress repealed the Clark Amendment, and they were free to assist UNITA openly.

By 1988, after many years of sporadic fighting, the situation in Angola had reached stalemate. The Angolan MPLA government, even with help from the Soviets and the Cubans (about 50 000 troops in the late 1980s), had failed to defeat UNITA. Equally UNITA, with South African and American assistance, had failed to defeat the government. The two sides were both exhausted. In one curious set of circumstances, the MPLA and the Cubans were willing to work with the Americans. In Cabinda, a province of Angola separated from the rest of the country by a strip of Zairean territory, the American oil company Chevron continued to work its oilfields. Neither the Angolan government nor the Soviets made any attempt to stop them; and on occasion Cuban troops actually guarded the American oilmen as they went about their work. It was an odd arrangement, but seems to have worked to everyone's satisfaction; and doubtless even a Marxist government was glad of the oil revenues.

By 1988 relations between the USA and USSR had been transformed out of recognition, and the Cold War was almost over. There was no point for either side to keep it going in the forests of Angola. Gorbachev was particularly anxious to end Soviet foreign entanglements, in Angola, Afghanistan and elsewhere. In December 1988 the external countries most directly involved in Angola reached an agreement in New York, in the corridors of the United Nations building. South Africa agreed to grant independence to Namibia, which ended its principal reason for intervening in Angola; and Cuba agreed to withdraw its forces from Angola by July 1991. Both were as good as their word: Namibia became independent in March 1990, and the Cuban troops left Angola by May 1991. At the same time, the opposing leaders in Angola (the President, Eduardo Dos Santos, and the UNITA leader, Jonas Savimbi) agreed on a cease-fire (22 June 1989), and even shook hands, though without conviction. The cease-fire failed, and fighting resumed. Portugal offered mediation (an initiative by the former colonial power which would have been unthinkable a few years earlier), and an agreement was reached at Estoril in May 1991, providing for an amalgamation of the military forces of the MPLA and UNITA into a single Angolan army, and for elections to be held under UN supervision in 1992. Elections were held in September 1992; UNITA lost, claimed that the elections had been unfair, and resumed its guerrilla warfare.

By that stage, foreign intervention in Angola had ceased. The Cubans had left; the Soviet Union had ceased to exist; the Americans had lost interest; the South African troops had long gone home and the regime which sent them was crumbling. But the war in Angola went on. A further attempt at a 'peace of national reconciliation' in 1994 failed. In 1999 government forces were still fighting UNITA in the forests of central Angola. The country had known no peace since 1975, and it appeared that warfare had become a way of life.

◆ Western Sahara: a war of succession and a wall of sand

In Western Sahara (formerly the Spanish colony of Rio de Oro, later Spanish Sahara) there developed a dispute of remarkable complexity and longevity, which has brought African states into conflict with one another, divided the Organization of African Unity, and ultimately brought about United Nations intervention. The territory concerned has an area of 102 680 square miles, with a population estimated in 1967 at 48 000 and in 1992 at 200 000, mostly nomadic. Its only economic asset lies in deposits of phosphates which were discovered in the north of the territory in 1963.[13]

When Morocco became independent in 1956, its government revived a claim dating back to the sixteenth century, to the whole of the Spanish Sahara, and parts of Algeria and Mauritania – all at the time under European control. In 1957 the Moroccans tried to invade part of the Spanish Sahara, but were driven back by Spanish forces. Spain continued to hold the territory, and in 1973 an independence movement was formed under the name Polisario (an abbreviation for the Popular Front for the Liberation of Saguia-el-Hamra and Rio de Oro.) In 1974 Morocco and Mauritania (a former French colony, now independent) agreed to partition the territory when the opportunity arose. Their chance came in 1975, when Spain decided to withdraw from its Saharan colony. On 14 November 1975 Spain, Morocco and Mauritania together signed an agreement providing for Spanish withdrawal, and the partition of the Western Sahara between Morocco and Mauritania. This was implemented in 1976, with Morocco taking the northern two-thirds of the country and Mauritania the remainder.

Polisario rejected this partition, and declared the independence of the Saharan Arab Democratic Republic, a move supported by Algeria, which opposed Moroccan claims in the area. The Democratic Republic was recognized quickly by ten African states (all left-wing in character) and by North

Korea – but no other communist states.[14] Mauritania, with help from the French air force, maintained its occupation of the southern territories for three years, but in 1979 dropped its claims and concluded a peace agreement with Polisario. Morocco, on the contrary, continued the war, and now laid claim to the whole of Western Sahara, including the southern sector formerly allotted to Mauritania. Between 1980 and 1985 the Moroccans (with some help from the Americans, who maintained a small base at Kenitra in Morocco) built a series of walls to protect the areas which they had occupied. One of these walls was 1600 miles long, from Zag in Morocco to Dakhla on the Atlantic coast, mostly built of sand and loose stones, but fortified with barbed wire, landmines and watch-towers, enclosing about half the territory of the Western Sahara, including the phosphate deposits, the frontier with Morocco, most of the coastline and nearly all the population. This fortification, variously called the Hassan Wall (after King Hassan of Morocco) and the Sahara Wall, marked a striking reversion to the frontier strategies of the Roman and Chinese empires.

Morocco thus established a military position which Polisario could not break. Diplomatically, on the other hand, Polisario secured some successes. They maintained a government in exile in Algeria, and in 1982 the Organization of African Unity accepted the membership of this government, under the name of Western Sahara. It took up its place in 1984, when Nigeria became the thirtieth member of the OAU to grant recognition. Morocco withdrew from the Organization of African Unity in protest, and in August 1984 sprang a surprise by signing a Treaty of Union with Libya. This was a somersault by Gadaffi, who had previously supported Polisario. The union, like others formed by Libya, had no substance, but it was of advantage to Morocco because it provided a link with a radical, left-wing and wealthy regime.

Both Morocco and Polisario advocated a referendum to decide the future of Western Sahara, but they could not agree on how such a vote should be conducted. Polisario insisted that the Moroccans must withdraw their forces before a referendum took place; Morocco refused. Polisario demanded that a referendum should be conducted by the Organization of African Unity; Morocco insisted that it should be organized by the United Nations. In 1988 direct negotiations between Algeria and Morocco achieved an agreement for a cease-fire, and a referendum to be conducted by the United Nations – a partial success for Morocco, and an illustration of the important role played by the Algerians. The cease-fire was frequently broken, and preparations for the referendum moved very slowly. Only in April 1991 was a United Nations Mission for the Referendum in Western Sahara (abbreviated obscurely to MINURSO) set up, to conduct a referendum choosing between independence and integration with Morocco. When the UN Mission arrived, it found great difficulty in compiling a list of voters in a largely nomadic population. As late as 1999 the Mission had registered

147 000 voters, and the two sides were presenting another 79 000 to be added to the list.[15]

What lies behind this lengthy dispute? Morocco has clung tenaciously to the occupied territory, and put a vast material and military effort into the Hassan Wall. Polisario has shown equal determination, winning diplomatic successes at the Organization for African Unity and claiming to deploy an army of 10 000 men. Casualties on both sides, over the sixteen years from 1975 to 1991, have been estimated at 10 000 dead. Yet the territory is barren and the population tiny. The only economic stake is the phosphate deposits, which Morocco has controlled throughout the dispute; but it is by no means certain that the profits from the phosphates (of which Morocco already held large resources) repaid the costs incurred in the conflict. There was some ideological element in the dispute; but it does not appear to have been decisive. Polisario was left-wing and 'progressive', as it signalled by calling itself a Popular Front and setting up a Democratic Republic; and its supporters were mostly left-wing African states. Morocco on the other hand was a conservative monarchy – though King Hassan did not shrink from a partnership with Gaddafi, a revolutionary militant. Strict Cold War divisions appear to have counted for little. By 1984 a total of 61 states had recognized Polisario as the government of an independent Western Sahara; but neither NATO nor Warsaw Pact members were among them. China too remained aloof.[16] For African states, there was an important issue of principle at stake, and the Organization of African Unity debated the respective merits of pre-colonial claims to territory (on which Morocco insisted) as against self-determination by the population. However, even when both sides in the Western Sahara dispute agreed on the principle of self-determination they were no nearer to a solution, because they could not agree on how that principle should be applied.

The most enduring, and probably the most important, element in the dispute has been a struggle of wills between Algeria and Morocco, in which both countries have committed their prestige. Morocco claimed the Western Sahara as soon as the country became independent in 1956; and the Moroccans later invested an immense effort in building the Hassan Wall. In these circumstances, Morocco could not afford to fail, for reasons of prestige rather than economics. Similarly, Algeria committed itself to support the Polisario, and remained reluctant to see its *protégé* lose.

One point is worth emphasizing. In this long and intractable dispute, there was almost no intervention from outside the continent. The whole extraordinary affair has been African in character.

◆ Southern Africa (I): Rhodesia/Zimbabwe

The British colony of Southern Rhodesia presented serious problems in the rush to independence by African colonies in the early 1960s. (See above, p.

234.) Southern Rhodesia included a substantial European minority in its population (221 000 out of a total of 3 800 000 in 1961) which controlled the internal politics of the country.[17] In the 1950s, the British government had tried to bring together Southern Rhodesia, Northern Rhodesia and Nyasaland in the East African Federation; but this broke down in 1963. When Northern Rhodesia and Nyasaland became independent in 1964, as Zambia and Malawi respectively, Southern Rhodesia was left alone as a colonial territory. The British government tried to negotiate a settlement leading rapidly to majority rule. The white population, long accustomed to internal self-rule, refused. On 11 November 1965 the Rhodesian Front government, led by Ian Smith, issued a Unilateral Declaration of Independence.

At that stage, a problem of decolonization became a complicated internal and international conflict. Inside Rhodesia, two nationalist guerrilla movements took shape: the Zimbabwe African People's Union (ZAPU), led by Joshua Nkomo, using bases in Zambia; and the Zimbabwe African National Union (ZANU), led by Robert Mugabe, using bases in Mozambique. Britain, as the colonial power, remained involved. The Labour government under Harold Wilson, which held office in 1965, opposed Rhodesian independence under white rule, because to accept it, even tacitly, would have offended Labour sentiment, broken up the Commonwealth, and created all kinds of difficulties in the Third World. But Wilson's government also ruled out the use of force in Rhodesia, as being difficult in military terms and virtually impossible politically, because a large part of British public opinion would not have stood for it. Britain therefore adopted the limited policy of imposing economic sanctions upon Rhodesia (cutting off supplies of oil and armaments, and restricting trade in other commodities); and at the same time appealed to the United Nations to take similar measures. In 1966 the British claimed that the Rhodesian situation presented a threat to peace (though so far there was virtually no sign of violence), and requested the United Nations Security Council to impose mandatory sanctions, i.e. measures binding upon all UN member states. After some delay, mandatory sanctions were introduced under Security Council Resolution No. 253, in May 1968. A British naval blockade was set up off the port of Beira, in what was then the Portuguese colony of Mozambique, to prevent oil supplies reaching Rhodesia by that route.

For some time, these measures had only limited effects. Militarily, the Rhodesian forces (including large numbers of black troops) held their own against the guerrillas. Support from South Africa and Mozambique meant that Rhodesian trade with the outside world continued, even with countries which in principle were imposing sanctions. Successive British governments (of both parties) offered steadily improving terms to Ian Smith for a negotiated end to independence. This situation changed radically in the mid-1970s. The first oil shock at the end of 1973 increased the price of oil fourfold, imposing a great strain on Rhodesian resources. In 1975 the Portuguese left Mozambique, which then became an open instead of a clandestine base for ZANU guerrillas. In 1976 the United States put pressure on South Africa to reduce its support for Rhodesia, in return for American concessions in other directions. And in October 1976 the two nationalist movements, ZANU and ZAPU, came together to form the Patriotic Front. (This proved only a temporary reconciliation, but was alarming to the Rhodesian government while it lasted.) Cumulatively, these events wore down the resistance of the white Rhodesians. The guerrilla war grew steadily more costly in resources and casualties. Sanctions created a sense of isolation which proved in many ways more damaging than their economic effects. The departure of the Portuguese and the slackening of South African support were decisive. In 1979 the British government was able to convene a conference at Lancaster House, in London, and arrive at an agreement on the end of UDI, a very short interim period of British rule, and then independence under universal suffrage, though with a proportion of parliamentary seats reserved for whites. Elections took place in February 1980, with Mugabe and ZANU victorious; and the new state of Zimbabwe became independent in April.

◆ Southern Africa (2): South Africa

South Africa presented an entirely different problem. The country was unique in Africa in a number of ways. Its population was unusually mixed, with a black majority, a large white minority, and substantial numbers of 'Cape coloured' (of mixed race) and Asians.

Year	Population of South Africa (millions)[18]				
	Total	Black	White	Coloured	Asian
1970	21.5	15.1	3.8	2.0	0.8
1992	38.4	29.1	5.0	3.3	1.0

The white population was made up principally of Afrikaners and British. The Afrikaners had been in the country for centuries. Their links with the Netherlands had long been severed, and unlike other Europeans in Africa, they had no other homeland to go to. They were sometimes described as 'the white tribe of Africa'. Following their own ideology, and to ensure their own political, cultural and economic supremacy, the South African Nationalist governments had set up the system of *apartheid*, imposing separation of the races and white domination. (See above, pp. 238–9.)

The *apartheid* regime provoked widespread and intense hostility; but at the same time South Africa had substantial assets. Its economy was the most varied and developed in Africa, and one of the richest. Mining yielded gold, diamonds and coal; manufacturing industry produced steel, cars and armaments; agriculture raised cereals, livestock, fruit and wine. In 1975 the gross domestic product of South Africa amounted to $35 290 000, with a GDP per head of $1353. (The only other African countries which could match this were the oil-producers, Libya and Gabon.) The figure for the average GDP per head was distinctly misleading, because most of the wealth was in white hands; but the wealth itself was real enough. Despite *apartheid*, many Africans from neighbouring countries were willing to work in South Africa and to gain at least something from its prosperity. Finally, South Africa maintained the strongest armed forces in Africa south of the Sahara – a well-disciplined and organized army of 50 000 men in 1978, together with an efficient fleet and a powerful air force.[19] South Africa could defeat any state in Africa in war (though the issue never in fact arose), and could intervene in other countries to great effect. The regime, like others, was vulnerable to occasional guerrilla attacks and sabotage, but was in no danger of being overthrown by its internal enemies, the African National Congress. The country could manufacture its own armaments, and even (with help from Israel and France) developed its own nuclear bomb, carrying out a successful test in 1979.

The South Africans needed all their strength, because their international situation was extremely difficult. The South African government and the system of *apartheid* became the targets of intense hostility from all Third World countries, the Soviet bloc, China, and most governments and a majority of public opinion in the Western world. This hostility was focussed in meetings of the Commonwealth (where the vast majority of members pressed Britain to impose severe sanctions upon South Africa); in conferences of non-aligned states, where South Africa was always high on the agenda; and above all at the United Nations. Article 27 of the United Nations Charter specifically excluded intervention in matters within the domestic jurisdiction of member states; but this provision was increasingly disregarded, on two main grounds: that the issue of human rights overrode all other considerations, and that the situation in South Africa was a threat to peace. Behind these arguments lay the deep emotions stirred by questions involving race and colonialism – which in South Africa were rolled into one.

In December 1960 the General Assembly of the United Nations adopted Resolution No. 1514, declaring that all peoples had the right to self-determination. In 1962 the Assembly set up a Special Committee on *Apartheid*, which in time produced a whole network of subsidiary organizations – for example, to deal with *apartheid* in sport. In 1963 the UN Security Council passed a resolution imposing a non-mandatory embargo on the export of arms to South Africa. In 1974 the General Assembly deprived South Africa of its seat in the Assembly, on a technicality arising from its credentials; a resolution in the Security Council to expel South Africa from the United

Nations altogether was accepted by a majority of members but vetoed by the USA, Britain and France. In 1977 the Security Council imposed a mandatory arms embargo on South Africa, specifically including assistance in the manufacture of nuclear weapons. For the vast majority of United Nations South Africa was a pariah state and the focus of intense hatred.

The practical effect of all these measures was for a long time very limited. South Africa was able to manufacture its own armaments, and was indeed stimulated to greater efforts by the arms embargoes. In December 1984 the Security Council had to admit the failure of its own policies by passing a resolution requesting UN members to stop *importing* arms from South Africa. The South Africans became skilled at evading sanctions, and were assisted by western governments and companies willing to invest in and trade with South Africa. British investment was of long standing, from Commonwealth days; the French government (under President Mitterrand) supplied two nuclear power plants; the Japanese would export anywhere on the right terms. American firms traded with South Africa, and American governments recognized the strategic importance of the Cape route for shipping, especially the super-tankers carrying oil from the Middle East to Europe and America.

International hostility to South Africa thus produced much sound and fury, but signified little in practical terms. The country's immediate situation was for a long time reasonably strong. South Africa was at first protected by buffer states to the north. Portugal maintained its colonies in Angola and Mozambique. Rhodesia, from 1965, was controlled by Ian Smith's white regime. South Africa itself occupied Namibia, the former German colony of South-West Africa, which South Africa had held as a mandate under the League of Nations and continued to administer despite United Nations opposition. This protective ring eventually crumbled. In 1975 the Portuguese withdrew from Angola and Mozambique. In 1980 Zimbabwe replaced Rhodesia. A new zone of 'front-line states' opposed to South Africa took shape – Zimbabwe, Botswana, Zambia, Malawi, Angola and Mozambique. In practice, these 'front-line states' were more hostile in word than in deed. Most of them were economically dependent on South Africa. In the 1970s, black workers were actually attracted to South Africa, in spite of *apartheid*, by the prospect of employment at higher wages than they could earn at home. South Africa at first made trouble in Angola and Mozambique by supporting rebels there; and later (in 1984) made agreements with the governments of both countries. By the Lusaka agreement with Angola (16 February 1984), South Africa undertook to withdraw its troops (about 1000 in number) from Angola. By the Nkomati accord with Mozambique, the two countries came to a form of non-aggression agreement, and undertook not to allow the use of their territories as bases for violence or terrorism. These agreements allowed South Africa to emerge from its isolation among neighbouring African states, and reduced the aid received by the African National Congress. At the same time, South Africa made common cause with other outcast states – notably Israel, which was also the target of hostility at the United Nations, where Zionism was condemned as racism.

In these circumstances, South Africa was able to survive, and even prosper. Yet gradually the strain of constant internal tension and external hostility took its toll. The effects of isolation were more psychological than economic, as was shown by the desperate attempts to attract touring sides to play rugby or cricket in South Africa. Eventually the regime came to an end more from a change of mind within rather than pressure from without – rather like the Soviet Union, and at the same time. It was the Afrikaner President F. W. de Klerk and the leader of the African National Congress, Nelson Mandela (imprisoned for 27 years by the South African government) who worked together in an astonishing combination to dismantle *apartheid* and establish majority rule in South Africa. These changes, which took place between 1989 and 1993, removed South Africa from the conspicuous place which it had held in world affairs for some thirty years.

The total number of conflicts in Africa, c.1960–1990, may be put at twenty-four in all (above, pp. 448–9). In a continent of some fifty states, mostly new and with little internal cohesion, this figure is perhaps not remarkable. African states maintained their existence (though they sometimes changed their names), and retained their boundaries intact; so that in some ways stability prevailed. Yet this impression was misleading. The combination of military coups, civil wars and wars between states in fact produced instability, and in some cases dissolution. The economic effects of war were disastrous, notably in Ethiopia and Somalia, where war and famine went hand in hand. This was part of a general economic decay which afflicted Africa.

◆ The African economy

In the 1950s it seemed likely that Africa as a whole could look forward to a favourable economic future, based on its mineral resources and a developing agriculture. These expectations were by no means fulfilled. For some thirty years Africa combined a high birth-rate with a diminishing death-rate, producing the highest rate of population growth in the world. The rate of population increase rose from an average of 2.7 per cent per year (1965–80) to 3 per cent per year (1980–90) – a rate which means, other things being equal, that the population doubles in 23 years.[20] Africa remained predominantly agrarian in its economy, and in many areas agricultural methods were not sufficiently developed to feed this rapidly growing population. In the 1960s there was a rough balance between production and consumption across the continent as a whole, but by 1990 there was a deficit estimated at about 20 per cent, and Africa became increasingly dependent on the receipt of food aid from outside.[21] At the same time, industry, with a few exceptions (mainly in South Africa) remained relatively undeveloped. Mining could produce heavy losses as well as high profits – which in any case did not always go to the country concerned.

African countries were for the most part primary producers, of crops or minerals – for example, coffee (Uganda), cocoa (Ivory Coast, Nigeria), copper (Zambia) and oil (Nigeria). Most of their products were subject to sometimes extreme fluctuations in market prices, which were largely out of the producers' control. The rising price of oil, which benefited a very few African countries, cost the vast majority dear. Nearly every African country south of the Sahara fell deeply into external debt, estimated at a total of $55 billion in 1980, and $155 billion in 1988.[22] Sub-Saharan Africa also became heavily dependent on foreign aid, to a far greater degree than any other part of the Third World. Sometimes this aid took a disguised form, as in most of the former French colonies, where the French government maintained convertibility between the French franc and the CFA (*Communauté Financière Africaine*) franc, which in a free market was worth only a fraction of the French currency. This involved a French subsidy to the countries concerned, but also a high degree of dependence by those countries on French influence.

The African countries made occasional efforts to diminish their economic dependence by co-operation with one another. The Organization of African Unity adopted as one of its aims the co-ordination of economic policy, but with very little practical effect. The West African Economic Community, formed in 1974 by five Francophone states in West Africa, sought to promote trade between its members, but with limited effect, attaining no more than 10 per cent of their total external trade. A similar organization, the Economic Community of West African States, made up of English-speaking countries, made very little progress in economic co-operation. The Southern African Development Community, set up by the 'front line' states against South Africa to redirect their trade towards one another rather than towards South Africa, was a complete failure – the magnetic pull of the South African economy was simply too strong to be resisted.

Failing co-operation with one another, African states looked outwards to the non-aligned movement and to the United Nations, working through the United Nations Conference on Trade and Development (UNCTAD), which was established as a permanent organ of the UN in 1964. A series of conferences between the developed countries and the rest of the world tried to secure the transfer of resources from the rich countries to the poor, or to create arrangements to stabilize commodity prices to the advantage of primary producers. These efforts, which met with little success, are part of a wider story.[23] African economic dependence increased rather than diminished.

◆ Outside powers and Africa

The role of outside powers in African affairs has to a large extent been considered elsewhere (see pp. 321–3 above), but it will be useful to recall the main concerns which caused these powers to be involved in the continent.

The Soviet Union had little history of involvement with Africa, but Soviet leaders in the 1960s and 1970s came to believe that the victory of socialism might well be achieved in the Third World, of which Africa formed a significant part. In North Africa, the Soviets developed relations with Algeria and Libya; and from 1974 onwards pursued active intervention in Somalia, Ethiopia, Angola and Mozambique, often using the Cubans as intermediaries. The result was an important growth of Soviet influence in Africa, and the acquisition of some useful naval stations, in almost nineteenth-century style. In a curious way, as we have seen, the Soviet interests and presence in Africa drew in the Chinese, to oppose the USSR and pursue the Sino-Soviet dispute even in this distant continent.

The United States was drawn into Africa by economic interests, especially mineral production and investments in South Africa, and by the strategic importance of the Cape route for shipping. The Americans also had commitments to Portugal as an ally in NATO and the provider of a valuable base in the Azores. NATO links did not formally extend to the Portuguese colonies in Africa, but they still caused the USA to look kindly on the Portuguese struggles there. Sections of American public opinion were also influenced by the intellectual and emotional concerns of Afro-Americans with the continent from which their ancestors had come as slaves. This aroused much sympathy with African liberation movements and the campaign against *apartheid*, at the same time as American governments tended to swing in the opposite direction, and support existing governments (even that of South Africa) if they were sufficiently anti-communist.

Among the former colonial powers, France and Britain retained close ties with Africa. For France, this was a matter of prestige, through the promotion of the French language and culture, by means of the association of *francophone* countries. Moreover, in Africa France could still behave as a great power, and French forces were ready to intervene all over Cental and West Africa – for example, as we have seen, in the long civil war in Chad. The British too had their own historical and cultural concerns, encouraged by the Commonwealth connection. Britain for long retained a strategic interest in the Simonstown base near the Cape of Good Hope. The long post-colonial entanglement in Rhodesia hung round the neck of successive British governments. If the French were on the whole keen to stay in Africa, the British eventually grew anxious to get out – at any rate from Rhodesia.

To some extent, African governments were able to use the involvement of external powers for their own ends, by playing the Soviets off against the Americans, or the Chinese against the Soviets. They could also use the worldwide reaction against *apartheid* to attract attention, and some assistance. At the beginning of the 1990s, with the almost simultaneous end of the Cold War and *apartheid,* these conditions came to and end. Africa ceased to be at the crossroads of world politics.

◆ Notes to Chapter 21

1. Chris Cook, *World Political Almanac* (London, 3rd edn, 1995), p. 22. See also above, pp. 241–2.
2. Chris Cook and David Killingray, *African Political Facts since 1945* (London, 1983), pp. 221–4; G.B.N. Ayittey, *Africa Betrayed* (New York, 1992), pp. 2–3.
3. Robert Chapuis and Thierry Brossard, *Les quatre mondes du Tiers Monde* (Paris, 1997), p. 187.
4. *Ibid.*, p. 191; Paul Johnson, *A History of the Modern World: From 1917 to the 1980s* (London, paperback edn, 1984), p. 518.
5. Ayittey, p. 116.
6. Obituaries of Mobutu in *Le Monde* and *The Times*, 9 September 1997.
7. *Le Monde*, 11–12 April 1999.
8. Cook, *Almanac*, pp. 291–6, 299–308.
9. *Oxford Economic Atlas* (Oxford, 4th. edn, 1974), p. 193.
10. Cook, *Almanac*, p. 304.
11. Cook and Killingray, *African Political Facts*, p. 204; *Oxford Economic Atlas*, p. 136. Life expectancy, 1963–64: 29 years men, 35 women; national income, 1963, US $192m; GNP per head, US$ 70; foreign trade, 1965, exports US$ 27m, imports US$ 31m.
12. Ayittey, p. 272.
13. Cook and Killingray, *African Political Facts*, p. 222.
14. The African states recognizing the Democratic Republic of Sahara were: Algeria, Angola, Benin, Bissau, Burundi, Madagascar, Mozambique, Rwanda, Seychelles and Togo.
15. *Le Monde*, 28 October 1999.
16. J.-B. Duroselle, *Histoire diplomatique de 1919 à nos jours* (Paris, 11th. edn, 1993), p. 870. They comprised 30 African states, 8 Asian, 16 Latin American, 6 Oceanian, and 1 European – Yugoslavia.
17. Cook and Killingray, *African Political Facts*, p. 220.
18. J. A. S. Grenville, *History of the World in the Twentieth Century* (London, 1998), p. 781.

19. Cook and Killingray, *African Political Facts*, pp. 188, 227.
20. Chapuis and Brossard, pp. 165–7.
21. *Ibid.*, pp. 168–9. By contrast, external food aid to Asia was reduced by one-half in the same period.
22. *Ibid.*, p. 161
23. For UNCTAD, see below, pp. 514–16.

CHAPTER

LATIN AMERICA IN THE WORLD, 1945–1990

Latin American contradictions – The United States and Latin America – Crises in Guatemala and Cuba, 1950–61 – The Alliance for Progress, 1961 – Cuba and Chile, 1961–73: 'No More Cubas' – Development and debt, c. 1965–85 – Latin American search for alternatives to the American connection – The United States takes a strong line, 1981–90 – The ambiguous case of Mexico

◆ Latin American contradictions

Latin America covers an enormous territory, stretching from the northern border of Mexico to the southern tip of South America. South America is itself a continent, with an area of 6 900 000 square miles and a population in 1992 of some 310 700 000, divided into only twelve sovereign states. (French Guiana is an Overseas Department of France.) Central America comprises seven small states, from the isthmus of Panama to the Mexican border. Mexico has a vast territory of nearly 760 000 square miles and a population of just over 86 000 000 in 1992. The Caribbean area includes a number of small island states, of which Cuba is the largest with some 11 000 000 people and Grenada the smallest with 87 000.

Almost all of these territories were colonized, intensively and over a long period, by Spain and Portugal. The principal languages are Portuguese in Brazil and Spanish everywhere else; though there are substantial indigenous populations, with their own languages, particularly in Mexico and some of the Andean countries. The predominant religion is Roman Catholicism. Latin America is thus an offshoot of European civilization which has been grafted deeply and firmly into the soil of a new continent.

Nearly all the Latin American states achieved independence from Spain and Portugal between 1816 and 1825. (Cuba, remaining a Spanish colony until 1898, was a notable exception.) After an early period of confusion and border conflicts between the new states, Latin America settled down into a remarkable territorial stability. (There were exceptions in the Chaco

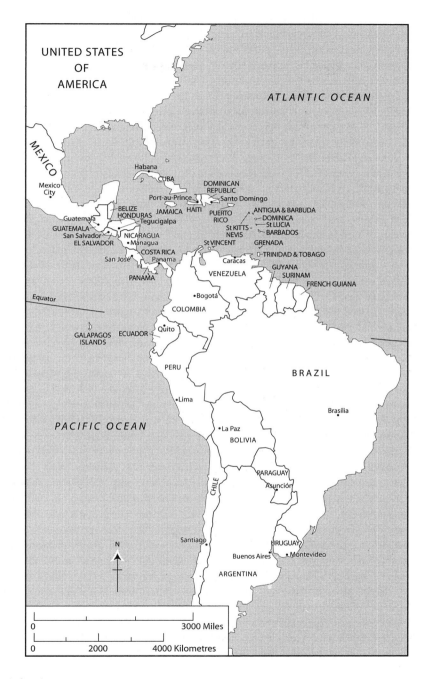

UNITED STATES
OF
AMERICA

ATLANTIC OCEAN

MEXICO

Habana
Mexico
City
CUBA

DOMINICAN
REPUBLIC
Port-au-Prince
Santo Domingo

BELIZE
HONDURAS
JAMAICA
HAITI
Guatemala
Tegucigalpa
PUERTO
RICO
ANTIGUA & BARBUDA
DOMINICA
GUATEMALA
San Salvador
NICARAGUA
St KITTS -
NEVIS
St LUCIA
BARBADOS
EL SALVADOR
Managua
St VINCENT
GRENADA
COSTA RICA
San José
Panama
TRINIDAD & TOBAGO
PANAMA
Caracas
GUYANA
VENEZUELA
SURINAM
FRENCH GUIANA

Equator

Bogotá

COLOMBIA

GALAPAGOS
ISLANDS
ECUADOR
Quito

PERU

B R A Z I L

Lima

Brasília

PACIFIC OCEAN

La Paz

BOLIVIA

PARAGUAY
Asunción

CHILE

N

Santiago

URUGUAY
Buenos Aires
Montevideo

ARGENTINA

0   3000 Miles
0   2000   4000 Kilometres

Latin America

conflict between Bolivia and Paraguay, and a border dispute between Peru and Colombia; but in so vast an area these served only to prove the rule.) As a result of this stability, most Latin American states are older than most European states in their present form – Germany and Italy, for example, are late nineteenth-century creations, and many states in eastern Europe date only from 1919, and in some cases much later.

Latin America is thus European in history and culture, but has been independent for so long and is separated by so great a distance from Europe that it has become a distinct entity. It also contrasts sharply with the other European transplants in North America, the United States and Canada, which have adopted very different forms of political tradition and economic development. This situation has produced some strange results. Latin American countries are highly conscious of their differences from the United States, and resentful of excessive American economic, political and cultural influence in their affairs. Yet they are also aware of their common European and Western heritage *with* the United States. In the great political and ideological divide of the Cold War, Latin American political, economic and cultural elites were usually on the same side as the Americans. The Catholic Church, despite the growth of left-wing 'liberation theology', was fundamentally opposed to communism. Culturally, Latin America had very little in common with official socialist realism. The dominant economic groups (banks, mining companies, the big producers of meat, sugar, fruit and coffee) were on the same side as their principal customers or investors. It is true that radical Latin American governments opposed the United States and sometimes looked to the Soviet Union for help; and that others chose to exaggerate their anti-communism in order to attract American assistance. But all in all there was a good deal of genuinely common ground between Latin America and the United States.

Large parts of Latin America are geographically remote from the rest of the world, separated by the vast expanses of the Atlantic and Pacific Oceans. But the nature of the Latin American economy has meant that the area has always been closely dependent on the outside world. In the long colonial period, the external trade of the various territories was almost exclusively directed towards Spain or Portugal. After independence a similar economic dependence prevailed, though in different circumstances and on different countries. Latin American countries became exporters of primary products – minerals, coffee, bananas, cereals, cattle. This meant heavy dependence on foreign investment for machinery (for example, sugar mills and refrigeration plant) and communications (especially railways); and on foreign customers to buy the products. In the late nineteenth century, Britain and Germany played a major role as both investors and customers; and gradually the United States came to join them. This situation was transformed, first by the great economic depression of the 1930s and then by the Second World War. The great depression brought a collapse in markets for primary products, and the drying up (sometimes the withdrawal) of foreign investments. The Second World War removed Germany from the Latin American economic scene, first by blockade and then by defeat. At the same time, British influence was drastically diminished, by the sale of investments during the war and economic exhaustion after it. After the Second World War, the external economic relations of Latin America were dominated almost exclusively by the United States.

In the latter half of the twentieth century Latin America underwent rapid population growth, though the *rate* of growth tended to diminish, falling to 1.9 per cent per annum in 1993, as against 2.8 per cent in 1965.[1] This population became increasingly urban in character. From about 1960 onwards, a majority of the Latin American population lived in towns, and by 1992 it was estimated that 73 per cent of the population was urban, with several cities of enormous size: for example, Mexico City, with a population of *c.*19 000 000, Rio de Janeiro with 10 000 000, and Buenos Aires with 11 000 000.[2] Many of these cities combined great wealth with extreme poverty, gleaming skyscrapers surrounded by shanty-towns, with consequent social and political strains. The rural population grew more slowly, but there was still pressure on the land and demand for agrarian reform. These internal problems, urban and rural, arose at the same time as the Cold War dominated international relations; and the United States and the Soviet Union, capitalism and socialism, offered very different solutions.

In international relations, Latin America offered the striking spectacle of an area almost free from war between states. From 1945 to the end of the century there were only three such wars, of small scale and brief duration. Two were between Central American states: Nicaragua and Honduras in 1957, and Honduras and El Salvador in 1965. The Nicaragua–Honduras war arose from a long-standing border dispute. In April 1957 Nicaraguan troops occupied the disputed territory; the Hondurans counter-attacked; and the Organization of American States (see below, p. 477) intervened to secure a cease-fire on 6 May, followed by a restoration of the status quo. The so-called 'Football War' between Honduras and El Salvador in 1969 broke out after a victory by El Salvador over Honduras in a World Cup soccer match (15 June 1969); but the underlying cause lay in Honduran resentment at Salvadoran immigration into the country. After the football match, there were riots in Honduras directed against Salvadoran immigrants; some were killed and many (perhaps 11 000) driven out of the country. On 14 July Salvadoran troops entered Honduras to assist their fellow-countrymen. The Organization of American States intervened and requested a cease-fire on 16 July; Honduras accepted but El Salvador did not. The OAS then declared El Salvador to be an aggressor, and agreed to impose sanctions (29 July). El Salvador then withdrew its forces, and completed its retreat by 5 August. The conflict was short, but deaths (military and in the rioting) were estimated at 2000.[3]

The third conflict was between Argentina and Great Britain in 1982, over the Falkland Islands (or under their Spanish name the Islas Malvinas). These islands had been claimed by both Spain and Britain in the eighteenth century. Argentina, on becoming independent, maintained the Spanish claim; while Britain annexed the islands in 1833. In April 1982 the then Argentinian military ruler, General Galtieri, sent an expedition to seize the islands, partly to make good this ancient claim and partly as a move in internal politics – the capture of the Malvinas was in fact greeted with delight in Argentina, and brought Galtieri an immense if short-lived popularity. The Argentinians invaded the islands on 2 April 1982, not expecting a military response. In fact the first British warships sailed for the South Atlantic almost at once, on 5 April; and thereafter the British fought a bold and resolute campaign. After brief but sometimes fierce fighting the last Argentinian troops surrendered at Port Stanley on 14 June. British losses were 255 killed and 777 wounded; Argentinian casualties are not known, but were certainly heavier.[4]

In this strange conflict, the territory at stake was of little material significance to either side. Each country fought essentially for pride and the vindication of right. Argentina lost, and General Galtieri's government was destroyed by the defeat. Britain won, and Margaret Thatcher's government reaped the political fruits of victory. There were wider consequences for Latin America as a whole. Latin American opinion was strongly on the side of Argentina. At a meeting of the Foreign Ministers of the Organization of American States, all but two Latin American governments voted for a resolution condemning the 'unjustified and disproportionate armed attack perpetrated by the United Kingdom'.[5] In terms of prestige, the Falklands/Malvinas War was a conflict between continents as well as between two countries; and Argentina's defeat, despite all its advantages of geography and numbers of men on the ground, was a humiliation for the whole South American continent.

Over a period of some fifty years, and in a territory the size of Latin America, these three small wars amount to very little, especially when compared to international conflicts in the rest of the world. But there was another side of the coin, in an endemic instability *within* states throughout Latin America – a constant succession of coups and revolutions, and abrupt swings from dictatorship to democracy and back again. The roots of this instability went back to the wars of independence, when the new states were established by force and became heavily dependent on their armies for internal security. In the nineteenth century, political change, particularly of a 'progressive' or radical nature was achieved by military means because no other methods would work. The pattern of armed coups and military rule remained predominant after 1945. The very absence of wars meant that armies had almost no occupation except politics. Instability reached a peak in Ecuador, which had no fewer than thirty presidents between 1952 and 1962. In Brazil, the giant of South America and a country with immense economic potential, a military coup overthrew the radical President Goulart in March 1964; he was replaced by a field marshal, who was himself followed by two generals in 1967 and 1969 respectively. There was a particularly dramatic case in Chile, where President Allende's left-wing Popular Unity government formed in 1970 was overthrown by a military coup led by General Pinochet in September 1973 – an act of unusual violence in a country noted for its stability and democratic traditions.[6] In the 1970s, military dictatorships took over in all the larger countries of Latin America except for Mexico, Venezuela and Colombia.

This endemic internal instability had important consequences in international affairs. The different sides in internal conflicts looked for support from outside, sometimes from neighbouring Latin American states (for example, in the 1950s Nicaragua provided shelter and assistance to rebels against the government of Costa Rica), but above all from the United States. The Brazilian army officers who deposed the President and seized power in 1964 knew in advance that they could rely on American help if they needed it, though in the event they did not. The American Central Intelligence Agency provided substantial support for Pinochet's coup in Chile in 1973. American intervention was not a one-way street – sometimes the Americans took the initiative, but on other occasions they were invited in. Either way, the internal politics of Latin American states became a battle-ground for international politics, and an arena of the Cold War.

Latin America was thus a bundle of contradictions. The area was geographically isolated from the rest of the world, but economically dependent upon it as a source of investment and a market for exports. Endemic economic weakness, arising from a high dependence on primary production, was combined with an immense economic potential – by 1993 Brazil's gross national product was the ninth largest in the world and Mexico's the eleventh.[7] Very close economic and political ties with the United States went alongside resentment against American influence and a constant search for an alternative to the American connection. Amid these various contradictions, our examination of Latin America in world affairs must start with relations with the United States.

◆ The United States and Latin America

The involvement of the United States in Latin America has deep historical roots. The Monroe Doctrine, embodied in President Monroe's message to Congress on 2 December 1823, declared that: 'The American continents, by the free and independent condition which they have assumed and maintain, are henceforth not to be considered as subjects for future colonization by any European powers.' This was a warning to the European powers against any future conquests on the American continent; but by implication it was more than that. Behind the emphatic negative, 'Thou shalt not intervene', lay a hidden positive, 'but we will'. In future, the United States was to be the predominant power in the hemisphere.[8] As the ninettenth century came to an end and the twentieth began, the Americans were able to make this implicit claim good. In 1898 the United States went to war with Spain, helped Cuba throw off Spanish rule, and ended by establishing a form of protectorate over the newly independent island. In 1903 President Theodore Roosevelt engineered a coup in the province of Panama, then part of Colombia; set up Panama as a new state; and then ensured that the Panama Canal ran through a Canal Zone under American control. In December 1904 Roosevelt announced what he called his Corollary to the Monroe Doctrine, asserting that brutal wrong-doing or dangerous impotence by a government in the western hemisphere might require intervention by a civilized nation – meaning the United States. Cuba and Panama showed that the United States regarded the Caribbean and Central America as its sphere of influence. The Roosevelt Corollary asserted a right of American intervention in the whole of Latin America.

The motives behind these claims were a mixed bag of strategy, economics, prestige and idealism. The Caribbean was so close to American territory as to affect the safety of the United States itself. In 1940, when Germany defeated France in Europe, the Americans would not allow the Germans to take control of the French Caribbean islands of Martinique and Guadeloupe; and United States warships were despatched to make sure that they did not do so – in very much the same way as the navy was to establish a blockade against the Soviets off Cuba in 1962. The Panama Canal linking the Atlantic and Pacific Oceans was vital to American strategic communications. Mexico and Venezuela provided secure sources for American oil imports. American commercial enterprises of various kinds (for example, mineral companies and fruit growers) promoted, or even imposed, favourable political conditions for their operations. In all these matters, American prestige came to be deeply involved, with consequences far outside the hemisphere – after all, if the Americans could not impose their will in their own backyard (as when they singularly failed to overthrow Castro in Cuba), they were bound to lose credibility elsewhere. Idealism added another element, and also a good deal of confusion. American governments often genuinely wanted to do good in Latin America – to promote human rights, encourage democracy and diminish poverty. Yet these aims were frequently in conflict with more material objectives, laying the Americans open to charges of hypocrisy. To combine the interests of a great power with the aspirations of liberal idealism was difficult, if not impossible; though the Americans were not deterred from trying.

American policy towards Latin America thus showed both the outstretched hand of friendship and the mailed fist of armed intervention. It also produced grandiose projects of aid and co-operation. After the Second World War, the United States set out to organize the American hemisphere under its own leadership, but using all the forms and language of co-operation. The Treaty of Rio de Janeiro (2 September 1947), between the United States and nineteen Latin American countries (all except Nicaragua and Ecuador) established an alliance for collective defence against armed attack, or to meet any situation which might endanger the peace of the continent – a provision directed against subversion by the Soviet Union, though no enemy was named.[9] This treaty was followed up by a Conference of American States (held at Bogota, 30 March–2 May 1948), which set up the Organization of American States (OAS). The Charter of the OAS laid down that the territory of a member state was inviolable, and was not to be the object of any military occupation or other measures of force, direct or indirect (Article 17); but at the same time it provided that an armed attack or other form of aggression, or 'any other fact or situation that might endanger the peace of America' would require measures to maintain peace and security (Article 25). The Charter thus closed the door against American intervention with one hand, and re-opened it with the other.[10] The OAS was also furnished with permanent Councils to deal with economic, social and cultural affairs; though little was done to add substance to this framework for inter-American co-operation – especially by comparison with the immense effort which the Americans put, at much the same time, into Marshall Aid for Western Europe.

The Americans supplemented these continent-wide agreements by working directly with various Latin American states. Between 1952 and 1954 the United States concluded military agreements with ten countries: Brazil, Chile, Colombia, Cuba, Dominica, Ecuador, Honduras, Nicaragua, Peru and Uruguay. The Americans agreed to supply military equipment and to train officers in the armed services; in return, the other governments agreed to supply strategic materials, and to restrict exports to the Soviet Union. The United States also tried to persuade all Latin American countries to cut off diplomatic relations with the Soviet Union; and eventually all did so, with the exception of Argentina, Mexico and Uruguay.

◆ Crises in Latin America: Guatemala and Cuba, 1950–62

The elaborate provisions of the Treaty of Rio and the Charter of the Organization of American States proved of only limited value in a number of crises which arose in the 1950s and early 1960s, notably in Guatemala and Cuba.

Guatemala is a Central American state, with a population in the 1950s of some 4 000 000 and of no great wealth. Its main trading partner was the United States, which in 1955 provided 65 per cent of its imports and purchased 74 per cent of its exports, mostly coffee and bananas.[11] In 1950 there was a presidential election, in which the two main candidates were army officers; one died in unexplained circumstances, leaving the field clear for his opponent, Jacobo Arbenz, who was elected. Arbenz was a radical politician, prepared to work with communists and accept them into his government; and his programme of reforms included an agrarian law (1952) providing for the expropriation of uncultivated land, much of it owned by the American United Fruit Company, at rates of compensation calculated according to the value declared by the owners for purposes of taxation – a shrewd device. The direct threat to American economic interests was not great. But Foster Dulles, the American Secretary of State, believed that Arbenz was under direct Soviet influence and thus presented a dangerous threat, on the principle of the thin end of the wedge. In March 1954, at a meeting of the Organization of American States at Caracas, Dulles secured the passage of a resolution declaring that the control of the political institutions of any American state by the international communist movement would be a threat to its own independence and to the peace of the hemisphere as a whole (Guatemala voted against the resolution, and Argentina and Mexico abstained.) In June 1954 a so-called Guatemalan 'army of liberation', directed and armed by the American Central Intelligence Agency, invaded Guatemala from the neighbouring states of Honduras and Nicaragua. Arbenz was overthrown, and the leader of the rebellion, Colonel Carlos Armas, became president.

The Americans thus partially covered their intervention in Guatemala by invoking the Organization of American States, but essentially this was a reversion to the common practice earlier in the century, when the United States had intervened by force in a number of Central American countries. But in the early 1950s the fear of communism had introduced a new element into the situation, which appears to have been decisive for American policy; as can be seen by comparing Guatemala with other Latin American crises of the same period. In Costa Rica, not far from Guatemala, José Figueres, who was president from 1952 to 1958, pursued a policy of social reform (including higher taxation and the abolition of the army). The United Fruit Company also operated in Costa Rica (as it did in Guatemala), and Figueres raised the tax on the company's profits from 10 to 30 per cent. But at the same time he outlawed the Communist Party, and was able to proceed with his radical measures without interference from the United States. In Bolivia in 1952 the National Revolutionary Movement took power, embarked on land reform and the nationalization of the tin mines, and appealed to the United States for help. President Eisenhower agreed. In 1953 the United States bought large quantities of Bolivian tin at high prices, and continued to provide economic aid over the next few years. It appears that the crucial distinction between these two cases and that of Guatemala was the American conviction that Arbenz was under direct Soviet influence, whereas the governments of Costa Rica and Bolivia were not.

In Guatemala the Americans used the iron hand; in Costa Rica and Bolivia the velvet glove. In Cuba for a long time they did almost nothing, while what were to prove decisive events took place. Cuba was the last Spanish colony in America to become independent (in 1898), and until the 1930s was virtually a protectorate of the United States. In the 1950s it was under the dictatorship of Fulgencio Batista, supported by the Americans. It was an island with a population of about 7 000 000 in the 1950s, and with an economy almost entirely reliant upon sugar (providing 80 per cent of its exports in 1955). In 1955 Fidel Castro, an aspiring revolutionary not yet 30 years old, landed in Cuba from Mexico, and began a guerrilla campaign against Batista in the hill country in the east of the island. His movement gradually gained ground, and by the autumn of 1958 Batista's army and regime were disintegrating. On 1 January 1959 Castro and his bearded troops entered Havana as victors. The United States had begun to withdraw its support from Batista as early as 1957, and ceased to supply him with arms in March 1958.

So far, there was nothing strikingly unusual about these events – neither dictators nor revolts were out of the ordinary in Latin America. It remained to be seen what sort of regime Castro would set up. He was certainly left-wing, an ardent Cuban nationalist, and strongly anti-American. He embarked at once on agrarian reform and the redistribution of land, state intervention in industry, and the imposition of rent control in the cities. It remains uncertain how far, at this stage, he was simply a revolutionary nationalist, and how far he was already a Marxist socialist who as yet preferred not to display his true colours.

At the time, and quite reasonably, the United States government did not know what to make of Castro. Eisenhower's Secretary of State, Christian Herter, met him in April 1959, and found him an enigma; Eisenhower himself (who had many other things to think about) was willing to wait and see. By March 1960 he had waited long enough, and concluded that Castro was fundamentally hostile to the United States. He approved a scheme to set up a Cuban rebel force in Guatemala to overthrow Castro's government, in the same way that Arbenz's government had been overthrown in Guatemala itself in 1954. In July 1960 the United States applied what was expected to be a decisive economic sanction by forbidding the importation of Cuban sugar. But already in February 1960 the Soviet Union had granted Cuba a credit of $100 million, and undertaken to purchase 4 million tons of sugar per year for four years (out of an average yearly crop of about 44 million tons). The Soviet government now offered to buy the whole Cuban sugar crop, which nullified the effect of the American embargo and transformed the political situation. The Cubans were now supported by a superpower.

President Kennedy, who took office in January 1961, allowed the CIA to go ahead with its plan for an attack on Cuba by the exiles based in Guatemala, in the hope of triggering off a revolt against Castro. A force of about 1500 Cubans, with ineffectual American support, landed at the Bay of Pigs on 17 April 1961, and was easily defeated within three days. As an example of how to use the mailed fist, it left much to be desired. (See above, pp. 136–40.)

The Americans turned next to a strange mixture of clandestine conspiracy and open diplomacy. Their conspiracies included a number of extraordinary schemes to overthrow or assassinate Castro, while diplomacy brought into play the machinery of continental co-operation. In February 1962 the Foreign Ministers of the Organization of American States met at Punta del Este and agreed to exclude Cuba from participation in the Organization's activities. The OAS also placed an embargo on all arms sales to Cuba, and recommended trade sanctions without making them mandatory. The United States also put pressure on all Latin American governments to break off diplomatic relations with Cuba, and by April 1962 fifteen states had done so. Eventually, in July 1964, the Organization of American states resolved that all members should break off diplomatic relations and cease all trade with Cuba. Only Mexico refused, maintaining diplomatic relations with Havana and keeping up an air service which was Cuba's only direct link with the rest of the continent.

◆ The Alliance for Progress, 1961

These widely different measures against Cuba were accompanied by an ambitious project designed to prevent any repetition of the Cuban revolution elsewhere by transforming the whole of Latin America. At the very same time that the Bay of Pigs adventure was being prepared, President Kennedy and his advisers devised a proposal for an 'Alliance for Progress', which was announced on 13 March 1961 and adopted at a meeting of the Inter-American Economic and Social Council (a section of the Organization of American States) at Punta del Este in the following August. It was the policy of the outstretched hand at its most generous. The Declaration which prefaced the so-called Charter of Punta del Este set out a formidable list of objectives. The Alliance for Progress would strengthen democratic institutions; accelerate economic and social development; carry out housing programmes and provide decent houses for all; encourage agrarian reform and redistribution of land; assure fair wages and working conditions; wipe out illiteracy; improve health and sanitation; reform tax laws so as to redistribute income to those in most need; and find a quick and lasting solution to the problem of excessive fluctuations in the prices of Latin American primary products. To help in achieving these aims, the United States undertook to provide the major part of the twenty billion dollars which would be required over the next ten years to supplement the efforts of the Latin American states themselves. Economic targets were set at an average growth rate of 2.5 per cent per year in gross national product per head, and a 50 per cent rise in living standards, over a period of ten years.[12]

It was an astonishing and utopian scheme, stopping barely short of promising a new heaven and a new earth. It is not surprising that it was not fully carried out. The United States met its financial commitments, providing $18 billion of government money and another $3 billion in private investment. But 90 per cent of these vast sums was used by the receiving states to service or repay their existing debts, which made a useful contribution to their finances but fell far short of the immense promises held out by the Declaration. The rate of economic growth achieved across the whole project was about 1.5 per cent per year, which was well worth while but short of the target set.[13] Again, the Alliance for Progress was intended to promote democratic regimes. The Americans made a start on this, and in 1961–63 they suspended economic aid, and/or broke off diplomatic relations, with various countries where military coups established dictatorships of various kinds – Argentina, Dominica, Ecuador, Guatemala, Honduras, Peru. But these measures were imposed only temporarily, for periods varying from three weeks to six months. In 1964, under Johnson's Presidency, the attempt to discriminate against dictatorial regimes was given up. In March 1964 the Americans approved in advance of a military coup in Brazil, and were prepared to help it if necessary. In several Latin American countries, the armed forces were strengthened by funds, equipment and training supplied under the Alliance for Progress. The United States also reverted to direct intervention by its own forces. In 1965 they despatched first 400 marines (28 April) and then a massive force of 24 000 troops to the Dominican Republic to forestall a possible left-wing take-over. They rapidly camouflaged this intervention by installing an Inter-American Peacekeeping Force, with troops from five Latin American countries as well as the USA, commanded by a Brazilian general; but the basis of the operation remained solidly American. The Alliance for Progress had not superseded more old-fashioned methods.

The vast and ambitious project of the Alliance for Progress achieved a short-lived public relations success, together with real but limited economic advances. But all in all it proved a failure, and the sheer scope of its ambitions raised hopes which were bound to be disappointed.

◆ Cuba, Chile and the United States, 1961–73: 'No More Cubas'

The Alliance for Progress certainly did not remove Castro, who survived, and developed Cuba into a fully-fledged communist state, with the

Communist Party as the sole political organization. In 1961 the Cuban government launched a Four-Year Plan for the economy, to diversify agriculture and reduce dependence on sugar, and to introduce new light industries. Collective farms were introduced, and industry and commerce were nationalized. In December 1961 Castro nailed his colours to the mast by publicly declaring his adherence to Marxism-Leninism. Rationing of food and other goods was introduced in 1962, as a demonstration of equality as much as to cope with the American economic blockade. Soviet economic assistance increased, though Soviet strategic support proved a mixed blessing. Khrushchev was prepared to defend Cuba against an American invasion, which after the Bay of Pigs was an unlikely contingency. He also, for his own purposes, installed Soviet missiles in Cuba, which led to the missile crisis of October 1962,[14] which ended in success for the United States in that the Soviets removed their missiles and most of their troops, but with a safeguard for Cuba in that Kennedy undertook not to invade the island, provided that Cuba took no aggressive action in the western hemisphere. In this crisis between the superpowers, Castro found himself relegated to the sidelines, not consulted by Khrushchev about the final decision to withdraw the missiles. But at the end of it Castro remained the unchallenged head of the Cuban state, with a Soviet brigade of some 2800 men still stationed in the island as a token of Moscow's support. (It was not withdrawn until 1991, in quite different circumstances.) Castro became an unmistakeable figure, known throughout the world by his shaggy beard, his camouflage uniform and his impressive presence – and his immensely long speeches. He was the man who had defied the United States in its own backyard, and lived to tell the tale.

Castro hoped (just as the Americans feared) that his revolution would be a model for others in Latin America. Régis Debray (at that time one of Castro's disciples, though he later reappeared in France as a devotee of General de Gaulle) produced a theory of 'foquismo', advocating the establishment of focal points round which revolutions would gather, as the Cuban revolution had gathered round Castro's stronghold in the mountains. The Cubans in fact tried to start revolutions in Venezuela and Guatemala, but without success. In 1966–67 Che Guevara himself, the embodiment of revolutionary zeal, tried to carry the spark of guerrilla warfare to the forests of Bolivia, only to be killed in a disastrous campaign. On the other hand, the Cubans achieved considerable influence by means of radio broadcasts, films and cultural propaganda; and Havana became a vigorous centre for left-wing conferences and literary awards. But such influence had its limits, and by the end of the 1960s the impetus was fading. There were no further revolutions. Cuba stood alone, in defiant isolation. In the 1970s, Castro was to turn his attention to Africa, with greater success.

In 1970 another socialist regime came to power in Latin America, not by revolution but by constitutional means, in Chile. Salvador Allende, who was variously described as a democratic socialist or a Marxist democrat, had previously stood three times as a candidate for the presidency and been defeated. In 1970 he stood for a fourth time, at the head of an alliance of socialists and communists under the name of Popular Unity. He gained 36.3 per cent of the popular vote, against 34.9 per cent for Alessandri, the conservative candidate; and under the constitution his election as President then required confirmation by the Chilean Congress. The Americans tried to prevent his election by bribing members of Congress; and they also supported an attempted military coup which failed as soon as it began. Allende was elected President, and embarked on a programme of national-izing the copper and coal mines, the steel industry, several banks, and many commercial firms, foreign as well as Chilean. In the countryside, the large estates were seized, and replaced either by state co-operatives or by small land-owners – a change which was imposed with great rapidity, causing a sharp drop in agricultural production. Opposition to these measures built up in Congress, and in 1972 Allende attempted to change the constitution by replacing Congress with an 'assembly of the people'. Congress (not unnaturally) rejected this proposal, and Allende did not press on with it.

The United States, having failed to prevent Allende coming to power, continued to oppose him. They blocked loans to Chile by the World Bank and the Inter-American Development Bank. Loans from private American banks also dried up. Chile looked elsewhere, to the Soviet Union, China and Western Europe; all promised loans in 1972, but were slow to produce them. By 1973 the Chilean economy was in confusion. The government could not cope with the enormous tasks which it had taken on by nation-alizing so many companies; price controls led to a widespread black market; inflation reached 150 per cent, and perhaps as much as 500 per cent at one stage.

In September 1973 a military coup, led by the Defence Minister, General Pinochet, and with assistance from the American Central Intelligence Agency, overthrew Allende's government. The coup itself was exceptionally violent by Latin American standards. Allende refused an offer of safe passage abroad, and stood his ground in the presidential palace, which was attacked by rocket-firing aircraft. Allende himself was killed, and the coup was followed by a long period of severe repression, with casualties variously estimated at 5000 to 15 000 dead. The American role in these events may not have been decisive, but it was prominent. The CIA provided large subsidies for opposition groups and newspapers, and worked closely with the the officers involved in the coup. In 1975 many of the details of American intervention were made public by the investigations of a US Senate Committee. There was no doubt that the United States had assisted in the violent overthrow of a constitutional left-wing government, for fear that Chile would become another Cuba.[15] There must be no more Cubas.

'No more Cubas' is widely seen as the key to United States policy in Latin America between 1961 and the mid-1970s, with much truth; though this apparently simple slogan covered widely different policies. Cuban-style revolutions might be forestalled, and the attraction of the Cuban example diminished, by spending vast quantities of American money on economic and social development in Latin America, and making sure that this largesse received wide publicity. This was the 'Alliance for Progress' approach. But there was another approach, based on early and forceful intervention. In Cuba, the United States had abandoned Batista without backing a suitable successor; they had allowed Castro to establish himself; and then they had bungled an attempt to overthrow him. In 1965, by contrast, the Americans despatched 24 000 troops to the Dominican Republic, which may indeed have been excessive, but was at least decisive. Again, the Pinochet coup in Chile in 1973 was violent and its consequences were bloody; but it was successful, and Pinochet remained president until 1990.

Were there likely to be more Cubas? Looking back, it seems unlikely. Chile might conceivably have followed the same road, but Allende was from a very different stable from Castro. He was a democratic politician, who fought four presidential elections and lost three of them, while Castro was a true revolutionary who was never elected to anything. At any rate, the Cuban example was not followed. How far this was due to American policy – the velvet glove or the iron hand – remains open to speculation.

◆ Development and debt c.1965–85

One reason why the Cuban example was less attractive than it might have been was that the period between the mid-1960s and mid-1970s was one of strong economic growth over most of Latin America. In the area as a whole, gross national product increased on average by about 6 per cent a year; and some of the large Latin American countries did much better, and for a longer period: between 1950 and 1980 the Brazilian GNP grew sixfold, that of Mexico fourfold, and that of Argentina threefold.[16] This growth came from a rapidly developing economy. Some sectors of agriculture flourished – coffee in Brazil, Colombia, Mexico and Central America; cattle-raising in Brazil and Argentina; and the less reputable crop of coca in Bolivia, Peru and Colombia, to feed the North American drugs habit. Mineral prices were generally good. Brazil diversified its economy by developing manufacturing industry; and several countries established rapidly growing tertiary sectors in banking, administration and office work of all kinds. This economic growth was patchy, but it was real, and sometimes dramatic.

At the end of 1973 came the oil shock, when the price of Middle East oil suddenly quadrupled inside a few weeks. (See Chapter 19 above.) The oil-importing countries of Latin America (which meant all except Venezuela, since even Mexico was no longer a net exporter) were faced with heavy expenditure to buy oil, and in most cases borrowed to meet it. At the same time a mass of petrodollars, accumulated by the Arab oil states and deposited in western banks, became available for loans. In consequence, the total external debt of Latin America more than tripled between 1975 and 1980, rising from 75 billion dollars to 229 billion. These debts were mostly incurred in US dollars at a time when the dollar was weak, and when interest rates were low. Between 1978 and 1980 these conditions changed radically. In 1978 the United States government began to tackle domestic inflation by putting up interest rates; by 1980 the dollar had strengthened, and interest rates reached 15 per cent or even in some circumstances as high as 20 per cent. This proved ruinous for the Latin American countries which had borrowed at the lower rates, and demonstrated again the heavy dependence of Latin America on the United States. In 1982 Mexico declared itself unable either to repay or to service its loans. The United States government intervened with a credit of 3.9 billion dollars to relieve the immediate crisis, and encouraged private banks to contribute another $5 billion.[17] In 1984 the International Monetary Fund, under the direction of the USA, came to the assistance of Brazil, though insisting in return on severe retrenchment by the Brazilian government.

This dependence, though apparently one-way, was in fact mutual. The possibility of a widespread default on debts, threatening the security of the commercial banks and thus the whole system of international credit, meant that the United States was every bit as dependent on the larger Latin American countries as the other way about. It was far from surprising that from 1984 onwards there was a general rescheduling (i.e. postponement) of debts, and in some cases a restructuring (i.e. reduction). Latin America and the United States were closely and apparently inescapably bound up with one another.

◆ Latin America in search of alternatives to the US connection

The ties binding Latin America and the United States together appeared inescapable, but the Houdini instinct was strong, and the Latin American countries tried hard to find an alternative. One obvious possibility was co-operation between the Latin American states themselves. As early as 1948 an Economic Commission for Latin America was set up as a Regional Agency under the United Nations, establishing its headquarters at Santiago in Chile, about as far from Washington as it was possible to go. Its first

Executive Secretary was Raul Prebisch, an Argentinian economist and banker who wanted to assist Latin American primary producers by securing agreements to protect them against extreme price fluctuations, and also to diversify the Latin American economies through the planned development of industry. These ideas, which were similar to the *dirigisme* practised in France under Jean Monnet's National Plan, were taken up by a number of states, notably Brazil, but Latin American governments lacked the continuity and authority to pursue them consistently. Moreover, the United States at first opposed Prebisch's plans, which ran counter to ideas of free enterprise and offered a threat to American economic predominance. Later, however, the thinking behind the Alliance for Progress drew on the Economic Commission's ideas; and stable commodity prices and diversification of the economy have remained the most likely solutions for Latin American economic problems.

Various groups of Latin American countries set up other organizations to promote economic co-operation, though usually with limited or short-lived effects. In 1958 a draft treaty for a Central American Common Market was signed by El Salvador, Guatemala, Honduras and Nicaragua, leading to a General Treaty of Central American Economic Integration concluded in December 1960, which Dominica and Panama joined later. In February 1960 the Treaty of Montevideo set up a Latin American Free Trade Association, including Argentina, Bolivia, Brazil, Chile, Colombia, Ecuador, Mexico, Paraguay, Peru, Uruguay and Venezuela; but this ambitious organization remained largely a paper exercise. On 26 May 1969 five countries (Bolivia, Chile, Colombia, Ecuador and Peru) concluded the Andean Pact, to reduce tariffs and improve economic co-operation (for example, by co-ordinating their manufacture of petro-chemical products, rather than competing against one another). Venezuela joined the Pact in 1973, and Mexico became an associate. Chile withdrew in 1976, in face of hostility against the Pinochet regime. A Caribbean Free Trade Association was formed in December 1968, and developed slowly into the Caribbean Common Market (CARICOM). Much later, in 1991, Argentina, Brazil, Paraguay and Uruguay signed the Treaty of Asuncion setting up the Common Market of the South (Mercosur), starting with a customs union and a common external tariff. The co-operation of Argentina and Brazil, the one Spanish-speaking and the other Portuguese, and often rivals in the past, was particularly important. The four members together comprised nearly half the total gross national product of the whole of Latin America. In contrast to earlier attempts at Latin American co-operation, which had usually been directed against the USA, the members of Mercosur sought to work with the Americans by attracting investment and selling in the American market.

All these organizations set out to work within the American hemisphere. Venezuela, on the other hand, set out to work with other oil-producers, notably in the Middle East. In 1960 Venezuela took a leading role in setting up the Organization of Petroleum Exporting Countries (OPEC), and remained the only permanent Latin American member of the Organization. Ecuador joined in 1973 but left in 1992; Mexico, though a substantial oil-producer, never joined at all.

A very different way of looking outside Latin America for an alternative to relations with the United States was to identify with the Third World. In the 1960s and 1970s there was a strong movement in this direction, following a theory of dependency which corresponded closely to Latin American conditions. In simple terms, 'dependency theory' argued that a 'core' of industrialized states was exploiting a 'periphery' of primary producing countries, by purchasing their commodities cheaply, accumulating profits for themselves rather than for the producing countries, and by working with elites in the producing countries at the expense of the population at large. These conditions in fact prevailed over large parts of Latin America. The United States was obviously a powerful industrialized state; Latin American countries relied heavily on primary products, whether crops or minerals, which mostly went to the USA; the profits of these transactions frequently went to American companies and their local partners, without reaching the mass of the population. This theory also corresponded with the obvious economic fact that primary producers were entirely dependent on the prices of their commodities on the world markets, which were liable to fluctuate wildly. There was a strong case for finding out whether the 'periphery' could negotiate better terms with the 'core', and whether fluctuations in commodity prices could somehow be controlled – which was what Raul Prebisch had argued in 1948.

A means of attaining these objectives appeared to be at hand in the Conferences of Non-Aligned States which began at Belgrade in 1961 with a meeting of 25 countries. At Belgrade, the only Latin American full member of the Conference was Cuba (masquerading under the banner of non-alignment, despite its links with the USSR); but Bolivia, Brazil and Ecuador were represented by observers. At the Algiers Conference in September 1973 there were three Latin American members (Chile, Cuba and Peru), and several Latin American observers. This Conference produced an ambitious proposal for a New International Economic Order, in which the primary producers would come together to negotiate with the industrialized states – which in principle was what the Latin Americans wanted.

This aspiration for a new economic order linked up with efforts being made separately by the United Nations Conference on Trade and Development (UNCTAD), which held its first meeting at Geneva, 23 March–15 June 1964, attended by 120 governments, of which 77 were from developing countries. The first UNCTAD failed to find agreement between different proposals for fixing prices for primary products; and the second, at New Delhi in February–March 1968, only produced hopeful recommendations for new tariff arrangements to favour developing countries. Latin American countries took part in both these conferences, and the third UNCTAD was actually held in Latin America, at Santiago (Chile), in April–May 1972; but it made no further progress. However, the 'Group of 77' which had come together at the first UNCTAD continued to be active in the General Assembly of the United Nations, and in 1974 made another demand for a New International Economic Order, in which the industrialized states would transfer wealth to the primary producers and other poor countries.[18]

In 1977 a new approach to the same problem was attempted at a conference convened in Paris by the President of France, Giscard d'Estaing, to discuss what was now called the 'North–South' division between industrialized and developing countries. Five Latin American countries (Argentina, Brazil, Mexico, Peru and Venezuela) were among those representing the 'South'. This conference eventually led to the setting up of the Brandt Commission, which published its report, *North–South: A Programme for Survival* in 1980, advocating a restructuring of world trade and the provision of subsidies by the industrialized countries to aid the others.[19] In the Brandt Report, the whole of Latin America was classified as part of the under-developed 'South'.

For Latin American countries, these forays into Non-Aligned Conferences, UNCTAD and North-South relations brought new contacts and some welcome publicity for their problems; but they produced almost nothing by way of substantial results. New commodity agreements were not forthcoming, and the terms of trade for primary producers remained subject to abrupt fluctuations. Taking part in the politics of the Third World came to have a diminishing appeal for several Latin American countries. Large parts of Latin America were moving rapidly away from Third World conditions, as defined by demographic and economic criteria. The Southern Cone (Argentina, Chile, Uruguay and Paraguay) by 1990 showed statistics for infant mortality, life expectancy, GNP per head, and numbers of motor vehicles in proportion to the population that were close to those of prosperous industrial states. Brazil and Mexico stood at ninth and eleventh respectively in the table of states according to their Gross National Product. By 1993, Latin America as a whole had an average GNP per head of $3100 – well above that in Russia, supposedly one of the 'core' industrialized states.[20] Averages of this kind concealed wide differences between countries and between individuals within countries; but no general identification between Latin America and the Third World could be made. Carlos Menem, who became President of Argentina in 1989, was reported as saying; 'I don't want to belong to the Third World. Argentina has to be in the First World, which is the only world that should exist.'[21] He probably spoke for many.

The Latin American search for an alternative to the close connection with the United States was lengthy, and covered much ground; but none of its ventures led very far. It appeared that Latin America and the United States were stuck with one another, and would have to make the best of it.

◆ United States policy under Carter and Reagan, 1976–88

Under Carter's presidency (1977–81), the United States changed its policy towards Latin America yet again. Carter's watchword was respect for human rights, and he set out to make American assistance (economic and military) to Latin American countries dependent on their human rights record. Latin Americans, for their part, saw this as intervention in their internal affairs. Argentina, Brazil, El Salvador and Guatemala rejected American military aid under these new conditions, and went to western Europe (particularly France) to buy military equipment. (For example, Argentina bought French Exocet missiles, which were used against British warships during the Falklands War of 1982.) In Nicaragua, Carter withdrew first military and then economic assistance from Anastasio Somoza's dictatorship, leading to Somoza's defeat by the Sandinista guerrillas in July 1989; whether the Sandinistas showed any more respect for human rights was open to grave doubt. Carter also took the remarkable step of preparing for American withdrawal from the Panama Canal Zone, concluding a treaty (ratified by the US Senate in 1978) providing for the end of the American-controlled Canal Zone by the year 2000. This foreshadowed the end of an arrangement which dated from 1903, and which had always previously been regarded as vital for American communications.

The result was an awkward mixture of ostentatious respect for Latin American sovereignty (as in the case of Panama) alongside officious attempts to impose American views of human rights on reluctant Latin American governments; so that no one knew quite where they stood. Reagan brought this uncertainty to an end. He made a gesture in the direction of economic aid by introducing the Caribbean Basin Initiative in February 1982, but this came to little. (See above, p. 345.) But for the most part he reverted to a policy of the mailed fist, by means of subversion and military force. Three examples stand out, all in Central America and the Caribbean.[22]

(1) In Nicaragua, the Soviet Union supplied arms to the Sandinista government set up in 1979; and the United States set up the Contra guerrilla movement to lead a revolt. American support for the Contras was maintained persistently throughout the 1980s, using all kinds of clandestine means, and from 1984 to 1986 in defiance of a ban imposed by Congress. The struggle in Nicaragua continued, without decisive success for either side, until the Cold War itself faded away. In 1989 the Americans and

Soviets withdrew their support from the Contras and Sandinistas respectively. The Sandinistas agreed to hold elections, and the Americans undertook to accept a Sandinista government provided that the elections were fairly conducted. The elections took place in February 1990; the opposition won; and both the Sandinistas and the Soviet Union accepted the verdict. Reagan had made Nicaragua a test case for American determination, and eventually (though after Reagan had ceased to be President) the United States achieved its objective. (2) In El Salvador the United States intervened to support the existing government against a left-wing revolt supported by Cuba and the Soviet Union. (3) In the most spectacular of his interventions, Reagan used overwhelming force to invade the tiny island of Grenada in October 1983, claiming that it was being turned into a Cuban and Soviet base for use against the United States. A vast naval force arrived off the island, and marines splashed ashore from their landing-craft. After the invasion, the USA provided $48.4 million in aid to Grenada in 1984, and the CIA is reported to have spent $675 000 on covert political action to ensure a pro-American result in the elections held that year.[23] All in all, the American intervention in Grenada used a sledgehammer to crack a nut, but the message sent by the expedition was designed for others besides the Grenadans. In all these three cases, Reagan chose to invest a minor conflict or problem with crucial significance, in the Cold War and in American policy towards Central America and the Caribbean.

This policy did not end with Reagan's presidency, nor with the end of the Cold War. In December 1989 the United States invaded Panama, in circumstances which had nothing to do with the Cold War, nor even with the normal working of international relations. In 1988 the dictator of Panama, General Manuel Noriega, had been indicted for drug trafficking by an American grand jury – itself an unusual step to take against the head of a foreign state. In an attempt to remove Noriega, the American government froze all Panamanian assets in the United States, and cut off the supply of banknotes to Panamanian banks, which used the US dollar as the national currency. Noriega stood firm, and in 1989 he won a presidential election – though in dubious circumstances. On 15 December 1989 Noriega announced that a state of war existed between Panama and the United States; and on the 16th an American marine officer (off duty from the Canal Zone) was killed at a road-block. An American invasion (using the grandiose code-name of Operation JUST CAUSE) began on 20 December. Panamanian opposition ceased by the 31st, after fighting in which 26 Americans were killed and 323 wounded; the Panamanians lost 314 soldiers killed, plus an unknown number of civilians – substantial figures for only ten days of fighting.[24] Noriega took refuge in the Vatican legation, where the Americans sought to unhinge him by playing loud rock music outside the building. He surrendered on 3 January 1990; was taken for trial in Florida on drugs charges; convicted in 1992, and sentenced to 40 years in prison.

The episode was partly Hollywood in character, and partly sheer farce; and yet its implications were serious. The Americans seem simply to have assumed that Panama was not an organized sovereign state; which may have been true, yet they also continued to observe the 1977 treaty on the Canal Zone, which assumed that Panama *was* a responsible state. To all appearances, the Americans had reverted to the practice of Theodore Roosevelt, carrying a big stick and treating Central America as their own backyard. Yet things were not quite what they used to be. The Organization of American States, which in earlier days could be relied on to support the USA, condemned the invasion of Panama. The General Assembly of the United Nations, with its majority of small Third-World countries which sympathized with Panama, did the same. These votes did nothing to change the situation on the ground in Panama, but they were serious blows to America's prestige and reputation.

◆ The ambiguous case of Mexico

Relations between Mexico and the United States offer a portrait of ambiguity which reveals something of the whole association between Latin America and the USA. Mexico is one of the largest of Latin American countries, with a population of some 86 000 000 in 1990. In 1900 its population had been only one-fifth of that of the United States; in 1990 it was almost one-third, and still rising.[25] The Mexican-American frontier is over 1200 miles long, from the Pacific to the Caribbean. The past of the two countries is full of conflict and dispute. In the Mexican War of 1846–48 the United States gained Texas, New Mexico and Upper California. In 1916 General Pershing led an American expeditionary force into Mexico before commanding another in France in 1917. Mexican domestic politics were frequently radical and revolutionary, leading to attacks on American businesses and residents. In 1938 President Cardenas of Mexico expropriated foreign (including American) oil companies, setting up a state oil company, Petroleos Mexicanos (PEMEX), amid an outburst of nationalist sentiment. In the 1960s Mexico was the only Latin American country to resist American pressure to break off relations with Cuba, and to keep an air service open to Havana.

Yet among all this hostility the Mexicans never broke completely with the United States, and they were sometimes willing to co-operate with the Americans. During the Second World War, Mexico declared war on Germany and Japan in 1942; sent a squadron of aircraft to serve in the Pacific; and by agreement with the United States government sent about 300 000 workers to replace Americans called up into the army. Mexico, though a substantial oil-producer, did not join the Organization of Petroleum Exporting Countries, which used the oil weapon against the

United States in 1973. In the 1970s the USA was the principal customer for Mexican oil; accounted for about two-thirds of all Mexican trade; and provided 90 per cent of its tourist revenues.[26] Whatever the state of Mexican sentiments about the Americans, Mexican prosperity was closely bound up with the United States.

In sum, Mexico nurses a deep-seated hostility to the United States, as a result of both history and geography; but Mexican dependence on the United States is inescapable. In the 1990s Mexican-American relations came to be dominated by two issues, one looming as a threat, the other offering a transformation for the better. The danger lay in the threat to the United States from Mexican immigration, much of it illegal. Each year, tens of thousands of Mexicans crossed the long frontier, which neither country controlled effectively – Mexico because it had no wish to do so, the USA probably because it could not, even if it wished. In 1990 the US Census Bureau put the Hispanic population of the country, mostly Mexican in origin, at 22 300 000. Hispanics formed about a quarter of the total population in California and Texas, two of the largest states of the union, and both gained from Mexico in the nineteenth century.[27] A sort of prolonged replay of the war of 1846–48 seemed to be under way, with unpredictable results. On the other hand, there has been a remarkable move towards closer relations between Mexico and the USA than have ever existed in the past. In 1990 President Carlos Salinas of Mexico announced that he intended to seek a free trade agreement with the United States, and received a favourable response from the Americans. In August 1992 Mexico, the United States and Canada signed the North American Free Trade Agreement (NAFTA), to come into operation on 1 January 1994, with the purpose of removing all tariffs and other trade barriers between the three countries over a period of twenty years. If pursued to its conclusion, this agreement will bind the developing economy of Mexico to the advanced economy of the United States, and encourage the movement of goods, capital and people in a way never previously attempted. Whether this can end the ambiguity of Mexican-American relations remains to be seen, but it seems highly unlikely.

At the end of the 1980s Latin America and the United States were in a state of uneasy balance. The Latin American debt crisis of the early 1980s had shown their dependence on one another. Latin American countries had been forced to ask the United States to bale them out of their difficulties; and the Americans had no choice but to do so, and to provide new loans, even if they privately thought they were throwing good money after bad. By 1988 total Latin American debt had risen to about $400 billion, including $113bn for Brazil, $108 billion for Mexico and $54 billion for Argentina, mostly owed to the United States.[28] The Americans had reasserted themselves in brusque fashion and sometimes with overwhelming force in

Central America and the Caribbean; and yet they remained uncertain whether they wanted to be feared or loved.

The Latin American countries for their part had looked in vain for escape from their over-close relations with the United States. Revolution no longer seemed a way out. There had been no more Cubas even when the Cuban alternative had seemed most attractive; by 1990 the communist camp in eastern Europe had dissolved and even the Soviet Union was looking shaky. The Latin Americans had tried the non-aligned movement, UNCTAD and the North–South negotiations without much success. Co-operation within Latin America was being revived in the Common Market of the South, but had yet to produce solid results. The United States still dominated the northern horizon, feared, disliked, and sometimes even despised; but also envied and admired, and offering an irresistible magnet for migrants. Latin America and the United States could not live apart, but the question of how they were to live together had still not been resolved.

◆ Notes to Chapter 22

1. Tulio Halperin Donghi, *The Contemporary History of Latin America* (Durham, N. Carolina, 13th edn, 1996), pp. 403–4; Robert Chapuis and Thierry Brossard, *Les quatre mondes du Tiers Monde* (Paris, 2nd edn, 1997), pp. 81–2.
2. *Ibid.*, pp. 83–4.
3. Chris Cook, *World Political Almanac* (London, 3rd edn, 1995), p. 324.
4. *Ibid,.* p. 325.
5. *Keesing's Contemporary Archives*, 1982, p. 31715. The resolution was carried by 17 votes to nil. Chile, Colombia, Trinidad and the United States abstained.
6. For Chile, see below, pp. 483–4.
7. Chapuis and Brossard, p. 91.
8. Monroe Doctrine quoted in Samuel Eliot Morison and Henry Steele Commager, *The Growth of the American Republic* (London, 4th edn, 1954), Vol. I, p. 462. For the comment on 'Thou shalt not', R.W. Van Alstyne, *The Rising American Empire* (London, 1960), pp. 98–9.
9. Abridged text of the Treaty of Rio, J. A. S. Grenville, *The Major International Treaties, 1914–1973* (London, 1974), pp. 325–8.
10. Abridged text of the Charter of the OAS, *ibid.*, pp. 328–30.
11. *Oxford Economic Atlas of the World* (London, 4th edn, 1972), p. 160.
12. Text of Declaration to the Peoples of America and abridged text of the Charter of Punta del Este, Grenville, *Treaties,* pp. 346–50.
13. J. P. T. Dunbabin, *The Post-Imperial Age: The Great Powers and the Wider World* (London, 1984), pp. 397–8.
14. For the Cuba missile crisis, see above, pp. 142–7.

15. For differing accounts of Allende's regime and the Pinochet coup, see Donghi, *Latin America*, pp. 344–51, and Gaddis Smith, *The Last Years of the Monroe Doctrine, 1945–1993* (New York, 1994), pp. 132–7.
16. Chapuis and Brossard, p. 75.
17. Dunbabin, *Post-Imperial Age*, pp. 426–7.
18. For UNCTAD and the proposals for a New International Economic Order, see below, pp. 514–16.
19. For the Brandt Commission, see below, pp. 515–16.
20. Figures in Chapuis and Brossard, pp. 77, 90–1.
21. Quoted in Thomas E. Skidmore and Peter H. Smith, *Modern Latin America* (Oxford, 4th edn, 1997), p. 113.
22. See above, pp. 345–8, for Reagan's interventions in Latin America.
23. Thomas Carothers, *In the Name of Democracy: US Policy toward Central America in the Reagan Years* (Oxford, 1991), pp. 112–13.
24. Cook, *Almanac*, p. 326.
25. Donghi, *Latin America*, pp. 403–4.
26. Fiona Venn, *Oil Diplomacy in the Twentieth Century* (London, 1986), pp.167–8.
27. Skidmore and Smith, p. 397.
28. *Ibid.*, p. 388.

PART III

THE CONDUCT AND MOTIVATION OF INTERNATIONAL AFFAIRS

So far this book has described the principal events in international affairs between 1945 and 1991, and analysed their immediate causes and consequences. Sometimes the resulting impression may be one of a merely random sequence of happenings. John Masefield once wrote a novel which he called *O.D.T.A.A.*, standing for *One Damned Thing After Another*; and a historian of international affairs may well be tempted to borrow his title. Yet when we look back over the whole period, and penetrate beneath the surface of events, we can discern some patterns among them, and observe underlying forces which influenced their course. It is time to take stock, and ask some deeper questions about how and why events happened as they did.

The next two chapters therefore ask the questions *How* and *Why*. *How* were international relations conducted? And *why* did states and people act as they did in their relations with one another?

CHAPTER 23

THE CONDUCT OF INTERNATIONAL AFFAIRS

**War: the use and threat of force – The new diplomacy: the United
Nations and other international organizations – Publicity and the
mass media**

Traditionally, relations between states have been personified in the symbolic
figures of the soldier and the ambassador, representing war and diplomacy.[1]
These figures still play their parts, though they have changed their appearance and their methods. In the world since 1945, the soldier may not always
wear uniform, and may fight in the jungle or the city streets rather than on
the open battlefield. The diplomat may now represent an international
organization – the United Nations, the International Monetary Fund, or the
European Union rather than a single state. But they are still there, and they
are accompanied by other figures, more prominent than they were in the
past – the journalist, the publicist and the propagandist, who bring their
influence to bear upon warfare and can sometimes conduct diplomacy more
rapidly and effectively than any ambassador.

When we ask how international affairs are conducted, three answers
stand out: by force and the threat of force; by international organizations
in increasing number and complexity; and by news, propaganda and
publicity. Let us examine these three elements.

◆ War: the use and threat of force

War is by definition *the collective use of force,* not simply a fight or a duel
between individuals. It starts at one end of the spectrum with the organized
armed forces of whole states, backed by their populations in the effort of
near-total war, and finishes at the other in an uncertain zone occupied by
guerrilla forces numbering no more than a few thousands, or even hundreds.
In the past, war usually had a juridical character: governments formally
declared war on one another; there were laws of war (for example, on the

treatment of prisoners); wars ended in peace conferences and treaties. In the half-century or so since 1945 such formalities have been abandoned, but the use of force itself has retained its place in international affairs.

The General Assembly of the United Nations was rash enough to designate 1986 as the 'International Year of Peace'. At the end of that year, the Stockholm International Peace Research Institute reviewed the situation, and found that no fewer than 41 countries were engaged in armed conflicts of one kind or another, totalling 36 conflicts in all and involving five-and-a-half million combatants.[2] These figures were not out of the ordinary. One authoritative work of reference has counted 80 wars between 1945 and 1989; another put the total at about 100 for the same period.[3] Casualties, on the unreliable estimates available, may amount to about 18 000 000 dead, many of them non-combatants.[4] It is the record of a half-century of conflict.

Why were these wars fought, and how did war influence the conduct of international affairs? It has become almost a commonplace in some circles to say that war is futile and settles nothing. In reality, and to a striking extent, war has been used in the classical sense defined by Clausewitz, the nineteenth-century philosopher of war, as the continuation of policy by other means. Wars have been fought to achieve political aims – with mixed results, but that has been their purpose. In 1950 North Korea sought to achieve the political aim of unifying Korea by war, by invading the South. It failed. From 1954 to 1962 the Algerian National Liberation Front could only achieve independence from France by war. It succeeded. In both Korea and Vietnam, the United States tried to contain communism by war. In Korea they succeeded, eventually holding a line very close to that on which the war began. In Vietnam they failed, giving up the struggle and seeing South Vietnam fall to their enemies. Thus the results differed, but in each case force was being used to achieve a political aim. The repeated wars between Israel and the Arab states furnish another revealing example. Israel is the child of war. The state came into existence in 1948 by victory in battle against the surrounding Arab states, and has since lived in an almost continuous state of siege, dependent on force and the threat of force for its continued existence. From time to time the Israelis have also used force to extend or safeguard their territory – to occupy the Sinai peninsula, to annex Jerusalem, to secure a more defensible frontier along the River Jordan, or to set up a buffer zone in south Lebanon. The Israelis have thus repeatedly used force to achieve political aims, including the most vital aim of all, the very existence of the state. Yet they have only partially achieved the ultimate political aim of a settled security against their Arab neighbours, and they are still engaged in a constant low-intensity war against the Palestinians. The *intifada* (Arabic: 'shaking off'), in which the simplest weapon is stone-throwing (the method once used by David against Goliath), has had a wearing-down effect on Israeli morale which may yet

prove of decisive importance. Other examples of the use of force for political ends may be found among the frequent civil wars of the period. For
example, Biafra fought to achieve separation from Nigeria (1967–70) and
failed; Eritrea fought to establish independence from Ethiopia (1963–91),
and ultimately succeeded.

There are exceptions. There have been some wars which have been so
confused that no coherent political objective can be discerned – the conflicts
in Chad (1965–88) and the Western Sahara (1975–91) appear to have
achieved their own momentum, detached from whatever political aim was
present at the start. The long war between Iraq and Iran (1980–88) began
with geographical and political aims on the part of Iraq (to secure an advantageous frontier line along the Shatt al-Arab waterway, and to strengthen
Saddam Hussein's position against a religious and political rival), but it
continued long after these aims had become unattainable, and both sides
persisted, at immense cost, out of sheer obduracy. But in general, war has
been used as an instrument of policy, demonstrating a striking degree of continuity with the past in a world where so much has changed, and even more
was *supposed* to have changed, and war was considered by many as being
outdated. War has continued to be waged, and sometimes has achieved much.

All this has referred, naturally enough, to wars which actually took place.
But we must also look at wars which *did not* take place, but whose very
possibility profoundly affected the conduct of international affairs. Never
have non-events been so important. There were two wars which seemed
possible but did not occur: a war in Europe between NATO and the
Warsaw Pact, and an outright nuclear war between the United States and
the Soviet Union.

War in Europe was technically possible at any time, as two formidable
forces confronted one another across the iron curtain. Each was armed with
conventional weapons (the tanks, guns and aircraft which had wrought
such havoc in the Second World War, now in more deadly forms), and also
with nuclear weapons (including the so-called 'tactical' nuclear artillery, of
immense destructive power). On the whole, the Soviets held the advantage
in tanks and guns, the Americans in tactical nuclear weapons. Fighting
might easily have broken out in tense situations, and would then have been
impossible to contain. For example, during the Berlin blockade of 1948–49,
if the Americans had tried to force a way through to West Berlin with an
armoured column, or if the Soviets had shot down a Western aircraft during
the airlift, war might well have ensued. In October 1961, after the building
of the Berlin Wall, American and Soviet tanks faced one another at
Checkpoint Charlie, and the chance of a violent incident lay in the hands of
a few junior officers and their men – who in fact behaved with great
restraint and good sense. (It should not be forgotten that soldiers can make
very good diplomats.)

In these circumstances, war was possible, perhaps by accident, or at any rate unintentionally. How far was there also a danger of war by design, by a Soviet invasion of Western Europe? It is now the conventional historical wisdom that any such threat was small, or even unreal – one well-informed writer dismisses as 'ridiculous' any thought that Soviet forces were capable of invading Western Europe in the late 1940s.[5] At the time, the danger did not appear in the least ridiculous, and allied commanders in the west had little hope of stopping the Red Army anywhere short of the Channel. The Warsaw Pact plans that have come to light were offensive, at any rate until the late 1980s, when Gorbachev insisted on some defensive planning. Plans made even in the early 1980s for an assault by some 60 divisions (38 of them Soviet) envisaged reaching the French border in 13–15 days, and the Atlantic and Pyrenees in 35 days. Nuclear weapons were to be used at an early stage, whether or not NATO used them.[6] NATO plans to resist a Soviet offensive consisted in the early years of a 'tripwire' strategy, using ground forces only as a 'tripwire' to trigger an instant and massive retaliation with nuclear weapons. This strategy was rigid, and by no means convincing – if Soviet forces advanced into certain areas, perhaps in northern Norway, would the United States really respond with nuclear weapons and risk the destruction of its own cities? The Americans replaced it in 1962 by the strategy of 'flexible response', envisaging action by conventional and nuclear forces according to circumstances. This looked better up to a point, but in all probability would still have meant an early use of tactical nuclear weapons. The West European governments in NATO feared that it would turn their countries into a nuclear battle-ground while the USA and the Soviet Union escaped attack; and NATO as a body did not accept 'flexible response' until 1967.

The existence of these plans tells us almost nothing about the likelihood of their being put into practice. It was the task of general staffs to prepare for war, and to consider various scenarios and possibilities, in which the 'worst case' was bound to figure, leading to an exaggeration of the enemy's strength and intentions. What we do know is that nothing actually happened. The great European war of the late twentieth century did not take place, for the fundamental reason that it would certainly have involved nuclear weapons.

That brings us to the second war which did not take place – the nuclear war between the United States and the Soviet Union; and so to the issue of the nuclear balance and deterrence. This has already been examined in the narrative chapters,[7] but certain fundamental points must be repeated here. The immense power and destructive capacity of atomic and nuclear weapons dominated thought and inspired terror. The scale of the new weapons was beyond imagination. As a basis for comparison, the heaviest bombs used in the Allied bombing offensive against Germany during the Second World War were 10-ton bombs, comprising 6 tons of TNT. The atomic bomb dropped on Hiroshima in August 1945 had an explosive power equal to about 15 000 tons of TNT; and that used against Nagasaki about 22 000 tons. Nuclear weapons were measured in megatons, so that a one-megaton bomb was equivalent to one million tons of TNT, and so up the scale. In February 1954 the United States tested a bomb at Bikini atoll which produced 15 megatons. In October 1961 the Soviet Union tested a weapon at Novaya Zemlya which produced 58 megatons. These tests produced a series of effects – a blinding flash on explosion, tremendous blast, searing heat, and nuclear radiation persisting for long periods.[8] The total effects of a number of nuclear weapons exploding in rapid sequence and close proximity, in an outright nuclear war, remained completely unknown.

The means of delivering these weapons were aircraft, ballistic missiles fired from bases on land, and similar missiles fired from submarines. The development of nuclear-powered submarines, of very long range and capacity to stay at sea for long periods, meant that almost no target would be safe from attack from a source which was itself hard to detect and destroy. The resulting balance of strength as missiles were developed between the 1960s and 1990 is worth recapitulating.

	1970		1980		1990	
Missiles[9]	USA	USSR	USA	USSR	USA	USSR
ICBM	1054	1465	1039	1330	990	1710
SLBM	656	229	576	937	624	930
TOTAL	1710	1694	1615	2267	1614	2640
Warheads[10]						
On ICBMs	1054	1465	2139	4388	2440	6955
On SLBMs	656	229	4880	1897	5376	3162
TOTALS	1710	1694	7019	6285	7816	10117

Note: ICBM: inter-continental ballistic missile; SLBM: submarine-launched ballistic missile

The exact relationship between these prodigious forces of destruction depended on a number of complicated variables, including reliability, accuracy and targetting policy, as well as the state of the weather – a slightly odd consideration among all this advanced science and technology. But the broad equilibrium, the balance of terror, far outweighed such detailed considerations. The two sides could destroy one another, with a wide margin to spare.

These nuclear arsenals were developed and refined by a series of tests,[11] at first mostly in the atmosphere. In August 1963 the United States, the Soviet Union and the United Kingdom signed a partial Test Ban Treaty, forbidding tests in the atmosphere, and underground tests became the norm.

Date	Environment	USA	USSR
16 7.45–5.8.63	Atmosphere	212	212
	Underground	114	—
	Underwater	5	3
6 8.63–1990	Atmosphere	—	—
	Underground	598	464
	Underwater	—	—
TOTALS		929	679

There was also a constant series of innovations in weapons and means of delivery. Atomic bombs were followed by nuclear bombs. Bombing aircraft were followed (and to a large degree superseded) by ballistic missiles. Missiles were installed on nuclear-powered submarines. Individual missiles were equipped with multiple warheads, each capable of being directed at a different target. Anti-missile missiles were developed. Cruise missiles were designed to fly low and at great speed, to penetrate defence systems. Technology never stood still, and the cost was enormous.[12]

In addition to the two superpowers, other countries developed nuclear weapons, though on a much smaller scale.[13]

Date	Environment	UK	France	China	India
16.8.45–5.8.63	Atmosphere	21	4	—	—
	Underground	2	4	—	—
6.8.63–1990	Atmosphere	41	23	—	
	Underground	20	134	13	1
TOTALS		43	183	36	1

The British tested their first atomic bomb in October 1952, and the RAF was equipped with its first atomic bombs in November 1953. The first British nuclear weapon was tested in April 1958. The first method of delivery was the V-bomber, followed by land-based missiles, and later by nuclear-powered submarines, each equipped with 16 Polaris missiles, which first came into service in 1968. The French conducted their first atomic test in October 1964, and their first thermonuclear explosion in August 1968. They too developed nuclear bombers (1964); land-based missiles (1971); and submarines (1972). By 1983 they could keep three nuclear-powered submarines at sea at any one time. China first tested an atomic bomb in

October 1964, and a thermonuclear weapon in June 1967. They brought nuclear bombers into service in 1970; an inter-continental ballistic missile in 1971; and a missile-carrying nuclear submarine in 1987.[14] India carried out an atomic test in 1974, but did not test a thermonuclear weapon until 1998, when they were at once matched by Pakistan. South Africa conducted a successful test in 1979, and it is generally understood that Israel has a bomb 'in the basement'.

How could these weapons, of a destructive power totally unknown in the previous history of the world, be used? In the early stages, between 1945 and 1949, when the United States had a monopoly of atomic weapons, which were few in number (13 in 1947, 50 in 1948), they were regarded simply as weapons of last resort, with no special theory or rules about their use. When the Soviet Union exploded its first atomic bomb in 1949, and then conducted its first thermonuclear test in 1953, a systematic strategy had to be worked out, by both sides. In essence, the possession of nuclear weapons by both sides meant that there could be no defence except the threat of reprisal. The result was the concept of nuclear deterrence: that a rational opponent would not attack if retaliation was certain, and the ensuing cost would be greater than any conceivable gain. The conditions necessary for deterrence were simple. (1) One's own nuclear weapons must be invulnerable to a pre-emptive strike, or at any rate capable of surviving in sufficient strength to permit retaliation in overwhelming force. (2) The enemy's nuclear weapons must be vulnerable to attack. (3) The retaliation against a first strike must be certain, or at any rate credible – the enemy must *believe* that nuclear reprisal would follow.

These conditions were simple, but the subsequent calculations and theories were not. As we have seen, the United States adopted in 1953 the strategy of 'massive retaliation', by which the Americans would respond with nuclear weapons against any Soviet attack, and would strike against any targets, with no safe areas. When the Soviet Union launched the Sputnik satellite (which was proof of its advanced rocket technology), and the Americans became afraid of a 'missile gap' (i.e. Soviet superiority in nuclear missiles – which did not in fact exist), this strategy lost its credibility. Would the United States really launch a nuclear war, and invite its own destruction, in response to a Soviet advance into a limited area, perhaps of minor importance? The answer seemed likely to be No. So in principle 'massive retaliation' was replaced in 1962 by the strategy of 'graduated response', by which the Americans would reply to an attack by a range of weaponry including conventional forces, tactical nuclear artillery, and strategic nuclear weapons. But even while this concept was being elaborated, and before it was formally adopted by NATO in 1967, it ceased to carry conviction. In February 1965 the American Secretary of Defence, Robert McNamara, declared that only the certainty of mutual assured destruction (which produced the singularly appropriate acronym MAD) could achieve deterrence.

The Soviet Union for its part for a long time claimed to follow its own path, and denied the principle of deterrence. Between 1945 and the first Soviet atomic test in 1949, Stalin maintained confidently that the atomic bomb changed nothing, though behind the scenes his scientists worked flat out to make one, and in public Soviet propaganda tried to influence Western public opinion to 'ban the bomb'. Later, Khrushchev continued to claim that the capitalist system would suffer more heavily than socialism in a nuclear war, and that victory would go to the Marxist–Leninist side. He threatened Britain and France with rocket attack during the Suez crisis in 1956. In September 1957 he attended the launch of a Soviet inter-continental ballistic missile, and told the press that the USSR would turn out missiles like sausages, though in fact this was only the second successful firing. In 1959 he set up Rocket Strategic Forces, though there were still only four long-range missiles ready for use.[15] All this was a sort of nuclear bluff, on a weak hand. In private and in practice, he understood that nuclear weapons meant that the United States and the Soviet Union could destroy one another. The Soviets, like the Americans, effectively adopted a strategy of deterrence. In 1962 Marshal Sokolovsky (who had been Chief of the General Staff from 1952 to 1960) published a book on strategy, which argued that a war between the superpowers would necessarily be nuclear, and that the Soviets would at once carry out nuclear strikes on all kinds of targets, while on land the Army would take the offensive with all types of forces. After the Cuban missile crisis, the Soviet government and high command accepted that a nuclear war would not necessarily mean the triumph of socialism, and in practice their views became very similar to the American theory of mutual assured destruction – in fact, deterrence.

The principle of deterrence gave rise to intense and frequently abstruse debate. The possibility of a surprise first strike; the capacity for a retaliatory second strike; the question of survival by means of nuclear shelters and civil defence; the long-term consequences of nuclear war – all these issues were discussed in elaborate detail, though mercifully they remained abstract questions. From this debate, two points emerged with important consequences for international relations. First, in a situation where everything depended on the success of deterrence, the development of an effective defence could actually have a *destabilizing* effect on relations between the superpowers. Second, the smaller nuclear powers could have an effect out of proportion to their actual weight.

The potentially destabilizing effects of the development of anti-missile defences had far-reaching consequences. If one superpower could launch a first strike on the other, in the confidence that its defences could defeat a retaliatory second strike, then the balance of terror was disturbed, and might be completely upset. This possibility began to arise in the late 1960s, as anti-ballistic missiles (ABMs) came into service on both sides. Far from increasing security, the ABMs undermined the security which had been achieved through the balance of terror. This led the two superpowers to negotiate on strategic arms limitation, and also to restrict their own capacities for defence. That was why the Strategic Arms Limitation Talks (SALT) which the Americans and Soviets began in 1969 led to two treaties in 1972. The first limited the number of offensive missiles. The second restricted the zones to be protected by anti-missile defences to two in each country, thus preserving the power of the deterrent by limiting the scope of the defence. So, by a devious route, the strengthening of the defence had more effect than the power of the attack in bringing the two superpowers together and persuading them to reach agreement on arms limitation.

Much the same process, but on a larger scale, took place during Reagan's presidency, when the Americans embarked on the Strategic Defence Initiative, an attempt to introduce a defensive shield for the United States which would provide a total defence against nuclear attack by destroying enemy missiles in flight. If successful, this would have nullified the power of the Soviet deterrent, and thus effectively destroyed the nuclear balance. Whether the Strategic Defence Initiative was a workable project was always doubtful, but even the prospect was sufficient to alarm the Soviets, who would either have to match the American effort (at enormous expense) or to reach an agreement with the Americans which would render the competition unnecessary. This alarm caused Gorbachev to try to stop the SDI before it really got under way, and so was one of the causes leading to the Soviet–American agreements of the late 1980s, and eventually to the end of the Cold War. Churchill had once speculated, in March 1955, that safety might be the sturdy child of terror, and so on this occasion it proved.

The possession of nuclear weapons by countries other than the superpowers (Britain, France and China) produced some important effects. Nuclear weapons were a form of 'equalizer', in that a comparatively small number could provide a very effective threat of destruction. They also exercised a destabilizing effect, which caused the two superpowers to unite to prevent the further spread of nuclear weapons. In July 1968 the United States, the Soviet Union and Britain signed a Nonproliferation Treaty, agreeing not to transfer nuclear weapons to other countries or to assist them to build such weapons. Non-nuclear states which adhered to the treaty undertook to prevent the diversion of civilian nuclear projects to military purposes. This treaty achieved only modest success. France and China did not sign. Nor did Israel, South Africa, India and Pakistan, which were all at work on nuclear weapons. Among the many states which adhered to the treaty, not all observed its terms – for example, Iraq set out to build a nuclear bomb, though the Israelis intervened by bombing their nuclear plant in June 1981. Despite these failings, the Nonproliferation Treaty formed an important common ground between the United States and the Soviet Union, and became one of the elements of détente.

In the event, the Cold War came to an end without atomic or nuclear weapons being used, but the possibility of nuclear war had been ever-present. At a famous press conference on 30 November 1950, President Truman carefully did not rule out the use of atomic weapons in the Korean War. In 1953 Eisenhower implicitly threatened that he might use the atomic bomb to bring the Chinese to the negotiating table and so secure an armistice in Korea. In 1954 John Foster Dulles and the American Chiefs of Staff considered the use of atomic bombs to save the situation at Dien Bien Phu, in Indo-China, but Eisenhower rejected the idea. In October 1962 the Cuba missile crisis brought the two superpowers to the verge of a nuclear war. In 1973, during the October (Yom Kippur) War in the Middle East, American nuclear forces were placed on full alert, to the alarm of the Soviets. There were other occasions when a war might have arisen out of a false alarm – for example, it was reported much later that on 26 September 1983 a Soviet satellite apparently detected the launching of an American missile attack, but the responsible officer concluded that it was an error and took no action.[16]

Nuclear war remained the war that did not happen. How then can we measure its influence upon the conduct of international affairs? Raymond Aron pointed out as early as 1962 that while the advent of nuclear weapons had changed *something* in relations between states, it had not changed either human nature or the nature of states themselves.[17] What had changed was that for the first time in history states were preparing for a war which they did not want and had no real intention of waging. By the late 1950s, nuclear war could not be fought without destroying, in large part or even totally, the states which took part in it, and wiping out most of their populations. The two nuclear superpowers therefore could not use their nuclear weapons against one another. This gave the United States and the Soviet Union much in common, because they both wanted to avoid nuclear war. Before the nuclear age, a situation in Europe where two alliances confronted one another across sensitive frontiers, and at any time an incident might have escalated into a conflict, would almost certainly have ended in war. During the Cold War, it did not, because neither side would accept nuclear war. This was a profound change. But at the same time much remained the same. Nuclear weapons proved powerless outside Europe and also in indirect confrontations between the superpowers. The United States, though a nuclear power, was defeated in Vietnam. The Soviet Union, though a nuclear power, was defeated in Afghanistan. In 1962 the danger of nuclear war caused the Soviets to withdraw their missiles from Cuba, but afterwards Castro's regime remained intact and American nuclear strength availed nothing against it. In the 1970s, nuclear weapons had no influence on guerrilla wars in Angola or Ethiopia. The possession of immense power could go hand in hand with impotence in certain circumstances.

How can we sum up the effects of war (meaning both the use and threat of force) on international affairs? Let us look at different kinds of war. Anti-colonial wars, or wars of liberation, were few in number – two big ones against the French in Indo-China and Algeria, smaller ones against the Dutch in Indonesia, the British in Palestine, Cyprus and Malaya, and against the Portuguese in Angola and Mozambique. But they were decisive in their effects. The great wave of decolonization which passed through Africa at the end of the 1950s and early 1960s was the result of earlier colonial defeats. The imperial powers (except for the Soviet Union, and for a long time Portugal) lost the will to fight and the belief in victory. Wars of liberation became unnecessary because the colonial powers withdrew without a fight. Conventional war too proved decisive on occasion. Israel owed its existence, and its later expansion, to wars fought by regular forces. The British recovered the Falkland Islands from Argentine occupation in 1982 by a well-organized amphibious operation. The Soviet Union imposed its will in Hungary in 1956 and Czechoslovakia in 1968 by the use of overwhelming military force. In wars fought by regular forces against mainly guerrilla opponents, the United States suffered defeat in Vietnam and the Soviet Union in Afghanistan, on both occasions with profound effects on the powers concerned. For a long time the United States was badly divided by the Vietnam War, and the Soviet Union suffered serious internal damage from the war in Afghanistan.

When we turn to the wars which might have been fought but were not, the results were equally significant. There was stability in Europe from 1947 to 1989 because the threat of force, and especially the atomic and nuclear deterrent, kept the peace. The balance of terror between the United States and the Soviet Union when both were nuclear powers produced dangerous rivalry, but also a form of stability and eventually common interest and détente.

Nuclear weapons have naturally produced a profound revulsion against their appalling destructive power, and against man's new capacity to destroy himself. Yet the disconcerting question arises as to whether the world would have been a more peaceful or a safer place if there had been no nuclear weapons, and states had been limited to the sort of weaponry which wrought such havoc during the Second World War. Since 1945, 'conventional' war has produced some devastating effects. But in Europe and between the superpowers, the nuclear deterrent preserved a precarious but priceless stability. Either way, no one could argue that the use and threat of force had lost its influence.

◆ The new diplomacy: the United Nations and other international organizations

Before the Second World War, relations between states were still mainly conducted by the conventions of the 'old diplomacy'. The major powers (still mostly European, plus the United States and Japan) maintained diplomatic services of very similar kinds, in which an elite of professional diplomats conducted foreign policy in secret and according to accepted customs. It is true that this pattern was already changing. President Wilson of the United States had proclaimed the need for 'open covenants, openly arrived at'. The League of Nations had introduced a new forum for the conduct of international affairs, and tried to mobilize what was vaguely called 'world opinion', for example in the cause of disarmament. The Soviet Union pursued a revolutionary policy through the Comintern as well as a foreign policy of a conventional (and often highly secret) kind – for example, in the Soviet–German Pact of August 1939. Nazi Germany and Fascist Italy often conducted their foreign policy by the same brutal methods which they used at home. But despite these exceptions the old diplomacy still survived, and maintained much of the influence which it had built up in the nineteenth century.[18]

In the period since 1945, the old diplomacy has retained some importance. One of the most influential documents in the history of American foreign policy, George Kennan's 'long telegram' of 1946 (see above, pp. 75–6) was written by a professional foreign service official. Later, the Soviet government kept the same Ambassador (Anatoly Dobrynin) in post in Washington for twenty-two years, from 1962 to 1984, in which time he built up a valuable knowledge of American affairs and developed confidential relations with a number of American leaders. On a narrower stage, one of the sharpest crises in Franco-British relations is always referred to as 'the Soames Affair' (1969), because it turned on the contents of a confidential conversation between President de Gaulle and the British Ambassador in Paris, Christopher Soames. In a very different context, Israel and the Palestine Liberation Organization reached an outline agreement in 1993 in negotiations conducted in complete secrecy under Norwegian auspices in Oslo – an achievement which ran into difficulties as soon as it was subjected to the glare of publicity. Moreover, even though relations between the superpowers came increasingly to be conducted at summit meetings between American and Soviet leaders, summits were usually prepared and their conclusions consolidated by the patient work of officials.

The old diplomacy thus continued to function. But to a large degree it became overshadowed by the role of international organizations, which increased in number and importance during the period after 1945. These organizations varied widely in character. Some were regional (the Organization of American States, the Organization of African Unity, the European Economic Community, later the European Union). Others were functional (the International Monetary Fund, the World Bank, the permanent organization related to the General Agreement on Tariffs and Trade). The Commonwealth, consisting almost entirely of former parts of the

British Empire, was partly functional and partly sentimental in character – and none the worse for that. The organization which has the widest membership, and despite many shortcomings retains a high reputation, is the United Nations. It is necessary to examine in some detail the role of the United Nations Organization, and its influence on the conduct of international affairs. (See above, pp. 41–4, for the structure of the United Nations Organization.)

When the United Nations was set up in 1945, its two main purposes were to preserve peace through collective security, and to promote economic and social progress, in the belief that war arose from economic rivalries and social conflicts. It accepted all member states as being equal in the General Assembly, where each had one vote; but also acknowledged the status and influence of the great powers by granting a right of veto in the Security Council to the five permanent members of the Council – the United States, the Soviet Union, China, Britain and France. From the beginning, in 1945, the Charter of the United Nations adopted the principle of non-intervention in the internal affairs of member states; but as early as December 1948, the General Assembly also accepted unopposed a Universal Declaration of Human Rights which pointed directly towards intervention in internal affairs. Thus the United Nations became subject to constant internal tensions. On the one hand, it asserted the sovereignty and dignity of its member states, and on the other it proclaimed universal rights which could only be achieved by the infringement of sovereignty. From this contradiction much difficulty followed.

The character of the United Nations was much altered over the years by changes in its membership. Its founder members in 1945 numbered 51, mostly European and from the American continent. When it attained its fiftieth birthday in 1995, the UN had 185 members, and the great majority of the additional 134 were new states, mostly former colonies in Asia, Africa and the Pacific. An institution whose structures and purposes were primarily shaped by the Western powers (the role of the Soviet Union in setting up the UN was largely passive) was thus transformed, and came to represent quite different concerns, notably a fierce demagogic hostility towards colonialism.

The United Nations thus began its life with two principal objectives: to secure peace and to promote economic progress. A third – the attainment of human rights – was quickly added. Within twenty years of the UN's foundation, a fourth objective – the mobilization of world opinion against colonialism – had become predominant, and changed the nature of the whole organization. Let us examine these four purposes, in an order which follows the logic of events rather than strict chronology: (1) the securing of peace; (2) the mobilization of opinion against colonialism; (3) the promotion of economic order; and (4) human rights.

The United Nations and the cause of peace

The idea of peace through collective security, ensured and if necessary imposed by the great powers working together in the Security Council, foundered rapidly. The coming of the Cold War meant that the two most important permanent members of the Security Council, the United States and the Soviet Union, were constantly opposed to one another. The Soviet Union vetoed American initiatives, and *vice versa*. Moreover, after 1949 Taiwan (not a great power by any definition) held the seat of China on the Security Council, and mainland China was not represented at the United Nations until 1971. The Security Council thus lost political coherence and moral authority. Only the Korean War (1950–53), fought under the authority of the United Nations and under the UN flag, fulfilled the purpose of collective security to thwart aggression; and even this was in practice an American operation, which only attained UN support through the absence of the Soviet Union from the Security Council at a vital moment. The Korean War must be seen as a part of American foreign policy rather than of United Nations peace-keeping.

In consequence, the preservation of peace by the United Nations came to be limited to two functions, of very different kinds and of much smaller importance than its original far-reaching purpose. First, the United Nations offered a point of contact between opponents, and an opportunity for mediation, usually in corridors, private offices or hotel rooms rather than in formal surroundings and public sessions. The United Nations became an assiduous arranger of cease-fires, starting in Palestine in 1948 and Kashmir in 1949. Since then there have been UN cease-fires all over Asia and Africa, often precarious and rarely developing into permanent peace settlements. Similarly, the United Nations has provided an escape route for countries which have got into difficulties and are looking for a way out which saves face or covers a retreat with a smoke-screen of fine phrases – what Conor Cruise O'Brien called a 'ritual at the brink'.[19] For example, in 1965 Pakistan and India wanted to find a way out of their renewed battles in Kashmir, and Pakistan in particular was in difficulties holding off an Indian attack on Lahore. The Security Council helped both parties by calling for a cease-fire. In 1988 Iran and Iraq had fought themselves to a standstill, and a Security Council resolution helped them to bring their eight-year conflict to an end. These were limited but useful achievements. But on the other hand, the United Nations has often stood by and done nothing in the face of civil wars (in Nigeria and Sudan, for example), massacres (e.g. in Uganda, Ethiopia and Burundi), and large-scale war (the Iran–Iraq War raged for eight years before the Security Council helped to bring it to an end). The United Nations has only a patchy record, even in providing an escape route to peace.

Second, the United Nations has provided a large number of peace-keeping bodies, to supervise a cease-fire, to keep watch on a newly-drawn

frontier, or occasionally to maintain order in a situation where government has broken down. These bodies are often referred to as UN
'Forces', and indeed they usually include soldiers under UN command;
but the intention is very rarely to use force. Words frequently used in
their titles are 'supervision' or 'observation'. Between 1948 and 1989,
the United Nations undertook fourteen such peace-keeping operations,
as follows[20]:

UN Truce Supervision Organization – UNTSO (to supervise armistices
between Israel, Egypt, Jordan, Syria, Lebanon, June 1948, continuing.)
UN Military Observer Group for India and Pakistan – UNMOGIP: to
supervise cease-fire between India and Pakistan in Kashmir, January
1949, continuing.
UN Commission for Indonesia – UNCI: to supervise truce between
Indonesia and the Netherlands, 1949–51
UN Emergency Force, Egypt–Israel Border – UNEF: to supervise cease-
fire between Egypt and Israel after the Suez War, November 1956–June
1967; withdrew at Egyptian request.
UN Observer Group in Lebanon – UNOGIL: established July 1958, at
the request of Lebanon, which accused Syria (United Arab Republic) of
intervention in its internal affairs; withdrew December 1958.
UN Congo Operation – UNCO: to maintain law and order, and essential services, in the Congo, at the request of the Congo government, July
1960–June 1964; the UN force reached a maximum strength of 19 825
in July 1961.
UN Temporary Executive Authority-Security Force, West Irian –
UNTEA-UNSF: to administer West Irian/Western New Guinea during
transfer from the Netherlands to Indonesia, September 1962–May 1963.
UN Yemen Observation Mission – UNYOM: to supervise the disen-
gagement of royalist and republican forces in Yemen civil war, July
1963–September 1964; withdrew after reporting that the disengagement
was minimal.
UN Force in Cyprus – UNFICYP: to keep the peace between Greeks and
Turks in Cyprus; established March 1964, continuing.
UN India–Pakistan Observation Mission – UNIPOM: to supervise cease-
fire between India and Pakistan, on the frontier line from Kashmir to the
Rann of Kutch on the Arabian Sea, September 1965–March 1966.
UN Emergency Force, Egypt-Israel Border – UNEF: to supervise cease-
fire after the Yom Kippur/October War, 1973, October 1973–July 1979,
ending with the conclusion of an Egypt-Israel peace treaty.
UN Disengagement Observer Force, Syria–Israel Border – UNDOF: to
supervise disengagement of Syrian and Israeli forces, Golan Heights,
May 1974, continuing.
UN Interim Force in Lebanon – UNIFIL: to confirm Israeli withdrawal

from south Lebanon, and assist Lebanese government in restoring law and order, March 1978, continuing.

UN Observer Group in Central America – ONUCA: to supervise the agreement ending the Nicaraguan civil war, operating in Nicaragua, El Salvador and Honduras, November 1989–January 1992.

These operations, with very few exceptions, have amounted to little more than holding a slender line between two combatants. Supervising the cease-fire line in Kashmir has been a full-time task from 1949 to the present day (written in 2000), but it has achieved no lasting success because the fundamental conflict between India and Pakistan remains unresolved. Everywhere, the work is dreary, thankless and often dangerous. The results are rarely more than a negative absence of fighting rather than any positive establishment of peace. The burden has fallen mainly upon the small and medium-sized countries (the Scandinavians – Danes, Finns, Norwegians and Swedes – are called on with particular frequency) rather than on the great powers which were at one time expected to keep the peace. It is a far cry from the high hopes of the founders of the United Nations, but all in all it is a record of steady achievement in arduous and complex conditions. We may adapt Voltaire's phrase about God, and reflect that if the United Nations did not exist, it would have to be invented, at least in this particular role. Strikingly, as the Cold War came to an end, the number of such operations increased sharply: six began in 1991, and a further three in 1992.[21]

The United Nations and world opinion: anti-colonialism and racism

In 1960 sixteen former African colonies attained independence, and total membership of the United Nations reached 99. A new majority of former colonies and anti-colonial states took over in the General Assembly. Moreover, at this stage even the imperial powers ceased to defend their own actions or positions. The Soviet Union sponsored in 1960 what emerged as General Assembly Resolution No.1514, to the effect that: 'All peoples have the right of self-determination', and that 'Inadequacy of political, economic, social or educational preparedness should never serve as a pretext for delaying independence.'[22] This resolution was passed without a single contrary vote, though with nine abstentions. An attempt to fix a universal date for independence at no later than the next year, 1961, was defeated; but even so this astonishing resolution proposed to dispense with any preparation for independence, without a single government daring to vote against it.

In 1961 the General Assembly set up a Special Committee on Decolonization to secure the implementation of this resolution. The remaining colonies in Africa, notably the Portuguese in Angola and Mozambique and the British in Rhodesia were subjected to constant criticism; as was

South Africa – an independent state, but ruled by a white minority. This situation led the United Nations to widen its attacks from colonialism to more general issues of race and racial discrimination. On 21 December 1965, the General Assembly adopted an International Convention on the Elimination of all forms of Racial Discrimination (Resolution No.2106A), which defined racial discrimination as meaning any distinction, exclusion, restriction or preference 'based on race, colour, descent, or national or ethnic origin which has the purpose or effect of nullifying or impairing the recognition, enjoyment or exercise, on an equal footing, of human rights and fundamental freedoms in the political, economic, social, cultural or any other field of human life'.[23] This is worth citing at length, because it shows the wide range of issues raised by the term racial discrimination, notably relating to human rights and economic freedom.

Once the racial issue was launched, there was no telling where it would stop. General Assembly Resolution No.3379 (10 November 1975) declared that 'Zionism is a form of racism and racial discrimination', and was passed by 72 votes against 35, with 32 abstentions.[24] This resolution was later revoked, but even so, the running together of anti-colonialism, anti-racism and anti-Zionism shows with particular force how the UN came to direct world opinion into new and unexpected directions. In the phrase of a weary British professional diplomat, 'the UN was for decades a home from home for Decolonization Man . . .'[25] This was undreamed of by the founders of the United Nations in 1945, but two decades later had become one of its principal activities and purposes.

The United Nations and international economic order

The founders of the United Nations believed that the preservation of peace required the removal of the economic causes of war. The Bretton Woods Conference of 1945 set up the International Monetary Fund, to secure a system of stable exchange rates, and the International Bank for Reconstruction and Development, later called the World Bank, which was first to finance post-war reconstruction and later to promote economic development in a wider manner. These two organizations became specialist agencies within the United Nations. The Bretton Woods Conference also proposed the setting up of an International Trade Organization. A conference of 23 states held at Geneva in 1947 concluded a General Agreement on Tariffs and Trade (GATT), which aimed at a systematic and progressive reduction of tariffs. At first, GATT was intended to be temporary, pending the creation of the International Trade Organization envisaged at Bretton Woods, but this did not come about, and a World Trade Organization did not come into existence until 1994.

Meanwhile GATT took on a permanent existence, with a Director-General and Secretariat based in Geneva. It held a series of long and complicated negotiations on tariff reductions, which moved forward in four main 'rounds'. The Dillon Round (1960–62, named after the US Secretary of the Treasury, Douglas Dillon) achieved a reduction of 20 per cent in certain tariffs on trade between the United States on the one hand and the European Economic Community and the United Kingdom on the other. The Kennedy Round (1963–67, named after President John F. Kennedy) aimed at the wider objective of securing tariff reductions by all member states on specific products; and in fact 46 governments agreed on reductions which averaged 36 per cent. The Tokyo Round (1973–79) dealt mainly with tariffs on industrial products. Eight of the major industrial states, plus the European Economic Community acting as a unit, agreed to reduce their tariffs, in some cases by as much as one-third; but the agreement left a significant loophole by allowing governments to restrict imports when they were causing serious injury to their own industries. The Uruguay Round (1986–93) set out to widen the scope of GATT to agriculture and the provision of services, and to increase its coverage from one-third to two-thirds of world trade. The United States also tried to tackle the EEC's practice of producing vast agricultural surpluses, which were then sold cheaply (dumped, in effect) to the detriment of other agricultural producers. This dispute caused a breakdown in the negotiations in 1992, but agreement was reached in 1993, and formally signed in 1994 by 120 governments.[26] At the conclusion of the Uruguay Round, agreement was finally reached to set up a World Trade Organization, first proposed as long ago as 1945. GATT was thus wound up, and the new World Trade Organization became a specialized agency of the United Nations.

GATT's immense labours were concentrated on the major sectors of international trade, and on the tariffs of the principal industrial and commercial countries. That was its brief. But to the Third World countries which came by 1960 to form a majority in the United Nations, GATT represented merely a club of rich countries working for their own benefit. In 1964 the UN General Assembly responded to this sentiment by setting up a United Nations Conference on Trade and Development (UNCTAD) as a permanent body. The new organization held its first conference (1st UNCTAD) at Geneva (23 March–15 June 1964), attended by 120 governments, of which 77 were developing countries. This Group of 77 (often abbreviated to G-77) came to assume an almost permanent status at the United Nations (though the actual numbers attached to it grew steadily). The first UNCTAD passed a resolution calling upon the industrialized states to devote one per cent of their gross national product to aid to the developing countries. It also agreed on various principles, of which No.14 was that 'complete decolonization' was a necessary condition for economic development, thus linking two great Third World themes. No agreement was reached on practical matters, and the conference paid no attention to such awkward facts as Hong Kong's continuing colonial status and rapidly advancing economy.[27] In 1967 the Group of 77 held a meeting at Algiers, and agreed on proposals for financial transfers from the developed to the underdeveloped states, measures to relieve or cancel debts, and preferential access for their products to markets in western industrialized states. At the second UNCTAD (held at New Delhi, 1 February–29 March 1968), the conference agreed on a system of preferences which would allow the G-77 countries to maintain their own tariffs while securing improved access to western markets. (In practice, several western countries dealt with what they regarded as unfair competition by using a range of non-tariff barriers; so the trade conditions for the developing countries were not necessarily improved.)

The third UNCTAD met in Santiago, Chile, from 13 April to 21 May 1972. The conference registered the fact that its efforts so far had achieved little, and embarked on a new course. The President of Mexico, Luis Echeverria, proposed the adoption of a Charter of the Economic Rights and Duties of States, which would extend the existing notion of human rights (which we shall come to later) by the assertion of rights for states. This proposal was accepted by the conference, and developed at a summit meeting of non-aligned states in Algiers in September 1973. This meeting, attended by 75 governments, mostly from Asia and Africa, framed a demand for a New International Economic Order to be put to the General Assembly of the United Nations. Again the issue of economic development was linked to colonialism, and the Algiers conference agreed that the essence of colonialism was the economic structure imposed by the industrialized states upon the others (or by the North upon the South, in the terms which were coming into use).

In 1974 the United Nations duly accepted a resolution (No.3201) for the establishment of a new international economic order. This claimed that the gap between developed and developing countries was continuing to widen, as the result of a system which had been set up at a time when most of the developing countries did not exist as independent states. This situation must be corrected by adopting a new economic order, and by extensive aid from the developed to the developing countries. But at the same time, every country retained the right to adopt any economic or social system it wished, without being subject to discrimination as a result, and without being denied aid. This was in effect an attempt to change the whole economic system in favour of the Third World.

The movement touched a nerve among the industrialized countries. There was a pervasive feeling of guilt among most of the former imperial powers, which felt vaguely that they should make up for their past exploitation of their colonies. It was widely accepted that the poverty of the developing countries was caused by the wealth of the industrialized states, and that somehow the Holy Grail of equality and economic justice should be attained by a new economic policy.[28] In 1974 President Giscard d'Estaing of France called for a conference to discuss the 'North–South divide'. The result was a curious gathering in Paris, in May–June 1977. The representatives of the 'North' were (in alphabetical order): Australia, Canada, the European Economic Community (made up of nine countries at that time), Japan, Spain, Sweden, Switzerland and the United States. The 'South' was made up of: Algeria, Argentina, Brazil, Cameroon, Egypt, India, Indonesia, Iran, Iraq, Jamaica, Mexico, Nigeria, Pakistan, Peru, Saudi Arabia, Venezuela, Yugoslavia, Zaire and Zambia.

Geographically, this division made little sense – Australia (as its very name denotes) is not in the north, and among the representatives of the 'South' 11 out of 19 are north of the equator. As to poverty, Iran, Iraq and Saudi Arabia were among the Arab oil states that had recently quadrupled the price of their petroleum, while Argentina and Brazil were the wealthiest countries in South America.[29] Despite these anomalies, the conference agreed to invite Willy Brandt (the former Chancellor of West Germany) to form a Commission to report on questions of international development. The Brandt Report, *North–South: A Programme for Survival*, published in 1980, advocated a transfer of resources from the industrialized states to the Third World, principally through a large-scale programme of aid.

The Brandt Report was welcomed throughout the western world. In 1980 the major industrialized countries reached a commodities agreement, setting up a fund to stabilize the prices of certain primary products, only to find that most of the Group of 77 were not interested in such limited practical measures. In the event, the Brandt Report proved the high-water mark of the UNCTAD and North–South pressure. The Reagan administration in the United States adopted a tougher line than that of its predecessors on the whole issue. In March 1984 the United States demanded the reform of UNCTAD, on the grounds that the organization was costly, inefficient, and devoted to its own form of ideology rather than practical results. The Americans received little support, but they persisted, and gradually achieved some success. In 1985 UNCTAD accepted a plan to set up a fund to purchase stocks of some primary products, and so prevent the more violent fluctuations in prices. The seventh UNCTAD, in 1987, met for only three weeks instead of the usual six; rejected a lengthy and extreme document drafted by Cuba; and agreed to a balanced final document in which Western governments acknowledged their responsibility to promote sustainable growth and to open their markets to Third World exports, while Third World governments accepted that each country had the responsibility to promote its own development. It was not simply a coincidence that this change of attitude on the part of UNCTAD and many of the Third World countries occurred when the Cold War was moving towards a close, and the Group of 77 could no longer call with certainty on the support of the Soviet Union. Later, in 1989–91, as first the Soviet bloc and then the Soviet Union itself broke up, the situation changed yet again. The problem of economic development remained, and Africa (alone among the continents) became steadily poorer. But the end of the Cold War had removed the ability of the developing countries to play one superpower against the other, and thus deprived them of much of their leverage.

The United Nations and human rights

When the United Nations was established, its founders intended it to prevent war and to promote peace, essentially after the fashion of the old League of Nations though (it was hoped) by improved methods. But under the terrible impulse of the crimes perpetrated by Nazi Germany the new organization also set out to protect the rights of the individual, in the belief that violation of personal rights was likely to escalate into violence between states. Article 56 of the Charter of the United Nations committed member states to promote respect for human rights, and on 10 December 1948 the General Assembly of the United Nations adopted unopposed a Universal Declaration of Human Rights.

This remarkable document set out in thirty-one articles rights which were claimed to be common to all members of the human family, and to be the foundation of liberty, justice and peace. The first article declared in ringing tones that all human beings are born free and equal in dignity and rights; and the second maintained that all rights must be observed without any discrimination on grounds of race, colour, sex, nationality, religion or any other condition. Others proclaimed that no one should be held in slavery or subjected to torture; that all had the right to equality before the law, and no one should be arrested or detained without trial; and all had the right to move freely within a country and to leave it. There was a right to marry, and marriage should only take place with the free and full consent of the couple concerned. Other articles asserted the right to own property; to freedom of thought and expression, and of religion and its practice. Another set of articles dealt with social rights: social security, the right to work and to leisure, and the right to education.[30]

This declaration was a striking departure in the conduct of international affairs and of international organizations. It left the United Nations with a contradiction between Article 2(7) of the Covenant, excluding intervention in matters within the sovereign jurisdiction of member states, and the Declaration of Human Rights, which required intervention in internal affairs unless it were to remain a mere set of pious hopes. The tension between these two opposed positions remained unresolved, and was indeed incapable of resolution.

The problems raised by the Universal Declaration of Human Rights were apparent from the start, and grew more difficult with time. Not a single vote was cast against the Declaration of Human Rights, which shows the weight of accepted opinion which it represented. But the Soviet bloc, South

Africa and Saudi Arabia abstained, revealing serious dissent in both principle and practice.

In the Soviet Union and other communist states, governments claimed that the rights of the state should prevail over the rights of the individual, and that economic rights exercised collectively outweighed rights to private property – for example, in the collectivization of agriculture. In South Africa, racial discrimination had long been established in law and in practice, and in 1948 the Nationalist Party had come to power and begun the systematic imposition of *apartheid*, as a matter of principle as well as of political and economic advantage to the white population. In Saudi Arabia, the government claimed that the Declaration of Human Rights, being based on a combination of Judaeo-Christian tradition and Enlightenment political thought, was incompatible with Islamic law and custom – for example, on non-discrimination between the sexes, marriage practices, and freedom of religion. Much later, in December 1984, Iran was actually to repudiate the Declaration of Human Rights on the ground that the concepts embodied therein had no validity in an Islamic Republic. In each of these cases, there were also powerful practical forces at work. The Soviet Union had long been accustomed to imprison vast numbers of its own people without trial, and to deprive almost everyone of freedom of information or the ability to leave the country. South Africa and Saudi Arabia, in their different ways, ran closed and authoritarian societies. It is striking that these countries were prepared to show their dissent, though only by abstaining. Many governments disregarded the human rights of their citizens as set out in the Declaration, but very few were willing to say so.

These difficulties were already signalled by the vote of December 1948. Others emerged with time, notably among the Third World countries which dominated the General Assembly from the 1960s onwards. In the 1970s and 1980s attention turned away from the rights of individuals, which were often regarded as essentially Western values, to collective rights. In 1973 the Non-Aligned Summit at Algiers, which demanded a New World Economic Order, also launched a claim for a New World Information and Communications Order, on the ground that freedom of information under existing conditions only meant freedom for the wealthy countries which possessed the advanced technology to control information. Again, in December 1987 the UN General Assembly adopted (by 146 votes to 1, with 8 abstentions) a Declaration on the right to development, by virtue of which each individual and each people should have the right to participate in and contribute to economic, social, cultural and political development.[31]

The United Nations had a mixed record on human rights. It was strong on resolutions and declarations. The Universal Declaration of 1948 was followed in 1966 by two Conventions, one dealing with economic, social and cultural rights, the other with civil and political rights. Later conventions asserted the right to political asylum, and condemned genocide and torture. But it was weak on action. Double standards were common. The United Nations Commission on Human Rights regularly spent a large proportion of its time in the 1970s and 1980s on condemning South Africa over *apartheid* and Israel for its actions in the West Bank territory, while the Chinese occupation of Tibet, with its destruction of a whole civilization in breach of several different human rights as laid down in 1948, went largely unchallenged. The UN Commission on Human Rights included members from, for example, the Sudan (where the southern population, largely Christian, was under constant attack by the Arab government) and Iraq (where Saddam Hussein practised a thoroughgoing dictatorship). Not until 1992 did the Commission pass a resolution condemning an African country for violations of human rights, and then it was Equatorial Guinea, not Rwanda where the massacre of Tutsis by the Hutu majority amounted to genocide.[32] (It should be added that the western democracies were sometimes no better: Britain supported Idi Amin in Uganda, France and the United States both supported Mobutu in Zaire.) But despite a good deal of hypocrisy and duplicity, and a vast mass of speeches and resolutions which were never intended to have any practical effect, the constant discussion of human rights had far-reaching effects on international affairs. Broadly speaking, these effects operated in two different areas and in divergent directions.

First, the western democracies, especially the United States, used human rights as an instrument against the Soviet Union. In the early 1970s, the US Congress and pressure groups raised the cases of Jews who were trying to leave the Soviet Union to migrate to Israel, and cited Article 13 of the Universal Declaration of Human Rights (on freedom of movement, including the right to leave one's own country). In 1975 the Helsinki Accords, which included a whole section on the rights of individuals, were actually accepted by the Soviet Union, and were then used by dissident groups within the Soviet bloc in ways which neither the Soviets nor the Americans had expected. This helped to weaken the Soviet bloc from within, and so worked to the advantage of the West.

But in other ways the human rights issue worked to the detriment of the West. In 1948, when the Universal Declaration of Human Rights was drawn up, what were essentially Western values prevailed. Even the colonial peoples who rebelled against imperialism did so in the name of liberal principles, claiming the rights of self-determination and self-government. But some forty years later the appeal of Western concepts of human rights was in decline. In 1990, Sweden (a country with impeccable neutralist and progressive credentials) proposed at the United Nations a resolution condemning the military government in Burma for breach of human rights, but was defeated by Third World votes. At a World Conference on Human Rights in Vienna in June 1993, some fifty countries opposed the existing concepts of rights, in the name of different principles and values. This group included Burma, China, Cuba, Indonesia, Iran, Iraq, Libya, Malaysia, Pakistan, Singapore, Sudan, Syria, Vietnam, and Yemen – a curious mixture of Islamic and communist states, which also brought together the thoroughly capitalist Singapore with the defiantly communist Cuba. Vocal advocates of cultural pluralism argued that the Western model of the Declaration of Human Rights was not, as it claimed to be, universal. The age of cultural pluralism, or relativism, had arrived, in which one country's or group of countries' values were as good as another's. The climate in which international organizations operated, and international affairs were conducted, had changed considerably.[33]

◆ The age of international organizations

The United Nations was the largest and most prominent of international organizations, but it was only one among a vast array that came into being in the half-century after the end of the Second World War. This was not a wholly novel development. In the nineteenth century the European states had set up international commissions to facilitate traffic along the Rhine and the Danube, and a similar organization for railways which passed through several countries. The International Postal Union provided vital, though usually unnoticed, services. An international commission for air traffic followed in 1919. The creation of the League of Nations, with its subsidiary bodies (the International Labour Office and the World Health Organization, for example) gave a further impulse to this development. Idealists aspired towards world government, but practical men knew that what was necessary was world *administration*, which these various organizations set out to provide.

After the Second World War this movement swelled from a stream to a flood. By 1992 over 350 inter-governmental organizations were in existence, all conforming broadly to a common type: they were permanent in character, with established structures (a secretariat, a standing committee or steering group, an annual or periodical conference), powers to take action, and often a juridical identity recognized in international law. This prodigious growth was partly a consequence of the Second World War and a belief that conflicts must be avoided by co-operation of all kinds. It arose also from the increasing technical complexity of the post-war world – for example, the development of communication by satellites. Perhaps above all it was caused by the sheer number of new states (there were 184 members of the United Nations by 1993). The United Nations itself set up over 50 specialized agencies. Regional organizations proliferated – in Europe, the Organization for European Economic Co-operation in the West, COMECON in the East; the Arab League; the Organization of American States; the Organization of African Unity; the Association of

South-East Asian Nations. Other Organizations were worldwide in character: the principal industrialized states formed the Group of Six in 1975, becoming the Group of Seven (G-7) in 1976, while the poorer, developing countries formed the Group of 77. A new form of alliance appeared, with permanent political bodies and integrated military structures – the North Atlantic Treaty Organization was the most complex and bureaucratic military alliance ever known. Several oil-producing states came together to form the Organization of Petroleum Exporting Countries (OPEC). Muslim states set up the Organization of the Islamic Conference, with 24 founder members in 1971 and 51 members or observers by 1994.

In nearly every case, these organizations sought to improve co-operation between governments by placing it on a permanent and institutional basis, while member states retained the final power of decision. The European Economic Community, later European Community, and in 1992 European Unity, was of a different character. Members of the EEC conferred certain powers on the European Commission (for example, the EEC negotiated as a single body within the General Agreement on Tariffs and Trade), and in case of conflict between European law and the laws of member states, European law prevails. This has led to the evolution of a hybrid body, which was (and is) much more than a customs union or common market, but not yet a super-state, because the powers exercised by European institutions are limited. The aspiration towards 'ever closer union', set out in the founding Treaty of Rome (1957) remained carefully undefined.

Organizations for co-operation between governments were numbered in hundreds. Non-governmental organizations were counted in thousands – over 3000 in 1986, or as many as 4500 if different criteria were adopted.[34] They came in all shapes and sizes. Political parties formed their own international groupings – communists in Cominform, and in world conferences of communist parties; socialists in the Socialist International which was revived in 1951. Christian Democratic parties set up their own international group in 1961. Trade unions have formed various unions among themselves – communist, Catholic, European, 'free'. The ecumenical movement among Christian churches set up the World Council of Churches. Humanitarian and charitable organizations abound, from the long-established International Red Cross to the more recent OXFAM and *Médecins sans Frontières*. Amnesty International takes up the cause of political prisoners and prisoners of conscience. Multinational companies deal in oil, chemicals, automobiles, electronics, communications and a multitude of other products and services. Often in opposition to them stand the environmental groups, notably Greenpeace and Friends of the Earth. The methods used by these organizations (open or secret, violent or pacific), and their impact on the conduct of international affairs, vary almost infinitely.

These complex webs of government and non-government bodies form an extra network, in addition to the long-established relations between states.

Their actual influence on the conduct of international affairs is difficult to establish. Members of the EEC/EC/EU have handed over control of large parts of their agricultural and commercial policies to European bodies. In the Warsaw Pact, the Soviet Union controlled the military policies and dispositions of the smaller members. On the other hand, the Arab League failed even to co-ordinate, never mind unify, the policies of its members. The Organization of African Unity has been largely ineffectual. Even the International Monetary Fund, with apparently far-reaching powers of financial coercion at its disposal, produced very uneven results. Dealing with Great Britain in 1976–77, the IMF advanced a large loan only on strict conditions, including substantial cuts in British public spending, which were duly observed; but dealing with Zaire in the 1980s the same IMF made loans on conditions of reforms and good management which were simply disregarded. All in all, it is probable that the enormous numbers of inter-governmental organizations have tended to modify rather than transform the conduct of international affairs, and to influence rather than decide policy. Their influence is probably strongest in western Europe, where NATO and the European Community have established firm and continuous systems of control over certain matters. Africa stands at the other extreme, with the Organization of African Unity exercising no more than fitful influence on a handful of issues. The Organization of American States is somewhere in the middle, with the Latin American countries varying widely in their attitude to the preponderance of the United States. No country, even the most powerful, isolated or self-confident, behaves as though these organizations did not exist. Even communist China wanted to participate in the General Agreement on Tariffs and Trade; Switzerland refuses to join the United Nations but is a member of the Organization for Economic Co-operation and Development. But in important issues of policy, very few countries are prepared to hand control over to one of these organizations; and in the last resort of national security and self-preservation, states keep decisions in their own hands.

◆ Publicity: news, propaganda and the mass media

In the second half of the twentieth century the mass media of communication changed out of recognition, and attained remarkable speed – amounting eventually to immediacy – in the transmission of news. Newspapers attained their highest point of circulation and influence by mid-century, and then entered a period of relative decline – though not in their readership among elites. Radio was immensely influential during the Second World War, but relied on receivers which were large, heavy and reliant on wires and plugs. From the 1950s, the advent of the transistor radio, small in size, powered by batteries, and easily transportable (and cheap), made radio reception almost ubiquitous except in the poorest countries. Television advanced swiftly. In 1970 there were some 250 million television sets in the world, of which about 100 million were in the United States. By 1988 there were reported to be 794 424 000, of which 195 000 000 were in the Soviet Union.[35] In 1962 the first communications satellite, Telstar, allowed television pictures to be transmitted directly from one continent to another. When Neil Armstrong took his first steps on the moon in July 1969, he was watched by television audiences across the world. News of events, transmitted as pictures, became available within hours of their taking place. By 1989 some crucial events (the fall of the Berlin Wall, Ceauşescu being shouted down on his balcony in Bucharest, the Chinese tanks going into action in Tiananmen Square, in Beijing) appeared on television screens as they happened.

These changes opened a new chapter in an old story. Propaganda and the manipulation of information have been instruments of politics and war for as long as we have written and pictorial records. The new technology offered fresh scope for an old craft. Messages transmitted publicly could be as important as secret communications between governments. In 1956, during the Suez crisis, Moscow Radio broadcast messages from the Soviet government to the governments of Britain and France, threatening them with rocket attack. During the Cuba missile crisis, in October 1962, President Kennedy and Khrushchev both used television broadcasts to make important communications to one another. The transistor radio provided a crucial new instrument for governments and their opponents alike – provided that they had the skill and the authority to use it. In April 1961 the President of France, General de Gaulle, was faced by a revolt by French generals in Algiers. He broadcast, on television and on radio, forbidding all Frenchmen and above all soldiers to obey the orders of the rebellious officers, and making a dramatic appeal: '*Françaises, Français, aidez-moi!*' Thanks to transistors, he was able to speak directly to the rank and file of the army in Algiers, and support for the revolt melted away. The Ayatollah Khomeini, the religious leader of opposition to the Shah of Persia, was able to work the other way about. Living in exile in Paris, Khomeini made cassette recordings attacking the Shah and his policies. Small in size, and reproduced in thousands of copies, these cassettes were smuggled into Iran and listened to on transistor radios with cassette players. In both these cases, the winning combination was that of modern technology with traditional authority – patriotism on the part of de Gaulle, religion on the part of Khomeini.

Television reporting, with its vividness, immediacy and apparent authenticity, could have a remarkable heightening effect in a crisis. During the Cuba missile crisis, a Soviet merchant vessel was filmed approaching an American blockading warship, and television audiences in the United States watched transfixed as the ships met and passed – without incident, as it happened. Sometimes, television coverage had a marked effect in changing public opinion. The television pictures of the communist Tet offensive in South Vietnam in 1968 shook their American audiences. In the Middle East, until the late 1980s, western (and especially American) opinion was broadly pro-Israeli, and the Israeli government had played its hand successfully as the best source of news for the western media. Then the *intifada*, the Arab rising in the West Bank and Gaza Strip beginning in December 1987, was filmed by western television crews, not through manipulation by the Palestinians but simply because they happened to be there. Arab youths with stones as their weapons confronted heavily armed Israeli soldiers, reversing the common conception of a tiny Israel at grips with bigger neighbours. It is hard to be certain about such matters, but it is likely that these television pictures marked a turning-point in western sentiments towards the Palestinians – even in the United States, where pro-Israeli feeling remained strong in some circles. Sometimes the pressure of television was applied directly to governments. During the famine in Somalia in 1992, what is well called 'the media drumbeat' created a public demand in the West for something to be done, and the United States launched 'Operation Provide Hope', with American troops arriving in Mogadishu in December 1992. (They left shortly afterwards, having provided almost nothing.) A British official once incautiously remarked that 'We are under no pressure to do something about crises that are not on television' – which was by no means wholly true, but had enough truth in it to be revealing.[36]

For most of the period since 1945, the sources of news and the means of its dissemination lay in the hands of the advanced industrial countries, which had developed a whole network of news-gathering and transmission. The Soviet Union had its own news agency, Tass; its own official press (notably *Pravda* and *Izvestia*), and the broadcasting power of Radio Moscow. But most of the world relied on the four great Western news agencies – Reuters, Associated Press, United Press International, and *Agence France-Presse* (formerly Havas Agency). It has been estimated that in the mid-1980s these four news agencies together provided some 80 per cent of the world's international news; that Reuters served the media of 158 countries, and Associated Press those of 115.[37] As the Third World and non-aligned states emerged into prominence in the 1960s and 1970s, they became acutely conscious that for many purposes they could only draw upon sources of information provided by the West, and that the presentation even of their own affairs to the world at large was in Western hands.

Third World and developing countries reacted against this situation in various ways. In the 1960s a Latin American news agency, the Inter Press Service, was set up to provide information about Latin America in addition to that of the main news agencies. In 1975 the Non-Aligned News Agency Pool was established, for the same purpose though with a wider constituency. In 1976 UNESCO (the United Nations Educational, Scientific and Cultural Organization), meeting at Nairobi, adopted a resolution to establish a New World Information and Communications Order – a proposal which had been launched at the Non-Aligned Summit at Algiers in 1973. The General Assembly of the United Nations formally took up the UNESCO proposal later in 1976. Like a number of other grandiose schemes put forward at the United Nations, the New Information Order remained largely a dead letter – as we have just seen, the big four news agencies retained their prominent positions in the 1980s. In any case, the Third World countries complained too much. Nearly every country had its own radio station which could be use for propaganda purposes – Radio Cairo broadcast to the whole Arabic-speaking world. Newspapers were perfectly capable of taking reports from the main news agencies and exploiting them after their own fashion. Even so, the issue was real, and the claim for a New Information Order reflected the importance of news and propaganda in international affairs.

Nowhere was this importance more obvious than in the conduct of the Cold War, which, because it remained 'cold' by avoiding military conflict between the superpowers, was a propaganda war as well as much else. For a long time, the main battleground was on the air-waves – radio broadcasting. On the Western side, the first in the field was not the United States but Britain. In March 1946 the BBC began to broadcast in Russian (which it had not done during the war), with three programmes each day totalling one-and-a-quarter hours, including a news bulletin. The tone maintained the objectivity which had been adopted with such success during the Second World War, which was perfectly compatible with skilled propaganda, though Solzhenitsyn was later to criticize the BBC for pulling its punches in its Russian-language broadcasts. (It was notable that the Soviets did not begin to jam the BBC until 1949.) On the American side, the Voice of America began broadcasts in Russian in February 1947, and by 1951 was broadcasting in several other languages within the Soviet Union – Estonian, Latvian, Lithuanian, Armenian, Azerbaijani, Georgian, Tartar and Turkmeni. In 1950 a new American radio station, Radio Free Europe, began transmissions from Munich to eastern Europe, using six languages: Polish, Hungarian, Czech, Slovak, Romanian, and Bulgarian. (Albanian was added for a brief period, from 1953 to 1955.) In 1953 another new station came on the air: Radio Liberation from Bolshevism, broadcasting to the peoples of the Soviet Union in Russian, Ukrainian, Estonian, Latvian, Lithuanian, Armenian, Azerbaijani, Georgian, Armenian, Turkmeni and Uzbek. In 1956 this station was renamed Radio Liberation, and in 1959 changed its name again to Radio Liberty – significantly dropping the idea of 'liberation', which had manifestly not been pursued during the Hungarian rising of 1956. The Voice of America was an American government venture, in the same pattern (though not the same style) as the BBC

World Service. Radio Free Europe and Radio Liberation/Liberty were run by the Central Intelligence Agency as part of psychological warfare.

On the other side, the Soviet Union started from a stronger position, in that communist ideas already circulated freely in Western countries. Communist parties all had their newspapers. Fellow-travellers supported the Soviet Union from an apparently independent position – in France, for example, Jean-Paul Sartre was immensely influential. There were a number of communist 'front' organizations (for example, the World Peace Council, founded in 1952), which attracted widespread support. Communism itself, and the determination to hold a dialogue with communism, took deep root in Western universities and in the churches. Therefore, the task of Soviet radio broadcasting was very different from that of Western radio, which had to try to infiltrate into a closed society. Radio Moscow also started with a fund of goodwill built up between 1941 and 1945, when Soviet broadcasts were popular in the occupied countries. After the war, the Soviets continued to broadcast in the principal west European languages, and also put out a world service in English designed to reach the English-speaking elites in Asia and Africa. Among the Soviet satellites, East Germany was the most active in radio broadcasting; in the 1960s, the East Germans had two stations broadcasting to West Germany, and also put out programmes in other languages, including Arabic and Swahili.

The effects of all these efforts are difficult to assess. Radio broadcasts could be jammed, though in fact this was one-way traffic. The Soviets jammed, the West did not; which reveals something about Soviet anxieties. Jamming of the Voice of America began in April 1948, that of the BBC in 1949. By 1962 the Soviets were using between two and three thousand stations to jam broadcasts from the West.[38] Suspensions of jamming of the Voice of America and the BBC became a sort of barometer of the state of the Cold War. The Soviets ceased jamming briefly in Spring 1956, and again during Khrushchev's visit to the United States in 1959. They stopped again in 1963, and resumed only in 1968, at the time of the Soviet invasion of Czechoslovakia. Jamming was again suspended in 1973, as détente with the United States developed, and resumed in 1980 with the invasion of Afghanistan and the renewed Cold War. Jamming of the Voice of America and the BBC was ended under Gorbachev in 1987, and not resumed. It is worth noting that Radio Liberty, the principal CIA station, was jammed consistently from its start in 1953 until the end of 1988 – there was no discharge in that particular part of the Cold War until hostilities were virtually at an end. Technically, jamming was never totally effective, and skilled hands could sometimes retune radios to evade it. Western broadcasts reached listeners in the Soviet bloc, though evidence on their numbers was necessarily patchy. Poland, Czechoslovakia and Hungary provided the largest audiences; numbers in the Soviet Union appear to have been small, except for Moscow, Leningrad and the Baltic states. Some estimates put the total audience for Western broadcasting as high as one-third of the adult population, and even three-quarters in exceptional circumstances; but these seem likely to be excessive.[39] In the West, there appears to have been only a small audience for Radio Moscow, made up partly of devotees and partly of specialists in search of information.

The contribution of all this to the eventual outcome of the Cold War remains uncertain. The very fact of Soviet jamming reflected a dangerous lack of self-confidence even at times of the greatest Soviet success, which may well have had a long-term effect. Western broadcasting gave its listeners in the Soviet bloc a link with the outside world, and an opportunity to escape (in however limited a degree) from enforced isolation. This influence was naturally strongest in the eastern European countries which only came under Soviet dominance after 1945. By 1987 and 1988, when jamming of broadcasting came to an end, other means of communication were also opening up. Direct television broadcasting by satellite allowed television receivers deep in the Soviet Union to pick up programmes from the West. Fax and electronic mail services between West and East began to operate. Philip Taylor sums up judiciously: 'It is impossible to attribute the changes of the period 1989–91 purely to live satellite television or to increased international communications. But it is equally difficult to see how such changes could have taken place without them.'[40]

There are at least two exceptions to the influence of communications and the mass media which should give us pause to reflect. In Tiananmen Square, Beijing, on 4 June 1989, the Chinese government demonstrated that power still grew out of the barrel of a gun, as Mao had written long before. 'Tanks, not television, decided the outcome.'[41] Western opinion was naturally shocked, but equally naturally the shock wore off with time. In Cuba, the United States has been broadcasting by radio since the 1960s and by television since 1990, with little apparent effect. China showed that force has not lost its influence. Cuba probably demonstrates the strength of a deep antipathy towards an over-mighty neighbour.

Radio and television are powerful, but they have their limits. Modern communications have brought changes in the conduct of international affairs, without utterly transforming them. Even in the most obvious aspects (such as the speed with which communications, including pictures, can be transmitted), the changes are less remarkable than they often appear. During the war crisis of July 1914, telegrams took only hours to reach a foreign capital, and news of the mobilization of armies was telephoned at once. It is probably the weight and multiplicity of channels of communication, and the extra vividness of television pictures, which had had the most effect in putting pressure on governments. States (except for the most inscrutable and thick-skinned) are more conscious of their *image* – that key word of modern times – than they were a hundred, or even fifty years ago; and in that respect international affairs have taken on a different aspect.

Among these means by which international affairs are conducted there are some strange contrasts. In the modern use and threat of force, the extremely simple (an ambush in guerrilla warfare, stone-throwing during the *intifada*) goes alongside the highly complex (nuclear weapons, and the sophisticated theories regarding their use). The old diplomacy co-exists with the new. Perhaps most remarkably, when many advantages lay with the great powers, with their modern armaments, advanced economies and well-organized governments, the balance was often redressed in favour of weaker countries, and sometimes of peoples who had yet to form a state. In warfare, guerrillas could defeat regular armies, as the Algerian nationalists did when fighting the French, and the Vietcong and North Vietnamese when fighting the Americans. The United Nations Organization, which was designed to give particular weight to the great powers, came to be dominated by the votes and the ambitions of the Third World countries, many of them with only tiny populations. The mass media which dominated publicity and communications in the world were mostly in the hands of the advanced industrial countries, and the Third World complained that it was discriminated against and marginalized; yet these same mass media focussed a degree of attention on the Third World (especially Africa) which it could never otherwise have secured. All three main elements in the conduct of international affairs thus conspired to shift the balance of influence (not power) towards the weaker countries. This was a curious and unexpected state of affairs.

◆ Notes to Chapter 23

1. Raymond Aron, *Peace and War* (London, 1966), p. 5.
2. Rosemary Righter, *Utopia Lost: The United Nations and World Order* (New York, 1995), p. 115.
3. Patrick Brogan, *World Conflicts: Why and Where they are happening* (London, 1989), p. vii; B. J. Bond, *The Pursuit of Victory: From Napoleon to Saddam Hussein* (Oxford, 1996), p. 171.
4. Figure of 18 080 000 compiled from the casualty figures in Brogan, *World Conflicts*, pp. 567–71 – which the author presents with grave warnings as to their unreliability.
5. Seweryn Bialer, *The Soviet Paradox: External Expansion, Internal Decay* (London, 1986), p. 277.
6. David Miller, *The Cold War: A Military History* (London, 1998), pp.359–61.
7. See above, pp. 156, 300–4, 319–21.
8. Miller, *Cold War*, pp. 71–2.
9. *Ibid.*, p. 159.

10. *Ibid.*, p. 160.
11. *Ibid.*, p. 81.
12. Daniel Colard, *Les relations internationales de 1945 à nos jours* (Paris, 6th edn, 1996), p. 194, provides a valuable summary; see also above, pp. 300–4.
13. Miller, *Cold War*, p. 81.
14. *Ibid.*, pp.136–48, 405.
15. Vladislav Zubok and Constantine Pleshakov, *Inside the Kremlin's Cold War* (Cambridge, Mass., 1996), pp.191–2.
16. Report in *Figaro*, 23 February 1999, based on the recollections of Stanislav Petrov, the Lieutenant-Colonel on duty that night.
17. See the discussion in Robert Colquhoun, *Raymond Aron*, Vol.II: *Sociologist in Society, 1955–1983* (London, 1986), p. 186.
18. It is still well worth reading Harold Nicolson, *Diplomacy* (London, 1939), and see also Thomas Otte, *Harold Nicolson and Diplomatic Theory* (Leicester, 1998). For the change which followed 1945, see Peter Marshal, *Positive Diplomacy* (London, 1997), pp. 9–19.
19. Quoted in Righter, *Utopia Lost*, p. 77. The two examples which follow are taken from the same source.
20. Chris Cook, *World Political Almanac* (London, 3rd edn, 1995), pp. 326–9. This list omits a number of operations (UN Special Commission in the Balkans, 1947–54; UN Good Offices Mission in Afghanistan, 1988–90; UN Group of Military Observers, Iran and Iraq, 1988–9; UN Mission of Verification in Angola, 1989–91; UN Assistance Group in Namibia and Angola) on the grounds that they were not strictly peace-keeping. But some definitions could include them, bringing the total to 19.
21. For UN peace-keeping since 1990, see below pp. 553–7.
22. Quoted in J. P. D. Dunbabin, *The Post-Imperial Age* (London, 1994), p. 6.
23. *Keesing's Contemporary Archives*, 1966, p. 21257A.
24. *Ibid.*, 1975, p. 27487A.
25. Anthony Parsons, *From Cold War to Hot Peace: UN Interventions 1947–1994* (London, 1995), p. viii.
26. See the valuable summary of the GATT negotiations in Segal, *World Affairs Companion*, pp. 36–8.
27. See P.T. Bauer, *Equality, the Third World and Economic Delusion* (London, 1981), pp. 185–90: 'The Lesson of Hong Kong'.
28. 'The Grail of Equality', in *ibid.*, pp. 8–25 – a severe and effective attack on the whole idea, concluding that the creation and maintenance of economic equality between states could only be achieved by massive coercion – by whom?
29. See the acid comments in Paul Johnson, *A History of the Modern World:From 1917 to the 1980s* (London, paperback, 1984), p. 692.

30. Text in *Keesing's Contemporary Archives*, 1988, p. 9699A; see also the UN website: www.un.org/overview/rights.htmk

31. *Keesing's*, 1987, p. 35035. The USA voted against; the abstentions included West Germany, Israel, Japan and the United Kingdom.

32. Righter, *Utopia Lost*, pp. 298–300.

33. *Ibid.*, p. 18; Samuel P. Huntington, *The Clash of Civilizations and the Remaking of World Order* (New York, 1996), pp. 194–6.

34. Colard, *Relations internationales*, p. 103, gives a figure of over 3000; Eric Hobsbawm, *Age of Extremes: The Short Twentieth Century, 1914–1991* (London, 1994), p. 461, gives 4615.

35. *Encyclopedia Britannica Book of the Year*, 1990, p.379.

36. The phrase 'media drumbeat', quoted in Philip M. Taylor, *Global Communications, International Affairs and the Media since 1945* (London, 1997), p. 75; British official's remark quoted *ibid.*, p. 93.

37. *Ibid.*, p. 48.

38. *Ibid.*, p. 42.

39. See Kenneth Short, ed., *Western Broadcasting over the Iron Curtain* (New York, 1986), chapters by E. Parta and M. McIntosh; Gabriel Partos, *The World that Came in from the Cold* (London, 1993), p. 90, puts the proportion at one-third to three-quarters, according to circumstances.

40. Taylor, *Global Communications*, p. 53.

41. *Ibid.*, p. 87.

CHAPTER
24

MOTIVATION: WHY DO STATES AND PEOPLES ACT AS THEY DO?

**Reasons of state and national interests – Ideas and beliefs:
ideologies, nationalism and religion**

We have seen *how* states and peoples conduct their relations with one another. There remains a deeper and more difficult question: *why* do they act as they do? As with individuals, the motives of governments and peoples are usually mixed – a combination of self-interest, beliefs and emotions. Let us look at the main elements in the mixture.

◆ Reasons of state and national interests

In the eighteenth and nineteenth centuries it was generally assumed that those who governed states should act according to reasons of state. That was, after all, their function, and the trade which they pursued was rightly called statecraft. Statesmen were expected to follow rational courses of action, designed to protect or advance the national interest, which should itself be the subject of reasonable assessment and calculation. This remains largely true for the period after 1945. There have been very few rulers so devoted to an ideal or an ideology, or perhaps so far gone in insanity, as to choose to wreck their own country – Hitler in his last days was one, and modern Africa has produced one or two.

It is therefore necessary to start an examination of why states and peoples act as they do in their relations with one another by discussing reasons of state and the concept of the national interest. Unhappily, these familiar terms at once present a problem of definition. What are national interests? A distinguished historian has argued that 'national interest is what people think it is'; and an experienced practitioner of diplomacy and statecraft reflected in his retirement that the interests of states 'exist only in the mind, or at least become effective only when thought about'.[1] It is true that national interest is to some degree subjective. Moreover, within any

country there are different individual or sectional interests, which sometimes claim to represent the whole country, or that their particular concerns
should override other considerations. For example, it may be to the advantage of a number of commercial firms, and their workers, and indeed the
national economy as a whole, to trade with a country which other people
regard, on political grounds, as hostile or evil. In such circumstances, where
does the national interest lie?

Such problems are real, but need not deter us. National interest may be
what people think it is, but at least we know what it is usually considered
to be. There is a widely agreed set of components, starting with security: the
safety of the state, including its independence, its territory and the lives of
its people. These three elements cannot be treated as equal. In war, lives are
sacrificed to secure independence, and in extreme circumstances countries
will surrender territory or even independence rather than incur unacceptable loss of life. For example, in 1940 Denmark yielded to German invasion
rather than attempt a hopeless resistance, and similarly the Baltic states of
Estonia, Latvia and Lithuania accepted Soviet annexation for the same
reason. Total security in all respects is a rare commodity, and has probably
not been attained by any state, great or small, in the period since 1945. The
strongest power in the world, the United States, was threatened by nuclear
attack from the Soviet Union and felt under a strange psychological challenge from Cuba. Nepal, though protected by the Himalayas, could not feel
safe from the Chinese, who had occupied Tibet. Even Switzerland, sheltered
by its traditional neutrality, would not have been immune if the Soviets had
invaded western Europe. So in fact every country has to settle for *relative*
security, based on military strength, or alliances, or neutrality, as seems
best.

After security, every state seeks economic advantage of some sort – to
maintain or increase its wealth, or at least escape from poverty. This
universal principle needs little illustration, though it has been put into
practice in many different ways – by setting up tariffs to protect home
industries and agriculture, by securing control of raw materials, or by the
attempts of poor countries to attract aid or to cancel their debts. Economic
advantage may sometimes conflict with security. For example, governments may well have to choose between military expenditure for security
and investment to promote prosperity or social services at home. More
specifically, in the 1960s west European members of NATO could buy oil
from the Soviet Union more cheaply than elsewhere, but the United States
tried to persuade them not to become dependent on imports from the
enemy in the Cold War, which might be cut off at any moment. A similar
dispute arose in the 1980s over the purchase of natural gas from Siberia,
and the west Europeans (even the British) eventually went ahead with the
project despite American arguments that it prejudiced their security and
increased Soviet revenues.

Economic advantage is material, and usually measurable; but the immaterial, in the unmeasurable form of prestige, can be every bit as important. Is there a country in the world which does not aspire to its own version of the Field of the Cloth of Gold, where Henry VIII of England met Francis I of France, amid great pomp and display, in 1520? The quest for prestige and national status symbols can eat up money and material resources. Some of the poorest African states feel they must have their own national airline. In Côte d'Ivoire, President Houphouet-Boigny built, in the new capital of Yamoussoukrou, the vast Basilica of Our Lady of Peace, rivalling St Peter's in Rome in some respects, in a country with only about a million Catholics in a population of fourteen million.[2] Countries bid against one another to stage the Olympic Games, even though the financial cost of doing so may never be recovered. At a more modest level, most countries practise some form of cultural diplomacy, to promote their language, literature and art. This may sometimes bring a practical return (particularly through the use of language), but is more usually a matter of prestige whose advantages are at best indirect and intangible.

Finally, most governments have to judge the national interest, even in foreign policy, in terms of internal politics and pressures. American presidents, in many respects immensely powerful, are subject to the constraints applied by Congress, the mass media and public opinion. In 1947 President Truman knew that his policy of aid to Greece and Turkey (the Truman Doctrine) depended entirely on Congressional support, which he won over by playing on anti-communist sentiment – Senator Vandenberg advised him to 'scare hell out of the country'.[3] In the next few years there was no need to scare the hell out of anyone, because they were scared already. Anticommunist feeling became so strong that no American president could afford to be accused of being 'soft on communism'. In the 1960s, President Johnson was determined not to be the man who 'lost' South Vietnam to the communists, as Truman had been accused of 'losing' China in 1949. Later still, domestic opinion changed, and pressure built up for the United States to withdraw from Vietnam, more or less whatever the consequences. In these circumstances, the American national interest became in the short term a matter of trying to pacify opposition at home, and in the long term to restore internal unity, rather than achieving any specific foreign policy objective. In a similar way, though in very different circumstances, Gorbachev's foreign policy in the late 1980s was largely determined by domestic considerations. His fundamental objective was reform at home, and to achieve it he desperately needed agreement with the United States, to avoid a new arms race and gain some economic flexibility. He was working against time, and to gain his objectives at home he needed to bring an end to the Cold War abroad. Many other cases could be cited, for example when governments are subject to the demands of pressure groups – to save the life of a national condemned by a foreign court; to impose an arms embargo on a dangerous or unpopular government; or even to secure the overthrow of an evil regime, e.g. the *apartheid* regime in South Africa. In such circumstances national interest can indeed become what some important group thinks it is, or a particular view of morality may prevail against the idea of national interest itself. Reasons of state might thus be subordinated to very different concepts of foreign policy, based on ideas and beliefs.

◆ Ideas and beliefs: ideologies, nationalism and religion

Ideology

The twentieth century was, by common consent, an age of ideology, but it is not so easy to find agreement on what the term means. For the purposes of international history rather than political theory, we may use Alan Cassels' working definition that an ideology is 'a set of closely related ideas held by a group', embodying 'a broad interpretation of the human condition'. As such it may vary from a carefully constructed world outlook devised by intellectuals to a vague set of general values held by a wider public.[4] Raymond Aron observed that an ideology is 'a secular religion', which strikes just the right note;[5] and it is interesting to see that Eric Hobsbawm, whose political standpoint is far removed from Raymond Aron's, describes the twentieth century as 'an era of religious wars' between ideologies whose divinities were politicians treated as gods.[6]

The period since 1945 has been one of constant ideological struggle, between between Marxism-Leninism on the one hand and liberal democracy plus capitalism (more or less modified) on the other. This situation was complicated by the split between the Soviet and the Chinese brands of Marxism-Leninism, producing a three-sided conflict and a good deal of confusion, not least because these struggles have been pursued *within* states as well as *between* them.

The ideological aspects of the Cold War and the Sino-Soviet dispute have already been discussed earlier in this book, but it is worth reviewing certain points here, and asking what role ideology played in the foreign policies of the Soviet Union, China and the United States.

The Soviet Union claimed that ideology was its *raison d'être*. Dostoyevsky once wrote that 'Every great people believes, and must believe if it intends to live long, that in it alone resides the salvation of the world.'[7] When the Bolsheviks seized power, that was what they believed. The Soviet state 'was created to fulfil a mission'.[8] With the passage of time, that mission changed in character and diminished in influence. In the 1930s Stalin put the interests of the Soviet state ahead of those of international communism – though he could always claim that in the long run the two were the same. Khrushchev grasped that nuclear weapons would pay no attention to the class system, and he therefore abandoned the Leninist doctrine of the inevitability of war between the socialist and imperialist camps. Even so, he appears not to have lost his faith in the eventual victory of socialism, finding new hope in the Third World. Similarly, Gorbachev understood the failures of the Soviet system, but he wanted to reform it, not abandon it. By the 1980s, ideology did not play the role which it had played in the 1920s, but it still retained an important influence. It provided categories of thought and expression – it was difficult for Soviet leaders, and the officials who advised them, to see the world except through Marxist–Leninist spectacles. It instilled a belief that socialism (whatever its temporary difficulties) was superior to capitalism, and would prevail in the end – history was on the side of the Soviets. And it nourished a sense of achievement, through victory in war and material advance in peace.[9]

All this meant that there was always an ambiguity in Soviet foreign policy. The Soviet Union could never behave simply as a great power (in so far as great powers ever behave 'simply' at all). This showed itself in all kinds of ways, not least in policy towards the Third World. The XXV Congress of the Communist Party of the Soviet Union in 1976 stressed the importance of strengthening co-operation with the developing countries and increasing their role in world development.[10] This was not mere window-dressing. Dobrynin (the Soviet Ambassador in Washington) observed rather wearily that almost any delegation could turn up in Moscow from a Third World country, spin a tale about socialism, and go home with a loan or a promise of arms supplies. In the Middle East, Soviet policy was much complicated by ideology. Islam represented a religion, and indeed a whole way of life which was inevitably opposed to socialism. The Soviets believed that Islam, like all religions, was reactionary, and would eventually die out – with some help from Centres for Scientific Atheism (one of which was set up in Tashkent as late as 1982). Yet Islam was also a force which could rally the masses against western imperialism, and should therefore be encouraged. The Soviet Union was thus placed in the awkward position of opposing Islam in some circumstances and encouraging it in others.[11]

The ideological element in Soviet policy led to the striking fact that in the period after the Second World War the Soviet Union used force directly against other communist countries – in Hungary in 1956, in Czechoslovakia in 1968, on the border with China in 1969, and in the invasion of Afghanistan in 1979, which was at first intended to replace one communist leader by a more reliable one. Soviet propaganda delivered ferocious attacks against Tito and Mao, who were regarded as renegade communists. Khrushchev and Brezhnev found it easier to talk to Eisenhower and Nixon than to Mao or other Chinese leaders. This was because heretics were more dangerous to the Soviets than unbelievers, because they threatened the whole legitimacy of the Soviet regime.[12] This did not mean that the Soviet Union could never deal with Yugoslavia and China, and reach some accommodation with them – at various times and to some degree they managed to do so; but the process was made much more difficult by considerations of ideology.

In short, ideology was by no means the sole determinant of Soviet foreign policy, but it was always an influence. There was no question of the Soviet Union being simply one state among others, conducting its policy on grounds of power politics and reason of state alone.

The same was true, and perhaps more so, of communist China. Mao Zedong rejected crucial Soviet doctrines in the conduct of foreign affairs. He condemned Khrushchev's acceptance of peaceful co-existence with the United States, maintaining instead the inevitability of war between the socialist and capitalist camps. Moreover, he refused to accept the simple division of the world into these two camps, claiming that in fact there were three, very differently composed: (1) the superpowers, the USA and the Soviet Union, which worked together to impose their will upon others; (2) other developed and industrialized states; and (3) the Third World in Asia, Africa and Latin America, of which China was the natural leader. This aggressive and idiosyncratic ideological stance had a profound influence on Chinese foreign policy. It did much to bring about the Sino-Soviet dispute, in which the ideological split was probably the most important single element. (The Chinese knew exactly how to irritate the Soviets. In 1966 they renamed the street in Beijing on which the Soviet Embassy stood 'The Street of the Struggle Against Revisionism', so that the Embassy had to put this taunt on its letterhead!)[13] This did not mean that Chinese foreign policy was completely inflexible. For example, the Chinese were willing to co-operate with Pakistan, an Islamic country frequently ruled by military dictators. In 1971–72 they even received visits by Kissinger and Nixon, and reached a working arrangement with the United States. But any attempt to understand Chinese policy *without* ideology would lead to distortion.

The appeal of Marxism-Leninism spread far beyond the Soviet Union and China. In the early 1980s other states professing Marxism-Leninism, in one form or another, comprised, in Asia: North Korea, Outer Mongolia, Vietnam, Laos, Cambodia, Afghanistan and South Yemen; in Africa: Ethiopia, Angola, Mozambique, and Zimbabwe; in Latin America: Cuba and Nicaragua; and in Europe the six Soviet satellites (East Germany, Poland, Czechoslovakia, Hungary, Romania, and Bulgaria), plus Albania and Yugoslavia. This made a total of twenty-two states, making up perhaps one-third of the population of the world. Moreover, for most of the period after 1945 the ideology of communism exerted a strong appeal to many intellectuals in the West, as well as to communist parties across the world. This appeal was reinforced by transposing the Marxist analysis of the class struggle onto a global basis, in the form of a 'development theory' in which the capitalist industrial states played the role of the bourgeoisie and the developing countries formed a worldwide proletariat. In these ways, there was scarcely any aspect of world affairs in which Marxist ideology did not play some part, thus living up to its universalist aspirations.

The United States also professed a form of universalist ideology, not in the shape of a tightly constructed intellectual outlook but of a general set of ideas and sentiments, made up of democracy, individualism and the free market. It has been well said that Franklin Roosevelt believed that everyone would adopt American values and the American way of life if they only had the chance; and most of his countrymen probably shared that belief. President Reagan thought much the same, putting it in his own way by invoking the American dream. 'The American dream lives – not only in the hearts and minds of our countrymen but ·. . . of millions of the world's people in both free and oppressed societies who look to us for leadership. As long as that dream lives, as long as we continue to defend it, America has a future, and all mankind has a reason to hope.'[14] A dream is by definition vague and insubstantial, and for that very reason it can appeal to all sorts and conditions of men. For most of the time, most Americans maintained a remarkable belief in their own destiny as 'the last, best hope of earth'. They would have agreed with Dostoyevsky that in them, as a great people, resided the salvation of the world.

Yet this went alongside what even a sympathetic observer has described as 'a strange lack of inner confidence'.[15] Government and people alike fell from time to time into an excessive fear of a powerful communist bloc abroad and a communist conspiracy at home, producing an almost obsessive anti-communist mind-set. This caused a division between the United States and its western European allies. The French and British, with their very different circumstances and experiences, refused to be frightened by what they often regarded as the bogeyman of communism. The French were not unduly perturbed when as much as a quarter of their electorate voted communist. The British refused to follow the Americans in not recognizing the communist government of China, applying the conventional pragmatic tests for diplomatic recognition rather than declaiming against an evil regime. The ideological rigidity of American anti-communism thus produced a rift in the North Atlantic alliance – even though the west Europeans were fundamentally on the same side as the Americans, and professed the same values. In the Western world, ideology therefore cut two ways, forming an important basis for the North Atlantic alliance and at the same time creating a fault line within it.

At the same time, a number of west European states were pursuing an ideological programme of their own in the development of European integration. In 1950 the Schuman Plan proposed to set up a High Authority to exercise supranational control over the coal and steel industries of its six member states (France, West Germany, Italy, Belgium, the Netherlands, and Luxembourg), which together formed the European Coal and Steel Community. In 1957 the same six states concluded the Treaty of Rome, setting up the European Economic Community, which took the process of integration further by creating (over a period of time) a single internal market, a common external tariff, and institutions exercising significant authority in the member states. The founding fathers of this movement (Jean Monnet and Robert Schuman in France, Konrad Adenauer in Germany, Alcide de Gasperi in Italy, Paul-Henri Spaak in Belgium) shared a common stock of thought and sentiment. They believed that in 1940 the nation state had failed in Europe, and also that Nazi Germany had perverted the ideals of nationalism beyond repair. It was therefore necessary to put something in the place of the nation state, and to rebuild western Europe on a new model. Schuman, Adenauer and de Gasperi were all Catholics, but the idea of west European unity was equally attractive to many socialists, with their own tradition of internationalism. The idea of European unification was far from new, but its embodiment in political, economic and legal structures was an immense departure. Thus a new ideology was brought to bear on international affairs.

Communists believed that the age of the nation state was over and that the unifying principle for everyone was no longer nationality, but class. Americans, in a much vaguer way, believed that everyone would become Americanized if they had the opportunity. The advocates of European integration started from the premiss that the nation state had failed, and must be replaced by a wider European entity. Reports of the death of the nation state came in from all directions. They were much exaggerated. Nations and nationalism proved to be very much alive.

Nations and nationalism

In common parlance, the words 'state' and 'nation' are often used interchangeably, which can be misleading and sometimes completely false. A state is a political entity, with a government and a territory defined by specific frontiers. As such, it may be be largely made up of a single nation (a nation-state), or it may contain several nations – for example, the Hapsburg Empire before 1918, or the Soviet Union (multi-national states). A nation is a group of people conscious of its own identity, and often seeking to create a state to embody that identity – hence the many demands for national self-determination in the nineteenth and twentieth centuries.

In 1945 the new world organization formally took the title of the United Nations, a misnomer which highlights this contrast. The United Nations was an organization of *states*, not nations; and there were many nations which had not yet succeeded in creating states for themselves. This issue soon came to dominate the political activities of the United Nations, as the

UN set out to assist the liberation of colonial peoples seeking to form their own states. In 1960 the General Assembly adopted Resolution No.1514, declaring that: 'All peoples have the right to self-determination; by virtue of that right they freely determine their political status and freely pursue their economic, social and cultural development.'[16]

This avoided the use of the word 'nation', but was otherwise a classic statement of the right of national self-determination. But when does a people become a nation? No one can say for certain, because there are no objective and generally accepted criteria for nationhood. Every test that can be applied (language, territory, race, common history and tradition, religion) breaks down in one case or another. In Europe, language was for a long time regarded as the strongest basis for a nation, but the Swiss with their four languages and the Belgians with two, at once appeared as exceptions. Outside Europe, Indian nationalism could never appeal to linguistic unity, but had to absorb hundreds of different languages. In Latin America, the common language of Spanish did not prevent the emergence of separate nations. Territory raises problems, because two nations may be in contention for the same territory, and in an extreme case Zionists claimed (up to 1948) that they formed a nation which had yet to attain a territory.

Again, there is no single means by which a nation comes into existence. Sometimes the nation is formed by the state, as in the long growth of France and England under their respective monarchies; sometimes the nation formed the state, as in the case of Italy and Germany in the nineteenth century – though with some help from Cavour, Bismarck and others. Some nations have been promoted by writers, intellectuals and politicians; others are rooted in ancient traditions, and persist in spite of intellectuals and politicians.

None of these difficulties of definition or criteria appear to matter much in practice, because the essence of nationalism lies in instinct and sentiment. 'Each nationalist proposes as the critical test whatever is closest to his heart.' The key to the appeal of nationalism is that it provides an answer to the question 'Who are we?' To that question, 'Every state has to have an answer'.[17] The answer is found in elements which are both ancient and modern. Every nation must have a history, and if it does not have a real history it will invent one. It must have a literature (folk-tales and poetry are best), heroes and martyrs. It must have an anthem – the French picked a winner in the *Marseillaise*; American baseball games begin with 'The Star-Spangled Banner'; and enthusiasts for a united Europe have seized on the last movement of Beethoven's Choral Symphony. New nations sometimes have a new capital – Washington, Canberra, Brasilia, Islamabad. Israel, *sui generis* as always, has two capitals, a new one in Tel Aviv and an ancient one in Jerusalem. The universal symbol of nationhood is a flag, which must be invented when a nation comes into being, preserved if it goes into eclipse, and transformed when it changes its character – as when South Africa adopted its present multi-coloured banner in place of the old flag which bore the Dutch colours and the Union Jack. Flags may also reveal the aspirations of the future. Samuel Huntington observed that in April October 1994 thousands of people marched in Los Angeles *under the Mexican flag* to protest against a referendum denying state benefits to illegal immigrants.[18]

Compared to other motives in the conduct of international affairs, nationalism has the strongest emotional appeal. Reason of state is a matter of calculation, and has to be cold-blooded if not actually cynical. Ideology is usually intellectual and cerebral. Nationalism appeals to the heart. Old nations have shown astonishing powers of endurance. Poland vanished from the map from 1795 to 1918, and again from 1939 to 1945, and then spent over forty years under Soviet domination, but Polish nationalism lived on. When the great frost of the Cold War melted, and the iron grip of Soviet power was removed from eastern Europe and the Soviet Union itself, nations emerged into the light of day and sought to form their own states, sometimes with surprising ease, sometimes only through fierce and bloody struggle. As late as the year 2000 the full weight of the Russian Army had not yet defeated the Chechens. Nationalists are rarely reluctant to shed blood, whether their own or other people's.

The result has been a plethora of nations, some old and some new, some tightly knit and others still in the process of being bound together. Some of the old European nations have perhaps grown weary. The Germans appear uncertain of their identity, and ready to take part in a new Europe. The British are adrift in a sea of devolution and multi-culturalism. Yet in western Europe the ancient nations of the Scots and Basques are reviving their claims to statehood, while in eastern Europe nations welcome their release from Soviet domination. Arab nationalism is torn between the aspirations of pan-Arabism, based on language and a largely common culture, and the development of separate Arab states – Egypt, Syria, Jordan and Iraq have developed strong identities, and the attempt at a union between Egypt and Syria did not last long (1958–61). Asian nations have often had a long history and an ancient civilization to build on, as in India, China, Thailand and Iran. Indonesia, on the other hand, inherited only the unity imposed by the Dutch as the colonizing power, and has attained little coherence. Most modern African states have scarcely been nations at all, by any criterion that is usually applied, but their politicians and intellectuals have tried to create a national self-consciousness to overcome tribal and linguistic divisions. How far this will succeed remains to be seen.

The right to national self-determination is widely accepted, at any rate in principle. Since no one can define a nation, except to say that a people constitutes a nation if it thinks it does (or even if an ardent minority thinks it does), there is potentially no limit to the divisions which may follow. Let us take two small but significant examples. In Sri Lanka, the majority of the population (74 per cent in the 1990s) is Sinhalese, but there is a substantial minority (variously estimated at 16–18 per cent) of Tamils, partly indigenous and partly from India. The Tamils are mostly Hindu (as against the majority religion of Buddhism), they speak their own language, and they are concentrated in the north of the island, in and around the city of Jaffna, on a peninsula almost cut off from the rest of the island. Since 1977 Tamil separatists have waged an incessant conflict, by terror, by guerrilla action, and sometimes by open, regular war. The sheer tenacity and fighting power of the Tamils is testimony to the strength of their national feeling. Successive Sri Lankan governments, dedicated to their own form of nationalism, have refused to allow the unity of their state to be broken up. The result has been a twenty-year war which in the year 2000 was still unresolved.

Cyprus provides a different example, with (so far) a different outcome. Cyprus, formerly a British colony, became independent in 1960, though its Greek population (amounting to about 80 per cent) wanted union with Greece (*Enosis*). After independence, both the Greek Cypriots and the government of Greece itself continued to demand *Enosis*. Turkey, the near neighbour of Cyprus to the north, considered itself the protector of the Turkish population in the island (about 18 per cent), and refused to permit *Enosis*. In July 1974 a group of Greek colonels seized power in Athens and set up a military dictatorship; at the same time, a pro-*Enosis* faction carried out a coup in Cyprus and deposed the president. Fearing a Greek take-over, Turkish forces landed in northern Cyprus, and by mid-August occupied just over one-third of the island. There was a cease-fire, followed by a forced transfer of populations, involving perhaps 225 000 people, mostly Greeks being expelled from the north. A United Nations force was interposed along the cease-fire line, the so-called 'Green Line'. On 15 November 1983 northern Cyprus declared its independence as the Turkish Republic of North Cyprus. It was recognized only by Turkey, and it was condemned by the Security Council of the United Nations, but even so, in the year 2000 the island remains divided along the cease-fire line of 1974, and the Turkish Republic of Northern Cyprus maintains its lonely existence.

How could the principle of self-determination be applied in these circumstances? In 1960, and doubtless in 1974, a majority of Cypriots would probably have voted for union with Greece, and presumably the Turks would have had to accept it or leave. Does the forcible partition of the island since 1974 create a new situation, in which a referendum in the north would certainly result in a vote for independence or possibly union with Turkey? The two nationalisms at grips here are Greek and Turkish; and the issue has been decided (so far) not on principle but by the successful use of force.

In Cyprus as in Sri Lanka, the strength of nationalism has divided two fairly small islands, Turk against Greek, Tamil against Sinhalese. Cyprus is split into two parts; Sri Lanka is subjected to endless civil war. Nationalism has proved a fatally divisive force. What appears in a United Nations resolution as the simple and over-riding principle of self-determination is not simple at all when it comes to be applied, nor is it necessarily over-riding.

Nationalism is powerful, because it commands great emotional commitment, capable of long endurance as well as fierce outbursts. Its appeal is widespread because it is protean, and can adapt to many different circumstances. Its effects are complicated and often unpredictable. As a motive force in international affairs it is at once a reality and a mystery. No theory can grasp it, no diplomacy can manage it, and even force cannot always contain it, because it has a power of its own.

In the latter part of the twentieth century nationalism was joined among the unpredictables of international affairs by religion.

Religion

In the first half of the twentieth century there was a widespread assumption in the developed, industrialized world that international politics were secular in nature. This was as true of the West, where religion continued to hold a place in public life, as in the communist East, where it was excluded and persecuted. (Except in times of dire emergency like the German invasion of the Soviet Union, when even Stalin was prepared to appeal for the help of the Orthodox Church.) When modern man, whether western or communist, no longer gave first place to religion in his own behaviour, he found it difficult to conceive that others could do so, or even could have done so in the past. Historians studying the Protestant Reformation or the Wars of Religion set out to find the deeper motives (usually believed to be economic) which had been hidden beneath the cloak of religion. Similarly, statesmen looking out at the Arab world found it easier to think in terms of Arab nationalism than of Islam. Even the Turkish elite, led by Kemal Ataturk, followed the same path after the collapse of the Ottoman Empire in 1919. They created a new Turkey on secular lines, in the belief that it was the only true pattern for a modern state.

In the second half of the century, this accepted wisdom came under severe challenge, from the widely different quarters of the papacy and Islam.

In 1934 Stalin is said to have remarked to Pierre Laval (the Premier of France, and a good match for Stalin in cynicism), 'The Pope! How many divisions has *he* got?' Churchill, when he related this story, commented that Laval might have mentioned 'a number of legions not always visible on parade'.[19] Stalin's successors came to discover the truth of this observation. In 1978 Karol Wojtyla, a Polish cardinal, was elected to the papacy, and in the next few years became a world statesman as well as religious leader. As early as 1979 Pope John Paul II returned to his native Poland and was greeted by vast crowds. He spoke of the spiritual unity of Europe, including eastern Europe, and gave opposition to Soviet domination a new focus and a fresh impetus, which became an important influence in the collapse of the Soviet bloc in 1989.

Gorbachev, when he set out on his reforming course, speedily grasped what he was up against. He was not the first Soviet statesman to make contact with the Vatican. Gromyko, that stern and cautious Foreign Minister, made eight visits to three different Popes between 1963 and 1985, even though the Soviet Union and the Vatican had no formal diplomatic relations. But Gorbachev, in this matter as in others, was willing to move fast and knew the value of gestures. In February 1988 the Red Army Choir was invited to visit the Vatican, and sang Schubert's *Ave Maria* in the presence of the Pope himself. Later that year the Soviet government held great ceremonies to mark the 1000th anniversary of the conversion of Russia to Christianity; Gorbachev invited the Vatican to send a delegation; and no fewer than ten cardinals attended in response. Each aspect of this event was remarkable – that the Soviet Union should mark a religious commemoration; that the Vatican should be invited; and that it should respond on such a scale. Nothing like this would have been conceivable under Stalin and Pius XII.

In December 1989 the change in relations was finalized by Gorbachev making a formal visit to the Vatican, and the establishment of diplomatic relations between the Soviet Union and the Holy See. It is plain that relations between the two men were more than simply diplomatic. In August 1991, when the old-guard communists mounted their coup against Gorbachev in Moscow, Pope John Paul was in Hungary. When he heard the news that the coup had failed, the Pope exclaimed 'Thank God', and at once sent Gorbachev a telegram of good wishes.[20]

These were remarkable events, signalling the impact of religion on international affairs in a dramatic and unexpected manner. The circumstances were exceptional. The election of a Polish Pope, and John Paul's charismatic appeal in his native land and elsewhere in eastern Europe, coincided with a crisis within the Soviet bloc. (John Paul was elected in 1978, the Soviets invaded Afghanistan at the end of 1979, Gorbachev came to power in 1985.) The two dominant personalities of John Paul and Gorbachev overlapped for only six years, from 1985 to 1991. After that, the situation changed. The Pope turned his attention to many other matters, and to other parts of the world. Religious issues, and relations between church and state, ceased to be central in eastern Europe and the former Soviet Union. It was as though a wave had risen, swept aside some old breakwaters, and then passed. But for a few years there had been no doubt that religion had its impact on international affairs.

There was another religious force which made an impact on world affairs: the revival of Islam. This might have become apparent as early as 1947,

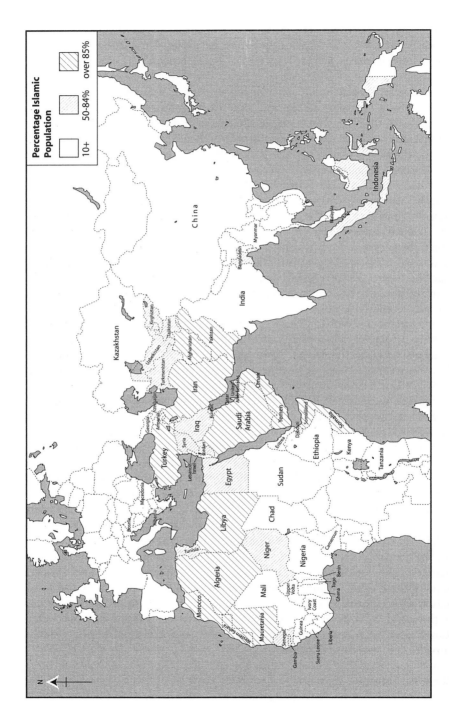

Percentage Islamic
Population

	10+
	50-84%
	over 85%

N

The Islamic World, c.1990

when Pakistan was founded as a new state whose sole reason for existence was religious – the successful demand by Jinnah and his supporters to partition British India along religious lines, and set up a Muslim state. But the significance of this event was not immediately obvious, and the Cold War dominated the political horizon. There was little unity within Islam itself. The ancient rift between Sunnis and Shi-ites (which may be defined as historical rather than doctrinal) goes back to the seventh century AD. The Sunnis form the great majority of Muslims in the modern world, amounting by some estimates to about 90 per cent; the Shi-ites comprise the remainder, mostly in Iran, Pakistan and the Indian sub-continent.[21] During the twentieth century there has been a division between 'modernizers', often among an educated elite, who have tried to redefine Islam in 'progressive' terms and direct religion towards social justice, and those (often called 'fundamentalists') who wished to preserve the whole Muslim tradition, and take Islam as the basis for the whole of politics and law – a specifically Islamic 'just society'.[22] Moreover, while Islam was professed by very large numbers (variously estimated at between 800 and 1000 million in 1990), forming a majority of the population in 36 states, it was for a long time not a political force.[23]

A movement to provide Islam with a political organization began in 1969, after the burning of the Al Aqsa mosque in Jerusalem, which aroused fears of a general attack on Muslim holy places. Leaders from 24 Muslim states met in Rabat, the capital of Morocco, on the initiative of King Faisal of Saudi Arabia, with support from King Hassan of Morocco. This summit conference proposed the creation of the Organization of the Islamic Conference, whose details and structures were agreed on at a series of meetings of foreign ministers, and which was finally established by the Jiddah Pact in 1972. The headquarters of the Organization were established at Jiddah in Saudi Arabia (which provided most of the funds from its vast oil revenues); a summit conference was to be held every three years, and a conference of foreign ministers annually. By 1994 there were 45 member states, plus the Palestine Liberation Organization and Zanzibar (which was part of Tanzania, and thus not itself a state) and a number of countries and organizations with observer status:[24]

Albania	Chad	Indonesia
Algeria	Comoros	Iran
Azerbaijan	Djibuti	Iraq
Bahrein	Egypt	Jordan
Bangladesh	Eritrea	Kuwait
Benin	Gabon	Kyrgyzstan
Brunei	Gambia	Lebanon
Burkina Faso	Guinea	Libya
Cameroon	Guinea-Bissau	Malaysia

Maldives	Palestine Liberation	Sudan
Mali	Organization	Syria
Mauritania	Qatar	Tunisia
Morocco	Saudi Arabia	Turkey
Niger	Senegal	Uganda
Oman	Sierra Leone	United Arab Emirates
Pakistan	Somalia	Yemen

Zanzibar (part of Tanzania, and thus not a state) became a member in 1992. Afghanistan was suspended from membership in January 1980, after the Soviet invasion.

Observers: Nigeria, the Turkish Republic of North Cyprus, Mozambique. The Moro National Liberation Front (Philippines) obtained observer status in 1972 and the Pattani United Liberation Front (Thailand) in 1976.

The Organization of the Islamic Conference was (and remains) the only one of the many international organizations in the world which is based on a religion. It had large funds at its disposal; in 1973 it set up the Islamic Development Bank, and in 1974 a special fund for Muslim minorities. However, in many ways it appeared a familiar entity on the world scene, with its secretariat and regular conferences.

The Iranian revolution of February 1979 introduced a different element altogether into the politics of Islam. The Ayatollah Khomeini set up an Islamic Republic, based on Islamic law and rejecting many of the conventions of the modern world. We have already seen that in December 1984 Iran repudiated the Universal Declaration of Human Rights, which no other state had previously done, whatever their actual practices may have been. The new regime in Iran supported the Hezbollah ('the Party of God', which operated in southern Lebanon in the 1980s, attacking the Israelis across the border; and also Hamas (the Islamic Resistance Movement), founded in December 1987, which organized the *intifada* and opposed what it regarded as the dangerous moderation of the Palestine Liberation Organization when the PLO began to negotiate with Israel. On 14 February 1989, the Ayatollah Khomeini issued his sentence, or *fatwa*, upon the writer Salman Rushdie for his novel *The Satanic Verses*. Khomeini called upon 'every zealous Muslim' to kill Rushdie and his publishers, so that no one else would dare to offend Muslim values. Anyone who was killed in such an attempt would achieve the status of a martyr.[25] This declaration aroused demonstrations in Pakistan, India, London and Bradford, which in turn awoke fears among western liberals and intellectuals. The example of Islamic fundamentalism set in Iran proved attractive in other Muslim countries. In Algeria, for example, the *Front Islamique du Salut* (FIS – Islamic Salvation Front), founded in 1989, gained support steadily, and in January 1992 was on the brink of an electoral victory when the army intervened to prevent the second ballot taking place and impose martial law. It was notable that the French government, acutely conscious of its own Algerian immigrant population, supported this interference with democracy rather than see an Islamic Republic emerge in Algeria. A fear of Islamic fundamentalism spread through much of western society. It was symptomatic that when an explosion destroyed a public building in Oklahoma City, in the Mid-West of the United States in April 1995, the first reaction was to look for Islamic terrorists, though the actual culprits turned out to be alienated Americans.

It remains uncertain how far this fear was justified. Iran settled down after the death of Khomeini, though it remained an Islamic republic. Algeria retained an uneasy stability. Islam has no great power to provide material resources and military leadership. Saudi Arabia is wealthy, but has only a small population (17 400 000 in 1994) and remains militarily dependent on the Americans – despite the USA representing the devil incarnate to many Islamic militants. Indonesia has a large population (193 000 000 in 1994), but is ill-organized and militarily weak. Pakistan is dominated by its conflict with India. Turkey is a member of the Organization of the Islamic Conference, but firmly maintains its status as a secular state. In these circumstances, Islam lacks a 'core state', round which it can unite.[26]

Religion has thus re-emerged as a motive force in international affairs, to general surprise in the 'advanced' and industrialized world, but it is not clear what this irruption will amount to. Pope John Paul II has been a world figure, on a par with Gorbachev, Reagan or George Bush, but much of his influence is personal, and may not be passed on to his eventual successor. The Iranian revolution produced shock waves, which – as after earthquakes – diminished with time. It remains to be seen whether there is another earthquake in store, or perhaps the less dramatic shifts produced by demography and movements of peoples. At any rate, Islam appears the most dynamic of the world religions, and the frontier of Islam includes much of Asia and Africa, and is moving almost imperceptibly into parts of Europe. It may well have more surprises in store.

Among the mixed motives which lie behind the actions of governments and peoples, reasons of state and national interests can often be calculated and even predicted. The movements inspired by ideas, beliefs and emotions cannot. For this reason if for no other, the study of international history is unlikely to become an exact science.

◆ Notes to Chapter 24

1. John Lukacs, *A New History of the Cold War* (New York, 3rd. edn, 1966), p. 354; Evan Luard, *International Society* (London, 1990), p. 253.
2. The basilica cost some $300 million to build, and its maintenance costs

are estimated at $1.5 million per year. Its dome is actually lower than that of St Peter's in Rome, but the addition of a cross of gold makes the total height greater.

3. Quoted in Robert H. Ferrell, *Harry S. Truman: A Life* (London, 1994), p. 251. See above, pp. 77–9.
4. Alan Cassels, *Ideology and International Relations in the Modern World* (London, 1996), p. 6; see pp. 1–8 for the problems of definition.
5. Quoted in Robert Colquhoun, *Raymond Aron*, Vol. II, *Sociologist in Society* (London, 1986), p. 269.
6. Eric Hobsbawm, *Age of Extremes: The Short Twentieth Century, 1914–1991* (London, 1994), p. 563.
7. Dostoyevsky, *The Diary of a Writer*, quoted in Adam Ulam, 'Russian Nationalism', in Seweryn Bialer, ed., *The Domestic Context of Soviet Foreign Policy* (London, 1981), p. 3.
8. Seweryn Bialer, 'Soviet Foreign Policy: Sources, Perceptions, Trends', *ibid.*, p. 418.
9. Raymond Aron, *Les dernières années du siècle* (Paris, 1984), p. 127.
10. Digest of Reports by the International Relations Section of the Central Committee to the Communist Party of the Soviet Union, printed in Franklin Griffiths, 'Ideological Development and Foreign Policy', in Bialer, *Domestic Context*, p. 22.
11. Galia Golan, *Soviet Policies in the Middle East, from World War Two to Gorbachev* (Cambridge, 1990), pp. 197–209.
12. Seweryn Bialer, *The Soviet Paradox: External Expansion, Internal Decline* (London, 1986), pp. 186–7.
13. Kenneth Minogue, *Nationalism* (London, 1967), p. 116.
14. Cassels, *Ideology*, p. 204 (Roosevelt), 219 (Reagan).
15. Lukacs, *Cold War*, p. 319.
16. *Keesing's Contemporary Archives*, 1960, p. 17993.
17. Minogue, *Nationalism*, p. 31; Samuel P. Huntington, *The Clash of Civilizations and the Remaking of World Order* (New York, 1996), p. 126.
18. *Ibid.*, pp. 19–20.
19. Winston S. Churchill, *The Second World War*, Vol.I: *The Gathering Storm* (London, 1948), pp. 105–6.
20. David Willey, *God's Politician: John Paul at the Vatican* (London, 1992), p. xiii; see also pp. 8–10 for relations with Gorbachev, and p. 14 for the Red Army Choir.
21. See Peter Mansfield, *A History of the Middle East* (London, 1991), pp.15, 136–7, for a clear summary of these complex questions.
22. Albert Hourani, *A History of the Arab Peoples* (London, 1992), pp. 391–9.
23. Figures in Daniel Colard, *Les relations internationales de 1945 à nos jours* (Paris, 6th. edn, 1996), p. 52.

24. Chris Cook, *World Political Almanac* (London, 3rd. edn, 1995), p. 28; Reinhard Schulze, *A Modern History of the Islamic World* (London, 2000), pp. 211–12.
25. Text of the *fatwa*, *ibid.*, p. 260.
26. Huntington, *Clash*, pp. 178–9.

Postscript
THE WORLD SINCE THE COLD WAR: NEW ORDER AND OLD CHAOS

The end of the Cold War and the collapse of the Soviet Union between 1989 and 1991 were political earthquakes which shook the whole world. For some forty-five years world events had taken their shape from the rivalry of the two superpowers and their opposing ideologies. What was to follow – a new world order, as President Bush hopefully forecast in a speech to the United States Congress on 6 March 1991, or the re-emergence of an old chaos? Some problems became easier to resolve (for example, the struggle between Sandinistas and Contras in Nicaragua faded away when there was no wider Cold War to sustain it); but other conflicts, which had been suppressed during the Cold War, emerged to replace them (notably in the break-up of Yugoslavia, which produced wars and massacres lasting for eight years). Great efforts were made to introduce new forms of international co-operation through the United Nations and trade associations, and even to create a new integration of states in the European Union. Yet at the same time the former Soviet Union and Yugoslavia disintegrated, with new states fighting for their boundaries or for their very existence; while elsewhere independence movements struggled to create more new states – for example, the Palestinians, or the Basque separatists. For a decade, the phrase 'international community' became a commonplace for western politicians and journalists, yet such community as existed seemed powerless to achieve much that was practical. What are we to make of these confused and contradictory events?

The greatest impulse to the belief that the Cold War would be replaced by a new world order arose from the Gulf War of 1990–91. On 2 August 1990 Iraq, ruled by Saddam Hussein, invaded the small neighbouring state of Kuwait, and annexed it by a proclamation on the 8th. There were a number of specific disputes between the two countries; but the principal reason for the invasion was that Iraq had accumulated vast debts during its long war against Iran, and wanted to seize the oil resources of Kuwait to supplement its own revenues. At once, the United Nations Security Council passed a resolution condemning the invasion and demanding the withdrawal of Iraqi forces from Kuwait. The new conditions produced by the end of the Cold War now came into play. The United States and the Soviet Union co-operated with one another diplomatically, so that the USSR did not use its veto on behalf of Iraq, as it almost certainly would have done in earlier circumstances. Moreover, the extinction of a state was a dangerous precedent, arousing widespread alarm. The German annexation of Austria in 1938 was much quoted as a parallel, and the old 'lessons' from appeasement were again rehearsed. In economic terms, the oil-consuming countries did not wish to see Saddam Hussein in control of the oil resources of Kuwait. All these considerations came together to cause the United States to take a lead which others were ready follow. The Americans immediately despatched forces to prevent Saudi Arabia from becoming the next victim of Iraqi attack. They then formed a wide coalition, including several Arab states, to oppose Iraq, and continued to use the United Nations to provide legitimacy for their policy. On 30 November 1990 the Security Council presented Iraq with an ultimatum, demanding withdrawal from Kuwait by 15 January 1991, with the threat that all necessary means would be used to enforce this demand.

Iraq did not withdraw. The United States, along with 27 other countries, concentrated large forces in Saudi Arabia and the Persian Gulf. The Americans supplied the vast majority of the aircraft and warships, but other allies provided about half the 600 000 troops which gathered in the area under American command. Saudi Arabia, Germany and South Korea made substantial contributions to the financial costs of the war.

On 16 January 1991 an air offensive was opened against Iraqi targets (including the capital, Baghdad, as well as forces in the field). During this phase, the Iraqis fired a number of missiles against Israel and Saudi Arabia, but despite this the conflict did not spread to other areas in the Middle East. The allied ground forces began their attack on 24 February, rapidly defeated the Iraqi army, and entered Kuwait City on the 26th. A cease-fire, ordered by the American command, came into effect on 28 February. The land war thus lasted just over four days, and was for the most part fought in the desert, in circumstances of unusual isolation. The United States deployed a crushing superiority in technology and fire-power, and the allied forces suffered only light casualties. The cease-fire left Saddam Hussein in power in Baghdad, though the Americans hoped he would be overthrown by a revolt within his own country. In the event, there was a rebellion by the Kurds in northern Iraq, and another by Shi-ite Muslims in the south, who for a time occupied Basra. These movements received no support from outside. Turkey, Syria and the Soviet Union all had Kurdish minorities in their own countries, and were not disposed to support Kurdish separatism in Iraq. The United States tended to regard Shi-ite Iraqis as pro-Iranian, and thus by extension anti-American. The large Iraqi armies which had survived the Gulf War were able to crush both Kurds and Shi-ites. In April 1991 a Security Council resolution condemned Saddam Hussein for persecuting his own people, and an attempt was made to provide 'safe havens' for some of the Kurds, with little success. Economic sanctions against Iraq were maintained, and occasional bombing attacks were continued, which appear to have harmed the population more than the regime.

The Gulf War was a remarkable achievement by the United States, its allies, and the United Nations. Kuwait was liberated and the invader driven out. The fighting was brief, and restricted in geographical area. Casualties on the winning side were slight. It was true that a number of Arab or Islamic states supported Iraq: Iran (even though it was Iraq's recent enemy), Jordan (King Hussein was particularly outspoken), Libya, Mauritania, Sudan, Tunisia and Yemen; and so did the Palestine Liberation Organization. Public opinion in several Arab countries was apparently

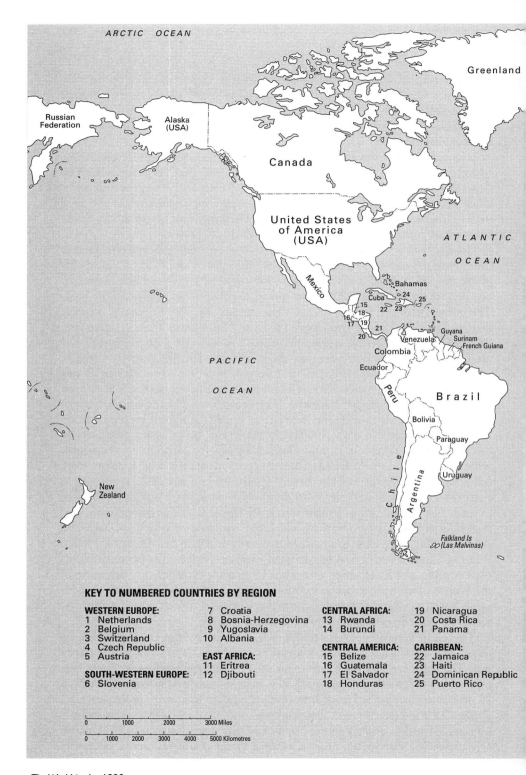

ARCTIC OCEAN

Greenland

Russian
Federation

Alaska
(USA)

Canada

United States
of America
(USA)

ATLANTIC

OCEAN

Mexico

Bahamas

Cuba   24
15   25
16   18   22   23
17   19
21
20   Guyana
Venezuela   Surinam
Colombia   French Guiana

PACIFIC

Ecuador

OCEAN

Peru   Brazil

Bolivia

Paraguay

Chile

Argentina   Uruguay

New
Zealand

Falkland Is
(Las Malvinas)

KEY TO NUMBERED COUNTRIES BY REGION

WESTERN EUROPE:
1 Netherlands
2 Belgium
3 Switzerland
4 Czech Republic
5 Austria

SOUTH-WESTERN EUROPE:
6 Slovenia

7 Croatia
8 Bosnia-Herzegovina
9 Yugoslavia
10 Albania

EAST AFRICA:
11 Eritrea
12 Djibouti

CENTRAL AFRICA:
13 Rwanda
14 Burundi

CENTRAL AMERICA:
15 Belize
16 Guatemala
17 El Salvador
18 Honduras

19 Nicaragua
20 Costa Rica
21 Panama

CARIBBEAN:
22 Jamaica
23 Haiti
24 Dominican Republic
25 Puerto Rico

0   1000   2000   3000 Miles

0   1000   2000   3000   4000   5000 Kilometres

The World in the 1990s

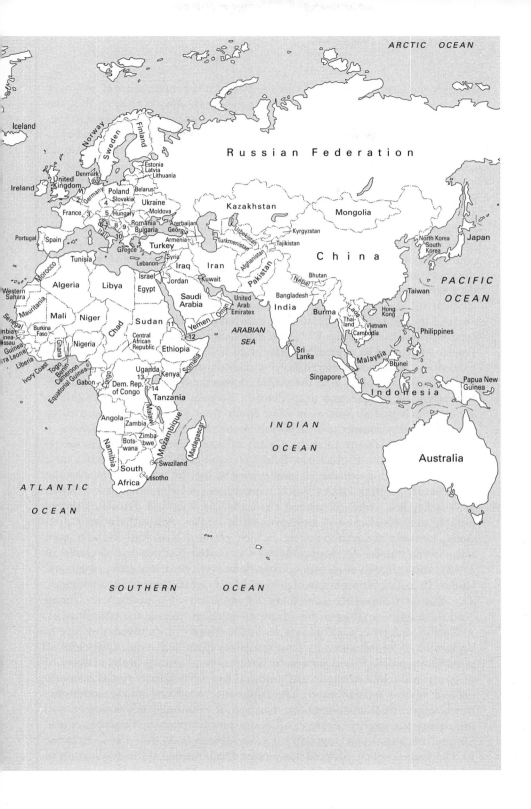

strongly in favour of Iraq, and there is evidence that after the war was over there was a revulsion of feeling against the West.[1] But in spite of this, the unity of the allied side was maintained for as long as was necessary to win the war. This, it seemed, was how collective security had been intended to work when the United Nations was set up in 1945. The 'international community' had come into its own.

This idea was always over-optimistic. The 'international community' had little real existence. It usually meant the United Nations, which comprised 184 members in 1993, when Andorra and Monaco joined the organization. It was impossible for a body of this size, with members ranging from China (population 1 200 million) to Monaco (population 28 000) to form a community or an international society in any true sense. The notion that the 'international community' could regularly act together, following the precedent set in the Gulf War, was implausible.

Even so, the early 1990s saw a number of vast conferences, under the aegis of the United Nations, to define global interests which were common to all countries. In June 1992 the Earth Summit took place at Rio de Janeiro, attended by representatives of 175 states, as well as by delegates from non-governmental organizations. This enormous meeting, reported by the mass media from across the world, debated environmental and ecological problems, revealing a deep division between many of the developed states, which had already as it were 'made their pile' and now wanted to protect the environment, and poorer countries which saw no reason to accept new restrictions upon the already difficult course of economic development. The Rio Conference adopted a so-called Earth Charter and Agenda 21, setting out targets and priorities for the environment into the 21st century. In June 1993 a World Conference on Human Rights convened at Vienna, less widely attended than that at Rio, but attracting many notable individuals and non-governmental bodies. Again there were divisions, between western countries which claimed that individual human rights were universally applicable (as the United Nations had declared in 1948), and others, which argued that there were Asiatic values, or Islamic values, or collective rights, which should prevail in certain circumstances. The Vienna Conference agreed on the creation of a permanent United Nations High Commission for Human Rights, to pursue the issue further. A World Conference on Population and Development followed, at Cairo in September 1994, attended by representatives from 172 states. Questions of population policy raised profound differences of principle on matters of morality and religion, where Catholic and Islamic countries found common ground against secular states. The conference produced a long and sometimes vague final document on matters of economic development and improving the quality of life in all countries. There ensued another World Summit on Social Development, at Copenhagen in March 1995, attended by 185 states, which adopted a ten-point Declaration on the eradication of world poverty. In September 1995 there took place in Beijing a World Conference on the position of women, which again revealed profound divisions between secular and religious countries, and between rich and poor states, which took widely different views on the role and rights of women.

These vast gatherings produced mountains of paper, but little by way of immediate results. Yet they showed the United Nations Organization trying to act as the guardian of a world order in ways that were not conceived of when it was founded in 1945. The United Nations also began to operate with greater intensity in more familiar areas. Between 1991 and 1995, no fewer than 20 peace-keeping operations were undertaken, which was more than in all the previous 45 years of the UN's existence. It was unhappily true that a number of these ended in failure, or even humiliation. For example, in 1994 the Security Council passed a resolution to withdraw UN troops from Rwanda, where they were monitoring a supposed peace agreement between the government and rebels, because their lives were in danger. In Somalia two UN operations broke down in failure. Even so, the United Nations was taking a more active role than at any previous time in its history.

At the same time, a number of constructive international moves were under way outside the United Nations. In Europe, the fifteen states of the European Union formed an area of stability at a time when much of the continent was in flux. On 1 January 1999 eleven of these countries adopted a single currency, the euro, though its appearance in everyday use was postponed until 2002. The success or otherwise of this venture remains to be seen; but in any event it is a remarkable step towards a new form of European integration – it is hard to see how a single currency can long be maintained for eleven countries without a single authority to control it. Across the Atlantic, the North American Free Trade Association, made up of the United States, Canada and Mexico, came into operation on 1 January 1994, with the objective of removing all tariffs and other trade barriers between the three countries over a period of twenty years. Even more striking than was the invitation by NATO, offered in July 1997 and subsequently accepted, for the Czech Republic, Hungary and Poland to join the Organization, thus extending the area covered by the North Atlantic Treaty to the Polish-Russian border. Again, it remains to be seen what effect this will have (it has certainly been unwelcome to Russia); but in intention it is a move towards greater stability in Europe and the North Atlantic area.

Over against these steps towards a new world order, and towards greater stability in Europe and North America, there occurred a dismaying display of war, massacre and crisis in the Balkans, Africa and Asia.

The break-up of Yugoslavia produced by far the most serious conflict in Europe since the end of the Second World War. In 1989 Yugoslavia, under the rule of Slobodan Milošević, was a federation of six Republics (Bosnia-Herzegovina, Croatia, Macedonia, Montenegro, Serbia and Slovenia), plus two autonomous provinces, Kosovo and Voivodine. Serbia was the largest of the republics, and there were also substantial Serbian populations in Croatia and Bosnia. The Serbs also had a deep historical and emotional link with Kosovo, the scene of a disastrous defeat at the hands of the Ottoman Turks in 1389.

In 1991 the country began to break up. Slovenia declared independence on 25 June 1991, and Croatia on the 26th. If all the republics were to become independent with their existing frontiers, the Serbs would be divided between three countries: Serbia itself, Croatia and Bosnia. Milošević (who had been elected President of Serbia by a large majority in a free election in December 1990) was determined to prevent this by securing a 'Greater Serbia'. He attempted to make acceptance of Croatian independence conditional upon Croatia surrendering territories with Serb majorities; which the President of Croatia, Franjo Tujman, refused to do. When Bosnia declared independence in 1992, the Bosnian Serbs, led by Radovan Karadzic and with assistance from Serbia, proclaimed their own separate Republic of Srpska. Croatia also claimed to take over areas of Bosnia with a Croat majority in their population – a sort of Greater Croatia. The result was a many-sided conflict – between Serbia and Croatia, between both of these and Bosnia, and within Bosnia itself, where the situation was further complicated by the presence of large Albanian and Muslim populations, making a very complex mixture indeed. In these conflicts, all the participants undertook what was called 'ethnic cleansing' – driving out or killing alien peoples, so as to establish areas of homogeneous population. Serbs drove out Croats, and Croats expelled Serbs.

Outside powers were almost inevitably concerned with these events, though for some time they were reluctant to intervene directly. Germany and Austria supported Croatia, a predominantly Catholic country. Russia supported Serbia, on historical grounds, and as another Orthodox country; so did Greece, for complicated reasons which included the religious connection. France for a time supported Serbia, but in 1991–92 dropped the Serbs in order to secure German co-operation in the completion of the Maastricht Treaty on further European unification. In general, the West European states denounced Serbian atrocities and 'ethnic cleansing', while disregarding Croatian actions of the same kind. Meanwhile, Turkey, Iran and Saudi Arabia provided support for the Muslim population in Bosnia. Everywhere, television pictures of suffering populations aroused a public demand (especially in western Europe) that governments should 'do something', though no one was sure what.

The result was a series of external interventions, of growing magnitude. The European Union attempted mediation between Serbia and Croatia. A mission headed by David Owen from Europe and Cyrus Vance from the United States attempted to negotiate a settlement in Bosnia. The United Nations imposed an arms embargo on all participants in the fighting

(September 1991), though this was easily circumvented. The UN also attempted a humanitarian intervention, sending troops whose sole mission was to ensure the passage of food and medical supplies to the suffering populations. The United States declined to take part in this operation; and the troops concerned (including British and French contingents) found themselves in a very precarious position in face of strong local forces. In September 1993 the United Nations proclaimed the establishment of 'safe areas' for refugees, which they were in fact powerless to protect.

For some time, the United States seemed content to allow the Europeans to muddle through, but eventually intervened on the side of Croatia in 1994–95, for reasons which were by no means clear. The Americans attempted in 1994 to set up a Croatian-Bosnian Federation; and then in 1995 used the NATO alliance to launch bombing attacks against the Serbs. This military intervention, accompanied by active diplomacy, resulted in an agreement signed at Dayton, Ohio, in November 1995 by Milošević for Serbia, Tudjman for Croatia, and Izetbegovic, the President of Bosnia. All three parties confirmed the independence of Bosnia, but only by dividing it into two parts, one Serbian, the other Croatian and Muslim, bound together in a loose federation.

In several years of conflict, the total of refugees was perhaps 3 000 000; the dead were uncounted, but may have amounted to 200 000. It was no great advertisement for a new world order, for European policy, or for American intervention. Nor had a final settlement been reached. Another war was soon to take place over Kosovo.

Kosovo was an autonomous province of the former Yugoslavia, inte-grated into Serbia in 1989. Some 90 per cent of its population of 2 000 000 were Albanians, but the Serbs regarded it as central to their history. In 1996 the Kosovo Liberation Army began an armed struggle against the Serbs; the Serbs in turn began to drive Albanians out of the province. In 1999 (from 23 March to 10 June) NATO forces, led by the United States, waged a war by aerial bombardment against Serbia on behalf of Kosovo. President Clinton of the United States, President Chirac of France, and Blair, the British Prime Minister, all insisted that NATO was fighting to prevent ethnic cleansing and to preserve human rights; they also indicated from time to time that they aimed to remove Milošević from power in Serbia. It was an extraordinary war, in which Serbia was attacked by cruise missiles and by bombers, some of which flew from bases in the United States, launched their bombs from a height of 15 000 feet, and then returned home. It was thus waged by one side without risks and without casualties – something unprecedented in the history of warfare. Finally, Milošević accepted NATO terms, and the war ended with the withdrawal of Serb forces from Kosovo and the deployment of United Nations force in the province, which was divided into five sectors, under American, British, French, German and Italian occupation. It was also agreed that refugees were to return to Kosovo (perhaps half-a-million had left during the fighting); but that proved difficult to carry out. Despite his defeat, Milošević remained as President of Serbia – as he does at the time of writing, in August 2000.

It was the only war actually fought by NATO, as distinct from the possible war against the Soviet Union which the alliance was designed to prepare for and also to prevent. NATO governments claimed that it was a war fought solely for humanitarian aims, and not for gain of any kind; and indeed it is hard to see that any of them secured significant advantage from the conflict. The war might therefore stand as an example of the new world order. On the other hand, it was also a war fought by a supposedly defensive alliance of sixteen countries, led by one, attacking about ten million Serbs, leaving ruin and refugees behind. Opinion in western Europe was, and remains, divided on the wisdom and morality of the operation. In any case, it was certainly an occasion when the aspirations of the new world order towards human rights and humanitarian missions met the very different forces of nationalism and religious conflict – which on the whole proved the stronger.

In Africa the situation was worse, because individual crises took place in a context of deepening poverty. A World Bank report of 31 May 2000 indicated a decline in GNP per head in sub-Saharan Africa between 1970 and 1997, when in Asia and Latin America the situation had been improving. When South African figures were taken out of the calculation, the decline for the rest of the area was almost one-third over the 27 years.[2] Economic decline was accompanied by widespread political confusion, among which a number of crises stand out.

Somalia proved a disastrous area, which neither the United Nations nor the United States could cope with. In 1991 government in the country disintegrated, and then remained non-existent for the next nine years. A president was finally inaugurated in August 2000, but even then the ceremony had to take place outside Somalia itself. Meanwhile, the country collapsed in civil war and famine. In 1992 the Security Council of the United Nations made an attempt to secure the distribution of food and humanitarian aid, through the presence of small numbers of UN troops. This proved a failure, and much of the aid was seized by the Somali warlords who controlled most of the country. As in Yugoslavia, the television cameras played their part, presenting appalling pictures of famine and disease; and under the impact of public opinion President Bush of the United States proposed the establishment of a large Intervention Force to secure the delivery of humanitarian aid. This proposal was taken up by the UN Secretary-General, and implemented by a Security Council resolution in December 1992. The force began to arrive in Somalia that same month, and eventually reached a total of about 37 000 men from 28 different countries. It was under American, not United Nations, command, and the operation was given an American code-name: RESTORE HOPE.

The operation was only a very partial success. Some famine relief and medical assistance was achieved, often by voluntary organizations; but the military aspects of the intervention encountered many difficulties against Somali irregular troops, and especially forces led by General Aidid, the most prominent Somali leader. On 5 June 1993 twenty Pakistani soldiers were killed by Aidid's men, and the next day the Security Council passed a resolution authorizing the troops in Somalia to capture Aidid. American special forces were sent to the country to help in this venture, but without result. In October, a number of American soldiers were captured by Somalis, and the mutilated corpses of 18 men were displayed in the capital, Mogadishu, for the benefit of the television cameras and horrified audiences in the United States. President Clinton quickly announced that American forces would be withdrawn from Somalia by 31 March 1994. Humanitarian intentions thus met brute force, and gave way. The Americans left the country by the end of March, along with most other contingents, leaving a force consisting of Indian, Pakistani and Bangladeshi troops. (This was, incidentally, a striking combination between armies which, in the case of India and Pakistan, might well have been in conflict on their own home ground.) These troops, now under UN command, remained until March 1995. Somalia remained in confusion and without a government. A committee of enquiry set up by the Security Council recommended that the United Nations should not attempt operations to impose peace in internal conflicts. The United Nations and the United States together had proved no match for Somali warlords, and the new world order obviously had some very definite limits.

There were other events elsewhere in Africa, sometimes exceeding those in Somalia in horror and disaster. In Rwanda in 1993–94 there were massacres of the Tutsi population by the majority Hutus, and retaliation by the Tutsis with support from Uganda. Deaths among the Tutsis were estimated at about a million, amounting to genocide. There were also heavy casualties among the Hutu, and perhaps a million Hutu took refuge in Congo. In these appalling events the United Nations and outside powers played little part. A small United Nations force in Rwanda, helpless and in danger, withdrew early in 1994. The French intervened, under United Nations cover, in June–August 1994 to set up a protective zone for Hutu refugees. This operation, code-named TURQUOISE, remains obscure in many of its details, but it appears that the French forces, while acting with humanitarian intentions, actually provided shelter for many of those who had perpetrated massacres. Meanwhile, in the neighbouring state of Burundi, also populated by Hutus and Tutsis, a civil war began in 1993 and was still in progress in 2000.

Elsewhere in Africa, the Democratic Republic of Congo (formerly Zaire) suffered rebellion and civil war from 1998 onwards, with intervention by neighbouring African states. Early in the year 2000, about 35 000 troops from six outside countries were engaged in the Congo – from Angola, Namibia and Zimbabwe in support of President Kabila, and from Burundi, Rwanda and Uganda in support of rebels against him. In Sierra Leone a civil war was waged by the United Revolutionary Front against the government from 1999 to 2000, reducing parts of the country to near-anarchy. A West African Force intervened under United Nations auspices in 1999, and was still present in August 2000, with only limited effect; a small British force also intervened in the summer of 2000. Between Eritrea and Ethiopia a fierce frontier war took place in 1999–2000, involving heavy casualties on both sides. Parts of Africa – usually the poorest, with apparently nothing to spare for warfare – were dissolving in conflict. There is no sign that any new world order, or vast United Nations conferences on development and the environment, can do much to check this slide.

In Asia, there has been little open warfare, but at least three dangerous crises persist. First, the conflict between India and Pakistan continues, with sporadic outbreaks of fighting in Kashmir. Both are now nuclear powers. China, another nuclear power, stands on the sidelines of this dispute, with a common frontier with both India and Pakistan. Second, China maintains its claim to Taiwan, with a constant if usually muted threat of military action. (In Quemoy, where the Chinese precipitated a crisis in 1958, the guns are now silent, but Taiwan still maintained a garrison of 20 000 men there in 2000.) Taiwan began in the late 1990s to assert its independence as a separate state from China, and has elected a new government with that objective. Yet even the possibility of China recognizing Taiwanese independence is unthinkable. Third, in Korea, North and South remain as separate and hostile states. In 1998 North Korean warships made incursions into South Korean and Japanese waters, causing Japanese warships to fire their first shots in anger since the end of the Second World War. There was something of a thaw in 2000, with a meeting between the two Presidents in June, and between long-separated families in August; but the fundamental problem remains.

On the other hand, China and Russia, after the long separation of the Sino-Soviet dispute, have improved their relations, on the significant basis of opposition to aspects of the 'new world order'. In August 1999 Boris Yeltsin and Jiang Zemin met in Biskek (the capital of Kyrgystan), along with representatives from Kyrgystan, Tajikistan and Kazakhstan. Jiang Zemin denounced the United States for trying to impose its hegemony on the rest of the world by force – referring to the Kosovo war against Serbia, in which the Americans had bombed the Chinese Embassy in Belgrade (presumably by accident). Yeltsin joined in declaring his opposition to Western hegemony. In December 1999 the Russian and Chinese leaders met again, this time in Beijing, and issued a statement condemning the use of of human rights as a pretext to destroy the sovereignty of independent states. China asserted its support for Russian military action in Chechnya (where the Americans had been expressing their anxiety about human rights violations); Yeltsin endorsed the Chinese claim to Taiwan. This was a significant combination against American policy in Kosovo, and against claims that human rights justified intervention in the internal affairs of states.

China had long taken its own view of human rights. 1999 saw the 40th anniversary of the rising in Lhasa against the Chinese occupation of Tibet – an occupation which still continues in 2000 and seems likely to be permanent. The position of China in international affairs since the end of the Cold War remained in some ways uncertain. China was becoming the dominant power in eastern Asia, and the centre of a 'bamboo network' of families and other relations. Overseas Chinese formed about one-third of the population of Malaysia, and one-tenth of that of Thailand, and played an important part in the economy of both countries.[3] The Chinese continue to intervene in Africa, where they have developed interests in oil in the Sudan and provide military support for the Sudanese government in its civil war against the Christians and blacks in the south. Outsiders have seen China as a sleeping giant for two centuries. It may be that the full awakening has yet to take place.

At the other end of Asia, the Arab–Israeli dispute still continues, concentrated in the 1990s in a long attempt to reconcile the positions of Israel and the Palestine Liberation Organization. In 1993 talks in total secrecy in the surprising surroundings of Oslo yielded an outline of a possible agreement, on the basis of Palestinian autonomy. In September 1993 the Israeli Prime Minister, Yitzhak Rabin, and the head of the PLO, Yasser Arafat, met in Washington and shook hands under the encouraging gaze of President Clinton, who had mediated between them. Arafat accepted that Israel should exist, in peace and security; Rabin accepted the PLO as the representative of the Palestinian people. This marked a considerable shift on both sides; but the difficulties became glaringly apparent when Rabin was assassinated (4 November 1995) by an Israeli opponent to all concessions. The Palestinian claim to a state, not just an autonomous region, and the difficult problem of Jerusalem, remain to be settled. After more than fifty years, the Arab–Israeli dispute has become narrower in scope, but remains intense in nature.

During the 1990s, world affairs lacked the shape which had previously been provided by the rivalry of the two superpowers – uncomfortable and dangerous though that strait-jacket had been. Russia was the principal successor to the Soviet Union, but did not really fill its shoes. The country was in economic confusion, grappling uncertainly with the transition from a command economy to a free market. Its political system was weak and untried, and Boris Yeltsin was an erratic leader, plagued by ill-health. Even the borders of the state were in places uncertain, and in the Caucasus the Russians fought a long and difficult war to prevent the secession of Chechnya – without final success at the time of writing. The armed forces frequently went unpaid, and showed signs of poor morale. The former ocean-going fleet lay decaying in its harbours – with some of its weaknesses suddenly revealed in public by the disaster of the submarine *Kursk* in August 2000. The new Russia, though still an important country with much influence, was no longer a superpower to match the United States.

The United States remained immensely strong in military terms – its victory in the Persian Gulf in 1991 was a formidable display of strength and expertise. The country was immensely wealthy, and in the late 1990s recovered its economic dynamism to a remarkable degree after a period of stagnation. Yet its use of military power was inhibited by an apparently total unwillingness to accept casualties; and even the desire to create a global economy working on American lines is limited by the generally inward-looking nature of American society. The United States hesitates between the reality of being the only remaining superpower and a reluctance to intervene if the costs are high – the brief foray into Somalia in 1993 was a disaster which no one wished to repeat.[4]

Moreover, in the division between the industrialized and developed 'North' and the mainly poor 'South', both have grown afraid. The 'South' is afraid of losing investment or aid, and can no longer play the Cold War card of appealing to one side against the other. But the 'North' is even more afraid, or at any rate nervous – of unrestrained immigration, of terrorism, and of the unfamiliar force of militant Islam. Europe in particular, having been the source of migration in the nineteenth century, sending millions of people to the United States, Canada, Australia and other colonies of white settlement, now confronts the opposite situation, in which immigrants move into Europe from Asia and Africa. It may be that the fears which these changes arouse will prove to be misplaced or exaggerated. (In the year 2000 a report to the European Commission argued that in the coming years Europe would *need* large numbers of immigrants for its own economic well-being.) But so far there is a nervousness about immigration, which even extends to the United States, a country which was made by migration.

The dichotomy between a new world order and an ancient chaos continues. The world after the Cold War still lacks a method of dealing with international crises, and lives from hand to mouth, in a constant state of flux.

◆ Notes to Postscript

1. Samuel P. Huntington, *The Clash of Civilizations and the Remaking of World Order* (New York, 1996), pp. 248–51.

2. *Le Monde*, 4–5 June 2000. The figures for GNP per head in sub-Saharan Africa, adjusted for changes in the value of the US dollar, were: 1970, $525 per head; 1997, $336 per head.
3. Huntington, *Clash of Civilizations*, p. 170.
4. Eric Hobsbawm, not always an admirer of European imperialism in all its aspects, observed acidly that Britain, France and Italy ruled their respective parts of Somaliland for decades without undue difficulty, but the Americans proved unable to stay for more than a year. Eric Hobsbawm, *Age of Extremes: The Short Twentieth Century, 1914–1991* (London, 1994), p. 562.

GUIDE TO FURTHER READING

The following is a selection from the vast literature that is available on the subject of this book. The choice has necessarily been somewhat arbitrary, but most of the works listed in the first section, dealing with world histories and books on international history, include extensive bibliographies that will provide ample supplementary information. The place of publication is London unless otherwise indicated.

◆ General: World histories and books on international history

Calvocoressi, Peter, *World Politics since 1945* (7th edn, 1996)
Conquest, Robert, *Reflections on a Ravaged Century* (1999)
Dunbabin, J. P. D., *International Relations since 1945*, Vol.1: *The Great Powers and their Allies;* Vol. 2: *The Post-Imperial Age: The Great Powers and the Wider World* (1994)
Grenville, J. A. S., *History of the World in the Twentieth Century* (revised edn, 1998)
——, *The Major International Treaties, 1914–1973: A History and Guide with Texts* (1974)
——, *The Major International Treaties since 1945: A History and Guide with Texts* (1987)
Hobsbawm, Eric, *Age of Extremes: The Short Twentieth Century, 1914–1991* (1994)
Holland, R. F., *European Decolonization: An Introductory Survey* (1985)
Huntington, Samuel P., *The Clash of Civilizations and the Remaking of World Order* (1996)
Jansen, G. H., *Afro-Asia and Non-Alignment* (1966)
Johnson, Paul, *A History of the Modern World: From 1917 to the 1980s* (1983)
Kennedy, Paul, *The Rise and Fall of the Great Powers* (1988)
Keylor, W. R., *The Twentieth-Century World: An International History* (4th edn, Oxford, 2000)
Kissinger, Henry, *Diplomacy* (1994)
Reynolds, David, *One World, Divisible: A Global History since 1945* (1999)
Segal, Gerald, *The World Affairs Companion.* (revised edn, 1993)
Vadney, T.E., *The World since 1945* (2nd edn, 1992)
Woods, Ngaire, ed., *Explaining International Relations since 1945* (Oxford, 1996)

◈ The Second World War

Alperovitz, Gar, *The Decision to Use the Bomb* (1995)

Dear, I. C. B and Foot, M. R. D., eds, *The Oxford Companion to the Second World War* (Oxford, 1995)

Gaddis, John Lewis, *The United States and the Origins of the Cold War, 1941–1947* (New York, 1972)

Hogan, Michael J., ed., *Hiroshima in History and Memory* (Cambridge, 1996)

Hoopes, Townsend and Brinkley, Douglas, *FDR and the Creation of the UN* (1997)

Kimball, Warren F., *The Juggler: Franklin Roosevelt as Wartime Statesman* (Princeton, 1991)

McCauley, Martin, *The Origins of the Cold War, 1941–1949* (2nd edn, 1995)

Maddox, Robert James, *Weapons for Victory: The Hiroshima Decision Fifty Years Later* (Columbia, Missouri, 1995)

Mastny, Vojtech, *Russia's Road to the Cold War* (New York, 1979)

◈ The Cold War and US–Soviet relations: general

Ashton, Stephen Richard, *In Search of Détente: The Politics of East–West Relations since 1945* (1989)

Barnet, Richard J., *Allies: America, Europe and Japan since the War* (1984)

Bialer, Seweryn, *The Soviet Paradox: External Expansion, Internal Decline* (1986)

Bialer, Seweryn, ed., *The Domestic Context of Soviet Foreign Policy* (1981)

Boyle, Peter G., *American-Soviet Relations: From the Russian Revolution to the Fall of Communism* (1993)

Crockatt, Richard, *The Fifty Years' War: The United States and the Soviet Union in World Politics, 1941–1991* (1996)

Gaddis, John Lewis, *The Long Peace: Inquiries into the History of the Cold War* (Oxford, 1987)

Gaddis, John Lewis, *We Now Know: Rethinking Cold War History* (Oxford, 1997)

Gorodetsky, Gabriel, *Soviet Foreign Policy, 1917–1991: A Retrospective* (1994)

Kolko, Gabriel, *Confronting the Third World: United States Foreign Policy 1945–1980* (New York, 1988)

Kramer, M. N., *From Dominance to Hegemony to Collapse: Soviet Policy in Eastern Europe, 1945–1991* (Pittsburg, 1996)

McCormick, Thomas J., *America's Half-Century: United States Foreign Policy in the Cold War* (1989)

Partos, Gabriel, *The World that Came in from the Cold* (1993)

Service, Robert, *A History of Twentieth Century Russia* (1997)

Young, John, *The Longman Companion to Cold War and Détente, 1941–91* (1993)

Note: *The Cold War International History Project Bulletin*, published by the Woodrow Wilson Center, Washington, DC, provides up-to-date research on the history of the Cold War.

◆ Cold War: First phase, to 1962

Ambrose, Stephen E., *Eisenhower*, Vol. II: *The President* (1984)

Aronson, Lawrence and Kitchen, Martin, *The Origins of the Cold War in Comparative Perspective* (1988)

Brinkley, D., ed., *Dean Acheson and the Making of US Foreign Policy* (1993)

Brogan, Hugh, *Kennedy* (1996)

Caute, David, *The Great Fear: The Anti-Communist Purge under Truman and Eisenhower* (1978)

Cohen, Warren I., *America in the Age of Soviet Power, 1945–1991* (1993)

Cook, Don, *Forging the Alliance: NATO, 1945–1950* (1989)

Ferrell, Robert H., *Harry S. Truman: A Life* (Columbia, Missouri, 1994)

Gaddis, John Lewis, *Strategies of Containment: A Critical Appraisal of Post-War American Security Policy* (Oxford, 1982)

Hogan, Michael J., *The Marshall Plan: America, Britain and the Reconstruction of Western Europe, 1947–1952* (New York, 1987)

Kennan, George F., *Memoirs*, Vol. I, *1925–1950* (1967); Vol. II: *1950–1963* (1972)

Kennan, George F. and Lukacs, John, *George F. Kennan and the Origins of Containment, 1944–1946: The Kennan–Lukacs Correspondence* (Columbia, Missouri, 1997)

Lukacs, John, *A New History of the Cold War* (New York, 3rd edn, 1966)

Miscamble, Wilson D., *George F. Kennan and the Making of American Foreign Policy, 1947–1950* (1992)

Molotov, V., *Molotov Remembers: Inside Kremlin Politics. Conversations with Felix Chuev*, ed. Albert Resis (Chicago, 1993)

Paterson, T., *Kennedy's Quest for Victory* (Oxford, 1989)

Pogue, Forrest C., *George C. Marshall*, Vol. IV: *Statesman, 1945–1959* (New York, 1987)

Reynolds, David, ed., *The Origins of the Cold War in Europe: International Perspectives* (1994)

Shlaim, Avi, *The United States and the Berlin Blockade, 1948–9* (Berkeley, 1983)

Tusa, Ann and John, *The Berlin Airlift* (1988)

Zubok, Vladislav and Pleshakov, Constantine, *Inside the Kremlin's Cold War* (Cambridge, Mass., 1996)

Korea

Cotton, James and Neary, Ian, eds, *The Korean War in History* (Manchester, 1989)

Cumings, Bruce, *The Origins of the Korean War*, Vol. 1: *Liberation and the Emergence of Separate Regimes*; Vol. 2: *The Roaring of the Cataract* (Princeton, 1981, 1990)

Hastings, Max, *The Korean War* (1987)

Lowe, Peter, *The Origins of the Korean War* (2nd edn, 1997)

MacDonald, Callum A., *Korea: The War Before Vietnam* (1986)

Stueck, William W., *The Necessary War: An International History of the Korean War* (Princeton, 1995)

Cuba

Beschloss, Michael R., *Kennedy v. Khrushchev: The Crisis Years, 1960–63* (1991)

Blight, James G., and Welsh, David A., eds, *On The Brink: Americans and Soviets Re-examine the Cuban Missile Crisis* (New York, 1989)

Fursenko, Aleksandr and Naftali, Timothy, *'One Hell of a Gamble': Khrushchev, Castro, Kennedy and the Cuban Missile Crisis, 1958–1964* (1997)

◆ Cold War: Second phase, 1963–91 (détente, new Cold War, end)

Ambrose, Stephen E., *Nixon*, Vol. II: *The Triumph of a Politician, 1962–72*; Vol. III: *Ruin and Recovery, 1973–90.* (New York, 1989, 1991)

Bell, Coral, *The Diplomacy of Détente* (1977)

Bell, Coral, *The Reagan Paradox: US Foreign Policy in the 1980s* (New Brunswick, 1989)

Brown, Archie, *The Gorbachev Factor* (Oxford, 1996)

Dobrynin, Anatoly, *In Confidence: Moscow's Ambassador to America's Six Cold War Presidents (1962–1986)* (New York, 1995)

Gaddis, John Lewis, *The United States and the End of the Cold War: Implications, Reconsiderations, Provocations* (Oxford, 1992)

Garthoff, Raymond L., *Détente and Confrontation: American-Soviet Relations from Nixon to Reagan* (Washington, DC, 1985)

Garthoff, Raymond L., *The Great Transition: American-Soviet Relations and the End of the Cold War* (Washington, DC, 1994)

Halliday, Fred, *The Making of the Second Cold War* (1984)

Hogan, Michael J., ed., *The End of the Cold War: Its Meaning and Implications* (Cambridge, 1992)

Kissinger, Henry, *The White House Years* (1979)

Kramer, M. N., *Crisis in Czechoslovakia, 1968: The Prague Spring and the Soviet Invasion* (New York, 1996)

Mervin, David, *Ronald Reagan and the American Presidency* (1990)

Oberdorfer, Don, *The Turn: From the Cold War to a New Era* (1991)

Pryce-Jones, David, *The War that Never Was: The Fall of the Soviet Empire, 1985–9* (1995)

Rubinstein, A. Z., *Moscow's Third World Strategy* (Princeton, 1988)

Vietnam

Braestrup, Peter, *Big Story: How the American Press and TV Reported and Interpreted the Crisis of Tet 1968 in Vietnam and Washington* (Boulder, Col., 1977)

Herring, George C., *America's Longest War: The United States and Vietnam,1950–1975* (New York, 1986)

Moss, George Donelson, *Vietnam: An American Ordeal* (Englewood Cliffs, 1992)

Short, Anthony, *The Origins of the Vietnam War* (1989)

Smith, R. B., *An International History of the Vietnam War*, Vol. I: *Revolution versus Containment* (1983); Vol. II: *The Kennedy Strategy* (1985); Vol. III:*The Making of a Limited War* (1991)

◆ Europe

Bartlett, C. J., *The Special Relationship: A Political History of Anglo-American Relations since 1945* (1992)

Crampton, Richard, *Eastern Europe in the Twentieth Century* (1995)

Davies, Norman, *God's Playground: A History of Poland*, Vol. II: *1795 to the Present* (1986)

Deighton, Anne, ed., *Britain and the First Cold War* (1990)

Hiden, John and Salmon, Patrick, *The Baltic Nations and Europe* (1994)

Hoensch, J. K., *A History of Modern Hungary, 1867–1994* (1995)

Lacouture, Jean, *De Gaulle*, Vol. II: *The Ruler, 1945–1970* (1992)

Louis, William R. and Bull, Hedley, eds, *The 'Special Relationship': Anglo-American Relations since 1945* (1989)

Maier, Charles S., ed., *The Cold War in Europe: Era of a Divided Continent* (3rd edn, Princeton, 1996)

Meier, V., *Yugoslavia: A History of its Demise* (1999)
Milward, Alan S., *The Reconstruction of Western Europe, 1945–51* (1987)
Nicholls, A. J., *The Bonn Republic: West German Democracy, 1945–1990* (1997)
Nicoll, William and Salmon, Trevor C., *Understanding the New European Community* (1994)
Pavlowitch, Stevan K., *Tito: Yugoslavia's Great Dictator: A Reassessment* (1992)
Turner, Henry Ashby Jr, *Germany from Partition to Unification* (1992)
Urwin, Derek W., *Western Europe since 1945: A Political History* (4th edn, 1989)
Varsori, Antonio, ed., *Europe 1945–1990s: The End of an Era?* (1995)
Williams, Charles, *Adenauer: The Father of the New Germany* (2000)
Young, John W., *Cold War Europe, 1945–1989: A Political History* (1991)

◆ The Middle East

Bill, James, *The Eagle and the Lion: The Tragedy of American-Iranian Relations* (1988)
Chubin, S. and Tripp, C., *Iran and Iraq at War* (1988)
Freedman, Lawrence and Karsh, Ephraim, *The Gulf Conflict, 1990–1991* (1993)
Golan, Galia, *Soviet Policies in the Middle East, from World War Two to Gorbachev* (Cambridge, 1990)
Hourani, Albert, *A History of the Arab Peoples* (1991)
Kuniholm, Bruce R., *The Origins of the Cold War in the Near East: Great Power Conflict and Diplomacy in Iran, Turkey and Greece* (Princeton, 1980)
Kyle, Keith, *Suez* (1991)
Long, D. E., *The United States and Saudi Arabia: Ambivalent Allies* (Boulder, Col., 1985)
Louis, William R. and Owen, Roger, eds, *Suez 1956: The Crisis and its Consequences* (Oxford, 1989)
McDowell, David, *A Modern History of the Kurds* (1996)
Mansfield, Peter, *A History of the Middle East* (1991)
Sayigh, Y. and Shlaim, A., eds, *The Cold War in the Middle East* (Oxford, 1997)
Shlaim, Avi, *The Iron Wall: Israel and the Arab World* (London, 2000)
Yapp, M. E., *The Near East since the First World War* (1996)

Arab–Israeli conflicts

Bailey, Sidney D., *Four Arab–Israeli Wars and the Peace Process* (revised edn, 1990)

Cobban, Helena, *The Palestinian Liberation Organization* (Cambridge, 1984)

Gilbert, Martin, *A History of Israel* (1998)

McDowell, David, *Palestine and Israel* (1989)

Morris, B., *1948 and After: Israel and the Palestinians* (Oxford, 1990)

Ovendale, Ritchie, *The Origins of the Arab–Israeli Wars* (2nd edn, 1992)

Schoenbaum, D., *The United States and the State of Israel* (Oxford, 1993)

Shlaim, Avi, *The Iron Wall: Israel and the Arab World* (London, 2000)

◆ Asia

Buckley, R., *US–Japan Alliance Diplomacy, 1945–1990* (Cambridge, 1992)

Buckley, R. and Horsley, W., *Nippon: New Superpower* (1997)

Burke, S. M., *Mainsprings of Indian and Pakistani Foreign Policies* (Minneapolis,1974)

Cohen, Warren I., *America's Response to China: A History of Sino-American Relations* (Oxford, 1990)

Cribb, Robert and Brown, Colin, *Modern Indonesia: A History since 1945* (1995)

Dower, John, *Japan in War and Peace: Essays on History, Culture and Race* (1995)

Edwardes, Michael, *Nehru: A Political Biography* (1971)

Harvey, Robert, *The Undefeated: The Rise, Fall and Rise of Greater Japan* (1994)

Hoffman, Steven A., *India and the China Crisis* (Berkeley, 1990)

Iriye, Akira, *China and Japan in the Global Setting* (Cambridge, Mass., 1992)

Iriye, Akira, *Japan and the Wider World: From the Mid-Nineteenth century to the Present* (1997)

Legge, J. D., *Sukarno: A Political Biography* (1972)

Maxwell, Neville, *India's China War* (1970)

Medvedev, Roy, *China and the Superpowers* (Oxford, 1986)

Moise, Edwin E., *Modern China: A History* (2nd edn, 1994)

Noman, O., *Pakistan: A Political and Economic History since 1947* (1988)

Quested, R K. I., *Sino-Russian Relations: A Short History* (1984)

Robinson, Thomas W. and Shambaugh, David, eds, *Chinese Foreign Policy: Theory and Practice* (Oxford, 1994)

Segal, Gerald, *Rethinking the Pacific* (Oxford, 1990)

Thompson, R., *The Pacific Basin: A History of the Foreign Relations of the Asian, Australasian and American Rim States and the Pacific Islands* (1995)

Wolpert, S., *A New History of India* (4th edn, Oxford, 1992)

◆ Africa

Ayittey, George B. N., *Africa in Chaos* (1999)
Crowder, Michael, ed., *Cambridge History of Africa*, Vol. VIII: *1940–1975* (Cambridge, 1984)
Davidson, Basil, *Black Star: A View of the Life and Times of Kwame Nkrumah* (Boulder, Col., 1989)
Decalo, Samuel, *Coups and Army Rule in Africa* (1976)
Fieldhouse, D. K., *Black Africa 1945–1980: Economic Decolonization and Arrested Development* (1986)
Hargreaves, John D., *Decolonization in Africa* (2nd edn, 1996)
Horne, Alistair, *A Savage War of Peace: Algeria 1954–1962* (1987)
Mazrui, A. and Tidy, M., *Nationalism and New States in Africa* (1984)
Naldi, G., *The Organization of African Unity* (1989)
Shillington, Kevin, *South Africa since 1945* (1996)
Somerville, K., *Foreign Military Intervention in Africa* (1990)

◆ Latin America

Balfour, Sebastian, *Castro* (2nd edn, 1994)
Carothers, Thomas, *In the Name of Democracy: US Policy towards Central America in the Reagan Years* (Oxford, 1991)
Donghi, Tulio Halperin, *The Contemporary History of Latin America* (Durham, N. Carolina, 1993)
Keen, B., *A History of Latin America*, Vol. II (4th edn, New York, 1992)
Lowenthal, Abraham F., ed., *Exporting Democracy: The United States and Latin America* (Baltimore, 1991)
Miller, Nicola, *The USSR and Latin America, 1959–1987* (Cambridge, 1989)
Skidmore, Thomas E. and Smith, Peter H., *Modern Latin America* (4th edn, Oxford,1997)
Smith, Gaddis, *The Last Years of the Monroe Doctrine, 1945–1993* (New York, 1994)
Thomas, Hugh, *Cuba: The Pursuit of Freedom* (1971)

◆ War, strategy and intelligence

Aldrich, R., ed., *British Intelligence, Strategy and the Cold War* (1993)
Andrew, Christopher, *For the President's Eyes Only: Secret Intelligence and the American Presidency from Washington to Bush* (1995)
Blum, William, *The CIA, A Forgotten History* (1986)

Bond, Brian, *The Pursuit of Victory: From Napoleon to Saddam Hussein* (Oxford,1996)

Brogan, Patrick, *World Conflicts* (1992)

Freedman, Lawrence, *The Evolution of Nuclear Strategy* (1981)

Freedman, Lawrence, *Terrorism and International Order* (1986)

Haslam, Jonathan, *The Soviet Union and the Politics of Nuclear Weapons in Europe, 1969–87* (1989)

Holloway, David, *Stalin and Bomb: The Soviet Union and Atomic Energy, 1939–1956* (1994)

Holloway, David, *The Soviet Union and the Arms Race* (1983)

Laqueur, Walter, *The Age of Terrorism* (1987)

Miller, David, *The Cold War: A Military History* (1998)

Moynihan, Brian, *The Claws of the Bear: A History of the Soviet Armed Forces from 1917 to the Present* (1989)

Porch, Douglas, *The French Secret Services: From the Dreyfus Affair to the Gulf War* (1996)

Ranelagh, John, *The Agency: The Rise and Decline of the CIA* (New York, 1986)

Ranelagh, John, *The CIA: A History* (1992)

◆ International organizations

Bailey, Sidney, *How Wars End: The United Nations and the Termination of Armed Conflict* (Oxford, 1982)

Bailey, Sidney, *The United Nations* (1989)

James, Alan, *Peacekeeping in International Politics* (1990)

Luard, Evan, *The United Nations* (1979)

Mansergh, Nicholas, *The Commonwealth Experience*, Vol. II: *From British to Multiracial Commonwealth* (1982)

Marshall, Peter, *Positive Diplomacy* (1997)

Miller, J. D. B., *Survey of Commonwealth Affairs: Problems of Expansion and Attrition, 1953–1969* (Oxford, 1974)

Moore, R.J., *Making the New Commonwealth* (Oxford, 1987)

Parsons, Anthony, *From Cold War to Hot Peace: UN Interventions 1947–1994* (1995)

Righter, Rosemary, *Utopia Lost: The United Nations and World Order* (1995)

◆ Media and propaganda

Friedland, Lewis, *Covering the World: International Television News Services* (1992)

Mickelson, S., *America's Other Voices: Radio Free Europe and Radio Liberty* (New York, 1983)
Short, Kenneth, ed., *Western Broadcasting over the Iron Curtain* (New York, 1986)
Taylor, Philip M., *Global Communications, International Affairs and the Media since 1945* (1997)
Taylor, Philip M., *Munitions of the Mind: A History of Propaganda from the Ancient World to the Present Day* (2nd edn, Manchester, 1995)

◆ Ideas and beliefs

Cassels, Alan, *Ideology and International Relations in the Modern World* (1996)
Chadwick, Owen, *The Christian Church and the Cold War* (1992)
Donnelly, J., *Universal Human Rights in Theory and Practice* (Ithaca, 1989)
Hobsbawm, E. J., *Nations and Nationalism since 1870* (2nd edn, Cambridge, 1992)
Kedourie, Elie, *Nationalism* (4th edn, Oxford, 1993)
Lewis, Bernard, *Islam in History* (1973)
Minogue, K. R., *Nationalism* (1967)
Rhodes, A. R. E., *The Vatican in the Age of the Cold War* (Norwich, 1992)
Schulze, Reinhard, *A Modern History of the Islamic World* (2000)
Willey, David, *God's Politician: John Paul at the Vatican* (1992)

◆ Economics

Ashworth, W., *A Short History of the International Economy since 1945* (4th edn, 1987)
Bauer, P. T., *Equality, the Third World and Economic Delusion* (1981)
Kunz, Diane B., *Butter and Guns: America's Cold War Economic Diplomacy* (New York, 1997)
Longrigg, S. H., *Oil in the Middle East* (3rd edn, 1968)
Odell, Peter R., *Oil and World Power* (6th edn, 1981)
Sampson, Anthony, *The Money Lenders: Bankers in a Dangerous World* (1981)
Sayigh, Yussif Abdallah, *The Economies of the Arab World*, 2 vols (1975)
Strange, Susan, *International Monetary Relations* (1976)
Venn, Fiona, *Oil Diplomacy in the Twentieth Century* (1986)
Yergin, Daniel, *The Prize: The Epic Quest for Oil, Money and Power* (1991)

INDEX